DOCUMENTS
ON
AMERICAN FOREIGN
RELATIONS

VOL. III
JULY 1940—JUNE 1941

EDITED BY

S. SHEPARD JONES

Director, World Peace Foundation

AND

DENYS P. MYERS

Director of Research
World Peace Foundation

WORLD PEACE FOUNDATION

BOSTON

1941

WORLD PEACE FOUNDATION

40 Mt. Vernon Street, Boston, Massachusetts

Founded in 1910

THE World Peace Foundation is a non-profit organization which was founded in 1910 by Edwin Ginn, the educational publisher, for the purpose of promoting peace, justice and good-will among nations. For many years the Foundation has sought to increase public understanding of international problems by an objective presentation of the facts of international relations. This purpose is accomplished principally through its publications and by the maintenance of a Reference Service which furnishes on request information on current international problems. Recently increased attention has been focused on American foreign relations by study groups organized for the consideration of actual problems of policy.

PREFACE

The year ending June 30, 1941 was a momentous one for the American people. It began with the nation enveloped in a cloud of gloom following the surrender of France at Compiègne. Fear of German air power as Göring's armada turned in its full fury toward a half-armed England did not break the morale of sturdy Britain; but in America the successive *Blitz* victories of the Nazis in Western Europe had, at least for the moment, aroused widespread alarm. So quick had been the collapse of France, so great had been the loss of British matériel, that the position of the last bulwark of democracy and friendly naval power in Europe seemed desperate. In the United States the cry went up for Defense — for Hemispheric Defense; for Aid to Britain.

Faced with this situation the program of the American Government naturally assumed the character of emergency action. Last year's volume carried the initial documents of the defense program, and in this third volume of the series *Documents on American Foreign Relations* the story rapidly unfolds in its many aspects.

Within the first three months following the French armistice the American Government responded with the following notable action. In July the Foreign Ministers of the American Republics drew up the Act of Havana and the Convention for the Provisional Administration of European Possessions in the Western Hemisphere. In August the President and the Canadian Prime Minister announced at Ogdensburg the creation of a Permanent Joint Board on Defense to safeguard the "northern half of the Western Hemisphere." In quick succession followed other milestones in the nation's history: the Destroyers-Bases deal with Great Britain and the enactment by Congress (despite an approaching national election) of the Selective Training and Service Act.

From the study of the official record of the diplomatic, executive and legislative papers herein, students of American policy will no doubt be impressed by the intimate relationship between the unfolding of events abroad and the action taken by our Government. It is hardly an exaggeration to say that the development of hostilities in Europe, Asia and on the high seas "called the tune" for further American measures.

Although both candidates for the Presidency in the autumn of 1940 sensed the nation's deep desire to stay out of war and talked in those

iii

terms, external developments, in particular the German-Italian-Japanese Treaty of military alliance directed against the United States, gave the nation an increased sense of the totalitarian threat to the Western World. It was not long before the re-elected President asked that America become the "arsenal of democracy." When in March 1941 Congress enacted the Lend-Lease legislation after a two months' public debate, the policy implied in the existing "Neutrality Act" was clearly overshadowed in the public mind. America would defend itself by sending aid to all those who resisted aggression and whose defense was vital to America's defense.

As the war spread to the Balkans, to the Middle East and Russia, and as Japanese encroachments continued in the Far East, the temper of the country hardened and the Government looked for other ways to resist the triumph of aggression. The "battle of production" was speeded, the outposts of hemispheric defense were strengthened and a new one, Greenland, was brought under American protection. In the Pacific Japan was cautioned by diplomatic, economic, financial and military actions. Aid to China was increased and by extended export control supplies to Japan were sharply curtailed. By June 1941 a program of economic warfare against all Axis Powers was gathering momentum. Axis assets in this country were frozen and the consuls of Germany and Italy were sent home. The nation, however reluctant to plunge into war, was clearly in no mood to overlook further encroachments on its interests. When Germany invaded the Soviet Union in June, Washington announced a willingness to send aid to Stalin — action which would have been politically unthinkable in 1940 before the collapse of France.

Documents on American Foreign Relations: July 1940–June 1941, like its predecessor, is a volume crowded with the record of great events. Unfortunately the percentage of pages treating of emergency or war problems is very large. But for those who wish to understand the issues facing this country both now and in the better era that is certain to come, these pages are not to be omitted. How clearly this record reveals that the American worker, taxpayer and citizen in 1941 is also a worker, taxpayer and citizen of the world! It is his concern — his vital concern — that the basis for a more stable and lasting world order be laid in the months that lie ahead.

The conditions of a world at war, the changing practice of governments in giving out information, coupled with the wish to bring out the finished work in time for the academic year, have led to the use of "unofficial" sources for documentary texts to a degree that would not

otherwise be necessary.   But to round out the year's picture, it seemed
desirable to include such texts when no better ones were available.

Again the editors wish to express a word of deep appreciation for the
invaluable assistance of their associates at the World Peace Foundation,
in particular to Miss Marie J. Carroll and Mrs. Ralph de Miranda, for
many hours of painstaking and thoughtful work in the preparation of
this book.

S. S. J. and D. P. M.

Boston, Massachusetts
September 15, 1941

CONTENTS

CONTENTS

PART III — NATIONAL ACTION

X. NEUTRALITY OF THE UNITED STATES

PART I

POLICY

PRINCIPLES AND POLICY:
GENERAL STATEMENTS

(1) *Treaty for Renunciation of War. Statement on the 12th Anniversary of the Signing, by the Secretary of State (Hull), August 29, 1940* [1]

Twelve years ago today, there was signed a solemn treaty outlawing war, to which this country and 60 other countries gave their unqualified adherence. In Article 1 of that treaty, the High Contracting Parties renounced war as an instrument of national policy in their relations with one another. In Article 2, the High Contracting Parties agreed that "the settlement or solution of all disputes or conflicts of whatever nature or of whatever origin they may be which may arise among them, shall never be sought except by pacific means." In exchanges of views preceding and accompanying the ratification of that treaty, it was accepted as a part of the general understanding that the right of self-defense is implicit in sovereignty and remains with each and all of the signatory and adhering states.

In recent years, the renunciation made in Article 1 of the Kellogg-Briand Pact has been disregarded by some of the signatories; and the pledge given in Article 2 of that treaty has been violated by those signatories. Several nations have sent their armed forces into and against other countries. In consequence, destruction of life and of property, of material values and of spiritual values — destruction on a vast scale — not alone in the countries invaded but also in the countries whose armies are the invaders, is going on in various parts of the world.

Some of the invaded nations have been destroyed, some are fighting desperately in self-defense, and every other country, perceiving the manner in which activities of conquest spread and become enlarged as operations of conquest proceed, finds itself forced to arm as speedily as possible and to the utmost of its capacity in preparation for self-defense — toward preserving its own security by preventing war from reaching and crossing its boundaries.

[1] Department of State, *Bulletin*, III, p. 175.

Today no country and no individual is secure against the destructive effects of the existing armed conflicts. No human being anywhere can be sure that he or she will be allowed for long to live in peace. Only by vigorous and adequate preparation for self-defense can any country, including our own, hope to remain at peace.

It was to spare the human race the untold suffering and indescribable tragedy of the kind we are witnessing today that the Kellogg-Briand Pact was signed. The soundness of its underlying principles has in no way been impaired by what has taken place since then. Sooner or later they must prevail as an unshakeable foundation of international relations unless war with its horrors and ravages is to become the normal state of the world and mankind is to relapse into the chaos of barbarism. And I am certain that there are in the human race resources of mind and of spirit sufficient to insure that these sane bases of civilized existence will become firmly established.

(2) *Radio Address to the Peoples of the Western Hemisphere by the President (Roosevelt), October 12, 1940* [1]

MY FRIENDS OF THE AMERICAS:

It is no mere coincidence that this radio broadcast to the entire Western Hemisphere — North America, Central America and South America — should take place on the anniversary of Christopher Columbus' discovery of the New World. No day could be more appropriate than this day on which we celebrate the exploits of the bold discoverer.

Today, all of us Americans of North and Central and South America join with our fellow citizens of Italian descent to do honor to the name of Columbus.

Many and numerous have been the groups of Italians who have come in welcome waves of immigration to this hemisphere. They have been an essential element in the civilization and make-up of all of the 21 republics. During these centuries Italian names have been high in the list of statesmen in the United States and in the other republics — and in addition, those who have helped to create the scientific, commercial, professional, and artistic life of the New World.

The Americas have excelled in the adventure of many races living together in harmony. In the wake of the discoverers came the first set-

---

[1] Department of State, *Bulletin*, III, p. 291; the address was delivered from the President's train at Dayton, Ohio, and was transmitted by long- and short-wave over national and world hookups. French, Italian and Spanish versions were broadcast after the English original; for those texts see *Congressional Record*, Vol. 86, p. 20609 (daily edition), October 15, 1940.

tlers, the first refugees from Europe. They came to plough new fields, build new homes, establish a new society in a new world. Later, they fought for liberty. Men and women of courage, of enterprise, of vision, they knew what they were fighting for; they gained it — and thereby "gave hope to all the world for all future time."

They formed, here in the Western Hemisphere, a new human reservoir, and into it has poured the blood, the culture, the traditions of all the races and peoples of the earth. To the Americas they came — the "masses yearning to be free" — "the multitudes brought hither out of many kindreds and tongues," cherishing common aspirations, not for economic betterment alone, but for the personal freedoms and liberties which had been denied to them in the Old World.

They came not to conquer one another but to live with one another. They proudly carried with them their inheritance of culture, but they cheerfully left behind the burden of prejudice and hatred.

In this New World were transplanted the great cultures of Spain and Portugal. In our own day the fact is that a great part of the Spanish and Portuguese culture of the entire world now comes from the Americas.

It is natural that all American citizens from the many nations of the Old World should kindly remember the lands where their ancestors lived and the great attributes of the old civilization in those lands. But in every single one of the American Republics, the first and final allegiance and loyalty of these citizens, almost without exception, is to the republic in which they live and move and have their being.

For when our forefathers came to these shores, they came with a determination to stay and to become citizens of the New World. As it established its independence, they wanted to become citizens of America — not an Anglo-Saxon America, nor an Italian, nor a German, nor a Spanish, nor a Portuguese — but just citizens of an independent nation of America.

Here, we do not have any dual citizenship. Here, the descendants of the very same races who had always been forced to fear or hate each other in lands across the ocean have learned to live in peace and in friendship.

No one group or race in the New World has any desire to subjugate the others. No one nation in this hemisphere has any desire to dominate the others. In the Western Hemisphere no nation is considered a second-class nation. And that is something worth remembering.

We know that attempts have been made — we know that they will continue to be made — to divide these groups within a nation and to divide these nations among themselves.

There are those in the Old World who persist in believing that here in this new hemisphere the Americas can be torn by the hatreds and fears which have drenched the battlegrounds of Europe for so many centuries. Americans as individuals, American republics as nations, remain on guard against those who seek to break up our unity by preaching ancient race hatreds, by working on old fears, or by holding out glittering promises which they know to be false.

"Divide and conquer" has been the battle-cry of the totalitarian powers in their war against the democracies. It has succeeded on the continent of Europe for the moment. On our continents it will fail.

We are determined to use our energies and our resources to counteract and repel the foreign plots and propaganda — the whole technique of underground warfare originating in Europe and now clearly directed against all the republics on this side of the ocean.

That propaganda repeats and repeats that democracy is a decadent form of government. They tell us that our old democratic ideal, our old traditions of civil liberties, are things of the past.

We reject this thought. We say that *we are* the future. We say that the direction in which they would lead us is backward, not forward — backward to the bondage of the Pharaohs, backward to the slavery of the Middle Ages.

The command of the democratic faith has been ever onward and upward. Never have free men been satisfied with the mere maintenance of any *status quo*, however comfortable or secure it may have seemed at the moment.

We have always held to the hope, the belief, the conviction that there is a better life, a better world, beyond the horizon.

That fire of freedom was in the eyes of Washington, and Bolívar, and San Martín, and Artigas, and Juárez, and Bernardo O'Higgins, and all the brave, rugged, ragged men who followed them in the wars of independence.

That fire burns now in the eyes of those who are fighting for freedom in the lands across the sea.

On this side of the ocean there is no desire, there will be no effort, on the part of any one race, or people, or nation, to control any other. The only encirclement sought is the encircling bond of good old-fashioned neighborly friendship. So bound together, we are able to withstand any attack from the east or from the west. Together we are able to ward off any infiltration of alien political and economic ideas which would destroy our freedom and democracy.

When we speak of defending this Western Hemisphere, we are speaking not only of the territory of North, Central, and South America and the immediately adjacent islands. We include the right to the peaceful use of the Atlantic and Pacific Oceans. That has been our traditional policy.

It is a fact, for example, that as far back as 1798 the United States found that its peaceful trade and commerce with other parts of the Americas were threatened by armed privateers sent to the West Indies by nations then at war in Europe. Because of this threat to peace in this hemisphere of ours, the United States Ships *Constellation, Constitution, United States,* and many others were fitted out; and they drove the armed vessels of Europe out of the waters to the south of us, and made commerce between the Americas once more peaceable and possible.

We of the Americas still consider that this defense of these oceans of the Western Hemisphere against acts of aggression is the first factor in the defense and protection of our own territorial integrity. We reaffirm that policy, lest there be any doubt of our intention to maintain it.

There are some in every single one of the 21 American Republics who suggest that the course the Americas are following is slowly drawing one or all of us into war with some nation or nations beyond the seas.

The clear facts have been stated over and over again. This country wants no war with any nation. This hemisphere wants no war with any nation. The American Republics are determined to work in unity for peace, just as we work in unity to defend ourselves from attack.

For many long years every ounce of energy I have had has been devoted to keeping this nation and the other republics at peace with the rest of the world. That is what continues uppermost in my mind today — the objective for which I hope and work and pray.

We arm to defend ourselves. The strongest reason for that is that it is the strongest guarantee for peace.

The United States of America is mustering its men and resources, arming not only to defend itself, but, in cooperation with the other American republics, to help defend the whole hemisphere.

We are building a total defense on land and sea and in the air, sufficient to repel total attack from any part of the world. Forewarned by the deliberate attacks of the dictators upon free peoples, the United States, for the first time in its history, has undertaken the mustering of its men in peacetime. Unprecedented dangers have caused the United States to undertake the building of a navy and an air force sufficient to defend all the coasts of the Americas from any combination of hostile powers.

We have asked for, and we have received, the fullest cooperation and assistance of industry and labor. All of us are speeding the preparation of adequate defense.

And we are keeping the nations of this hemisphere fully advised of our defense preparations. We have welcomed the military missions from neighboring republics; and in turn our own military experts have been welcomed by them.[1] We intend to encourage this frank interchange of information and plans.

We shall be all for one and one for all.

This idea of a defense strong enough and wide enough to cover this half of the world had its beginnings when the Government of the United States announced its policy with respect to South America. It was the policy of the good neighbor, the neighbor who knew how to mind his own business, but was always willing to lend a friendly hand to a friendly nation which sought it, the neighbor who was willing to discuss in all friendship the problems which will always arise between neighbors.

From the day on which that policy was announced, the American Republics have consulted with each other; they have peacefully settled their old problems and disputes; they have grown closer and closer to each other; until at last in 1938 at Lima, their unity and friendship were sealed.

There was then adopted a declaration that the New World proposed to maintain collectively the freedom upon which its strength had been built. It was the culmination of the good-neighbor policy, the proof of what was said by that famous Argentinian of Italian birth, Alberdi — "The Americas are a great political system: the parts draw life from the whole; and the whole draws life from its parts."

Through the acquisition of eight naval bases in territories of the British Empire lying within the sphere of the New World, from Newfoundland to Guiana, we have increased the immediate effectiveness of the great Navy which we now have and of the greater Navy we have under construction. These bases were acquired by the United States; but not for the protection of the United States alone. They were acquired for the protection of the whole Western Hemisphere. The unity of the American Republics was proven to the world when these naval bases were promptly opened by the United States to the other republics for cooperative use. In that act was typified the good-neighbor conception of hemispheric defense through cooperation by and for all of us.

American radio stations will play their part in the new unity which has been built so solidly between the American nations during the past eight years. They must be effective instruments for the honest exchange and communication of ideas. They must never be used as stations in other lands are used, to send out on the same day one false story to one country, and a different false story to another.

[1] See p. 144.

The core of our defense is the faith we have in the institutions we defend. The Americas will not be scared or threatened into the ways the dictators want us to follow.

No combination of dictator countries of Europe and Asia will halt us in the path we see ahead for ourselves and for democracy.

No combination of dictator countries of Europe and Asia will stop the help we are giving to almost the last free people fighting to hold them at bay.

Our course is clear. Our decision is made. We will continue to pile up our defense and our armaments. We will continue to help those who resist aggression, and who now hold the aggressors far from our shores. Let no American in any part of the Americas question the possibility of danger from overseas. Why should we accept assurances that we are immune? History records that not long ago those same assurances were given to the people of Holland and Belgium and Norway.

It can no longer be disputed that forces of evil which are bent on conquest of the world will destroy whomever and whenever they can destroy. We have learned the lessons of recent years. We know now that if we seek to appease them by withholding aid from those who stand in their way, we only hasten the day of their attack upon us.

The people of the United States, the people of all the Americas, reject the doctrine of appeasement. They recognize it for what it is — a major weapon of the aggressor nations.

I speak bluntly. I speak the love the American people have for freedom and liberty and decency and humanity.

That is why we arm. Because, I repeat, this nation wants to keep war away from these two continents. Because we all of us are determined to do everything possible to maintain peace on this hemisphere. Because great strength of arms is the practical way of fulfilling our hopes for peace and for staying out of this war or any other war. Because we are determined to muster all our strength so that we may remain free.

The men and women of Britain have shown how free people defend what they know to be right. Their heroic defense will be recorded for all time. It will be perpetual proof that democracy, when put to the test, can show the stuff of which it is made.

I well recall during my recent visit to three great capital cities in South America, the vast throngs which came to express by their cheers their friendship for the United States. I especially remember that above all the cheers I heard one constant cry again and again — one shout above all others: " !Viva la Democracia!" — "Long live democracy!"

Those three stirring words cry out the abiding conviction of people in all the democracies that freedom shall rule in the land.

As I salute the peoples of all the nations in the western world, I echo that greeting from our good neighbors of the Americas: "¡Viva la Democracia!" — "Long live democracy!"

(3) Our Foreign Policy.   Address by the Secretary of State (Hull), October 26, 1940 [1]

[Excerpt]

It is with no light heart that I address you and any others who may be listening tonight on the subject of our international relations. I should be lacking in candor if I did not emphasize the gravity of the present situation.

Only once before in our national existence has as grave a danger from without threatened this Nation as the danger which looms today on the international horizon. That was in the stirring days when the founders of this Republic staked everything on their unshakable conviction that a nation of free men could be established and would endure on the soil of America. Theirs was a struggle and a victory the fruits of which have been the proud inheritance of succeeding generations of Americans for more than a century and a half. These generations, including our own, have enjoyed this inheritance in a world where human freedom, national independence, and order under law were steadily becoming more and more firmly established as a system of civilized relations among nations and among individuals.

Today that system and all peaceful nations, including our own, are gravely menaced. The danger arises out of the plans and acts of a small group of national rulers who have succeeded in transforming their peoples into forceful instruments for widespread domination by conquest.

To understand the significance of this danger and to prepare to meet it successfully we must see clearly the tragic lessons taught by what has occurred since the protagonists of conquest began their march across the earth. I ask you to review with me the whirlwind developments of one of the saddest and most crucial decades in the history of mankind — that of the nineteen-thirties.

[Here follows the review indicated.]

· ·

[1] Department of State, Bulletin, III, p. 331; delivered at the National Press Club dinner, Washington, and broadcast over the blue network of the National Broadcasting Co.

The appalling tragedy of the present world situation lies in the fact that peacefully disposed nations failed to recognize in time the true nature of the aims and ambitions which have actuated the rulers of the heavily arming nations. Recoiling from the mere contemplation of the possibility of another widespread war, the peoples of the peaceful nations permitted themselves to be lulled into a false sense of security by the assurances made by these rulers that their aims were limited. This continued even as succeeding events left less and less room for doubt that, behind the screen of these assurances, preparations were being made for new attempts at widespread conquest. To mask still further this monstrous deception, these rulers and their satellites attempted to brand as "war mongers" and "imperialists" all who warned against the clearly emerging dangers, and poured upon them vituperation and abuse.

The United States, together with most other nations, has stood firmly for the basic principles underlying civilized international relations — peace, law, justice, treaty observance, non-intervention, peaceful settlement of differences, and fair-dealing, supported by the fullest practicable measure of international cooperation. The advocacy of these principles has won for us the friendship of all nations, except those which, vaguely describing themselves as the "have-nots" and claiming a superior right to rule over other peoples, are today on the march with great armies, air fleets, and navies to take by force what they say they need or want.

The rulers of these nations have repudiated and violated in every essential respect the long-accepted principles of peaceful and orderly international relations. Merciless armed attack; unrestrained terrorization through slaughter of non-combatant men, women, and children; deceit, fraud, and guile; forced labor; confiscation of property; imposed starvation and deprivations of every sort — all these are weapons constantly used by the conquerors for the invasion and subjugation of other nations.

They adhere to no geographic lines and they fix no time limit on their programs of invasion and destruction. They cynically disregard every right of neutral nations, and, having occupied several such countries, they then proceed to warn all peaceful nations that they must remain strictly neutral until an invading force is actually crossing their borders. They have as a fixed objective the securing of control of the high seas. They threaten peaceful nations with the direst consequences if those nations do not remain acquiescent, while the conquerors are seizing the other continents and most of the seven seas of the earth.

Let no one comfort himself with the delusion that these are mere excesses or exigencies of war, to be voluntarily abandoned when fighting ceases. By deed and by utterance, the would-be conquerors have made it abundantly clear that they are engaged upon a relentless attempt to transform the civilized world as we have known it into a world in which mankind will be reduced again to the degradation of a master-and-slave relationship among nations and among individuals, maintained by brute force.

The hand of crushing assault has struck again and again at peaceful nations, complacent and unprepared in their belief that mere intention on their part to keep peace was an ample shield of security.

There can be nothing more dangerous for our Nation than for us to assume that the avalanche of conquest could under no circumstances reach any vital portion of this hemisphere. Oceans give the nations of this hemisphere no guaranty against the possibility of economic, political, or military attack from abroad. Oceans are barriers but they are also highways. Barriers of distance are merely barriers of time. Should the would-be conquerors gain control of other continents, they would next concentrate on perfecting their control of the seas, of the air over the seas, and of the world's economy; they might then be able with ships and with planes to strike at the communication lines, the commerce, and the life of this hemisphere; and ultimately we might find ourselves compelled to fight on our own soil, under our own skies, in defense of our independence and our very lives.

These are some of the governing facts and conditions of the present-day international situation. These are the dangers which must be recognized. Against these dangers, our policies and measures must provide defense.

V

We are in the presence not of local or regional wars, but of an organized and determined movement for steadily expanding conquest. Against this drive for power no nation and no region is secure save as its inhabitants create for themselves means of defense so formidable that even the would-be conquerors will not dare to raise against them the hand of attack.

The first need for all nations still masters of their own destiny is to create for themselves, as speedily and as completely as possible, impregnable means of defense. This is the staggering lesson of mankind's recent experience.

To meet that need, we are bringing our military, naval, and air establishments to maximum practicable strength. Production of military supplies is being brought to a greater and greater pitch of speed and effectiveness. Wherever necessary for the carrying out of the defense program, export of essential materials is being stringently regulated. Arrangements are being carried forward to provide military and technical training for the youth of this country. We intend to continue and intensify our effort in all these directions.

We are taking measures toward dealing with subversive activities in this country directed from abroad. The experience of many other countries has brought us the shocking realization of the manner in which, and the extent to which, such activities are employed to undermine social and political institutions and to bring about internal disintegration and decay in the countries which they plan to make their victims. We intend to act in this field with unremitting vigor.

We are seeking to advance by every appropriate means the spirit of inter-American solidarity and the system of continental defense. In conformity with the procedure set up at Buenos Aires and Lima, the Panama Consultative Meeting of the Ministers of Foreign Affairs of the American Republics adopted important measures to safeguard the national and collective interests of the American nations, their peace, and their economic security. Last summer they met again, at Havana, to consult with regard to several threats to the peace and security of the Americas, the danger of which, they unanimously agreed, existed. To ward off these threats, they took positive steps to prevent any transfer of sovereignty in the Western Hemisphere from one non-American nation to another, embodied in an international convention and in the Act of Havana. They also agreed upon procedures for combating subversive activities in the American nations and they adopted measures of economic defense and collaboration.

We have concluded an arrangement with Great Britain under which we have acquired long-time leases of eight strategically located naval and air bases which will enable us to create a protective girdle of steel along the Atlantic seaboard of the American Continent — bases which will be available for use by all of the American Republics. We are engaged in defense consultations with our neighbors to the south, and we have created facilities for such consultations with Canada. In all these fields, we intend to continue vigorous effort.

We have sought in every appropriate way to discourage conquest and to limit the area of war. We have followed consistently the policy of refusing recognition of territorial changes effected by force or threat of force. We have taken every opportunity to express our concern over threatened changes by force in the existing political status of colonial possessions, disturbance of which would extend the area of hostilities.

We have placed under license the funds of invaded countries. In these respects, too, we intend to continue our activities.

We believe that the safety and the primary interests of the United States must be upheld with firmness and resolution — supported by the speediest and fullest possible armament for all defensive purposes. In view of the unprecedented character of menacing developments abroad, we have frankly recognized the danger involved and the increasing need for defense against it. As an important means of strengthening our own defense and of preventing attack on any part of the Western Hemisphere, this country is affording all feasible facilities for the obtaining of supplies by nations which, while defending themselves against barbaric attack, are checking the spread of violence and are thus reducing the danger to us. We intend to continue doing this to the greatest practicable extent. Any contention, no matter from what source, that this country should not take such action is equivalent, in the present circumstances, to a denying of the inalienable right of self-defense.

VI

In our democracy the basic determination of foreign policy rests with the people. As I sense the will of our people today, this Nation is determined that its security and rightful interests shall be safeguarded.

The dangers with which we are confronted are not of our making. We cannot know at what point, or when, we may possibly be attacked. We can, however, be prepared, first, to discourage any thought of assault upon our security and, if any such assault should be attempted, to repel it.

The people of this country want peace. To have peace, we must have security. To have security, we must be strong. These are times that test the fiber of men and of nations.

Our system of defense must, of necessity, be many-sided, because the dangers against which safeguards are imperatively required are manifold. Essential to effective national defense are constant and skilful use of political and economic measures, possession of military weapons, and continuous exercise of wisdom and of high moral qualities. We must have planes and tanks and ships and guns. We must have trained men. We must hold to the ideal of a world in which the rights of all nations are respected and each respects the rights of all; in which principles of law and order and justice and fair-dealing prevail. Above all, we must be a united people — united in purpose and in effort to create impregnable defense.

Thus can we maintain our inheritance. Thus will we continue to make this country's high contribution toward the progress of mankind on the roadway of civilized effort.

(4) *Armistice Day Address by the President (Roosevelt), Amphi-theater, Arlington National Cemetery, November 11, 1940* [1]

On this day which commemorates the end of fighting between human beings in a world war, it is permissible for me to search far back in the history of civilization in order to visualize important trends.

On the Great Seal of the United States, which, for a century and a half, has reposed in the loving care of a long line of Secretaries of State of the United States, appear these words: "*novus ordo seclorum,*" which means: "a new order of the ages."

In almost every century since the day that recorded history began, people have thought that they were creating or establishing some kind of "new order of the ages."

But in the scheme of civilization from which ours descends I suppose that we can properly recognize that in 2,500 years there have been only a very few "new orders" in the development of human living under a thing called government.

Without question, the philosophy of orderly government in which the governed had some form of voice in a civilized society goes back to the days of ancient Greece. We must remember, however, that while the philosophy of democracy was there first expressed in words and on paper, the practice of it was by no means consistent and was confined to a relatively small number of human beings and to a relatively small geographical area.

We came to the age of Rome — an age of a strange admixture of elections and laws and military conquest and personal dictatorship. It was an age which extended the civilization of the period to the greater part of the then known world. It was an age which forced its own conception of laws and ways of life on millions of less civilized people who previously had lived under tribal custom or centralized direction. Definitely, Rome was an age.

With Rome's collapse and the overrunning of Europe by vast population movements from farther east, orderly progress deteriorated and the sword drove learning into hiding. That dark period could hardly be called an age because it was an interim between ages.

Then, with the reawakening of a thousand years ago, with the crusades, the feudal system, the guilds, the kings, and the Renaissance, that

[1] Department of State, *Bulletin*, III, p. 417.

age which immediately preceded our own was born and grew and flourished. That was an era of enormous distinction — arts and literature and education and exploration — marching armies, barons, and empires. Human security was still non-existent — democracy was not permitted.

Toward its close, however, the appearance of tiny movements in tiny places, led by tiny people, forecast the next vast step forward — the era of 1776 — the age in which, thank God, we still live.

Those beginnings originated, it is true, in the old world — among the philosophers, among the seekers of many kinds of freedom forbidden by those who governed.

Those beginnings found their freest development in the colonies that were organized along the seaboard of North America. There, by the processes of trial and error, democracy as it has since been accepted in so many lands had its birth and its training.

There came into being the first far-flung government in all the world whose cardinal principle was democracy — the United States of America.

We must accept that as fact because, truly and fundamentally, it was a new order — nothing like it had ever been seen before. We must accept it because the new order spread into almost every part of the civilized world. It spread in many forms — and over the next century almost all peoples had acquired some form of popular expression of opinion, some form of election, of franchise, of the right to be heard. The Americas and the British Isles led the world in spreading the gospel of democracy among peoples great and small.

And the world as a whole felt with much right that it had discarded feudalism, conquest, and dictatorship.

People felt that way until 1914, when a definite effort was made in a part of the world to destroy this existing "new order of the ages" — to destroy it after its relatively short trial, and to substitute for it the doctrine that might makes right. The attempt failed 22 years ago today.

You and I who served in the period of the World War have faced in later years unpatriotic efforts by some of our own countrymen to make us believe that the sacrifices made by our own Nation were wholly in vain.

A hundred years from now, historians will brand such efforts as puny and false.

A hundred years from now, historians will say rightly that the World War preserved the new order of the ages for at least a whole generation — a full 20 years — and that if the axis of 1918 had been successful in military victory over the associated nations, resistance on behalf of democracy in 1940 would have been wholly impossible.

America, therefore, is proud of its share in maintaining the era of democracy in that war in which we took part. America is proud of you who served — and ever will be proud.

I, for one, do not believe that the era of democracy in human affairs can or will be snuffed out in our lifetime. I, for one, do not believe that mere force will be successful in sterilizing the seeds which had taken such firm root as a harbinger of better lives for mankind. I, for one, do not believe that the world will revert either to a modern form of ancient slavery or to controls vested in modern feudalism or modern emperors or modern dictators or modern oligarchs in these days. The very people under their iron heels will, themselves, rebel.

What are a few months or even a few years in the lifetime of any of us? We, alive today, live and think in terms of our grandparents, and our own parents, and ourselves, and our children — yes, and our grandchildren. We, alive today — not in the existent democracies alone, but also among the populations of the smaller nations already overrun — are thinking in the larger terms of the maintenance of the new order to which we have been accustomed and in which we intend to continue.

We recognize certain facts of 1940 which did not exist in 1918 — a need for the elimination of aggressive armaments, a need for the breaking down of barriers in a more closely knitted world, a need for restoring honor in the written and spoken world. We recognize that the processes of democracies must be greatly improved in order that we may attain those purposes.

But over and above the present, we recognize and salute the eternal verities that lie with us in the future of mankind.

You, the men of 1917 and 1918, helped to preserve those truths of democracy for our generation.

We still unite, we still strive mightily to preserve intact that new order of the ages founded by the Fathers of America.

(5) Address on National Security by the President (Roosevelt), December 29, 1940 [1]

This is not a fireside chat on war. It is a talk on national security; because the nub of the whole purpose of your President is to keep you now, and your children later, and your grandchildren much later, out of a last-ditch war for the preservation of American independence and

[1] From the office of the Secretary to the President. The broadcast from the White House at 9 : 30 P.M., December 29, was carried by all principal radio networks in the United States and Canada, and was rebroadcast by long- and short-wave throughout the world in English, French, German, Italian and Spanish.

all of the things that American independence means to you and to me and to ours.

Tonight, in the presence of a world crisis, my mind goes back eight years ago to a night in the midst of a domestic crisis. It was a time when the wheels of American industry were grinding to a full stop, when the whole banking system of our country had ceased to function.

I well remember that while I sat in my study in the White House, preparing to talk with the people of the United States, I had before my eyes the picture of all those Americans with whom I was talking. I saw the workmen in the mills, the mines, the factories; the girl behind the counter; the small shopkeeper; the farmer doing his Spring plowing; the widows and the old men wondering about their life's savings.

I tried to convey to the great mass of American people what the banking crisis meant to them in their daily lives.

Tonight, I want to do the same thing, with the same people, in this new crisis which faces America.

We met the issue of 1933 with courage and realism.

We face this new crisis — this new threat to the security of our nation — with the same courage and realism.

Never before since Jamestown and Plymouth Rock has our American civilization been in such danger as now.

For, on September 27, 1940,[1] by an agreement signed in Berlin, three powerful nations, two in Europe and one in Asia, joined themselves together in the threat that if the United States interfered with or blocked the expansion program of these three nations — a program aimed at world control — they would unite in ultimate action against the United States.

The Nazi masters of Germany have made it clear that they intend not only to dominate all life and thought in their own country, but also to enslave the whole of Europe, and then to use the resources of Europe to dominate the rest of the world.

Three weeks ago their leader stated "There are two worlds that stand opposed to each other." Then in defiant reply to his opponents, he said this: "Others are correct when they say: With this world we cannot ever reconcile ourselves. . . . I can beat any other power in the world." So said the leader of the Nazis.

In other words, the Axis not merely admits but proclaims that there can be no ultimate peace between their philosophy of government and our philosophy of government.

In view of the nature of this undeniable threat, it can be asserted,

[1] See p. 304.

properly and categorically, that the United States has no right or reason to encourage talk of peace, until the day shall come when there is a clear intention on the part of the aggressor nations to abandon all thought of dominating or conquering the world.

At this moment, the forces of the states that are leagued against all peoples who live in freedom, are being held away from our shores. The Germans and Italians are being blocked on the other side of the Atlantic by the British, and by the Greeks, and by thousands of soldiers and sailors who were able to escape from subjugated countries. The Japanese are being engaged in Asia by the Chinese in another great defense.

In the Pacific is our fleet.

Some of our people like to believe that wars in Europe and in Asia are of no concern to us. But it is a matter of most vital concern to us that European and Asiatic war-makers should not gain control of the oceans which lead to this hemisphere.

One hundred and seventeen years ago the Monroe Doctrine was conceived by our government as a measure of defense in the face of a threat against this hemisphere by an alliance in Continental Europe. Thereafter, we stood on guard in the Atlantic, with the British as neighbors. There was no treaty. There was no "unwritten agreement."

Yet, there was the feeling, proven correct by history, that we as neighbors could settle any disputes in peaceful fashion. The fact is that during the whole of this time the Western Hemisphere has remained free from aggression from Europe or from Asia.

Does anyone seriously believe that we need to fear attack while a free Britain remains our most powerful naval neighbor in the Atlantic? Does anyone seriously believe, on the other hand, that we could rest easy if the Axis powers were our neighbor there?

If Great Britain goes down, the Axis Powers will control the continents of Europe, Asia, Africa, Australasia, and the high seas — and they will be in a position to bring enormous military and naval resources against this hemisphere. It is no exaggeration to say that all of us in the Americas would be living at the point of a gun — a gun loaded with explosive bullets, economic as well as military.

We should enter upon a new and terrible era in which the whole world, our hemisphere included, would be run by threats of brute force. To survive in such a world, we would have to convert ourselves permanently into a militaristic power on the basis of war economy.

Some of us like to believe that even if Great Britain falls, we are still safe, because of the broad expanse of the Atlantic and of the Pacific.

But the width of these oceans is not what it was in the days of clipper ships. At one point between Africa and Brazil the distance is less than from Washington to Denver — five hours for the latest type of bomber. And at the north of the Pacific Ocean America and Asia almost touch each other.

Even today we have planes which could fly from the British Isles to New England and back without refueling. And the range of the modern bomber is ever being increased.

During the past week many people in all parts of the nation have told me what they wanted me to say tonight. Almost all of them expressed a courageous desire to hear the plain truth about the gravity of the situation. One telegram, however, expressed the attitude of the small minority who want to see no evil and hear no evil, even though they know in their hearts that evil exists. That telegram begged me not to tell again of the ease with which our American cities could be bombed by any hostile power which had gained bases in this Western Hemisphere. The gist of that telegram was: "Please, Mr. President, don't frighten us by telling us the facts."

Frankly and definitely there is danger ahead — danger against which we must prepare. But we well know that we cannot escape danger, or the fear of it, by crawling into bed and pulling the covers over our heads.

Some nations of Europe were bound by solemn nonintervention pacts with Germany. Other nations were assured by Germany that they need never fear invasion. Nonintervention pact or not, the fact remains that they were attacked, overrun and thrown into the modern form of slavery at an hour's notice or even without any notice at all. As an exiled leader of one of these nations said to me the other day — "The notice was a minus quantity. It was given to my government two hours after German troops had poured into my country in a hundred places!"

The fate of these nations tells us what it means to live at the point of a Nazi gun.

The Nazis have justified such actions by various pious frauds. One of these frauds is the claim that they are occupying a nation for the purpose of "restoring order." Another is that they are occupying or controlling a nation on the excuse that they are "protecting it" against the aggression of somebody else.

For example, Germany has said that she was occupying Belgium to save the Belgians from the British. Would she hesitate to say to any South American country, "We are occupying you to protect you from aggression by the United States"?

Belgium today is being used as an invasion base against Britain, now fighting for its life. Any South American country, in Nazi hands, would always constitute a jumping off place for German attack on any one of the other Republics of this Hemisphere.

Analyze for yourselves the future of two other places even nearer to Germany if the Nazis won. Could Ireland hold out? Would Irish freedom be permitted as an amazing exception in an unfree world? Or the Islands of the Azores which still fly the flag of Portugal after five centuries? We think of Hawaii as an outpost of defense in the Pacific. Yet, the Azores are closer to our shores in the Atlantic than Hawaii is on the other side.

There are those who say that the Axis powers would never have any desire to attack the Western Hemisphere. This is the same dangerous form of wishful thinking which has destroyed the powers of resistance of so many conquered peoples. The plain facts are that the Nazis have proclaimed, time and again, that all other races are their inferiors and therefore subject to their orders. And most important of all, the vast resources and wealth of this Hemisphere constitute the most tempting loot in all the world.

Let us no longer blind ourselves to the undeniable fact that the evil forces which have crushed and undermined and corrupted so many others are already within our own gates. Your government knows much about them and every day is ferreting them out.

Their secret emissaries are active in our own and neighboring countries. They seek to stir up suspicion and dissension to cause internal strife. They try to turn capital against labor, and vice-versa. They try to re-awaken long slumbering racial and religious enmities which should have no place in this country. They are active in every group that promotes intolerance. They exploit for their own ends our natural abhorrence of war. These trouble-breeders have but one purpose. It is to divide our people into hostile groups and to destroy our unity and shatter our will to defend ourselves.

There are also American citizens, many of them in high places, who, unwittingly in most cases, are aiding and abetting the work of these agents. I do not charge these American citizens with being foreign agents. But I do charge them with doing exactly the kind of work that the dictators want done in the United States.

These people not only believe that we can save our own skins by shutting our eyes to the fate of other nations. Some of them go much further than that. They say that we can and should become the friends and even the partners of the Axis powers. Some of them even suggest that we should imitate the methods of the dictatorships. Americans never can and never will do that.

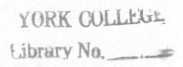

The experience of the past two years has proven beyond doubt that no nation can appease the Nazis. No man can tame a tiger into a kitten by stroking it. There can be no appeasement with ruthlessness. There can be no reasoning with an incendiary bomb. We know now that a nation can have peace with the Nazis only at the price of total surrender.

Even the people of Italy have been forced to become accomplices of the Nazis; but at this moment they do not know how soon they will be embraced to death by their allies.

The American appeasers ignore the warning to be found in the fate of Austria, Czecho-Slovakia, Poland, Norway, Belgium, the Netherlands, Denmark, and France. They tell you that the Axis powers are going to win anyway; that all this bloodshed in the world could be saved, and that the United States might just as well throw its influence into the scale of a dictated peace, and get the best out of it that we can.

They call it a "negotiated peace." Nonsense! Is it a negotiated peace if a gang of outlaws surrounds your community and on threat of extermination makes you pay tribute to save your own skins?

Such a dictated peace would be no peace at all. It would be only another armistice, leading to the most gigantic armament race and the most devastating trade wars in history. And in these contests the Americas would offer the only real resistance to the Axis powers.

With all their vaunted efficiency and parade of pious purpose in this war, there are still in their background the concentration camp and the servants of God in chains.

The history of recent years proves that shootings and chains and concentration camps are not simply the transient tools but the very altars of modern dictatorships. They may talk of a "new order" in the world, but what they have in mind is but a revival of the oldest and the worst tyranny. In that there is no liberty, no religion, no hope.

The proposed "new order" is the very opposite of a United States of Europe or a United States of Asia. It is not a government based upon the consent of the governed. It is not a union of ordinary, self-respecting men and women to protect themselves and their freedom and their dignity from oppression. It is an unholy alliance of power and pelf to dominate and enslave the human race.

The British people are conducting an active war against this unholy alliance. Our own future security is greatly dependent on the outcome of that fight. Our ability to "keep out of war" is going to be affected by that outcome.

Thinking in terms of today and tomorrow, I make the direct statement to the American people that there is far less chance of the United

States getting into war, if we do all we can now to support the nations defending themselves against attack by the Axis than if we acquiesce in their defeat, submit tamely to an Axis victory, and wait our turn to be the object of attack in another war later on.

If we are to be completely honest with ourselves, we must admit there is risk in *any* course we may take. But I deeply believe that the great majority of our people agree that the course that I advocate involves the least risk now and the greatest hope for world peace in the future.

The people of Europe who are defending themselves do not ask us to do their fighting. They ask us for the implements of war, the planes, the tanks, the guns, the freighters which will enable them to fight for their liberty and our security. Emphatically we must get these weapons to them in sufficient volume and quickly enough, so that we and our children will be saved the agony and suffering of war which others have had to endure.

Let not defeatists tell us that it is too late. It will never be earlier. Tomorrow will be later than today.

Certain facts are self-evident.

In a military sense Great Britain and the British Empire are today the spearhead of resistance to world conquest. They are putting up a fight which will live forever in the story of human gallantry.

There is no demand for sending an American Expeditionary Force outside our own borders. There is no intention by any member of your government to send such a force. You can, therefore, nail any talk about sending armies to Europe as deliberate untruth.

Our national policy is not directed toward war. Its sole purpose is to keep war away from our country and our people.

Democracy's fight against world conquest is being greatly aided, and must be more greatly aided, by the rearmament of the United States and by sending every ounce and every ton of munitions and supplies that we can possibly spare to help the defenders who are in the front lines. It is no more unneutral for us to do that than it is for Sweden, Russia and other nations near Germany, to send steel and ore and oil and other war materials into Germany every day.

We are planning our own defense with the utmost urgency; and in its vast scale we must integrate the war needs of Britain and the other free nations resisting aggression.

This is not a matter of sentiment or of controversial personal opinion. It is a matter of realistic military policy, based on the advice of our military experts who are in close touch with existing warfare. These military and naval experts and the members of the Congress and the

Administration have a single-minded purpose — the defense of the United States.

This nation is making a great effort to produce everything that is necessary in this emergency — and with all possible speed. This great effort requires great sacrifice.

I would ask no one to defend a democracy which in turn would not defend everyone in the nation against want and privation. The strength of this nation shall not be diluted by the failure of the Government to protect the economic well-being of all citizens.

If our capacity to produce is limited by machines, it must ever be remembered that these machines are operated by the skill and the stamina of the workers. As the Government is determined to protect the rights of workers, so the nation has a right to expect that the men who man the machines will discharge their full responsibilities to the urgent needs of defense.

The worker possesses the same human dignity and is entitled to the same security of position as the engineer or manager or owner. For the workers provide the human power that turns out the destroyers, the airplanes and the tanks.

The nation expects our defense industries to continue operation without interruption by strikes or lock-outs. It expects and insists that management and workers will reconcile their differences by voluntary or legal means, to continue to produce the supplies that are so sorely needed.

And on the economic side of our great defense program, we are, as you know, bending every effort to maintain stability of prices and with that the stability of the cost of living.

Nine days ago I announced the setting up of a more effective organization to direct our gigantic efforts to increase the production of munitions. The appropriation of vast sums of money and a well coordinated executive direction of our defense efforts are not in themselves enough. Guns, planes and ships have to be built in the factories and arsenals of America. They have to be produced by workers and managers and engineers with the aid of machines which in turn have to be built by hundreds of thousands of workers throughout the land.

In this great work there has been splendid cooperation between the government and industry and labor.

American industrial genius, unmatched throughout the world in the solution of production problems, has been called upon to bring its resources and talents into action. Manufacturers of watches, of farm implements, linotypes, cash registers, automobiles, sewing machines, lawn mowers and locomotives are now making fuses, bomb packing crates, telescope mounts, shells, pistols and tanks.

But all our present efforts are not enough. We must have more ships, more guns, more planes — more of everything. This can only be accomplished if we discard the notion of "business as usual." This job cannot be done merely by superimposing on the existing productive facilities the added requirements for defense.

Our defense efforts must not be blocked by those who fear the future consequences of surplus plant capacity. The possible consequences of failure of our defense efforts now are much more to be feared.

After the present needs of our defense are past, a proper handling of the country's peacetime needs will require all of the new productive capacity — if not more.

No pessimistic policy about the future of America shall delay the immediate expansion of those industries essential to defense.

I want to make it clear that it is the purpose of the nation to build now with all possible speed every machine and arsenal and factory that we need to manufacture our defense material. We have the men — the skill — the wealth — and above all, the will.

I am confident that if and when production of consumer or luxury goods in certain industries requires the use of machines and raw materials essential for defense purposes, then such production must yield to our primary and compelling purpose.

I appeal to the owners of plants — to the managers — to the workers — to our own government employees — to put every ounce of effort into producing these munitions swiftly and without stint. And with this appeal I give you the pledge that all of us who are officers of your government will devote ourselves to the same whole-hearted extent to the great task which lies ahead.

As planes and ships and guns and shells are produced, your government, with its defense experts, can then determine how best to use them to defend this hemisphere. The decision as to how much shall be sent abroad and how much shall remain at home must be made on the basis of our over-all military necessities.

We must be the great arsenal of democracy. For us this is an emergency as serious as war itself. We must apply ourselves to our task with the same resolution, the same sense of urgency, the same spirit of patriotism and sacrifice as we would show were we at war.

We have furnished the British great material support and we will furnish far more in the future.

There will be no "bottlenecks" in our determination to aid Great

Britain. No dictator, no combination of dictators, will weaken that determination by threats of how they will construe that determination.

The British have received invaluable military support from the heroic Greek army, and from the forces of all the governments in exile. Their strength is growing. It is the strength of men and women who value their freedom more highly than they value their lives.

I believe that the Axis powers are not going to win this war. I base that belief on the latest and best information.

We have no excuse for defeatism. We have every good reason for hope — hope for peace, hope for the defense of our civilization and for the building of a better civilization in the future.

I have the profound conviction that the American people are now determined to put forth a mightier effort than they have ever yet made to increase our production of all the implements of defense, to meet the threat to our democratic faith.

As President of the United States I call for that national effort. I call for it in the name of this nation which we love and honor and which we are privileged and proud to serve. I call upon our people with absolute confidence that our common cause will greatly succeed.

(6) *Annual Message of the President (Roosevelt) to the Congress, January 6, 1941* [1]

To the Congress of the United States:

I address you, the Members of the Seventy-Seventh Congress, at a moment unprecedented in the history of the Union. I use the word "unprecedented," because at no previous time has American security been as seriously threatened from without as it is today.

Since the permanent formation of our government under the Constitution, in 1789, most of the periods of crisis in our history have related to our domestic affairs. Fortunately, only one of these — the four-year War between the States — ever threatened our national unity. Today, thank God, one hundred and thirty million Americans, in forty-eight States, have forgotten points of the compass in our national unity.

It is true that prior to 1914 the United States often had been disturbed by events in other Continents. We had even engaged in two wars with European nations and in a number of undeclared wars in the West Indies, in the Mediterranean and in the Pacific for the maintenance of

---

[1] Text from the office of the Secretary to the President; House Doc. No. 1, 77th Cong., 1st sess. This message contains the President's definition of the "Four Freedoms," see p. 33, and also p. 38.

American rights and for the principles of peaceful commerce. In no case, however, had a serious threat been raised against our national safety or our independence.

What I seek to convey is the historic truth that the United States as a nation has at all times maintained opposition to any attempt to lock us in behind an ancient Chinese wall while the procession of civilization went past. Today, thinking of our children and their children, we oppose enforced isolation for ourselves or for any part of the Americas.

That determination of ours was proved, for example, during the quarter century of wars following the French Revolution.

While the Napoleonic struggles did threaten interests of the United States because of the French foothold in the West Indies and in Louisiana, and while we engaged in the War of 1812 to vindicate our right to peaceful trade, it is, nevertheless, clear that neither France nor Great Britain nor any other nation was aiming at domination of the whole world.

In like fashion from 1815 to 1914 — 99 years — no single war in Europe or in Asia constituted a real threat against our future or against the future of any other American nation.

Except in the Maximilian interlude in Mexico, no foreign power sought to establish itself in this hemisphere; and the strength of the British fleet in the Atlantic has been a friendly strength. It is still a friendly strength.

Even when the World War broke out in 1914, it seemed to contain only small threat of danger to our own American future. But, as time went on, the American people began to visualize what the downfall of democratic nations might mean to our own democracy.

We need not over-emphasize imperfections in the Peace of Versailles. We need not harp on failure of the democracies to deal with problems of world reconstruction. We should remember that the Peace of 1919 was far less unjust than the kind of "pacification" which began even before Munich, and which is being carried on under the new order of tyranny that seeks to spread over every continent today. The American people have unalterably set their faces against that tyranny.

Every realist knows that the democratic way of life is at this moment being directly assailed in every part of the world — assailed either by arms, or by secret spreading of poisonous propaganda by those who seek to destroy unity and promote discord in nations still at peace.

During sixteen months this assault has blotted out the whole pattern of democratic life in an appalling number of independent nations, great and small. The assailants are still on the march, threatening other nations, great and small.

Therefore, as your President, performing my constitutional duty to "give to the Congress information of the state of the Union," I find it necessary to report that the future and the safety of our country and of our democracy are overwhelmingly involved in events far beyond our borders.

Armed defense of democratic existence is now being gallantly waged in four continents. If that defense fails, all the population and all the resources of Europe, Asia, Africa and Australasia will be dominated by the conquerors. The total of those populations and their resources greatly exceeds the sum total of the population and resources of the whole of the Western Hemisphere — many times over.

In times like these it is immature — and incidentally untrue — for anybody to brag that an unprepared America, single-handed, and with one hand tied behind its back, can hold off the whole world.

No realistic American can expect from a dictator's peace international generosity, or return of true independence, or world disarmament, or freedom of expression, or freedom of religion — or even good business.

Such a peace would bring no security for us or for our neighbors. "Those, who would give up essential liberty to purchase a little temporary safety, deserve neither liberty nor safety."

As a nation we may take pride in the fact that we are soft-hearted; but we cannot afford to be soft-headed.

We must always be wary of those who with sounding brass and a tinkling cymbal preach the "ism" of appeasement.

We must especially beware of that small group of selfish men who would clip the wings of the American eagle in order to feather their own nests.

I have recently pointed out how quickly the tempo of modern warfare could bring into our very midst the physical attack which we must expect if the dictator nations win this war.

There is much loose talk of our immunity from immediate and direct invasion from across the seas. Obviously, as long as the British Navy retains its power, no such danger exists. Even if there were no British Navy, it is not probable that any enemy would be stupid enough to attack us by landing troops in the United States from across thousands of miles of ocean, until it had acquired strategic bases from which to operate.

But we learn much from the lessons of the past years in Europe — particularly the lesson of Norway, whose essential seaports were captured by treachery and surprise built up over a series of years.

The first phase of the invasion of this hemisphere would not be the landing of regular troops. The necessary strategic points would be occupied by secret agents and their dupes — and great numbers of them are already here, and in Latin America.

As long as the aggressor nations maintain the offensive, they — not we — will choose the time and the place and the method of their attack.

That is why the future of all American Republics is today in serious danger.

That is why this Annual Message to the Congress is unique in our history.

That is why every member of the Executive branch of the government and every member of the Congress face great responsibility — and great accountability.

The need of the moment is that our actions and our policy should be devoted primarily — almost exclusively — to meeting this foreign peril. For all our domestic problems are now a part of the great emergency.

Just as our national policy in internal affairs has been based upon a decent respect for the rights and dignity of all our fellow-men within our gates, so our national policy in foreign affairs has been based on a decent respect for the rights and dignity of all nations, large and small. And the justice of morality must and will win in the end.

Our national policy is this:

First, by an impressive expression of the public will and without regard to partisanship, we are committed to all-inclusive national defense.

Second, by an impressive expression of the public will and without regard to partisanship, we are committed to full support of all those resolute peoples, everywhere, who are resisting aggression and are thereby keeping war away from our hemisphere. By this support, we express our determination that the democratic cause shall prevail; and we strengthen the defense and security of our own nation.

Third, by an impressive expression of the public will and without regard to partisanship, we are committed to the proposition that principles of morality and considerations for our own security will never permit us to acquiesce in a peace dictated by aggressors and sponsored by appeasers. We know that enduring peace cannot be bought at the cost of other people's freedom.

In the recent national election there was no substantial difference between the two great parties in respect to that national policy. No issue was fought out on this line before the American electorate. Today, it is abundantly evident that American citizens everywhere are demanding and supporting speedy and complete action in recognition of obvious danger.

Therefore, the immediate need is a swift and driving increase in our armament production.

Leaders of industry and labor have responded to our summons. Goals of speed have been set. In some cases these goals are being reached ahead of time; in some cases we are on schedule; in other cases there are slight but not serious delays; and in some cases — and I am sorry to say very important cases — we are all concerned by the slowness of the accomplishment of our plans.

The Army and Navy, however, have made substantial progress during the past year. Actual experience is improving and speeding up our methods of production with every passing day. And today's best is not good enough for tomorrow.

I am not satisfied with the progress thus far made. The men in charge of the program represent the best in training, ability and patriotism. They are not satisfied with the progress thus far made. None of us will be satisfied until the job is done.

No matter whether the original goal was set too high or too low, our objective is quicker and better results.

To give two illustrations:

We are behind schedule in turning out finished airplanes; we are working day and night to solve the innumerable problems and to catch up.

We are ahead of schedule in building warships; but we are working to get even further ahead of schedule.

To change a whole nation from a basis of peacetime production of implements of peace to a basis of wartime production of implements of war is no small task. And the greatest difficulty comes at the beginning of the program, when new tools and plant facilities and new assembly lines and shipways must first be constructed before the actual matériel begins to flow steadily and speedily from them.

The Congress, of course, must rightly keep itself informed at all times of the progress of the program. However, there is certain information, as the Congress itself will readily recognize, which, in the interests of our own security and those of the nations we are supporting, must of needs be kept in confidence.

New circumstances are constantly begetting new needs for our safety. I shall ask this Congress for greatly increased new appropriations and authorizations to carry on what we have begun.

I also ask this Congress for authority and for funds sufficient to manufacture additional munitions and war supplies of many kinds, to be turned over to those nations which are now in actual war with aggressor nations.

Our most useful and immediate role is to act as an arsenal for them as well as for ourselves. They do not need man power. They do need billions of dollars' worth of the weapons of defense.

The time is near when they will not be able to pay for them in ready cash. We cannot, and will not, tell them they must surrender, merely because of present inability to pay for the weapons which we know they must have.

I do not recommend that we make them a loan of dollars with which to pay for these weapons — a loan to be repaid in dollars.

I recommend that we make it possible for those nations to continue to obtain war materials in the United States, fitting their orders into our own program. Nearly all of their matériel would, if the time ever came, be useful for our own defense.

Taking counsel of expert military and naval authorities, considering what is best for our own security, we are free to decide how much should be kept here and how much should be sent abroad to our friends who by their determined and heroic resistance are giving us time in which to make ready our own defense.

For what we send abroad, we shall be repaid, within a reasonable time following the close of hostilities, in similar materials, or, at our option, in other goods of many kinds which they can produce and which we need.

Let us say to the democracies: "We Americans are vitally concerned in your defense of freedom. We are putting forth our energies, our resources and our organizing powers to give you the strength to regain and maintain a free world. We shall send you, in ever-increasing numbers, ships, planes, tanks, guns. This is our purpose and our pledge."

In fulfillment of this purpose we will not be intimidated by the threats of dictators that they will regard as a breach of international law and as an act of war our aid to the democracies which dare to resist their aggression. Such aid is not an act of war, even if a dictator should unilaterally proclaim it so to be.

When the dictators are ready to make war upon us, they will not wait for an act of war on our part. They did not wait for Norway or Belgium or the Netherlands to commit an act of war.

Their only interest is in a new one-way international law, which lacks mutuality in its observance, and, therefore, becomes an instrument of oppression.

The happiness of future generations of Americans may well depend upon how effective and how immediate we can make our aid felt. No one can tell the exact character of the emergency situations that we may be called upon to meet. The Nation's hands must not be tied when the Nation's life is in danger.

We must all prepare to make the sacrifices that the emergency — as serious as war itself — demands. Whatever stands in the way of speed and efficiency in defense preparations must give way to the national need.

A free nation has the right to expect full cooperation from all groups. A free nation has the right to look to the leaders of business, of labor, and of agriculture to take the lead in stimulating effort, not among other groups but within their own groups.

The best way of dealing with the few slackers or trouble makers in our midst is, first, to shame them by patriotic example, and, if that fails, to use the sovereignty of government to save government.

As men do not live by bread alone, they do not fight by armaments alone. Those who man our defenses, and those behind them who build our defenses, must have the stamina and courage which come from an unshakeable belief in the manner of life which they are defending. The mighty action which we are calling for cannot be based on a disregard of all things worth fighting for.

The Nation takes great satisfaction and much strength from the things which have been done to make its people conscious of their individual stake in the preservation of democratic life in America. Those things have toughened the fiber of our people, have renewed their faith and strengthened their devotion to the institutions we make ready to protect.

Certainly this is no time to stop thinking about the social and economic problems which are the root cause of the social revolution which is today a supreme factor in the world.

There is nothing mysterious about the foundations of a healthy and strong democracy. The basic things expected by our people of their political and economic systems are simple. They are:

Equality of opportunity for youth and for others.

Jobs for those who can work.

Security for those who need it.

The ending of special privilege for the few.

The preservation of civil liberties for all.

The enjoyment of the fruits of scientific progress in a wider and constantly rising standard of living.

These are the simple and basic things that must never be lost sight of in the turmoil and unbelievable complexity of our modern world. The inner and abiding strength of our economic and political systems is dependent upon the degree to which they fulfill these expectations.

Many subjects connected with our social economy call for immediate improvement.

As examples:

We should bring more citizens under the coverage of old-age pensions and unemployment insurance.

We should widen the opportunities for adequate medical care.·

We should plan a better system by which persons deserving or needing gainful employment may obtain it.

I have called for personal sacrifice. I am assured of the willingness of almost all Americans to respond to that call.

A part of the sacrifice means the payment of more money in taxes. In my budget message I recommend that a greater portion of this great defense program be paid for from taxation than we are paying today. No person should try, or be allowed, to get rich out of this program; and the principle of tax payments in accordance with ability to pay should be constantly before our eyes to guide our legislation.

If the Congress maintains these principles, the voters, putting patriotism ahead of pocketbooks, will give you their applause.

In the future days, which we seek to make secure, we look forward to a world founded upon four essential human freedoms.

The first is freedom of speech and expression — everywhere in the world.

The second is freedom of every person to worship God in his own way — everywhere in the world.

The third is freedom from want — which, translated into world terms, means economic understandings which will secure to every nation a healthy peacetime life for its inhabitants — everywhere in the world.

The fourth is freedom from fear — which, translated into world terms, means a world-wide reduction of armaments to such a point and in such a thorough fashion that no nation will be in a position to commit an act of physical aggression against any neighbor — anywhere in the world.

That is no vision of a distant millennium. It is a definite basis for a kind of world attainable in our own time and generation. That kind of world is the very antithesis of the so-called new order of tyranny which the dictators seek to create with the crash of a bomb.

To that new order we oppose the greater conception — the moral order. A good society is able to face schemes of world domination and foreign revolutions alike without fear.

Since the beginning of our American history we have been engaged in change — in a perpetual peaceful revolution — a revolution which goes on steadily, quietly adjusting itself to changing conditions — without the concentration camp or the quick-lime in the ditch. The world order which we seek is the cooperation of free countries, working together in a friendly, civilized society.

This nation has placed its destiny in the hands and heads and hearts of its millions of free men and women; and its faith in freedom under the guidance of God. Freedom means the supremacy of human rights everywhere. Our support goes to those who struggle to gain those rights or keep them. Our strength is in our unity of purpose.

To that high concept there can be no end save victory.

FRANKLIN D. ROOSEVELT

THE WHITE HOUSE
   January 6, 1941.

(7) *Address by the President (Roosevelt) to the White House Correspondents' Association, March 15, 1941* [1]

This dinner of the White House Correspondents' Association is unique. It is the first one at which I have made a speech in all these eight years. It differs from the press conferences that you and I hold twice a week. You cannot ask me any questions; and everything I have to say is word for word "*on* the record."

For eight years you and I have been helping each other. I have been trying to keep you informed of the news of Washington and of the Nation and of the world from the point of view of the Presidency. You, more than you realize it, have been giving me a great deal of information about what the people of this country are thinking.

In our press conferences, as at this dinner tonight, we include reporters representing papers and news agencies of many other lands. To most of them it is a matter of constant amazement that press conferences such as ours can exist in any nation in the world.

That is especially true in those lands where freedoms do not exist— where the purposes of our democracy and the characteristics of our country and of our people have been seriously distorted.

Such misunderstandings are not new. I remember that in the early days of the first World War the German Government received solemn assurances from their representatives in the United States that the people of America were disunited; that they cared more for peace at any

---

[1] Release of the Office of the Secretary to the President; reprinted in Department of State, *Bulletin,* IV, p. 277. The address, delivered at the annual dinner of the Association, was broadcast throughout the United States by all radio networks and broadcast, or rebroadcast, throughout the world in nine languages on long- and short-wave circuits.

price than for the preservation of ideals and freedom; that there would even be riots and revolutions in the United States if this Nation ever asserted its own interests.

Let not dictators of Europe and Asia doubt our unanimity now.

Before the present war broke out on September 1, 1939, I was more worried about the future than many people — most people. The record shows I was not worried enough.

That, however, is water over the dam. Do not let us waste time reviewing the past or fixing or dodging the blame for it. History cannot be rewritten by wishful thinking. We, the American people, are writing new history today.

The big news story of this week is this: The world has been told that we, as a united nation, realize the danger which confronts us — and that to meet that danger our democracy has gone into action.[1]

We know that although Prussian autocracy was bad enough, Nazism is far worse.

Nazi forces are not seeking mere modifications in colonial maps or in minor European boundaries. They openly seek the destruction of all elective systems of government on every continent — including our own; they seek to establish systems of government based on the regimentation of all human beings by a handful of individual rulers who have seized power by force.

These men and their hypnotized followers call this a new order. It is not new. It is not order. For order among nations presupposes something enduring — some system of justice under which individuals, over a long period of time, are willing to live. Humanity will never permanently accept a system imposed by conquest and based on slavery.

These modern tyrants find it necessary to their plans to eliminate all democracies — eliminate them one by one. The nations of Europe, and indeed we ourselves, did not appreciate that purpose. We do now. The process of the elimination of the European nations proceeded according to plan through 1939 and 1940, until the schedule was shot to pieces by the unbeatable defenders of Britain.

The enemies of democracy were wrong in their calculations for a very simple reason. They were wrong because they believed that democracy could not adjust itself to the terrible reality of a world at war.

They believed that democracy, because of its profound respect for the rights of men, would never arm itself to fight.

They believed that democracy, because of its will to live at peace with its neighbors, could not mobilize its energies even in its own defense.

[1] See Lend-Lease legislation, p. 711.

They know now that democracy can still remain democracy, and speak, and reach conclusions, and arm itself adequately for defense.

From the bureaus of propaganda of the Axis powers came the confident prophecy that the conquest of our country would be "an inside job" — a job accomplished not by overpowering invasion from without, but by disrupting confusion and disunion and moral disintegration from within.

Those who believed that knew little of our history. America is not a country which can be confounded by the appeasers, the defeatists, the backstairs manufacturers of panic. It is a country which talks out its problems in the open, where any man can hear them.

We have just now engaged in a great debate.[1] It was not limited to the halls of Congress. It was argued in every newspaper, on every wave length — over every cracker barrel in the land. It was finally settled and decided by the American people themselves.

The decisions of our democracy may be slowly arrived at. But when that decision is made, it is proclaimed not with the voice of any one man but with the voice of 130 millions. It is binding on all of us. And the world is no longer left in doubt.

This decision is the end of any attempts at appeasement in our land; the end of urging us to get along with the dictators; the end of compromise with tyranny and the forces of oppression.

The urgency is *now*.

We believe firmly that when our production output is in full swing, the democracies of the world will be able to prove that dictatorships cannot win.

But, now, the time element is of supreme importance. Every plane, every other instrument of war, old and new, which we can spare now, we will send overseas. That is commonsense strategy.

The great task of this day, the deep duty which rests upon us is to move products from the assembly lines of our factories to the battle lines of democracy — Now!

We can have speed and effectiveness if we maintain our existing unity. We do not have and never will have the false unity of a people browbeaten by threats and misled by propaganda. Ours is a unity which is possible only among free men and women who recognize the truth and face reality with intelligence and courage.

Today, at last, ours is not a partial effort. It is a total effort and that is the only way to guarantee ultimate safety.

Beginning a year ago, we started the erection of hundreds of plants and we started the training of millions of men.

[1] See Lend-Lease legislation, p. 711.

Then, at the moment the aid-to-democracies bill was passed we were ready to recommend the seven-billion-dollar appropriation[1] on the basis of capacity production as now planned.

The articles themselves cover the whole range of munitions of war and of the facilities for transporting them.

The aid-to-democracies bill was agreed to by both Houses of the Congress last Tuesday afternoon. I signed it one half hour later. Five minutes later I approved a list of articles for immediate shipment. Many of them are on their way. On Wednesday, I recommended an appropriation for new material to the extent of seven billion dollars; and the Congress is making patriotic speed in making the appropriation available.

Here in Washington, we are thinking in terms of speed, and speed now! And I hope that that watchword will find its way into every home in the Nation.

We shall have to make sacrifices — every one of us. The final extent of those sacrifices will depend upon the speed with which we act Now!

I must tell you tonight in plain language what this undertaking means to you — to your daily life.

Whether you are in the armed services; whether you are a steel worker or a stevedore; a machinist or a housewife; a farmer or a banker; a storekeeper or a manufacturer — to all of you it will mean sacrifice in behalf of country and your liberties. You will feel the impact of this gigantic effort in your daily lives. You will feel it in a way which will cause many inconveniences.

You will have to be content with lower profits from business because obviously your taxes will be higher.

You will have to work longer at your bench or your plow or your machine.

Let me make it clear that the Nation is calling for the sacrifice of some privileges but not for the sacrifice of fundamental rights. Most of us will do that willingly. That kind of sacrifice is for the common national protection and welfare; for our defense against the most ruthless brutality in history; for the ultimate victory of a way of life now so violently menaced.

A half-hearted effort on our part will lead to failure. This is no part-time job. The concepts of "business as usual" and "normalcy" must be forgotten until the task is finished. This is an all-out effort — nothing short of all-out effort will win.

[1] See "Defence Aid Supplemental Appropriation Act," approved March 27, 1941, p. 727.

We are now dedicated, from here on, to a constantly increasing tempo of production — a production greater than we now know or have ever known before — a production that does not stop and should not pause.

And so, tonight, I am appealing to the heart and to the mind of every man and every woman within our borders who loves liberty. I ask you to consider the needs of our Nation at this hour and to put aside all personal differences until our victory is won.

The light of democracy must be kept burning. To the perpetuation of this light, each must do his own share. The single effort of one individual may seem very small. But there are 130 million individuals over here. There are many more millions in Britain and elsewhere bravely shielding the great flame of democracy from the blackout of barbarism. It is not enough for us merely to trim the wick or polish the glass. The time has come when we must provide the fuel in ever-increasing amounts to keep the flame alight.

There will be no divisions of party or section or race or nationality or religion. There is not one among us who does not have a stake in the outcome of the effort in which we are now engaged.

A few weeks ago I spoke of four freedoms — freedom of speech and expression, freedom of every person to worship God in his own way, freedom from want, freedom from fear. They are the ultimate stake. They may not be immediately attainable throughout the world but humanity does move toward those ideals through democratic processes. If we fail — if democracy is superseded by slavery — then those four freedoms or even the mention of them will become forbidden things. Centuries will pass before they can be revived.

By winning now, we strengthen their meaning, we increase the stature of mankind and the dignity of human life.

There is a vast difference between the word "loyalty" and the word "obedience." Obedience can be obtained and enforced in a dictatorship by the use of threat and extortion or it can be obtained by a failure on the part of government to tell the truth to its citizens.

Loyalty is different. It springs from the mind that is given the facts, that retains ancient ideals and proceeds without coercion to give support to its own government.

That is true in England and in Greece and in China and in the United States today. And in many other countries millions of men and women are praying for the return of a day when they can give that kind of loyalty.

Loyalty cannot be bought. Dollars alone will not win this war. Let us not delude ourselves as to that.

Today, nearly a milllion and a half American citizens are hard at work in our armed forces. The spirit and the determination of these men of our Army and Navy are worthy of the highest traditions of our country. No better men ever served under Washington, or John Paul Jones, or Grant, or Lee, or Pershing. That is a boast, I admit — but it is not an idle one.

Upon the national will to sacrifice and to work depends the output of our industry and our agriculture.

Upon that will depends the survival of the vital bridge across the ocean — the bridge of ships which carry the arms and food for those who are fighting the good fight.

Upon that will depends our ability to aid other nations which may determine to offer resistance.

Upon that will may depend practical assistance to people now living in nations which have been overrun, should they find the opportunity to strike back in an effort to regain their liberties.

This will of the American people will not be frustrated either by threats from powerful enemies abroad or by small, selfish groups or individuals at home.

The determination of America must not be obstructed by war profiteering.

It must not be obstructed by unnecessary strikes of workers, by short-sighted management, or by deliberate sabotage.

For, unless we win, there will be no freedom for either management or labor.

Wise labor leaders and wise business managers will realize how necessary it is to their own existence to make common sacrifice for this great common cause.

There is no longer the slightest question or doubt that the American people recognize the extreme seriousness of the present situation. That is why they have demanded, and got, a policy of unqualified, immediate, all-out aid for Britain, Greece, China, and for all the governments in exile whose homelands are temporarily occupied by the aggressors.

From now on that aid will be increased — and yet again increased — until total victory has been won.

The British are stronger than ever in the magnificent morale which has enabled them to endure all the dark days and the shattered nights of the past 10 months. They have the full support and help of Canada, and the other dominions, of the rest of their Empire, and non-British people throughout the world who still think in terms of the great freedoms.

The British people are braced for invasion whenever the attempt may come — tomorrow — next week — next month.

In this historic crisis, Britain is blessed with a brilliant and great leader in Winston Churchill. But, no one knows better than Mr. Churchill himself, that it is not alone his stirring words and valiant deeds which give the British their superb morale. The essence of that morale is in the masses of plain people who are completely clear in their minds about the one essential fact — that they would rather die as free men than live as slaves.

These plain people — civilians as well as soldiers and sailors and airmen — women and girls as well as men and boys — are fighting in the front line of civilization, and they are holding that line with a fortitude which will forever be the pride and the inspiration of all free men on every continent and on every island of the sea.

The British people and their Grecian allies need ships. From America, they will get ships.

They need planes. From America, they will get planes.

They need food. From America, they will get food.

They need tanks and guns and ammunition and supplies of all kinds. From America, they will get tanks and guns and ammunition and supplies of all kinds.

China likewise expresses the magnificent will of millions of plain people to resist the dismemberment of their Nation. China, through the Generalissimo, Chiang Kai-shek, asks our help. America has said that China shall have our help.

Our country is going to be what our people have proclaimed it must be — the arsenal of democracy.

Our country is going to play its full part.

And when dictatorships disintegrate — and pray God that will be sooner than any of us now dares to hope — then our country must continue to play its great part in the period of world reconstruction.

We believe that the rallying cry of the dictators, their boasting about a master-race, will prove to be pure stuff and nonsense. There never has been, there isn't now, and there never will be, any race of people fit to serve as masters over their fellow-men.

The world has no use for any nation which, because of size or because of military might, asserts the right to goose-step to world power over other nations or other races. We believe that any nationality, no matter how small, has the inherent right to its own nationhood.

We believe that the men and women of such nations, no matter what size, can, through the processes of peace, serve themselves and serve the world by protecting the common man's security; improve the standards of healthful living; provide markets for manufacture and for agriculture. Through that kind of peaceful service every nation can increase its happiness, banish the terrors of war, and abandon man's inhumanity to man.

Never, in all our history, have Americans faced a job so well worthwhile. May it be said of us in the days to come that our children and our children's children rise up and call us blessed.

(8) *The Need for Spiritual Rebirth. Statement of the Secretary of State (Hull), March 22, 1941* [1]

There are at work in the world today powerful forces the significance of which no individual and no nation can ignore without falling into a position of the gravest danger and of the utmost jeopardy. These forces are not new in the experience of mankind. They rose on many occasions in the past and, for varying periods and with varying intensity, held sway over human affairs. They spring today from the same source from which they have always sprung in the past — from godless and soulless lust for power which seeks to hold men in physical slavery and spiritual degradation and to displace a system of peaceful and orderly relations among nations by the anarchy of wanton violence and brute force.

These massed forces of lust for tyrannical power are directed against the very bases of the way of life which has come to be the cherished ideal of a preponderant majority of mankind — against the moral, spiritual, social, political, and economic foundations of modern civilization. Nation after nation has been crushed into surrender, overrun and enslaved by the exercise of brute force combined with fraud and guile. And as the dismal darkness descends upon more and more of the earth's surface, its menacing shadow falls blacker and blacker athwart our continent. The very instinct of self-preservation bids us beware.

We have the power to meet that menace successfully. For that we need material means of defense. These means we are determined to create, and we are creating them. But more than that is needed.

Men will defend to the utmost only that in which they have complete faith. No more vital test has ever confronted the American people than that which confronts it today. There are difficult and dangerous times ahead. Our national independence and our cherished institutions are not immune from the challenge of the lust for power that already stalks so much of the earth's surface. Unprecedented effort and heavy sacrifices

[1] Department of State, *Bulletin*, IV, p. 335.

will be required of us as the price of preserving, for ourselves and for our posterity, the kind of America that has been fostered and preserved for us by the vigilance, courage, and sacrifice of those who preceded us. We shall succeed if we retain unimpaired the most precious heritage which they bequeathed us — an unshakable faith in the everlasting worth of freedom and honor, of truth and justice, of intellectual and spiritual integrity, a triumphant faith in God.

Without that faith, no material means of defense will suffice. With it, we need fear no enemy outside or within our borders.

We need today a resurgence of spiritual purpose and of moral stamina. We must re-dedicate ourselves to the service, the defense, and the nurturing of freedom under justice and law. Our homes, our schools, our churches, our leaders in every walk of life must inculcate this faith and this spirit.

Our churches, particularly, have an exceptionally important role to play in this work of spiritual rebirth. The terrible misfortunes which are being visited upon mankind have been the result of a dangerous deterioration of standards of personal and of national conduct. We desperately need today a revival of religious fervor, a renewed humility before God in support of wholehearted adherence to high standards of individual and group behavior.

In times of grave crises, there are always some who fall a prey to doubt and unreasoning fear; some who seek refuge in cynicism and narrow self-interest; some who wrap themselves in the treacherous cloak of complacency. All these are dangers that lie within us.

Each and every one of us must search his mind and his heart for these signs of fatal weakness. The stern realities of the crisis which is upon us call, as never before, for vision and for loyalty. They call for all the strength of hand, of mind, and of spirit that we can muster. They call for self-reliance, for self-restraint, for self-imposed and freely accepted discipline. They call for the kind of national unity that can be achieved only by free men, invincible in their resolve that human freedom must not perish. They call for unselfish service today if we are to win through to a secure and bright tomorrow.

A responsibility seldom equalled in gravity and danger rests upon each and every one of us. Neglect or delay in assuming it, willingly and fully, would place in mortal danger our way of life and the sacred cause of human freedom. Were we to fail in that responsibility, we would fail ourselves; we would fail the generations that went before us; we would fail the generations that are to come after us; we would fail mankind; we would fail God.

I am supremely confident that we shall not fail. I am certain that in the minds and hearts of our people still lie welling springs — inexhaustible and indestructible — of faith in the things we cherish, of courage and determination to defend them, of sacrificial devotion, of unbreakable unity of purpose. I am certain that, however great the hardships and the trials which loom ahead, our America will endure, and the cause of human freedom will triumph.

(9) *Address by the Secretary of the Navy (Knox), April 24, 1941* [1]

[Excerpt]

As Secretary of the Navy, of course, I do have access to intimate details of information, from all parts of the world, that are not available to all, but this larger and more intimate knowledge in nowise changes the general aspect of the world situation as it is set forth daily in your publication and mine.

What we all see is an America which is gradually becoming encircled by military powers whose ideals, institutions and methods are all of them irreconcilably antagonistic to our ideals, institutions and methods. These same powers have also openly and repeatedly proclaimed themselves our enemies, and these openly avowed enemies have joined themselves together in a pact which they do not hesitate to say is aimed at us, and at us alone!

The only reason that this hostile pact, admittedly aimed at us, has not resulted in open warfare upon us has been because it does not suit the present purpose of these powers to engage in war with us. Whenever, in the judgment of the Axis powers, it better suits their purpose to begin hostilities, hostilities will begin, and nothing that we can do, save prostrating ourselves in abject surrender, will change this.

For months, there has been almost complete suspension of all direct contact between the United States and all of Europe, save Britain alone. Across the course of the ships that ply this single route have been flung an enlarged fleet, no one knows how numerous, of submarines — submarines which, due to scientific discoveries, are vastly more effective than they were in the last war. The sea-going range of these submarines has been immensely increased, and the field of their activity steadily expands westward, far over the line which divides the Atlantic between Europe and America.

[1] Navy Department release. The address was delivered at the annual dinner of the Bureau of Advertising of the American Newspaper Publishers' Association, Waldorf-Astoria, New York City.

Possession of convenient bases on the French Coast has added a whole fleet of surface raiders — ships of high speed, and some of them of great gun power, which prey disastrously upon the commerce between Britain and America. Finally, from bases in northern Norway and western France, huge fleets of heavy bombers circle back and forth to add terror from the skies to the dangers that lurk along the sea lanes leading to a beleaguered England. Steadily the toll of lost ships mounts far faster than replacements can be made.

To the southward of conquered Europe lies the Mediterranean, an accustomed highway for our ocean commerce in times of peace. Today the Mediterranean is forbidden waters. On its bosom ply only the craft that carry supplies to fighting armies, and the British and Italian men-of-war who fight for its control. Gone is all of our contact with the nations that border that sea.

The great continent of Africa, itself a field for contending armies, offers no ports for our merchantmen's trade. Its western coast, which thrusts itself halfway across the South Atlantic, affording an excellent base for operations against the southern half of the Western Hemisphere, is denied our commerce. Whether we swing eastward around the Cape of Good Hope or to the westward through the Straits of Magellan, we find enemy raider-infested seas. At the end of our journey, go we westward or eastward, we encounter an Axis partner who openly proclaims he entered that partnership in an effort to prevent us from interfering with their policies of ruthless military aggression.

The latest link in this chain of encirclement that is being forged by the Axis powers is the recently announced agreement between Russia and Japan.[1]

Russia was not in any peril of attack by Japan. Japan not only has her hands full, and more than full, in her attempt to subjugate Southern China by force of arms, but her aspirations are not northward. They are southward. Japan imperatively needed assurance that she would not be attacked in the north while she was pressing her designs in the south. Just how much assurance Japan feels that her Manchukuo border is safe, I do not know, but whatever that assurance may be it enhances the likelihood of an expansion of hostilities by Japan into a region which is one of the sources of critical war materials for both Great Britain and ourselves. The conclusion of this pact is certain to strengthen the hand of the war party in Japan.

Japan's promise, on the other hand, not to help Hitler if Hitler should attack Russia, is an empty promise. Japan could not help Russia in

[1] See Neutrality Pact between Japan and Soviet Union, p. 291.

Europe if she wanted to, and Hitler does not need the help of Japan for such a purpose.

The end, therefore, of this deal between Russia and Japan which tightens the circle around us, leaves Russia quite as likely an object of attack by Hitler as she was before the deal was made, and leaves Japan free from any Russian interference in the Far East. Summed up in military terms, the Russo-Japanese agreement makes Japan more secure as she pursues her dream of domination of all Eastern Asia and leaves Russia no stronger in the event of an attempted Nazi seizure of the Ukraine.

Thus, everywhere as we estimate the situation the world around, the pressure on us grows — through Libya; through Egypt and the Suez; through Yugoslavia and across to the sea; from the western coast of Africa to South America; through the Pacific to the Dutch Netherlands, and, most vital of all, across the broad North Atlantic from German bases in France and Norway now to Greenland. German strategy — world strategy, carefully planned and efficiently executed — is becoming clearer each day. German aspirations for world dominion can no longer be mistaken. The jaws of the Nazi trap are closing.

How long will we remain bemused and stupefied while the Axis powers press their plans for our isolation and ultimate defeat? Wherein lies the difference between what Germany has done to her earlier victims and what she is doing to us? First, the bland and hypocritical assurance that she has no hostile plans. That is what she told Poland when she signed the Polish nonaggression pact. Then, the organization of a skillfully integrated information service that would lay bare our weaknesses, our internal divisions and our vulnerable spots just as she did in France; and then, the organization of her Fifth Columns, not yet loosed to the maximum but sufficiently active to warn us unmistakably of their presence, just as she did in Norway. Next, a steady encirclement and seizure of vantage points from which to launch her attack, just exactly as she has just done in Yugoslavia. Why, we even emulate the Axis victims in our psychology. We think we can escape while all the rest of the world suffers. We keep alive a wretched partisanship when a united patriotism should characterize our thinking. We refuse to believe that the Axis powers even intend to attack us, or could be successful if they did. We refuse to face the realities of the situation in South America, the protection of which from successful invasion is a primary condition of our defense.

In that great region to the south of us, readily available as a base for an attack upon us, there is neither the military nor naval power to resist against invasion. In our fatuous complacency we ignore that in the present economic set-up, the tug of self-interest comes from Europe and not from North America. We fail to give due consideration to the size and significance of the subversive, pro-Nazi elements in many of the countries in that region — subversive elements that would speedily promote revolutionary chaos to the advantage of the Axis itself. Many of us fail to face what it will mean to our security if the Axis powers once gained a foothold close to our borders. We ignore what that might mean to the safety of the Panama Canal, the most vital line of communication under the American flag. Too few of us realize, and still fewer acknowledge, the size of the disaster to American hemispheric safety if Germany, already the conqueror of France, should establish herself in Dakar, a French colonial possession. From there, with her surface ships, submarines and long-range bombers, a victorious Germany could substantially cut us off from all commerce with South America and make of the Monroe Doctrine a scrap of paper.

Finally, some of the very blind among us refuse to see what will be the inevitable result if the final link in the chain of our encirclement is forged and the battle of the Atlantic is lost and England succumbs with her fleet sunk or captured.

This is but a partial, withal a brutally blunt, summary of the strategy of encirclement of which we are the victims.

Before we attempt an inventory of the measures we could take to meet this growing menace, this obvious encirclement, let us thoroughly digest this fact: Suppose this should happen — that our encirclement and isolation were complete and England had fallen, we then will be given but two choices — the choice of surrender or the choice of fighting. We won't surrender and we will fight. No one who knows about America and Americans doubts that. Consequently, we must fight ultimately unless we find and put into effect measures that will enable Britain to win without our fighting. We have already gone far in this direction. We have declared that the fight that England is making is our fight. We have likewise affirmed that the enemies she is fighting are our enemies. We have denounced, without reserve, Axis aggression, Axis faithlessness to treaties, Axis brutal and murderous disregard of international good faith, and we have said, with an overwhelming public approval of this statement, that we are in the fight to stay until victory for human liberty, for justice and for good faith is won.

We have made our productive facilities available to those who are fighting the Axis. We have loaned them much of our military equipment although we had insufficient for our own defense. We have passed the

Lease-Lend Bill and appropriated seven billion dollars to implement that bill by an almost unanimous vote of our Congress. We have opened up our yards and docks for the repair of British men-of-war and merchantmen. We have assumed protection of Greenland. We have removed restrictions on American flagships sailing to zones where fighting is over so that we might relieve Britain of the burden of supplying the armies fighting in that theatre.

We have gone a long way, and all of it with the support of an overwhelming public opinion. Incidentally, the latest test of public opinion discloses the American nation to be approximately 70 per cent for aid to Britain even at the risk of war.

Having gone thus far, we cannot back down. There is no retracing our steps. We have committed ourselves in this world struggle. If we should attempt to back down now, England would go down to catastrophic defeat and we would face a world-wide victorious Germany and her allies whom we should have to fight alone.

We have declared that the aggressor nations must not be permitted to win. We have irrevocably committed ourselves to see that that is prevented. We have put all of our resources into the scales to bring defeat to those who would rule the world by force. We have acknowledged that our destiny just as much as the destiny of the British Empire and the ultimate destiny of the conquered peoples of the Low Countries, of Scandinavia, of France and of the Balkans are at stake.

Having gone thus far, we can only go on.

Hitler cannot allow our war supplies and food to reach England — he will be defeated if they do. We cannot allow our goods to be sunk in the Atlantic — we shall be beaten if they do. We must make our promise good to give aid to Britain. We must see the job through. All of this is needed for our own safety and our future security. This is our fight. The American people have recognized the catastrophic quality of a totalitarian victory and by overwhelming majority they have endorsed every step along the progress we have made to our present posture.

Proclaiming, as we do, our faith in the ultimate victory of the good over evil, our devotion to the cause of human liberty, our century and a half of the pursuit of justice between men on terms of equality, we can no longer occupy the immoral and craven position of asking others to make all the sacrifice for this victory which we recognize as so essential to us. Our manhood and our self-respect demand that we shall assume our part of the burden.

(10) *Address by the President* (*Roosevelt*), *May 27, 1941* [1]

I am speaking tonight from the White House in the presence of the Governing Board of the Pan American Union, the Canadian Minister, and their families. The members of this Board are the Ambassadors and Ministers of the American Republics in Washington. It is appropriate that I do this. Now, as never before, the unity of the American Republics is of supreme importance to each and every one of us and to the cause of freedom throughout the world. Our future independence is bound up with the future independence of all of our sister Republics.

The pressing problems that confront us are military problems. We cannot afford to approach them from the point of view of wishful thinkers or sentimentalists. What we face is cold, hard fact.

The first and fundamental fact is that what started as a European war has developed, as the Nazis always intended it should develop, into a world war for world domination.

Adolf Hitler never considered the domination of Europe as an end in itself. European conquest was but a step toward ultimate goals in all the other continents. It is unmistakably apparent to all of us that, unless the advance of Hitlerism is forcibly checked now, the Western Hemisphere will be within range of the Nazi weapons of destruction.

For our own defense we have accordingly undertaken certain obviously necessary measures.

First, we joined in concluding a series of agreements with all the other American Republics. This further solidified our hemisphere against the common danger.

And then, a year ago, we launched, and are successfully carrying out, the largest armament production program we have ever undertaken.

We have added substantially to our splendid Navy, and we have mustered our manpower to build up a new Army which is already worthy of the highest traditions of our military service.

We instituted a policy of aid for the democracies — the nations which have fought for the continuation of human liberties.

This policy had its origin in the first month of the war, when I urged upon the Congress repeal of the arms embargo provisions in the Neutrality Law. In that message of September 1939, I said, "I should like to be able to offer the hope that the shadow over the world might swiftly

---

[1] Text from the Office of the Secretary to the President. The address was broadcast over all national networks, transmitted during delivery in Spanish and Portuguese to Latin America and rebroadcast in the German, Italian, French, Polish and Serbian languages. (Department of State, *Bulletin*, V, p. 647).

pass. I cannot. The facts compel my stating, with candor, that darker periods may lie ahead."

In the subsequent months, the shadows deepened and lengthened. And the night spread over Poland, Denmark, Norway, Holland, Belgium, Luxemburg, and France.

In June 1940, Britain stood alone, faced by the same machine of terror which had overwhelmed her allies. Our Government rushed arms to meet her desperate needs.

In September 1940, an agreement was completed with Great Britain for the trade of fifty destroyers for eight important off-shore bases.

In March 1941, the Congress passed the Lend-Lease Bill and an appropriation of seven billion dollars to implement it. This law realistically provided for material aid "for the government of any country whose defense the President deems vital to the defense of the United States."

Our whole program of aid for the democracies has been based on hard-headed concern for our own security and for the kind of safe and civilized world in which we wish to live. Every dollar of material we send helps to keep the dictators away from our own hemisphere. Every day that they are held off gives us time to build more guns and tanks and planes and ships.

We have made no pretense about our own self-interest in this aid. Great Britain understands it — and so does Nazi Germany.

And now — after a year — Britain still fights gallantly, on a "far-flung battle line." We have doubled and redoubled our vast production, increasing, month by month, our material supply of tools of war for ourselves and Britain and China — and eventually for all the democracies.

The supply of these tools will not fail — it will increase.

With greatly augmented strength, the United States and the other American Republics now chart their course in the situation of today.

Your Government knows what terms Hitler, if victorious, would impose. They are, indeed, the only terms on which he would accept a so-called "negotiated" peace.

Under those terms, Germany would literally parcel out the world — hoisting the swastika itself over vast territories and populations, and setting up puppet governments of its own choosing, wholly subject to the will and the policy of a conqueror.

To the people of the Americas, a triumphant Hitler would say, as he said after the seizure of Austria, and after Munich, and after the seizure of Czechoslovakia: "I am now completely satisfied. This is the last territorial readjustment I will seek." And he would of course add:

"All we want is peace, friendship, and profitable trade relations with you in the New World."

And were any of us in the Americas so incredibly simple and forgetful as to accept those honeyed words, what would then happen?

Those in the New World who were seeking profits would be urging that all that the dictatorships desired was "peace." They would oppose toil and taxes for more American armament. Meanwhile, the dictatorships would be forcing the enslaved peoples of their Old World conquests into a system they are even now organizing — to build a naval and air force intended to gain and hold and be master of the Atlantic and the Pacific as well.

They would fasten an economic stranglehold upon our several nations. Quislings would be found to subvert the governments in our Republics; and the Nazis would back their Fifth Columns with invasion, if necessary.

I am not speculating about all this. I merely repeat what is already in the Nazi book of world conquest. They plan to treat the Latin American nations as they are now treating the Balkans. They plan then to strangle the United States of America and the Dominion of Canada.

The American laborer would have to compete with slave labor in the rest of the world. Minimum wages, maximum hours? Nonsense! Wages and hours would be fixed by Hitler. The dignity and power and standard of living of the American worker and farmer would be gone. Trade unions would become historical relics, and collective bargaining a joke.

Farm income? What happens to all farm surpluses without any foreign trade? The American farmer would get for his products exactly what Hitler wanted to give. He would face obvious disaster and complete regimentation.

Tariff walls — Chinese walls of isolation — would be futile. Freedom to trade is essential to our economic life. We do not eat all the food we can produce; we do not burn all the oil we can pump; we do not use all the goods we can manufacture. It would not be an American wall to keep Nazi goods out; it would be a Nazi wall to keep us in.

The whole fabric of working life as we know it — business, manufacturing, mining, agriculture — all would be mangled and crippled under such a system. Yet to maintain even that crippled independence would require permanent conscription of our manpower; it would curtail the funds we could spend on education, on housing, on public works, on flood control, on health. Instead, we should be permanently pouring our resources into armaments; and, year in and year out, standing day and night watch against the destruction of our cities.

Even our right of worship would be threatened. The Nazi world does not recognize any God except Hitler; for the Nazis are as ruthless as the Communists in the denial of God. What place has religion which preaches the dignity of the human being, of the majesty of the human soul, in a world where moral standards are measured by treachery and bribery and Fifth Columnists? Will our children, too, wander off, goose-stepping in search of new gods?

We do not accept, and will not permit, this Nazi "shape of things to come." It will never be forced upon us, if we act in this present crisis with the wisdom and the courage which have distinguished our country in all the crises of the past.

The Nazis have taken military possession of the greater part of Europe. In Africa they have occupied Tripoli and Libya, and they are threatening Egypt, the Suez Canal, and the Near East. But their plans do not stop there, for the Indian Ocean is the gateway to the East.

They also have the armed power at any moment to occupy Spain and Portugal; and that threat extends not only to French North Africa and the western end of the Mediterranean, but also to the Atlantic fortress of Dakar, and to the island outposts of the New World — the Azores and Cape Verde Islands.

The Cape Verde Islands are only seven hours' distance from Brazil by bomber or troop-carrying planes. They dominate shipping routes to and from the South Atlantic.

The war is approaching the brink of the Western Hemisphere itself. It is coming very close to home.

Control or occupation by Nazi forces of any of the islands of the Atlantic would jeopardize the immediate safety of portions of North and South America, and of the island possessions of the United States, and of the ultimate safety of the continental United States itself.

Hitler's plan of world domination would be near its accomplishment today, were it not for two factors: One is the epic resistance of Britain, her colonies, and the great Dominions, fighting not only to maintain the existence of the Island of Britain, but also to hold the Near East and Africa. The other is the magnificent defense of China, which will, I have reason to believe, increase in strength. All of these, together, prevent the Axis from winning control of the seas by ships and aircraft.

The Axis powers can never achieve their objective of world domination unless they first obtain control of the seas. This is their supreme purpose today; and to achieve it, they must capture Great Britain.

They could then have the power to dictate to the Western Hemisphere. No spurious argument, no appeal to sentiment, and no false pledges like those given by Hitler at Munich, can deceive the American people into believing that he and his Axis partners would not, with Britain defeated, close in relentlessly on this hemisphere.

But if the Axis powers fail to gain control of the seas, they are certainly defeated. Their dreams of world domination will then go by the board; and the criminal leaders who started this war will suffer inevitable disaster.

Both they and their people know this — and they are afraid. That is why they are risking everything they have, conducting desperate attempts to break through to the command of the ocean. Once they are limited to a continuing land war, their cruel forces of occupation will be unable to keep their heel on the necks of the millions of innocent, oppressed peoples on the Continent of Europe; and in the end, their whole structure will break into little pieces. And the wider the Nazi land effort, the greater the danger.

We do not forget the silenced peoples. The masters of Germany — those, at least, who have not been assassinated or escaped to free soil — have marked these peoples and their children's children for slavery. But those people — spiritually unconquered: Austrians, Czechs, Poles, Norwegians, Dutch, Belgians, Frenchmen, Greeks, Southern Slavs — yes, even those Italians and Germans who themselves have been enslaved — will prove to be a powerful force in disrupting the Nazi system.

Yes, all freedom — meaning freedom to live, and not freedom to conquer and subjugate other peoples — depends on freedom of the seas. All of American history — North, Central and South American history — has been inevitably tied up with those words, "freedom of the seas."

Since 1799, when our infant Navy made the West Indies and the Caribbean and the Gulf of Mexico safe for American ships; since 1804 and 1805 when we made all peaceful commerce safe from the depredations of the Barbary pirates; since the War of 1812, which was fought for the preservation of sailors' rights; since 1867, when our sea power made it possible for the Mexicans to expel the French Army of Louis Napoleon, we have striven and fought in defense of freedom of the seas — for our own shipping, for the commerce of our sister Republics, for the right of all nations to use the highways of world trade — and for our own safety.

During the first World War we were able to escort merchant ships by the use of small cruisers, gunboats and destroyers; and this type of convoy was effective against submarines. In this second World War, however, the problem is greater, because the attack on the freedom of the seas is now fourfold: first — the improved submarine; second — the much greater use of the heavily armed raiding cruiser or hit-and-run battleship; third — the bombing airplane, which is capable of destroying merchant ships seven or eight hundred miles from its nearest base; and fourth — the destruction of merchant ships in those ports of the world which are accessible to bombing attack.

The battle of the Atlantic now extends from the icy waters of the North Pole to the frozen continent of the Antarctic. Throughout this huge area, there have been sinkings of merchant ships in alarming and increasing numbers by Nazi raiders or submarines. There have been sinkings even of ships carrying neutral flags. There have been sinkings in the South Atlantic, off West Africa and the Cape Verde Islands; between the Azores and the islands off the American coast; and between Greenland and Iceland. Great numbers of these sinkings have been actually within the waters of the Western Hemisphere.

The blunt truth is this — and I reveal this with the full knowledge of the British government: the present rate of Nazi sinkings of merchant ships is more than three times as high as the capacity of British shipyards to replace them; it is more than twice the combined British and American output of merchant ships today.

We can answer this peril by two simultaneous measures: first, by speeding up and increasing our great shipbuilding program; and second, by helping to cut down the losses on the high seas.

Attacks on shipping off the very shores of land which we are determined to protect, present an actual military danger to the Americas. And that danger has recently been heavily underlined by the presence in Western Hemisphere waters of Nazi battleships of great striking power.

Most of the supplies for Britain go by a northerly route, which comes close to Greenland and the nearby island of Iceland. Germany's heaviest attack is on that route. Nazi occupation of Iceland or bases in Greenland would bring the war close to our continental shores; because they are stepping-stones to Labrador, Newfoundland, Nova Scotia, and the northern United States, including the great industrial centers of the north, east and the middle west.

Equally, the Azores and the Cape Verde Islands, if occupied or controlled by Germany, would directly endanger the freedom of the Atlantic and our own physical safety. Under German domination they would become bases for submarines, warships, and airplanes raiding the waters which lie immediately off our own coasts and attacking the shipping in the South Atlantic. They would provide a springboard for actual attack against the integrity and independence of Brazil and her neighboring Republics.

I have said on many occasions that the United States is mustering its men and its resources only for purposes of defense — only to repel attack. I repeat that statement now. But we must be realistic when we use the word "attack"; we have to relate it to the lightning speed of modern warfare.

Some people seem to think that we are not attacked until bombs actually drop on New York or San Francisco or New Orleans or Chicago. But they are simply shutting their eyes to the lesson we must learn from the fate of every nation that the Nazis have conquered.

The attack on Czechoslovakia began with the conquest of Austria. The attack on Norway began with the occupation of Denmark. The attack on Greece began with occupation of Albania and Bulgaria. The attack on the Suez Canal began with the invasion of the Balkans and North Africa. The attack on the United States can begin with the domination of any base which menaces our security — north or south.

Nobody can foretell tonight just when the acts of the dictators will ripen into attack on this hemisphere and us. But we know enough by now to realize that it would be suicide to wait until they are in our front yard.

When your enemy comes at you in a tank or a bombing plane, if you hold your fire until you see the whites of his eyes, you will never know what hit you. Our Bunker Hill of tomorrow may be several thousand miles from Boston.

Anyone with an atlas and a reasonable knowledge of the sudden striking force of modern war, knows that it is stupid to wait until a probable enemy has gained a foothold from which to attack. Old-fashioned common sense calls for the use of a strategy which will prevent such an enemy from gaining a foothold in the first place.

We have, accordingly, extended our patrol in north and south Atlantic waters. We are steadily adding more and more ships and planes to that patrol. It is well known that the strength of the Atlantic Fleet has been greatly increased during the past year, and is constantly being built up.

These ships and planes warn of the presence of attacking raiders, on the sea, under the sea, and above the sea. The danger from these raiders is greatly lessened if their location is definitely known. We are thus being forewarned; and we shall be on our guard against efforts to establish Nazi bases closer to our hemisphere.

The deadly facts of war compel nations, for simple self-preservation, to make stern choices. It does not make sense, for instance, to say, "I believe in the defense of all the Western Hemisphere," and in the next breath to say, "I will not fight for that defense until the enemy has landed on our shores." And if we believe in the independence and integrity of the Americas, we must be willing to fight to defend them just as much as we would to fight for the safety of our own homes.

It is time for us to realize that the safety of American homes even in the center of our country has a definite relationship to the continued safety of homes in Nova Scotia or Trinidad or Brazil.

Our national policy today, therefore, is this:

First, we shall actively resist wherever necessary, and with all our resources, every attempt by Hitler to extend his Nazi domination to the Western Hemisphere, or to threaten it. We shall actively resist his every attempt to gain control of the seas. We insist upon the vital importance of keeping Hitlerism away from any point in the world which could be used and would be used as a base of attack against the Americas.

Second, from the point of view of strict naval and military necessity, we shall give every possible assistance to Britain and to all who, with Britain, are resisting Hitlerism or its equivalent with force of arms. Our patrols are helping now to insure delivery of the needed supplies to Britain. All additional measures necessary to deliver the goods will be taken. Any and all further methods or combination of methods, which can or should be utilized, are being devised by our military and naval technicians, who, with me, will work out and put into effect such new and additional safeguards as may be needed.

The delivery of needed supplies to Britain is imperative. This can be done; it must be done; it will be done.

To the other American nations — twenty Republics and the Dominion of Canada — I say this: the United States does not merely propose these purposes, but is actively engaged today in carrying them out.

I say to them further: you may disregard those few citizens of the United States who contend that we are disunited and cannot act.

There are some timid ones among us who say that we must preserve peace at any price — lest we lose our liberties forever. To them I say: never in the history of the world has a nation lost its democracy by a successful struggle to defend its democracy. We must not be defeated by the fear of the very danger which we are preparing to resist. Our freedom has shown its ability to survive war, but it would never survive surrender. "The only thing we have to fear is fear itself."

There is, of course, a small group of sincere, patriotic men and women whose real passion for peace has shut their eyes to the ugly realities of international banditry and to the need to resist it at all costs. I am sure they are embarrassed by the sinister support they are receiving from the enemies of democracy in our midst — the Bundists, and Fascists, and

Communists, and every group devoted to bigotry and racial and religious intolerance. It is no mere coincidence that all the arguments put forward by these enemies of democracy — all their attempts to confuse and divide our people and to destroy public confidence in our Government — all their defeatist forebodings that Britain and democracy are already beaten — all their selfish promises that we can "do business" with Hitler — all of these are but echoes of the words that have been poured out from the Axis bureaus of propaganda. Those same words have been used before in other countries — to scare them, to divide them, to soften them up. Invariably, those same words have formed the advance guard of physical attack.

Your Government has the right to expect of all citizens that they take loyal part in the common work of our common defense — take loyal part from this moment forward.

I have recently set up the machinery for civilian defense. It will rapidly organize, locality by locality. It will depend on the organized effort of men and women everywhere. All will have responsibilities to fulfill.

Defense today means more than merely fighting. It means morale, civilian as well as military; it means using every available resource; it means enlarging every useful plant. It means the use of a greater American common sense in discarding rumor and distorted statement. It means recognizing, for what they are, racketeers and Fifth Columnists, who are the incendiary bombs of the moment.

All of us know that we have made very great social progress in recent years. We propose to maintain that progress and strengthen it. When the nation is threatened from without, however, as it is today, the actual production and transportation of the machinery of defense must not be interrupted by disputes between capital and capital, labor and labor, or capital and labor. The future of all free enterprise — of capital and labor alike — is at stake.

This is no time for capital to make, or be allowed to retain, excess profits. Articles of defense must have undisputed right of way in every industrial plant in the country.

A nation-wide machinery for conciliation and mediation of industrial disputes has been set up. That machinery must be used promptly — and without stoppage of work. Collective bargaining will be retained, but the American people expect that impartial recommendations of our Government services will be followed both by capital and by labor.

The overwhelming majority of our citizens expect their Government to see that the tools of defense are built; and for the very purpose of preserving the democratic safeguards of both labor and management, this Government is determined to use all of its power to express the will of its people, and to prevent interference with the production of materials essential to our nation's security.

Today the whole world is divided between human slavery and human freedom — between pagan brutality and the Christian ideal.

We choose human freedom — which is the Christian ideal.

No one of us can waver for a moment in his courage or his faith.

We will not accept a Hitler dominated world. And we will not accept a world, like the postwar world of the 1920's, in which the seeds of Hitlerism can again be planted and allowed to grow.

We will accept only a world consecrated to freedom of speech and expression — freedom of every person to worship God in his own way — freedom from want — and freedom from terrorism.

Is such a world impossible of attainment?

Magna Carta, the Declaration of Independence, the Constitution of the United States, the Emancipation Proclamation and every other milestone in human progress — all were ideals which seemed impossible of attainment — yet they were attained.

As a military force, we were weak when we established our independence, but we successfully stood off tyrants, powerful in their day, who are now lost in the dust of history.

Odds meant nothing to us then. Shall we now, with all our potential strength, hesitate to take every single measure necessary to maintain our American liberties?

Our people and our Government will not hesitate to meet that challenge.

As the President of a united and determined people, I say solemnly:

We reassert the ancient American doctrine of freedom of the seas.

We reassert the solidarity of the twenty-one American Republics and the Dominion of Canada in the preservation of the independence of the hemisphere.

We have pledged material support to the other democracies of the world — and we will fulfill that pledge.

We in the Americas will decide for ourselves whether, and when, and where, our American interests are attacked or our security threatened.

We are placing our armed forces in strategic military position.

We will not hesitate to use our armed forces to repel attack.

We reassert our abiding faith in the vitality of our constitutional republic as a perpetual home of freedom, of tolerance, and of devotion to the word of God.

Therefore, with profound consciousness of my responsibilities to my countrymen and to my country's cause, I have tonight issued a proclamation[1] that an unlimited national emergency exists and requires the strengthening of our defense to the extreme limit of our national power and authority.

The nation will expect all individuals and all groups to play their full parts, without stint, and without selfishness, and without doubt that our democracy will triumphantly survive.

I repeat the words of the Signers of the Declaration of Independence — that little band of patriots, fighting long ago against overwhelming odds, but certain, as are we, of ultimate victory: "With a firm reliance on the protection of Divine Providence, we mutually pledge to each other our lives, our fortunes, and our sacred honor."

(11) *Message of the President* (*Roosevelt*) *to Congress on the Sinking of the* Robin Moor, *June 20, 1941* [2]

The correspondence respecting the sinking of the *Robin Moor* is printed at p. 417. The message is presented here because the occasion was taken to derive from the incident a formal commitment of general policy.

TO THE CONGRESS OF THE UNITED STATES OF AMERICA:

I am under the necessity of bringing to the attention of the Congress the ruthless sinking by a German submarine on May 21 of an American ship, the *Robin Moor*, in the South Atlantic Ocean (25° 40′ West, 6° 10′ North) while the vessel was on the high seas en route to South Africa.

According to the formal depositions of survivors the vessel was sunk within 30 minutes from the time of the first warning given by the Commander of the submarine to an officer of the *Robin Moor*.

The submarine did not display its flag, and the Commander did not announce its nationality.

The *Robin Moor* was sunk without provision for the safety of the passengers and crew.

It was sunk despite the fact that its American nationality was admittedly known to the Commander of the submarine and that its nationality was likewise clearly indicated by the flag and other markings.

The sinking of this American ship by a German submarine flagrantly violated the right of United States vessels freely to navigate the seas subject only to a belligerent right accepted under international law.

---

[1] For text, see p. 754.

[2] Department of State, *Bulletin*, IV, p. 741; S. Doc. 71 and H. Doc. 285, 77th Cong., 1st sess.

This belligerent right, as is known to the German Government, does not include the right deliberately to sink a merchant vessel, leaving the passengers and crew to the mercies of the elements. On the contrary the belligerent is required to place the passengers and crew in places of safety.

The passengers and crew of the *Robin Moor* were left afloat in small lifeboats from approximately two to three weeks when they were accidentally discovered and rescued by friendly vessels. This chance rescue does not lessen the brutality of casting the boats adrift in midocean.

The total disregard shown for the most elementary principles of international law and of humanity brands the sinking of the *Robin Moor* as the act of an international outlaw.

The Government of the United States holds Germany responsible for the outrageous and indefensible sinking of the *Robin Moor*. Full reparation for the losses and damages suffered by American nationals will be expected from the German Government.

Our Government believes that freedom from cruelty and inhuman treatment is a natural right. It is not a grace to be given or withheld at the will of those temporarily in a position to exert force over defenseless people.

Were this incident capable of being regarded apart from a more general background, its implications might be less serious — but it must be interpreted in the light of a declared and actively pursued policy of frightfulness and intimidation which has been used by the German Reich as an instrument of international policy.

The present leaders of the German Reich have not hesitated to engage in acts of cruelty and many other forms of terror against the innocent and the helpless in other countries, apparently in the belief that methods of terrorism will lead to a state of affairs permitting the German Reich to exact acquiescence from the nations victimized.

This Government can only assume that the Government of the German Reich hopes through the commission of such infamous acts of cruelty to helpless and innocent men, women and children to intimidate the United States and other nations into a course of non-resistance to German plans for universal conquest — a conquest based upon lawlessness and terror on land and piracy on the sea.

Such methods are fully in keeping with the methods of terrorism hitherto employed by the present leaders of the German Reich in the policy which they have pursued toward many other nations subsequently victimized.

The Government of the German Reich may however be assured that the United States will neither be intimidated nor will it acquiesce in the plans for world domination which the present leaders of Germany may have.

We are warranted in considering whether the case of the *Robin Moor* is not a step in a campaign against the United States analogous to campaigns against other nations. We cannot place reliance on official declarations to the contrary.

Like statements, declarations, and even solemn pledges have been forthcoming in respect of many nations, commencing with the statement that the Government of the German Reich considered its territorial aspirations satisfied when it seized Austria by force. Evidence that the Government of the German Reich continues to plan further conquest and domination is convincing, and, indeed, scarcely disputed.

Viewed in the light of the circumstances the sinking of the *Robin Moor* becomes a disclosure of policy as well as an example of method. Heretofore, lawless acts of violence have been preludes to schemes of land conquest. This one appears to be a first step in assertion of the supreme purpose of the German Reich to seize control of the high seas, the conquest of Great Britain being an indispensable part of that seizure.

Its general purpose would appear to be to drive American commerce from the ocean wherever such commerce was considered a disadvantage to German designs; and its specific purpose would appear to be interruption of our trade with all friendly countries.

We must take it that notice has now been served upon us that no American ship or cargo on any of the seven seas can consider itself immune from acts of piracy. Notice is served on us, in effect, that the German Reich proposes so to intimidate the United States that we would be dissuaded from carrying out our chosen policy of helping Britain to survive.

In brief, we must take the sinking of the *Robin Moor* as a warning to the United States not to resist the Nazi movement of world conquest. It is a warning that the United States may use the high seas of the world only with Nazi consent.

Were we to yield on this we would inevitably submit to world domination at the hands of the present leaders of the German Reich.

We are not yielding and we do not propose to yield.

FRANKLIN D. ROOSEVELT

THE WHITE HOUSE
June 20, 1941.

PART II

RELATIONS WITH FOREIGN STATES

CHAPTER II

THE WESTERN HEMISPHERE

1. INTER-AMERICAN RELATIONS

A. Second Meeting of the Ministers of Foreign Affairs of the American Republics, Havana, Cuba, July 21-30, 1940

(1) *Resolutions Incorporated in the Final Act, July 30, 1940* [1]

The following resolutions, recommendations and declarations were incorporated in the Final Act of the Conference and are here printed as a separate series, with the exception of Resolution XX (The "Act of Havana"), which was printed in *Documents on American Foreign Relations, II, 1939–1940*, p. 93. [Hereinafter referred to as *Documents*, etc.] The Final Act appears in the English, Spanish, Portuguese and French languages.

[Excerpt]

I. INTER-AMERICAN NEUTRALITY COMMITTEE

The Second Meeting of the Ministers of Foreign Affairs of the American Republics

Resolves:

One. To urge the Inter-American Neutrality Committee to draft a preliminary project of convention dealing with the juridical effects of the Security Zone and the measures of international cooperation which the American States are ready to adopt to obtain respect for the said Zone.

Two. To entrust the Inter-American Neutrality Committee, which functions at Rio de Janeiro, with the drafting of a project of inter-American convention which will cover completely all the principles and

---

[1] Department of State, *Bulletin*, III, p. 127–48, corrections p. 178; *Report . . . submitted to the Governing Board of the Pan American Union by the Director General* (Pan American Union, Congress and Conference Series No. 32, p. 27 *ff.*).

Second Meeting of the Ministers of Foreign Affairs of the American Republics, Havana, July 21–30, 1940. Report of the Secretary of State (Department of State, Conference Series 48, Publication 1575).

rules generally recognized in international law in matters of neutrality, and especially those contained in the Resolutions of Panama,[1] in the individual legislation of the different American States, and in the recommendations already presented by the same Committee.

Three. When the aforementioned project has been drafted, it shall be deposited in the Pan American Union, in order to be submitted for the signature, adhesion and ratification of the respective Governments of the American Republics.

Four. Pending the drafting, acceptance and ratification of the project, it is recommended that the American States adopt in their respective legislations concerning neutrality, the principles and rules contained in the Declarations of Panama and in the recommendations already drafted, or which may hereafter be drafted by the Inter-American Neutrality Committee, it being suggested that the incorporation of the said resolutions and recommendations in the respective legislations be made, in so far as practicable, in a codified and joint form.

Five. To direct that the aforementioned Inter-American Neutrality Committee submit, whenever it may deem advisable, its recommendations direct to the Governments of the American Republics, provided, however, that it shall report also concerning them to the Pan American Union.

Six. To recommend that the Pan American Union circulate, among the Governments of the American States the minutes of the Inter-American Neutrality Committee of Rio de Janeiro, and that the minutes be published by the Pan American Union, when the said Committee deems it opportune.

Seven. That the Inter-American Neutrality Committee may function with the attendance of a minimum of five members, and that, whatever be the number of members present at the meetings, resolutions shall be adopted with the favorable vote of at least four members.

Eight. That even though the Committee is permanent in nature, it is authorized to hold periodical meetings and to adjourn for a specified time, without prejudice to the calling of extraordinary sessions by the President, when some urgent and important question is to be considered.

Nine. To extend a vote of applause and congratulations, for its meritorious work, to the Inter-American Neutrality Committee of Rio de Janeiro, and to its members, Their Excellencies Afranio de Mello Franco, L. A. Podestá Costa, Mariano Fontecilla, A. Aguilar Machado, Charles G. Fenwick, Roberto Córdoba, Gustavo Herrera, Manuel Francisco Jiménez and S. Martínez Mercado.

[1] For text see *Documents, II, 1939–40,* p. 109.

Reservation of the Bolivian Delegation [1]

The Bolivian delegation desires that the peculiar situation of its country be borne in mind, mediterranean state lacking coasts, whose right to free transit has been recognized in the Convention of Havana, of 1928, on Maritime Neutrality [2] and by bilateral treaties entered into with frontier nations.

The application of the principles suggested by the Inter-American Committee on Neutrality, in so far as respects internment, would signify a disregard of the rights of Bolivia on this subject, which has surely not been in the minds of the authors of the project, and would lead to the danger that, in the event of war, the internment of the members of the armed forces of its country, who were forced to cross into neutral territory would take place.

Reservation of the Chilean Delegation

The Delegation of Chile, convinced of the need of giving practical application to continental solidarity, approves the agreements with the understanding that Chile will only assume obligations and responsibilities when the aforementioned agreements are ratified by its constitutional bodies.

II. Norms Concerning Diplomatic and Consular Functions

Whereas:

1. One of the bases of the spiritual unity of the Americas has its roots in the firm adherence by the peoples of the Continent to the principles of international law.

2. The American Republics on February 20, 1928 signed, at Havana, a Convention on Diplomatic Officers [3] which contains the principles generally accepted by all nations.

3. The said Convention establishes, among others, the following principles:

(a) Foreign diplomatic officers shall not participate in the domestic or foreign politics of the State in which they exercise their functions.

(b) They must exercise their functions without coming into conflict with the laws of the country to which they are accredited.

(c) They should not claim immunities which are not essential to the fulfillment of their official duties.

(d) No State shall accredit its diplomatic officers to other States without previous agreement with the latter.

[1] Originally Reservation 4 annexed to the Final Act.
[2] *Treaties, Conventions*, etc., 1923–1937, IV, p. 4743.
[3] Hudson, Manley O., *International Legislation*, IV, p. 2385.

(e) States may decline to receive a diplomatic officer from another, or, having already accepted him, may request his recall without being obliged to state the reasons for such a decision,

The Second Meeting of the Ministers of Foreign Affairs of the American Republics

Resolves:

To urge the Governments of the American Republics to prevent, within the provisions of international law, political activities of foreign diplomatic or consular agents, within the territory to which they are accredited, which may endanger the peace and the democratic tradition of America.

III. Coordination of Police and Judicial Measures for the Defense of Society and Institutions of Each American State

Whereas:

1. The First Meeting of the Ministers of Foreign Affairs of the American Republics held at Panama, approved on October 3, 1939 a recommendation [1] on the coordination of police and judicial measures for the maintenance of neutrality, article 1 of which states as follows:

That action be taken, as soon as possible, through an exchange of views between the Foreign Offices, or through an inter-American conference, for the formulation between themselves of coordinated rules and procedure of a useful, opportune and effective manner, that will facilitate the action of the police and judicial authorities of the respective countries in preventing or repressing unlawful activities that individuals, whether they be nationals or aliens, may attempt in favor of a foreign belligerent State;

2. Experience has shown that it is not only desirable to formulate such rules and procedure with reference to neutrality, but it has also demonstrated the need to organize in the most effective manner possible the defense of society and of the institutions of each State not only against common crimes, but likewise with respect to certain unlawful activities which may affect them;

3. Such defense must be undertaken by the authorities of each State, but its efficacy depends to a large extent upon a common orientation, as uniform as possible, as well as upon an adequate and constant cooperation between such authorities,

The Second Meeting of the Ministers of Foreign Affairs of the American Republics

[1] See *Documents, II, 1939–40*, p. 114.

Resolves:

One. The Governing Board of the Pan American Union shall convoke the States which are members of the Union to an international conference at such place and date as it may determine to draft the international conventions and recommendations which it deems necessary to assure through the action of the proper authorities in each State, and through the coordination of such action with that of other States in the Continent, the most complete and effective defense against acts of an unlawful character, as well as against any other unlawful activities which may affect the institutions of American States.

Two. In the said conference, each State shall be represented by a jurist with plenipotentiary powers accompanied, if deemed advisable, by experts on matters pertaining to the police authorities.

Three. Before the conference is convoked, the Pan American Union shall undertake the preparatory work by means of an inquiry among the Governments of the Continent with regard to the existing legislative or administrative provisions, as well as with respect to their opinions on the various topics which it is deemed advisable to consider.

IV. INTER-AMERICAN LEAGUE OF NATIONAL RED CROSS SOCIETIES

WHEREAS:

It is America's unavoidable duty, for reasons of human solidarity, to contribute to the alleviation of the suffering and misery of victims of war,

The Second Meeting of the Ministers of Foreign Affairs of the American Republics

Recommends:

That the Fourth Pan American Red Cross Conference, which will meet at Santiago, Chile, next December, consider the desirability of organizing, along the general lines of the League of National Red Cross Societies, an Inter-American League of National Red Cross Societies, which shall coordinate the action of the said Red Cross Societies of the American countries and the cooperation of the Inter-American League and its Executive Committee with the League and the International Committee of the Red Cross.

V. PRECAUTIONARY MEASURES WITH REFERENCE TO THE ISSUANCE OF PASSPORTS

WHEREAS:

1. A passport is essentially an identification document which accredits in foreign countries the holder thereof as a national of the country which issues it;

2. Such document has an eminently international character, inasmuch as its possessor uses it solely as a document of identification outside the territory of his country of origin or of adoption;

3. The States of the American Continent must exercise the utmost care in issuing passports for the use of their respective nationals, in order that they may find greater facilities in traveling through the countries of America;

4. It is their duty to prevent the use of counterfeit passports,

The Second Meeting of the Ministers of Foreign Affairs of the American Republics

Resolves:

One. To recommend to the Governments of the American Republics the adoption of the precautionary measures in the issuance of passports which each deems appropriate.

Two. To recommend to the countries of America the adoption of uniform punitive measures against the use of counterfeit or altered passports or passports of more than one country.

VI. Activities Directed from Abroad Against Domestic Institutions

The Second Meeting of the Ministers of Foreign Affairs of the American Republics

Resolves:

One. That having in mind the equal concern and equal responsibility of the American Republics for the preservation of the peace and security of the hemisphere, each one of the Governments of the American Republics shall adopt within its territory all necessary measures in accordance with its constitutional powers to prevent and suppress any activities directed, assisted or abetted by foreign governments, or foreign groups or individuals, which tend to subvert the domestic institutions, or to foment disorder in their internal political life, or to modify by pressure, propaganda, threats, or in any other manner, the free and sovereign right of their peoples to be governed by their existing democratic systems.

In the event that the peace of any of the American Republics is menaced by such activities, the respective Governments agree that they will immediately consult together, if the State directly interested wishes to request it, taking into account the provisions of this resolution and the special circumstances which may affect the peace or the tranquillity of the American Republics.

The American Republics being juridically equal as sovereign and independent States, each shall act in its individual capacity in any steps undertaken in this connection.

Two. In order to make such consultation more efficacious, the Governments of the American Republics further declare that the fullest interchange of information between them is essential with regard to the aforementioned activities within their respective jurisdictions.

Three. The Governments of the American Republics agree that any government which obtains information purporting to show that activities of the aforementioned character are taking place, or are threatening to take place, within the territory of one or more of the American Republics, shall at once communicate in the strictest confidence to the Foreign Minister of such nation or nations the information so obtained.

Four. The Governments of the American Republics declare that, under existing world conditions, the fullest interchange between them of all information of the character described, is in the common interest of them all, and will assist in the preservation of the peace and integrity of the Americas.

VII. Diffusion of Doctrines Tending to Place in Jeopardy the Common Inter-American Democratic Ideal or to Threaten the Security and Neutrality of the American Republics

Whereas:

1. At the First Meeting of the Ministers of Foreign Affairs held at Panama the American Republics once more affirmed their adherence to the democratic ideal that prevails in this Continent, considering that this ideal might find itself endangered by virtue of the action of foreign ideologies inspired by diametrically opposed principles;

2. That the General Declaration of Neutrality of the American Republics, signed at Panama on October 3, 1939,[1] recognized as one of the principles of neutrality, admitted by the American States, that they "shall prevent in accordance with their internal legislation, the inhabitants of their territories from engaging in activities capable of affecting the neutral status of the American Republics";

3. The Convention on the Rights and Duties of States in the event of Civil Strife [2] was signed at the Sixth International Conference of American States at Havana in 1928, which has been ratified by the majority of the American States;

[1] See *Documents, II, 1939–40*, p. 109.
[2] *Treaties, Conventions*, etc., 1923–1937, IV, p. 4725.

4. The exclusion of foreigners from the enjoyment and exercise of strictly political rights is a general rule of internal public law incorporated in the constitutions and laws of States;

5. The Sánchez de Bustamante Code of Private International Law, accepted and put into force through the Convention concluded and signed at the Sixth Inter-American Conference on February 20, 1928, establishes an identical rule excepting, of course, special provisions contained in the internal legislation of the American States;

6. The aforesaid exclusion from the enjoyment of political rights implies the tacit prohibition for foreigners to engage in political activities within the territory of the State in which they reside;

7. The present European conflict has revealed the existence of foreign political organizations in certain neutral States with the deliberate purpose of making attempts against public order, the system of government and the very personality of such States;

8. Such foreign political organizations would constitute in the American States a denial of the latter's democratic institutions, a menace to their right of self-preservation and a threat of violation of their regime of neutrality, and

9. In order to protect the security and neutrality of the American Republics in so far as they might be affected by illicit activities on the part of individuals or associations, either national or foreign, tending to foment civil strife or internal disturbances and to propagate subversive ideologies, it is advisable to coordinate the measures which may be adopted either in common or individually to combat these dangers,

The Second Meeting of the Ministers of Foreign Affairs of the American Republics

Resolves:

One. To reiterate the recommendation made at the First Consultative Meeting held at Panama to the effect that the Governments of the American Republics "take the necessary measures to eradicate from the Americas the spread of doctrines that tend to place in jeopardy the common inter-American democratic ideal," [1] and also that they take the measures which may be advisable to prevent any activities susceptible of jeopardizing American neutrality.

Two. To recommend to the Governments of the American Republics the following rules with respect to civil strife, internal disturbances, or the spread of subversive ideologies:

[1] See *Documents, II, 1939–40*, p. 107.

a. To use the necessary means to prevent the inhabitants of their territory, nationals or aliens, from participating in, collecting supplies, crossing the boundary or sailing from their territory for the purpose of starting or promoting civil strife, internal disturbances, or spreading subversive ideologies in another American country;

b. To disarm and intern every rebel force crossing their boundaries. There shall be observed, in so far as they are applicable, the rules of internment drafted by the Inter-American Neutrality Committee at Rio de Janeiro; [1]

c. To forbid the traffic in arms and war matériel, except when intended for the Government, unless the belligerency of the rebels has been recognized, in which latter case the rules of neutrality shall be applied, and

d. To prevent that within their jurisdiction there be equipped, armed or adapted for warlike purposes any vessel intended to operate in favor of the rebellion.

Three. To reiterate the recommendation of the First Consultative Meeting, held at Panama, to the effect that action be taken, as soon as possible for the adoption of the rules and procedure that may be judged useful to facilitate the action of the police and judicial authorities of the respective countries in repressing unlawful activities that individuals, either nationals or foreigners, may attempt at any time in favor of a foreign State.

Four. To recommend to the Governments of the American States that they adopt the following legislative or administrative norms, without prejudice to the respect due to their individual and sovereign right to regulate the juridical status of foreigners:

a. Effective prohibition of every political activity by foreign individuals, associations, groups or political parties, no matter what form they use to disguise or cloak such activity;

b. Rigorous supervision of the entry of foreigners into national territory, particularly in the case of nationals of non-American States;

c. Effective police supervision of the activities of foreign non-American groups established in the American States;

d. Creation of an emergency penal system for the offenses set forth in this article.

Five. To encourage the reciprocal communication, directly or through the Pan American Union, of information and data concerning the entry,

[1] Pan American Union, *Decrees and Regulations on Neutrality* . . ., Supplement No. 1 (Law and Treaty Series No. 13), p. 53.

rejection and expulsion of foreigners and the adoption of the preventive and repressive measures provided for in the previous article;

Six. Any of the American Republics directly affected by the activities referred to in this resolution may initiate the procedure of consultation.

VIII. Project on Extension of Territorial Waters

The Second Meeting of the Ministers of Foreign Affairs of the American Republics

Resolves:

That the project presented by the Delegation of Uruguay, concerning the extension of territorial waters, together with the modifications introduced by the present Consultative Meeting be transmitted for study to the Committee of Experts for the Codification of International Law; and that there also be requested the opinion of the Inter-American Neutrality Committee at Rio de Janeiro regarding the same project.

IX. Project on Refugees

The Second Meeting of the Ministers of Foreign Affairs of the American Republics

Resolves:

That the projects presented to the Meeting by the Delegations of Argentina, Uruguay and Mexico (Projects Nos. 35, 36 and 42) concerning refugees and assistance to minors proceeding from evacuated areas be referred for consideration to the Pan American Union.

X. Interoceanic Railway Between Arica and Santos by Way of Bolivia

The Second Meeting of the Ministers of Foreign Affairs of the American Republics

Resolves:

To recognize the importance and usefulness for continental defense of the Arica (Chile)–Santos (Brazil) interoceanic railway, through Bolivia, and to recommend to the American nations, especially to those directly interested in the project, the advisability of proceeding as soon as possible with the financing of the section still to be constructed.

XI. Codification of International Law

Whereas:

1. The Eighth International Conference of American States approved several resolutions with the purpose of coordinating, intensifying and accelerating the work of codification of international law in America;[1]

2. The said Conference also adopted other resolutions on the coordination and improvement of the inter-American peace instruments;

3. According to historical tradition and the most profound convictions of the American peoples it is urgent at this time, when the bases of law and of pacific relations among peoples are the object of serious attacks, that the nations of America once again reaffirm their effective support of the principles of international law and of the pacific settlement of international controversies and prove their firm intention to work for the maintenance and preservation of those principles,

The Second Meeting of the Ministers of Foreign Affairs of the American Republics

Resolves:

One. To recommend to the Governments of the American Republics that they adopt the necessary measures to carry out the resolutions approved by the Eighth International Conference of American States relative to the codification of international law and the improvement and coordination of the inter-American peace instruments.

Two. To urge the various organizations in charge of the study of matters to which the above mentioned resolutions refer, to submit, as soon as possible, their recommendations and observations so that the Governing Board of the Pan American Union may convoke the meeting of the International Conference of American Jurists within the next two years.

Three. To request the Pan American Union to communicate the present resolution to all Governments members of the Union, together with a report on the present status of the work provided for in the above mentioned resolutions of the Eighth Conference.

XII. Promotion of Continental Solidarity

Whereas:

The sentiment of solidarity between the American Republics constitutes a genuine force for continental defense, to which all of them should

---

[1] Among the resolutions referred to Nos. VII, XIV, XV, XVII, XVIII, XXIX–XXXII may be mentioned.

lend unreservedly their maximum cooperation, removing any obstacle that might jeopardize this principle of American public law, in order that no State of this Continent may find itself deterred from offering its fullest and most decided cooperation, both in the political and economic fields, to the fulfillment of that ideal,

The Second Meeting of the Ministers of Foreign Affairs of the American Republics

Resolves:

To recommend to the American States that in any case in which internal legislation or contractual acts in force constitute a hindrance to the fullest cooperation which a State should lend to the principle of continental solidarity, it initiate, through legal means, the revision of such acts, in so far as this may be possible.

XIII. Hostile Acts in Territorial Waters and in the Security Zone

Whereas:

1. At the First Meeting of the Ministers of Foreign Affairs held at Panama for the purpose of preserving peace, the neutrality of the American Republics was established,[1] during the war begun in Europe; the irrevocable purpose was asserted of complying strictly with those duties within the principles of international law and the clauses of the conventions codifying them, and due respect was demanded for the situation created by those norms;

2. Within this purpose of maintaining security on this Continent, a maritime zone, adjacent to the territorial area of each nation was established,[2] excluding such zone from hostile acts from the land, sea, or air;

3. In the hostilities, belligerency has transgressed the principles of international law, has disregarded the duties imposed by neutrality, and has also brought about hostile acts, not only in the zone excluded by the XV Resolution of Panama, but also contrary to sovereignty in the maritime zone of some of the Republics;

4. Without prejudice to the juridical procedure and settlement which should be given in each case to the claims raised because of these transgressions, it is necessary and opportune that the voice of the Republics of America condemn them and state the irrevocable purpose of practicing

---

[1] General Declaration of Neutrality, October 3, 1939, *Documents, II, 1939–40,* p. 109.

[2] The Declaration of Panama, October 3, 1939, *ibid.,* p. 115.

and demanding respect to the fullest extent for the norms regulating the existence of the international community,

The Second Meeting of the Ministers of the Foreign Affairs of the American Republics

Declares:

One. That it condemns hostilities within territorial waters, as contrary to the right of sovereignty of the nation having jurisdiction over them and to the tenets of international law.

Two. That it considers such hostilities within the Security Zone to be prejudicial to the votes and joint resolutions of the Republics of America for the preservation of peace on this Continent.

XIV. THE PEACEFUL SOLUTION OF CONFLICTS

WHEREAS:

In behalf of the closest possible unity of the Continent, it is imperative that differences existing between some of the American nations be settled,

The Second Meeting of the Ministers of Foreign Affairs of the American Republics

Resolves:

To recommend to the Governing Board of the Pan American Union that it organize, in the American capital deemed most suitable for the purpose, a Committee composed of representatives of five countries, which shall have the duty of keeping constant vigilance to insure that States between which any dispute exists or may arise, of any nature whatsoever, may solve it as quickly as possible, and of suggesting, without detriment to the methods adopted by the parties or to the procedures which they may agree upon, the measures and steps which may be conducive to a settlement.

The Committee shall submit a report to each Meeting of the Ministers of Foreign Affairs and to each International Conference of American States regarding the status of such conflicts and the steps which may have been taken to bring about a solution.

RESERVATION OF THE PERUVIAN DELEGATION [1]

Peru accepts the proposal of the Haitian Delegation with the reservation that the Committee shall function only at the request of the interested parties.

[1] Department of State, *Bulletin*, III, p. 144; the reservation was originally attached to the Final Act as No. 9.

XV. Reciprocal Assistance and Cooperation for the Defense of the Nations of the Americas

The Second Meeting of the Ministers of Foreign Affairs of the American Republics

Declares:

That any attempt on the part of a non-American State against the integrity or inviolability of the territory, the sovereignty or the political independence of an American State shall be considered as an act of aggression against the States which sign this declaration.

In case acts of aggression are committed or should there be reason to believe that an act of aggression is being prepared by a non-American nation against the integrity or inviolability of the territory, the sovereignty or the political independence of an American nation, the nations signatory to the present declaration will consult among themselves in order to agree upon the measure it may be advisable to take.

All the signatory nations, or two or more of them, according to circumstances, shall proceed to negotiate the necessary complementary agreements so as to organize cooperation for defense and the assistance that they shall lend each other in the event of aggressions such as those referred to in this declaration.

Reservation of the Colombian Delegation

I vote affirmatively with the statement that I shall sign the Act of Havana and the Declaration concerning Reciprocal Assistance and Cooperation for the Defense of the Nations of the Americas, subject to approval by my Government and to the constitutional norms of my country.

XVI. Maintenance of Peace and Union among the American Republics

The Second Meeting of the Ministers of Foreign Affairs of the American Republics

Declares:

One. That the Governments of the American Republics are irrevocably determined to maintain and strengthen their union, in order that America may fulfill its high mission on behalf of civilization;

Two. That they will, therefore, omit no effort to prevent any controversy which might impair their solidarity;

Three. That they will also make every effort to settle in a friendly manner and as soon as possible the differences which exist between them, in order that their reciprocal confidence and their cooperation for continental defense against any foreign aggression may be further strengthened;

Four. That they reaffirm their strong desire to avoid the use of force in this Continent as a means of solving differences between nations and, therefore, to resort exclusively to juridical and pacific methods;

Five. That they consider it essential to extend the sphere of action of these methods, so that in all cases they may be decisively effective for the preservation of peace;

Six. That they will, likewise, make every effort to the end that these principles and aspirations may be adopted in the relations between the nations of America and those of other continents;

Seven. That during the present period of hostilities they will strive for the maintenance of law and justice, in accordance with the Declaration of Panama;

Eight. That they vehemently desire that peace be established on bases which will be lasting and inspired by the common welfare of all peoples;

Nine. That they are disposed to maintain international relations on juridical bases resting on the solid foundation of moral forces, in order to reestablish definitely the bonds of human community; and

Ten. That, faithful to their ideals, they will coordinate their own interests with the duties of universal cooperation.

XVII. PROCEDURE ON CONSULTATION

WHEREAS:

1. It is incumbent upon the present Meeting, as provided in paragraph 3 of Chapter II of the Agenda, to examine the functioning of the system of consultation among the Governments of the American Republics established by the resolutions of the Inter-American Conference for the Maintenance of Peace and of the Eighth International Conference of American States, for the purpose of suggesting measures susceptible of perfecting it;

2. The high motives which led the American Republics to put the aforementioned system into effect will continue to make advisable the convoking of other Meetings such as those of Panama and of Havana, whenever the lofty interests of the Continent so require;

3. Future Meetings, as in the case of the present one, will have to be convoked under the pressure of events and under emergency conditions which will make it difficult and inadvisable to determine in advance the most appropriate time and country for the Meeting;

4. Prior to the First and the Second Consultative Meetings, the experience and knowledge of the Governing Board of the Pan American Union was resorted to, and in convoking future Meetings, it would be advisable to take advantage of the collaboration of that body,

The Second Meeting of the Ministers of Foreign Affairs of the American Republics

Resolves:

One. The Government which desires to initiate consultation in any of the cases contemplated in the conventions, declarations and resolutions of the Inter-American Conferences, and to propose a Meeting of the Ministers of Foreign Relations or of their representatives, shall address the Governing Board of the Pan American Union indicating the questions with which it desires the consultation to deal, as well as the approximate date on which the Meeting should be held.

Two. The Governing Board shall immediately transmit the request, together with a list of the subjects suggested, to the other Governments, members of the Union, and invite the observations and suggestions which the respective Governments may desire to present.

Three. On the basis of the answers received, the Governing Board of the Pan American Union will determine the date for the Meeting, prepare the appropriate Agenda, and adopt, in accordance with the respective Governments, all other measures advisable for the preparation of the Meeting.

Four. The Governing Board of the Pan American Union shall proceed to draft regulations for Consultative Meetings which shall be submitted to all the American Governments for their approval.

Five. The Third Meeting of the Ministers of Foreign Affairs of the American Republics will be held at Rio de Janeiro, the capital of Brazil.

Six. After the next Meeting, the designation of the country where each Consultative Meeting shall be held, shall be made by the Governing Board of the Pan American Union in accordance with the procedure set forth in the present resolution.

XVIII. RELATIONS BETWEEN THE GOVERNMENTS OF CHILE AND SPAIN

The Second Meeting of the Ministers of Foreign Affairs of the American Republics

Pursuant to the Declaration of Continental Solidarity proclaimed at the Eighth Pan American Conference held at Lima and ratified at the Consultative Meeting at Panama in 1939,[1]

[1] *Documents, I, 1938–39*, p. 44; *II, 1939–40*, p. 104.

Declares:

That it has followed with concern the conflict which has arisen between Chile and Spain, and that, notwithstanding its cordial sentiments toward Spain it expresses its lively sympathy and fraternal solidarity with the attitude assumed by the Government of Chile in defense of principles fundamental for the free peoples of America, and that it expresses its hope that the relations between the two States will be reestablished as soon as possible.

Reservation of the Mexican Delegation [1]

The Delegation of Mexico adheres to the declaration which has been approved only because it expresses its lively sympathy and fraternal solidarity with the attitude which the Government of the Sister Republic of Chile has assumed in defense of principles fundamental for the free peoples of America.

XIX. The Question of Belize

The Second Meeting of the Ministers of Foreign Affairs of the American Republics

Resolves:

To express the keen desire and wishes of the American countries in favor of a just, peaceful, and prompt solution of the question of Belize between Guatemala and Great Britain.

XX. Act of Havana

See *Documents, II, 1939–40*, p. 93.

For the text in the four languages of signature, with the reservations of the Argentine, Uruguayan, Chilean, Colombian and Venezuelan delegations, all relating to constitutional conditions for acceptance, see Provisional Administration of European Colonies and Possessions in the Americas, Act of Havana contained in the Final Act of the Second Meeting of the Ministers of Foreign Affairs of the American Republics, Executive Agreement Series 199, Department of State Publication 1607.

XXI. Inter-American Sanitary Cooperation

Whereas:

1. According to reports received by the Meeting the principal epidemic diseases, such as bubonic plague, yellow fever and malignant malaria,

[1] Department of State, *Bulletin*, III, p. 143; originally appeared as No. 1 attached to the Final Act.

which were an international menace and could be spread through international commerce, have been effectively controlled to such an extent that for all practical purposes the danger of their international propagation is believed to have been eliminated;

2. Diseases and epidemics are intensified in cases of alterations in the normal life of peoples, reaching alarming degrees whenever wars between nations are unleashed; and

3. The satisfactory results obtained have been due to effective cooperation between various countries, the Pan American Sanitary Bureau and the Rockefeller Foundation, pursuant to the sanitary treaty known as the Pan American Sanitary Code, which has been ratified by all the Governments,

The Second Meeting of the Ministers of Foreign Affairs of the American Republics

Resolves:

To express its satisfaction for the efficient results obtained to date and to recommend that cooperation with relation to sanitary activities continue and, as far as possible, be extended with a view to further improving sanitary, social and economic conditions, recognized as essentially interdependent and beneficial nationally as well as internationally.

XXII. Project Regarding Cooperation Between Pan American Institutions

The Second Meeting of the Ministers of Foreign Affairs of the American Republics

Resolves:

That the project presented by the Dominican Delegation regarding cooperation between official Pan American institutions in defense of the continental principles of peace and democracy be transmitted for consideration to the Pan American Union.

XXIII. Pan American Highway [1]

Whereas:

1. It has been the invariable desire of all the American Republics, expressed since the First Inter-American Conference, to make effective and practical their solidarity by means of the construction of a network

[1] See p. 117, 119.

of highways to unite all of their capital cities, and the satisfaction of this desire, as a result of world circumstances, has become a vital and urgent need;

2. In carrying out these aims, the American Republics signed at Buenos Aires, on December 23, 1936, at the Inter-American Conference for the Maintenance of Peace, a convention to advance the financing, the technical studies, and the construction of the highway referred to; [1]

3. The recommendations contained in Resolution III, approved at the First Meeting of the Ministers of Foreign Affairs of the American Republics, held at Panama in 1939, included the following:

10. To make every effort in order to complete their respective sections of the Pan American Highway and to recommend to the countries which have ratified the Buenos Aires convention that they designate as soon as possible one or more experts to expedite the fulfillment of the recommendations of the Third Pan American Highway Congress. [2]

4. The Pan American Highway, by promoting close relations and commerce between nations, would benefit equally all the inhabitants of the Americas; and

5. The distribution of the cost of constructing the Highway among the nations which it crosses on the sole basis of the territorial extension of each country, in addition to not being equitable, makes impossible or delays indefinitely its construction,

The Second Meeting of the Ministers of Foreign Affairs of the American Republics

Resolves:

One. To invite the American nations which as yet have not ratified the Convention of Buenos Aires relating to the Pan American Highway, to do so as soon as possible.

Two. To recommend to the Financial Commission created by that Convention that, in drafting the plans for financing the construction of the Highway, it study the desirability of taking into account, in distributing the total cost among the nations linked by it, the following factors: the economic capacity of the individual nations; their population; their revenues; the length of the Highway in the territory of each of them; and the benefits which each nation will derive from the Highway. The said Commission should also take into account the right of those nations which have constructed all or part of their respective sections to have the estimated value of the work completed by them accepted as

[1] United States, *Treaty Series* No. 927.
[2] *Documents, II, 1939–40*, p. 103.

all or part of the contribution which would be allocated to the particular country as its share in the total cost of the Pan American Highway.

Three. To recommend to the Inter-American Financial and Economic Advisory Committee that it collaborate fully with the Pan American Highway Financial Commission with a view to the prompt and efficacious accomplishment of its task.

XXIV. INSURANCE AND REINSURANCE

WHEREAS:

1. The Delegation of the Dominican Republic has presented to this Second Meeting a draft resolution recommending to the American nations that they encourage by appropriate legislation the development of insurance, and especially of reinsurance facilities; and

2. Because of its complex technical character, a detailed study of the various aspects of this recommendation is required, which this Meeting is not in a position to undertake in view of the shortness of the time at its disposal,

The Second Meeting of the Ministers of Foreign Affairs of the American Republics

Resolves:

To transmit to the Inter-American Financial and Economic Advisory Committee, at Washington, the project of the Dominican Republic to the end that it proceed to make a study of it and to report its conclusions to the Governments of the American Republics.

XXV. ECONOMIC AND FINANCIAL COOPERATION

WHEREAS:

1. At the First Consultative Meeting held at Panama it was resolved to declare that in view of existing circumstances, it had become more desirable and necessary than ever to establish a close and sincere cooperation between the American Republics in order that they might protect their economic and financial structure, maintain their fiscal equilibrium, safeguard the stability of their currencies, promote and expand their industries, intensify their agriculture, and develop their commerce;

2. In order to attain the objectives of the preceding paragraph, it was agreed to create an Inter-American Financial and Economic Advisory Committee, in Washington; [1]

---

[1] *Documents, II, 1939–40*, p. 100.

3. The war now in progress has increased the disruption in the channels of international commerce and the curtailment of markets for certain products of the Americas;

4. The existence of surpluses of commodities, the exportation of which is essential to the economic life of the countries of the Americas, is economically, socially, financially, and in other respects a matter of great importance to the masses of the population, and especially to those groups participating in the production and distribution of wealth in each country, and, finally, to the Governments of the entire Continent;

5. It must be anticipated that these difficulties will exist as long as the war continues and that some of them, as well as other new ones, will exist after the war ends; and

6. It is of great importance that the economic development of the American countries be directed toward a diversification of their production and, at the same time, toward an increase in their consumption capacity,

The Second Meeting of the Ministers of Foreign Affairs of the American Republics

Resolves:

One. To declare:

(*a*) That the American nations continue to adhere to the liberal principles of international trade, conducted with peaceful motives and based upon equality of treatment and fair and equitable practices;

(*b*) That it is the purpose of the American nations to apply these principles in their relations with each other as fully as present circumstances permit;

(*c*) That the American nations should be prepared to resume the conduct of trade with the entire world in accordance with these principles as soon as the non-American nations are prepared to do likewise;

(*d*) That, in the meantime, the American nations shall do everything in their power to strengthen their own economic position; to improve further the trade and other economic relations between and among themselves; and to devise and apply appropriate means of effective action to cope with the difficulties, disadvantages and dangers arising from the present disturbed and dislocated world conditions; and

(*e*) That the American nations consider it necessary to maintain or improve the normal economic situation established between them in order to assure the preservation or improvement of the position enjoyed in their respective markets.

Two. To strengthen and expand the activities of the Inter-American Financial and Economic Advisory Committee as the instrument for continuing consultation among the American Republics with respect to economic and trade matters and arrangements, having in mind especially the immediate situations which must be met as a result of the curtailment and changed character of important foreign markets. For the purpose of dealing with special problems, there may be organized subcommittees, composed of representatives of the interested countries, which should meet at such places as may be deemed most appropriate for their effective functioning.

Three. Specifically, to instruct the said Committee that it proceed forthwith.

(*a*) To cooperate with each country of this Continent in the study of possible measures for the increase of the domestic consumption of its own exportable surpluses of those commodities which are of primary importance to the maintenance of the economic life of such countries;

(*b*) To propose to the American nations immediate measures and arrangements of mutual benefit tending to increase trade among them without injury to the interests of their respective producers, for the purpose of providing increased markets for such products and of expanding their consumption;

(*c*) To create instruments of inter-American cooperation for the temporary storing, financing and handling of any such commodities and for their orderly and systematic marketing, having in mind the normal conditions of production and distribution thereof;

(*d*) To develop commodity arrangements with a view to assuring equitable terms of trade for both producers and consumers of the commodities concerned;

(*e*) To recommend methods for improving the standard of living of the peoples of the Americas, including public health and nutrition measures;

(*f*) To establish appropriate organizations for the distribution of a part of the surplus of any such commodity, as a humanitarian and social relief measure;

(*g*) To consider, while these plans and measures are being developed, the desirability of a broader system of inter-American cooperative organization in trade and industrial matters, and to propose credit measures and other measures of assistance which may be immediately necessary in the fields of economics, finance, money, and foreign exchange.

Four. To reaffirm Resolution XIII of the Inter-American Financial and Economic Advisory Committee, and to recommend that, in order to promote the economic development of the American nations under the terms of said resolution, each nation, upon its own initiative and in consonance with the program of the Inter-American Development Commission, establish appropriate enterprises with government or private capital provided by two or more American Republics. Such enterprises may deal directly with the Inter-American Bank or other official or private credit institutions, it being recommended that the said Bank give its sympathetic consideration to the possibility of granting them financial aid.

RESERVATION OF THE CHILEAN DELEGATION [1]

The Delegation of Chile, as it did at the First Consultative Meeting of Panama, qualifies its vote in respect of "liberal principles of international trade" to which reference is made in paragraphs *a*, *b* and *c* of Section 1, for the reasons stated before the Committee which dealt with this project. It requests that record of this qualification be made in the appropriate document.

(2) *Convention on the Provisional Administration of European Colonies and Possessions in the Americas* [2]

Signed at Havana, July 30, 1940; advice and consent of the United States Senate, September 27, and ratification by the President, October 10, 1940.

The Governments represented at the Second Meeting of Ministers of Foreign Affairs of the American Republics,

Considering:

One. That the American Republics have formulated at the Second Consultative Meeting the Act of Havana [3] with regard to the destiny of colonies of non-American countries located in this hemisphere as well as with respect to the provisional administration of such colonies;

Two. That as a result of the events which are taking place in the European continent situations may develop in the territories of the possessions which some of the belligerent nations have in the Americas which may extinguish or materially impair the sovereignty which they

---

[1] Department of State, *Bulletin*, III, p. 144; originally appeared as No. 6 attached to the Final Act.

[2] Department of State, *Bulletin*, III, p. 145; *Congressional Record*, Vol. 86, p. 19290 (daily edition).

[3] See *Documents, II, 1939–40*, p. 93.

exercise over them, or leave their government without a leader, thus creating a state of danger to the peace of the continent and a state of affairs in which the rule of law, order, and respect for life, liberty and the property of inhabitants may disappear;

Three. That the American Republics consider that force cannot constitute the basis of rights, and they condemn all violence whether under the form of conquest, of stipulations which may have been imposed by the belligerents in the clauses of a treaty, or by any other process;

Four. That any transfer, or attempted transfer, of the sovereignty, jurisdiction, possession or any interest in or control over any such region to another non-American State, would be regarded by the American Republics as against American sentiments and principles and the rights of American States to maintain their security and political independence;

Five. That no such transfer or attempt to transfer or acquire any interest or right in any such region, directly or indirectly, would be recognized or accepted by the American Republics no matter what form was employed to attain such purposes;

Six. That by virtue of a principle of American international law, recognized by various conferences, the acquisition of territories by force cannot be permitted;

Seven. That the American Republics, through their respective government agencies, reserve the right to judge whether any transfer or attempted transfer of sovereignty, jurisdiction, cession or incorporation of geographic regions in the Americas, possessed by European countries up to September 1, 1939, has the effect of impairing their political independence even though no formal transfer or change in the status of such region or regions shall have taken place;

Eight. That in the cases foreseen, as well as any others which might leave the government of such regions without a leader, it is, therefore, necessary to establish a provisional administrative regime for such regions until such time as their definitive regime is established by the free determination of their people;

Nine. That the American Republics, as an international community which acts strongly and integrally, using as a basis political and juridical principles which they have applied for more than a century, have the unquestionable right, in order to preserve their unity and security, to take such regions under their administration and to deliberate as to their destinies, in accordance with their respective degrees of political and economic development;

Ten. That the provisional and transitory character of the measures agreed to does not imply an oversight or abrogation of the principle of non-intervention which regulates inter-American life, a principle proclaimed by the American Institute, recognized by the meeting of jurists held at Rio de Janeiro and fully reaffirmed at the Seventh International American Conference held at Montevideo;

Eleven. That this community has therefore international juridical capacity to act in this manner;

Twelve. That in this case, the most appropriate regime is that of a provisional administration; and that this system entails no danger because the American Republics do not entertain any purpose whatsoever of territorial aggrandizement;

Thirteen. That the establishment of a special provisional regime in the present convention and in the Act of Havana concerning the provisional administration of European colonies and possessions in the Americas does not eliminate or modify the system of consultation agreed upon at Buenos Aires, confirmed at Lima, and practiced at Panama and Havana;

Fourteen. Being desirous of protecting their peace and safety and of promoting the interests of any of the regions herein referred to which may fall within the purview of the foregoing recitations, have resolved to conclude the following convention:

I. If a non-American State shall directly or indirectly attempt to replace another non-American State in the sovereignty or control which it exercised over any territory located in the Americas, thus threatening the peace of the continent, such territory shall automatically come under the provisions of this convention and shall be submitted to a provisional administrative regime.

II. The administration shall be exercised, as may be considered advisable in each case, by one or more American States, with their previous approval.

III. When the administration shall have been established for any region it shall be exercised in the interest of the security of the Americas, and for the benefit of the region under administration, with a view to its welfare and progress, until such time as the region is in a position to govern itself or is restored to its former status, whenever the latter is compatible with the security of the American Republics.

IV. The administration of the region shall be exercised under conditions which shall guarantee freedom of conscience and of worship, subject to the regulations which public order and good habits may demand.

V. The administration shall enforce the local laws coordinating them with the purposes of this convention, but it may furthermore adopt such measures as may be necessary to meet situations in which such laws do not exist.

VI. In all that concerns commerce and industry, the American nations shall enjoy the same situation and benefits, and the administrator is forbidden to establish a privileged position for itself or its nationals or for certain states. Open economic relations shall be maintained with all countries on a reciprocity basis.

VII. Natives of the region shall participate, as citizens, in public administration and in the courts of justice without further qualification than their capacity so to do.

VIII. To the extent that it may be practicable, rights of every sort shall be governed by local law and custom, and vested rights shall be protected in accordance with such law.

IX. Forced labor shall be abolished in the regions where it exists.

X. The administration shall provide facilities for education of all kinds with the two-fold purpose of developing the wealth of the region and improving the living conditions of the population, especially as regards public and individual hygiene and preparation for the exercise of political autonomy as soon as possible.

XI. The natives of a region under administration shall have their own Organic Act which the administration shall establish, consulting the people in whatever manner is possible.

XII. The administration shall submit an annual report to the inter-American organization entrusted with the control of the regions under administration, of the manner in which it has fulfilled its functions, attaching thereto copies of its accounts and of the measures adopted in the region during the year.

XIII. The organization referred to in the preceding article shall be competent to take cognizance of the petitions submitted by inhabitants of the region through the medium of the administration, with reference to the exercise of the provisional administration. The administration shall transmit, with this petition, such observations as it may deem proper.

XIV. The first administration shall be granted for a period of three years; at the end of this period, if necessary, it shall be renewed for successive periods not longer than ten years.

XV. The expenses incurred in the exercise of the administration shall be defrayed with the revenues of the region under administration but in case they are insufficient the deficit shall be met by the State or States which act as administrators.

XVI. A commission to be known as the "Inter-American Commission for Territorial Administration" is hereby established, to be composed of a representative from each one of the States which ratifies this convention; it shall be the international organization to which this convention refers. Once this convention has become effective, any country which ratifies it may convoke the first meeting proposing the city in which it is to be held. The Commission shall elect its chairman, complete its organization and fix its definitive seat. Two-thirds of the members of the Commission shall constitute a quorum and two-thirds of the members present may adopt decisions.

XVII. The Commission is authorized to establish a provisional administration in the regions to which the present convention refers; allow such administration to be exercised by the number of States which it may determine in each case, and supervise its exercise under the terms of the preceding articles.

XVIII. None of the provisions contained in the present convention refers to territories or possessions which are the subject of dispute or claims between European powers and one or more of the Republics of the Americas.

XIX. The present convention is open for signature by the American Republics at the city of Havana and shall be ratified by the High Contracting Parties in conformity with their constitutional procedures. The Secretary of State of the Republic of Cuba shall transmit at the earliest possible date authentic certified copies to the governments for the aforementioned purpose of ratification. The instrument of ratification shall be deposited in the archives of the Pan American Union in Washington, which shall notify the signatory governments of said deposit. Such notification shall be considered as an exchange of ratifications.

XX. The present convention shall enter into force when two-thirds of the American Republics have deposited their respective instruments of ratification.

IN WITNESS WHEREOF, the undersigned Plenipotentiaries, having deposited their full powers found to be in due and proper form, sign this convention on behalf of their respective Governments and affix thereto their seals on the dates appearing opposite their signatures.

RESERVATIONS [1]

RESERVATION OF THE CHILEAN DELEGATION

1. The Chilean Delegation, convinced of the necessity of effecting practically the continental solidarity, approves the resolution, making clear that Chile shall only acquire commitments and responsibilities when the said resolutions shall have been ratified by its constitutional organisms.

[1] Department of State, *Bulletin*, III, p. 148.

Reservation of the Argentine Delegation

2. The Delegate of the Argentine Republic in signing this Act places on record that it does not refer to or include the Malvinas Islands, because the latter do not constitute a colony or possession of any European nation, since they are a part of the Argentine territory and are included within its dominion and sovereignty, as was stated at the Panama meeting, which statement he considers reiterated hereby in its entirety, and also with reference to other southern Argentine regions as he has stated in the deliberations of this Commission. He likewise states that the signing of this Act and Resolution does not affect and leaves intact his Government's powers established in the constitutional norms which obtain in Argentina, with respect to the procedure applicable in order that this Act and Resolution may acquire validity, force, and effectiveness.

Reservation of the Colombian Delegation

3. I vote in the affirmative with the suggestion that I shall sign the Convention, subject to the approval by my Government and the constitutional standards of my country.

Reservation of the Venezuelan Delegation

4. The Venezuelan Delegation signs with the understanding that the Convention concerning the colonial possessions remains subject to the public powers of the nation, in accordance with its constitutional provisions.

Additional Reservation of the Chilean Delegation

5. The Chilean Delegation, at the time of signing this Convention, in addition to the reservation set forth at yesterday's Meeting, makes reservation of Chile's rights in Antarctica.

[Here follow signatures.]

The Convention signed at Havana on July 30, 1940 will go into effect when two thirds of the American Republics shall have ratified it. Six ratifications had been deposited by June 30, 1941 and legislative action had been taken by three other States.

Countries which have deposited instruments of ratification with the Pan American Union, as of June 30, 1941:

United States	October 24, 1940
Dominican Republic	November 28, 1940
Costa Rica	December 17, 1940
Brazil	January 14, 1941
Peru	April 4, 1941
Panama	May 13, 1941

Countries which have acted on the Convention, but have not yet deposited the instruments of ratification:

Colombia — Convention approved by Chamber of Representatives, October 2, 1940.

El Salvador — Convention approved by Legislative Assembly and ratification signed by the President, November 27, 1940.

Honduras — In Congressional Decree No. 8 of December 23, 1940, National Legislature gave its approval to the ratification of the Convention.

(a) **Message Transmitted by the President (Roosevelt), September 13, 1940** [1]

To THE SENATE OF THE UNITED STATES:

To the end that I may receive the advice and consent of the Senate to ratification I transmit herewith, in certified form, a Convention entitled "Convention on the Provisional Administration of European Colonies and Possessions in the Americas," signed at Havana on July 30, 1940. Also enclosed, for the information of the Senate, but not requiring ratification, is a copy of the "Act of Havana," [2] signed on the same date at the Second Meeting of the Ministers of Foreign Affairs of the American Republics and a report concerning the Convention and Act, from the Secretary of State.

I commend the Convention to the early consideration of the Senate.

FRANKLIN D. ROOSEVELT

THE WHITE HOUSE,
September 13, 1940.

(b) **The Secretary of State (Hull) to the President (Roosevelt), September 12, 1940** [3]

DEPARTMENT OF STATE,
Washington, September 12, 1940.

THE PRESIDENT,
The White House.

The undersigned, the Secretary of State, has the honor to lay before the President, in certified form, with a view to its transmission to the Senate to receive the advice and consent of that body to ratification, if his judgment approve thereof, a Convention entitled "Convention on the Provisional Administration of European Colonies and Possessions in the Americas," signed at Havana on July 30, 1940. The Convention is accompanied by the "Act of Havana" which is included in the Final Act of the Conference, signed at the same time. This Act is important as information and as a part of the record.

Permit me also to make the following statement concerning the background and provisions of the Convention.

It will be recalled that the primary purpose of the American republics in convoking the Meeting of Foreign Ministers at Havana last July was to consider the possibility that developments in Europe might affect the status of the European possessions in the Western Hemisphere in such a manner as to constitute a threat to the peace and security of the American republics. Sovereignty over these possessions has been maintained for many generations and in some cases for several centuries by the French, British and Netherlands Governments. These geographic regions have not heretofore constituted a menace to the peace of the Americas and we have maintained the most cordial relations with their respective administrations.

[1] Department of State, *Bulletin*, III, p. 269; Sen. Exec. O, 76th Cong., 3d sess.
[2] *Documents, II, 1939–40*, p. 93. The Act of Havana is annex No. XX to the Final Act of the Second Meeting of the Ministers of Foreign Affairs of the American Republics.
[3] Department of State, *Bulletin*, III, p. 269.

It would not, however, be consistent with the policy of the United States or desirable from the point of view of the defense of the Western Hemisphere to permit these regions to become a subject of barter in the settlement of European difficulties, or a battleground for the adjustment of such difficulties. Either situation could only be regarded as a threat to the peace and safety of this hemisphere, as would any indication that the possessions under consideration might be used to promote systems alien to the inter-American system. Any effort, therefore, to modify the existing status of these possessions whether by cession, by transfer, or by any impairment whatsoever in the control heretofore exercised would be of profound and immediate concern to all the American Republics.

The foregoing views are entirely consonant with the basic principle of foreign policy of the United States as enunciated over a century ago by President Monroe.

This doctrine continues to represent the policy of the United States; it is fundamental to our national defense. Moreover, as I have pointed out to the Congress in connection with legislation designed to strengthen the defense of this country, the war at present raging in Europe is the result in part of the abandonment by certain European powers of those principles of respect for the pledged word and of peaceful negotiation of agreements for the modification of the established order to which the American Republics adhere.

The progress of that war to date has obliged the government of one of the countries having possessions in the American Republics to abandon its homeland; the government of a second of these countries has been forced to sign an armistice involving, among other conditions, the hostile occupation of more than one-half of its territory. The third of the governments with whose possessions in this hemisphere we are now concerned is engaged in a struggle in which its very existence may be at stake.

It was therefore altogether appropriate that the United States in company with the other free and sovereign republics of the Western Hemisphere, should consider the consequences which might result from the transfer of sovereignty over any of these British, French or Netherland possessions, especially if that transfer were made to a country which has demonstrated a lack of adherence to the established principles of international law. It was equally obvious that such a transfer, by giving a foothold in the Americas to the representatives of a system of government and of international politics entirely alien to the traditions and practice of the American republics, would constitute a very serious danger to the peace and security of the two continents.

It must also be recognized that this threat may become a reality, not only through a formal transfer of territory, but also through circumstance arising out of the relative status of victor and vanquished, without there having been any formal expression regarding the disposition of these territories.

On June 17, 1940, the Secretary of State, after the Government of the United States had been informed that the Government of France had requested of the German Government the terms of an armistice, directed the representatives of the United States at Berlin and Rome to make a communication to the German and Italian Governments the pertinent paragraph of which is the following:

" The Government of the United States feels it desirable, in order to avoid any possible misunderstanding, to inform Your Excellency that in accordance with its traditional policy relating to the Western Hemisphere, the United States would not recognize any transfer, and would not acquiesce in any attempt to transfer, any geographic region of the Western Hemisphere from one non-American power to another non-American power." [1]

The Governments of France, Great Britain, and the Netherlands were informed in the same sense.

The Senate itself has also given evidence of its adherence to the policy which I have outlined above through the passage of S. J. Resolution 271 on June 17, 1940, "approving nonrecognition of the transfer of any geographic region in the Western Hemisphere from one non-American power to another non-American power, and providing for consultations with other American Republics in the event that such transfer should appear likely."

On July 21, 1940 there assembled at Havana the Second Meeting of the Ministers of Foreign Affairs of the American Republics for purposes of consultation in accordance with the procedure established at the Inter-American Conference for the Maintenance of Peace held at Buenos Aires in December 1936 and the Eighth International Conference of American States held at Lima in December 1938.

It was recognized that it would be contrary to the interests of the American Republics to permit the European possessions in the New World to become a subject of barter in the settlement of European differences and that such a situation would involve a threat to the peace and security of the hemisphere. Even in the absence of an actual transfer of sovereignty, it was evident that the use of these possessions to promote systems alien to the inter-American system could not be countenanced. Furthermore, in approaching this matter, it appeared desirable that any solution which might be reached should not carry with it the creation of any special interest for the benefit of any particular American Republic or Republics but that the solution should further the legitimate interests of all the American Republics as well as the interests of the possessions that might be involved. It was therefore agreed that in the event that conditions should so permit, such possessions as might be taken under control by, or on behalf of, the American Republics should be returned to their original sovereigns or declared independent, as soon as possible after the passing of the emergency which furnished the basis for the assumption of control over them.

To give effect to the foregoing, two measures were adopted at Havana, the Act of Havana, and the Convention submitted herewith. The former, a copy of which, as already stated, I enclose as essential information but not as requiring ratification, provides for the emergency establishment of a regime of provisional administration under specified conditions "when islands or regions in the Americas now under the possession of non-American nations are in danger of becoming the subject of barter of territory or change of sovereignty." The determination of the necessity for establishing such a provisional regime is entrusted to an emergency committee consisting of one representative of each of the American Republics, although provision is also made for individual or joint action on the part of any of the American Republics should the need be so urgent that consideration by the committee cannot be awaited. In other words, full freedom of action is retained by each of the American Republics, should the circumstances be such

---

[1] *Documents, II, 1939–40*, p. 90.

as in its estimation to require it to take provisional steps without prior submission of its views to the Committee.

The purpose of the Convention is to obtain the acceptance in treaty form of the mutual obligations recognized by the American Republics with respect to the situation envisaged in the "Act of Havana." It is my belief that this convention should be brought into force at the earliest possible date.

Respectfully submitted,

CORDELL HULL

B. European Possessions in the Western Hemisphere — Further Developments

The passage by the House of Representatives of H. J. Res. 556, 76th Cong., 3d sess., on June 18, 1940 preceded by the Senate's passage of S. J. 271 on June 17, provided a legislative approbation for announcing the United States policy of defense of the Western Hemisphere [1] and for its participation in the negotiation at Havana of the Act and Convention concerning the Provisional Administration of European Colonies and Possessions in the Americas, adopted July 30, 1940.[2] Prompt advice and consent by the Senate to ratification of the convention further committed the Congress to the policy involved. Failure of the 76th Congress, however, to reconcile the resolutions passed by the separate houses on June 17 and 18, 1940 left no legislative expression of that policy. Public Law 32, approved April 10, 1941 provided that formal commitment.

(1) *Joint Resolution Affirming and Approving Nonrecognition of the Transfer of Any Geographic Region in This Hemisphere from One Non-American Power to Another Non-American Power, and Providing for Consultation with Other American Republics in the Event That Such Transfer Should Appear Likely, Approved April 10, 1941* [3]

Whereas our traditional policy has been to consider any attempt on the part of non-American powers to extend their system to any portion of this hemisphere as dangerous to the peace and safety not only of this country but of the other American Republics; and

Whereas the American Republics agreed at the Inter-American Conference for the Maintenance of Peace held in Buenos Aires in 1936 and at the Eighth International Conference of American States held in Lima in 1938 to consult with one another in the event that the peace, security, or territorial integrity of any American republic should be threatened; and

Whereas the Meeting of the Foreign Ministers of the American Republics at Panama October 3, 1939, resolved "That in case any geographic

[1] *Documents, II, 1939–40*, p. 86–93.

[2] See p. 85.

[3] Public Law 32, 77th Cong.; originating as S. J. Res. 7, reported by chairman of the Committee on Foreign Relations, March 3, 1941; Sen. Report No. 76; passed Senate March 10; House Report No. 251, March 13.

region of America subject to the jurisdiction of any non-American state should be obliged to change its sovereignty and there should result therefrom a danger to the security of the American Continent, a consultative meeting such as the one now being held will be convoked with the urgency that the case may require": Therefore be it

Resolved by the Senate and House of Representatives of the United States of America in Congress assembled, (1) That the United States would not recognize any transfer, and would not acquiesce in any attempt to transfer, any geographic region of this [1] hemisphere from one non-American power to another non-American power; and

(2) That if such transfer or attempt to transfer should appear likely, the United States shall, in addition to other measures, immediately consult with the other American Republics to determine upon the steps which should be taken to safeguard their common interests.

(2) *French Possessions. Letter from the Secretary of State (Hull) to Senator James M. Mead, of New York, June 2, 1941* [2]

I have received your letter of May 21, 1941, setting forth the desirability, from a national defense standpoint, of the acquisition by the United States of French possessions in the Western Hemisphere and suggesting that this Government may undertake negotiations with the Government at Vichy for the establishment of defense bases in the French Islands of the Antilles, St. Pierre-Miquelon, as well as on French territory in French Guiana.

The Department is giving full and careful consideration to all aspects of the problem presented by these French territories in this Hemisphere and its possible implications as regards national security and defense. As you are no doubt aware, the policy of this Government as regards the French West Indies, which includes all territories subject to the jurisdiction of the High Commissioner for French territories in the Western Hemisphere, is governed by an agreement entered into at the Havana Conference in 1940 by all of the American Republics, including the United States, as well as by the arrangement entered into between the High Commissioner and Admiral Greenslade, U.S.N., and later confirmed by both Governments. This arrangement provides certain guar-

---

[1] The difference in the two resolutions of the 76th Congress was that S. J. Res. 271 employed the expression "Western Hemisphere" and H. J. Res. 556 used the expression "this hemisphere." The Under Secretary of State on January 28, 1941 informed Senator Tom Connally (Texas) that both phrases "mean the same thing and are used interchangeably" (Senate Report No. 76, 77th Cong., 1st sess.).

[2] Department of State, *Bulletin*, IV, p. 720.

antees regarding the movement of French vessels in American waters and commits the French Government to prior notification regarding any shipments of gold. It also permits the establishment of a daily patrol by vessel and by plane of the Islands of Martinique and Guadeloupe, and a Naval observer is at present stationed at Fort de France, Martinique, to check its observance.

This Government is also releasing on a monthly basis a restricted amount from French funds blocked in this country to permit the Islands to make purchases in this country of foodstuffs and essential supplies to maintain the economic structure of the Islands and French Guiana. It has been agreed that supplies purchased through the use of these funds shall be limited to products urgently required on the Islands themselves and shall not be for reexport from the Islands to French North Africa or Metropolitan France.

Should evidence develop so that further action by this Government in the interests of national defense be required, you may be assured that any action contemplated will accord with the agreement reached with the other American Republics at the Havana Conference.

(3) *Emergency Committee for the Provisional Administration of European Colonies and Possessions in the Americas, as of June 30, 1941*

The "Act of Havana" adopted by the Second Meeting of the Ministers of Foreign Affairs of the American Republics at Havana on July 30, 1940 provides for an Emergency Committee composed of a representative of each of the American Republics which is to be constituted as soon as two-thirds of the American Republics shall have appointed their members. On October 24, 1940 the Pan American Union was notified that Ecuador had appointed its member, whereupon the Committee may have been said to exist, inasmuch as Ecuador's appointment was the fourteenth to be made. By June 30, 1940 sixteen appointments had been made. The Committee shall assume the administration of any region in the Western Hemisphere now controlled by a European power whenever an attempt shall be made to transfer the sovereignty or control of such territory to another non-American nation. It is to function only until the Convention on the Provisional Administration of European Colonies and Possessions in the Americas shall come into effect. The purpose of the "Act of Havana" in establishing the Emergency Committee was to give immediate effect to the main provisions of the convention, also signed at Havana, regarding the setting up of a provisional administrative regime over any of the possessions now under the jurisdiction of a non-American government whenever an attempt may be made to transfer control or sovereignty thereof to another non-American government.

The "Act of Havana" also contains the important provision that, should the need for emergency action be so urgent that action by the Committee cannot be awaited, any of the American Republics may act individually or jointly with others in the manner which its own defense or that of the continent requires. The American Republic or Republics taking action under these circumstances must place the matter before the Committee immediately in order that it may adopt appropriate measures.

Bolivia	Señor Dr. Don Luis Fernando Guachalla, Minister at Washington
Brazil	Senhor Doutor Mauricio Nabuco
Costa Rica	Dr. Don Luis Fernández Rodriguez, Minister at Washington
Cuba	Dr. Aurelio Fernández Concheso, Ambassador at Washington
Dominican Republic	Señor Don Andres Pastoriza, Minister at Washington
Ecuador	Señor Capitán Colón Eloy Alfaro, Ambassador at Washington
El Salvador	Señor Dr. Don Hector David Castro, Minister at Washington
Guatemala	Señor Dr. Don Adrian Recinos, Minister at Washington
Haiti	Mr. Elie Lescot, Minister at Washington
Honduras	Señor Dr. Don Julian R. Caceres, Minister at Washington
Mexico	Dr. Francisco Castillo Nájera, Ambassador at Washington
Nicaragua	Señor Dr. Don Leon Bayle, Minister at Washington
Panama	Señor Dr. Don Jorge E. Boyd, Ambassador at Washington
Peru	Señor Don Manuel de Freyre y Santander, Ambassador at Washington
United States	The Honorable Sumner Welles, Under Secretary of State
Venezuela	Señor Dr. Don Diógenes Escalante, Ambassador at Washington

C. Coffee Marketing Agreement

The international adjustment of trade in specific commodities has become common since 1919. In the study of such problems by the League of Nations it became possible to envisage a system by which producing, marketing and consuming interests might be articulated by an international treaty which would take account of the actual commodity situation and establish a body to follow experience and to modify the arrangements from time to time within specified limits. A series of commodities was included in the agenda of the Monetary and Economic Conference convened at London in July 1933. Agreements on wheat and silver [1] were concluded subsequently in 1933 and an agreement on sugar [2] on May 6, 1937

The principles thus given international standing were in 1940 applied to coffee, of which the world production in 1939–40 amounted to 22,000,000 quintals (220 lbs.), with Central and South America accounting for 18,980,000 quintals, or 81% of that total. The United States takes for consumption substantially 40% of the approximately 5,000,000,000 lbs. of world production.

The Inter-American Coffee Marketing Agreement signed on November 28, 1940 on behalf of 15 of the republics, including the United States, was the first of its kind in the economic history of the American republics. The study of the coffee problem was entrusted to the Inter-American Financial and Economic Advisory Committee by a resolution of the Havana Meeting of the Ministers of Foreign Affairs of the American Republics (resolution XXV [3]). The American Republics that signed the agreement are the United States of America, Brazil, Colombia, Costa Rica, Cuba, Dominican Republic, Ecuador, El Salvador, Guatemala, Haiti, Honduras, Mexico, Nicaragua, Peru, and Venezuela.

The principal object of the agreement, which was drafted by the Inter-American Financial and Economic Advisory Committee, is to allocate equitably the market of the United States and that of the rest of the world among the various coffee-producing countries through the adoption of basic annual export quotas for each country.

[1] *Treaties, Conventions,* etc., 1923–1937, IV, p. 5507.   [2] *Ibid.,* p. 5599.   [3] See p. 82.

(1) Inter-American Coffee Agreement, Signed at Washington, November 28, 1940 [1]

In force April 16, 1941 by virtue of the protocol [2] of April 15, 1941 (as provided in Article XX) for Brazil, Colombia, Costa Rica, El Salvador, Guatemala, Haiti, Honduras, Mexico, Peru and the United States; for Ecuador, April 30, 1941; for the Dominican Republic, May 1, 1941; for Nicaragua, May 14, 1941.

The Governments of Brazil, Colombia, Costa Rica, Cuba, the Dominican Republic, Ecuador, El Salvador, Guatemala, Haiti, Honduras, Mexico, Nicaragua, Peru, the United States of America and Venezuela,

CONSIDERING THAT

in view of the unbalanced situation in the international trade in coffee affecting the economy of the Western Hemisphere, it is necessary and desirable to take steps to promote the orderly marketing of coffee, with a view to assuring terms of trade equitable for both producers and consumers by adjusting the supply to demand,

Have accordingly agreed as follows:

ARTICLE I. In order to allocate equitably the market of the United States of America for coffee among the various coffee producing countries, the following quotas are adopted as basic annual quotas for the exportation of coffee to the United States of America from the other countries participating in this Agreement:

Producing Country	Bags of 60 Kilograms [3] Net, or Equivalent Quantities
Brazil	9,300,000
Colombia	3,150,000
Costa Rica	200,000
Cuba	80,000
Dominican Republic	120,000
Ecuador	150,000
El Salvador	600,000
Guatemala	535,000
Haiti	275,000
Honduras	20,000
Mexico	475,000
Nicaragua	195,000
Peru	25,000
Venezuela	420,000
Total	15,545,000

[1] Department of State, *Bulletin,* III, p. 483.
[2] Text in Department of State, *Bulletin,* IV, p. 487.
[3] Executive Order No. 8758, May 21, 1941 (6 *Fed. Reg.,* p. 2535) establishes the conversion factors of 132.276 pounds per 60 kilograms and 1.2 pounds of green to 1 pound of roasted coffee.

For the control of the quotas for the United States market, the official import statistics compiled by the United States Department of Commerce shall be used.

ARTICLE II. The following quotas have been adopted as basic annual quotas for the exportation of coffee to the market outside the United States from the other countries participating in this Agreement:

Producing Country	Bags of 60 Kilograms Net, or Equivalent Quantities
Brazil	7,813,000
Colombia	1,079,000
Costa Rica	242,000
Cuba	62,000
Dominican Republic	138,000
Ecuador	89,000
El Salvador	527,000
Guatemala	312,000
Haiti	327,000
Honduras	21,000
Mexico	239,000
Nicaragua	114,000
Peru	43,000
Venezuela	606,000
Total	11,612,000

ARTICLE III. The Inter-American Coffee Board provided for in Article IX of this Agreement shall have the authority to increase [1] or decrease the quotas for the United States market in order to adjust supplies to estimated requirements. No such increase or decrease shall be made oftener than once every six months nor shall any change at any one time exceed 5 per cent of the basic quotas specified in Article I. The total increase or decrease in the first quota year shall not exceed 5 per cent of such basic quotas. Any increase or decrease in the quotas shall remain in effect until superseded by a new change in quotas, and the quotas for any quota year shall be calculated by applying to the basic quotas the weighted average of the changes made by the Board during the same year. Except as provided in Articles IV, V and VII, the percentage of each of the participating countries in the total quantity of coffee which these countries may export to the United States market shall be maintained unchanged.

The Board shall also have the authority to increase or decrease the export quotas for the market outside the United States to the extent

[1] By resolution of the Inter-American Coffee Board, May 28, 1941, these quotas were increased by 5% amounting to a total increase of 259,757 bags.

that it deems necessary to adjust supplies to estimated requirements, maintaining unchanged the percentage of each of the participating countries in the total quantity of coffee to be exported to that market, except as provided in Articles IV, V and VII. Nevertheless, the Board shall not have the authority to distribute these quotas among determined countries or regions of the market outside the United States.

ARTICLE IV. Each producing country participating in this Agreement undertakes to limit its coffee exports to the United States of America during each quota year, to its respective export quota.

In the event that, due to unforeseen circumstances, a country's total exports of coffee to the United States of America exceed in any quota year its export quota for the United States market, that quota for the following year shall be decreased by the amount of the excess.

If any producing country participating in this Agreement has exported in any quota year less than its quota for the United States market, the Board may increase that country's quota for the immediately following quota year by an amount equal to the deficiency for the preceding quota year, up to the limit of 10 per cent of the quota for such previous year.

The provisions of this Article shall also apply to the export quotas for the market outside the United States.

Any exportation of coffee to the market outside the United States which may be lost by fire, inundation or any other accident, before arriving at any foreign port, shall not be charged against the quota of the respective country corresponding to the date of shipment, provided that the loss is duly established before the Inter-American Coffee Board.

ARTICLE V. In view of the possibility of changes in the demand for coffee of a particular origin in the market outside the United States, the Board is empowered, by a two-thirds vote, to transfer, on the request of any participating country, a part of that country's quota for the United States market to its quota for the market outside the United States in order to bring about a better balance between supply and demand in special types of coffee. In such cases, the Board is authorized to make up the resulting deficiency in the total quota for the United States market by increasing the quotas of the other producing countries participating in this Agreement in proportion to their basic quotas.

ARTICLE VI. Each producing country participating in this Agreement shall take all measures necessary on its part for the execution and operation of this Agreement and shall issue for each coffee shipment an official document certifying that the shipment is within the corresponding quota fixed in accordance with the provisions of this Agreement.

ARTICLE VII. The Government of the United States of America shall take all measures necessary on its part for the execution and operation of this Agreement and shall limit, during each quota year, the entry for consumption into the United States of America of coffee produced in the countries listed in Article I to the quotas as established in the said Article or as modified pursuant to other provisions of this Agreement, it being understood that notice of any modified quotas will be communicated by the Board to the Governments of the countries participating in this Agreement.

The Government of the United States of America also undertakes to limit the total entry for consumption of coffee produced in countries other than those listed in Article I of this Agreement to a basic annual quota of 355,000 bags of 60 kilograms net or equivalent quantities. The quota on such coffee shall be increased or decreased by the same proportion and at the same time as the global quota of the participating countries for the United States market.

In the event that due to unforeseen circumstances any quota is exceeded during any quota year, that quota for the following year shall be decreased by the amount of the excess.

ARTICLE VIII. In the event that there should be foreseen an imminent shortage of coffee in the United States market in relation to its requirements, the Inter-American Coffee Board shall have the authority, as an emergency measure, to increase the quotas for the United States market, in proportion to the basic quotas, up to the quantity necessary to satisfy these requirements even though in this manner the limits specified in Article III may be exceeded. Any member of the Board may request such an increase and the increase may be authorized by a one-third vote of the Board.

When, owing to special circumstances, it may be necessary for the purposes of the present Agreement to reduce the quotas for the United States market by a percentage greater than that established in Article III, the Inter-American Coffee Board shall also have the authority to exceed the percentage of reduction beyond the limits established by the said Article III, provided that this is approved by the unanimous vote of the Board.

ARTICLE IX. The present Agreement shall be under the administration of a Board, which shall be known as the "Inter-American Coffee Board," and which shall be composed of delegates representing the Governments of the participating countries.

Each Government shall appoint a delegate to the Board upon approval of the Agreement. In the absence of the delegate of any participating country, his Government shall appoint an alternate who shall act in place of the delegate. Subsequent appointments shall be communicated by the respective Governments to the Chairman of the Board.

The Board shall elect from among its members a Chairman and a Vice-Chairman who shall hold office for such period as it may determine.

The seat of the Board shall be in Washington, D. C.

ARTICLE X. The Board shall have the following powers and duties in addition to those specifically set forth in other Articles of this Agreement:

(*a*) The general administration of the present Agreement;

(*b*) To appoint any employees that it may consider necessary and determine their powers, duties, compensation and duration of employment;

(*c*) To appoint an Executive Committee and such other permanent or temporary committees as it considers advisable, and to determine their functions and duties;

(*d*) To approve an annual budget of expenses and fix the amount to be contributed by each participating Government in accordance with the principles laid down in Article XIII;

(*e*) To seek such information as it may deem necessary to the proper operation and administration of this Agreement; and to publish such information as it may consider desirable;

(*f*) To make an annual report covering all of its activities and any other matters of interest in connection with this Agreement at the end of each quota year. This report shall be transmitted to each of the participating Governments.

ARTICLE XI. The Board shall undertake, as soon as possible, a study of the problem of coffee surpluses in the producing countries participating in this Agreement, and shall also take appropriate steps with a view to working out satisfactory methods of financing the storage of such surpluses in cases where such action is urgently needed to stabilize the coffee industry. Upon request, the Board shall assist and advise any participating Government which may desire to negotiate loans in connection with the operation of this Agreement. The Board is also authorized to render assistance in matters relating to the classification, storage and handling of coffee.

ARTICLE XII. The Board shall appoint a Secretary and take all other necessary measures to establish a Secretariat which shall be entirely free and independent of any other national or international organization and institution.

ARTICLE XIII. The expenses of delegates to the Board shall be defrayed by their respective Governments. All other expenses necessary for the administration of the present Agreement, including those of the

Secretariat, shall be met by annual contributions of the Governments of the participating countries. The total amount, manner and time of payment shall be determined by the Board by a majority of not less than two-thirds of the votes. The contribution of each Government shall be proportionate to the total of its respective basic quotas, except that the Government of the United States of America will accept as its contribution an amount equal to 33⅓ per cent of the total required contribution.

ARTICLE XIV. Regular meetings of the Board shall be held on the first Tuesday of January, April, July and October. Special meetings shall be called by the Chairman at any other time at his discretion, or upon written request of delegates representing not less than five of the participating Governments, or fifteen per cent of the quotas specified in Article I, or one-third of the votes established in Article XV. Notice of all special meetings shall be communicated to the delegates not less than three days before the date fixed for the meeting.

The presence of delegates representing not less than 75 per cent of the total votes of all the participating Governments shall be necessary to constitute a quorum for a meeting. Any participating Government may, through its delegate, by written notice to the Chairman, appoint the delegate of another participating Government to represent it and to vote on its behalf at any meeting of the Board.

Except as otherwise provided in this Agreement, decisions of the Board shall be taken by a simple majority of the votes, it being understood that, in every case, the computation shall be calculated on the basis of the total votes of all the participating Governments.

ARTICLE XV. The votes to be exercised by the delegates of the participating Governments shall be as follows:

Brazil	9
Colombia	3
Costa Rica	1
Cuba	1
Dominican Republic	1
Ecuador	1
El Salvador	1
Guatemala	1
Haiti	1
Honduras	1
Mexico	1
Nicaragua	1
Peru	1
United States of America	12
Venezuela	1
Total	36

ARTICLE XVI. The official reports of the Board to the participating Governments shall be written in the four official languages of the Pan American Union.

ARTICLE XVII. The participating Governments agree to maintain, in so far as possible, the normal and usual operation of the coffee trade.

ARTICLE XVIII. The Board is authorized to appoint advisory committees in the important markets, to the end that consumers, importers and distributors of green and roasted coffee, as well as other interested persons, may be given an opportunity to express their views concerning the operation of the program established under this Agreement.

ARTICLE XIX. If the delegate of any participating Government alleges that any participating Government has failed to comply with the obligations of the present Agreement, the Board shall decide whether any infringement of the Agreement has taken place, and, if so, what measures shall be recommended to correct the situation arising therefrom.

ARTICLE XX. The present Agreement shall be deposited with the Pan American Union at Washington, which shall transmit authentic certified copies thereof to the signatory Governments.

The Agreement shall be ratified or approved by each of the signatory Governments in accordance with its legal requirements and shall come into force when the instruments of ratification or approval of all the signatory Governments have been deposited with the Pan American Union. As soon as possible after the deposit of any ratification the Pan American Union shall inform each of the signatory Governments thereof.

If, within ninety days [1] from the date of signature of this Agreement, the instruments of ratification or approval of all the signatory Governments have not been deposited, the Governments which have deposited their instruments of ratification or approval may put the Agreement into force among themselves by means of a Protocol. Such Protocol shall be deposited with the Pan American Union, which shall furnish certified copies thereof to each of the Governments on behalf of which the Protocol or the present Agreement was signed.

ARTICLE XXI. As long as the present Agreement remains in force, it shall prevail over provisions inconsistent therewith which may be contained in any other agreement previously concluded between any of the participating Governments. Upon the termination of the present Agreement, all the provisions which may have been temporarily suspended by virtue of this Agreement shall automatically again become

[1] The 90-day period ended February 26, 1941; the protocol was opened for signature on April 15, 1941.

operative unless they have been definitely terminated for other reasons.

ARTICLE XXII. The present Agreement shall apply, on the part of the United States of America, to the customs territory of the United States. Exports to the United States of America and quotas for the United States market shall be understood to refer to the customs territory of the United States.

ARTICLE XXIII. For the purpose of this Agreement the following definitions are adopted:

(1) "Quota year" means the period of twelve months beginning October 1, and ending September 30 of the following calendar year.

(2) "Producing countries participating in this Agreement" means all participating countries except the United States of America.

(3) "The Board" means the Inter-American Coffee Board provided for in Article IX.

ARTICLE XXIV. Subject to the eventuality covered by Article XXV, the present Agreement shall remain in force until October 1, 1943.

Not less than one year prior to October 1, 1943 the Board shall make recommendations to the participating Governments as to the continuation or otherwise of the Agreement. The recommendations, if in favor of continuation, may suggest amendments to the Agreement.

Each participating Government shall signify to the Board its acceptance or rejection of the recommendations referred to in the immediately preceding paragraph within six months after the date of the receipt of such recommendations. This period may be extended by the Board.

If said recommendations are accepted by all the participating Governments, the participating Governments undertake to take such measures as may be necessary to carry out said recommendations. The Board shall draw up a declaration certifying the terms of said recommendations and their acceptance by all the participating Governments, and the present Agreement shall be deemed to be amended in accordance with this declaration as from the date specified therein. A certified copy of the declaration together with a certified copy of the Agreement as amended shall be communicated to the Pan American Union and to each of the participating Governments.

The same procedure for making amendments or for the continuation of the Agreement may be followed at any other time.

ARTICLE XXV. Any of the participating Governments may withdraw from the present Agreement after prior notification of one year to the Pan American Union which shall promptly inform the Board. If one or more participating Governments representing 20 per cent or more of

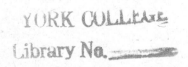

the total quotas specified in Article I of this Agreement withdraw therefrom, the Agreement will thereupon terminate.

ARTICLE XXVI. In the event that because of special and extraordinary circumstances the Board should believe that the period fixed by Article XXIV for the duration of this Agreement might be reduced, it shall immediately notify all the participating Governments which, by unanimous agreement, may decide to terminate this Agreement prior to October 1, 1943.

TRANSITORY ARTICLE. All coffee entered for consumption into the United States of America between October 1, 1940 and September 30, 1941, both inclusive, shall be charged against the quotas for the first quota year.

All coffee exported to the market outside the United States between October 1, 1940 and September 30, 1941, both inclusive, shall be charged against the quotas for the first quota year.

Done at the City of Washington, in English, Spanish, Portuguese and French, the 28th day of November, 1940.

(2) *Joint Resolution to Carry Out the Obligations of the United States under the Inter-American Coffee Agreement, Signed at Washington on November 28, 1940, and for Other Purposes, Approved April 11, 1941* [1]

Whereas an Inter-American Coffee Agreement was signed at Washington on November 28, 1940, by representatives of the Governments of the United States of America, Brazil, Colombia, Costa Rica, Cuba, the Dominican Republic, Ecuador, El Salvador, Guatemala, Haiti, Honduras, Mexico, Nicaragua, Peru, and Venezuela; and

Whereas the said agreement contemplates the cooperation of the Government of the United States in a joint effort to promote the orderly marketing of coffee in international trade, with a view to assuring equitable terms for both producers and consumers by adjusting supply to demand: Therefore be it

Resolved by the Senate and House of Representatives of the United States of America in Congress assembled, That on and after the entry into force of the Inter-American Coffee Agreement, as proclaimed by the President, and during the continuation in force of the obligations of the United States thereunder, no coffee imported from any foreign country may be entered for consumption except as provided in the said agreement.

SEC. 2. The President is authorized to make such allocations of the

[1] Public Law 33, 77th Cong. 1st sess.; originating as S. J. Res. 43; Senate Report No. 74; House Report No. 330, pts. 1 and 2.

quota provided in the agreement for countries not participating in the said agreement as he finds necessary or appropriate in order to afford any such country or countries an opportunity to supply a fair share of the quota, whether or not required by any international obligation of the United States, or in order to make available the types of coffee usually consumed in the United States. The President is also authorized to make such rules and regulations as he finds necessary or appropriate to carry out the provisions of this joint resolution and of the said agreement, and with respect to any provision of such regulations for any act or performance by an importer of coffee, compliance therewith shall be a condition to the entry for consumption of the coffee in respect of which the act or performance is required.

(3) *Executive Order No. 8738 Allocating the Quota under the Inter-American Coffee Agreement for Countries Not Signatories of the Agreement, April 21, 1941* [1]

WHEREAS under the Inter-American Coffee Agreement signed on November 28, 1940, and the joint resolution of Congress approved April 11, 1941 (Public Law 33, 77th Cong., 1st sess.), the entry for consumption in the United States of coffee produced in countries which are not signatories of the Inter-American Coffee Agreement is limited to a basic annual quota of 355,000 bags of 60 kilograms net or equivalent quantities; and

WHEREAS I find that it is necessary to allocate the said quota in order to make available the types of coffee usually consumed in the United States:

Now, THEREFORE, by virtue of the authority vested in me by section 2 of the said joint resolution of April 11, 1941, it is hereby ordered as follows:

1. No more than the following-named quantities (in bags of 60 kilograms net or equivalent quantities) of the types of coffee specified below, produced in countries not signatories of the Inter-American Coffee Agreement, may be entered for consumption in the United States from the effective date of this order to August 31, 1941, inclusive:

   (*a*) Arabica:

   (1) Mocha, 20,000 bags.[2]

   (2) Other Arabica, 20,000 bags.

   (*b*) Species other than Arabica: The number of bags calculated by deducting from 315,000, the number of bags of coffee produced in such countries and entered for consumption from and including October 1, 1940, to the effective date of this order, as determined and made public by the Secretary of the Treasury.

2. This order shall become effective on the day following the day it is filed in the Division of the Federal Register, the National Archives.

FRANKLIN D. ROOSEVELT

THE WHITE HOUSE,
   April 21, 1941.

---

[1] Department of State, *Bulletin,* IV, p. 518; 6 *Fed. Reg.,* p. 2047.

[2] Executive Order No. 8774 of June 10, 1941 (6 *Fed. Reg.,* p. 2845) adjusts this quota up to August 31, 1941.

(4) *Organization and Activities of the Inter-American Coffee Board* [1]

The Inter-American Coffee Board organized and issued a statement April 17, 1941. The membership consists of representatives of the states for which the agreement is in force, the chairmanship falling to the United States and the vice-chairmanship to Brazil. The Executive Committee consists of the representatives of El Salvador, Brazil, Colombia, Guatemala and the United States.

(a) *Resolution of April 23, 1941 on Sales Statistics*

WHEREAS:

1. It is advisable to maintain up-to-date information on coffee sales registered in the producing countries, within the export quota; and

2. Having this information in due time would avoid all difficulties and would make it possible for the Board to follow the course of the sales of coffee in each country, and to know at all times the unfilled balance on their respective quotas;

Resolves:

1. To request of all the signatory governments of the Inter-American Coffee Agreement to communicate the amount of all coffee sales registered since the first of October last, in bags of 60 kgs.;

2. To request that henceforth they communicate through the most rapid medium, on Monday of each week, the amount of the sales registered up to and including Saturday of the previous week.

(b) *Resolution of May 15, 1941 on Evasive Practices*

The Inter-American Coffee Board has taken cognizance of the fact that efforts have been made to evade the intentions of the Inter-American Coffee Agreement through false representations to authorities in producing countries that particular lots of coffee were intended for sale in countries other than the United States, whereas the actual intention was to enter the coffee for consumption in the United States.

The Board condemns this practice and intends to take effective steps to terminate it, in cooperation with the governments of the countries participating in the Inter-American Coffee Agreement.

(c) *Resolutions of May 28, 1941 on Increase of Quotas*

WHEREAS:

An emergency situation is presented due to the possible scarcity of means of transportation to the United States in the future, which might lead to an imminent shortage of coffee in the market of the United States in relation to its needs;

In these circumstances it is deemed convenient to authorize the forward shipment of a reasonable amount of coffee belonging to the next quota year, making use of the faculties which for cases of emergency are conferred upon the Board by Article VIII of the Inter-American Coffee Agreement;

Therefore Resolves:

1. To authorize the participating producing countries, once they have exported the total amount of their respective quotas for the current quota year, to export

[1] Excerpted from Department of State, *Bulletin*, IV, p. 720–2. English versions of resolutions by State Department.

to the United States before next September 30, to be charged to their respective quotas for the next quota year, an amount of coffee not to exceed 15 per cent of their respective basic quotas, on condition that the coffee so exported be warehoused under the supervision of the United States customs authorities so that it is not entered for consumption before October 1, 1941.

2. To recommend that the necessary measures be taken to prevent the reserve stock existing in the custom houses of the United States next October 1, due to the exportations authorized above, from disturbing the normal course of the coffee market at the beginning of the next quota year.

WHEREAS:

1. The consumption of coffee in the United States has shown a steady increase during recent years, and appears to be still increasing; and

2. It is desirable that adequate supplies of coffee be available to meet estimated requirements of the United States market;

Resolves:

1. To increase, as of June 1, 1941, the quotas for the United States market by 5 per cent of the basic quotas, in accordance with the provisions of Article III of the Inter-American Coffee Agreement; . . .

D. Office for Coordination of Commercial and Cultural Relations Between the American Republics [1]

(1) *Order Establishing the Office, August 16, 1940* [2]

Pursuant to authority vested in it by section 2 of the Act of August 29, 1916 (39 Stat. 649), the Council of National Defense, with the approval of the President, hereby establishes as a subordinate body to the Council an office to be known as the Office for Coordination of Commercial and Cultural Relations Between the American Republics, at the head of which there shall be a Coordinator of Commercial and Cultural Relations Between the American Republics (hereinafter referred to as the Coordinator). The Coordinator shall serve as such without compensation but shall be entitled to actual and necessary transportation, subsistence and other expense incidental to the performance of his duties.

The Coordinator shall:

(1) establish and maintain liaison between the Advisory Commission, the several departments and establishments of the Government and with such other agencies, public or private, as the Coordinator may deem

---

[1] Other releases issued by the Office appear at p.111, 115.

[2] Department of State, *Bulletin*, III, p. 151. The Coordinator of Commercial and Cultural Relations Between the American Republics announced on November 14, 1940 the names of the advisers appointed to serve on the Policy Committee, the Scholarship Committee, the Literary Committee, Publications Committee, Music Committee and Art Committee. (Release from Office, November 14, 1940.)

necessary or desirable to insure proper coordination of, and economy and efficiency in, the activities of the Government with respect to hemisphere defense, with particular reference to the commercial and cultural aspects of the problem, and shall also be available to assist in the coordination and carrying out of the purposes of Public Resolution No. 83 — 76th Congress (H. J. Res. 367); [1]

(2) be a member and chairman of the Inter-Departmental Committee on Inter-American affairs, which shall include the President of the Export-Import Bank, one designate from each of the following Departments: State, Agriculture, Treasury, and Commerce, and such representatives from other agencies and departments as may be needed from time to time, the Committee to consider and correlate proposals of the Government with respect to hemisphere defense, commercial and cultural relations and to make recommendations to the appropriate Government departments and agencies;

(3) be responsible directly to the President, to whom he shall submit reports and recommendations with respect to the activities of his office;

(4) review existing laws, coordinate research by the several Federal agencies, and recommend to the Inter-Departmental Committee such new legislation as may be deemed essential to the effective realization of the basic objectives of the Government's program;

(5) be charged with the formulation and the execution of a program in cooperation with the State Department which, by effective use of Governmental and private facilities in such fields as the arts and sciences, education and travel, the radio, the press, and the cinema, will further national defense and strengthen the bonds between the nations of the Western Hemisphere.

Nelson A. Rockefeller is hereby appointed Coordinator of Commercial and Cultural Relations between the American Republics.

> HENRY L. STIMSON, *Secretary of War;*
> FRANK KNOX, *Secretary of the Navy;*
> HAROLD L. ICKES, *Secretary of the Interior;*
> H. A. WALLACE, *Secretary of Agriculture;*
> ROBERT H. HINCKLEY, *Acting Secretary of Commerce;*
> C. V. McLAUGHLIN, *Acting Secretary of Labor.*

Approved:

> FRANKLIN D. ROOSEVELT,
> *The White House,*
> *August 16, 1940.*

[1] *Documents, II, 1939–1940,* p. 173.

(2) *Representation of United States Business in American Republics.* *Statement of the Coordinator (Rockefeller), January 8, 1941* [1]

As a defense measure, the Office of the Coordinator has undertaken a continuing study of the representation of United States business in the other American Republics in cooperation with the Department of State and other interested Government agencies. The first phase of the study is now completed, and its results are being made available to the interested Government departments.

Shortly after the Office of the Coordinator was established on August 16, 1940, a mission sponsored by this Office undertook a comprehensive study in Central and South America in cooperation with United States Foreign Service officers. The mission was headed by Percy L. Douglas, on leave of absence from the Otis Elevator Company, International Division, and included John Lockwood, New York lawyer, and George H. Butler, of the State Department, as well as a group of technical assistants. The mission returned to the United States in December after visits to 18 of the other 20 American Republics and has reported to the Coordinator.

The work of correlating the findings on a hemisphere basis is nearing completion. Examination of the country-by-country reports discloses the following facts:

1. That United States business is frequently represented in Central and South America by firms and individuals now known to support objectives contrary to the best interests of the American Republics.

2. That these representatives often use advertising appropriations of United States business firms to force newspapers and in some instances radio stations to adopt anti-American editorial policies.

3. That many employees of United States companies or their affiliates in Central and South America are known members of local anti-American organizations.

4. That many anti-American firms, which formerly sold only European products, have now succeeded in obtaining agencies for United States business. These new connections are keeping them alive and enabling them to maintain their trade contacts. In many instances, they openly declare they will return to their former lines at the expiration of the war.

5. That many of these agents who now represent United States firms are obtaining through this medium confidential trade information which is made available to anti-American powers.

[1] Department of State, *Bulletin*, IV, p. 63.

6. That profits thus derived from representation of United States firms are being used to finance operations of propaganda agencies in Central and South America.

7. That many of the firms representing United States companies also serve as centers for distribution of anti-American literature and propaganda.

8. Many of the larger anti-American firms have established their own purchasing agents in the United States and with the goods obtained in this market remain in business.

9. Officers and employees of a number of firms, representing United States businesses, are officials of anti-American powers.

The purpose of the mission was to discover the extent of such practices and their effect on hemisphere defense. The mission's findings indicate that the majority of our exporting firms are not represented in Central and South America by agents with non-American connections, but that there are a sufficient number to make this a serious concern from a defense point of view. It should be emphasized also that in many cases the firms involved have had no knowledge of the anti-American activities of their agents, and thus they have unwittingly contributed to our own difficulties and to those of our neighbors. In many cases, the connections are traceable to recent non-American pressures, the application of which could not have been foreseen when the connection was established.

Many United States companies have already taken steps to remedy the situation by cooperating with the nationals in the countries in which they operate to appoint agents friendly to inter-American solidarity. It is confidently anticipated that our exporting firms as a whole will cooperate as soon as they are apprised of the situation as it relates to their interests.

E. Inter-American Development Commission and the National Councils [1]

(1) *Statement on the Establishment of the Commission (June 3, 1940) and the South American Councils*

The Inter-American Development Commission was established on June 3, 1940 as a working unit of the Inter-American Financial and Economic Advisory Committee, which was organized following the meeting of Foreign Ministers at Panama in 1939.[2] Whereas the parent body is composed of representatives of the 21 American Republics, the Commission consists of only five members, who are:

[1] Compiled from Department of State, *Bulletin*, III, p. 464; IV, p. 14, 181, 287, 373, 423, 635, 700.

[2] *Documents, II, 1939–40*, p. 100–4.

Nelson A. Rockefeller, chairman, Coordinator of Commercial and Cultural
Relations Between the American Republics, Office for Emergency Management in the Executive Office of the President;

J. Rafael Oreamuno, vice chairman, former Minister of Costa Rica in Washington;

George W. Magalhaes, special representative of the Westinghouse Electric
International Co., New York City;

Renato de Azevedo, New York representative of the Lloyd Brasileiro Navigation
Co.;

Carlos Campbell del Campo, commercial counselor of the Embassy of Chile
in the United States.

The Commission is designated as a permanent commission which shall
compile basic information, establish contacts between interested parties,
and recommend in each case or in general the facilities and assurances
which these enterprises should obtain from the Latin American governments. These enterprises are devoted to (a) the exploration and exploitation of the mineral resources in Latin America; (b) the cultivation and
marketing of agricultural and forest products; and (c) the establishment
and development of industrial plants.

The Commission is carrying out the assignment along the following
lines: (1) by stimulating the increase of non-competitive imports from
Latin America to the United States; (2) by stimulating and increasing
trade between the Latin American countries themselves; and (3) by
encouraging development of industry in Latin America, particularly
along the lines of production of consumer goods.

Messrs. Oreamuno and Magalhaes were designated on November 27,
1940 to establish national councils throughout South America, and left
New York immediately thereafter for Rio de Janeiro. The mission
visited the following countries: Argentina, Bolivia, Brazil, Chile, Colombia, Ecuador, Paraguay, Peru, Uruguay, and Venezuela. In each of these
South American countries they organized a five-man group which will
carry out the program of the Inter-American Development Commission
in Washington. These groups are drafted from the ranks of industry,
finance, agriculture, and the professions in each country. All governments concerned gave their assent to the proposed expansion.

The National Councils were organized between December 1940 and
June 1941 under chairmen as follows:

1. Brazil: Chairman, Leonardo Truda, member of the Conselho do Comercio
   do Brasil; chairman of commercial and economic mission to Caribbean
   countries, 1940; former president Bank of Brazil;
2. Argentina: Chairman, Dr. Raul Prebisch, general manager of the Banco
   Central;

3. Uruguay: Chairman, Fermin Silveira Zorzi, general manager of the Banco de la República;
4. Paraguay: Chairman, Oscar Perez Uribe, president of the Centro de Importadores;
5. Chile: Chairman, Dr. Guillermo del Pedregal, vice president of the Corporación de Fomento;
6. Bolivia: Chairman, Jesús Lozada, of the Ministry of Finance;
7. Peru: Chairman, Benjamin Roca, former Minister of Finance;
8. Colombia: Chairman, Mariano Roldán, Minister of Economia Nacional, chairman of the Instituto de Fomento Industrial;
9. Ecuador: Chairman, Dr. Antonio Queredo, former Minister of Foreign Affairs, director of the Central Bank of Ecuador;
10. Venezuela: Chairman, Dr. Oscar Augusto Machado, director of the Compañía Anónima de la Electricidad de Caracas.

At a later date, a second mission will establish similar agencies in Costa Rica, Cuba, the Dominican Republic, El Salvador, Guatemala, Haiti, Honduras, Mexico, Nicaragua, and Panama.

F. Shipping and Communications

(1) Inter-American Maritime Conference, Washington, November 25–December 2, 1940 [1]

The Inter-American Maritime Conference adjourned December 2 after unanimously adopting 12 resolutions on shipping problems of the American Republics. All the resolutions were directed to the Inter-American Financial and Economic Advisory Committee, under whose auspices the Conference was held.

The 12 resolutions adopted as the Final Act of the Conference were drawn up by a special committee which was named to coordinate the 38 resolutions that had been introduced by the various delegations. This committee was presided over by the Delegate of El Salvador, Dr. Hector David Castro.

In closing the Conference Assistant Secretary of State Henry F. Grady, Chairman of the Conference, thanked the delegates for the serious attention given to the shipping problems before the Conference and said he considered it a "splendid example of the real work which can be accomplished at a meeting of this sort."

The subjects dealt with in the 12 resolutions adopted are as follows:
1. Inter-American Steamship and Transshipment Facilities.
2. Maintenance of Present Inter-American Maritime Services.

[1] Department of State, *Bulletin*, III, p. 517. For the Proceedings of the Inter-American Maritime Conference, see Pan American Union, Congress and Conference Series No. 34.

3. Transportation of Perishable Products.

4. Free Ports.

5. Tourist Travel.

6. Ocean Freight-Rate Problems.

7. General Average and York-Antwerp Rules.

8. Full-Time Service of Inspection and Visit.

9. Port Dues, Charges, Taxes, and Other Imposts on Shipping.

10. Transportation of Cargo in National Vessels.

11. Uniformity in Shipping Statistics.

12. Establishment of a Permanent Inter-American Maritime Organization.

(2) *Creation of the Committee for Coordination of Inter-American Shipping* [1]

With a view to assuring adequate tonnage for continued movement of inter-American products, there has been created, with the approval of the President, a Committee for Coordination of Inter-American Shipping, composed of James V. Forrestal, Under Secretary of the Navy, Rear Admiral Emory S. Land, Chairman of the Maritime Commission, and Nelson A. Rockefeller, Coordinator of Commercial and Cultural Relations Between the American Republics.

The Committee will seek to coordinate the shipping requirements of the Central and South American trades with the supply of vessel tonnage under the jurisdiction of the Maritime Commission and with the needs of the military branches of the Government. The Committee proposes, through cooperation with the shipping companies, to plan use of available tonnage in an effort to ensure adequate transportation for cargoes to be moved in both directions during 1941.

Estimates of the Maritime Commission indicate that adequate shipping will be available to handle the requirements of inter-American trade in 1941 if the vessels now operating are retained in this service and with the addition of certain vessels now intended for the trade. At present there are, the Maritime Commission estimates, approximately 119 vessels regularly serving the east and west coasts of South America. Fifty-four of these fly the flag of the United States, 22 are of Norwegian ownership, and the balance are operated under other flags, including those of Central and South America.

In establishing this Committee the Government does so with the recognition that the uninterrupted flow of commerce between the United

[1] Department of State, *Bulletin*, IV, p. 163, released to the press by the Office for Coordination of Commercial and Cultural Relations Between the American Republics, February 7, 1941.

States and Central and South American nations is directly related to the national defense program and to the economic welfare of the American Republics.

(3) *Requisitioning of Foreign-Flag Vessels in American Ports. Resolution of the Inter-American Financial and Economic Advisory Committee, April 26, 1941* [1]

[See Chapter VIII for Requisitioning of Ships, p. 629.]

WHEREAS:

Subparagraph (D) of Article 2, Resolution IV,[2] on economic cooperation, of the Meeting of Foreign Ministers of the American Republics at Panama in 1939 charged the Inter-American Financial and Economic Advisory Committee with studying and proposing to the Governments the most effective measures for mutual cooperation to lessen or offset dislocations in the trade of the American Republics resulting from the present war;

The commerce of the American Republics has normally been carried on in large measure in merchant vessels of non-American powers, many of which are not available for such trade because of the increasing rate of destruction of the means of maritime transportation by the belligerent nations, the consequent increased diversion of such vessels to other trades, and the prolonged stationing by their owners of a large number of such vessels in American ports interrupting their normal commercial activities; and

The resulting shipping shortage has prejudiced and is prejudicing the commerce of and among the American Republics, creating a very grave problem for the fundamental right of the nations of the Americas to preserve the trade which is essential to their normal existence;

Some of the American Republics have already been forced to take steps with a view to remedying this situation; and

Bearing in mind the recommendations of the Inter-American Neutrality Committee, which were adopted by Resolution I [3] of the Second Meeting of the Ministers of Foreign Affairs of the American Republics at Havana in July 1940,

The Inter-American Financial and Economic Advisory Committee

Resolves:

To recommend to the Governments of the American Republics:

a. That they declare that the foreign flag vessels in American ports, the normal commercial activities of which have been interrupted as a

---

[1] Department of State, *Bulletin*, IV, p. 531.

[2] *Documents, II, 1939–40*, p. 101; resolution III is referred to.   [3] See p. 63.

consequence of the war, may now be utilized by the American Republics in accordance with the rules of international law and the provisions of their respective national legislations, in such a manner as to promote the defense of their economies as well as the peace and security of the continent. The utilization of said vessels may be effected by the American Republics either through agreements with the owners of the vessels or by virtue of the right of each of the American Republics to assume complete jurisdiction and control over such vessels, and as they may deem it convenient to satisfy their own requirements.

b. That just and adequate compensation for the utilization of the said vessels be made in accordance with the commonly accepted rules of international law and the national legislations of each of the American Republics. In the determination of this compensation, the damages which might have been caused and the other obligations resulting by the presence of these ships in the ports in which they may be, shall be taken into consideration.

c. That they reaffirm their full right to the free navigation of those vessels, both in their national and international trade, once they are under the flag of any one of the American republics, and that they agree upon measures tending to facilitate the effective exercise of said right.

(4) *Proposed Inter-American Highway. Historical Release of the Department of State, May 10, 1941* [1]

The President on May 1, 1941 transmitted to the Congress of the United States a draft of proposed legislation authorizing the appropriation of a sum not to exceed 20 million dollars to enable the United States to cooperate with the Governments of the Republics in Central America, that is with the Governments of the Republics of Costa Rica, El Salvador, Guatemala, Honduras, Nicaragua, and Panama, in the survey and construction of the proposed inter-American highway within the borders of those republics.

The Secretary of State, in his report transmitting the draft bill to the President, stated that the section of the highway in question is approximately 1,550 miles in length, reaching from the Panama Canal to the border between Guatemala and Mexico, where it would connect with the Mexican section of the highway and provide direct transportation from Laredo, Tex., to the Canal Zone.

Principal reasons why it is considered desirable for the United States to make a direct contribution in the completion of the highway were set forth by the Secretary of State as follows: (1) Improved transportation

[1] Department of State, *Bulletin*, IV, p. 557.

within and between the several countries and the United States; (2) development of new lands and new natural resources, and increased consumption of American imports; (3) increased employment and maintenance of economic structures; (4) increased tourist traffic; (5) increased market for American automobiles, parts, garage equipment, etc.; (6) defense value; and (7) the fact that from 80 to 90 per cent or more of the amounts appropriated under this bill would be spent for the purchase of American machinery and equipment, for transportation thereof on American vessels, and for salaries of American engineers, resulting in between 16 and 18 million dollars of additional American exports, not to mention increased employment afforded thereby in the United States and Central America.

The report stated in part:

The definite advantages which the United States, as well as the Central American countries, would derive from the completion of the highway, at least as far south as the Panama Canal, have long been recognized and, during the past few months, increased consideration has been given to the ways and means of completing this road in the near future. This highway has been the subject of numerous conferences between the Departments of State, War, and Navy, and the Public Roads Administration. The conclusion has been reached that the road cannot be completed within the forseeable future without the assumption of a substantial part of the necessary expenditures by the Government of the United States, and that the completion of the road is of such interest to this Government that such direct participation by it is justified. . . . While defense considerations have not motivated the suggestion for an outright contribution by this Government to the construction of the highway, the War and Navy Departments believe that a through highway from the United States to the Panama Canal would be of real value from the standpoint of the defense of the Caribbean area. The importance of political stability in all the countries of the Western Hemisphere at this time can hardly be exaggerated and this is in turn largely dependent upon the maintenance of economic stability. The project contemplated by this proposed legislation will contribute directly to the maintenance of order, as improved communications will give the established governments in these countries materially more effective control over any attempted subversive activities within their borders and the actual work of construction would substantially assist in safeguarding the economic situation in these countries.

The first official cooperative action directed toward the construction of an all-American highway took the form of a resolution passed by the Fifth International Conference of American States at Santiago, Chile, as early as 1923. Since that time the United States has participated in a number of highway conferences, several of which have had as their primary purpose promoting the development of an inter-American highway. At the Inter-American Conference for the Maintenance of Peace, held at Buenos Aires in 1936, a Convention on the Pan American Highway was signed by the 21 American Republics and has since been ratified by 11 of the signatory governments. The Fourth Pan American Highway Congress, which will be held in Mexico City from September 15 to 24 of this year, will be attended by a delegation from the United States.

The Government of the United States has at various times appropriated sums to cover its share of survey and construction work on the proposed highway. In 1930, $50,000 was appropriated by Congress to enable the Secretary of State to cooperate with the several governments members of the Pan American Union in carrying out a reconnaissance survey of the route of the proposed inter-American highway. A further sum of $1,000,000 was appropriated in 1934 to enable the United States to cooperate with those governments in the survey and construction of the highway, subject to "the receipt of assurances satisfactory to the President from such governments of their cooperation in such survey and construction." In the same year an additional sum of $75,000 was made available to the Secretary of Agriculture for making location surveys, plans, and estimates. In 1938, $34,000 from accumulated administrated funds was made available to the Secretary of Agriculture for the continuation of cooperation. In the same year $50,000 was appropriated to enable the Secretary of State to continue in the collaboration, but was limited by the terms of the act to expenditures for engineering advice and assistance and, as in the case of previous appropriations, was subject to the receipt of assurances satisfactory to the President of the continued cooperation of the governments concerned in the project.

A loan of $2,000,000 was made to Nicaragua in 1939 for construction of a section of the Inter-American Highway. In 1940 a loan of $4,600,000 was made to Costa Rica for the same purpose. These loans are being expended under the supervision of officials of the Public Roads Administration of the United States.

A credit of $1,150,000 was recently extended by the Export-Import Bank to the Government of Ecuador, $900,000 of which was intended for expenditure on road construction, with preference being given to highways that will complete an international highway through Ecuador. . . .

(a) Appropriation for the Inter-American Highway, Approved April 5, 1941 [1]

For all necessary expenses to enable the President to utilize the services of the Public Roads Administration in fulfilling the obligations of the United States

[1] *Independent Offices Appropriation Act, 1942*, Public Law No. 28, 77th Cong., approved April 5, 1941; originated as H.R. 2788; hearings by Committee on Appropriations; House Report No. 15; Senate Report No. 69; House (conf.) Rep. No. 335.

under the Convention on the Pan American Highway between the United States and other American Republics, signed at Buenos Aires, December 23, 1936, and proclaimed September 16, 1937 (51 Stat. 152), for the continuation of cooperation with several governments, members of the Pan American Union, in connection with the survey and construction of the Inter-American Highway as provided in Public Resolution, approved March 4, 1929 (45 Stat. 1697), as amended or supplemented, and for performing engineering service in pan-American countries for and upon the request of any agency or governmental corporation of the United States, $100,000 to be derived from the administrative funds provided under the Act of July 11, 1916, as amended or supplemented (23 U.S.C. 21), or as otherwise provided.

G. Financial Relations

1. STABILIZATION ARRANGEMENT WITH ARGENTINA

(1) *Joint Statement of the Secretary of the Treasury (Morgenthau), the Argentine Ambassador (Espil) and the General Manager of the Central Bank of Argentina, December 27, 1940* [1]

As another practical proof that the good-neighbor policy is a living force among American Republics, the United States and Argentina have completed a stabilization arrangement by which $50,000,000 of the United States Stabilization Fund is set aside to promote stability between the United States dollar and the Argentine peso.

The agreement provides, under conditions acceptable to both parties, for the purchase of Argentine pesos with dollars, and for the exchange of information and of views bearing on the proper functioning of such a program.

This is a cooperative arrangement between old and good friends. It has been discussed and formulated in this spirit by representatives of the Argentine Government and the Central Bank of Argentina, and by the officials of the United States Treasury. The monetary authorities of the two countries expect to hold further discussions in the same friendly spirit during the coming year; and it is hoped that these conversations will enable both countries to reap the greatest possible benefit from the workings of the present agreement.

2. DOMINICAN REPUBLIC

(1) *Convention Relating to Customs Revenues between the Dominican Republic and the United States, Washington, September 24, 1940* [2]

In force March 10, 1941

This convention replaces that of December 27, 1924, under which a general receiver of Dominican customs appointed by the President of the United States

[1] Department of State, *Bulletin*, III, p. 590; Treasury Department, Press Service No. 23–25.   [2] Senate, Executive P, 76th Cong., 3d sess.

was charged with ensuring service on the Dominican external debt, and substitutes for him a bank depository of all Dominican public funds obligated first to service the public debt under the scrutiny of a representative of the bondholders, both the bank and the person to be designated by the Governments of the Dominican Republic and of the United States in common accord. The convention relieves the Dominican Republic of the control exercised by a foreign official over its customs revenues, a long-desired ambition, and changes the security behind the $15,400,000 of outstanding bonds from the customs receipts to all revenues of the republic. The Foreign Bondholders Protective Council, Inc., on behalf of bondholders, opposed the change on the ground that the United States, in withdrawing its guaranty of the bonds, altered the bond contract to the potential detriment of the holders.

The intervention of the United States in Dominican affairs was defined by the treaty of February 8, 1907, which established the general receivership of customs as a guaranty of service on bond issues of 1908 and 1918. From 1916 to 1924 military officers of the United States conducted the Dominican Government, which was remitted to Dominican control by a convention of June 12, 1924, ratifying the action of the military government. That government had signed a bond contract for a refunding loan in 1922, while a further contract in 1926 completed the refunding of former issues and consolidated the Dominican public debt under the revised guaranties of the convention of December 27, 1924.

In 1931 the Dominican Government became unable to meet amortization payments on the 1922 and 1926 bond issues. It accepted a proposal of the Foreign Bondholders Protective Council, Inc., dated August 10, 1934, to reduce the amortization rate so that the two issues would be liquidated, not in 1942 and 1941, but in 1969 and 1961 respectively.

Negotiations for a revision of the 1924 convention began in 1936 and continued "through various drafts of a possible convention from A to the letter X." [1] The treaty signed September 24, 1940 was submitted to the Senate for its advice and consent on October 9, 1940 by the President. On October 15, 1940 the Foreign Bondholders Protective Council, Inc.,[2] objected to the convention in a letter to the Secretary of State as changing "a bilateral contract without the consent of one of the parties" [the bondholders]. On October 29, 1940 it made further representations in a letter and historical memorandum to the Senate Committee on Foreign Relations. The committee held hearings and made a favorable report to the Senate on the convention.[3] The Senate advised and consented to ratification on February 14, 1941 and the exchange of ratifications took place March 10, 1941.

Among the exchanges of notes accompanying the convention one provided for pensioning two officials of the General Receivership and another for annual payments in liquidation of claims by American nationals against the Dominican Government.

WHEREAS at the City of Washington, D. C., on the twenty-seventh day of December of 1924 a Convention was concluded and signed

---

[1] U. S. Congress, Senate, Committee on Foreign Relations, *Dominican Republic — Convention relating to Customs Revenues;* Hearings . . . 76th Cong., 3d sess. . . . November 27 and December 4, 1940, p. 5. The statement was by Harold D. Finley, Assistant Chief, Division of American Republics, Department of State.

[2] This council is a private, non-profit corporation organized to perform the general functions contemplated for the Corporation of Foreign Security Holders by the act of May 27, 1933 (U. S. Code, title 15, secs. 77 bb–77 mm).

[3] Senate Executive Report No. 3, 77th Cong., 1st sess.

between the Plenipotentiaries of the United States of America and the Dominican Republic, providing for the assistance of the United States of America in the collection and application of the customs revenues of the Dominican Republic; and

WHEREAS the Government of the United States of America and the Government of the Dominican Republic have performed their obligations under the said Convention of 1924 in a manner satisfactory to both parties; and

WHEREAS the Government of the United States of America and the Government of the Dominican Republic are both desirous of modifying the said Convention to the advantage of both parties and at the same time of safeguarding the rights of the holders of the bonds of the issues of 1922 and 1926;

The President of the United States of America, represented by Cordell Hull, Secretary of State of the United States of America, and

The President of the Dominican Republic, represented by Generalissimo Rafael Leonidas Trujillo Molina, Benefactor of the Country, Ambassador Extraordinary on Special Mission,

Who, having communicated to each other their respective full powers, found to be in good and due form, have agreed upon the following Articles:

ARTICLE I. The Government of the Dominican Republic shall collect through its appropriate national officials the customs revenues of the Dominican Republic and all revenues pertaining to the customs duties. The General Receivership of the Dominican Customs provided for in the Convention of December 27, 1924, shall cease to operate on the day on which the Dominican Government undertakes the collection of customs revenues.

All property and funds of the General Receivership shall be turned over on that day to the Government of the Dominican Republic.

No claim shall be advanced by either Government against the other on account of any act of the General Receivership.

ARTICLE II. The Government of the United States of America and the Government of the Dominican Republic, in common accord, shall designate a Bank, with establishment in the Dominican Republic, as sole depository of all revenues and public funds of whatsoever nature of the Dominican Government.[1] They likewise shall designate, by common

---

[1] By an exchange of notes accompanying the convention the following interpretation is determined:

"The term 'all revenues and public funds of whatsoever nature of the Dominican Government' employed in the Convention signed between us today to replace the

accord, an official who shall act in the said Bank as representative of the holders of the bonds of the external debt of 1922 and 1926, in all matters that concern the service of the said external debt. If at any time the Bank so designated ceases for any reason to function in this capacity or if either Government shall deem a change advisable, a successor shall be designated under the procedure stipulated above. If the representative of the holders of the bonds of the external debt of 1922 and 1926 shall, for any reason, be unable to continue in that capacity, or if either Government shall deem a change advisable, his successor shall be designated in accordance with the same procedure established for the original designation. In the event that it should become necessary to designate a successor to either the Bank or the official representing the holders of the bonds of the external debt of 1922 and 1926, and in the further event that the two Governments should be unable to reach mutual accord on such designation within a period of three months, the Foreign Bondholders Protective Council, Incorporated, shall be requested to nominate said successor, and in the event of its failure to make such nomination the President or a Vice President of the American Bankers Association, or his duly authorized representative, shall be requested to make the nomination; provided, however, that neither a Bank nor a person previously rejected by either Government may be so nominated. In the event that a Bank or person is nominated in accordance with this procedure, the two Governments shall designate such nominee.

The official representing the holders of the bonds of the external debt of 1922 and 1926 shall, with the approval of the two Governments, designate a deputy to serve in his stead in the event of his temporary absence or incapacity.

ARTICLE III. During the first ten days of each calendar month the representative of the holders of the bonds of the external debt of 1922 and 1926 or his deputy shall receive, by endorsement and orders of payment which shall be issued to the Depository Bank by the Dominican Government through the intermediary of the Secretary of State for

---

Convention of December 27, 1924, embraces the deposit and pledge of any and all income and receipts of the Dominican Government, from whatsoever source derived, whether known as revenues, customs, duties, excises, fees, fines, imposts, charges, levy or any other kind of similar income, receipts or funds which belong to and are under the control of the Government of the Dominican Republic. It is understood that such term does not include funds under the control of the Dominican Government which, under existing laws, are collected for, belong to, and are distributed among the municipalities, which are autonomous under the constitution of the State."

Treasury and Commerce, the sum necessary to cover monthly payments as follows:

(1) the payment of one-twelfth of the annual interest charges of all of the outstanding bonds of the external debt of 1922 and 1926;

(2) the payment of one-twelfth of the annual amounts designated for the amortization of the said bonds, including the interest of all the bonds which are or may be retained in the sinking fund. The said amortization shall be computed and effected in accordance with the loan contracts as modified by the agreement between the Dominican Republic and the Foreign Bondholders Protective Council, Incorporated, concluded on August 16, 1934, and by the provisions of Article V of the present Convention;

(3) the payment of one-twelfth of the annual cost of the services rendered by the representative of the holders of the bonds of the external debt of 1922 and 1926, or his deputy, who shall receive salaries which are the subject of an exchange of notes attached hereto,[1] which shall be given full force and effect as integral parts of this Convention, and a reasonable amount for expenses incurred in the performance of their duties, and the payment of one-twelfth of the annual amount agreed upon between the Dominican Government and the Depository Bank as the compensation for the services of the said Bank.

No disbursements of funds of the Dominican Government shall be made by the Depository Bank until the payments provided for in this Article shall have been made.

The sums received by the above-mentioned representative for the service of the bonds shall be immediately transmitted by him to the Fiscal Agent or Agents of the loans.

ARTICLE IV. The Government of the Dominican Republic declares that the interest and amortization service of the bonds of the external debt of 1922 and 1926 as well as the payments stipulated in the third numbered paragraph of Article III of the present Convention, constitute an irrevocable first lien upon all of its revenues of whatsoever nature.

ARTICLE V. In case the total collections from all the revenues of whatsoever nature of the Dominican Government should in any calendar year exceed twelve million five hundred thousand dollars ($12,500,000) there shall be applied to the sinking fund for the redemption of bonds of the external debt of 1922 and 1926 which may be outstanding, ten per cent (10%) of the excess above twelve million five hundred thousand

---

[1] The salary of the representative is fixed at $10,000 annually by an exchange of notes accompanying the convention, and that of a deputy at $5,000.

dollars ($12,500,000) but less than thirteen million five hundred thousand dollars ($13,500,000), and in addition five per cent (5%) of all sums exceeding thirteen million five hundred thousand dollars ($13,500,000).

ARTICLE VI. The representative of the holders of the bonds of the external debt of 1922 and 1926 shall have complete access to all records and books of the Depository Bank relating to the public revenues.

The Secretary of State for Treasury and Commerce of the Dominican Government shall supply monthly to the representative of the holders of the bonds of the loans of 1922 and 1926 complete and detailed reports, duly certified, of all the revenues and disbursements and other fiscal operations of the Dominican Government.

ARTICLE VII. The system of deposit of all revenues of the Dominican Republic shall be carried out in accordance with the Dominican laws of accounting and of the Treasury now governing such matters, and these laws as well as the powers conferred by this Convention upon the representative of the holders of the bonds of the loans of 1922 and 1926, shall not be modified by the Dominican Government during the life of this Convention without the previous consent of both Governments.

ARTICLE VIII. Any controversy which may arise between the Government of the United States of America and the Government of the Dominican Republic in relation to the execution of the provisions of the present Convention shall, if possible, be settled through diplomatic channels. Upon notification by either the Government of the United States of America or the Government of the Dominican Republic that, in its opinion, possibilities of settlement by this means have been exhausted, such controversies shall be settled in accordance with the procedure stipulated in the Inter-American Arbitration Convention signed at Washington, January 5, 1929, notwithstanding the provisions of Article 2 (a) thereof.

ARTICLE IX. The Convention signed by the United States of America and the Dominican Republic on December 27, 1924, shall cease to have effect, and the present Convention shall enter into force upon the exchange of ratifications which shall take place in the City of Washington within thirty days following ratification by the Government which ratifies the later in point of time; provided, however, that Articles I, II and V of the said Convention of December 27, 1924, shall continue in full force and effect until the two Governments agree that there have been adopted and put into operation all the measures necessary for the execution of the present Convention.

The present Convention shall continue in full force and effect during the existence of the outstanding external bonds of 1922 and 1926. After the redemption or cancellation of the said bonds, the provisions of this Convention shall automatically cease to have effect.

In witness whereof the respective Plenipotentiaries have signed the present Convention in duplicate in the English and Spanish languages, both texts being equally authoritative, and have hereunto affixed their seals.

Done in the City of Washington the twenty-fourth day of September, 1940.

CORDELL HULL   [SEAL]

RAFAEL L. TRUJILLO [SEAL]

(a) *Payment of Claims of American Nationals. Exchange of Notes, Washington, September 24, 1940* [1]

DEPARTMENT OF STATE,

Washington, September 24, 1940.

His Excellency, Dr. RAFAEL L. TRUJILLO,
> *Ambassador Extraordinary of the*
> *Dominican Republic on Special Mission.*

EXCELLENCY: I have the honor to acknowledge the receipt of your note of today's date relating to the agreement arrived at by our two Governments in relation to the policy of the Dominican Government concerning the liquidation of its unfunded indebtedness to nationals of the United States of America in which you confirm your Government's understanding of the agreement in the following terms:

> The Dominican Government desires to seize this propitious moment to settle a further matter outstanding between the two Governments, thus reinforcing the harmonious relations already existing between our two peoples.

> The Dominican Republic will include in its next annual budget and in ensuing budgets as long as may be necessary, an annual appropriation of one hundred and twenty-five thousand dollars ($125,000) which shall be paid out each year exclusively to the liquidation of *bona fide* claims by American nationals against the Government of the Dominican Republic.

Your statement of the agreement represents my understanding of the arrangement and is satisfactory to the Government of the United States of America.

Accept, Excellency, the renewed assurances of my highest consideration.

CORDELL HULL

(2) *Exchange of Telegrams Concerning the Termination of the General Receivership of Dominican Customs, April 2, 1941* [2]

Notes were exchanged on March 31 between the two Governments at the capital of the Dominican Republic agreeing that all the necessary measures have now been taken by both Governments to put the provisions of the new convention into operation.

[1] Senate Executive P, 76th Cong., 3d sess. The proposing note of the exchange is omitted.   [2] Department of State, *Bulletin*, IV, p. 437.

The branch of the National City Bank of New York, located at Ciudad Trujillo, has been designated as the sole depository bank, and Mr. Oliver P. Newman, of Washington, D. C., has been named as the official representing the bondholders. These designations were made by the two Governments acting in accord.

(a) The Secretary of State (Hull) to the Minister for Foreign Affairs of the Dominican Republic (Despradel), April 2, 1941

I desire on this day which begins a new era in the friendly and neighborly relations between our countries, to send my felicitations and good wishes to Your Excellency and to the Dominican Government and people.

CORDELL HULL

(b) The Minister for Foreign Affairs of the Dominican Republic (Despradel) to the Secretary of State (Hull), April 2, 1941

[Translation]

APRIL 2, 1941.

I have the honor to express to Your Excellency my deep gratification for the cordial congratulations which you have conveyed to the people and Government of the Dominican Republic and for your kind wishes on the occasion of the putting into operation of the Trujillo-Hull agreement. This transcendental event strengthens the sincere friendship existing between our two countries, reaffirming the high ideals of justice and good understanding in which these friendly relations are inspired.

ARTURO DESPRADEL

(c) The Secretary of State (Hull) to the Deputy General Receiver of Dominican Customs (Pearson), April 2, 1941

On the termination of the General Receivership of Dominican Customs, I desire to express my appreciation for the fine record of service rendered by you and the many officers and employees of the Receivership, both Dominican and American, during the last third of a century. I extend to all of you the thanks of this Government and my best wishes for your future success and happiness.

CORDELL HULL

3. HAITI

(1) *Supplementary Agreement between the United States and Haiti, Port-au-Prince, February 13, 1941* [1]

Relaxation of the control by the Fiscal Representative over Haitian finances has been proceeding for some years. A general receiver and a financial adviser nominated by the President of the United States were appointed by the President of Haiti under the treaty of September 16, 1915. Until 1933 the United States exercised extensive control over the Haitian administration, through military officers and later through a high commissioner. The Haitianization agreement of August 5, 1931 provided for the transfer of some services to the Government of Haiti and the agreement of August 7, 1933 completed the remission of administrative authority. On January 1, 1934 the financial adviser-receiver general was succeeded by the Fiscal Representative, whose powers were of a lesser order but whose tenure extends until the amortization of the 6% 30-year gold bonds of 1922 and 1923. Beginning in 1938 a series of agreements has been continued whereby the original authority of the Fiscal Representative has been progressively suspended in certain respects. The agreement of July 8, 1939 (Executive Agreement Series 150) included in the amounts to be paid to the Fiscal Representative an amortization account of $20,000; that of September 27, 1940 (Executive Agreement Series 183) continued to include in those amounts all receipts, additional to regular budgets, to be expended to meet serious emergencies. The present agreement eliminates both of these provisions.

The undersigned plenipotentiaries, duly authorized by their respective governments, have agreed upon the following Executive Agreement supplementary to the Agreement between the United States of America and the Republic of Haiti, signed at Port-au-Prince on August 7, 1933:

ARTICLE 1. On and after February 1, 1941, and until and including September 30, 1941, all monies received by or for the Haitian Government shall be deposited in the National Bank of the Republic of Haiti to the credit of the Haitian Government with the exception of the following sums which will be deposited to the credit of the Fiscal Representative:

1. The five per centum of customs revenues foreseen in Article 9 of the Accord of August 7, 1933,[2] and

2. The amounts needed to pay two-thirds of the sums due and payable on the coupons maturing April 1, 1941, and October 1, 1941, on all outstanding bonds issued under the loan contracts of October 6, 1922, and May 26, 1925, which amounts shall be credited to the Fiscal Representative.

Signed at Port-au-Prince, in duplicata, in the English and French languages, this 13 day of February nineteen hundred and forty-one.

EDWARD J. SPARKS [SEAL]

FERNAND DENNIS [SEAL]

[1] Executive Agreement Series 201, Department of State Publication 1582.

[2] Executive Agreement Series 46; see also the modifying agreements of January 13 and July 1, 1938, July 8, 1939 and September 27, 1940 (Executive Agreement Series 117, 128, 150, and 183).

(2) *Statement of the Department of State, February 14, 1941* [1]

[Excerpt]

The Department of State announces that it has reached an agreement in principle with the Government of the Republic of Haiti which, when formalized and ratified by the necessary legislation in Haiti, will suspend certain past undertakings of the Government of Haiti to the Government of the United States to the extent necessary to permit the fiscal representative at Port-au-Prince to postpone remittance to the fiscal agents of the loans of 1922 and 1923 (National City Bank of New York) of one-third the interest at the rate of 6 per cent, due on the outstanding bonds of the Republic of Haiti on April 1 and October 1, 1941. It is expected that an accord will soon be reached between the United States and Haitian Governments providing for this postponement and modifying the accord concluded between them on August 7, 1933 to that extent.

The Republic of Haiti, in inviting the attention of the bondholders — through the medium of the Foreign Bondholders Protective Council, Incorporated — to its long record of punctual payment of the interest on its outstanding debt and, until in recent years, of full amortization thereon, has stated that the closing of European markets to Haitian agricultural products, particularly coffee, cotton, and sugar, has resulted in serious repercussions on Haitian economy. Thus, the failure this year of European countries to purchase Haitian coffee has resulted in an unsold present surplus of about 200,000 bags (of 60 kilos each) which can be disposed of neither in Europe on account of war conditions, nor in the United States because of the coffee-quota arrangement which limits the exports of Haitian coffee to the United States to 275,000 bags (an amount considerably greater than any past marketings in the United States). Simultaneously, European markets have been closed to Haitian cotton, the crop of which this year amounts to about 3,000,000 kilograms, as well as to a portion of the Haitian sugar production, about 35,000 tons, which can find little market elsewhere owing to war conditions.

Foreseeing the difficulties which these restrictions were apt to bring about in its economy, the Haitian Government several months ago reduced its budgetary expenditures by about 20 per cent and has reduced all Government salaries from 5 per cent to 25 per cent. In spite of these economies, which have reduced the essential services of the Government to a bare minimum, the present forecast is nevertheless for a deficit in operating expenses during the present fiscal year ending September 30, 1941. In these circumstances, and with its cash position reduced, the

[1] Department of State, *Bulletin*, IV, p. 179.

Haitian Government has reluctantly appealed to the Foreign Bond-holders Protective Council, Incorporated, which has now expressed itself as accepting a postponement in the payment of one-third of the interest at the rate of 6 per cent due on the coupons of the bonds which are payable April 1 and October 1, 1941. In view of the situation as thus explained, the Department is entering into the agreement with the Haitian Government described above.

4. PANAMA

The United States Government presented to the public the case for the refunding of Panamanian bonds proposed in 1940 and effected in 1941. Panama had not transmitted the income from four internal revenues pledged to the service of the 5% bonds since partial payment of the coupon of May 15, 1933. Another reason for Panama being in default was the reduction of the weight of the United States gold dollar by the President's proclamation of January 31, 1934. The Canal annuity of $250,000 payable by the United States under the convention of November 18, 1903 was stipulated in gold and Panama declined to accept dollars of the reduced weight as proper payment. A second charge on the annuity was the service of the Panamanian 5% bonds, the first charge on the annuity being service on an issue of $5\frac{1}{2}$% bonds. By Article VII of the general treaty of March 2, 1936,[1] which was in force July 27, 1939, the Canal annuity was fixed at 430,000 balboas of the same gold content as the dollar. There was thus $180,000 additional available for debt service. An offer was made of $3\frac{1}{4}$% bonds due December 1, 1994, in lieu of the 5% bonds due May 15, 1963. This offer was not assented to by a sufficient number of bondholders and the Department of State supported the plan in a public statement when the original period of assent was extended to February 24, 1941.

Under the Plan for the Readjustment of External Debt of the Republic of Panama dated January 31, 1940, other bond issues of Panama and the arrears certificates accumulated since 1933 were also refunded.

(1) *Statement on Debt Refunding by the Department of State, February 3, 1941* [2]

On April 4, 1940 the Republic of Panama, through a prospectus duly registered with the Securities and Exchange Commission, made an offer to holders of Republic of Panama 5-per cent 35-year bonds, Series A, due May 15, 1963, pursuant to a Plan for the Readjustment of the External Debt of the Republic of Panama. This Plan was to become effective when so declared by the Republic on or before October 25, 1940 after the holders of at least 80 per cent of the principal amount of 5-per cent bonds should have assented to the Plan by depositing their bonds under the Plan.

---

[1] *Documents, II, 1939–40*, p. 206.
[2] Department of State, *Bulletin*, IV, p. 163.

Apparently due in part to conditions resulting from the war in Europe, including the invasion and occupation of countries in which substantial amounts of the 5-per cent bonds are held, deposits of 80 per cent of the principal amount of the bonds were not received by October 25, and the Panamanian Government has since extended the offer by successive periods of one month. By an announcement published January 24, 1941, the Ambassador of Panama gave notice to holders of the 5-per cent bonds that the Republic of Panama had agreed to an extension of the period of the Plan and Deposit Agreement to and including February 24, 1941, adding that the Republic believes that with this extension sufficient time has been given to all bondholders to make a decision, and does not intend to grant any further extension of time within which the necessary assents to the Plan may be received in order to enable the Republic to declare it effective. The announcement also suggested that in order that sufficient time be available for the preparation of all documents in connection with essential parts of the Plan, holders of 5-per cent bonds, Series A, who desire to assent to the Plan, deposit their bonds not later than February 10, 1941. The Ambassador of Panama has supplemented this formal announcement by a statement on the same lines issued to the press on February 3, 1941.

The Foreign Bondholders Protective Council has issued a statement discussing the Plan and saying that the Council feels that it is to the interest of the bondholders to accept the Plan offered and recommends that they do so. Holders of very close to 80 per cent of the bonds have deposited or agreed to deposit their bonds. It is believed that part of the delay in obtaining assents may be due to the difficulty of communication with widely scattered holders of the bonds. It is therefore hoped that wide publicity can be given to the Panamanian Government's announcement of January 24 and statement of February 3.

The consummation of the Plan, which involves the application to the service of Panamanian dollar bonds of the full amount of the increased annuity payable to Panama by the United States Government under the treaty of March 2, 1936 and of the income of the constitutional fund of Panama established by the Constitution of the Republic in 1904, would be a very helpful development in the relations between the two countries.

5. COLOMBIA

The Republic of Colombia advertised on June 5, 1941 an issue of 3% 30-year external sinking fund dollar bonds dated October 1, 1940 in exchange at par for the 6% external sinking fund gold bonds dated July 1, 1927 and April 1, 1928. The offer extends to October 1, 1943. The bonds at present issued were in default in 1935 and for several years the Foreign Bondholders Protective Council, Inc., has not approved of a settlement or refunding on the 3% basis offered by the Colombian Government on the ground that it does not adequately represent Colombia's capacity to pay. In 1940 Colombia paid interest at 3% and purchased $400,000 of bonds in the market. The statement of the Department of State at the end of the year was calculated to forward a settlement. The refunding offer of June 1941 represented a new effort to adjust the matter by substituting new bondholders' contracts for the old ones.

(1) *Statement on Debt Refunding by the Department of State, December 31, 1940* [1]

The Government of the Republic of Colombia, after maintaining full debt service on its 6-per cent bonds, $25,000,000 of which were issued through the usual private financial channels in 1927, and $35,000,000 in 1928, finally, in 1933, was forced to suspend payments. However, before suspending payments, approximately $3,800,000 of the first issue and $5,000,000 of the second issue had been paid, reducing the amount of bonds then outstanding from $60,000,000 to approximately $51,200,000. In 1933 the Colombian Government made an additional payment in non-interest-bearing, deferred-interest certificates of $1,799,534, which were redeemed at maturity in 1937, and in 1934 a further payment in 12-year 4-per cent funding certificates of $3,743,145, which it has regularly serviced.

Since that time the Colombian Government has carried on prolonged negotiations with representatives of the bondholders, in an effort to reach an agreement as to payment and an interest rate that the Colombian Government felt it would be able to meet. No permanent agreement has yet been reached.

About a year ago the Department of State, with the cooperation of the Treasury Department and the Federal Loan Administrator, acting merely as friendly intermediaries, began meeting with representatives of the Colombian Government and the Foreign Bondholders Protective Council, Inc., of New York, in the hope of finding some common ground of adjustment that would be acceptable to both parties.

Some progress was made, and in the expectation of reaching a permanent agreement during 1940 the Colombian Government this year has paid 3 per cent on both issues, amounting to approximately $1,350,000, and has expended approximately $400,000 in the purchase and retirement of bonds. These bonds and approximately $6,000,000 face value of bonds theretofore purchased by the Colombian Government have been canceled so that the total outstanding amount at the present time

[1] Released to the press by the Department of State, December 31, 1940; Department of State, *Bulletin*, IV, p. 12.

on both issues is about $44,000,000, with accrued interest at 6 per cent of $12,200,000.

The Colombian Government now offers to refund the principal of $44,000,000 and accumulated interest at 3 per cent amounting to $6,100,000, a total of about $50,100,000, with new 3-per cent bonds of a maturity of 25 to 30 years, the exact date to be indicated in the formal detailed offer to be issued shortly. To service the new bonds it offers to make available $1,800,000 per year for five years and $2,000,000 per year thereafter. The amounts not required for interest at 3 per cent per annum are to be devoted entirely to the purchase in the market and cancellation of the new bonds.

While the Government of the United States has no direct interest in the matter, the Department of State, the Treasury Department, and the Federal Loan Administrator have acted as friendly intermediaries to assist the parties in reaching an agreement, and they are of the opinion that in view of conditions that have prevailed since 1932, the offer of the Colombian Government constitutes a fair effort on its part to adjust its obligations. They recognize, of course, that the bondholders must make their own decision.

6. MEXICO

(1) *Payment on Agrarian Claims, June 30, 1941* [1]

The Mexican Ambassador at Washington on June 30 handed to the Acting Secretary of State the Mexican Government's check for one million dollars in payment of the amount due June 30, 1941 on account of the claims of American citizens whose lands in Mexico have been expropriated since August 30, 1927 under the Mexican agrarian program. The arrangement under which the payment became due was effected by this Government's note of November 9, 1938 and the Mexican Government's reply of November 12, 1938.[2]

This represents the third payment by Mexico on account of these claims, the first and second payments of one million dollars having been made on May 31, 1939 and June 29, 1940, respectively, under the arrangement of November 9–12, 1938.

The claims in question are under active consideration by the Agrarian Claims Commission, United States and Mexico.

[1] Department of State, *Bulletin*, V, p. 9.
[2] For history of agrarian claims see *Documents, I, 1938–39*, p. 87.

H. Mutual Defense

1. USE OF DOMINICAN REPUBLIC FACILITIES

(1) *The Dominican Minister (Pastoriza) to the Secretary of State (Hull), December 4, 1939* [1]

WASHINGTON, D. C., *December 4, 1939.*

Hon. CORDELL HULL,
      Secretary of State of the
            United States of America,
                  Washington, D. C.

MY DEAR MR. SECRETARY OF STATE: I have the honor to inform Your Excellency that the Dominican Government is glad to offer the greatest facilities in order that public vessels and airplanes of the Government of the United States, in charge of special patrol duties, may make use, as often as they desire and without attending to any previous formalities, of the harbors, bays, and territorial waters of the Dominican Republic, entering same and remaining therein as often and as long as the Government of Your Excellency may deem necessary or expedient.

The Dominican Government thus ratifies, in an ample spirit of solidarity, its irrevocable determination to cooperate with the Government of the United States of America in everything that tends to ensure the continental defense, and to maintain the peace and feelings of international harmony, which today serve as a standard in the foreign policy of all the countries of the Western Hemisphere. The Dominican Government — as I have had the opportunity of proving to Your Excellency on other occasions — has kept, and will continue to keep up, its willingness to offer the Government of the United States its modest but sincere and decided support without reservations of any kind, in order that the continental security may become more and more effective in the face of the hatreds and conflicts which, on other continents, threaten civilization of mankind.

These sentiments of cooperation with the Government of the United States of America, upon which the foreign policy of the Dominican Government has been based ever since Generalissimo Rafael Leonidas Trujillo Molina, benefactor of the fatherland, became the leader of the

[1] *Congressional Record,* Vol. 87, p. 1012, February 13, 1941 (daily edition).

nation, do not constitute a mere reaffirmation of our inter-American rapprochement policy but answer the conviction of the Dominican Government that this policy is the only one compatible with the necessity of preserving the spirit of international appeasement and the democratic ideology, which constitute the greatest of the noble features of American civilization.

I avail myself of this opportunity to express to Your Excellency the renewed assurances of my highest consideration.

ANDRÉS PASTORIZA,
Envoy Extraordinary and Minister Pleni-
potentiary of the Dominican Republic.

2. AIR AND NAVAL BASES IN URUGUAY

In June 1940 the United States heavy cruiser *Quincy* made a courtesy visit to Montevideo, Uruguay, shortly after the discovery of an alleged Nazi plot to seize the country. At a luncheon on June 23 in honor of the officers of the *Quincy* Edwin C. Wilson, United States Minister to Uruguay, emphasized the need of the Americas to reaffirm their determination to defend the hemisphere against any intervention and said that he was authorized to state "that it is the intention and avowed policy of my Government to cooperate fully, whenever such cooperation is desired, with all of the other American governments in crushing all activities which arise from non-American sources and which imperil our political and economic freedom."

In November 1940 explorations by United States officials were taking place in South and Central America concerning arrangements for hemisphere defense to be made with American Governments. Rumors as to the character and scope of such arrangements were given currency in the press, which reported various journalistic impressions and remarks of political personages. In Uruguay the question became involved in a political controversy between the Government of President Alfredo Baldomír and the Nationalist party under the leadership of Luis Alberto Herrera, which held three posts in the cabinet and half the seats in the Senate. The controversy was based upon an assumed issue that the United States desired to establish naval and air bases instead of using bases to be constructed if and when an actual threat of aggression should exist.

The Uruguayan Minister for Foreign Affairs defined the situation on November 11, the United States made a statement on November 13, but the controversy widened with the resignation of one of the three Herrerista cabinet ministers in Uruguay on November 15, and a motion for a vote of censure on November 19 in the Senate at Montevideo.

While the Uruguayan Congress was debating the question, another element that is always latent but seldom apparent in Spanish America came to public attention. On November 18 the rector of the University of Madrid, in the name of all Spanish universities, sent all universities of South and Central America a message asking "all intellectuals of our (*sic*) America not to consent, either in spirit or body, that any foreign power should install itself in the body of our Hispanidad." Other Spanish organizations and interests took a similar stand. These activities were discussed by the Uruguayan Minister at Madrid with the Spanish Minister for Foreign Affairs.[1]

(1) *Communiqué of the Uruguayan Minister for Foreign Affairs (Guani), November 11, 1940* [2]

Regarding published reports relative to the establishment of foreign military bases in Uruguay, what has been said in previous communiqués of this Chancellery must be reiterated.

Certainly, consideration has not been given nor is it being given to permitting the establishment of such foreign bases on our territory. The President of the Republic has consulted with the National Defense Minister and the Minister for Foreign Affairs regarding the program for the common defense of the continent and has considered the study of these problems with the other American governments.

In this respect there have been held various technical consultations between the high commands of the armies of the American nations, among them Uruguay, in accord with resolutions adopted at the last Pan American conferences.

Extensive correspondence published upon this matter these days states exactly how far coordination in military defensive action is carried in behalf of solidarity by the nations of this continent, but they believe it to be always fundamental that they can interpret in what way foreign interference, direct or indirect, of some States with respect to others, may affect thus their respective sovereignties.

The resulting program has in view naval or air bases constructed in our case by Uruguayan authorities, directed, maintained and controlled by and placed only at the disposition of an American country in a pressing continental military defense necessity upon conditions established by the government of the republic.

In an equal manner Uruguay could make use of similar bases to be in determined spaces in other American States always considered necessary for collective defense.

The accords to which we refer respond to the concept of the resolutions adopted at the Inter-American conferences, in which the continental governments declared forcefully the decision to maintain and to strengthen the union of the countries of this hemisphere in the face of whatever foreign aggression may be attempted upon their territorial integrity and sovereignty.

[1] *New York Times*, November 20, 1940, p. 2.
[2] *Ibid.*, November 12, 1940, p. 12.

(2) *Intentions of the United States. Statement by the Acting Secretary of State (Welles), November 13, 1940* [1]

I want to make it very clear that the United States Government has never sought directly or indirectly to obtain the lease or cession of air and naval bases in Uruguay. As Secretary Hull has frequently stated, in none of our conversations with any of the other American Republics has there ever been involved the possibility of any suggestions on our part which would affect in any sense the sovereignty of any other American nation.

(3) *Statement of Acting Secretary of State (Welles) at Press Conference Colloquy, November 22, 1940* [2]

At the press conference of the Acting Secretary of State November 22, a correspondent said:

"Mr. Secretary, all of us here consider that you have from time to time made fairly clear our position on the bases in Latin America, but recently there seems to have been a flood of propaganda from Spain and continued misunderstanding in some of the Latin American countries, and we have, as a result, the action of the Uruguayan Senate refusing to approve of any agreement that might be made on bases and so forth down there. I think there is a general misunderstanding in some countries concerning our position, and I wonder if you would care again to clarify both our position and our policy."

The Acting Secretary replied:

"I am relieved when you say that you gentlemen think I have made it clear. I have seen, as you have, a great deal of propaganda which was undoubtedly intended to confuse the issues and to make out something which was not the case, and, therefore, I again repeat that at no time has this Government discussed with the government of any other American Republic the cession through sale or lease of any naval or other bases, nor has it made any suggestion which would in any sense, if carried out, have infringed in any degree the sovereignty of any of the other American Republics."

---

[1] Department of State, *Bulletin*, III, p. 432; volunteered at the press conference with reference to a published story of some purported agreement between the United States and the Government of Uruguay with regard to air and naval bases.

[2] *Ibid.*, p. 452.

(4) *Statement of the Uruguayan Minister at Madrid to the Spanish Press* [1]

In relation to the comments of the Spanish press in respect of the negotiations which the Uruguayan Cabinet is carrying on at the present time in matters within its competence, the Minister of Uruguay considers himself obliged to note that according to the telegraphic information which he has just received from his Government the version of the cession of naval bases to any country is completely inexact. It is a question of steps in connection with "collective continental military defense" which are being taken in the same form with the Argentine Republic and the other American states.

In the telegraphic despatch which the Uruguayan Chancellery received from Montevideo it is added that far from there being discrepancies between the American countries there exists a solidarity of purpose among them also improving the resolutions of the Pan American conference.

(5) *Vote of Confidence of the Uruguayan Chamber of Representatives, November 27, 1940* [2]

The Chamber of Representatives, after hearing the information of delegations from the executive branch of the Government, manifests its most absolute adhesion to the international policy followed by the Government in the matters that were the object of this afternoon's deliberation, and [asserts] that it is in agreement with the principles that Uruguay has sustained in all international conferences and with the policy of inter-American cooperation and solidarity.

3. ARGENTINA AND CONTINENTAL DEFENSE

(1) *Interview of President Roberto M. Ortiz of the Argentine Republic by the United Press, November 19, 1940* [3]

Regardless of my personal situation,[4] which you will understand, I have been following events very closely, and I am watching over develop-

[1] Department of State, *Bulletin*, III, p. 452. The statement was reported to the Department of State by the Ambassador to Spain (Weddell), November 23, 1940.

[2] *New York Times*, November 28, 1940, p. 4. The vote was 53 to 21 and was interpreted as a disapproval of criticism of the Government expressed in the Senate debate of November 21, whose resolutions did not directly deal with naval and air bases.

[3] Text supplied by United Press Associations, New York City. The interview was reported by William Pozzo, the correspondent at Buenos Aires. The narrative portion of the dispatch is omitted.

[4] The President was just resuming his functions after an illness which had caused him to delegate his powers to Vice President Ramon S. Castillo for a period of some five months.

ments both within and without the country with the result that I am impressed by the fact that the world is passing through a period of great crisis.

It is the duty of chiefs of governments to seek to obtain the happiness and well-being of their peoples, and to this end they must maintain the greatest serenity and vision to permit them to foresee coming events as far in advance as possible.

We are faced with grave events, and we can affirm that the development of ideals is not keeping pace with the military successes of arms, while we see in many cases that victorious arms are preventing the evolution of the ideals of the vanquished.

The danger does not lie so much in the physical occupation of our continent, but rather it is found in the ideas of dissolution which are fermenting in an enormous social group. To combat these disintegrating ideas, it is more necessary than ever to maintain a profound and sincere democratic faith so that the light of liberty will continue to shine.

The community of ideals between the peoples of America, cooperation and spiritual unity of thought, in a word, coordination in a plan of action, must be the principal elements to guide the peoples of America in forming a single unit for the establishment of their defense against foreign perils.

Naturally this plan of community of thought and spirit must be considered as only a complement to technical cooperation, and in this connection I hold the conviction that the recent visit to the United States of the South American army chiefs, including General Mohr, of Argentina, has served to indicate that the branches of the different governments have arrived at a better understanding.

My thought regarding the matter of bases is that under no consideration, and always taking into account the principles of ample collaboration supported by the American nations at Lima, Panama, and Havana, can there possibly develop points of friction in treating with these problems of defense, the principal objective of which, I repeat, must be directed against the peril of subversive and exotic ideas.

(2) *Comment by the Acting Secretary of State (Welles), November 22, 1940* [1]

I have read the interview granted by President Ortiz of Argentina to the United Press on November 19 with the utmost interest and attention. I hope it will be studied by every section of public opinion in this country. It sets forth clearly and succinctly the true interpretation of

[1] Department of State, *Bulletin*, III, p. 453; in response to a request by newspaper correspondents.

enlightened Pan Americanism as evidenced by the agreements reached by the American Republics at Buenos Aires, Lima, Panama, and Havana. The statements contained in the interview constitute an inspiration to all of those who are working for Pan American collaboration and the maintenance of our democratic institutions in the New World.

(3) *Statement of the Argentine Ministry of Foreign Relations on Pan American Aerial and Naval Bases, November 22, 1940* [1]

Regarding the problem of Pan American aerial and naval bases, the Foreign Offices of Argentina and Uruguay have exchanged opinions opportunely on this problem and on other economic problems of mutual interest. These conversations are continuing in an atmosphere of close and loyal collaboration befitting the relations of both countries.

The problems of the River Plate, in which are bound the permanent interests of Argentina and Uruguay, must be considered henceforth among the proposals of continental defense inspired by the resolutions of the last Pan American Conference.

4. DEFENSE SITES IN PANAMA

(1) *Manifesto of the Government of Panama, March 5, 1941* [2]

The Governments of Panama and the United States recently exchanged ideas, on the initiative of the American Government, on the situation created by the European war in so far as it may affect the safety of the Panama Canal.

The conversations were held in an atmosphere of ample and perfect understanding and in the light of the Arias-Roosevelt treaty of March 2, 1936.[3]

The Panama Government, desirous of harmonizing the fulfillment of its contractual obligations with its inherent duty of safeguarding its own rights, has given long and careful consideration to the requests of the North American Government.

The Government of the United States requests the use of a number of areas outside the Canal Zone, in Panama territory, for the installation of air bases, searchlights and aircraft detectors, which the Washington Government considers indispensable for the defense of the Panama Canal. These requests were made under Article 10 of the 1936 treaty.

The Panama Government, after studying the situation at a number of cabinet meetings, has decided to accede to the United States Govern-

---

[1] United Press version, *New York Times*, November 23, 1940, p. 4.

[2] *New York Times*, March 6, 1941, p. 7. The manifesto was signed by President Arnulfo Arias and all the Ministers of the Government.

[3] *Documents, II, 1939–40*, p. 199.

ment's request in view of the fact that "an international conflagration has broken out carrying with it the possibility of a threat to the security of the Panama Canal, which threat makes it necessary for the United States to adopt measures for defense" under the terms of the treaty.

The desire to defend the legal rights of Panama from the viewpoint of territorial integrity and political independence, taken together with the terms of the 1936 treaty, has led the Government of the Republic to grant the use of the aforementioned areas, subject to certain conditions as follows:

The military authorities of the United States will occupy the said territories only for as long as the present European war lasts and will cease occupation as soon as that war ends.

The United States Government will give adequate compensation to Panama.

The Republic of Panama will retain and exercise jurisdiction over civilians in the occupied areas, in accordance with conditions which in the opinion of both governments may be necessary for the defense of the canal.

In view of the urgency shown by the United States Government, the Panama Government has given the Canal Zone authorities its consent for the initiation of military preparations that may be required.

The Panama Government believes the aforementioned conditions and final agreements between the two Governments ensure that the future negotiations will be completed without the least difficulty and in accordance with the letter and spirit of the treaty of 1936.

(2) *Statement of the Secretary of State (Hull), March 6, 1941* [1]

I was most gratified, as will be all the people of this country as well as those of our sister republics in this hemisphere, to learn from the manifesto issued yesterday by the Panamanian Government that Panama will make available immediately to our military authorities certain sites in the Republic of Panama which are considered essential for the protection and security of the Panama Canal. In taking this action, Panama has shown that the spirit of partnership in the defense of the Canal, which is one of the fundamentals of the General Treaty between the two countries ratified in 1939, is a tangible and practical thing.

In accordance with the manifesto, our military authorities will proceed immediately to the preliminary preparation of these defense sites. I am

[1] Department of State, *Bulletin*, IV, p. 265.

confident that the negotiations which are now in progress with regard to the details involved will be worked out to the mutual satisfaction of both our Governments.

5. UNITED STATES–MEXICAN AGREEMENT FOR TRANSIT OF MILITARY AIRCRAFT

This is an agreement desired by the State Department, for the purpose of promoting the common defense of the Western Hemisphere, and by the War Department, expressly for the purpose of procuring an inland route for the passage of military aircraft across the country of Mexico and its territorial waters, to the Panama Canal or to the lower Caribbean.

(1) *Agreement between the United States and Mexico to Facilitate the Reciprocal Transit of Military Aircraft through the Territories and Territorial Waters of the Two Countries, Signed at Washington, April 1, 1941* [1]

In force April 25, 1941

The Under Secretary of State of the United States of America, Sumner Welles, and the Ambassador Extraordinary and Plenipotentiary of Mexico, Dr. Francisco Castillo Nájera, the former appointed by the President of the United States, Franklin D. Roosevelt, and the latter by the President of Mexico, General Manuel Avila Camacho, after having communicated to each other their respective full powers, which were found to be in due and proper form, and following instructions from their Governments, declare: that both countries, the United States and Mexico, in view of the exceptional circumstances which have arisen from the present European conflict, and taking into consideration the necessity of ensuring conditions of maximum speed for the movements required in the defense of the American Continent in matters of aviation, and desirous of organizing a substantial and efficient collaboration by both countries in their task to defend the Americas, and with the highest regard for their juridical equality and respect for the sovereignty of both countries, have agreed to permit the reciprocal transit of military aircraft through their territories and territorial waters, pursuant to the following clauses: —

First. The mutual concessions which the High Contracting Parties grant each other under this Agreement will be effective only for the duration of the present state of possible threats of armed aggression against either of them and, if so required, in the opinion of both Governments, by the needs of their mutual defense.

[1] United States, *Treaty Series*, No. 971. Advice and consent to the ratification given by the United States Senate, April 3, 1941.

Second. In view of the resolutions of the Second Meeting of Ministers of Foreign Relations, held at Havana, the United States and Mexico will grant free transit through their respective territories and territorial waters of military airplanes and seaplanes of the other country, without restrictions as to type, number, frequency of flights, personnel or material carried.

Third. Each Government agrees to give to the other, official notice, at least twenty-four hours in advance, of the departure from its territory of any such aircraft which it is desired shall fly over the territory of the other, and such notice shall specify the number and type of the aerial units, the flight routes, the land and sea airports on which the airplanes and seaplanes contemplate making regular landings, and the number of their crew and individuals carried.

Fourth. The airplanes and seaplanes of each Government shall use only the routes previously determined by the other Government with regard to the flights over land and territorial waters of the latter. The Governments will also determine the regular landing places within their respective territorial boundaries.

The flights to which this Agreement refers shall not be made until the routes and places referred to in the preceding paragraph shall have been designated.

Fifth. Each Government assumes the obligation that none of its aircraft shall take more than 24 hours to transit the territory of the other, including the use of all land and sea airports within the latter's territory or territorial waters, except in case of *force majeure* when the stay may be prolonged for the time deemed necessary by the Government whose territory is being traversed.

Sixth. Any military aircraft of one of the Contracting Parties, landing on any of the points designated for that purpose in the territory of the other Party, will have the right to be furnished only such fuel, food, provisions, etc., as the latter country may be willing to furnish according to its own legislation. But in no event shall an aircraft be denied fuel, food, provisions, supplies, etc., sufficient to enable it to reach the nearest source of supply within the jurisdiction of its own country.

Seventh. Each Government, within its own territory and by means of its own forces, shall protect the points designated on land or sea for the landing of aircraft. Should either Government be in need of material or equipment for this purpose which the other Government may be in a position to furnish, the matter shall form the subject of discussion and any material or equipment furnished shall be on such terms and conditions as may be agreed upon.

Eighth. Present conditions of possible threats of armed aggression against the American Continent will exist, in so far as the reciprocal concessions emanating from this Agreement are concerned, so long as the Governments of the United States and Mexico shall jointly deem them to exist; and it is expressly understood that the mere notification by one of the High Contracting Parties to the other that it considers that the state of affairs that has brought about this Agreement has disappeared, will suffice for the complete termination of the concessions and obligations herein contained. Such notification may be given through the usual diplomatic channels, or direct by one Government to the other. Aircraft of either Party in transit at the time such unilateral notification is given shall have twenty-four hours within which to leave the territory of the other.

Ninth. This Agreement, when ratified by the Constitutional branch of each Government, will become effective as of the date of the exchange of ratifications, which shall take place in the city of Washington as soon as possible.

IN WITNESS WHEREOF, and with the powers hereinbefore stated, the Under Secretary of State of the United States of America and the Ambassador of Mexico, sign and cause their seals to be affixed to this Agreement, made in duplicate, in the English and Spanish languages, in the city of Washington, on the first day of April of the year nineteen hundred forty-one.

SUMNER WELLES   [SEAL]
Under Secretary of State of the United States
F. CASTILLO NÁJERA   [SEAL]
Ambassador of Mexico.

6. TOUR OF CHIEFS OF NAVAL GENERAL STAFFS OF AMERICAN REPUBLICS

At the invitation of Admiral Harold R. Stark, Chief of Naval Operations, the Chiefs of the Naval General Staffs of the American Republics which maintain naval forces came to "observe the development in activities of the United States Navy." The tour of inspection extended to various naval establishments from coast to coast. The party arrived in Washington on May 7, 1941 and remained there until May 12. A list of the Chiefs of the Naval General Staffs follows: Vice Admiral José Machado de Castro e Silva, Brazil; Vice Admiral Julio Allard P., Chile; Vice Admiral José Guisasola, Argentina; Rear Admiral Gustavo A. Schröder, Uruguay; Rear Admiral Carlos Rotalde G. del V., Peru; Commodore David Coello Ochoa, Mexico; Capt. Julio Díez Argüelles y Fernandez Castro, Cuba; Col. Francisco Tamayo Cortes, Colombia; Comdr. Cesar A. Mogollón Cárdenas, Ecuador; Comdr. Antonio Picardi, Venezuela; and Comdr. Ramón Díaz Benza, Paraguay.

(1) *Welcome by the Secretary of State (Hull), May 8, 1941* [1]

I am very pleased to welcome you.   If our naval forces needed stimulation more than they have been stimulated, they would get it from contacts with you.   I know it will be a source of pleasure and satisfaction for all our officials to extend every possible courtesy and facility to you. You come here not only at a most interesting but a most important time from the standpoint of our mutual welfare and safety.

I have for long years emphasized in conferences here and with you in Latin America the viewpoint that any threat to the safety of any one among our 21 Republics was a threat to the safety of all of them.   For some years that was minimized by many statesmen and even Army and Navy men, but new developments of unprecedented nature, which signified a world-wide movement of conquest, have brought more sharply to each the actual danger or threat not only to one but to all of the American Republics.

As we see this threat of danger the more important we find it to collaborate together and to cooperate in every practical way for the purpose of increasing the effectiveness of our agencies and means of common defense against the common danger, which has no geographical limits in its ultimate objectives.   We shall have a common objective in resisting a common danger.

I wish each of you a most satisfactory visit.   I am sure we shall profit from this exchange of ideas as much if not more than you.

(2) *Toast of the Under Secretary of State (Welles) to the Visiting Officers, Sulgrave Club, Washington, May 10, 1941* [2]

I am deeply conscious of the privilege of having with us tonight as our honored guests, these distinguished officers in whom are vested the command of the Navies of the Western Hemisphere.

It is needless for me to say that their visit at any time would be a source of the greatest pleasure to the Government of the United States.

But at a moment such as this, I know that we all realize that the visit with which we are honored is of outstanding importance.   It is a further and convincing demonstration of the determination of the Americas to collaborate together for the advancement and protection of their mutual interests.

[1] Department of State, *Bulletin*, IV, p. 553.
[2] *Ibid.*, p. 554.   Mr. Welles was host at the dinner.

During these latter years, the American Republics — the sovereign and independent associates of the Western Hemisphere — have, I am thankful to say, been drawn very closely together.

Five years ago our Governments had the wisdom to interpret correctly the sinister significance of the storm clouds that were already then fast arising on the world horizon.

At the Inter-American Conference for the Maintenance of Peace held at Buenos Aires, the great Capital of the Argentine Republic, in December of 1936, the American nations, by common accord, agreed upon the steps which they considered necessary to enable them to maintain the peace of the Americas and to insure the security of the Western Hemisphere.

Today the peoples of the Americas know that they confront powers bent upon world domination, and upon the obliteration of all of the freedoms which we Americans most dearly cherish — freedom of worship, freedom of speech, and freedom of thought. And yet the American nations are confident of their own strength as they face the conflagration which is fast spreading in the west, and in the east, because of their knowledge that there is no misunderstanding which separates them and no fears or suspicions which divide them.

We all of us recognize that in our unity lies our strength.

We have pledged ourselves to the defense of our New World and to the preservation of our liberties. It is incumbent upon us to make this pledge a reality so strong, so powerful, that no alien forces, however powerful, will ever be enabled to encroach upon this hemisphere.

My country throws open its portals to you. We appreciate this opportunity to show you why we are supremely confident that no successful assault can be made upon the security of any American country.

We want you to see our ships and our shipyards, our airplanes and our airplane factories, our equipment and the industry that makes it.

We want you to see the scope and extent of our present defenses and to learn of the plans for their improvement and enlargement.

In the name of my Government I can assure you that to the utmost extent of its ability, the United States stands prepared to play its full part in the defense of the Western Hemisphere and to assist its neighbors to the limits of its power, should that task ever become necessary.

My Government is grateful for your visit. It trusts that your stay among us will be as useful and as satisfactory to you as it is to us. We hope that we may have the privilege of seeing you often in our midst.

I ask you to join with me in a toast to the Presidents of the 21 American Republics and to the freedom and liberty of our nations which can be and which will be, because of our continued cooperation, rendered secure.

(3) *Reply of Vice Admiral José Guisasola, Argentina* [1]

MR. UNDER SECRETARY OF STATE:

Your presence here on this happy occasion and the fortunate fact that I have been requested by my colleagues of the nations of Latin America to reply to your kind words of welcome enable me to phrase words of thanks for your amiable reception at dinner, and, prizing the distinction with which my friends, the other Chiefs of Naval General Staffs of the Americas, have honored me, I desire to express my feelings in these few words.

Gentlemen, interpreting the feeling of those we represent from the American navies, although at the same time it is a very obvious thing, as we all know how the kind invitation of Admiral Stark, the Chief of Naval Operations, has warmed our hearts, I desire to call attention to and make public our recognition of our sincere appreciation of this wonderful invitation, especially as it comes to us from the American Navy which as an organization reflects the virtues and warm hospitality which is such an outstanding trait of their people.

Our navies are closely and intimately associated; a common viewpoint of ideals and ends guides us; the same very love of our profession makes us kin; one common hope of progress and development unites us in the struggle for those things which are common to all of us, and for the continued advance towards those objectives which constitute the fundamental bases of our institutions and freedom.

Confirmation of these concepts is the interesting program conceived by our kind host. Its realization will be for us without doubt an example of efficiency and fitting testimony of the power of the United States.

It is a matter of innermost satisfaction to me that they have entrusted these matters to the wise direction and matchless efficiency of their sailors, so closely related many of them with ours in their daily labors and pursuits. And leaving for a moment my main theme I wish to thank them and their higher authorities for the efficient collaboration which without stint they have always given us.

In these times in which we live, complex and transitional as they are, marking the end of one epoch and the beginning of another, this visit, or rather this assembly, of the senior representatives of our navies, now that mutual understanding and frank speech between the people of this,

---

[1] Department of State, *Bulletin*, IV, p. 555.

our Western Hemisphere, is so clearly necessary, assumes a significant value.

If we seek in the American way of life for reasons which may explain this truth we will find that history, the directives of the right and international justice, and a close interlinking of interests makes us kin, proving the existence of feeling common to all our peoples.

I speak of this America that takes such legitimate pride in having made human harmony an invariable rule in their relations with each other; in this America which, becoming free, opened its gates wide to all men who, attracted by the fertility of its soil and protected by the most liberal laws, came to enrich its soil with their toil and energy, and thus to fashion their and America's future. With their strength of soul and manly energy they have worked for the progress of the generous land that gave them shelter.

I believe with you, Sir, that the common understanding and mutual knowledge of people one with another, their respect for each other's institutions and culture, and their innermost feelings, paves the way to true bonds of friendship; this indeed is a creative policy of sincerity without suspicions, neighborliness without inhibitions, friendship without conditions.

This hour, fateful as it is in history, goes beyond that; it fosters a very profound sentiment and makes for a oneness of understanding and affection.

Mr. Under Secretary of State, thanking you again in the name of the Chiefs of the Naval General Staffs of the American navies and for myself for your presence here, which we so highly appreciate for its true worth, I wish you as much happiness as you have given us by your so cordial welcome.

7. MILITARY, NAVAL AND AIR MISSIONS

(1) *List of Agreements Made by the United States*

Agreement between the United States and Argentina.   Signed June 29, 1940.
To place at the disposal of Argentina military aviation instructors when so requested by the Argentine Minister of War. The term of contract is one year. It supersedes the agreement signed September 12, 1939. Executive Agreement Series No. 175.

Agreements between the United States and Peru. Signed July 31, 1940.
Renewal by the United States of a naval mission and agreement to furnish an aviation mission to cooperate with the Ministry of Marine and Aviation of the Republic of Peru. The two missions function in an advisory capacity to the Peruvian Navy and Naval Aviation Force respectively. The term of each contract is for four years. Executive Agreement Series Nos. 177 and 178.

Agreements between the United States and Ecuador. Signed December 12, 1940, and April 30, 1941. Agreement by the United States to furnish a naval mission and a military aviation mission to cooperate with the Minister of National Defense of the Republic of Ecuador. The two missions function in an advisory capacity to the Ecuadoran Navy and Air Force respectively. The term of each contract is four years. Executive Agreement Series Nos. 188, 189, 206.

Agreement between the United States and Brazil. Signed January 17, 1941. Providing a military and military aviation mission to cooperate in technical matters with the Brazilian Ministry of War with the object of increasing and perfecting the efficiency of the Brazilian Army in Coast Artillery and Aviation and in the various subjects correlated with both. The term of the mission is for four years. Executive Agreement Series No. 202.

Agreement between the United States and Venezuela. Signed March 24, 1941. Providing a naval mission to cooperate with the Ministry of War and Navy of the Republic of Venezuela. The mission functions in an advisory capacity to the Venezuelan Navy. The term of the contract is four years. Executive Agreement Series No. 203.

Agreement between the United States and Peru. Signed April 15, 1941. Places at the disposal of Peru a military adviser to the Remount Service of the Peruvian Army. The term of the contract is three years. Executive Agreement Series No. 205.

I. Cultural Relations

A program of cultural cooperation necessarily proceeds on a hundred fronts to embrace almost innumerable human interests. The active inter-American interchanges can never be completely indicated within a few pages for they result from private, institutional and official initiatives. Only a few of the most significant activities can be noticed here.

For a list of the amounts to be spent for cooperation with the American Republics under the Department of State Appropriation Act, 1942 (Public Law 135, 77th Cong.), see Department of State, *Bulletin*, V, p. 49. The total of 30 projects called for $600,300, as compared with a similar appropriation of $370,500 for the fiscal year 1941.

1. EXCHANGE OF PROFESSORS AND STUDENTS

The primary purpose of the exchange program of students, teachers, and professors is to develop a more realistic understanding between the peoples of the Western Hemisphere. By emphasizing the essential reciprocity of cultural relations, the exchanges are designed to make available to the people of the American republics a more accurate knowledge of progress in the fields of the humanities, social sciences, natural sciences, law, medicine, pharmacy, journalism, technology, engineering, and other studies.

This official exchange of students and professors is indicative of the interest of the various governments concerned. The provisions of the Buenos Aires convention serve to supplement the efforts of private organizations and institutions in the field of cultural relations.

(1) *Announcement of March 15, 1941* [1]

On February 15, 1941 Mexico deposited with the Pan American Union the instrument of ratification of the Convention for the Promotion of Inter-American Cultural Relations signed by the 21 American Republics at Buenos Aires December 23, 1936 (Treaty Series 928) [2] bringing to 15 the number of countries which have agreed to carry out the terms of the convention, the provisions of which are administered by the Department of State on behalf of the United States. The convention provides for the annual exchange of two graduate students or teachers and the biennial exchange of professors by the United States and each of the other ratifying republics.

2. STUDENTS FROM THE OTHER AMERICAN REPUBLICS

Figures showing the enrollment of students from the other American republics in the colleges and universities of the United States were recently made available to the Department by the Committee on Friendly Relations Among Foreign Students. These statistics reveal that the total number of such students during the present academic year is 1,421, an increase of 159 over the 1939–40 academic year. The majority of these students have come to study in this country at their own expense.

An analysis of these figures reveals the significant fact that the greatest increase is in the number of students from South America. Every country of that continent except Argentina and Bolivia showed a rise in the number of students sent to the United States during the past year. On a percentage basis, the increase of students from South America amounted to 26.8 per cent, while those from Central America increased 12.5 per cent, those from Mexico, 5.5 per cent, and those from the West Indies, no increase. The proportionately larger increase from South America is in accordance with the Department's policy of encouraging the reduction of travel costs for students, particularly from the more distant republics, who wish to study in the United States. Reductions in travel costs for students have already helped materially in stimulating student visits to this country.

The statistical chart opposite shows the number of students from the other American Republics who have studied in the United States during the past 10 years.

3. VISIT TO UNITED STATES OF LEADERS IN THE PROFESSIONS, THE ARTS, AND EDUCATION

(1) *Announcements of January 11 and 16, 1941* [3]

The Division of Cultural Relations of the Department of State has extended invitations to 30 distinguished educational, professional, and artistic leaders of the other American Republics to visit the United States. Funds to defray the cost of these trips were provided in the Second Deficiency Act of 1940. Arrangements for the itineraries of the visitors are being worked out in cooperation with the colleges and universities of the United States.

[1] Department of State, *Bulletin*, IV, p. 289.
[2] *Documents, II, 1939–40*, p. 194.
[3] Department of State, *Bulletin*, IV, pp. 62, 96.

United States, 1931–41 [1]

COUNTRY	1931–32	1932–33	1933–34	1934–35	1935–36	1936–37	1937–38	1938–39	1939–40	1940–41
WEST INDIES:										
Cuba	152	151	167	149	255	340	359	363	315	299
Dominican Republic	4	4	3	3	6	7	10	8	7	18
Haiti	23	3	8	2	4	3	9	9	19	24
Total	179	158	178	154	265	350	378	380	341	341
MEXICO	258	204	181	161	185	209	222	198	244	257
CENTRAL AMERICA:										
Costa Rica	23	29	25	23	23	16	26	25	47	52
Guatemala	13	11	11	10	13	10	10	13	20	32
Honduras	23	25	20	18	21	24	24	41	36	42
Nicaragua	16	21	17	12	13	21	15	17	16	19
Panama	47	64	58	58	59	73	77	94	111	118
Salvador	4	4	3	5	4	6	7	9	14	16
Unspecified	7	4	4	3	7	3	11	2	4	—
Total	133	158	138	129	140	153	170	201	248	279
SOUTH AMERICA:										
Argentina	27	20	24	25	25	22	25	31	46	44
Bolivia	24	16	14	4	4	10	7	5	10	10
Brazil	26	20	22	12	23	21	36	45	77	88
Chile	14	23	11	8	12	14	14	25	41	69
Colombia	78	42	43	50	49	47	51	54	95	129
Ecuador	12	9	7	5	11	13	14	13	15	17
Paraguay	2	2	1	1	1	3	1	1	—	3
Peru	34	27	23	16	18	17	33	31	46	72
Uruguay	2	1	2	3	3	—	4	6	6	9
Venezuela	32	17	17	13	19	25	47	51	84	100
Unspecified	22	33	14	20	13	14	14	23	8	3
Total	273	210	178	157	178	186	246	285	429	544
Grand Total	843	730	675	601	768	898	1,016	1,064	1,262	1,421

[1] Department of State, *Bulletin*, IV, p. 386; compiled from publications of the Committee on Friendly Relations Among Foreign Students.

The interests of the persons invited include writing and journalism, education, history, architecture, engineering, physiology, sociology and anthropology, music and the fine arts, and classical studies. Most of the visits will be made between January and April 1941 since the summer-vacation periods in the South American countries usually run from the end of December to the last of March.

A group of 85 students, teachers, and professional men and women from Chile, Peru, Ecuador, and Colombia arrived in New York Monday, January 13, on the *Santa Lucia* of the Grace Line to attend the special winter session of the University of North Carolina, organized for South Americans. This is the first time that an American university has arranged for a six-weeks session devoted to courses and work of specific interest to persons from the other American Republics.

This large group includes university students, professors, architects, physicians, lawyers, literary men, and members of congress.

4. ROLE OF THE MOTION PICTURE

(1) *Cooperation of the Motion-Picture Industry in Promotion of Inter-American Relations. Announcement of January 15, 1941* [1]

[Excerpt]

Nelson A. Rockefeller, Coordinator of Commercial and Cultural Relations Between the American Republics, announced January 14 a wide-scale program for the use of motion pictures as a medium for promotion of closer relations and better understanding among the American Republics. He announced the appointment of Hollywood committees representative of the producers, stars, writers, and directors, to cooperate in carrying out the program, and detailed initial steps taken to date.

"The motion-picture industry," said Mr. Rockefeller, "was among the first to organize itself for cooperation with the Coordinator's Office. In conferences over the past few weeks with John Hay Whitney, Director of the Motion Picture Division of the Coordinator's Office, representatives of the industry have formed cooperating committees to make more effective the whole range of its contribution; in feature films, short subjects, and newsreels."

Several pictures scheduled for production in the near future may be photographed either in whole or in part in Central and South America. A special committee has been formed to investigate production facilities now available in Central and South America, as well as desirable locales.

Mr. Whitney, who is now on the Coast holding conferences with leaders of the industry, said that the Motion Picture Producers and Distributors of America have agreed to appoint an expert on ways of life in the other American Republics to serve in the office of the Code Administrator in Hollywood. This person will cooperate with all of the producers to insure authenticity in films involving Central and South America and to advise on language and historical problems. Mr. Whitney also said that the leading studios in Hollywood have appointed, or

[1] Department of State, *Bulletin*, IV, p. 95. Released to the press by the Office for Coordination of Commercial and Cultural Relations Between the American Republics on January 15, 1941.

will appoint, special representatives who will concentrate on South and Central American aspects of production. In certain cases, companies have already sent for representatives in Central and South America to confer on this problem.

"The program outlined by the industry is to be based solely on the presentation of entertainment films," said Mr. Whitney. "Our American screen has always attracted the greatest audiences in the world because of its freedom of expression and expression of freedom. The producers feel that through sympathetic study of the cultural bonds existing among the American Republics, elements of screen entertainment, heretofore undiscovered or not fully utilized, can be found and brought to life on the screen and this, we know, will do much to create a better understanding among the nations of this hemisphere."

(2) *Distribution of Educational Motion Pictures in the American Republics. Announcement of March 22, 1941* [1]

In a recent release to the newspapers, Nelson A. Rockefeller, Coordinator of Commercial and Cultural Relations Between the American Republics, announced an extensive program for the collection, distribution, and, when necessary, the production of informative and educational non-theatrical motion pictures for use in the American Republics.

Films made available as a result of this program, which is being carried out in cooperation with the Department of State, will be offered for showing before schools, universities, cultural institutions, and other appropriate organizations and groups in the other American Republics.

The Film Library, Inc., of the Museum of Modern Art in New York, under the direction of the Coordinator's Office will gather desirable films from all sources and, after reviewing them, will cut and edit them for sound-tracking in Spanish and Portuguese. Distribution of the prints to the other American Republics will be undertaken in cooperation with the Department of State.

The Film Library has in its files 13,000,000 feet of film. In 1940 it circulated 174 different titles among 280 colleges, study groups, and museums in 41 States. All of this material will be made available for use in the new program. The Museum of Modern Art will also arrange for the production of new films on special subjects should this prove necessary because of a lack of appropriate existing films.

In order to make available in the United States educational motion pictures of the other American Republics the Library will purchase suitable foreign-made film for the Coordinator's Office and will arrange for its distribution in the United States in cooperation with the Department of State.

(3) *Address by the President (Roosevelt), February 27, 1941* [2]

[Excerpt]

We have been seeking to affirm our faith in the western world through a wider exchange of culture, of education, of thought, and of free expression among the

[1] Department of State, *Bulletin*, IV, p. 340.

[2] Delivered by radio in connection with the Thirteenth Annual Awards Dinner of the Academy of Motion Picture Arts and Sciences, Hollywood, California. Department of State, *Bulletin*, IV, p. 229.

various nations of this hemisphere. Your industry has utilized its vast resources of talent and facilities in a sincere effort to help the people of this hemisphere to come to know each other.

In carrying on this program of advancing the spirit of inter-American solidarity and continental defense our Government has established machinery to coordinate our growing commercial and cultural relations with the American Republics. Our Government has invited you to do your share of the job of interpreting the people of the Western Hemisphere to one another. And all of us in all the 21 American Republics are grateful that your response is so immediate and so wholehearted.

I do not minimize the importance of the motion-picture industry as the most popular medium of mass entertainment. But tonight I want to place the chief emphasis on the service you can render in promoting solidarity among all the people of the Americas.

For all this and for your splendid cooperation with all who are directing the expansion of our defense forces, I am glad to thank you. In the weeks and months that lie ahead we in Washington know we shall have your continued aid and support.

(4) Motion-Picture-Projection Equipment for United States Missions. Statement Released March 15, 1941 [1]

The Office of the Coordinator of Commercial and Cultural Relations Between the American Republics has made available twenty 16 mm. sound-motion-picture projectors for distribution by the Department of State to United States embassies and legations in the other American Republics. The projectors are to be used for the showing of cultural and educational films to interested groups. They will be lent for this purpose to schools, clubs, and other organizations.

Various approved films, from different sources, will be transmitted to the missions for use with the projection equipment. Of particular interest will be the 12 reels recently selected by the Interdepartmental Committee on Cooperation with the American Republics. These films, chosen from among the films produced by various Government agencies, will be sound-tracked with Spanish and Portuguese narrations.

5. INSTITUTES ENGAGED IN PROMOTION OF CULTURAL RELATIONS

(1) Announcement of Department of State, March 22, 1941 [2]

The following institutes in the other American republics are engaged in the promotion of cultural relations between those countries and the United States:

Argentina: Buenos Aires. Instituto Cultural Argentino-Norteamericano — Dr. Cupertino del Campo, *President;* Dr. Amaranto A. Abeledo, *Secretary.* Maipú, 686, Buenos Aires.

Córdoba. Instituto Cultural Argentino-Norteamericano — Señor Don Exequiel Feigín, *President;* Dr. Enrique Gaviola. Colón, 769, Córdoba.

---

[1] Department of State, *Bulletin*, IV, p. 288.   [2] *Ibid.*, p. 342.

Brazil: Rio de Janeiro. Instituto Brasil-Estados Unidos — Capt. Francisco Radler de Aquino, *President;* Senhor Adhemar de Canindé Jobim, *Secretary.* Rua Mexico, 90, Rio de Janeiro.

Porto Alegre. Instituto Cultural Brasileiro Norteamericano — Senhor Erico O. Mello, *President;* Senhor Placido Puccini, *First Secretary.* Rua 7 de setembro, N. 1156, 4o. andar, Sala 2, Porto Alegre.

São Paulo. União Cultural Brasil-Estados Unidos — Dr. A. C. Pacheco e Silva, *President.* Rua dos Ingelezes, 258, São Paulo.

Chile: Santiago. Instituto Cultural Chileno-Norteamericano — Dr. Ernesto Barros Jarpa, *President;* Señor Eugenio Pereira Salas, *Secretary.* Casilla, 9286, Santiago.

Honduras: Tegucigalpa. Instituto Hondureño de Cultura Interamericana — Dr. Jorge Fidel Durón, *President;* Señorita Ofelia Mendoza, *Secretary.* Tegucigalpa.

Peru: Lima. Instituto Cultural Peruano-Norteamericano — Dr. Alfredo Alvárez Calderón, *President;* Dr. Manuel Beltroy, *Secretary.* Jirón Carabaya, 780, Lima.

Uruguay: Montevideo. Alianza Cultural Uruguay-Estados Unidos de Norte América — Dr. Eduardo Blanco Acevedo, *President;* Dr. Carlos Alberto Estapé, *Secretary.* Piso, 2, 217, Edificio de la Bolsa de Comercio, Montevideo.

On September 5, 1940, a Colombian-North American Cultural Institute was established at Bogotá on the initiative of Dr. Jorge Bejarano, a leading medical doctor. Activities and program are in process of formation. Dr. Baldomero Sanín Cano is the president.

6. INTER-AMERICAN UNION OF THE CARIBBEAN

The Inter-American Union of the Caribbean [1] which has its headquarters at Havana, Cuba, was organized for the purpose of convening meetings "to further closer relations and to contribute toward the development of cultural as well as economic and tourist relations among the nations in this portion of the New World." The first meeting was convened by the "Sociedad Colombista Panamericana" of Havana in October 1939, while the second meeting was held in Ciudad Trujillo from May 31 to June 6, 1940.[2] A third meeting convened at Port-au-Prince on April 22, 1941, to consider an agenda covering social, cultural, and scientific questions. Following is a statement describing the general characteristics of this organization.

(1) General Characteristics of the Union [3]

The Inter-American Meetings of the Caribbean are designed to produce periodically and regularly, in a given city, the attendance of representatives of the cultural, scientific and economic institutions, both official and private, most expressive of the thought and of the material progress of those nations of America, in order that such delegates, meeting in Assembly shall jointly fraternize,

[1] Department of State, *Bulletin,* IV, p. 469 (April 19, 1941).

[2] Unión interamericana del Caribe, Segunda reunión; memoria. Habana, Secretaria general, 1940.

[3] Reprinted from the *Agenda* issued by the Secretariat, Havana, Cuba.

study and resolve the adoption of any measures deemed proper to promote facilities for the peace, culture and union thereof.

The members of the Meetings of the Caribbean shall be of three kinds: (a) governmental, (b) corporative, (c) individual.

The Governments of Colombia, Costa Rica, Cuba, the Dominican Republic, El Salvador, Guatemala, Haiti, Honduras, Mexico, Nicaragua, Panama, the United States of America and Venezuela, shall freely appoint their representatives to such meetings, and they shall be considered *Governmental Members* of the Assembly.

The delegates of Cultural Corporations, Organizations and Institutions shall be considered *Corporative Members* of the Assembly.

The following entities may be participants in said meetings: Universities, Institutions of High Social, Political and Economic Studies, Literary, Scientific, Artistic, Historical and Geographical Academies, Athenaeums, Lyceums and other similar institutions of learning and study, Libraries and Archives, Superior, Technologic and Polytechnic centers, Physical Culture and Sport centers, Professional Schools and Associations, Chambers of Commerce, National Tourism Organizations and establishments, and any organization of an official or private character not comprised within the foregoing specifications, created for the purposes of coordination or defense of the collective interest, and the cooperation of which may be useful or beneficial to the high aims of union and fraternity among the Caribbean nations.

By special invitation extended by the permanent Secretary General of the Inter-American Meetings of the Caribbean, any person who, by reason of his merits and his well-known Americanistic callings is worthy of such noted distinction, shall be considered as an *Individual Member*.

J. Boundary Dispute between Ecuador and Peru

The boundary dispute between Ecuador and Peru, like most other territorial controversies in Latin America, harks back to the indefinite delimitations and provincial descriptions in the Spanish colonial documents. It involves some 40,000 square miles of land, the principal area lying both sides of the Marañón River. The King of Spain withdrew from an arbitration in 1910, and Argentina, Brazil and the United States as mediators made proposals. Their efforts bore fruit in the protocol of June 21, 1924 [1] by which the parties were to undertake direct negotiations in Washington and, if not successful, should submit certain questions to the arbitration of the President of the United States. The operation of the protocol was contingent upon the settlement of the Tacna-Arica question between Chile and Peru. Negotiations were therefore begun only in 1930 and hinged for several years upon the scope of the direct settlement and the arbitration methods prescribed in the 1924 protocol. Ecuador and Peru signed an agreement at Lima July 6, 1936 whereby the potential arbitration was defined "as arbitration according to law" and delegations of three plenipotentiaries each were to meet at Washington, September 30; the territorial *status quo* was to be maintained, without prejudice to the rights of either party, until the termination of the negotiations and arbitral proceedings. The inability of the delegations to attain results either in a negotiated settlement or in agreeing to the terms of questions to be arbitrated led to a cessation of the negotiations. On October 10,

[1] League of Nations, *Treaty Series*, XXVII, p. 345.

1938, the Provisional President of Ecuador invited the Presidents of Argentina, Brazil, Chile, the United States and Uruguay to extend their mediation in view of their successful termination of the Chaco dispute. The mediatory governments of 1910 resumed their task by the démarche made in the notes which follow. According to the press, hostilities between armed forces of the two nations broke out on July 5, 1941 in the disputed frontier area.

(1) *The Secretary of State (Hull) to the Ministers of Ecuador (Donoso) and Peru (Solf y Muro), May 8, 1941* [1]

The Governments of Argentina, Brazil and the United States are deeply concerned by the continuance, particularly at a time when continental solidarity is vital, of the difficulties which for over a century have perturbed the relations between Peru and Ecuador.

The Governments of the two countries involved have given many proofs of their earnest desire to remove this cause of friction between them. They have been in almost constant discussion and negotiation over a period of many years in an effort to agree upon a common boundary. However, in spite of the fact that some progress has been made and that the two parties have agreed to submit the matter to arbitration, it must be recognized that as of the present date the controversy contains serious possibilities of dangerous developments.

Other continents are aflame with hate and violence. Every day the theater of war extends to wider horizons.

Confronted with a crisis in world affairs of a magnitude heretofore totally unknown, the American Republics have frequently declared, and at the meeting of Foreign Ministers held at Havana in July 1940 reiterated, their irrevocable determination to omit no effort to prevent any controversy which might impair their solidarity. The continuance of any situation that results in the impairment of harmonious relations between two of the American Republics diminishes and undermines the strength of that solidarity.

Conscious of the desire of both the Government of Peru and the Government of Ecuador to settle their long-standing boundary dispute, as repeatedly evidenced by both countries, and impressed by the necessity, in this critical hour, of the American Republics drawing ever closer together in an unshakable determination to maintain unimpaired their peace, territorial integrity, and security, the Governments of Argentina, Brazil and the United States tender their friendly services in furthering the prompt, equitable and final settlement of the dispute to the Government of Peru and to the Government of Ecuador to be availed of by those Governments, together with the services of such other Govern-

[1] Department of State, *Bulletin*, IV, p. 596.

ments as they are both desirous of inviting, in such manner as may be deemed appropriate and advantageous.

The Governments of Argentina, Brazil and the United States earnestly and sincerely hope that the Governments of Peru and Ecuador, appreciative of the high motives which have inspired this action, will give the proposal their most attentive and urgent consideration.

Accept [etc.]   CORDELL HULL

(2) *The Minister of Foreign Affairs of Ecuador (Donoso) to the Secretary of State (Hull)* [1] *[Released to the Press, May 13, 1941]*

The Ecuadoran Government has had the honor of receiving a message in which Your Excellency so graciously communicated to it that the Governments of the United States of America, Argentina and Brazil, motivated by the necessity in this critical hour of a closer *rapprochement* between the American republics, disturbed by the continuation of the difficulties which for more than a century have disturbed the relations between Ecuador and Peru and fully cognizant of the desire of both parties to solve their ancient difference over boundaries, offered them friendly services together with those of any other Governments that it might seem desirable to invite in order to promote the prompt, equitable and final solution of this controversy. My Government, which concurs fully with the sentiments, desires and proposals expressed in this message and persuaded that this solution is, as Your Excellency says so eloquently, a vital factor for the unity and solidarity of the continent in this moment of disquieting expectations, and being under an obligation to show itself especially worthy of the motives of your pacific offer, accepts with pleasure the generous services of the illustrious Governments of the United States of America, Argentina and Brazil. I am honored in being able to assure the American Government of the gratitude of Ecuador and to applaud so fine an act of fellowship and high understanding of the necessities and destinies of America. I trust fully that Peru is equally devoted to those same ideals of fraternity for the glory and benefit of the continent and honor of our countries now called to a close-knit union and mutual aid for the future. [I believe with absolute faith] that the assistance of these Governments and that of others which might be designated will have the most complete and prompt success in the equitable and final solution of the controversy.

I present [etc.]   JULIO TOBAR DONOSO

(3) *The Minister of Foreign Affairs of Peru (Solf y Muro) to the Secretary of State (Hull)* [2] *[Released to the Press, May 13, 1941]*

The Government of Peru has received the cablegram in which Your Excellency is good enough to advise it that the Governments of the Argentine Republic, Brazil and the United States of America offer "their friendly services in furthering the prompt, equitable and final settlement of the [boundary] dispute" pending between Ecuador and Peru, in the hope of removing, under these grave

[1] Department of State, *Bulletin*, IV, p. 596.   [2] *Ibid.*, p. 597.

circumstances, any situation which by prejudicing "the harmonious relations between two of the American Republics diminishes and undermines the strength of that [continental] solidarity."

My Government, highly appreciating these proposals, recalls that it is the second time that Argentina, Brazil and the United States of America have taken this position. In 1910, a serious condition of tension having been caused by the Ecuadoran rejection of the Spanish arbitration, the three countries succeeded in removing the danger of a conflict. They then asked for the withdrawal of the forces encamped on the frontiers and proposed the final settlement of the dispute through the mediation, which Ecuador rejected, affirming "that Ecuador is the only one who has to decide whether or not the dispute with Peru affects her vital interests, the national honor and the sovereignty of the State itself." According to the Ecuadoran Government direct arrangements were the "most decorous means" and "most fitting for sister nations" to put an end to the dispute, "with no other judge than the good offices of our most illustrious and great friends."

While noting these facts, which constitute the best proof that Peru is not responsible for the prolongation of the dispute, my Government must re-state, in the first place, the unwavering juridical position of my country of respect for the popular will from which our nationalities emerged, the basic principle in the argument maintained by Peru in the arbitration proceedings at Madrid and repeated in the Washington conferences. It is therefore an unavoidable duty to declare that my Government cannot admit that, at any time, the sovereign rights of Peru over the provinces of Túmbez, Jaén and Mainas which, in 1821, swore the independence of Peru under the aegis of General San Martín and which afterward participated in the definitive establishment of the Peruvian State, and have been represented in the congresses of Peru up to the present time, be made a matter of argument. Peru is disposed to settle her boundary dispute,— but not to admit a controversy concerning the nationality of provinces which have been a part of Peru for one hundred and twenty years, and in which are large Peruvian populations which have expressed their energetic protest against the separatist claims of Ecuador. Peru's position is one of the most fervent adherence to peace, but she demands, also, respect for her international personality. To discuss the nationality of three Peruvian provinces or merely to begin with an assumed right to do so, would imply the intention to disintegrate the personality of Peru, formed by her constituent parts since her independence, to revise the work of American independence and the principles of obedience to the popular will in the formation of nationalities and to introduce a grave confusion in the international order, which is based on respect for the personality of States fixed by their sacred initial constitution. The situation created by regrettable incidents which lead the friendly Governments to fear "the possibility of dangerous developments" will readily disappear, as has happened on previous occasions, with the simple observance of Ecuador of the *status quo* guaranteed by agreements concluded since independence. In consonance with the principles stated, which Your Excellency will probably appreciate, the Government of Peru accepts the good offices offered by the Governments of Argentina, Brazil and the United States of America, to the end that the atmosphere of cordiality and sincere collaboration between the two countries may be restored.

I avail [etc.] ALFREDO SOLF Y MURO

(4) *Statement of the Secretary of State (Hull), May 16, 1941* [1]

The friendly offices extended by the three governments met a varied reception in Ecuador and Peru. Critical comment in Peru alleged that the proffer was not entirely disinterested, and unofficially implied that the United States was making a side deal with Ecuador in connection with the tender. To an inquiry as to that reaction, the Secretary of State made this reply.

I am glad to have the opportunity of reiterating once again that this Government was motivated in offering to Ecuador and Peru its friendly offices solely by the most friendly desire to assist in settling, once and for all, the long-standing boundary dispute between those two neighboring countries. This Government is happy to have been associated with the Governments of Argentina and Brazil in this tender of friendly offices.

In some quarters it has been insinuated that this Government participated in this friendly initiative in order to obtain bases on the Galapagos Islands. I wish to take this opportunity to state categorically and definitely that the United States has not, in any way, discussed with Ecuador the question of bases on the Galapagos Islands. Moreover, the willingness of this Government to consider making available to Ecuador two coastal patrol vessels and military supplies has absolutely no relation to the offer of friendly good offices but derives solely from a general policy of this Government made known to each and every one of the American Republics, to cooperate so far as possible in military and naval matters for the purpose of strengthening the defense of the Western Hemisphere.

2. CANADIAN–AMERICAN RELATIONS

A. Mutual Defense : Military and Economic

(1) *"Ogdensburg Agreement." Joint Statement of the President (Roosevelt) and the Prime Minister of Canada (Mackenzie King), Ogdensburg, N. Y., August 18, 1940* [2]

The Prime Minister and the President have discussed the mutual problems of defense in relation to the safety of Canada and the United States.

It has been agreed that a Permanent Joint Board on Defense shall be set up at once by the two countries.

This Permanent Joint Board on Defense shall commence immediate studies relating to sea, land, and air problems including personnel and matériel.

[1] Department of State, *Bulletin*, IV, p. 598.
[2] *Ibid.*, III, p. 154. See Scott, F. R. *Canada and the United States.* (Boston, World Peace Foundation, 1941.)

It will consider in the broad sense the defense of the north half of the Western Hemisphere.

The Permanent Joint Board on Defense will consist of four or five members from each country, most of them from the services. It will meet shortly.

(a) *Joint Permanent Board on Defense, United States and Canada, Appointed August 22, 1940* [1]

For the United States:

Hon. Fiorello H. La Guardia, President, United States Conference of Mayors

Lt. Gen. Stanley D. Embick, Commanding the Fourth Corps Area, Headquarters, Atlanta, Ga.

Capt. Harry W. Hill, United States Navy, War Plans Division, Office of Chief of Naval Operations

Comdr. Forrest P. Sherman, United States Navy

Lt. Col. Joseph T. McNarney, United States Army Air Corps

Mr. John D. Hickerson, Assistant Chief, Division of European Affairs, Department of State, to be Secretary of the American section of the Joint Board

For Canada:

Mr. O. M. Biggar, K.C.

Brigadier K. Stuart, D.S.O., M.C., Deputy Chief, General Staff

Captain L. W. Murray, R.C.N., Deputy Chief, Naval Staff

Air Commander A. A. L. Cuffe, Air member, Air Staff, Royal Canadian Air Force

Mr. Hugh L. Keenleyside, Counselor, Department of External Affairs, to be Secretary of the Canadian section of the Joint Board

(2) *"Hyde Park Declaration." Joint Statement of the President (Roosevelt) and the Prime Minister of Canada (Mackenzie King), Hyde Park, N. Y., April 20, 1941* [2]

The President and the Canadian Prime Minister spent seven hours in consultation on April 20 at a time when the surveys of the Permanent Joint Board on Defense were well in hand. Their purpose was to lay down the general principles of mobilizing the resources of the continent, taking account of the operation of the Lend-Lease Act and the conditions of the currency exchanges among the United States, the United Kingdom and Canada. The joint statement outlines the general principles on which technical and financial arrangements are based.

Among other important matters, the President and the Prime Minister discussed measures by which the most prompt and effective utilization might be made of the productive facilities of North America for the

[1] Department of State, *Bulletin*, III, p. 154. The first meeting of the Board was held at Ottawa, August 26, 1940.   [2] *Ibid.*, IV, p. 494.

purposes both of local and hemisphere defense and of the assistance which, in addition to their own programs, both Canada and the United States are rendering to Great Britain and the other democracies.

It was agreed as a general principle that in mobilizing the resources of this continent, each country should provide the other with the defense articles which it is best able to produce, and, above all, produce quickly, and that production programs should be coordinated to this end.

While Canada has expanded its productive capacity manyfold since the beginning of the war, there are still numerous defense articles which it must obtain in the United States, and purchases of this character by Canada will be even greater in the coming year than in the past. On the other hand, there is existing and potential capacity in Canada for the speedy production of certain kinds of munitions, strategic materials, aluminum and ships, which are urgently required by the United States, for its own purposes.

While exact estimates cannot yet be made, it is hoped that during the next twelve months Canada can supply the United States with between $200,000,000 and $300,000,000 worth of such defense articles. This sum is a small fraction of the total defense program of the United States, but many of the articles to be provided are of vital importance. In addition, it is of great importance to the economic and financial relations between the two countries that payment by the United States for these supplies will materially assist Canada in meeting part of the cost of Canadian defense purchases in the United States.

Insofar as Canada's defense purchases in the United States consist of component parts to be used in equipment and munitions which Canada is producing for Great Britain, it was also agreed that Great Britain will obtain these parts under the Lease-Lend Act and forward them to Canada for inclusion in the finished article.

The technical and financial details will be worked out as soon as possible in accordance with the general principles which have been agreed upon between the President and the Prime Minister.

(a) Statement of the Prime Minister of Canada (Mackenzie King), Concerning the Hyde Park Declaration, House of Commons, April 28, 1941 [1]

[Excerpt]

On March 12, I described the United States Lease-Lend Act as one of the milestones of freedom, pointing the way to ultimate and certain victory. The Lease-Lend Act settled the principle of United States assistance to Britain and the other

[1] Issued by Director of Public Information, Ottawa, 1941.

democracies. It did not, however, solve all of the complex economic problems involved in the mobilization of the resources of the United States and Canada in order to render to Britain, in the speediest manner, the most effective assistance and support.

One of the reasons for my recent visit to the United States and my conferences with the President, was the urgent need for Canada to find an immediate solution of some of the problems involved in our wartime economic relations with the United States and with the United Kingdom. Before indicating the extent to which a solution has been found in the Hyde Park Declaration, I shall outline briefly the problems themselves.

The War Exchange Problem

It will be readily recognized that we, in Canada, could not possibly have embarked upon our existing program of war production if we had not lived side by side with the greatest industrial nation in the world. Without ready access to the industrial production of the United States, and particularly the machine tools and other specialized equipment so necessary in producing the complex instruments of modern war, Canada's war effort would have been seriously retarded. We would have been forced to embark upon the production of many articles which, because of limited demand, could only have been produced at high cost, and over a considerable period of time. Canada also lacks certain essential raw materials which must be procured from the United States. Since the outbreak of war, we have steadily expanded our purchases in the United States of these essential tools, machines and materials which were required both for our own Canadian war effort, and in the production of war supplies for Britain.

Even in normal times Canada purchases much more from the United States than we sell to our neighbors. In peacetime we were able to make up the deficit by converting into United States dollars the surplus sterling we received as a result of the sale of goods to Britain. But from the outset of war, this has been impossible. The Government realized at once that Canada would be faced with a growing shortage of United States dollars to pay for our essential war purchases. To conserve the necessary exchange the Foreign Exchange Control Board was established on September 15, 1939. As the need has grown, increasingly stringent measures have been adopted to reduce the unessential demands for United States dollars in order to conserve sufficient funds to make our payments for essential weapons and supplies of war. These war purchases could not be reduced without a corresponding, or perhaps an even more serious reduction in our war effort. Despite the drastic measures taken to conserve exchange, the lack of United States dollars was becoming, as one writer expressed it, one of the most serious "bottlenecks" in Canada's war effort.

Risk of Wasteful Duplication of Production

The problem of exchange was the most urgent problem we faced in our economic relations with the United States. But we also realized a growing danger of possible unnecessary duplication of production facilities on the North American continent, with consequent undue pressure on scarce labor and materials if

Canada and the United States each tried to make itself wholly self-sufficient in the field of war supplies. We felt it imperative to avoid such waste, which might well have had the most serious consequences. The experience of the Department of Munitions and Supply, and the studies of the Permanent Joint Board on Defense, both suggested the same solution. That solution was the coordination of the production of war materials of Canada and the United States. This was in reality a simple and logical extension, to the economic sphere, of the Ogdensburg Agreement.

The practical experience of a year and a half of organizing and developing war production in Canada revealed that many of the essentials of war could be made in the comparatively small quantities required by Canada only at a prohibitive cost. They could, however, be produced economically in the United States where the demand was large enough to result in the economies of large-scale production. On the other hand, the production of other weapons and materials had been developed in Canada to the point where output could be expanded more quickly, and probably more economically, than new production facilities could be organized in the United States. It was, therefore, only common sense to extend to the production of war materials the same reciprocity in which, at Ogdensburg in August last, our two countries had permanently placed their defense.

Visit to the United States

During my Easter visit, I had the opportunity of preliminary discussions with the Secretary of State, Mr. Cordell Hull, and the Secretary of the Treasury, Mr. Morgenthau, at Washington. I also, later, had an opportunity of conferring with Mr. Harry Hopkins, who has been entrusted with immediate direction and supervision of the measures to be taken under the Lease-Lend Act. On Sunday, April 20, I spent the day with the President at Hyde Park. At the close of the visit, I gave to the press a statement of the understanding which the President and I had reached regarding the problems I have mentioned. That statement it is proposed to call the Hyde Park Declaration.

[Here follows the text of the Declaration.[1]]

Immediate Purpose of the Declaration

The immediate purpose of the joint Declaration is set out in its first paragraph, which might be described as the preamble. It states that the President and I discussed measures by which the most prompt and effective utilization might be made of the productive facilities of North America. Let me emphasize the two words: prompt and effective. They indicate that, while recognizing the short-run necessity of speed, the vital importance of the time factor, we have not lost sight of the long-run necessity of the utmost efficiency in the organization of our war production.

The preamble goes on to recognize a twofold object in ensuring this prompt and effective utilization of the productive facilities of both countries. Not only does it envisage the extension of the scope of our joint defense arrangements to

[1] See p. 161.

the economic sphere, but it recognizes the advantages of coordinating the use of the resources of both countries as a means of speeding up and increasing the volume of aid to Britain from this continent.

Let me state this in another way. The Hyde Park Declaration is more than an extension of the Ogdensburg Agreement for hemispheric defense. It is also a joint agreement between Canada and the United States for aid to Britain.

The Basic Principle: Cooperation in Production

The basic principle underlying the agreement is set out in the second paragraph. It is a recognition of the fact that each country has special advantages for the production of certain war materials which are lacking in the other, and that both countries will benefit by each producing for the other, as well as for itself, the defense articles which it is best able to produce. It constitutes an acceptance of the economic interdependence of Canada and the United States as the foundation of the program of war production in both countries. It represents the application to war production of the principle, recognized by Canada and the United States in the trade agreements of peace time, that the exchange of goods is of mutual benefit.

The third paragraph of the Declaration is an amplification of the basic principle of the agreement. It recognizes, on the one hand, the vital necessity, for Canada's war program, of obtaining certain defense articles from the United States; on the other hand, it indicates the possibilities of the speedy expansion of Canadian production of other defense articles, munitions and strategic materials. It is not without significance that aluminium and ships are specified by name in the declaration.

Practical Operation of the Agreement

One question which may arise in connection with the Hyde Park Declaration is: how can Canada spare to the United States any defense articles or munitions? Surely, it will be said, all our war production is needed either for Canada or for Britain! The answer is that we have advanced so far in the production of certain articles that expansion beyond British and Canadian needs can be readily accomplished. That is true of certain types of small arms, guns and ammunition, certain explosives and chemicals, certain armed fighting vehicles, aluminium and certain other metals and materials, merchant ships and naval vessels of the type we have been building, namely, corvettes and mine-sweepers. There are in addition certain types of clothing and textiles, certain leather, rubber and timber products, and certain secret devices in which Canada could probably make an important contribution, if these were desired. On the other hand, the production of engines for aircraft in Canada would be a slow process, costly both in time and in those types of skilled labor and specialized equipment of which no surplus exists. Moreover, this is a field in which not one but many types are needed to fill the varied demands and improvements in designs that are constantly occurring.

The fact that Canadian war production is so well organized in many fields as to enable Canada to meet speedily many United States requirements is a high tribute to Canadian industry and Canadian labor.

Alleviation of the Exchange Problem

In the Declaration itself a rough estimate was made of the value of the defense articles which it is hoped Canada will be in a position to supply to the United States in the next twelve months. The estimate is between $200,000,000 and $300,000,000 worth. We may be able to do better than this, but obviously detailed negotiations will be necessary with the appropriate purchasing departments or agencies of the United States Government, in order to determine how best they can use the surplus capacity, existing and potential, of Canadian industry. The immediate significance to Canada of the sale of these defense articles is, of course, the provision of the United States dollars to help us in paying for Canada's essential war purchases in the United States.

While these United States purchases will assist us very materially in meeting our deficit, they alone will not solve the whole problem. A further important contribution to its solution is contained in another paragraph of the Declaration which provides that Canadian purchases in the United States of materials or components to be used in equipment and munitions being produced by Canada for Britain will be made available to Britain under the terms of the Lease-Lend Act. Hitherto it has been necessary to Canada to find United States dollars to pay for these purchases on British account. These purchases have materially added to the growing deficit in our balance of trade with the United States.

The combination of United States purchases in Canada and the lease-lending of defense articles for Britain will go a very long way toward the solution of Canada's acute exchange problem. It is, however, not anticipated that the whole deficit will be covered in this way. Essential Canadian purchases in the United States will still exceed United States purchases in Canada. There would, therefore, appear to be little prospect of relaxing any of the existing foreign exchange conservation restrictions without causing a new deficit which would imperil Canada's war effort.

The final paragraph of the Declaration provides for the working out of the technical and financial details as soon as possible in accordance with the general principles set out in the Declaration itself. Officials of the two governments are at present engaged upon the task of working out these details. Until that task is completed it will not be possible to say exactly what Canada will supply the United States or what the United States will supply Canada. I have already indicated certain articles which it is anticipated will be included in the list to be supplied by Canada.

Significance of the Declaration

Hon. members will, I am sure, be more interested in the broad significance of the Hyde Park Declaration than in its technical aspects.

Its most immediate significance is that, through the coordination of war production in both countries, it will result in the speeding up of aid to Britain by the United States and Canada. As a result of the better integration of North American industry, the proposed arrangement will, through increasing total production, have the further effect of increasing the total volume of aid to Britain. It will have a corresponding effect upon Canada's war effort. Full utilization of the production facilities we have built up, and specialization on those things which we are best fitted to produce, will increase both our national income and our own armed strength, as well as increasing our capacity to aid Britain.

As I have already said, the agreement will go a long way toward the solution of the exchange problem and, in this way, will remove one of the financial obstacles to the maximum war production program of Canada and the United States. We, in Canada, have reason to be gratified at the understanding shown by the President and by the Secretary of the Treasury, of Canada's difficult exchange problem. We may, I am sure, feel an equal confidence that in the working out of the detailed technical and financial arrangements, Canadian officials will find the same generous measure of understanding and the same spirit of cooperation.

The Economic Corollary of Ogdensburg

I have spoken thus far of the immediate significance of the Declaration, of the effect it will have in speeding up aid to Britain in the critical months ahead, and of its importance in assisting us to meet our exchange problem. But beyond its immediate significance the Hyde Park Declaration will have a permanent significance in the relations between Canada and the United States. It involves nothing less than a common plan of the economic defense of the Western Hemisphere. When we pause to reflect upon the consequences, in Europe, of the failure of the peace-loving nations to plan in concert their common defense, while yet there was time, we gain a new appreciation of the significance for the future of both Canada and the United States of the Ogdensburg Agreement and of this new Declaration which might well be called the economic corollary of Ogdensburg.

For Canada, the significance of the Hyde Park Declaration may be summarized briefly as follows: first, it will help both Canada and the United States to provide maximum aid to Britain and to all the defenders of democracy; second, it will increase the effectiveness of Canada's direct war effort; and finally, through the increased industrial efficiency which will result, it will increase our own security and the security of North America.

It is appropriate at this point to emphasize the fact that, while the agreement will increase the effectiveness of our war effort and our assistance to Britain, the self-imposed burden upon the Canadian people will nevertheless remain as great as ever. The sacrifices which we are called upon to make will not be reduced by the Hyde Park Declaration, but the results achieved by our sacrifices will, we believe, be considerably greater. At the same time, the risks of delays and breakdowns will be materially reduced. The utmost effort of the Canadian people is more than ever needed in the present phase of this terrible struggle; but in making that effort we shall have, as the result of the agreement, the added satisfaction of knowing that we are making a greater contribution than otherwise would be possible to the cause of freedom.

Foundations of a New World Order

In referring to the passage of the Lease-Lend Act, I expressed in this house the view that "Canada's example, as a nation of the new world, actively participating to the utmost limit in the present struggle, has also had its influence in arousing the people of the United States to their present realization that freedom itself is at stake in this war."

Unhesitatingly, to-day, I would go one step farther and would say that the example given by Canada has, I believe, aroused the admiration of our neighbors and made them ready to accept this new partnership.

Last November, I said to hon. members of this house that the link forged by the Ogdensburg Agreement was no temporary axis, formed by nations whose common tie was a mutual desire for the destruction of their neighbors. The Hyde Park Declaration is, I believe, a further convincing demonstration that Canada and the United States are indeed laying the enduring foundations of a new world order, an order based on international understanding, on mutual aid, on friendship and good will.

(3) *Formation of Joint Economic Committees, United States and Canada. Statement of the Department of State, June 17, 1941* [1]

The Government of Canada and the Government of the United States of America announced on June 17 that they have established joint committees of inquiry to explore the possibility of a greater degree of economic cooperation between Canada and the United States. They will be known as the Joint Economic Committees.

The Committees have been instructed to study and to report to their respective governments on the possibilities of (1) effecting a more economic, more efficient, and more coordinated utilization of the combined resources of the two countries in the production of defense requirements (to the extent that this is not now being done) and (2) reducing the probable post-war economic dislocation consequent upon the changes which the economy in each country is presently undergoing.

It is the common belief of the two governments that such studies and reports should assist the governments and peoples of each country in formulating policies and actions for the better utilization of their productive capacities for the mutually greater welfare of each, both in the present emergency period and after the emergency has passed.

This joint inquiry marks one further step in the implementation of the declaration made by President Roosevelt and Prime Minister Mackenzie King at Hyde Park on April 20, 1941.

The members of the United States Committee will be Mr. William L. Batt, Mr. Harry D. White, Prof. Alvin H. Hansen, and Mr. E. Dana Durand. Mr. Adolf A. Berle, Jr., Assistant Secretary of State, will sit with the Committee from time to time as occasion may render desirable.

[1] Department of State, *Bulletin*, IV, p. 747.

The members of the Canadian Committee will be Mr. R. A. C. Henry, Prof. W. A. Mackintosh, Mr. J. G. Bouchard, and Mr. Alex Skelton. Mr. H. L. Keenleyside of the Department of External Affairs will sit with the Committee from time to time as occasion may render desirable.

In order that the Secretary of State and the Secretary of State for External Affairs may be kept closely in touch with the activities of the Committees, Mr. Leroy D. Stinebower has been appointed as liaison officer from the Department of State, and a liaison officer from the Department of External Affairs will shortly be designated.

B. Limitation of Naval Vessels on the Great Lakes

The agreement concerning naval force on the Great Lakes effected between Great Britain and the United States by exchange of notes at Washington April 28, 29, 1817 [1] has proved to be one of the most effective instruments in political history. This Rush-Bagot Agreement confined the naval force of each party on the Great Lakes and Lake Champlain to four vessels "not exceeding 100 tons burden, and armed with 1 18-pound cannon." In the waters affected the British had had 30 vessels of all kinds capable of carrying 393 guns and the United States 38 vessels capable of carrying 527 guns. The vessels to which the parties limited themselves were obsolete in type within a few decades, but the spirit of the limitation was tacitly and loyally maintained in the replacements which occurred. More remarkable than the agreement was its effect. The removal of tension on the border waters seems to have established a general policy of non-protection of the American-Canadian frontier. It served to inhibit fortification of the land boundary as it existed and as it came to exist. The same principle was applied after the acquisition of Alaska in 1867 to the Alaskan-Canadian boundary. The boundaries between Canada and United States territory are the best administered in the world. The principal reason is the complete absence in policy and purpose of any strategic consideration in the functions of the International Boundary Commission, United States and Canada and Alaska and Canada, and its predecessors. Land and water boundaries of a total length of 5,527 miles, marked by 8,143 monuments,[2] are without any fortified place and without military establishment because of the cumulative psychological effect of the agreement of 1817.

Though the actual terms of the 1817 agreement have been obsolete for a century and have for many years been technically disregarded in practice, the intention of the agreement has been fully maintained and no important controversy has ever materialized around it.[3] The understandings reached in 1939-40 as set forth in the notes here printed are a modern interpretation of its terms.

---

[1] *Treaties, Conventions*, etc., 1776–1909, I, p. 628.

[2] Data as of September 30, 1940 (U. S. Congress, House of Representatives, Committee on Appropriations, *Department of State Appropriation Bill for 1942, Hearings* . . . 77th Cong., 1st sess., p. 276.

[3] For incidents which involved the agreement see Callahan, James M., *The Neutrality of the American Lakes* (Baltimore, Johns Hopkins University, 1898); Levermore, Charles H., *The Anglo-American Agreement of 1817 for Disarmament on the Great Lakes*.(Boston, World Peace Foundation, 1914).

(1) *The American Minister to Canada (Roper) to the Canadian Under Secretary for External Affairs (Skelton), June 9, 1939* [1]

OTTAWA, CANADA,
June 9, 1939.

MY DEAR DR. SKELTON:

In a confidential letter addressed to the Secretary of State on January 31, 1939, Admiral Leahy, the Acting Secretary of the Navy, raised certain questions regarding the Rush-Bagot Agreement of 1817. Among other things, Admiral Leahy requested the views of Mr. Hull concerning the mounting of two 4-inch guns on each of the American naval vessels on the Great Lakes, to be used in firing target practice in connection with the training of naval reserves. He inquired, if this was considered improper, concerning the possibility of modifying the Rush-Bagot Agreement to permit this practice. The question was subsequently the subject of informal conversations between officers of our State and Navy Departments.

After careful consideration of the problem, Mr. Hull is inclined to the opinion that a modification of the Rush-Bagot Agreement would be undesirable at this time. It is clear from a study of the documents relating to the negotiation of the Agreement and its early history that the objective of the negotiators was to provide a solution of an immediate and urgent problem arising out of the war of 1812 and the terms of the Agreement themselves support the view that its indefinite continuation in force was not anticipated. Consequently, from a naval standpoint, its provisions have long been out of date, but in spite of numerous vicissitudes the Agreement itself has survived unchanged for more than one hundred and twenty years and, with the passage of time, has assumed a symbolic importance in the eyes of our own and Canadian citizens. It is true that shortly after the World War modification of the Agreement was studied in this country and in Canada, with a view to making its provisions conform more closely to modern conditions, and a stage was even reached where the Governments exchanged drafts of suggested changes. The proposed changes were never actually agreed upon, however, and Mr. Hull is inclined to think that the two Governments were wise to allow the matter to fall into abeyance, since it is highly debatable whether the realization of their limited objectives would have compensated for the disappearance of the 1817 Agreement as a symbol of the friendly relations between the two countries for over a century.

[1] Department of State, *Bulletin*, IV, p. 366.

It was perhaps inevitable that an agreement, the technical provisions of which became obsolete more than half a century ago, should from time to time have been subjected to what may have been considered technical violations by both parties, and of such instances there is a clear record. We believe it can be successfully maintained, however, that without a degree of tolerance the Agreement could scarcely have survived to the present day in its original form. But it is a fact of equal significance that even when the two Governments felt compelled to depart from a strict observance of its terms they were concerned that the spirit underlying it should be preserved.

I understand from information furnished by our Navy Department that the following five vessels of the United States Navy are now serving on the Great Lakes:

Ship	Launched	Present Location	Displacement	Battery
Dubuque . . .	1905	Detroit . . .	1085	None
Hawk . . .	1891	Michigan City .	375	None
Paducah . . .	1905	Duluth . . .	1085	None
Wilmington . .	1897	Toledo. . . .	1392	None
Wilmette . . .	1903	Chicago . . .	2600	4-4"/50 2-3"/50 A. A. 2-1 pdr.

In a number of respects the presence there of these vessels may not be considered entirely in keeping with a literal interpretation of the Rush-Bagot Agreement. On the other hand, it seems proper to take into account the fact that the vessels of our Navy now on the Great Lakes are there with the knowledge of the Canadian Government, written permission having been obtained for the passage of four of them through the Canadian canals en route to their stations. The case of the *Wilmette* is somewhat different, this vessel having been constructed on the lakes as a commercial vessel and subsequently taken over by our Navy during the World War.

In considering the number and size, disposition, functions and armaments of naval vessels in relation to the provisions of the Rush-Bagot Agreement, it is Mr. Hull's view, with which I feel sure you will agree, that the primary concern of both Governments is to maintain at all costs the spirit which underlies that Agreement and which is representative of the feelings of the Canadian and American people toward each other. With that clear objective in mind, Mr. Hull wishes me to make the following observations.

(1) *Number and Size of Vessels.* As indicated above, the United States Navy now has five vessels, all "unclassified," on the Great Lakes. In the discussion of this problem between officials of the State and Navy Departments, the fact was brought out that approximately one third of the national naval reserve personnel in the United States is concentrated in the region of which Chicago is the center. The need for adequate training of this personnel is clear and I am given to understand that even with our present five vessels on the Great Lakes our facilities are strained. A possible alternative would be to transport these reserves to the Atlantic Coast every summer for the customary two weeks' training period, but I am told that the cost of so transporting even a small fraction of these reserves would in all probability be prohibitive. In the circumstances and in view of the fact that these five vessels have been maintained on the Great Lakes since the war without objection on the part of the Canadian Government, Mr. Hull is inclined to think that the withdrawal of one of them would not be necessary.

Mr. Hull would be reluctant, however, to see American vessels on the Great Lakes increased beyond the present number, omitting from this calculation vessels which are "retained immobile" and used solely as floating barracks for naval reserves. The Canadian Government has in the past given permission for vessels of the latter category to be maintained on the Great Lakes and, it is hoped, would give sympathetic consideration to any similar requests which might be made in the future.

It is my understanding that the *Sacramento*, a vessel of 1,140 tons launched in 1914 and similar in size and type to vessels already on the Great Lakes, is now returning from China, her usefulness as an active naval vessel in regular commission having passed. I am informed that the Navy Department will probably wish this vessel to take the place of the *Hawk*, but that this will not involve an increase in the number of our naval vessels on the lakes. A formal request of your Government for permission for this vessel to proceed to the Great Lakes through Canadian waters will be made in due course.

With regard to the size of these vessels, it has been noted that all are of more than one hundred tons burden, the limit imposed by the Agreement. The change from wood to steel around the middle of the last century, along with other factors, contributed toward rendering this part of the Agreement obsolete. To our knowledge no objection has been taken by the Canadian Government to the presence on the Great Lakes of naval vessels of more than one hundred tons burden and there would be no inclination to question the maintenance by Canada of vessels similar to ours now operating there. It appears to have been the practice of our Navy Department for many years to station on the Great Lakes only "unclassified" vessels that have long since outlived their usefulness in terms of modern warfare and that have a draft of not more than fourteen feet. I understand that these vessels have and could have no use except to provide elementary training for naval reserves. Mr. Hull believes that it would be desirable to continue this policy, which goes beyond the objectives of the 1817 Agreement, but which is so clearly in keeping with the present temper of public opinion. He is so informing the Navy Department.

(2) *Disposition of Vessels.* At the time the Rush-Bagot Agreement was nego-tiated the Great Lakes were independent inland waters with no navigable connec-tion between them and the ocean or, in most cases, between the lakes themselves. This geographical fact was no doubt largely responsible for the provision of the Agreement which allotted one vessel to Lake Champlain, one to Lake Ontario and two to the so-called "Upper Lakes." That situation, of course, no longer exists, and Mr. Hull would not regard it as unreasonable or contrary to the spirit of the Rush-Bagot Agreement to have the naval vessels of each party move freely in the Great Lakes basin or to "maintain" them at any port or ports in the Lakes. Were the Canadian Government to act in accordance with such an interpretation, it is certain that no objection would be taken.

(3) *Functions of the Vessels.* In his letter of January 31, last, Admiral Leahy inquired whether the firing of target practice on the Great Lakes was consistent with the provisions of the Rush-Bagot Agreement. Since the Agreement is silent with respect to the functions of the naval vessels maintained by the two parties on the Great Lakes, other than to state that the naval force of each party is to be restricted to such services as will in no respect interfere with the proper duties of the armed vessels of the other party, it is clearly within the letter as well as the spirit of the Agreement for the naval vessels of both parties to be employed in the training of naval reserves or in any other normal activity, including the firing of target practice, within their respective territorial waters. Mr. Hull is so informing the Navy Department.

(4) *Armaments.* In Admiral Leahy's letter, the hope was expressed that the Rush-Bagot Agreement might be modified so as to permit each of our naval vessels to carry not over two 4-inch guns.

The Agreement itself provides that each of the naval vessels maintained by each Government may carry one 18-pound cannon. It is my understanding that the shell for a 3-inch gun weighs approximately fourteen pounds and the shell for a 4-inch gun approximately thirty pounds. It would therefore be within the scope of the Agreement for each of the naval vessels in question to carry one 3-inch gun. In the discussions between officers of the State and Navy Depart-ments, however, it was brought out that since the 4-inch gun is now what is considered "standard equipment," whereas the 3-inch gun is not, the use of the former is much more desirable from the point of view of giving adequate training to our naval reserves.

After careful consideration of this problem, Mr. Hull is of the opinion that the following proposal would be in harmony with the spirit of the Rush-Bagot Agree-ment; namely, the placing of two 4-inch guns on each of three naval vessels on the Great Lakes, and the removal of all other armaments, subject to certain conditions. These are that the firing of target practice be confined to the territorial waters of the United States, and that the 4-inch guns be dis-mantled except in the summer season during the period of the training of naval reserves.

There remains a question which is of definite interest to both Govern-ments, namely, the construction of naval vessels in shipyards situated on the Great Lakes. The State Department has recently received renewed inquiries on this question.

The Rush-Bagot Agreement, after providing for the maintenance of four naval vessels of each party on the Great Lakes, stipulated that

"All other armed vessels on those lakes shall be forthwith dismantled and no other vessels of war shall be there built or armed."

The provision just quoted should, Mr. Hull believes, be read in the light of the geographical factor to which reference has already been made. At a time when there was no navigable connection between the Great Lakes and the Atlantic Ocean, it was obvious that naval vessels constructed on the lakes could only be intended for use in those waters. Mr. Hull is satisfied that it was this contingency alone which the contracting parties wished to guard against, for no evidence whatever exists to suggest that either party at any time considered that the Agreement should affect the naval forces of the two countries outside the Great Lakes area.

In the circumstances, Mr. Hull believes that it would be entirely in harmony with the intent of the negotiators and the spirit of the Agreement for either country to permit naval vessels, unquestionably intended for tidewater service only, to be constructed in shipyards situated on the Great Lakes. In order carefully to preserve the intent of the Agreement, however, it is believed that prior to the commencement of construction each Government should provide the other with full information concerning any naval vessels to be constructed at Great Lakes ports; that such vessels should immediately be removed from the lakes upon their completion; and that no armaments whatever should be installed until the vessels reach the seaboard.

I shall be happy to receive for Mr. Hull's informal and confidential information any observations which you may wish to make with regard to the questions touched on in this letter.

Sincerely yours,
DANIEL C. ROPER

(2) The Canadian Under Secretary for External Affairs (Skelton) to the American Minister to Canada (Roper), June 10, 1939 [1]

OTTAWA, 10th June, 1939.

MY DEAR MR. ROPER:

I have consulted the Acting Prime Minister and Secretary of State for External Affairs and the Department of National Defense concerning your informal letter of June 9, 1939, which conveys the observations of the Secretary of State of the United States upon certain questions

---

[1] Department of State, *Bulletin*, IV, p. 369.

raised by the United States Navy Department regarding the Rush-Bagot Agreement of 1817.

The Canadian Government concur fully in the desirability of preserving this long-standing Agreement which has been of such inestimable value in furthering the ideals of good neighborhood in this region of the world. It is also recognized that the great changes in technical, industrial, water transport and population conditions which have occurred in the meantime, while in no sense altering the desire of both peoples to maintain the underlying spirit and objective of the Agreement, have rendered its technical scheme and definitions somewhat out of date. It might be urged that the logical method of dealing with the changed situation would be the conclusion of some formal revision of the Agreement, but it is further recognized that the drafting of a new document which would cover present and future considerations of interest to both countries might present difficulties at the present time, and it is noted that Mr. Hull is inclined to the opinion that this would be undesirable.

If formal revision is, as we agree, impracticable, it is nevertheless recognized that there are certain measures which are mutually considered to be practically necessary or desirable and, at the same time, to be consistent with the underlying objective of the Agreement though not strictly consistent with its technical scheme or definitions. In the case of various instances of this character which have occurred in the past, the two Governments have consulted and made appropriate dispositions by means of correspondence. It is felt that such procedure, which appears to be essentially inherent in the underlying spirit and objective, should be pursued as regards any new practical measures concerning naval vessels on the Great Lakes which may be contemplated at the present moment or in the future.

In the light of these general considerations it will be convenient to give you the views of the Canadian Government regarding the particular measures which your Government now consider desirable and which have been described in your letter under separate headings.

(1) *Number and Size of Vessels.* I note that there is no proposal to increase the present number of United States naval vessels on the Great Lakes. As regards the proposed substitution of the *Hawk*, which is now on the Lakes, by another vessel, the *Sacramento*, it is noted also that a formal request of the Canadian Government for permission for the latter vessel to proceed into the Great Lakes through Canadian waters will be made in due course. The Canadian authorities will be agreeable to this substitution, and I assume that at the time particular information will be given as to the disposition of the *Hawk* as well as a description of the *Sacramento* and the purpose of the substitution.

(2) *Disposition of Vessels.* It is recognized, for the reasons indicated in your letter, that it would be consistent with the underlying purpose of the Agreement to have the naval vessels of each party move freely in the Great Lakes or to maintain them at any of its ports in the Lakes.

(3) *Functions of the Vessels.* The Rush-Bagot Agreement, as your letter points out, is silent with respect to the functions of the naval vessels maintained by the two parties on the Great Lakes other than to state that the naval force of each party is to be restricted to such services as will in no respect interfere with the proper duties of the armed vessels of the other party. The Canadian Government accordingly recognize that it is within the letter as well as the spirit of the Agreement for such naval vessels of both parties to be employed in the training of naval reserves, or in any other normal activity, including the firing of target practice, within their respective territorial waters.

(4) *Armaments.* It appears that in view of present-day technical conditions, the United States naval authorities regard 3-inch guns as no longer adequate for the purpose of training naval reserves, whereas 4-inch guns, though not strictly within the technical definition of the Agreement, would be suitable for that purpose. Accordingly Mr. Hull suggests the following proposal as being in harmony with the spirit of the Agreement, namely, the placing of two 4-inch guns on each of three of the United States naval vessels on the Great Lakes and the removal of all other armaments, subject to certain conditions. These conditions are that the firing of target practice be confined to the territorial waters of the United States and that the 4-inch guns be dismantled except in the summer season during the period of the training of naval reserves. The Canadian naval authorities concur in the view of the United States naval authorities above indicated, and the Canadian Government agree that Mr. Hull's proposal is consistent with the underlying purpose and spirit of the Agreement. It is assumed that in due course the Canadian Government will be informed of the names of the vessels upon which the 4-inch guns have been placed. It is also assumed that, should any alteration as regards armament take place in any of the five vessels in the future, particulars will be furnished.

A further particular question is raised by your letter, namely, the construction of naval vessels in shipyards situated on the Great Lakes. Careful consideration has been given to Mr. Hull's observations regarding the changes in actual conditions that have occurred in this regard during the past century, and to the suggestion he has made in order to preserve the intent of the Agreement. The suggestion is that prior to the commencement of construction, each Government should provide the other with full information concerning any naval vessels to be constructed at Great Lakes ports; that such vessels should immediately be removed from the Lakes upon their completion; and that no armaments whatever should be installed until the vessels reach the seaboard. The Canadian Government appreciate the force of Mr. Hull's observations, and they agree that his particular suggestion would be consistent with the underlying objective of the Agreement. They would understand that in the case of each vessel so constructed, when the time came for her removal to the seaboard, the Government concerned would make the usual request through diplomatic channels for permission to pass through the other party's waters.

As regards all these matters and particular measures, the Canadian Government assume it would be understood that the foregoing observations and understandings so far as they have been expressed only with relation to United States naval vessels maintained on the Great Lakes or to naval vessels to be constructed in United States shipyards there, will apply equally to the case of any Canadian naval vessels that may be maintained on the Great Lakes or of naval vessels to be constructed in Canadian shipyards there.

Yours sincerely,

O. D. SKELTON

(3) The Canadian Under Secretary for External Affairs (Skelton) to the American Minister to Canada (Moffat), October 30, 1940 [1]

OTTAWA, *October 30, 1940.*

MY DEAR MR. MOFFAT:

May I refer to your predecessor's letter of June 9, 1939, and to my letter to Mr. Roper of the 10th June of the same year concerning certain questions raised by the United States Navy Department regarding the Rush-Bagot Agreement of 1817.

2. At that time it was recognized that there were certain measures which were mutually considered to be practically necessary or desirable and, at the same time, to be consistent with the underlying objective of the Rush-Bagot Agreement, though not strictly consistent with its technical scheme or definitions. In various instances of this character which had occurred in the past, the two Governments had concurred and made appropriate dispositions by means of correspondence. It was also agreed that such a procedure, which appeared to be essentially inherent in the underlying spirit and objective of the Agreement, should be pursued as regards any new practical measures, concerning naval vessels on the Great Lakes, which might be contemplated.

3. Certain special questions including "number and size of the vessels," "disposition of the vessels," "functions of the vessels," and "armaments" were discussed and dealt with in the correspondence. A further particular question was also raised, namely, the construction of naval vessels in shipyards situated on the Great Lakes. The practice and procedure that should be followed in the case of such construction was formulated along lines that met with the approval of the two Governments.

[1] Department of State, *Bulletin,* IV, p. 371.

4. The practice that was then approved included the following elements:

(a) That each Government should provide the other with full information concerning any naval vessels to be constructed in Great Lakes ports prior to the commencement of construction.

(b) That such vessels should be removed from the Lakes upon their completion.

(c) That no armaments whatever should be installed until the vessels reached the seaboard.

5. A new aspect of this question has arisen owing to the congestion at the Atlantic seaboard shipyards and it is the desire of the Canadian Government to have the vessels in the most complete form practicable while still on the Great Lakes. This might involve equipment with gun mounts and with guns which would be so dismantled as to be incapable of immediate use so long as the vessels remained in the Great Lakes.

6. It is therefore suggested that a further interpretation of the Rush-Bagot Agreement might be made in conformity with the basic intent of the Agreement that important naval vessels should not be built for service on the Great Lakes. This would involve recognition that armament might be installed on naval vessels constructed on the Great Lakes provided that:

(a) The vessels are not intended for service on the Great Lakes;

(b) Prior to commencement of construction, each Government furnish the other with full information concerning any vessel to be constructed at Great Lakes ports;

(c) The armaments of the vessels are placed in such condition as to be incapable of immediate use while the vessels remain in the Great Lakes; and

(d) The vessels are promptly removed from the Great Lakes upon completion.

I should be grateful if you would let me know, in due course, whether the above suggestion commends itself to your Government.

Yours sincerely,

O. D. SKELTON

(4) *The American Minister to Canada (Moffat) to the Canadian Under Secretary for External Affairs (Skelton), November 2, 1940* [1]

[Excerpt]

. . . . . .

In reply, I am authorized to inform you that the United States Government agrees to this further interpretation of the Rush-Bagot Agreement.

Sincerely yours,

PIERREPONT MOFFAT

[1] Department of State, *Bulletin*, IV, p. 372.

C. Great Lakes–St. Lawrence Waterway Project

The International Joint Commission, established by the convention concerning the boundary between the United States and Canada, January 11, 1909,[1] was invited by sec. 6 of the appropriation act for public works on rivers and harbors approved March 2, 1919 (40 Stat. 1288) to investigate what further improvement of the St. Lawrence River between Montreal and Lake Ontario was necessary to make the river navigable for ocean-going vessels. The Governments of the United States and Canada on January 21, 1920 referred to the Commission by agreement the question as defined by a memorandum of the Canadian-United States engineers dated November 11, 1919.[2] The report of the Commission with conclusions and recommendations was completed December 19, 1921 and in the United States was submitted to the Senate.[3]

A treaty for the completion of the Great Lakes–St. Lawrence deep waterway was signed at Washington July 18, 1932 with an exchange of notes dated January 13, 1933, and was reported favorably to the 72d and then to the 73d Congresses from the Senate Committee on Foreign Relations.[4] The treaty had concurrently been the subject of hearings before the Senate Committee on Foreign Relations between November 14, 1932 and February 10, 1933.[5] On January 10, 1934 the President transmitted to the Senate a message requesting the consideration of the treaty by the Senate and a summary of data prepared by the Interdepartmental Board on the Great Lakes–St. Lawrence Project.[6] The resolution of advice and consent failed in the Senate on March 14, 1934 by a vote of 46 yeas and 42 nays,[7] the treaty remaining in the Senate.

New negotiations were initiated in 1936.[8] The outbreak of the war in 1939 and the events of 1940, which compelled adoption of a policy of hemispheric defense, made it obvious that an agreement was of major importance. Accordingly, the technical features of the project were reviewed by experts from both Canada and the United States. On October 17, 1940, President Roosevelt allocated $1,000,000 of one of the early special defense appropriations to the Federal Power Commission and the Corps of Engineers of the United States Army for preliminary investigations, particularly engineering surveys, of the International Rapids Section of the St. Lawrence River. At the same time the President established a St. Lawrence Advisory Committee consisting of Messrs. Leland Olds, Chairman of the Federal Power Commission, Adolf A. Berle, Jr., Assistant Secretary of State; Brig. Gen. Thomas M. Robins, Corps of Engineers,

---

[1] *Treaties, Conventions,* etc., 1910–1923, III, p. 2607.

[2] Department of State, *Foreign Relations of the United States,* 1920, I, p. 411.

[3] *St. Lawrence Waterway. Message from the President of the United States . . . submitting the Report of the International Joint Commission . . .* (Sen. Doc. No. 114, 67th Cong., 2d sess., January 16, 1922).

[4] Submitted by message of the President January 19, 1933, Sen. Exec. C, 72d Cong., 2d sess.; Sen. Exec. Rept. No. 1, 72d Cong., 2d sess., February 21, 1933; Sen. Exec. Rept. No. 1, 73d Cong., 1st sess., March 28, 1933; pt. 2 (minority), May 3, 1933; pt. 3 (individual views), January 10, 1934. The treaty papers are also in *Great Lakes–St. Lawrence Deep Waterway Treaty* (Department of State Publication No. 347).

[5] U. S. Congress, Senate, Committee on Foreign Relations, *St. Lawrence Waterway, Hearings . . .* 72d Cong., 2d sess., on S. Res. 278.

[6] Sen. Doc. No. 110, 73d Cong., 2d sess.

[7] *Congressional Record,* Vol. 78, pt. 4, p. 4474.

[8] The following information is extracted from Department of State press release, March 21, 1941; Department of State, *Bulletin,* IV, p. 306.

United States Army; and Gerald V. Cruise, Executive Secretary and Acting Chief Engineer of the New York State Power Authority.[1] The function of this Committee was to advise the President in the necessary preliminary planning and to cooperate with the appropriate agencies of the Canadian Government, particularly the Canadian Temporary Great Lakes-St. Lawrence Basin Committee, a comparable body designated to assist the Canadian Government. These two Committees on January 3, 1941, completed a Joint Report to President Roosevelt and Prime Minister King. In this Joint Report the results of engineering investigations are submitted.[2] The principal conclusion contained in the report is that the so-called "238-242" Single Stage Control Project is the plan best adapted for the development of the International Rapids Section of the St. Lawrence River. Such a project, according to the Joint Report, "combines the essential features which have been continuously advocated by the representatives of both countries throughout the long period of study and negotiation devoted to the undertaking," and involves a construction program arranged "so that delivery of power can be begun and navigation provided within four years of the time when active work is initiated." Accompanying the Joint Report there were analyses of the main features of the Single Stage Project and a revised series of cost estimates which take into account rising construction costs and additional expense likely to be incurred in expediting the work in the interests of national defense.

According to the cost estimates, the total cost of the project in the International Rapids Section will be $266,170,000. This will provide for completion of the 2,200,000-horsepower power project as well as for the deep waterway improvement in this section of the river. In addition, there will be expenditures for the improvement of navigation channels, both below and above the International Rapids Section, in order that a waterway to accommodate vessels requiring 27-foot draft may be provided throughout the Great Lakes-St. Lawrence System, from Lake Superior to Montreal.

1. EXCHANGE OF NOTES ON STEPS FOR IMMEDIATE DEVELOPMENT

(1) *The Secretary of State (Hull) to the Minister of Canada (Christie), October 14, 1940* [3]

OCTOBER 14, 1940.

The Honorable
    LORING C. CHRISTIE,
        Minister of Canada.
SIR:

I have the honor to refer to the conversations which have taken place recently between officials of the Governments of the United States and Canada in regard to the desirability of taking immediate steps looking to the early development of certain portions of the Great Lakes-St. Lawrence Basin project. These conversations have indicated that there is apprehension in both countries over the possibility of a power shortage;

---

[1] See *Message of President to Congress*, October 17, 1940, Department of State *Bulletin*, III, p. 316; and Executive Order No. 8568, October 16, 1940; *ibid.*, p. 317.

[2] For the Joint Report and accompanying data, see Department of State, *Bulletin*, IV, p. 3316-30.

[3] Department of State, *Bulletin*, III, p. 430.

these apprehensions have been heightened by the necessity for increased supplies of power in consequence of Canada's war effort and of the major national defense effort in the United States.

In the light of these considerations the Government of the United States proposes that each Government appoint forthwith a Temporary Great Lakes–St. Lawrence Basin Committee consisting of not more than five members. These two Committees would cooperate in preliminary engineering and other investigations for that part of the project which is located in the International Rapids Section of the St. Lawrence River, in order that the entire project may be undertaken without delay when final decision is reached by the two Governments. The Government of the United States is prepared to advance the necessary funds up to $1,000,000 to pay for these preliminary engineering and other investigations on the understanding that their cost shall ultimately be prorated by agreement between the two Governments.

Meanwhile, to assist in providing an adequate supply of power to meet Canadian defense needs and contingent upon the Province of Ontario's agreeing to provide immediately for diversions into the Great Lakes System of waters from the Albany River Basin which normally flow into Hudson Bay, the Government of the United States will interpose no objection, pending the conclusion of a final Great Lakes–St. Lawrence Basin agreement between the two countries, to the immediate utilization for power at Niagara Falls by the Province of Ontario of additional waters equivalent in quantity to the diversions into the Great Lakes Basin above referred to.

I shall be glad if you will let me know if your Government is in accord with the foregoing proposals.

Accept [etc.]

For the Secretary of State:
ADOLF A. BERLE, Jr.

(2) *The Minister of Canada (Christie) to the Secretary of State (Hull),
October 14, 1940* [1]

No. 316

CANADIAN LEGATION,
Washington, October 14, 1940.

The Honorable CORDELL HULL,
Secretary of State of the United States,
Washington, D. C.

SIR:

I have the honor to refer to your note of October 14, in which you proposed that the Governments of Canada and the United States take

[1] Department of State, *Bulletin*, III, p. 431.

immediate steps looking to the early development of certain portions of the Great Lakes–St. Lawrence Basin project.

I am instructed to inform you that the Canadian Government is in accord with the proposals which you have made.

I have [etc.]

LORING C. CHRISTIE

2. ADDITIONAL DIVERSION OF WATERS

(1) *The Minister of Canada (Christie) to the Secretary of State (Hull), October 31, 1940* [1]

No. 340   CANADIAN LEGATION,
                                               Washington, October 31, 1940.

The Honorable CORDELL HULL,
    Secretary of State of the United States,
        Washington, D. C.

SIR:

I have the honor to refer to the third paragraph of your note of October 14 [2] concerning the Great Lakes–St. Lawrence Basin project, in which you state that to assist in providing an adequate supply of power to meet Canadian defence needs and contingent upon the Province of Ontario's agreeing to provide immediately for diversions into the Great Lakes System of waters from the Albany River Basin which normally flow into Hudson Bay, the Government of the United States would interpose no objection, pending the conclusion of a final Great Lakes–St. Lawrence Basin agreement between the two countries, to the immediate utilization for power at Niagara Falls by the Province of Ontario of additional waters equivalent in quantity to the diversions into the Great Lakes Basin above referred to.

I am instructed to inform you that the Canadian Government has received appropriate assurances that the Hydro-Electric Power Commission of Ontario is prepared to proceed immediately with the Long Lac-Ogoki diversions and that this action has been approved by the Government of the Province.

The Canadian Government is therefore giving appropriate instructions to authorize the additional diversion of 5,000 cubic feet per second at Niagara by the Hydro-Electric Power Commission of Ontario.

I have [etc.]

LORING C. CHRISTIE

[1] Department of State, *Bulletin*, III, p. 431.
[2] See *ibid.*, p. 430–1.

(2) *The Secretary of State (Hull) to the Minister of Canada (Christie),* *November 7, 1940* [1]

NOVEMBER 7, 1940.

The Honorable
 LORING C. CHRISTIE,
  Minister of Canada.
SIR:

I have the honor to acknowledge the receipt of your Note No. 340 of October 31, 1940, stating that the Hydro-Electric Power Commission of Ontario is prepared to proceed immediately with the Long Lac–Ogoki diversions of waters from the Albany River Basin into the Great Lakes System and that this action has been approved by the Government of the Province.

I note also that the Canadian Government is giving appropriate instructions to authorize the additional diversion of 5,000 cubic feet per second of water at Niagara Falls by the Hydro-Electric Power Commission of Ontario.

Accept [etc.]

For the Secretary of State:
 A. A. BERLE, Jr.

3. RENEWED CONSIDERATION OF THE ST. LAWRENCE PROJECT

(1) *The Prime Minister of Canada (Mackenzie King) to the American* *Minister to Canada (Moffat), March 5, 1941* [2]

DEPARTMENT OF EXTERNAL AFFAIRS,
 OTTAWA, *March 5, 1941.*
SIR:

I have the honor to refer to certain questions which have arisen in the course of the St. Lawrence Waterway negotiations, and which we have discussed recently.

2. As you are aware, my colleagues and I have been giving prolonged consideration to the problems presented by the St. Lawrence Waterway project. We have noted the progress made in the preparation of the engineering plans for the International Section and in the drafting of the general agreement. There is, however, one consideration of a fundamental character to which we desire to call attention.

[1] Department of State, *Bulletin*, III, p. 431.
[2] *Ibid.*, IV, p. 313.

3. The growing intensity of the war operations and the apprehension that still more serious perils will have to be faced in the very near future, necessitate the most careful examination of any proposed expenditure from the point of view of public need and in the light of war requirements.

4. In existing circumstances, the Canadian Government desires to know whether the Government of the United States is of the opinion, in view of the position in Canada, and, of course, the position in the United States as well, that the project as outlined in the State Department's proposals of 1936 and 1938 and under consideration since that time should now be proceeded with.

5. We have, of course, been fully aware of the desire of the Government of the United States to have a treaty or agreement respecting the St. Lawrence Waterway concluded at as early a date as possible, and negotiations which have been carried on more or less continuously for some time past have had in view the desire on our part to arrive, at the earliest possible date, at terms of agreement which would be mutually advantageous. We are also aware of the pronouncements which have been made from time to time by the President, respecting the added emphasis given by the war to the importance alike of power and navigation developments in the Great Lakes–St. Lawrence Waterway project. We are also duly appreciative of the agreement recently reached between our respective governments, whereby the Province of Ontario has obtained the right to the immediate use of additional power at Niagara, and the diversion of the waters of the Ogoki and Long Lac Rivers into Lake Superior, in consideration of which, authority was given for the immediate investigation by United States engineers of the project in the International Section of the St. Lawrence River in Ontario, in order to enable work of future development to proceed with the least possible delay, once an agreement between the two Governments, respecting the St. Lawrence development was concluded.

6. We would naturally be prepared to give every consideration to power or navigation developments which the United States may deem necessary to the prosecution of measures calculated to aid Great Britain Canada, and other parts of the British Commonwealth of Nations in the present war, or to further the security of the United States itself against possible future events which, at the moment cannot be foreseen but of which in times like the present full account must be taken. We realize that the Government of the United States will be as solicitou as our own Government to appraise the project at the present time in terms of its contribution to the efforts which are being put forward by our respective countries to preserve and to restore freedom.

It is from this point of view and in this spirit that we would ask that the St. Lawrence project be again reviewed by the Government of the United States before an agreement or treaty be finally entered into.

Accept [etc.]

W. L. MACKENZIE KING

(2) *The American Minister to Canada (Moffat) to the Prime Minister of Canada (Mackenzie King), March 10, 1941* [1]

LEGATION OF THE
UNITED STATES OF AMERICA,
OTTAWA, *March 10, 1941.*

SIR:

I lost no time in bringing to the attention of my Government your note of March 5 in regard to the St. Lawrence Waterway negotiations. In view of the importance of the question you raised, the matter was laid before the President, and I have been instructed, by way of reply, to transmit the following personal message from him to you:

"I have given careful consideration to your recent request that in view of the growing intensity of current war operations and the apprehension over perils which may have to be faced in the near future, the Government of the United States review the St. Lawrence project and give you an indication of its views as to whether, in the existing circumstances, this project as outlined in the State Department's proposals of 1936 and 1938 should now be proceeded with.

"May I say at the outset that I am aware of Canada's increasing war effort and I readily agree that it must have first call upon your country's resources and manpower. I also agree that in view of the existing situation the most careful examination of any proposed expenditure is necessary from the point of view of the public need and in the light of defense requirements.

"With these considerations in mind, the Government of the United States has, as you requested, reviewed the St. Lawrence project. We have welcomed this occasion to review this project because of the fact that our own defense program renders it desirable that all public expenditures in the United States be weighed in the light of considerations similar to those set forth in your communication. The Government of the United States is engaged in a great defense program. It is determined to supply such aid in material to Great Britain, the members of the Commonwealth, and their Allies as may be necessary to enable them to bring the war to a successful termination. Simultaneously, our own defenses are being strengthened to the extent necessary to prevent any foe from menacing the security of this hemisphere. It is indispensable that all public projects contemplated by the Government of the United States be considered from the standpoint of their relationship to these supreme objectives.

"The Government of the United States regards the Great Lakes–St. Lawrence project as directly associated with the accomplishment of the foremost national

[1] Department of State, *Bulletin*, IV, p. 314.

objectives of this Government. It believes that the project should be proceeded with and that construction should commence at the earliest possible moment. It regards the construction of this project as a matter of vital necessity.

"You refer to the engineering investigation now being conducted in the International Section of the St. Lawrence River. I need hardly say that I directed the release of $1,000,000 from the special defense funds for this purpose only because of my conviction that the completion of this project by 1945 might prove of vital importance to our defense effort. It is gratifying that there has been sufficient progress to make possible the initiation of construction this spring.

"I am sure you will agree with me that, while our countries must put forth the maximum immediate defense effort, we must also prepare for the possibility of a protracted emergency which will call upon the industries on both sides of the border to meet constantly expanding demands. The combination of advantages offered by the St. Lawrence project makes it imperative that we undertake it immediately.

"In terms of the time factor, the St. Lawrence project as a part of our defense program is not exceptional, since we are today appropriating money for construction of vessels of war which will not be ready for service until the completion of the St. Lawrence undertaking.

"I am convinced of the urgent need for the large increment in low cost electric power which the St. Lawrence project will provide. Already the demand for power is running ahead of expectations. In fact, one of the most serious handicaps to the rapid expansion of airplane production is the difficulty of finding the large supplies of high-load factor power required for aluminum production. We are, of course, expanding our electric facilities for this purpose as fast as practicable, but by the time the St. Lawrence power is available other sources of cheap power will have been largely allocated.

"The St. Lawrence project offers by far the soundest and most economical provision for the power requirements of certain portions of our long range defense program, more particularly for certain high-load factor defense industries. Furthermore, the manufacturing facilities and skilled labor available for the construction of steam turbines and electric equipment will be needed to meet the requirements of the vast areas of our continent where water power is not so economically available.

"I am also convinced that the opening of the St. Lawrence deep waterway to afford an outlet for naval and cargo ships constructed in Great Lakes shipyards, far from representing a diversion of funds and resources from the defense effort, would have the opposite effect. Our shipbuilding program, to meet the requirements of defense, will call for a great expansion of shipyards with their associated machine shops and adequate supplies of skilled labor. The extent to which intensified submarine and air attacks on convoys may necessitate an expansion of the program is still unknown. If the war is protracted, however, it seems certain that the number of shipyards required will have to be several times those at present available. In terms of our present industrial arrangements many of these can be made most readily and economically available in the Great Lakes area.

"If the full burden of our expanding ship construction must fall on seaboard shipyards, the time required to complete the vessels themselves must, in many instances, be increased by the period necessary to construct new shipyards and facilities. With this in mind it is apparent that the deep waterway could be completed in time to provide an outlet to the sea for many of the new vessels included in the present program.

"In the light of these facts, it is my belief that the funds and manpower required for the earliest possible completion of the St. Lawrence project could not be better spent for our joint defense effort, including aid to Great Britain. It is my feeling that failure to take advantage of the possibilities of this project would be shortsighted, in no way contributing to an increase in our immediate defense effort, while limiting our defense program in the difficult years which lie ahead."

Accept [etc.] PIERREPONT MOFFAT

4. ST. LAWRENCE WATERWAY AGREEMENT OF MARCH 19, 1941

(1) *Agreement in Relation to Utilization of the Water in the Great Lakes–St. Lawrence Basin between the United States and Canada, Ottawa, March 19, 1941* [1]

By the Message of the President to Congress, March 21, 1941,[2] the text of the following agreement was transmitted for the information of Congress.

The terms of the agreement contemplate that it shall be made effective by concurrent legislation of the Canadian Parliament and of the Congress of the United States.

The President of the United States of America and His Majesty the King of Great Britain, Ireland and the British dominions beyond the Seas, Emperor of India, in respect of Canada, have decided to conclude an Agreement in relation to the utilization of the water in the Great Lakes–St. Lawrence Basin and to that end have named as their respective plenipotentiaries:

The President of the United States of America:

JAY PIERREPONT MOFFAT,

Envoy Extraordinary and Minister Plenipotentiary of the United States of America to Canada;

ADOLF AUGUSTUS BERLE, Jr.,

Assistant Secretary of State;

LELAND OLDS,

Chairman of the Federal Power Commission;

---

[1] Department of State, *Bulletin*, IV, p. 307. For a tabular comparison of the texts of the original treaty of 1933 which was before the Senate in 1934, the proposed treaty of 1938, and the agreement of 1941 see " Analysis of St. Lawrence Seaway Treaties and Agreement," *Congressional Record*, Vol. 87, p. A1615 (March 31, 1941, daily edition).

[2] House Doc. No. 153, 77th Cong., 1st sess.; Department of State, *Bulletin*, IV, p. 307.

His Majesty the King of Great Britain, Ireland and the British dominions beyond the Seas, Emperor of India, for Canada:

The Right Honorable W. L. MACKENZIE KING,
> Prime Minister, President of the Privy Council and Secretary of State for External Affairs;

The Honorable CLARENCE D. HOWE,
> Minister of Munitions and Supply;

JOHN E. READ,
> Legal Adviser, Department of External Affairs;

Who, after having communicated to each other their full powers, found in good and due form, have agreed upon the following Articles:

PRELIMINARY ARTICLE

For the purposes of the present Agreement, unless otherwise expressly provided, the expression:

(a) "Joint Board of Engineers" means the board appointed pursuant to an agreement between the Governments following the recommendation of the International Joint Commission, dated December 19, 1921;

(b) "Great Lakes System" means Lakes Superior, Michigan, Huron (including Georgian Bay), Erie and Ontario, and the connecting waters, including Lake St. Clair;

(c) "St. Lawrence River" includes the river channels and the lakes forming parts of the river channels from the outlet of Lake Ontario to the sea;

(d) "International Section" means that part of the St. Lawrence River through which the international boundary line runs;

(e) "Canadian Section" means that part of the St. Lawrence River which lies wholly within Canada and which extends from the easterly limit of the International Section to Montreal Harbor;

(f) "International Rapids Section" means that part of the International Section which extends from Chimney Point to the village of St. Regis;

(g) "Governments" means the Government of the United States of America and the Government of Canada;

(h) "countries" means the United States of America and Canada;

(i) "Special International Niagara Board" means the board appointed by the Governments in 1926 to ascertain and recommend ways and means to preserve the scenic beauty of the Niagara Falls;

(j) "deep waterway" means adequate provision for navigation

requiring a controlling channel depth of 27 feet with a depth of 30 feet over lock sills, from the head of the Great Lakes to Montreal Harbor via the Great Lakes System and St. Lawrence River, in general accordance with the specifications set forth in the Report of the Joint Board of Engineers, dated November 16, 1926.

ARTICLE I. 1. The Governments agree to establish and maintain a Great Lakes–St. Lawrence Basin Commission, hereinafter referred to as the Commission, consisting of not more than ten members of whom an equal number shall be appointed by each Government. The duties of the Commission shall be:

(a) to prepare and to recommend plans and specifications for the construction of works in the International Rapids Section in accordance with and containing the features described in the Annex attached to and made part of this Agreement,[1] with such modifications as may be agreed upon by the Governments;

(b) upon approval of the plans and specifications by the Governments, to prepare a schedule allocating the construction of the works in the International Rapids Section on such a basis that each Government shall construct the works within its own territory or an equivalent proportion of the works so approved;

(c) to approve all contracts entered into on behalf of either Government for the works in the International Rapids Section;

(d) to supervise the construction of the works and to submit reports to the Governments from time to time, and at least once each calendar year, on the progress of the works;

(e) upon satisfactory completion of the works, to certify to the Governments that they meet the plans and specifications drawn up by the Commission and approved by the Governments;

(f) to perform the other duties assigned to it in this Agreement.

2. The Commission shall have the authority to employ such persons and to make such expenditures as may be necessary to carry out the duties set forth in this Agreement. It shall have the authority to avail itself of the services of such governmental agencies, officers and employees of either country as may be made available. The remuneration, general expenses and all other expenses of its members shall be regulated and paid by their respective Governments; and the other expenses of the Commission, except as provided for under Article III, paragraph (b) of this Agreement, shall be borne by the Governments in equal moieties.

3. The Governments agree to permit the entry into their respective countries, within areas immediately adjacent to the Niagara River and

[1] See p. 196.

the International Section to be delimited by exchange of notes, of personnel employed by the Commission or employed in the construction of the works, and to exempt such personnel from the operation of their immigration laws and regulations within the areas so delimited. In the event that the Commission, pursuant to the provisions of paragraph 1 (b) of this Article, allocates to either of the Governments the construction of works, any part of which is within the territory of the other Government, the latter Government shall make provision for the according, within the area in which such a part is situated, of such exemption from customs, excise and other imposts, federal, state and provincial, as may be reasonably practicable for the effective and economical prosecution of the work. Regulations providing for such exemptions may be settled by the Governments by exchange of notes.

4. The Governments shall, by exchange of notes, prescribe rules and regulations for the conduct of the Commission. They may by the same means extend or abridge its powers and duties; and reduce or after reduction increase the number of members (provided that there must always be an equal number appointed by each Government and that the total number of members shall at no time exceed ten); and upon completion of its duties, the Governments may terminate its existence.

ARTICLE II. The Government of Canada agrees:

(a) in accordance with the plans and specifications prepared by the Commission and approved by the Governments, to construct the works in the International Rapids Section allocated to Canada by the Commission; and to operate and maintain or arrange for the operation and maintenance of the works situated in the territory of Canada;

(b) to complete, not later than December 31, 1948, the essential Canadian links in the deep waterway, including the necessary deepening of the new Welland Ship Canal and the construction of canals and other works to provide the necessary depth in the Canadian section of the St. Lawrence River: provided that, if the continuance of war conditions or the requirements of defense justify a modification of the period within which such works shall be completed, the Governments may, by exchange of notes, arrange to defer or expedite their completion as circumstances may require.

ARTICLE III. The Government of the United States of America agrees:

(a) in accordance with the plans and specifications prepared by the Commission and approved by the Governments, to construct the works in the International Rapids Section allocated to the United States of America by the Commission; and to operate and maintain or arrange for the operation and maintenance of the works situated in the territory of the United States of America;

(b) to provide, as required by the progress of the works, funds for the construction, including design and supervision, of all works in the International Rapids Section except (1) machinery and equipment for the development of power, and (2) works required for rehabilitation on the Canadian side of the international boundary;

(c) not later than the date of completion of the essential Canadian links in the deep waterway, to complete the works allocated to it in the International Rapids Section and the works in the Great Lakes System above Lake Erie required to create essential links in the deep waterway.

ARTICLE IV. The Governments agree that:

(a) they may, in their respective territories, in conformity with the general plans for the project in the International Rapids Section, install or arrange for the installation of such machinery and equipment as may be desired for the development of power and at such time or times as may be most suitable in terms of their respective power requirements;

(b) in view of the need for coordination of the plans and specifications prepared by the Commission for general works in the International Rapids Section with plans for the development of power in the respective countries, the Commission may arrange for engineering services with any agency in either country, which may be authorized to develop power in the International Rapids Section;

(c) except as modified by the provisions of Article VIII, paragraph (b) of this Agreement, each country shall be entitled to utilize one-half of the water available for power purposes in the International Rapids Section;

(d) during the construction and upon the completion of the works provided for in the International Rapids Section, the flow of water out of Lake Ontario into the St. Lawrence River shall be controlled and the flow of water through the International Section shall be regulated so that the navigable depths of water for shipping in the Harbor of Montreal and throughout the navigable channel of the St. Lawrence River below Montreal, as such depths now exist or may hereafter be increased by dredging or other harbor or channel improvements, shall not be injuriously affected by the construction or operation of such works, and the power developments in the Canadian Section of the St. Lawrence River shall not be adversely affected;

(e) upon the completion of the works provided for in the International Rapids Section, the power works shall be operated, initially, with the water level at the power houses held at a maximum elevation 238.0, sea level datum as defined in the Report of the Joint Board of Engineers, for a test period of ten years or such shorter period as may be approved by any board or authority designated or established under the provisions of paragraph (f) of this Article; and, in the event that such board or authority considers that operation with the water level at the power houses held to a maximum elevation exceeding 238.0 would be practicable and could be made effective within the limitations prescribed by paragraphs (c) and (d) of this Article, the Governments may, by exchange of notes, authorize operation, subject to the provisions of this Article, and for such times and subject to such terms as may be prescribed in the notes, at a maximum elevation exceeding 238.0.

(f) the Governments may, by exchange of notes, make provision for giving effect to paragraphs (c), (d) and (e) of this Article;

(g) during the construction of the works provided for in the International Rapids Section, facilities for 14 foot navigation in that Section shall be maintained.

ARTICLE V. The Governments agree that nothing done under the authority of this Agreement shall confer upon either of them proprietary rights, or legislative, administrative or other jurisdiction in the territory of the other, and that the works constructed under the provisions of this Agreement shall constitute a part of the territory of the country in which they are situated.

ARTICLE VI. The Governments agree that either of them may proceed at any time to construct, within its own territory and at its own cost, alternative canal and channel facilities for navigation in the International Section or in waters connecting the Great Lakes, and to utilize the water necessary for the operation of such facilities.

ARTICLE VII. The High Contracting Parties agree that the rights of navigation accorded under the provisions of existing treaties between the United States of America and His Majesty shall be maintained notwithstanding the provisions for termination contained in any of such treaties, and declare that these treaties confer upon the citizens or subjects and upon the ships, vessels and boats of each High Contracting Party, rights of navigation in the St. Lawrence River, and the Great Lakes System, including the canals now existing or which may hereafter be constructed.

ARTICLE VIII. The Governments, recognizing their common interest in the preservation of the levels of the Great Lakes System, agree that

(a) each Government in its own territory shall measure the quantities of water which at any point are diverted from or added to the Great Lakes System, and shall place such measurements on record with the other Government semi-annually;

(b) in the event of diversions being made into the Great Lakes System from other watersheds lying wholly within the borders of either country, the exclusive rights to the use of waters which are determined by the Governments to be equivalent in quantity to any waters so diverted shall, notwithstanding the provisions of Article IV paragraph (c) of this Agreement, be vested in the country diverting such waters, and the quantity of water so diverted shall be at all times available to that country for use for power below the point of entry, so long as it constitutes a part of boundary waters;

(c) if any diversion of water from the Great Lakes System or the International Section, other or greater in amount than diversions permitted in either of the countries on January 1, 1940, is authorized, the Government of such country agrees to give immediate consideration to any representations respecting the matter which the other Government may make; if it is impossible otherwise to reach a satisfactory settlement, the Government of the country in which the diversion of water has been authorized agrees, on the request of the other Government, to submit the matter to an arbitral tribunal which shall be empowered to direct such compensatory or remedial measures as it may deem just and equitable; the arbitral tribunal shall consist of three members, one to be appointed by each of the Governments, and the third, who will be the chairman, to be selected by the Governments;

(d) the Commission shall report upon the desirability of works for compensation and regulation in the Great Lakes System, and, upon the approval by the Governments of any such works, shall prepare plans and specifications for their construction and recommend to the Governments an equitable allocation of their cost; the Governments shall make arrangements by exchange of notes for the construction of such works as they may agree upon.

ARTICLE IX. The Governments, recognizing their primary obligation to preserve and enhance the scenic beauty of the Niagara Falls and River, and consistent with that obligation, their common interest in providing for the most beneficial use of the waters of that River, as envisaged in the Final Report of the Special International Niagara Board, agree that:

(a) the Commission shall prepare and submit to the Governments plans and specifications for works in the Niagara River designed to distribute and control the waters thereof, to prevent erosion and to ensure at all seasons unbroken crest lines on both the American Falls and the Canadian Falls and to preserve and enhance their scenic beauty, taking into account the recommendations of the Special International Niagara Board; the Governments may make arrangements by exchange of notes for the construction of such works in the Niagara River as they may agree upon, including provision for temporary diversions of the waters of the Niagara River for the purpose of facilitating construction of the works; the cost of such works in the Niagara River shall be borne by the Governments in equal moieties;

(b) upon the completion of the works authorized in this Article, diversions of the waters of the Niagara River above the Falls from the natural course and stream thereof additional to the amounts specified in Article 5 of the Boundary Waters Treaty of 1909 may be authorized and permitted by the Governments to the extent and in the manner hereinafter provided:

(1) the United States may authorize and permit additional diversion within the State of New York of the waters of the River above the Falls for power purposes, in excess of the amount specified in Article 5 of the Boundary Waters Treaty of 1909, not to exceed in the aggregate a daily diversion at the rate of five thousand cubic feet of water per second;

(2) Canada may authorize and permit additional diversion within the Province of Ontario of the waters of the River above the Falls for power purposes, in excess of the amount specified in Article 5 of the Boundary Waters Treaty of 1909, not to exceed in the aggregate a daily diversion at the rate of five thousand cubic feet of water per second;

(c) upon completion of the works authorized in this Article, the Commission shall proceed immediately to test such works under a wide range of conditions, and to report and certify to the Governments the effect of such works, and to make recommendations respecting diversions of water from Lake Erie and the Niagara River, with particular reference to (1) the perpetual preservation of the scenic beauty of the Falls and Rapids, (2) the requirements of navigation in the Great Lakes System, and (3) the efficient utilization and equitable apportionment of such waters as may be available for power purposes; on the basis of the Commission's reports and recommendations, the Governments may by exchange of notes and concurrent legislation determine the methods by which these purposes may be attained.

ARTICLE X. The Governments agree that:

(*a*) each Government undertakes to make provision for the disposition of claims and for the satisfaction of any valid claims arising out of damage or injury to persons or property occurring in the territory of the other in the course of and in connection with construction by such Government of any of the works authorized or provided for by this Agreement;

(*b*) each Government is hereby released from responsibility for any damage or injury to persons or property in the territory of the other, which may be caused by any action authorized or provided for by this Agreement, other than damage or injury covered by the provisions of paragraph (*a*) of this Article;

(*c*) each Government will assume the responsibility for and the expense involved in the acquisition of any lands or interests in land in its own territory which may be necessary to give effect to the provisions of this Agreement.

ARTICLE XI. This Agreement shall be subject to approval by the Congress of the United States of America and the Parliament of Canada. Following such approval it shall be proclaimed by the President of the United States of America and ratified by His Majesty the King of Great Britain, Ireland and the British dominions beyond the Seas, Emperor of India, in respect of Canada. It shall enter into force on the day of the exchange of the instrument of ratification and a copy of the proclamation, which shall take place at Washington.

IN WITNESS WHEREOF the respective plenipotentiaries have signed this Agreement in duplicate and have hereunto affixed their seals.

DONE at Ottawa, the nineteenth day of March in the year of our Lord one thousand nine hundred and forty-one.

[SEAL] JAY PIERREPONT MOFFAT
[SEAL] ADOLF A. BERLE, Jr.
[SEAL] LELAND OLDS
[SEAL] W. L. MACKENZIE KING
[SEAL] C. D. HOWE
[SEAL] JOHN E. READ

Annex

CONTROLLED SINGLE STAGE PROJECT (238–242) FOR WORKS IN THE
INTERNATIONAL RAPIDS SECTION

(See Article I, Paragraph 1 (a))

The main features of the Controlled Single Stage Project (238–242),[1] described in detail with cost estimates in the report of the Temporary Great Lakes–St. Lawrence Basin Committees dated January 3, 1941, are as follows:

(1) A control dam in the vicinity of Iroquois Point.
(2) A dam in the Long Sault Rapids at the head of Barnhart Island and two power houses, one on either side of the international boundary, at the foot of Barnhart Island.
(3) A side canal, with one lock, on the United States mainland to carry navigation around the Control Dam and a side canal, with one guard gate and two locks, on the United States mainland south of Barnhart Island to carry navigation from above the main Long Sault Dam to the river south of Cornwall Island. All locks to provide 30 ft. depth of water on the mitre sills and to be of the general dimensions of those of the Welland Ship Canal. All navigation channels to be excavated to 27 ft. depth.
(4) Dykes, where necessary on the United States and Canadian sides of the international boundary, to retain the pool level above the Long Sault Dam.
(5) Channel enlargement from the head of Galop Island to below Lotus Island designed to give a maximum velocity in the navigation channel south of Galop Island not exceeding four feet per second at any time.
(6) Channel enlargement between Lotus Island and the Control Dam and from above Point Three Points to below Ogden Island designed to give a maximum mean velocity in any cross-section not exceeding two and one-quarter feet per second with the flow and at the stage to be permitted on the 1st of January of any year, under regulation of outflow and levels of Lake Ontario.
(7) The necessary railroad and highway modifications on either side of the international boundary.
(8) The necessary works to permit the continuance of 14 ft. navigation on the Canadian side around the Control Dam and from the pool above the Long Sault Dam to connect with the existing Cornwall Canal.
(9) The rehabilitation of the towns of Iroquois and Morrisburg, Ontario.

All the works in the pool below the Control Dam shall be designed to provide for full Lake Ontario level but initially the pool shall be operated at maximum elevation 238.0.

(a) Character of the Executive Agreement

The Constitution empowers the President to conduct relations with foreign governments as a function inherent in the Executive. It also provides that he has

[1] For an earlier project see Great Lakes–St. Lawrence Deep Waterway Treaty. Detailed estimates of Crysler Island Two-Stage Project (Project C-217); Appendix I to the Report of the Joint Board of Engineers (reconvened) on Improvement of the International Section of the St. Lawrence River, dated April 9, 1932 (Department of State Publication No. 401).

"Power, by and with the Advice and Consent of the Senate, to make Treaties, provided two-thirds of the Senators present concur." Instruments evidencing formal understandings between states are generically called treaties, but are also known by other technical names, of which "agreement" is one. It has been customary in the United States to employ a special form, the "executive agreement," which does not require the advice and consent of the Senate, to effect understandings which the President is authorized to make by virtue of legislation or other power possessed by him. The subjoined correspondence deals with an agreement made by the Executive for which subsequent approval in the form of enabling legislation was planned.

(i) *The Secretary of State (Hull) to the Attorney General (Jackson),
March 13, 1941* [1]

MARCH 13, 1941.

MY DEAR MR. ATTORNEY GENERAL:

I enclose for your consideration a memorandum prepared by the Legal Adviser of this Department, together with a copy of a proposed agreement between the United States and Canada regarding the Great Lakes–St. Lawrence Deep Waterway Project. It is hoped that an agreement may be signed within the next few days.

I should appreciate it if you would advise me whether you agree that the arrangement may be effectuated by an agreement signed under the authority of the Executives of the two countries and approved by legislative enactments by the Congress and the Canadian Parliament.

Sincerely yours,

CORDELL HULL

[Enclosure]

Memorandum by the Legal Adviser of the Department of State

For several years the United States and Canada have had under consideration the feasibility of a joint undertaking for the improvement of the Great Lakes–St. Lawrence Basin so as to make these waters available to sea-going vessels, the development of hydro-electric power, etc. The Legal Adviser of the Department of State, in a memorandum dated February 10, 1939, expressed the opinion that an arrangement between the United States and Canada concerning the project could be effected by a simple agreement between the two countries and approval of the agreement by legislation in the United States and in Canada. The negotiations have progressed to the point where an agreement is about ready to be signed, but before proceeding to signature it is thought desirable to ascertain whether the Attorney General concurs in the view that the purposes may be accomplished in this fashion.

It is not necessary here to enter into a discussion of the treaty-making power or of the power of the President to enter into executive agreements with foreign countries. It is sufficient to say that a very large number of such agreements on various subjects have been entered into from time to time throughout the history of this country. Some of them have been specifically authorized by acts of Congress; others, though not specially authorized, have been within the frame-

[1] Department of State, *Bulletin*, IV, p. 364.

work of acts of Congress; and still others have been concluded without enabling legislation on the subject.

Following the failure of the Senate to approve a treaty for the annexation of Texas, the annexation was accomplished by a joint resolution approved on March 1, 1845 (5 Stat. 797), after passage by a simple majority vote of the two houses of Congress. Likewise, in the case of Hawaii, a treaty of annexation had been signed on June 16, 1897, and approved by the Hawaiian Legislature, but there was not sufficient support in the United States Senate to obtain approval by a two-thirds vote. Thereafter Congress passed a joint resolution to accomplish the same purpose, which was approved July 7, 1898 (30 Stat. 750).

Of interest in this connection is action by Congress with respect to the construction of bridges across the international boundary — United States and Canada, subject to similar authorization by Canada. For example, Public Resolution No. 117, 75th Congress, 3d session, created the Niagara Falls Bridge Commission and authorized it to construct and operate bridges across the Niagara River, subject to "the approval of the proper authorities in the Dominion of Canada." (52 Stat. 767.)

On November 11, 1927, President Coolidge issued a presidential license to the Detroit-Ontario Subway, Inc., authorizing the company to construct, operate, and maintain a tunnel from a point in or near Brush or Randolph Street in the City of Detroit to a point on the international boundary line under the Detroit River. It is understood that corresponding authorization was given on the part of Canada by an Order in Council.

The improvement of the Great Lakes–St. Lawrence Basin for navigation and other purposes would seem clearly to fall within the commerce clause of the Constitution, giving the Congress the authority to regulate interstate and foreign commerce. Where the undertaking with respect to interstate and foreign commerce involves boundary waters over which this country does not have exclusive jurisdiction, there would seem to be no reason why the Congress should not within its Constitutional power enact legislation, contingent upon a like legislative enactment in the other country, signifying its approval of a joint undertaking signed by both Governments. The signing of an agreement by the two Governments would be but a convenient way of bringing about in advance of legislative enactments a joint understanding by the two Governments on a complicated question which could hardly be handled without such advance understanding. The agreement would contain provisions which might otherwise be incorporated in a treaty, but would not take the treaty form or follow the treaty process. It would not constitute a binding international agreement until Congress and the Canadian Parliament had indicated their approval.

GREEN H. HACKWORTH

(ii) *The Attorney General (Jackson) to the Secretary of State (Hull), March 14, 1941* [1]

MARCH 14, 1941.

MY DEAR MR. SECRETARY:

I have your letter of March 13 and concur in the conclusion reached by your Legal Adviser that it is legally unobjectionable so far as this country is concerned

[1] Department of State, *Bulletin*, IV, p. 365.

for the executives of the United States and Canada to enter into an agreement regarding the Great Lakes–St. Lawrence Deep Waterway project conditioned for its effectiveness upon the subsequent enactment of necessary legislation by the Congress and by the Canadian Parliament.

If an Agreement is executed and approved in this manner, its provisions would be binding upon the United States as respects Canada.

Respectfully,

ROBERT H. JACKSON

5. FURTHER UTILIZATION OF POWER OF NIAGARA WATERS. EXCHANGE OF NOTES, MAY 20, 1941 [1]

This exchange of notes amends in its application Article 5 of the treaty signed January 11, 1909 between the United States and Great Britain concerning boundary waters and boundary questions. It was submitted by the President to the Senate May 29, 1941 and on June 12 the Senate gave its advice and consent to ratification. The President approved the arrangement on June 13, 1941.[2]

(1) *The Secretary of State (Hull) to the Canadian Minister to the United States (McCarthy), May 20, 1941*

DEPARTMENT OF STATE,
Washington, May 20, 1941.

The Honorable LEIGHTON MCCARTHY,
Minister of Canada.

SIR: I have the honor to refer to conversations which have taken place recently between officials of the Governments of the United States and Canada with respect to the immediate and pressing needs for additional power in the Niagara Falls area for national defense purposes. Throughout these conversations, as well as in previous conversations during the course of years, on the general subject of the Falls at Niagara, two objectives have been kept in mind: first, the scenic beauty of this great heritage of the two countries; and second, the utilization of the power resources available there, consistent with the primary obligation of preserving the scenic beauty of the Falls.

Recent surveys have indicated that there is now idle equipment available and set up which could utilize at once an additional diversion for power purposes of 5,000 cubic feet per second on the United States side. I am informed by the defense authorities of this Government and by

[1] Department of State, *Bulletin*, IV, p. 709.
[2] *Ibid.*, p. 736.

the Federal Power Commission that this additional power is urgently needed in connection with the Government's National Defense Program. It is likewise understood from conversations with the appropriate Canadian officials that 3,000 cubic feet per second could be used immediately on the Canadian side in connection with the furtherance of the war efforts of Canada. These figures represent the immediate needs of the two Governments and do not pretend to take into consideration all industrial requirements of the two countries in the area by reason of the present emergency.

In view of the above, and having in mind assurances of engineers that there will be no material adverse effect to the scenic beauty of the Falls, I propose through this exchange of notes that for the duration of the emergency and in all events subject to reconsideration by both Governments on October 1, 1942, an additional diversion for power purposes of 5,000 cubic feet per second be utilized on the United States side of the Niagara River above the Falls. In making this proposal this Government is prepared to give assurances that no objection will be raised to an additional diversion of 3,000 cubic feet per second on the Canadian side of the Niagara River above the Falls. It is also proposed that the engineers of the two Governments be instructed to take such steps as may be necessary with a view to initiating forthwith the construction of works designed to distribute the flow of water over the Falls in such a manner as to preserve their scenic beauty.

Moreover, the American Government proposes that upon the entry into effect of the Agreement for the Utilization of the Water in the Great Lakes–St. Lawrence Basin signed on March 19, 1941, the foregoing arrangements will be subject to the provisions of Article IX of the Agreement, and that it will be open to the Commission appointed under the provisions of the Agreement and carrying out the duties imposed upon it, to take such action as may be necessary, and as may come within the scope of the Agreement with regard to diversions at Niagara.

If the foregoing is acceptable to the Government of Canada, this note and your reply thereto, when approved by the Senate, shall be regarded as placing on record the understanding arrived at between the two Governments concerning this matter.

Accept [etc.]

For the Secretary of State:

A. A. BERLE, Jr.

(2) *The Canadian Minister to the United States (McCarthy) to the Secretary of State (Hull), May 20, 1941*

CANADIAN LEGATION,
Washington, May 20, 1941.

The Honorable CORDELL HULL,
    Secretary of State of the United States,
        Washington, D. C.

SIR: With reference to your note of May 20, 1941, concerning the immediate and pressing needs for additional power in the Niagara Falls area for national defense purposes, I have the honor to inform you that the Government of Canada concurs in the arrangements set forth in your note and is prepared to give assurances that no objection will be raised by the Government of Canada to an additional diversion of 5,000 cubic feet per second on the United States side of the Niagara River above the Falls.

I have [etc.]

H. H. WRONG
(For the Minister).

6. AUTHORIZATION OF CONSTRUCTION

(1) *Message of the President to the Congress, June 5, 1941* [1]

TO THE CONGRESS OF THE UNITED STATES:

I recommend authorization of construction of the St. Lawrence Seaway and Power Project, pursuant to the agreement of March 19, 1941, with Canada, as an integral part of the joint defense of the North American continent.

Production and more production is the keynote of our all-out race for national defense. Electric power and transportation are limiting factors in the production of planes, guns, tanks and ships.

The enemies of democracy are developing every hydroelectric resource and every waterway from Norway to the Dardanelles. Are we to allow this continent to be out-matched because shortsighted interests oppose the development of one of our greatest resources?

Your action on this project will either make available or withhold 2,200,000 horsepower of low-cost electric power for the joint defense of North America.

[1] H. Doc. No. 245, 77th Cong.; Department of State, *Bulletin*, IV, p. 697.

Your action on this project will either open or keep bottled up one of the greatest transportation resources ever offered a people.

Both countries need the power. Both face power shortages which threaten to grow more serious as the demands of the defense program multiply with almost incredible rapidity.

Let us remember that it takes tens of thousands of kilowatt-hours of electricity to produce the materials that go into a single airplane. Our present aluminum program alone calls for more than ten billion kilowatt-hours a year. It is constantly expanding with the need for more planes to outstrip the aggressors.

Steam power plant construction offers no substitute for St. Lawrence power. No steam plants can provide the large blocks of low-cost electric energy required for certain essential defense industries. Furthermore, we are going to need all our capacity to produce steam power plant equipment to meet the tremendous demands which are growing in other parts of the country and to build power installations to drive our merchant and naval vessels.

Our defense production is a gigantic assembly line. Transportation is its conveyor belt. If raw materials cannot flow freely to our great industrial plants and the products cannot move continuously to the front, defense breaks down. Bottlenecks in transportation are as serious as shortages of power.

Expanding production is going to burden the railroads to the limit. We are expanding their rolling stock as fast as we can, but even the present orders for new cars and locomotives are competing for manufacturing capacity which could otherwise produce tanks and other items of heavy armament.

The Seaway will help prevent transportation bottlenecks. It will provide a great highway to and from important defense production areas. It will cut by more than a thousand miles the stretch of dangerous open water which must be traveled by supplies to Great Britain and strategic North Atlantic bases. It will increase our capacity to build ships.

The Great Lakes today hold many shipways and dry docks, as well as resources of men and materials for shipbuilding. They are bottled up because we have delayed completing the Seaway. If we start the Seaway now, scores of additional merchant ships may be built in coastal yards freed by transferring a portion of the longer-term naval program to the Great Lakes.

The St. Lawrence Project must be expedited. No comparable power, shipbuilding and transportation facilities can be made available in the time required to construct this project.

In dealing with the present emergency, too many people have under-estimated the degree to which our resources will be taxed. We cannot afford to make any more mistakes of that kind.

I am advised that we can build the St. Lawrence Project in four years. Under emergency pressure it may be completed in less time. I should like to agree with the people who say that the country's danger will be over sooner than that. But the course of world events gives no such assurance; and we have no right to take chances with the national safety.

I know of no single project of this nature more important to this country's future in peace or war. Its authorization will demonstrate to the enemies of democracy that, however long the effort, we intend to outstrip them in the race of production. In the modern world, that race determines the rise and fall of nations.

I hope that authorization will not be delayed.

THE WHITE HOUSE,   FRANKLIN D. ROOSEVELT
June 5, 1941.

3. LEASING OF NAVAL AND AIR BASES FROM THE UNITED KINGDOM

A. Arrangement by Exchange of Notes for the Leasing of Naval and Air Bases and the Transfer of Destroyers, Washington, September 2, 1940

This arrangement is incorporated as Annex I in the Agreement for the Use and Operation of Naval and Air Bases, signed March 27, 1941, printed at p. 216.

(1) *The British Ambassador (Lothian) to the Secretary of State (Hull),
September 2, 1940* [1]

BRITISH EMBASSY,
*Washington, D. C.,
September 2, 1940.*

SIR:

I have the honor under instructions from His Majesty's Principal Secretary of State for Foreign Affairs to inform you that in view of the friendly and sympathetic interest of His Majesty's Government in the United Kingdom in the national security of the United States and their desire to strengthen the ability of the United States to cooperate effectively with the other nations of the Americas in the defense of the Western Hemisphere, His Majesty's Government will secure the grant to the Government of the United States, freely and without considera-

[1] Department of State, *Bulletin*, III, p. 199; Executive Agreement Series No. 181. The notes are printed in full with the Message of the President of September 3, 1940 in House Doc. No. 943, 76th Cong., 1st sess.

tion, of the lease for immediate establishment and use of naval and air bases and facilities for entrance thereto and the operation and protection thereof, on the Avalon Peninsula and on the southern coast of Newfoundland, and on the east coast and on the Great Bay of Bermuda.

Furthermore, in view of the above and in view of the desire of the United States to acquire additional air and naval bases in the Caribbean and in British Guiana, and without endeavoring to place a monetary or commercial value upon the many tangible and intangible rights and properties involved, His Majesty's Government will make available to the United States for immediate establishment and use naval and air bases and facilities for entrance thereto and the operation and protection thereof, on the eastern side of the Bahamas, the southern coast of Jamaica, the western coast of St. Lucia, the west coast of Trinidad in the Gulf of Paria, in the island of Antigua and in British Guiana within fifty miles of Georgetown, in exchange for naval and military equipment and material which the United States Government will transfer to His Majesty's Government.

All the bases and facilities referred to in the preceding paragraphs will be leased to the United States for a period of ninety-nine years, free from all rent and charges other than such compensation to be mutually agreed on to be paid by the United States in order to compensate the owners of private property for loss by expropriation or damage arising out of the establishment of the bases and facilities in question.

His Majesty's Government, in the leases to be agreed upon, will grant to the United States for the period of the leases all the rights, power, and authority within the bases leased, and within the limits of the territorial waters and air spaces adjacent to or in the vicinity of such bases, necessary to provide access to and defense of such bases, and appropriate provisions for their control.

Without prejudice to the above-mentioned rights of the United States authorities and their jurisdiction within the leased areas, the adjustment and reconciliation between the jurisdiction of the authorities of the United States within these areas and the jurisdiction of the authorities of the territories in which these areas are situated, shall be determined by common agreement.

The exact location and bounds of the aforesaid bases, the necessary seaward, coast and anti-aircraft defenses, the location of sufficient military garrisons, stores and other necessary auxiliary facilities shall be determined by common agreement.

His Majesty's Government are prepared to designate immediately experts to meet with experts of the United States for these purposes.

Should these experts be unable to agree in any particular situation, except in the case of Newfoundland and Bermuda, the matter shall be settled by the Secretary of State of the United States and His Majesty's Secretary of State for Foreign Affairs.

I have [etc.]   LOTHIAN

The Honorable CORDELL HULL,
Secretary of State of the United States, Washington, D. C.

(2) *The Secretary of State (Hull) to the British Ambassador (Lothian),*
September 2, 1940

DEPARTMENT OF STATE,
Washington, September 2, 1940.

EXCELLENCY:

I have received your note of September 2, 1940, of which the text is as follows:

[Here follows text of the note, printed above.]

I am directed by the President to reply to your note as follows:

The Government of the United States appreciates the declarations and the generous action of His Majesty's Government as contained in your communication which are destined to enhance the national security of the United States and greatly to strengthen its ability to cooperate effectively with the other nations of the Americas in the defense of the Western Hemisphere. It therefore gladly accepts the proposals.

The Government of the United States will immediately designate experts to meet with experts designated by His Majesty's Government to determine upon the exact location of the naval and air bases mentioned in your communication under acknowledgment.

In consideration of the declarations above quoted, the Government of the United States will immediately transfer to His Majesty's Government fifty United States Navy destroyers [1] generally referred to as the twelve hundred-ton type.

Accept [etc.]   CORDELL HULL

His Excellency
The Right Honorable
THE MARQUESS OF LOTHIAN, C.H.,
British Ambassador.

[1] The 50 destroyers were turned over to the United Kingdom between September 9 and November 26, 1940. Originally commissioned in 1917–21, they were in a category in which "over-age" is 16 years. The total original cost of the destroyers was $75,-477,348 and the total recommissioning cost $20,478,445 (U. S. Congress, House of Representatives, Committee on Appropriations, *Navy Department Appropriation Bill for 1942; Hearings before the Subcommittee* . . . 77th Cong., 1st sess., p. 21).

(3) *Message of the President (Roosevelt) Informing the Congress of the Arrangement of September 2, 1940, Transmitted September 3, 1940* [1]

To the Congress of the United States:

I transmit herewith for the information of the Congress notes exchanged between the British Ambassador at Washington and the Secretary of State on September 2, 1940, under which this Government has acquired the right to lease naval and air bases in Newfoundland, and in the islands of Bermuda, the Bahamas, Jamaica, St. Lucia, Trinidad, and Antigua, and in British Guiana; also a copy of an opinion of the Attorney General dated August 27, 1940, regarding my authority to consummate this arrangement.

The right to bases in Newfoundland and Bermuda are gifts — generously given and gladly received. The other bases mentioned have been acquired in exchange for fifty of our over-age destroyers.

This is not inconsistent in any sense with our status of peace. Still less is it a threat against any nation. It is an epochal and far-reaching act of preparation for continental defense in the face of grave danger.

Preparation for defense is an inalienable prerogative of a sovereign state. Under present circumstances this exercise of sovereign right is essential to the maintenance of our peace and safety. This is the most important action in the reinforcement of our national defense that has been taken since the Louisiana Purchase. Then as now, considerations of safety from overseas attack were fundamental.

The value to the Western Hemisphere of these outposts of security is beyond calculation. Their need has long been recognized by our country, and especially by those primarily charged with the duty of charting and organizing our own naval and military defense. They are essential to the protection of the Panama Canal, Central America, the Northern portion of South America, The Antilles, Canada, Mexico, and our own Eastern and Gulf Seaboards. Their consequent importance in hemispheric defense is obvious. For these reasons I have taken advantage of the present opportunity to acquire them.

Franklin D. Roosevelt

The White House,
September 3, 1940.

[1] Department of State, *Bulletin*, III, p. 201; printed for the Congress as House Doc. No. 943, 76th Cong., 1st sess.

(a) Opinion of the Attorney General (Jackson), August 27, 1940 [1]

AUGUST 27, 1940.

THE PRESIDENT,
   The White House,
MY DEAR MR. PRESIDENT:
   In accordance with your request I have considered your constitutional and statutory authority to proceed by Executive Agreement with the British Government immediately to acquire for the United States certain off-shore naval and air bases in the Atlantic Ocean without awaiting the inevitable delays which would accompany the conclusion of a formal treaty.
   The essential characteristics of the proposal are:
   (a) The United States to acquire rights for immediate establishment and use of naval and air bases in Newfoundland, Bermuda, the Bahamas, Jamaica, St. Lucia, Trinidad and British Guiana; such rights to endure for a period of 99 years and to include adequate provisions for access to, and defense of, such bases and appropriate provisions for their control.
   (b) In consideration it is proposed to transfer to Great Britain the title and possession of certain over-age ships and obsolescent military materials now the property of the United States, and certain other small patrol boats which though nearly completed are already obsolescent.
   (c) Upon such transfer all obligation of the United States is discharged. The acquisition consists only of rights, which the United States may exercise or not at its option, and if exercised may abandon without consent. The privilege of maintaining such bases is subject only to limitations necessary to reconcile United States use with the sovereignty retained by Great Britain. Our Government assumes no responsibility for civil administration of any territory. It makes no promise to erect structures, or maintain forces at any point. It undertakes no defense of the possessions of any country. In short it acquires optional bases which may be developed as Congress appropriates funds therefor, but the United States does not assume any continuing or future obligation, commitment or alliance.
   The questions of constitutional and statutory authority, with which alone I am concerned, seem to be these.
   First. May such an acquisition be concluded by the President under an Executive Agreement or must it be negotiated as a Treaty subject to ratification by the Senate?
   Second. Does authority exist in the President to alienate the title to such ships and obsolescent materials, and if so, on what conditions?
   Third. Do the statutes of the United States limit the right to deliver the so-called "mosquito boats" now under construction or the over-age destroyers by reason of the belligerent status of Great Britain?

I

   There is, of course, no doubt concerning the authority of the President to negotiate with the British Government for the proposed exchange. The only

[1] Department of State, *Bulletin,* III, p. 201; House Doc. No. 243, 76th Cong., 1st sess.

questions that might be raised in connection therewith are (1) whether the arrangement must be put in the form of a treaty and await ratification by the Senate or (2) whether there must be additional legislation by the Congress. Ordinarily (and assuming the absence of enabling legislation) the question whether such an agreement can be concluded under Presidential authority or whether it must await ratification by a two-thirds vote of the United States Senate involves consideration of two powers which the Constitution vests in the President.

One of these is the power of the Commander-in-Chief of the Army and Navy of the United States, which is conferred upon the President by the Constitution but is not defined or limited. Happily, there has been little occasion in our history for the interpretation of the powers of the President as Commander-in-Chief of the Army and Navy. I do not find it necessary to rest upon that power alone to sustain the present proposal. But it will hardly be open to controversy that the vesting of such a function in the President also places upon him a responsibility to use all constitutional authority which he may possess to provide adequate bases and stations for the utilization of the naval and air weapons of the United States at their highest efficiency in our defense. It seems equally beyond doubt that present world conditions forbid him to risk any delay that is constitutionally avoidable.

The second power to be considered is that control of foreign relations which the Constitution vests in the President as a part of the Executive function. The nature and extent of this power has recently been explicitly and authoritatively defined by Mr. Justice Sutherland, writing for the Supreme Court. In 1936, in *United States* v. *Curtiss-Wright Export Corp.*, *et al.*, 299 U. S. 304, he said:

"It is important to bear in mind that we are here dealing not alone with an authority vested in the President by an exertion of legislative power, but with such an authority plus the very delicate, plenary and exclusive power of the President as the sole organ of the federal government in the field of international relations — a power which does not require as a basis for its exercise an act of Congress, but which, of course, like every other governmental power, must be exercised in subordination to the applicable provisions of the Constitution. It is quite apparent that if, in the maintenance of our international relations, embarrassment — perhaps serious embarrassment — is to be avoided and success for our aims achieved, congressional legislation which is to be made effective through negotiation and inquiry within the international field must often accord to the President a degree of discretion and freedom from statutory restriction which would not be admissible were domestic affairs alone involved. Moreover, he, not Congress, has the better opportunity of knowing the conditions which prevail in foreign countries, and especially is this true in time of war. He has his confidential sources of information. He has his agents in the form of diplomatic, consular and other officials. Secrecy in respect of information gathered by them may be highly necessary, and the premature disclosure of it productive of harmful results."

The President's power over foreign relations while "delicate, plenary and exclusive" is not unlimited. Some negotiations involve commitments as to the future which would carry an obligation to exercise powers vested in the Congress. Such Presidential arrangements are customarily submitted for ratification by a two-thirds vote of the Senate before the future legislative power of the country is committed. However, the acquisitions which you are proposing to accept are without express or implied promises on the part of the United States to be performed in the future. The consideration, which we later discuss, is completed upon transfer of the specified items. The Executive Agreement obtains an opportunity to establish naval and air bases for the protection of our coastline but it imposes no obligation upon the Congress to appropriate money to improve the opportunity. It is not necessary for the Senate to ratify an opportunity that entails no obligation.

There are precedents which might be cited, but not all strictly pertinent. The proposition falls far short in magnitude of the acquisition by President Jefferson of the Louisiana Territory from a belligerent during a European war, the Congress later appropriating the consideration and the Senate later ratifying a treaty embodying the agreement.

I am also reminded that in 1850, Secretary of State Daniel Webster acquired Horse Shoe Reef, at the entrance of Buffalo Harbor, upon condition that the United States would engage to erect a lighthouse and maintain a light but would erect no fortification thereon. This was done without awaiting legislative authority. Subsequently the Congress made appropriations for the lighthouse, which was erected in 1856. *Malloy, Treaties and Conventions*, Vol. 1, p. 663.

It is not believed, however, that it is necessary here to rely exclusively upon your constitutional power. As pointed out hereinafter (in discussing the second question), I think there is also ample statutory authority to support the acquisition of these bases, and the precedents perhaps most nearly in point are the numerous acquisitions of rights in foreign countries for sites of diplomatic and consular establishments — perhaps also the trade agreements recently negotiated under statutory authority and the acquisition in 1903 of the coaling and naval stations and rights in Cuba under the act of March 2, 1901, c. 803, 31 Stat. 895, 898. In the last-mentioned case the agreement was subsequently embodied in a treaty but it was only one of a number of undertakings, some clearly of a nature to be dealt with ordinarily by treaty, and the statute had required "that by way of further assurance the government of Cuba will embody the foregoing provisions in a permanent treaty with the United States."

The transaction now proposed represents only an exchange with no statutory requirement for the embodiment thereof in any treaty and involving no promises or undertakings by the United States that might raise the question of the propriety of incorporation in a treaty. I therefore advise that acquisition by Executive Agreement of the rights proposed to be conveyed to the United States by Great Britain will not require ratification by the Senate.

II

The right of the President to dispose of vessels of the Navy and unneeded naval material finds clear recognition in at least two enactments of the Congress and a decision of the Supreme Court — and any who assert that the authority does not exist must assume the burden of establishing that both the Congress and the Supreme Court meant something less than the clear import of seemingly plain language.

By section 5 of the act of March 3, 1883, c. 141, 22 Stat. 582, 599–600 (U. S. C., title 34, sec. 492), the Congress placed restrictions upon the methods to be followed by the Secretary of the Navy in disposing of naval vessels, which have been found unfit for further use and stricken from the naval registry, but by the last clause of the section recognized and confirmed such a right in the President free from such limitations. It provides:

"But no vessel of the Navy shall hereafter be sold in any other manner than herein provided, or for less than such appraised value, *unless the President of the United States shall otherwise direct in writing.*" (Underscoring [this print, italics] supplied)

In *Levinson* v. *United States*, 258 U. S. 198, 201, the Supreme Court said of this statute that "the power of the President to direct a departure from the statute is not confined to a sale for less than the appraised value but extends to the manner of the sale," and that "the word 'unless' qualifies both the requirements of the concluding clause."

So far as concerns this statute, in my opinion it leaves the President as Commander-in-Chief of the Navy free to make such disposition of naval vessels as he finds necessary in the public interest, and I find nothing that would indicate that the Congress has tried to limit the President's plenary powers to vessels already stricken from the naval registry. The President, of course, would exercise his powers only under the high sense of responsibility which follows his rank as Commander-in-Chief of his nation's defense forces.

Furthermore, I find in no other statute or in the decisions any attempted limitations upon the plenary powers of the President as Commander-in-Chief of the Army and Navy and as the head of the State in its relations with foreign countries to enter into the proposed arrangements for the transfer to the British Government of certain over-age destroyers and obsolescent military material except the limitations recently imposed by section 14 (*a*) of the act of June 28, 1940 (Public No. 671). This section, it will be noted, clearly recognizes the authority to make transfers and seeks only to impose certain restrictions thereon. The section reads as follows:

"Sec. 14. (*a*) Notwithstanding the provision of any other law, no military or naval weapon, ship, boat, aircraft, munitions, supplies, or equipment, to which the United States has title, in whole or in part, or which have been contracted for, shall hereafter be transferred, exchanged, sold, or otherwise disposed of in any manner whatsoever unless the Chief of Naval Operations in the case of naval material, and the Chief of Staff of the Army in the case of military material, shall first certify that such material is not essential to the defense of the United States."

Thus to prohibit action by the constitutionally-created Commander-in-Chief except upon authorization of a statutory officer subordinate in rank is of questionable constitutionality. However, since the statute requires certification only of matters as to which you would wish, irrespective of the statute, to be satisfied, and as the legislative history of the section indicates that no arbitrary restriction is intended, it seems unnecessary to raise the question of constitutionality which such a provision would otherwise invite.

I am informed that the destroyers involved here are the survivors of a fleet of over 100 built at about the same time and under the same design. During the year 1930, 58 of these were decommissioned with a view toward scrapping and a corresponding number were recommissioned as replacements. Usable material and equipment from the 58 vessels removed from the service were transferred to the recommissioned vessels to recondition and modernize them, and other usable material and equipment were removed and the vessels stripped. They were then stricken from the navy register, and 50 of them were sold as scrap for prices ranging from $5,260 to $6,800 per vessel, and the remaining 8 were used for such purposes as target vessels, experimental construction tests, and temporary barracks. The surviving destroyers now under consideration have been reconditioned and are in service, but all of them are over-age, most of them by several years.

In construing this statute in its application to such a situation it is important to note that this subsection as originally proposed in the Senate bill provided that the appropriate staff officer shall first certify that "such material is not essential to and cannot be used in the defense of the United States." Senator Barkley and others objected to the subsection as so worded on the ground that it would prevent the release and exchange of surplus or used planes and other supplies for sale to the British and that it would consequently nullify the provisions of the bill (see section 1 of the act of July 2, 1940, H. R. 9850, Public No. 703) which the Senate had passed several days earlier for that very purpose. Although Senator Walsh stated that he did not think the proposed subsection had that effect, he agreed to strike out the words "and cannot be used." Senator Barkley observed that he thought the modified language provided "a much more elastic term." Senator Walsh further stated that he would bear in mind in conference the views of Senator Barkley and others, and that he had "no desire or purpose to go beyond the present law, but to have some certificate filed as to whether the property is surplus or not." (Cong. Rec., June 21, 1940, pp. 13370–13371)

In view of this legislative history it is clear that the Congress did not intend to prevent the certification for transfer, exchange, sale or disposition of property merely because it is still used or usable or of possible value for future use. The statute does not contemplate mere transactions in scrap, yet exchange or sale except as scrap would hardly be possible if confined to material whose usefulness is entirely gone. It need only be certified as not essential, and "essential," usually the equivalent of vital or indispensable, falls far short of "used" or "usable."

Moreover, as has been indicated, the congressional authorization is not merely of a sale, which might imply only a cash transaction. It also authorizes equipment to be "transferred," "exchanged" or "otherwise disposed of"; and in connection with material of this kind for which there is no open market value is never absolute but only relative — and chiefly related to what may be had in exchange or replacement.

In view of the character of the transactions contemplated, as well as the legislative history, the conclusion is inescapable that the Congress has not sought by section 14 (a) to impose an arbitrary limitation upon the judgment of the highest staff officers as to whether a transfer, exchange or other disposition of specific items would impair our essential defenses. Specific items must be weighed in relation to our total defense position before and after an exchange or disposition. Any other construction would be a virtual prohibition of any sale, exchange or disposition of material or supplies so long as they were capable of use, however ineffective, and such a prohibition obviously was not, and was not intended to be, written into the law.

It is my opinion that in proceeding under section 14 (*a*) appropriate staff officers may and should consider remaining useful life, strategic importance, obsolescence, and all other factors affecting defense value, not only with respect to what the Government of the United States gives up in any exchange or transfer, but also with respect to what the Government receives. In this situation good business sense is good legal sense.

I therefore advise that the appropriate staff officers may, and should, certify under section 14 (*a*) that ships and material involved in a sale or exchange are not essential to the defense of the United States if in their judgment the consummation of the transaction does not impair or weaken the total defense of the United States, and certainly so where the consummation of the arrangement will strengthen the total defensive position of the nation.

With specific reference to the proposed agreement with the Government of Great Britain for the acquisition of naval and air bases, it is my opinion that the Chief of Naval Operations may, and should, certify under section 14 (*a*) that the destroyers involved are not essential to the defense of the United States if in his judgment the exchange of such destroyers for such naval and air bases will strengthen rather than impair the total defense of the United States.

I have previously indicated that in my opinion there is statutory authority for the acquisition of the naval and air bases in exchange for the vessels and material. The question was not more fully treated at that point because dependent upon the statutes above discussed and which required consideration in this section of the opinion. It is to be borne in mind that these statutes clearly recognize and deal with the authority to make dispositions by sale, transfer, exchange or otherwise; that they do not impose any limitations concerning individuals, corporations or governments to which such dispositions may be made; and that they do not specify or limit in any manner the consideration which may enter into an exchange. There is no reason whatever for holding that sales may not be made to or exchanges made with a foreign government or that in such a case a treaty is contemplated. This is emphasized when we consider that the transactions in some cases may be quite unimportant, perhaps only dispositions of scrap, and that a domestic buyer (unless restrained by some authorized contract or embargo) would be quite free to dispose of his purchase as he pleased. Furthermore, section 14 (*a*) of the act of June 28, 1940, *supra*, was enacted by the Congress in full contemplation of transfers for ultimate delivery to foreign belligerent nations. Possibly it may be said that the authority for exchange of naval vessels and material presupposes the acquisition of something of value to the Navy or, at least, to the national defense. Certainly I can imply no narrower limitation when the law is wholly silent in this respect. Assuming that there is, however, at least the limitation which I have mentioned, it is fully met in the acquisition of rights to maintain needed bases. And if, as I hold, the statute law authorizes the exchange of vessels and material for other vessels and material or, equally, for the right to establish bases, it is an inescapable corollary that the statute law also authorizes the acquisition of the ships or material or bases which form the consideration for the exchange.

III

Whether the statutes of the United States prevent the dispatch to Great Britain, a belligerent power, of the so-called "mosquito boats" now under construction or the over-age destroyers depends upon the interpretation to be placed on section 3 of title V of the act of June 15, 1917, c. 30, 40 Stat. 217, 222. This section reads:

"During a war in which the United States is a neutral nation, it shall be unlawful to send out of the jurisdiction of the United States any vessel, built, armed, or equipped as a vessel of war, or converted from a private vessel into a vessel of war, with any intent or under any agreement or contract, written or oral, that such vessel shall be delivered to a belligerent nation, or to an agent, officer, or citizen of such nation, or with reasonable cause to believe that the said vessel shall or will be employed in the service of any such belligerent nation after its departure from the jurisdiction of the United States."

This section must be read in the light of section 2 of the same act and the rules of international law which the Congress states that it was its intention to implement. (H. Rep. No. 30, 65th Cong., 1st Sess., p. 9) So read, it is clear that it is inapplicable to vessels, like the over-age destroyers, which were not built, armed, equipped as, or converted into, vessels of war with the intent that they should enter the service of a belligerent. If the section were not so construed, it would render meaningless section 2 of the act which authorizes the President to detain any armed vessel until he is satisfied that it will not engage in hostile operations before it reaches a neutral or belligerent port. The two sections are intelligible and reconcilable only if read in light of the traditional rules of international law. These are clearly stated by Oppenheim in his work on International Law, 5th ed., Vol. 2, sec. 334, pp. 574–576:

"Whereas a neutral is in no wise obliged by his duty of impartiality to prevent his subjects from selling armed vessels to the belligerents, such armed vessels being merely contraband of war, a neutral is bound to employ the means at his disposal to prevent his subjects from building, fitting out, or arming, to the order of either belligerent, vessels intended to be used as men-of-war, and to prevent the departure from his jurisdiction of any vessel which, by order of either belligerent, has been adapted to warlike use. The difference between selling armed vessels to belligerents and building them to order is usually defined in the following way: —

"An armed ship, being contraband of war, is in no wise different from other kinds of contraband, provided that she is not manned in a neutral port, so that she can commit hostilities at once after having reached the open sea. A subject of a neutral who builds an armed ship, or arms a merchantman, not to the order of a belligerent, but intending to sell her to a belligerent, does not differ from a manufacturer of arms who intends to sell them to a belligerent. There is nothing to prevent a neutral from allowing his subject to sell armed vessels, and to deliver them to belligerents, either in a neutral port or in a belligerent port. . . .

"On the other hand, if a subject of a neutral builds armed ships *to the order of a belligerent*, he prepares the means of naval operations, since the ships, on sailing outside the neutral territorial waters and taking in a crew and ammunition, can at once commit hostilities. Thus, through the carrying out of the order of the belligerent, the neutral territory has been made the base of naval operations; and as the duty of impartiality includes an obligation to prevent either belligerent from making neutral territory the base of military or naval operations, a neutral violates his neutrality by not preventing his subjects from carrying out an order of a belligerent for the building and fitting out of men-of-war. This distinction, although of course logically correct, is hair-splitting. But as, according to the present law, neutral States need not prevent their subjects from supplying arms and ammunition to belligerents, it will probably continue to be drawn."

Viewed in the light of the above, I am of the opinion that this statute does prohibit the release and transfer to the British Government of the so-called "mosquito boats" now under construction for the United States Navy. If these boats were released to the British Government, it would be legally impossible for that Government to take them out of this country after their completion, since to the extent of such completion at least they would have been built, armed, or equipped with the intent, or with reasonable cause to believe, that they would enter the service of a belligerent after being sent out of the jurisdiction of the United States.

This will not be true, however, with respect to the over-age destroyers, since they were clearly not built, armed, or equipped with any such intent or with reasonable cause to believe that they would ever enter the service of a belligerent.

In this connection it has been noted that during the war between Russia and Japan in 1904 and 1905, the German Government permitted the sale to Russia of torpedo boats and also of ocean liners belonging to its auxiliary navy. See Wheaton's International Law, 6th ed. (Keith), Vol. 2, p. 977.

IV

Accordingly, you are respectfully advised:

(a) That the proposed arrangement may be concluded as an Executive Agreement, effective without awaiting ratification.

(b) That there is presidential power to transfer title and possession of the proposed considerations upon certification by appropriate staff officers.

(c) That the dispatch of the so-called "mosquito boats" would constitute a violation of the statute law of the United States, but with that exception there is no legal obstacle to the consummation of the transaction, in accordance, of course, with the applicable provisions of the Neutrality Act as to delivery.

Respectfully submitted,

ROBERT H. JACKSON,
Attorney General.

(4) Instruction Sent by the Secretary of State (*Hull*) to Diplomatic Missions in the American Republics, September 6, 1940 [1]

It is desired that you formally notify the Government to which you are accredited that the United States has acquired the right to lease naval and air bases in Newfoundland, and in the islands of Bermuda,

[1] Department of State, *Bulletin*, III, p. 196.

the Bahamas, Jamaica, St. Lucia, Trinidad, and Antigua, and in British Guiana.

The Government of the United States has taken this step to strengthen its ability not only to defend the United States but in order the more effectively to cooperate with the other American Republics in the common defense of the hemisphere.

The resulting facilities at these bases will, of course, be made available alike to all American Republics on the fullest cooperative basis for the common defense of the hemisphere and in entire harmony with the spirit of the pronouncements made and the understandings reached at the conferences of Lima, Panama, and Havana.

B. Agreement for the Use and Operation of Naval and Air Bases

(1) *Message of the President (Roosevelt) Transmitting the Agreement, March 27, 1941* [1]

TO THE CONGRESS OF THE UNITED STATES:

On September 3, 1940, I transmitted for the information of the Congress notes [2] exchanged between the British Ambassador at Washington and the Secretary of State on the preceding day, under which this Government acquired the right to lease naval and air bases in Newfoundland and in the islands of Bermuda, the Bahamas, Jamaica, St. Lucia, Trinidad, and Antigua, and in British Guiana. I now transmit for the information of the Congress a copy of an agreement for the use and operation of these bases, which was signed in London on March 27, 1941, together with the notes exchanged in connection therewith. These bases are for American defense against attack and their construction is consistent with such defense. International developments since my message to the Congress of September third last [3] have emphasized the value to the Western Hemisphere of these outposts of security.

FRANKLIN D. ROOSEVELT

THE WHITE HOUSE,
March 27, 1941

---

[1] House Doc. No. 158, 77th Cong., 1st sess.; Department of State, *Bulletin*, IV, p. 387.

[2] See p. 203.

[3] See p. 206.

(2) *Text of the Agreement for the Use and Operation of Naval and Air Bases between the United Kingdom and the United States, London, Signed March 27, 1941* [1]

[Excerpt]

Whereas the Government of the United Kingdom of Great Britain and Northern Ireland, in consultation with the Government of Newfoundland, are desirous at this time of further effectuating the declarations made on their behalf by His Excellency the Most Honorable the Marquess of Lothian, C.H., His Majesty's Ambassador Extraordinary and Plenipotentiary, in his communication of the 2nd September, 1940, to the Secretary of State of the United States of America, a copy of which is set out in Annex I hereto and made a part hereof;

And whereas it is agreed that leases in respect of the naval and air bases to be leased to the United States of America in Newfoundland, Bermuda, Jamaica, St. Lucia, Antigua, Trinidad and British Guiana, respectively, shall forthwith be executed substantially in the forms of the leases set out in Annex II hereto which are hereby approved, and that a similar lease in respect of a base in the Bahamas shall be executed as soon as possible;

And whereas it is desired to determine by common agreement certain matters relating to the lease of the said bases, as provided in the communication of the 2nd September, 1940, and the reply thereto of the same date from the Honorable Cordell Hull, Secretary of State of the United States, set out in Annex I and made a part hereof;

And whereas it is desired that this agreement shall be fulfilled in a spirit of good neighborliness between the Government of the United Kingdom and the Government of the United States of America, and that details of its practical application shall be arranged by friendly cooperation; the undersigned, duly authorized to that effect, have agreed as follows:

ARTICLE I. GENERAL DESCRIPTION OF RIGHTS. (1) The United States shall have all the rights, power and authority within the leased areas which are necessary for the establishment, use, operation and defense thereof, or appropriate for their control, and all the rights, power and authority within the limits of territorial waters and air spaces adjacent to, or in the vicinity of, the leased areas, which are necessary to provide access to and defense of the leased areas, or appropriate for control thereof.

[1] House Doc. No. 158, 77th Cong., 1st sess.; Department of State, *Bulletin*, IV, p. 387.

(2) The said rights, power and authority shall include, *inter alia*, the right, power and authority:

(A) To construct (including dredging and filling), maintain, operate, use, occupy and control the said bases.

(B) To improve and deepen the harbors, channels, entrances and anchorages, and generally to fit the premises for use as naval and air bases.

(C) To control, so far as may be required for the efficient operation of the bases, and within the limits of military necessity, anchorage, moorings, and movements of ships and water-borne craft and the anchorage, moorings, landings, take-offs, movements and operations of aircraft.

(D) To regulate and control within the leased areas all communications within, to and from the areas leased.

(E) To install, maintain, use and operate under-sea and other defenses, defense devices and controls, including detecting and other similar facilities.

(3) In the exercise of the above-mentioned rights, the United States agrees that the powers granted to it outside the leased areas will not be used unreasonably or, unless required by military necessity, so as to interfere with the necessary rights of navigation, aviation, or communication to or from within the territories, but that they shall be used in the spirit of the fourth clause of the preamble.

(4) In the practical application outside the leased areas of the foregoing paragraphs there shall be, as occasion requires, consultation between the Government of the United States and the Government of the United Kingdom.

ARTICLE II. SPECIAL EMERGENCY POWERS. When the United States is engaged in war or in time of other emergency the Government of the United Kingdom agree that the United States may exercise in the territories and surrounding waters or air spaces all such rights, power and authority as may be necessary for conducting any military operations deemed desirable by the United States, but these rights will be exercised with all possible regard to the spirit of the fourth clause of the preamble.

ARTICLE III. NON-USER. The United States shall be under no obligation to improve the leased areas or any part thereof for use as naval or air bases, or to exercise any right, power or authority granted in respect of the leased areas, or to maintain forces therein, or to provide for the defense thereof; but if and so long as any leased area, or any part thereof, is not used by the United States for the purposes in this agreement set forth, the Government of the United Kingdom or the Government of the

Territory may take such steps therein as shall be agreed with the United States to be desirable for the maintenance of public health, safety, law and order, and, if necessary, for defense.

ARTICLE IV. JURISDICTION. (1) In any case in which

(A) A member of the United States forces, a national of the United States or a person who is not a British subject shall be charged with having committed, either within or without the leased areas, an offense of a military nature, punishable under the law of the United States, including, but not restricted to, treason, an offense relating to sabotage or espionage, or any other offense relating to the security and protection of United States naval and air bases, establishments, equipment or other property or to operations of the Government of the United States in the territory; or

(B) A British subject shall be charged with having committed any such offense within a leased area and shall be apprehended therein; or

(C) A person other than a British subject shall be charged with having committed an offense of any other nature within a leased area, the United States shall have the absolute right in the first instance to assume and exercise jurisdiction with respect to such offense.

(2) If the United States shall elect not to assume and exercise such jurisdiction the United States authorities shall, where such offense is punishable in virtue of legislation enacted pursuant to Article V or otherwise under the law of the territory, so inform the Government of the territory and shall, if it shall be agreed between the Government of the Territory and the United States authorities that the alleged offender should be brought to trial, surrender him to the appropriate authority in the territory for that purpose.

(3) If a British subject shall be charged with having committed within a leased area an offense of the nature described in paragraph (1)(A) of this article, and shall not be apprehended therein, he shall, if in the territory outside the leased areas, be brought to trial before the courts of the territory; or, if the offense is not punishable under the law of the territory, he shall, on the request of the United States authorities, be apprehended and surrendered to the United States authorities and the United States shall have the right to exercise jurisdiction with respect to the alleged offense.

(4) When the United States exercises jurisdiction under this article and the person charged is a British subject, he shall be tried by a United States court sitting in a leased area in the territory.

(5) Nothing in this agreement shall be construed to affect, prejudice or restrict the full exercise at all times of jurisdiction and control by the

United States in matters of discipline and internal administration over members of the United States forces, as conferred by the law of the United States and any regulations made thereunder.

ARTICLE V. SECURITY LEGISLATION. The Government of the Territory will take such steps as may from time to time be agreed to be necessary with a view to the enactment of legislation to ensure the adequate security and protection of the United States naval and air bases, establishments, equipment and other property, and the operations of the United States under the leases and this agreement and the punishment of persons who may contravene any laws or regulations made for that purpose. The Government of the Territory will also from time to time consult with the United States authorities in order that the laws and regulations of the United States and the territory in relation to such matters may, so far as circumstances permit, be similar in character.

[ARTICLE VI, Arrest and Service of Process; ARTICLE VII, Right of Audience for United States Counsel; ARTICLE VIII, Surrender of Offenders, omitted.]

ARTICLE IX. PUBLIC SERVICES. The United States shall have the right to employ and use all utilities, services and facilities, roads, highways, bridges, viaducts, canals and similar channels of transportation belonging to, or controlled or regulated by, the Government of the Territory or the Government of the United Kingdom, under conditions comparable to and no less favorable than those applicable from time to time to the Government of the United Kingdom.

ARTICLE X. SURVEYS. (1) The United States shall have the right, after appropriate notification has been given to the Government of the territory to make topographic and hydrographic surveys outside the leased areas in any part of the territories and waters adjacent thereto. Copies, with title and triangulation data, of any surveys so made will be furnished to the Government of the territory.

(2) Notification and copies will be given to the United States authorities of any such surveys carried out by the Government of the United Kingdom or the Government of the Territory.

ARTICLE XI. SHIPPING AND AVIATION. (1) Lights and other aids to navigation of vessels and aircraft placed or established in the leased areas and the territorial waters adjacent thereto or in the vicinity thereof shall conform to the system in use in the territory. The position, characteristics and any alterations thereof shall be notified in advance to the appropriate authority in the territory.

(2) United States public vessels operated by the War or Navy Departments, by the Coast Guard or by the Coast and Geodetic Survey, bound to or departing from a leased area shall not on entering or leaving the leased area or the territorial waters in the vicinity thereof be subject to compulsory pilotage or to light or harbor dues in the territory. If a pilot is taken pilotage shall be paid for at appropriate rates.

(3) British commercial vessels may use the leased areas on the same terms and conditions as United States commercial vessels.

(4) It is understood that a leased area is not a part of the territory of the United States for the purpose of coastwise shipping laws so as to exclude British vessels from trade between the United States and the leased areas.

(5) Commercial aircraft will not be authorized to operate from any of the bases (save in case of emergency or for strictly military purposes under supervision of the War or Navy Departments) except by agreement between the United States and the Government of the United Kingdom, provided that in the case of Newfoundland such agreement shall be between the United States and the Government of Newfoundland.

[ARTICLE XII, Motor Traffic, omitted.]

ARTICLE XIII. IMMIGRATION. (1) The immigration laws of the territory shall not operate or apply so as to prevent admission into the territory for the purposes of this agreement of any member of the United States forces posted to a leased area or any person (not being a national of a power at war with His Majesty the King) employed by, or under a contract with, the Government of the United States in connection with the construction, maintenance, operation or defense of the bases in the territory; but suitable arrangements will be made by the United States to enable such persons to be readily identified and their status to be established.

(2) If the status of any person within the territory and admitted thereto under the foregoing paragraph shall be altered so that he would no longer be entitled to such admission, the United States authorities shall notify the Government of the Territory and shall, if such person be required to leave the territory by that Government, be responsible for providing him with a passage from the territory within a reasonable time, and shall in the meantime prevent his becoming a public responsibility of the territory.

ARTICLE XIV. CUSTOMS AND OTHER DUTIES. (1) No import, excise, consumption or other tax, duty or impost shall be charged on

(A) Material, equipment, supplies or goods for use in the construction, maintenance, operation or defense of the bases, consigned to, or destined for, the United States authorities or a contractor;

(B) Goods for use or consumption aboard United States public vessels of the Army, Navy, Coast Guard or Coast and Geodetic Surveys;

(C) Goods consigned to the United States authorities for the use of institutions under Government control known as Post Exchanges, Ships' Service Stores, Commissary Stores or Service Clubs, or for sale thereat to members of the United States forces, or civilian employees of the United States being nationals of the United States and employed in connection with the bases, or members of their families resident with them and not engaged in any business or occupation in the territory;

(D) The personal belongings or household effects, of persons referred to in sub-paragraph (C) and of contractors and their employees, being nationals of the United States employed in the construction, maintenance or operation of the bases and present in the territory by reason only of such employment.

(2) No export tax shall be charged on the material, equipment, supplies or goods mentioned in paragraph (1) in the event of reshipment from the territory.

(3) This article shall apply notwithstanding that the material, equipment, supplies or goods pass through other parts of the territory en route to or from a leased area.

(4) Administrative measures shall be taken by the United States authorities to prevent the resale of goods which are sold under paragraph (1)(C), or imported under paragraph (1)(D) of this article, to persons not entitled to buy goods at such Post Exchanges, Ships' Service Stores, Commissary Stores or Service Clubs, or not entitled to free importation under paragraph (1)(D); and generally to prevent abuse of the customs privileges granted under this article. There shall be cooperation between such authorities and the Government of the Territory to this end.

ARTICLE XV. WIRELESS AND CABLES. (1) Except with the consent of the Government of the territory, no wireless station shall be established or submarine cable landed in a leased area otherwise than for military purposes.

(2) All questions relating to frequencies, power and like matters, used by apparatus designed to emit electric radiation, shall be settled by mutual arrangement.

ARTICLE XVI. POSTAL FACILITIES. The United States shall have the right to establish United States Post Offices in the leased areas for the exclusive use of the United States forces, and civilian personnel (including contractors and their employees) who are nationals of the United States and employed in connection with the construction, maintenance, operation or defense of the bases, and the families of such persons, for domestic use between United States Post Offices in leased areas and between such Post Offices and other United States Post Offices and Post Offices in the Panama Canal Zone and the Philippine Islands.

[ARTICLE XVII, Taxation, omitted.]

ARTICLE XVIII. BUSINESSES AND PROFESSIONS. Unless the consent of the Government of the Territory shall have been obtained —

(1) No business shall be established in a leased area; but the institutions referred to in Article XIV (1)(C) offering goods, under a prohibition against resale, exclusively to the persons mentioned in the said Article XIV (1)(C) shall not be regarded as businesses for the purposes of this article;

(2) No person shall habitually render any professional services in a leased area, except to, or for, the Government of the United States or the persons mentioned in Article XIV (1)(C).

ARTICLE XIX. FORCES OUTSIDE LEASED AREAS. (1) United States forces stationed or operating outside the leased areas under separate agreement with the Government of the United Kingdom or the Government of the territory shall be entitled to the same rights and enjoy the same status as United States forces stationed within the leased areas.

(2) The United States shall be under no obligation to maintain forces outside the leased areas by virtue of such agreement.

ARTICLE XX. HEALTH MEASURES OUTSIDE LEASED AREAS. The United States shall have the right, in collaboration with the Government of the Territory and, where necessary, with the local authority concerned, to exercise, without other consideration than just compensation to private owners, if any, such powers as such Government and local authority and the Government of the United Kingdom may possess of entering upon any property in the vicinity of the leased areas for the purpose of inspection, and of taking any necessary measures to improve sanitation and protect health.

ARTICLE XXI. ABANDONMENT. The United States may at any time abandon any leased area or any part thereof, without thereby incurring any obligation, but shall give to the Government of the United Kingdom as long notice as possible and in any case not less than one year, of its intention so to do. At the expiration of such notice the area abandoned shall revert to the lessor. Abandonment shall not be deemed to have occurred in the absence of such notice.

ARTICLE XXII. REMOVAL OF IMPROVEMENTS. The United States may at any time before the termination of a lease, or within a reasonable time thereafter, take away all or any removable improvements placed by or on behalf of the United States in the leased area or territorial waters.

ARTICLE XXIII. RIGHTS NOT TO BE ASSIGNED. The United States will not assign or underlet or part with the possession of the whole or any part of any leased area, or of any right, power or authority granted by the leases or this agreement.

ARTICLE XXIV. POSSESSION. (1) On the signing of this agreement, leases of the leased areas, substantially in the forms respectively set out in Annex II hereto, shall be forthwith executed, and all rights, power, authority and control under such leases and under this agreement (including transfer of possession where it shall not previously have been transferred) shall thereupon become effective immediately, and pending execution of such leases they may be exercised ad interim and possession of the leased areas shall be immediately given so far as the location thereof is then ascertained. Where the precise location of a portion of any leased area is not ascertainable until more detailed descriptions are available, possession of such portion shall be given as rapidly as possible. This article shall not require occupiers of buildings in a leased area to be removed from such buildings until reasonable notice to vacate has been given and expired, due regard being had to the necessity of obtaining alternative accommodation.

(2) The foregoing paragraph shall not apply in relation to the Bahamas, but a lease of the leased area therein, in terms similar to those of the leases set out in Annex II hereto, and subject to such special provisions as may be agreed to be required, will be granted to the United States of America as soon as the location of that area shall have been agreed, whereupon this agreement shall apply thereto.

ARTICLE XXV. RESERVATIONS. (1) All minerals (including oil), and antiquities and all rights relating thereto and to treasure trove, under, upon, or connected with the land and water comprised in the leased areas or otherwise used or occupied by the United States by virtue of this agreement, are reserved to the Government and inhabitants of the territory; but no rights so reserved shall be transferred to third parties, or exercised within the leased areas, without the consent of the United States.

(2) The United States will permit the exercise of fishing privileges within the leased areas in so far as may be found compatible with military requirements, and in the exercise of its rights will use its best endeavors to avoid damage to fisheries in the territory.

ARTICLE XXVI. SPECIAL PROVISIONS FOR INDIVIDUAL TERRITORIES. The provisions contained in Annex III hereto shall have effect in relation to the territories to which they respectively appertain.

ARTICLE XXVII. SUPPLEMENTARY LEASES. The United States may, by common agreement, acquire by supplementary lease for the unexpired period of the lease granted in a territory, such additional areas, sites and locations as may be found necessary for the use and protection of the bases upon such terms and conditions as may be agreed, which shall unless there are special reasons to the contrary be on the basis of those contained in this agreement.

ARTICLE XXVIII. MODIFICATION OF THIS AGREEMENT. The Government of the United States and the Government of the United Kingdom agree to give sympathetic consideration to any representations which either may make after this agreement has been in force a reasonable time, proposing a review of any of the provisions of this agreement to determine whether modifications in the light of experience are necessary or desirable. Any such modifications shall be by mutual consent.

ARTICLE XXIX. The United States and the Government of the Territory respectively will do all in their power to assist each other in giving full effect to the provisions of this agreement according to its tenor and will take all appropriate steps to that end. During the continuance of any lease, no laws of the territory which would derogate from or prejudice any of the rights conferred on the United States by the lease or by this agreement shall be applicable within the leased area, save with the concurrence of the United States.

ARTICLE XXX. INTERPRETATION. In this agreement, unless the context otherwise requires, the following expressions have the meanings hereby respectively assigned to them:

"Lease" means a lease entered into in pursuance of the communications set out in Annex I hereto, and in relation to any territory means a lease entered into in respect of an area therein.

"Leased Area" means an area in respect of which a lease is or will be entered into.

"Base" means a base established in pursuance of the said communications.

"Territory" means a part of His Majesty's Dominions in which a lease is entered into in pursuance of the communications set out in Annex I hereto; and,

"The Territory" means the territory concerned.

"The United States Authorities" means the authority or authorities from time to time authorized or designated, by the Government of the United States of America, for the purpose of exercising the powers in relation to which the expression is used.

"United States Forces" means the naval and military forces of the United States of America.

"British Subject" includes British protected person.

Signed in London in duplicate this twenty-seventh day of March, 1941.

On behalf of the United States of America:

JOHN G. WINANT, *Ambassador of the United States of America*, CHARLES FAHY, HARRY J. MALONY, HAROLD BIESEMEIER

On behalf of the Government of the United Kingdom of Great Britain and Northern Ireland:

WINSTON CHURCHILL, *Prime Minister;* LORD CRANBORNE, *Secretary of State for Dominions;* LORD MOYNE, *Secretary of State for Colonies.*

ANNEX I

[THE LOTHIAN-HULL EXCHANGE OF NOTES, SEPTEMBER 2, 1940, see p. 203-5.]

ANNEX II.   FORMS OF LEASES [1]

The schedules of the areas taken under the leases are omitted as of only technical surveying interest.[2] The leases are of the same form, but since they severally apply to territories of various status in the British Commonwealth of Nations or Empire certain distinctions are made in naming the lessors.

Newfoundland is a self-governing Dominion, the government of which is "in commission," that is, administered directly by commissioners responsible to the Secretary of State for Dominion Affairs; the Governor and Commander-in-chief is the lessor. The Governor of the colony is the lessor in the case of Jamaica and British Guiana, which are self-governing under constitutions. His Majesty the King is the lessor in the case of Bermuda, Saint Lucia (one of the Windward Islands), Antigua (one of the Leeward Islands) and Trinidad, all Crown colonies. The leases for all except Newfoundland are omitted.

[Excerpt]

1. NEWFOUNDLAND.[3]

[1] Department of State, *Bulletin,* IV, p. 396.

[2] A general description of the areas and a summary of the provisions of the leases was printed in *New York Times,* March 28, 1941.

[3] An exchange of notes on March 27, 1941 attached to the agreement confirms that "it is the intention of the Government of the United Kingdom of Great Britain and Northern Ireland that upon the resumption by Newfoundland of the constitutional status held by it prior to February 16, 1934, the words 'The Government of the United Kingdom' wherever they occur in relation to a provision applicable to Newfoundland in the said agreement shall be taken to mean, so far as Newfoundland is concerned, the Government of Newfoundland, and the agreement shall then be construed accordingly."

This indenture of lease made the _____ day of _____, nineteen hundred and forty-one, between His Excellency Sir Humphrey Walwyn, K.C.S.I., K.C.M.G., C.B., D.S.O., Governor and Commander-in-chief in and over the island of Newfoundland and its dependencies, in commission, hereinafter referred to as the Newfoundland Government, of the first part, and the United States of America, of the other part:

Whereas by notes exchanged on the second day of September, nineteen hundred and forty (copies of which are appended to the agreement herein after referred to), between His Majesty's Ambassador at Washington and the Secretary of State of the United States of America, His Majesty's Government in the United Kingdom undertook to secure the grant to the United States of America of the lease of certain naval and air bases and facilities in certain localities, including Newfoundland, for a period of ninety-nine years, free from all rent and charges other than compensation to be mutually agreed on to be paid by the United States in order to compensate the owners of private property for loss by expropriation or damage arising out of the establishment of the said bases and facilities; and,

Whereas in furtherance of the said notes an agreement between the Government of the United Kingdom and the United States of America was signed on the 27th day of March, nineteen hundred and forty-one; and,

Whereas in compliance with the undertaking of the Government of the United Kingdom hereinbefore referred to the Newfoundland Government has agreed to demise and lease the several pieces or parcels of land hereinafter described. Now this indenture witnesseth that in consideration of the premises the Newfoundland Government hath demised and leased and by these presents doth demise and lease unto the United States of America all those six several pieces or parcels of land (hereinafter referred to as the leased areas) described in the schedule to these presents and delineated on the plans hereto annexed:

To have and to hold the same for the full end and term of ninety-nine years to begin and to be computed from the date of these presents free from the payment of all rent and charges other than compensation as aforesaid. And the United States of America agrees that it will not during the term hereby granted use the leased areas nor permit the use thereof except for the purposes specified and on the terms and conditions contained in the aforesaid notes and agreement, which are incorporated in and form part of these presents except such parts thereof as refer specifically to territory other than Newfoundland.

[Here follows Schedule.]

ANNEX III. SPECIAL PROVISIONS FOR INDIVIDUAL TERRITORIES

[These provisions, of local interest only, relate to Bermuda, Jamaica, St. Lucia, Antigua, Trinidad and British Guiana.]

(a) United States Post Offices in Leased Areas. Letter from the British Secretary of State for Foreign Affairs (Eden) to the American Ambassador at London (Winant), March 27, 1941 [1]

LONDON, *March 27, 1941.*

I have the honor to acknowledge the receipt of Your Excellency's note of today's date concerning censorship, the terms of which are as follows:

[1] House Doc. No. 158, 77th Cong., 1st sess.; Department of State, *Bulletin*, IV, p. 410. Only the confirming note of the exchange is printed.

I have the honor to inform Your Excellency that my Government has agreed to the following understanding in respect of Article XVI of the Agreement signed this day between our respective Governments concerning the lease of bases:

(1) Mails passing between United States Post Offices shall not be subject to censorship except by the United States.

(2) In connection with the establishment of any United States Post Offices in a leased area, the United States will arrange administratively, for such time as Great Britain may be at war, for the examination of all nonofficial incoming or outgoing mail destined for or originating in a leased area.

(3) The use of these post offices will be strictly limited to persons entitled under Article XVI to use them and any mail deposited in such a post office which may be found by the United States examiners to be from a person not entitled to use it will, if required, be made available to the authorities of the territory for examination.

(4) Should the United States be at war and Great Britain be neutral, the British Government will insure that a similar procedure is adopted, with respect to incoming or outgoing mail destined for or originating in the territory in which a leased area is located, to safeguard the interests of the United States in the leased area.

(5) The United States and British authorities will collaborate to prevent their respective mails, in the leased areas or in the territories in which they are located, being used prejudicially to the security of the other.

(6) There will be no examination of official mail of either Government by the other under any conditions.

2. In reply, I have the honor to inform Your Excellency that the Government of the United Kingdom of Great Britain and Northern Ireland agree to this understanding, and, in accordance with Your Excellency's suggestion, Your Excellency's note and this reply will be regarded as placing on record the understanding between the two governments in this matter.

(3) *Protocol Respecting Newfoundland between the United States, United Kingdom and Canada, London, March 27, 1941* [1]

LONDON, *March 27, 1941.*

The undersigned Plenipotentiaries of the Governments of Canada, the United Kingdom of Great Britain and Northern Ireland and the United States of America having been authorized by their respective Governments to clarify certain matters concerning the defense of Newfoundland arising out of the Agreement signed this day concerning the bases leased to the United States, have drawn up and signed the following protocol.

It is recognized that the defense of Newfoundland is an integral feature of the Canadian scheme of defense and as such is a matter of special concern to the Canadian Government, which has already assumed certain responsibilities for this defense.

[1] House Doc. No. 158, 77th Cong., 1st sess.; Department of State, *Bulletin*, IV, p. 411.

It is agreed, therefore, that in all powers which may be exercised and in such actions as may be taken under the Agreement for the use and operation of the United States Bases, dated March 27, 1941 in respect of Newfoundland, Canadian interests in regard to defense will be fully respected.

Nothing in this Agreement shall affect the arrangements relative to the defense of Newfoundland already made by the Governments of the United States and Canada in pursuance of recommendations submitted to those Governments by the Permanent Joint Board on Defense — United States and Canada.[1]

It is further agreed that in all consultations concerning Newfoundland arising out of Articles I (4), II, and XI (5) of the Agreement, or of any other Articles involving considerations of defense the Canadian Government as well as the Government of Newfoundland will have the right to participate.

On behalf of the United States of America:

JOHN G. WINANT, *Ambassador of the United States of America;* CHARLES FAHY, HARRY J. MALONY, HAROLD BIESEMEIER.

On behalf of Canada:

VINCENT MASSEY, *Canadian High Commissioner at London;* L. W. MURRAY, L. B. PEARSON.

On behalf of the Government of the United Kingdom of Great Britain and Northern Ireland:

WINSTON CHURCHILL, *Prime Minister;* LORD CRANBORNE, *Secretary of State for Dominions;* LORD MOYNE, *Secretary of State for Colonies.*

4. GREENLAND

A. Defense of Greenland [2]

The German invasion of Denmark on April 9, 1940 evoked prompt disapproval by the President of the United States [3] and raised a question as to the status of Greenland, which is held to be within the area of the Monroe Doctrine. The United States established a consular post in Greenland.[4]

On May 3, 1940 the Greenland Councils, meeting at Godhavn, adopted a resolution in the name of the people of Greenland reaffirming their allegiance to

[1] See p. 160.
[2] Department of State, *Bulletin,* IV, p. 445. Several paragraphs of this prefatory note are lifted from the release of April 10, 1941.
[3] *Documents, II, 1939–40,* p. 410.
[4] See p. 764.

King Christian X of Denmark, and expressed the hope that, so long as Greenland remained cut off from the mother country, the Government of the United States would continue to keep in mind the exposed position of the Danish flag in Greenland and of the native and Danish population of Greenland. The Government of the United States expressed its willingness to assure that the needs of the population of Greenland would be taken care of.

On July 25, 1940,[1] the consultation of American Foreign Ministers at Havana declared that any attempt on the part of a non-American state against the integrity or inviolability of the territory, the sovereignty, or the political independence of an American state should be considered an act of aggression, and that they would cooperate in defense against any such aggression. In a further declaration, known as the Act of Havana, it declared that the status of regions in this continent belonging to European powers was a subject of deep concern to all of the governments of the American Republics.

During the summer of 1940 German activity on the eastern coast of Greenland became apparent. Three ships proceeding from Norwegian territory under German occupation arrived off the coast of Greenland, ostensibly for commercial or scientific purposes; and at least one of these ships landed parties nominally for scientific purposes, but actually for meteorological assistance to German belligerent operations in the north Atlantic. These parties were eventually cleared out. In the late fall of 1940, air reconnaissance appeared over East Greenland under circumstances making it plain that there had been continued activity in that region.

On January 9, 1941, the Department of State issued a release setting forth the Government's policy with respect to Greenland and pointing out that the United States had sent no troops to nor established any air or naval bases in Greenland. The Department pointed out, however, that the Government of the United States, with the full agreement of the Greenland authorities, had taken the following steps, "none of which has operated to the injury of any legitimate interest":

1. An American Consulate was provisionally established at Godthaab[2] to facilitate the handling of the numerous questions which have arisen with respect to the purchase in the United States of food and other supplies for Greenland and of the sale of Greenland products in this country.

2. An American Red Cross representative was sent to Greenland to determine on the spot and in consultation with the Greenland authorities what relief was needed by the inhabitants of Greenland.

3. In view of the heavy demands from many parts of the world for arms and ammunition manufactured in this country, the Government of the United States has facilitated the purchase in the United States by the Greenland authorities of a quantity of arms for the use of the small number of policemen employed by the Greenland authorities to patrol the cryolite mine at Ivigtut, which is Greenland's major economic asset.

On March 27, 1941, a German bomber flew over the eastern coast of Greenland and on the following day another German war plane likewise reconnoitered the same territory. Under these circumstances it appeared that further steps for the defense of Greenland were necessary to bring Greenland within the system of hemispheric defense envisaged by the Act of Havana.

The United States Government took the initiative in negotiating an agreement that would obviate Greenland from being made a base of aggression, defend the Western Hemisphere from that quarter and preserve Danish sovereignty over the island by insuring its rendition after the war ends.

[1] See *Documents, II, 1939–40*, p. 93; see further, p. 85 above.
[2] *Documents, II, 1939–40*, p. 87.

The release explaining the circumstances of the negotiation states: "The Government of the United States announces its policy of maintenance of the *status quo* in the Western Hemisphere." [1]

(1) *The Secretary of State (Hull) to the Minister of Denmark (Kauffmann), April 7, 1941* [2]

DEPARTMENT OF STATE,
Washington, April 7, 1941.

SIR:

I have the honor to refer to the informal conversations which you have had with officers of the Department of State during which the concern of the Government of the United States was expressed over the effect of recent military developments, particularly affecting Greenland, upon the maintenance of the peace and security of the United States and the rest of the American Continent.

You are also aware of the interest of the Government of the United States in maintaining unimpaired the safety of Greenland and the sovereignty of Denmark over that island. My Government has continuously had in mind the desire expressed by the United Greenland Councils at their meeting at Godhavn on May 3, 1940 that the Government of the United States of America would continue to hold in mind the exposed position of the Danish flag in Greenland and of the native Greenland and Danish population of the island.

My Government has taken note of the unusual situation in which Greenland now finds itself. The Kingdom of Denmark is at present under occupation by a foreign army. The Government of the United States has condemned that invasion as a violation of Danish sovereign rights, and has repeatedly expressed its friendly concern and its most earnest hope for the complete and speedy liberation of Denmark. Although the Government of the United States fully recognizes the sovereignty of the Kingdom of Denmark over Greenland, it is unhappily clear that the Government in Denmark is not in a position to exercise sovereign power over Greenland so long as the present military occupation continues.

Greenland is within the area embraced by the Monroe Doctrine and by the Act of Havana, with which you are familiar, and its defense against attack by a non-American power is plainly essential to the preservation of the peace and security of the American continent, and of the traditional policies of this Government respecting the Western Hemisphere.

[1] Department of State, *Bulletin*, IV, p. 444.
[2] *Ibid.*, p. 447.

My Government has consequently proposed measures for the adequate defense of Greenland consistent with the obligations of the United States under the Act of Havana signed on July 30, 1940. In doing so it is animated by sentiments of the completest friendliness for Denmark, and believes that by taking these steps it is safeguarding the eventual re-establishment of the normal relationship between Greenland and the Kingdom of Denmark.

I have the honor to enclose a draft of the proposed agreement relating to the defense of Greenland, which I believe embodies the ideas agreed upon in the course of our various conversations.

Accept [etc.] CORDELL HULL

(2) *The Minister of Denmark (Kauffmann) to the Secretary of State (Hull), April 9, 1941* [1]

ROYAL DANISH LEGATION,
Washington, D. C., April 9, 1941.

SIR:

I have received your note of the seventh instant concerning the defense of Greenland together with a draft of a proposed agreement regarding the same subject.

It is with appreciation that I note your renewed assurance that, although the present circumstances prevent the Government in Denmark for the time being from exercising its powers in respect of Greenland, your Government fully recognizes the Sovereignty of the Kingdom of Denmark over the island. At the same time I wish to convey to you my feelings of gratitude for the expression of friendly concern of your Government and its earnest hope for the complete and speedy liberation of Denmark.

I share your view that the proposed agreement, arrived at after an open and friendly exchange of views, is, under the singularly unusual circumstances, the best measure to assure both Greenland's present safety and the future of the island under Danish Sovereignty.

Furthermore, I am of the opinion that the terms of the agreement protect, as far as possible, the interests of the native population of Greenland whose welfare traditionally has been the paramount aim of Denmark's policy in Greenland.

I, therefore, shall accept and sign the agreement as proposed, acting on behalf of His Majesty, the King of Denmark, in His capacity of Sovereign over Greenland, whose authorities in Greenland have concurred herein.

I avail [etc.] HENRIK KAUFFMANN

[1] Department of State, *Bulletin*, IV, p. 448.

(3) *Agreement Relating to the Defense of Greenland, Washington, April 9, 1941* [1]

Whereas:

ONE. After the invasion and occupation of Denmark on April 9, 1940 by foreign military forces, the United Greenland Councils at their meeting at Godhavn on May 3, 1940 adopted in the name of the people of Greenland a resolution [2] reiterating their oath of allegiance to King Christian X of Denmark and expressing the hope that, for as long as Greenland remains cut off from the mother country, the Government of the United States of America will continue to hold in mind the exposed position of the Danish flag in Greenland, of the native Greenland and Danish population, and of established public order; and

TWO. The Governments of all of the American Republics have agreed that the status of regions in the Western Hemisphere belonging to European powers is a subject of deep concern to the American Nations, and that the course of military events in Europe and the changes resulting from them may create the grave danger that European territorial possessions in America may be converted into strategic centers of aggression against nations of the American Continent; and

THREE. Defense of Greenland against attack by a non-American power is essential to the preservation of the peace and security of the American Continent and is a subject of vital concern to the United States of America and also to the Kingdom of Denmark; and

FOUR. Although the sovereignty of Denmark over Greenland is fully recognized, the present circumstances for the time being prevent the Government in Denmark from exercising its powers in respect of Greenland.

Therefore,

The undersigned, to wit: CORDELL HULL, Secretary of State of the United States of America, acting on behalf of the Government of the United States of America, and HENRIK DE KAUFFMANN, Envoy Extraordinary and Minister Plenipotentiary of His Majesty the King of Denmark at Washington, acting on behalf of His Majesty the King of Denmark in His capacity as sovereign of Greenland, whose authorities in Greenland have concurred herein, have agreed as follows:

ARTICLE I. The Government of the United States of America reiterates its recognition of and respect for the sovereignty of the Kingdom

---

[1] Department of State, *Bulletin,* IV, p. 445; Executive Agreement Series 204, Department of State Publication No. 1602.

[2] See p. 235.

of Denmark over Greenland. Recognizing that as a result of the present European war there is danger that Greenland may be converted into a point of aggression against nations of the American Continent, the Government of the United States of America, having in mind its obligations under the Act of Havana signed on July 30, 1940, accepts the responsibility of assisting Greenland in the maintenance of its present status.

ARTICLE II. It is agreed that the Government of the United States of America shall have the right to construct, maintain and operate such landing fields, seaplane facilities and radio and meteorological installations as may be necessary for the accomplishment of the purposes set forth in Article I.

ARTICLE III. The grants of the rights specified in Article II shall also include the right to improve and deepen harbors and anchorages and the approaches thereto, to install aids to navigation by air and by water, and to construct roads, communication services, fortifications, repair and storage facilities, and housing for personnel, and generally, the right to do any and all things necessary to insure the efficient operation, maintenance and protection of such defense facilities as may be established.

ARTICLE IV. The landing fields, seaplane, harbor and other defense facilities that may be constructed and operated by the Government of the United States of America under Articles II and III will be made available to the airplanes and vessels of all the American Nations for purposes connected with the common defense of the Western Hemisphere.

ARTICLE V. It is agreed that the Government of the United States of America shall have the right to lease for such period of time as this Agreement may be in force such areas of land and water as may be necessary for the construction, operation and protection of the defense facilities specified in Articles II and III. In locating the aforesaid defense areas, the fullest consideration consistent with military necessity shall be given to the welfare, health and economic needs of the native population of Greenland. It is agreed, however, that since the paramount objective sought is the early attainment of an adequate defense establishment in Greenland, the utilization of any area deemed by the Government of the United States of America to be needed for this purpose shall not be delayed pending the reaching of an agreement upon the precise terms of a formal lease. A description of such areas, by metes and bounds, and a statement of the purpose for which they are needed shall in each case be communicated to the Danish authorities in Greenland as soon as practicable, and the negotiation of a formal lease shall be undertaken within a reasonable period of time thereafter.

ARTICLE VI. The Kingdom of Denmark retains sovereignty over the defense areas mentioned in the preceding articles. So long as this Agreement shall remain in force, the Government of the United States of America shall have exclusive jurisdiction over any such defense area in Greenland and over military and civilian personnel of the United States, and their families, as well as over all other persons within such areas except Danish citizens and native Greenlanders, it being understood, however, that the Government of the United States may turn over to the Danish authorities in Greenland for trial and punishment any person committing an offense within a defense area, if the Government of the United States shall decide not to exercise jurisdiction in such case. The Danish authorities in Greenland will take adequate measures to insure the prosecution and punishment in case of conviction of all Danish citizens, native Greenlanders, and other persons who may be turned over to them by the authorities of the United States, for offenses committed within the said defense areas.

ARTICLE VII. It is agreed that the Government of the United States of America shall have the right to establish and maintain postal facilities and commissary stores to be used solely by military and civilian personnel of the United States, and their families, maintained in Greenland in connection with the Greenland defense establishment. If requested by the Danish authorities in Greenland, arrangements will be made to enable persons other than those mentioned to purchase necessary supplies at such commissary stores as may be established.

ARTICLE VIII. All materials, supplies and equipment for the construction, use and operation of the defense establishment and for the personal needs of military and civilian personnel of the United States, and their families, shall be permitted entry into Greenland free of customs duties, excise taxes, or other charges, and the said personnel, and their families, shall also be exempt from all forms of taxation, assessments or other levies by the Danish authorities in Greenland.

ARTICLE IX. The Government of the United States of America will respect all legitimate interests in Greenland as well as all the laws, regulations and customs pertaining to the native population and the internal administration of Greenland. In exercising the rights derived from this Agreement the Government of the United States will give sympathetic consideration to all representations made by the Danish authorities in Greenland with respect to the welfare of the inhabitants of Greenland.

ARTICLE X. This Agreement shall remain in force until it is agreed that the present dangers to the peace and security of the American Continent have passed. At that time the modification or termination of the Agreement will be the subject of consultation between the Government of the United States of America and the Government of Denmark. After due consultation has taken place, each party shall have the right to give the other party notice of its intention to terminate the Agreement, and it is hereby agreed, that at the expiration of twelve months after such notice shall have been received by either party from the other this Agreement shall cease to be in force.

Signed at Washington in duplicate, in the English and Danish languages, both texts having equal force, this 9th day of April, nineteen hundred and forty-one.

[SEAL]   CORDELL HULL
           Secretary of State of the United States of America
[SEAL]   HENRIK KAUFFMANN
           *Envoy Extraordinary and Minister Plenipotentiary of
           His Majesty the King of Denmark at Washington*

(a) Address of the Greenland Provincial Councils to the President of the United States, Godhavn, May 3, 1940 [1]

To THE PRESIDENT OF THE UNITED STATES:

The people of Greenland have with the deepest sorrow witnessed the use of force that has been exerted against Greenland's mother country, Denmark. With anxiety we also see Denmark cut off from exercising the administration which for over two hundred years now it has exercised over the people of Greenland. We hope that it will not be long until the day when peace and justice are restored again and a free Denmark can continue such administration.

Under these circumstances, when it is necessary for the responsible Greenland authorities to seek to maintain in new ways the country's communications with the outside world, which are necessary to life, we have learned with great joy of the sympathy that has been expressed officially and unofficially by the Government of the United States and the American people, most recently by the appointment of a Consul to Greenland and the sending of a Coast Guard ship. It is our hope that the Government of the United States in future also, as long as lines of communication with our mother country are cut, will pay heed to the exposed status of the Danish flag in Greenland, the Greenland and Danish population here in the country and the prevailing administration at the present time, and that the Government in consideration of Greenland's isolated situation will for the time being provide means for furnishing the country with supplies and for marketing its products.

After giving an inviolable oath of loyalty to our lawful King, Christian X of Denmark, we wish at this hour to present to the President of the United States

[1] Unofficial translation from "De Forenede grønlanske Landsraads Forhandlinger 1940" (Minutes of the United Provincial Councils of Greenland for 1940) printed in the publication *Nalunaerutit*, 1940. Translation supplied by the Department of State, Division of Research and Publications.

the deep felt thanks of the people of Greenland for the sympathy for our cause and respect for our freedom, of which the great American nation has given us proof in these dark days.

B. Continued Recognition of the Minister of Denmark

The fundamental assumption in diplomatic intercourse is that a government is a completely free agent and that ambassadors and ministers accredited by it to other governments, and received by them, faithfully represent the wishes and policy of their own government. If conditions of fact are contrary to that assumption, the customary credence given both to governments and their representatives is affected. The United States took cognizance of the existing facts in concluding the Agreement relating to the Defense of Greenland, on April 9, 1941 with the Danish Minister, who acted in behalf of the normal interests of Denmark.

(1) *Statement of the Department of State, April 14, 1941* [1]

The Danish Minister, Mr. Henrik de Kauffmann, on April 14 informed the Secretary of State that he had received a telegram from the Foreign Office in Copenhagen recalling him as Envoy Extraordinary and Minister Plenipotentiary of the Kingdom of Denmark accredited to the Government of the United States, and that his action and authority in signing as the official representative of his Government the agreement relating to Greenland had been disclaimed by the purported official authorities in Copenhagen.

On August 26, 1939, the President received Mr. de Kauffmann's letters of credence as Danish Minister to the United States, and he has since been recognized in that capacity as the official representative of the Kingdom of Denmark.

On April 9, 1940, Denmark was invaded by the German army. Since that date an army of occupation, understood to total 200,000 German troops, has remained in subjugation of that country, and no act of the Danish Government since that time has been taken or can be taken save with the consent of the occupying power or as a result of its dictation.

In view of the foregoing, the Government of the United States has consistently held since April 9, 1940, and now holds, that the Government of Denmark can only be regarded as a government which is patently acting under duress and which is in no sense a free agent.

The agreement recently entered into by the Secretary of State and by the Danish Minister was entered into by this Government, as made clear at that time, because of the desire of the United States in this time of world emergency to insure the security and integrity of Greenland

[1] Department of State, *Bulletin*, IV, p. 469.

as a part of the Western Hemisphere, and at the same time to assist the local authorities of Greenland in preserving intact the territory of that Danish colony so that once the present world emergency has passed, the Government of Denmark might once more be enabled to exercise fully its sovereign powers over that territory.

The Government of the United States feels confident that the Danish Government and people will unquestionably recognize that the measures undertaken by this Government have been taken in their interest and with full recognition of the sovereignty of Denmark over Greenland, as well as with the hope and belief that the time is not far distant when that sovereignty can once more be freely exercised by a free and independent Danish Government.

The Danish Minister has informed the Secretary of State that he regards the orders of recall issued to him by the authorities in Copenhagen as issued under duress and that he consequently believes it his duty to disregard such orders.

The Secretary of State by direction of the President has informed the Danish Minister that because of the reasons above set forth, this Government will continue to recognize him as the duly authorized Minister of Denmark in Washington.

(2) *The Minister of Denmark (Kauffmann) to the Secretary of State (Hull), April 13, 1941* [1]

APRIL 13, 1941.

SIR:

Point four in the preamble to the agreement relating to the defense of Greenland signed by you and by me on the ninth instant reads:

Although the sovereignty of Denmark over Greenland is fully recognized, the present circumstances for the time being prevent the Government in Denmark from exercising its powers in respect of Greenland . . .

With this situation in mind and in accordance with our understanding I informed the Government in Denmark of the agreement only when it was made public at noon on April 10.

I did this in a telegraphic message to the Foreign Office in Copenhagen that was delivered after some delay on April 11.

I indicated that I had signed the agreement

. . . acting on behalf of His Majesty the King of Denmark in His capacity as sovereign of Greenland, whose authorities in Greenland have concurred herein, . . .

[1] Department of State, *Bulletin*, IV, p. 470.

and I explained the reasons for my action, adding

Under the circumstances, there was, to me, no doubt but that I must, in the interests of Denmark and Greenland, take this unusual step. The Government in Denmark will not, as long as Denmark is occupied, be able to obtain full information as to the background and necessity for this action. I, therefore, request that judgment of my decision be withheld until Denmark again is free, and the Danish Government and public can come to know the situation that made the step necessary. I earnestly beg His Majesty the King and the Danish Government to be assured that I have acted in the way which I felt to be right, after careful consideration and according to my best belief and the dictates of my conscience, fulfilling my allegiance to His Majesty the King.

I thereupon received from the Foreign Office in Copenhagen at 4 : 30 P.M. Saturday, April 12, 1941, a telegram, the English translation of which reads as follows:

The Government strongly disapproves the fact that you, without authorization from here, and contrary to the constitution, have concluded an agreement with the Government of the United States regarding the defense of Greenland. You are, therefore, by Royal Decree of April 12, 1941 recalled from your post as Denmark's Minister to Washington. The Legation will temporarily be in charge of Mr. Blechingberg, Counselor of Legation, as Chargé d'Affaires. You are requested immediately to notify the President of the above, and to add that letters of recall will be forwarded later. You are requested to return at once to Copenhagen. Acknowledge receipt by telegram.

From press reports I have furthermore learned that the Government in Denmark yesterday also declared the agreement of April 9, 1941 relating to the defense of Greenland to be considered as void, but this Legation has hitherto received no official communication from Copenhagen to that effect.

On April 10, 1940, the day after the occupation of Denmark by German military forces, I issued a public statement declaring, that I would work for one thing, the reestablishment of a free and independent Denmark. Since that time as before my conduct has been dictated solely by what I have believed to be to the true interest of my King and my country. My work would have been impossible without the sympathetic understanding and cooperative attitude of the American Government for which I am deeply grateful.

My conduct in the situation that has arisen now will be dictated by the same convictions. I believe the action taken in Copenhagen with regard to my recall and in respect to the agreement of the 9th instant to have been taken under duress. Consequently I consider it to be invalid both from the point of view of Danish and of generally recognized common law.

I believe it to be my duty towards my King and my country to carry on the work that was entrusted to me when I was appointed Danish Minister to Washington by a free Danish Government and to let myself be guided by the same principles as hitherto. This attitude of mine has the full support of all the other members of the Danish Foreign service stationed in the United States.

I have the honor, Mr. Secretary, to ask you please to bring this to the knowledge of the President.

The earnest hope for a speedy liberation of Denmark, expressed by President Roosevelt when the agreement relating to the defense of Greenland was made public three days ago will have brought encouragement to all Danes. I beg leave to ask you, Sir, to convey to the President the gratitude of my countrymen.

I avail [etc.] HENRIK KAUFFMANN

(3) *The Secretary of State (Hull) to the Minister of Denmark (Kauffmann), April 14, 1941* [1]

APRIL 14, 1941.

SIR:

Acknowledgment is made of your note of April 13, 1941 advising that the Government in Denmark purports to have recalled you from your post as Minister of Denmark. Cognizance has likewise been taken of your statement that you consider this action to have been taken under duress and to be invalid both from the point of view of Danish and of generally recognized common law, in view of the existing occupation of Denmark by German military forces.

My Government considers it to be the fact that the Government in Denmark in this respect is acting under duress, and in consequence I have the honor to advise that it continues to recognize you as the duly authorized Minister of Denmark in Washington. It renews its hope for the speedy liberation of Denmark.

Accept [etc.] CORDELL HULL

[1] Department of State, *Bulletin*, IV, p. 471.

CHAPTER III

THE FAR EAST

1. UNITED STATES–CHINESE RELATIONS

[See Chapter I for other references to China in the speeches of President Roosevelt.]

Assistance from the United States to China against Japanese aggression, definite but restrained since 1937, became more positive with the passage of the "Export Control Act" on July 2, 1940 [1] and since the President's Annual Message of January 6, 1941 the conflict in Asia has been specifically included in the national determination to compass the defeat of alleged "new orders" which the President had branded as counterfeit on November 11, 1940. China is receiving increasing aid which the "arsenal of democracy" is supplying to those countries which resist the aggressors.

Aid to China being within the national defense policy of the United States, most of the relations of the two countries fall within the bounds of the active American program. Special phases of Chinese-American relations between the two countries are recorded here.

A. Extraterritoriality

(1) *Statement of the Acting Secretary of State* (*Welles*), *July 19, 1940* [2]

The most recent statement of this Government on this subject is contained in a note presented on December 31, 1938,[3] to the Japanese Government, which mentions *inter alia* the progress made toward the relinquishment of certain rights of a special character which the United States together with other countries has long possessed in China. In 1931 discussions of the subject between China and each of several other countries, including the United States, were suspended because of the occurrence of the Mukden incident and subsequent disrupting developments in 1932 and 1935 in the relations between China and Japan. In 1937 this Government was giving renewed favorable consideration to the question when there broke out the current Sino-Japanese hostilities,

[1] Sec. 6 of Public No. 703, 76th Cong., 54 Stat. 714; quoted in Proclamation No. 2413, p. 474.

[2] Department of State, *Bulletin*, III, p. 36. See also p. 248.

[3] *Documents, I, 1938–39*, p. 246.

as a result of which the usual processes of government in large areas of China were widely disrupted.

It has been this Government's traditional and declared policy and desire to move rapidly by process of orderly negotiation and agreement with the Chinese Government, whenever conditions warrant, toward the relinquishment of extraterritorial rights and of all other so-called "special rights" possessed by this country as by other countries in China by virtue of international agreements. That policy remains unchanged.

(a) Statement of the Prime Minister (Churchill) to the House of Commons, July 18, 1940 on the Anglo-Japanese Agreement Prohibiting the Shipment of Arms to China through Hong Kong and Burma [1]

[Excerpt]

We wish for no quarrel with any nation of the Far East. We desire to see China's status and integrity preserved, and as indicated in our note of January 14, 1939,[2] we are ready to negotiate with the Chinese Government after the conclusion of peace for the abolition of extraterritorial rights, the rendition of concessions and the revision of treaties on a basis of reciprocity and equality.

B. Loans and Credits to the Chinese Government

[For record of previous credits since 1938 in the total amount of $70,000,000 see *Documents I, 1938–39*, p. 271; *II, 1939–40*, p. 554.]

(1) Statement of the President (Roosevelt), November 30, 1940 [3]

The discussions between the American and the Chinese authorities in the field of financial cooperation have progressed. There is contemplated a credit to the Chinese Government of $100,000,000. Of this, a credit for general purposes to the amount of $50,000,000 has been decided upon by this Government. Arrangements for early allocation of the balance, namely, $50,000,000, for purposes of monetary protection and management as between American and Chinese currencies are now in process in consultation with the appropriate Committees of the Congress.

The Secretary of the Treasury will appear Monday forenoon before a joint session of the Senate Committee on Banking and Currency and

---

[1] *New York Times*, July 19, 1940.
[2] *Documents, I, 1938–39*, p. 252.
[3] Department of State, *Bulletin*, III, p. 521.

the House Committee on Coinage, Weights and Measures.[1] At this time, he will bring to their attention the proposed extension of a $50,000,000 stabilization arrangement with the Central Bank of China.

(a) The Federal Loan Administrator (Jones) to the President (Roosevelt), November 30, 1940 [2]

DEAR MR. PRESIDENT:

In connection with the purchase of critical and strategic materials in our national defense program, the Metals Reserve Company,[3] a subsidiary of the RFC, is arranging for additional purchase of wolframite, antimony and tin from the National Resources Commission of China to the value of $60,000,000, to be delivered during the next few years at prices commensurate with market conditions as the metals are delivered.

To assist China in meeting her present financial problems, the Export-Import Bank has agreed to lend the Government of China an additional $50,000,000, the loans to be guaranteed by the Central Bank of China and retired through deliveries in this country of the metals covered by the above referred to contracts.

It is contemplated that disbursements on the loan will be made in cooperation with a representative of the Secretary of the Treasury in connection with further assistance to China by the Treasury of a like amount, thus providing China with additional credits in this country at this time of $100,000,000.

You will be interested to know that China is up to her schedule in deliveries of wood oil and tin to the United States through which method she is making payments on previous loans made against her commitment to sell us these essential materials.

Sincerely yours,

JESSE H. JONES

(2) Grant by the Government of the United Kingdom. Announcement of December 10, 1940 [4]

The United States Government announced on November 30 their intention to extend to the Government of China large credits for strengthening the United States dollar resources available to the Chinese monetary authorities and for other purposes.

His Majesty's Government for their part, having regard to the importance of their financial and economic relations with China, have now decided to grant further financial assistance to that country.

[1] The Committees unanimously approved (New York Times, December 3, 1940). They subsequently reported out H. R. 4646, which was enacted as Public Law 142, 77th Cong., approved June 30, 1941, and which extended the life of the stabilization fund to June 30, 1943.

[2] Department of State, Bulletin, III, p. 522.   [3] See p. 738.

[4] Parliamentary Debates, House of Commons, 5th series, 367, col. 796. The announcement was made December 10, 1940 by the Under Secretary of State for Foreign Affairs in the House of Commons and by the Secretary of State for Foreign Affairs in the House of Lords.

It is, of course, necessary for his Majesty's Government to conserve their gold and dollar assets for the essential war needs of the sterling area, and they cannot offer to China United States dollars or sterling which is convertible into United States dollars. Provided, however, that suitable arrangements can be made to ensure that sterling held in China is available only for use in the sterling area, his Majesty's Government are prepared in principle to make an advance of £5,000,000 to the Chinese stabilization fund and, with the concurrence of the Dominion Governments concerned, to grant credits which will be available for purchases in any part of the sterling area within a maximum of a further £5,000,000.

This decision has been communicated to the Chinese Government, with a request that they will make arrangements for the early negotiation of the preliminary technical agreement on which the possibility of these further sterling credits depends.

(3) Joint Statement of the Secretary of the Treasury (Morgenthau) and the President of the Central Bank of China (Soong), April 25, 1941 [1]

Another important step has been taken in the field of monetary cooperation between the United States and China by the signing of a stabilization agreement involving the purchase of Chinese yuan by the United States stabilization fund to the amount of United States $50,000,000. The agreement provides, under conditions acceptable to both parties, for the establishment by China of a United States dollar-Chinese yuan stabilization fund. Included in the fund's resources will be the dollars acquired from the United States through the purchase of Chinese yuan and a further sum of 20,000,000 United States dollars contributed by Chinese Government banks.

This is a cooperative agreement between friendly nations that are working together in many ways to preserve the basic freedoms. Apart from the obvious purposes of stabilizing the relationship between the currencies concerned, it will be an important factor in fostering the welfare of the participating countries.

China has also entered into an agreement with the British Treasury under which five million pounds sterling are provided for currency stabilization in addition to the existing Sino-British stabilization fund which was set up in 1939. This agreement closely parallels the agreement between the United States and China.

[1] *New York Times*, April 26, 1941, p. 7.

These stabilization funds will be managed by a five-man board which China is creating. The Board will consist of three Chinese, an American appointed by China on the recommendation of the Secretary of the Treasury, and a British national appointed on the recommendation of the British Treasury.

—

At the invitation of the Chinese Government, Lauchlin Currie,[1] Administrative Assistant to the President, is taking a short leave of absence for the purpose of visiting Chungking. He expects to return about the first of March. He will be accompanied by Emile Despres, Senior Economist in the Division of Research and Statistics of the Board of Governors of the Federal Reserve System. The purpose of their visit is to secure first-hand information on the general economic situation in China and to consult with the Chinese Government on matters pertaining to this situation. Mr. Currie bears personal greetings from the President to Generalissimo Chiang Kai-shek.

(4) *Statement of the British Embassy, Washington, April 26, 1941* [2]

It will be remembered that in 1939 a fund was set up, of which £5,000,000 was guaranteed by His Majesty's Treasury under the China (currency stabilization) Act, 1939, in order to check undue fluctuation in the sterling value of the Chinese yuan, and that in December last His Majesty's Government decided, in addition, to make available a credit of £5,000,000 to the Chinese Government for the same purpose.

Negotiations have been proceeding on the technical measures to carry this offer into effect. These negotiations have resulted in the conclusion of an agreement which has been signed in Washington today by Sir Frederick Phillips on behalf of His Majesty's Treasury and by His Excellency T. V. Soong, on behalf of the Government of China. This constitutes a further important step in the field of monetary cooperation between the United Kingdom and China and symbolizes the friendly relations between the two countries.

This agreement is closely parallel to the agreement which, as announced by the Secretary of the United States Treasury and His Excellency T. V. Soong, has also been signed today between the United States and China and which involves the establishment by China of a United States dollar-Chinese yuan stabilization fund and the purchase of Chinese yuan by the United States to the amount of fifty million United States dollars.

[1] Statement released by the White House, January 23, 1941. Department of State, *Bulletin*, IV, p. 110. Upon his return from his special mission no report was made public.

[2] *New York Times*, April 26, 1941, p. 7.

These stabilization funds will be managed by the stabilization board which is being set up by the Chinese Government. The board will consist of five members, three of whom will be Chinese, one American appointed by China on the recommendation of the Secretary of the United States Treasury and one British appointed upon the recommendation of His Majesty's Treasury.

———

A. Manuel Fox, member of the United States Tariff Commission, was recommended by the Secretary of the Treasury as the American member of the Board, with William A. Taylor, Treasury Division of Economic Research, as alternate. Cyril Rogers, who went to China with the Leith-Ross mission in 1935, was nominated as the British member. (Treasury Department, Press Service No. 24-92; *The Times* (London), May 1, 1941, p. 8.)

———

The following loans and credits have been extended to China in addition to the American and United Kingdom credits noted above:[1]

United States
$25,000,000, December 1938, extended by the Export-Import Bank. China to buy non-military supplies and to pay in wood oil.
$20,000,000, March 1939, extended by the Export-Import Bank. China to buy non-military supplies and to pay in tin.
$25,000,000, September 1940, extended by the Export-Import Bank for "foreign exchange needs," to be liquidated through the sale of tungsten.
In addition to these, China received a commercial credit of $12,800,000 and an aviation credit of $15,000,000 in March 1939.

United Kingdom
£5,000,000, March 1939, for the purpose of currency stabilization, guaranteed by the British Treasury.
£3,000,000, June 1939, commercial credit advanced by the British Export Credits Guarantee Department.
£10,000,000, reported to have been negotiated for the purpose of building the Burma Railway (now under construction).

Soviet
The Soviet Union by its barter agreements sends general supplies to China and receives tea and other agricultural products.
250,000,000 rubles, October 1938
250,000,000 rubles, February 1939
750,000,000 rubles, August 1939
250,000,000 rubles, December 1940

European
400,000,000 francs, September 1937, advanced by France for the purpose of monetary protection as between French and Chinese currencies.
150,000,000 francs, August 1938, advanced by France for the building of the Annam-Chennankwan Railway (between French Indo-China and Kwangsi).

[1] Trans-Pacific News Service, *Contemporary China*, No. 1, May 25, 1941.

480,000,000 francs, December 1938, extended by France for the building of
the Hsufu-Kunming Railway (between Szechuan and Yunnan).

£10,000,000, 1937, extended by Czechoslovakia for general supplies.

£20,000,000, March 1939, purchase credit extended by Belgium.

C. Aid under the Lend-Lease Act

(1) Message of Generalissimo Chiang Kai-shek to the President (Roosevelt), March 18, 1941

In his address to the White House Correspondents Association on March 15,
1941,[1] President Roosevelt said: "China likewise expresses the magnificent will
of millions of plain people to resist the dismemberment of their Nation. China,
through the Generalissimo Chiang Kai-shek, asks our help. America has said
that China shall have our help."

Three days later Generalissimo Chiang Kai-shek sent a message to President
Roosevelt, the text of which follows:[2]

The people of China, whether engaged in fighting the aggressor or
toiling in the fields and workshops in the rear in support of the defenders,
will be immeasurably heartened by your impressive reaffirmation of
the will of the American people to assist them in their struggle for
freedom from foreign domination, and in the resumption of their march
towards democracy and social justice for all.

D. Visit of Chinese Minister for Foreign Affairs

The Chinese Minister for Foreign Affairs designate, Quo Tai-chi, arrived in
New York April 23 from London, where he had been the Ambassador of his
country for several years. Before proceeding to Chungking to assume office he
made several public appearances in the United States and consulted with United
States authorities.

(1) The Appointed Chinese Minister for Foreign Affairs (Quo Tai-chi) to the Secretary of State (Hull), May 26, 1941 [3]

SAN FRANCISCO, *May 26, 1941.*

MY DEAR MR. SECRETARY:

I am shortly to depart from the United States for China and wish
to send you a word of farewell and of thanks for the cordial hospitality
extended to me during my brief stay in Washington.

[1] See p. 40.

[2] Department of State, *Bulletin*, IV, p. 335.

[3] *Ibid.*, p. 661.

It was very gratifying to me to receive in person during our conversations the extended account which you were so good as to give me of the attitude and policy of the United States in regard to problems, both economic and political, which are of concern to the whole world, and especially to your Government and mine, in this unhappy period of disturbance, violence and distress.

With the general principles of the foreign policy of the United States, which were set forth in your public statement of July 16, 1937,[1] I have long been familiar. I could, therefore, readily appreciate the importance which, as you indicated in our conversations, your Government attaches to the principles of world order under law and of equality of treatment among nations, and to general recognition of the need for freer international trade and for broader cultural exchange. My Government shares the desire and the hope of your Government that there may be brought about by processes of agreement conditions in world affairs in which those principles will be universally accepted and applied.

You will recall that on August 12, 1937,[2] there was sent to you a communication from my Government endorsing the principles, enumerated in your statement of July 16, 1937, and stating that China's policy was therefore in full harmony with the views of the Government of the United States. Such was the position of China then, and such is its position now.

My country has for nearly four years been fighting in self-defense. During this period the Government and people of the United States have shown great friendship and sympathy for the Government and people of China. The Chinese Government and people deeply appreciate the attitude, the policy, and the action of the Government of the United States. We feel, moreover, that our attitude, objectives and policies are constantly evolving along lines more and more completely in harmony with those of the United States.

My people are traditionally believers in nondiscrimination in international commercial relations and in the broad principles of cooperation and fair-dealing among nations which are implicit in the faithful observance of international agreements and the adjustment of problems in international relations by processes of peaceful negotiation and agreement freely arrived at. We believe in and subscribe to the principle of equality of commercial opportunity and nondiscriminatory treatment. Our Government gave clear indication of this nearly a century ago when there were being negotiated the first treaties between China and Occidental countries.

[1] *Documents, I, 1938–39*, p. 3.   [2] *Ibid.*, p. 151.

Upon restoration of peace, the Chinese Government desires and expects to seek and to effect the fullest application of those principles in its own economy and in its political and economic relations with other countries.

With many pleasant recollections of my visit to Washington, and with my kindest personal regards, I am, my dear Mr. Secretary,

Yours sincerely,

QUO TAI-CHI

(2) *The Secretary of State (Hull) to the Appointed Chinese Minister for Foreign Affairs (Quo Tai-chi), May 31, 1941* [1]

DEPARTMENT OF STATE,
Washington, May 31, 1941.

MY DEAR MR. MINISTER:

I acknowledge the receipt of and thank you for your letter of May 26, 1941 in regard to your visit to Washington and to our conversations during your short sojourn here.

We greatly enjoyed your visit.

It is very gratifying to receive in your letter reaffirmation of the endorsement by the Chinese Government and people of the general and fundamental principles which this Government is convinced constitute the only practical foundation for an international order wherein independent nations may cooperate freely with each other to their mutual benefit.

As you know, the program in which the Government and people of the United States put their trust is based upon and revolves about the principle of equality of treatment among nations. This principle comprehends equality in international relations in a juridical sense, nondiscrimination and equality of opportunity in commercial relations, and reciprocal interchange in the field of cultural developments. Implicit in this principle is respect by each nation for the rights of other nations, performance by each nation of established obligations, alteration of agreements between nations by processes not of force but of orderly and free negotiation, and fair dealing in international economic relations essential to peaceful development of national life and mutually profitable growth of international trade. One of the purposes of this program is to effect the removal of economic and other maladjustments which tend to lead to political conflicts.

As you are also aware, the Government and people of the United States have long had a profound interest in the welfare and progress of China

[1] Department of State, *Bulletin*, IV, p. 662.

It goes without saying that the Government of the United States, in continuation of steps already taken toward meeting China's aspirations for readjustment of anomalies in its international relations, expects when conditions of peace again prevail to move rapidly, by processes of orderly negotiation and agreement with the Chinese Government, toward relinquishment of the last of certain rights of a special character which this country, together with other countries, has long possessed in China by virtue of agreements providing for extraterritorial jurisdiction and related practices.

This Government welcomes and encourages every advance made by lawful and orderly processes by any country toward conditions of peace, security, stability, justice and general welfare. The assurances given in Your Excellency's letter under acknowledgment of China's support of the principle of equality of treatment and nondiscrimination in economic relations should have wholesome effect both during the present period of world conflict and when hostilities shall have ceased.

The Government of the United States is dedicated to support of the principles in which the people of this country believe. Without reservation, we are confident that the cause to which we are committed along with China and other countries — the cause of national security, of fair dealing among nations and of peace with justice — will prevail.

With kindest regards and best wishes, I am, my dear Mr. Minister,

Sincerely yours,

CORDELL HULL

2. EVOLUTION OF JAPANESE POLICY

Japan in 1940 attained the 2600th anniversary of the Imperial house, according to the accepted legend. The country's affairs were continuously in a state of emergency that impelled it to experiment in new directions both in internal and external policy. The military hierarchy dominated the conduct of public affairs. In August 1940 the Minister for Foreign Affairs replaced some 40 experienced members of the foreign service with persons more amenable to the prevailing tone of the government.

The regime of Prince Fumimaro Konoe, which began on July 22, 1940, undertook a "renovation of the national political structure" through a cabinet controlled by the Premier, the War, Navy and Foreign Ministers. It set out internally to abolish political parties, which were dissolved in August 1940, on the ground that they were "incompatible with our national polity" since they were "founded upon liberty, democracy or socialism." [1] Internally the drain on the economy created a social strain that portended exhaustion and an effort was futilely made to create a new structure of Yamato society. A shadowy scheme was launched for an Imperial Rule Assistance Association (Taisei Yokusan Kai) which received a subsidy of 1,580,000 yen for the period October 1940 to March 1941 and of 8,000,000 yen for the fiscal year 1941–42. Other

[1] *Tokyo Gazette*, IV, p. 45.

proposals for a body to support the government and to approve its decisions in lieu of the Diet multiplied after the "final reorganization" of the Association in April 1941.[1]

Japan's hope of advantageously bringing the "China Affair" to an end in order to release its energies for further expansion was defeated by increasingly effective Chinese resistance, and lack of progress in getting Chinese support for the Wang Ching-wei regime, which became bound to the Japanese program by the arrangements of November 30, 1940, and was recognized July 1, 1941 by Japan's partners in the Axis grouping. The determined stand of the Chinese Republic was supplemented by United States action to restrict Japanese supplies, to pronounce against new external moves of Japan and by increased and more open aid to China. Occupation of Chinese centers was curtailed, and bombing raids continued, but the Chinese saw to it that Japanese troops decreasingly occupied areas and were isolated at the points where they were.[2]

[1] *Japan Weekly Chronicle*, April 10, 1941, p. 431.

[2] After May 1940 the Japanese retired from various positions they had held in China, so that month represented the maximum extent of the occupation. The Japanese were in occupation, and occasionally control, of most of the maritime and riverain municipalities and had garrisons or guards in many areas where their control extended to the limit of a sentry's sight. In a large number of the administrative districts (*hsien* or counties) nominally occupied by the Japanese, the administration was by Chinese except in the area actually dominated physically by Japanese soldiers.

PROVINCES	NUMBERS OF HSIEN AND (MUNICIPALITIES) [a]		
	Total [b]	Free	Occupied
Suiyuan	17 (1)	2	15 (1)
Chahar	16*	3	13
Shantung	109 (2)	5	104 (2)
Hopei	132 (2)	5	127 (2)
Kiangsu	64 (3)	7	57 (3)
Shansi	105	18	87
Anhwei	62	36	26
Hupeh	72 (2)	42	30 (2)
Fukien	63 (1)	60	3 (1)
Chekiang	77 (1)	60	17 (1)
Kiangsi	84 (1)	73	11 (1)
Hunan	76 (1)	74 (1)	2
Kwangtung	99 (2)	75	24 (2)
Honan	111	76	35
Kwangsi	99	98	1
Total	1,186 (16)	634 (1)	552 (15)
Grand Total for China [c]	1,973 (23)	1,421 (8)	552 (15)

Percentage of occupied to total number of *hsien* 28%.

NOTE: [a] Figures in parentheses represent municipalities.
   [b] *Hsien* and municipalities in the Four Eastern Provinces (Manchuria) are not listed.   [c] Excluding Tibet and Mongolia.
   * Excluding Mongolian banners.

China Information Committee, *News Release*, July 29, 1940, p. 579.

The cabinet and the military hierarchy concentrated externally upon how to forward the "co-prosperity sphere of Greater East Asia" without running foul of the United States. Japan, said the Premier in a broadcast of July 23, 1940, "in its foreign relations should walk in a way of its own." Its subsequent activities took two directions, safe moves of word or action in the Far East and political association for such advantage as might appear. The character and timing of both were influenced by actual or presumed manifestations of the United States and the United Kingdom. The new spokesman of the Cabinet Information Board was as free with comment concerning and directed at the United States as his predecessor of the Foreign Office. Scarcely a week passed without their contribution to the news dispatches. This color to the news from Japan was based upon whatever was at hand. In the United States the press conferences of the President and Secretary of State are informal, verbal exchanges with correspondents providing them with tips, interpretations, background and "trial balloons"; anything that either official wishes to make formal is given out textually. The Japanese spokesman talked of that informal kind of outgiving as frequently as of official statements and action.

Japan was emboldened to undertake a southward movement of expansion, seeing opportunity in the collapse of France and the disruption of the Netherlands and new possibilities in its partnership with Germany and Italy under the treaty of September 27, 1940. The Japanese Government's pride in being a party to this treaty was shown by the issuance of an Imperial Rescript, which to the Japanese mind makes an irrevocable act. The alignment stiffened the attitude of the United States and the United Kingdom. The Burma road was reopened; the Netherlands East Indies maintained its independent negotiating position; Indo-China remained under French control, but less able itself to resist Japanese ambitions; Thailand gained by Japanese mediation and fell to some extent into step with the Nipponese program.

The Minister for Foreign Affairs, Yosuke Matsuoka, an open-spoken official, visited the Axis partners in March and April 1941 and left Europe with a "Neutrality Pact" concluded with the Soviet Union on April 13. His great expectations from that accomplishment were but slightly reflected among the Japanese people, whose economic condition and morale had steadily deteriorated for months and whose political confusion was an element of Imperial concern. The expectations were dissipated by the German attack on the Soviet Union beginning June 22, 1941. The United States became less and less a source of supply for Japan, and the supplies obtained required exchange and thus severely aggravated the financial stability of the country. The Government which assumed office July 22, 1940 resigned its task on July 16, 1941 without having realized the "lofty spirit of *Hakkō Itiu*" (the world as one family).

Japanese efforts in various directions responded to the idea expressed by the Minister for Foreign Affairs (Matsuoka) to the Budget Committee of the Diet February 18, 1941:[1] "Ultimately diplomacy is force, and it goes without saying that diplomacy not backed by strength can accomplish nothing." The United States repeatedly disapproved of Japanese attempts at negotiation with third Powers by ultimatum and at agreement under duress; it disregarded Japan's contentions of possessing superior rights in the Far East and of bilateral arrangements being justified *per se*.

[1] *The Times* (London), February 19, 1941, p. 3.

(1) *Japan and the Monroe Doctrine. Statement of the Spokesman of the Foreign Office, Tokyo, July 10, 1940* [1]

In his note of July 5, 1940 to the German Government [2] the Secretary of State (Hull) said that the Monroe Doctrine "contains within it not the slightest vestige of any implication, much less assumption, of hegemony on the part of the United States." It bore no resemblance to "policies which appear to be arising in other geographical areas of the world," alleged to be similar to it, which "would in reality seem to be only the pretext for the carrying out of conquest by the sword, of military occupation and of complete economic and political domination by certain powers of other free and independent peoples." Speaking for the President on July 6 his secretary (Early) made a statement to press correspondents suggesting the principle of the Monroe Doctrine as applicable to the settlement of territorial questions in Europe and Asia through consultation of the countries in the area concerned. The United States had no intention of interfering in territorial adjustments in Europe or Asia, Indo-China being given as an example. The "administrative or ultimate disposition" of American territories of conquered states should be settled by all of the American Republics, not by the United States alone. On July 8 the Secretary of State announced that his note of the 5th embodied the correct statement of United States foreign policy and that the President and he were agreed that the remarks of July 6 did not define policy.

Regardless of whether or not President Roosevelt's statement on the Monroe Doctrine constitutes a new definition and modification of that doctrine, the fact cannot be disputed that the attitude taken by the President and the Secretary of State of the United States on the question shows that the United States Government has converted the primarily passive and defensive character of the Monroe Doctrine to a positive one.

Hitherto the Monroe Doctrine has been applied to prevent the extension of the European system of Government to the Americas, as well as to forestall aggression of outside Powers on the Western Hemisphere. Now it is claimed that "the United States very sincerely believes and maintains the position that the administration or ultimate disposition of such islands and territorial possessions should be and is properly a question to be decided by and among all of the republics of the Western Hemisphere."

If this is the real attitude of the United States, it naturally coincides with the idea of regional structure which has recently been suggested by Mr. Arita, the Foreign Minister. [3] In fact, President Roosevelt declared that "the United States Government wants to see and thinks there should be application of a Monroe Doctrine in Europe and Asia, similar to the interpretation and application of those principles in this hemisphere."

[1] The Trans-Pacific, July 13, 1940, p. 8.
[2] See Documents, II, 1939-40, p. 91.
[3] Broadcast of June 29, 1940, Documents, II, 1939-40, p. 287.

Here we cannot help feeling that Mr. Hull discussed "the" Monroe Doctrine, while Mr. Roosevelt dwelt upon "a" Monroe Doctrine applicable to all geographical areas including the Americas. This we wish to take note of with special interest.

(2) Fundamental National Policies. Announcement of the Japanese Government, August 1, 1940 [1]

The world stands at a momentous, historic turning point, and it is about to witness the creation of new forms of government, economy, and culture, based upon the growth and development of sundry groups of nations. Japan, too, is confronted by the greatest trial she has ever experienced. In order to carry out fully at this juncture our national policy in keeping with the lofty spirit in which the nation was founded, it is a task of urgent necessity and importance that we should grasp the inevitable trends in the development of world history, expedite fundamental renovations in all phases of government, and strive for the perfection of the State structure for national defense. Accordingly, the general lines of the country's fundamental policies have been formulated as follows:

1. *Basic Policy*

The basic aim of Japan's national policy lies in the firm establishment of world peace in accordance with the lofty spirit of *Hakkō Itiu*,[2] in which the nation was founded, and in the construction, as the first step, of a new order in Greater East Asia, resting upon the solidarity of Japan, Manchoukuo and China.

Japan will, therefore, devote the total strength of the nation to the fulfilment of the above policy by setting up speedily an unshakable national structure and stand of her own adapted to meet the requirements of new developments both at home and abroad.

2. *National Defense and Foreign Policy*

The Government will strive, in view of the latest world and domestic developments, for the repletion of armaments adequate for the execution of national policies, armaments founded upon the State structure for national defense organized in such manner as to bring into full play the total strength of the nation.

Japan's foreign policy, which aims ultimately at the construction of a new order in Greater East Asia, will be directed, first of all, toward a complete settlement of the China Affair, and to the advancement of

---

[1] *Tokyo Gazette*, IV, p. 89.
[2] "The world as one family."

the national fortune by taking a farsighted view of the drastic changes in the international situation and by formulating both constructive and flexible measures to meet these changes.

3. *Renovation of Internal Structure*

What is urgently required in internal administration is the laying of the foundation for a State structure for national defense through a complete renovation of the domestic administration in general, for which purpose the Government expect the realization of the following points:

A. Renovation of education completely in harmony with the fundamental principles of national polity and the establishment of national morality which stresses, above all, service to the State and renounces all selfish and materialistic ideas.

B. Establishment of a powerful new political structure and a unified control of government affairs.

(*a*) Establishment of a new national structure, of which the keynote lies in service to the State through cooperation between Government and people, every man in accordance with his ability and within the sphere of his vocational activities.

(*b*) Renovation of the Diet as an organ for assisting the Throne, so as to adapt it to the new national structure.

(*c*) Fundamental renovation in the operation of administrative organs and the reformation of the bureaucracy aiming at the unity and efficiency of those organs.

C. Laying of the foundation of national defense economy based on the autonomous development of the economy of Japan, Manchoukuo and China [1] with Japan as the center.

(*a*) Establishment of a sphere of cooperative economies, with the Japan-Manchoukuo-China group as one of the units.

(*b*) Inauguration of a planned economy through the cooperation of Government and people, and especially the perfection of a unitary control system covering the production, distribution and consumption of important goods.

(*c*) Establishment of a financial program and reinforcement of control of finance and banking, directed toward the development of the nation's total economic strength.[2]

(*d*) Renovation of the foreign trade policy so as to adapt it to the new world situation.

[1] See the Joint Declaration of November 30, 1940, p. 287.

[2] See Department of Commerce. Bureau of Foreign and Domestic Commerce, *Economic Conditions in Japan during 1940 and early 1941* (International Reference Service, I, No. 33, June 1941). The total government bond issues outstanding June 30, 1941 amounted to 31,892,256,000 yen.

(*e*) Establishment of measures for self-sufficiency in respect of the people's daily necessities, especially in the principal foodstuffs.

(*f*) An epoch-making expansion of the vital industries — especially the heavy, chemical and machine industries.

(*g*) An epoch-making promotion of science and rationalization of production.

(*h*) Perfection and extension of the communication and transportation facilities so as to adapt them to the new developments at home and abroad.

(*i*) Establishment of land development plans aiming at the enhancement of the total national strength.

(*j*) Inauguration of permanent measures for the promotion of the stamina and physical strength of the nation, and particularly the fundamental measures for the security and development of agriculture and agricultural communities.

(*k*) Rectification of the inequality in individual sacrifices incident to the execution of national policies; full operation of various welfare measures, and renovation of the mode of living of the nation, and the maintenance of such standard of living as will enable the nation to lead a plain, solid and vigorous life and to surmount the national crisis by persevering truly through years of hardship.

(a) *"New Structure" of the Japanese State. Address of Premier Prince Konoe at First Session of the Preparatory Committee for the New National Structure, Tokyo, August 28, 1940* [1]

In the midst of a world upheaval of unprecedented magnitude Japan is today going forward with the unparalleled task of creating a new order in East Asia. If she is to bring the China Affair to a successful conclusion while adjusting herself to the international situation, and take a leading part in the establishment of a new world order, she must concentrate upon the accomplishment of this task the moral and material resources of the nation to the utmost degree so as to be in a position to take independently, swiftly and resolutely appropriate measures to meet whatever situation may arise. To this end Japan must perfect a highly organized national defense structure, the basis of which is a powerful internal structure. Consequently, there has arisen the pressing demand for the setting up of a new structure in politics, economy, education, culture and in all phases of the life of the State and of the people.

This demand is indeed the expression of the will of the nation, transcending Cabinet, faction or individual; nor is it of an ephemeral character for the carrying out of a specific policy, but rather of a lasting nature for rendering possible the energetic pursuance of any policy when the necessity arises. Whether or not Japan can firmly set up such a strong national structure will decide the rise or fall of the nation.

[1] *Tokyo Gazette*, IV, p. 133.

Among those matters which require to be considered in this new organization of the nation must be mentioned the harmonious cooperation between the High Command and the administrative branches of the Government, the consolidation of the mechanism of State and the heightening of efficiency, the institution of a new parliamentary structure for assisting the Throne. The Government, on their part, are exerting serious efforts toward the achievement of these ends; but of far greater importance is the firm establishment of that "national structure" which is to serve as their very foundation and by which the people are to fulfil effectively their duty of assisting the Throne. It is with this end in view that the present Preparatory Committee has been convened and that I request your deliberations and collaboration.

The aim of the new national structure is to unite all the forces of the State and people, welding into one living whole our hundred million fellowcountrymen and enabling them to fulfil in the highest degree their duty as subjects of the Throne. The realization of this purpose can only reside in the due performance by each of his appointed task. It is but natural when, as has been the case in the past, the majority of the people have no other opportunity of taking part in government than by casting a vote as the occasion arises once every three or four years, that the nation as a whole should find itself unable to take to heart the destiny of the country.

The organization of the nation is to be that in which the people serve the State in their everyday life, and must therefore embrace the economic and cultural spheres. There must be a solid nation-wide structure in which each component part is organized vertically and yet work in coordinated unity in a horizontal plane. It is because there does not exist such a structure, in which the people can effectively assist the Throne, that we see today a tendency toward conflict between those who govern and those who are governed; an absence on the part of the authorities who formulate the nation's policies of a true understanding of the people's real activities; and an indifference on the part of the people toward the formulation of State policies.

In view of this state of things, the essentials of the national structure are manifest: the people should be enabled to take a direct part from within in establishing the country's economic and cultural policies, which policies should embrace every sphere of national life to its very periphery. It is only under such conditions that the will and ideas of both those who govern and those who are governed can be fully appreciated by each other and that the entire strength of the nation can be concentrated on carrying out the national policies.

For the successful realization of this national structure a national movement is necessary. Such a movement should spring spontaneously from the people themselves. Where it is planned or guided by the Government, or where it is given an administrative structure, it may hinder the spontaneous manifestation of the total strength of the nation. The present circumstances, however, do not allow us to rely solely on the spontaneous development of such a movement. Moreover, undirected efforts from below are liable to degenerate into factional strife and fail to develop into a really national movement. The Government have thus found it necessary to take positive steps for fostering and directing this movement.

Viewed in this light, this movement is a common undertaking of the Government and of the people; it is a nation-wide movement to assist the Throne. It is not merely a spiritual movement in the narrow sense but one aiming at uplifting the political ideals and enhancing the political consciousness of the nation. And the choosing of men of talent, reputed or otherwise, from all strata of society to form the nucleus of the movement and thus to obtain for it a strong political power and driving force is the first and indispensable step that should be taken.

The movement is highly political in nature, but it is by no means a movement for a political party. Individual and sectional interests and attitudes are necessarily in the very nature of a political party. It is true that there can be no whole without a part; to condemn parties, however, because they comprise sectional elements is not sufficient. It may be said that in those times when liberalism was the basis of economic activities, the existence of political parties was justified. It must be acknowledged that in Japan too the parties stood up against the clannish and bureaucratic influences to make heard the voice of the people. Nevertheless it cannot be denied that the past activities of the parties were often not in keeping with the essential function of the Diet, which is to assist the Throne.

The new national structure movement aims at superseding the old party politics predicated upon liberalism. It is essentially national, all-embracing and public-spirited in character. It aims at the concentration and unification of all the forces and resources of the nation. Its activities extend to the whole life of the nation. Even were this movement to rise as a popular movement, its character would not be that of a political party in the old sense. It would, on the contrary, be a national movement standing above any political party, embracing all parties and factions, economic and cultural bodies, and uniting all in the spirit of public service. When such a movement is led by the Government, those who hold the reins of government and are entrusted with the task of assisting the Throne, are always placed in a position where they must seek the welfare of the whole but never be permitted to indulge in party politics which, in their very nature, contain elements of sectional antagonism and conflict.

As I have just stated, the national structure cannot take the form of a political party, especially when it is led by the Government. Nor can it be allowed to take the form of a single party system. Such a political system takes a "part" and makes of it a "whole"; it considers the State and the Party as one and the same thing, and views any opposition to the Party as a revolt against the State; it renders permanent the ruling position of one Party, with the head of that Party as a permanent wielder of the power to govern. No matter what brilliant results such a system may have reaped in other lands, it is not acceptable in Japan as it is contrary to the basic principle of our national polity of "One Sovereign over all." In Japan, it is the privilege of every one of His Imperial Majesty's subjects to assist the Throne, and that privilege cannot be monopolized by the power of either a single person or a single Party.

If there should arise a difference of opinion concerning the assistance to be offered, the final decision would rest with the Throne. And once an Imperial decision has been given, all the subjects of the Throne should unite in obeying His Majesty's Command. That is the very essence of Japanese polity.

Briefly, the new national structure is a nation-wide and permanent organization in which the Japanese people in all walks of life are to fulfil their duty of assisting the Throne.

Although the perfection of this structure is in no wise an easy task, the Government are convinced that it provides the best means for surmounting the difficulties which face the nation today.

His Imperial Majesty the Emperor was pleased to grant a Message on February 11 of this year, pointing to His subjects the way in which they should meet the present situation. The Government, in obedience to the Imperial Command, are taking the lead in this national movement to assist the Throne. They are resolved to overcome the serious obstacles confronting our country and to fulfil the heavy responsibilities which are theirs to "guard and maintain the prosperity of the Imperial Throne."

I have invited eminent authorities from the Government, from the Army and Navy, and from circles outside of the Government to join this Preparatory Committee for the National Structure, and I ask that you will study and collaborate in solving the questions relating to the general lines of the organization, the creation of a central organ for the national movement and the adjustment of its relations with existing organizations as well as its coordination with the structure of the State.

(3) Japan's Foreign Policy. Statement of the Minister for Foreign Affairs (Matsuoka), August 1, 1940 [1]

I have always said that the mission of Japan is to proclaim and demonstrate kodo [2] throughout the world. Viewed from the standpoint of international relations, this amounts, I think, to enabling all nations and races to find each its proper place in the world. Accordingly the immediate aim of our foreign policy at present is to establish, in accordance with the lofty spirit of kodo, a great East Asian chain of common prosperity with the Japan-Manchoukuo-China group as one of the links. We shall thus be able to demonstrate kodo in the most effective manner, and pave the way for the establishment of an equitable world peace. We should be resolved to surmount all obstacles, both material and spiritual, lying in our path. Furthermore, in concert with those friendly Powers which are prepared to cooperate with us, we should strive with courage and determination for the fulfilment of the ideal and the heaven-ordained mission of our country.

(4) Program for Economic Construction Embracing Japan, Manchoukuo and China. Announced by the Japanese Cabinet Information Bureau, November 5, 1940 [3]

[Excerpt]

For the purpose of realizing the task of constructing a new East Asiatic order and thereby ensuring the lasting peace of the world, the processes of the renovation of her internal structure and of the enlarge-

[1] Tokyo Gazette, IV, p. 118.

[2] Literally, "the Imperial way," whereby the Japanese people, achieving a unity of mind, with the Emperor as Master and serving Him with loyalty and devotion, endeavor to establish a highly moral nation through whose moral influence they hope to contribute to the peace and welfare of the world.　[3] Ibid., p. 214.

ment and organization of her living sphere must be brought into perfect unity. Her basic economic policies must accordingly be established upon the organized planning of the three following processes:

1. Perfection of the reorganization of national economy.

2. Organization and strengthening of Japanese-Manchoukuo-Chinese economy.

3. Enlarged organization of the East Asiatic sphere of common prosperity.

Basic Lines of Policy

1. The objective of the program for economic construction embracing Japan, Manchoukuo and China is to establish a self-supporting, self-sufficient economic structure within about ten years, in order to strengthen the position of East Asia in the world economy by accelerating the construction of the East Asiatic sphere of common prosperity.

2. Guiding principles on which Japan is to undertake the economic construction program embracing the three countries lie in the promotion of the general welfare in an ideal state of co-existence and common prosperity through the unitary cooperation of the three countries, in accordance with the high and broad spirit of *Hakkō Itiu*.[1]

3. In order to expedite the economic construction Japan will endeavor to uplift the morale of the nation, renovate the internal structure, augment national strength while rendering assistance to the economic reconstruction of Manchoukuo and China. For this purpose she will strive for the promotion of science and technique and undertake the development of pioneer industries.

4. Manchoukuo, being in an inseparable relationship with Japan, is expected to swiftly perfect and develop important basic industries.

5. China is expected to develop her resources and reconstruct her economic system in collaboration with Japan and Manchoukuo; in particular, progress in communications and transport services, smooth exchange of goods, and development of essential industries and resources are called for. Thus she is expected to contribute to the establishment of the East Asiatic sphere of common prosperity.

6. With a view to adjusting and accelerating the organized planning of economic construction embracing Japan, Manchoukuo and China the administrative machinery relating thereto shall be speedily perfected.

(a) Comment of the Cabinet's Intelligence Bureau [2]

Japan's guiding policy in establishing the Greater East Asian sphere of common prosperity with the creation of a new world order in view has entered on a

[1] "The world as one family." [2] *The Japan Weekly Chronicle*, November 14, 1940, p.601.

new stage through the conclusion of the tripartite pact among Germany, Italy and herself. In order to meet the new situation, the Government has fixed the outlines of Japan-Manchoukuo-Chinese economic construction, forming part of the fundamental economic policy, at a recent Cabinet meeting, and future policy is to be shaped and carried out along these lines.

The object of this policy is to compass the vigorous development of the Greater East Asian sphere of common prosperity, which is to be founded on the collective advance of Japanese, Manchoukuoan and Chinese economy in conformity with the conception of a new economic order. Present world economy based on free trade, which aims at the free exchange of goods between nations is crumbling before our eyes together with the old order. Japan's economy must be free from the old structure dependent on the old order so that it may be reorganized on a new basis. By this reorganization, Japanese economy must be made higher, wider and stronger, thereby elevating the standard of living for all East Asian peoples and enabling them to have their proper place. To make it higher means to give higher productivity to the national vitality; to make it wider means to extend the sphere of mutual economic dependence among Japan, Manchoukuo and China to Greater East Asia so as to establish a strong sphere of mutual prosperity covering Greater East Asia; and to make it stronger means to establish the national economy so firmly by reducing the degree of dependence on outside Powers to the minimum that it can stand the strain of any situation that may arise. In order to make the Japanese economy higher, wider and stronger in this way, the entire resources of the nation must be put together and while overcoming at home all hardships attendant on reforms by dint of a strong national will, all kinds of pressure and menace from other Powers must be resisted stoutly, so that the new East Asian economic order in which Japan exercises the directive influence may be completed within the next ten years. Only under this new order can all East Asian countries including Manchoukuo and China achieve a brilliant economic development.

(5) *Address by the Japanese Minister for Foreign Affairs* (*Matsuoka*) *to the Diet, Tokyo, January 21, 1941* [1]

It gives me a great pleasure to have this opportunity of explaining at the reopening of the 76th session of the Diet the recent trends in our country's foreign affairs.

Needless to say, the aim of Japan's foreign policy is that of enabling all nations of the world to take their own proper places, in accordance with the spirit of *Hakkō Itiu*, the very ideal which inspired the foundation of our Empire. The object of the Three-Power Pact concluded between Japan, Germany and Italy on September 27 last is none other than the realization of the same great ideal. We are, one and all, profoundly moved by the Imperial Rescript His Majesty the Emperor was graciously pleased to grant on the conclusion of the Pact, clearly indicating to the nation the path which they should follow.

[1] *Tokyo Gazette*, IV, p. 367. The address of the Premier at the same time (*ibid.*, p. 364) covered much the same ground from a national point of view.

The Three-Power Pact stipulates that Germany and Italy recognize and respect the leadership of Japan in the establishment of a new order in Greater East Asia. It is our avowed purpose to bring all the peoples in that region to revert to their inherent and true character, promoting conciliation and cooperation among them, and thereby setting an example of universal concord. The Pact also provides that Japan recognizes and respects the leadership of Germany and Italy in their similar endeavors in Europe. Far from antagonizing any country, the Pact is the embodiment of a peaceful but powerful cooperation directed toward the establishment of a new world order. In accordance with the provisions of the treaty, arrangements have already been made for setting up mixed commissions at the capitals of the three countries. Friendly relations between the three nations are thus becoming increasingly closer, politically, militarily, economically and culturally. During the month of November last year, the Pact was adhered to by Hungary, Rumania and Slovakia. It need not be repeated that the keynote of Japan's diplomacy is the idea of *Hakkō Itiu* and that it revolves round the Three-Power Pact as its axis. In this connection, I should like to touch briefly upon Article 3 of the Three-Power Pact. The article provides that the Contracting Parties undertake to assist one another with all political, economic and military means should one of the Contracting Parties be attacked by a Power at present not involved in the European War or in the Sino-Japanese conflict. In case such an attack should be made, the obligation stipulated by this article would, of course, fall upon us. Reference may be made, in passing, to Italy's military operations. There appear to be various species of malicious propaganda circulated on this subject, but I have no doubt that Italy, our ally, will attain her objective before long.

Of the nations in Greater East Asia, Manchoukuo has special and inseparable relations with this country. As you are aware, during the 10 years which have already elapsed since her emergence as an independent nation, her national foundations have become strong and secure while her international position has been greatly enhanced, and her people have been enjoying an increasing measure of prosperity. In June last year, the Emperor of Manchoukuo paid a visit to Japan to offer his felicitations personally to our Imperial House on the auspicious occasion of the 2,600th anniversary of the foundation of our Empire.[1] This is a source of genuine congratulation for the people of Japan and

---

[1] The German Führer on the formal anniversary, November 15, in a congratulatory message predicted for Japan "a glorious peace in a secure *Lebensraum.*" (*Japan Weekly Chronicle*, November 21, 1940, p. 637.)

Manchoukuo, as it is a conspicuous manifestation of the unique relations existing between the two nations, sharing, as they do, common aims and aspirations. By the Sino-Japanese Basic Treaty concluded with the National Government at Nanking, and by the Joint Declaration made by Japan, Manchoukuo and China, the Republic of China [1] recognized Manchoukuo, with the result that an exchange of ambassadors has been arranged between them.

Inasmuch as an early settlement of the China Affair is desirable for the establishment of the sphere of common prosperity throughout Greater East Asia, our present Government, ever since its formation, have urged the Chiang Kai-shek regime, to reconsider and reverse its attitude, with a view to bringing about its amalgamation with the Nanking Government; but it persists in struggling against Japan. The Chiang regime, however, is riddled with internal disruption and friction which are rapidly growing acute, while the masses under its control are suffering from high prices, a dearth of commodities and other hardships and privations. While the armed resistance of Chiang's regime has notably declined, the Chinese Communist troops have greatly gained in influence, with the result that they are steadily encroaching upon the sphere of influence of Chungking's armies. The leader in Chungking now seems to be greatly harassed by the growing strength and outlawry of the Communist forces. Despite its being in such a miserable plight, the Chiang regime is still advocating national reconstruction through its continued resistance against Japan. This is due to its misplaced hopes in assistance from Great Britain and the United States, especially the latter, and also to the force of past circumstances from which that regime cannot easily escape. In June last year, Great Britain temporarily suspended the traffic of goods destined for the Chiang regime through the Hong Kong and Burma routes. On October 18 of the same year, however, following the announcement of the Three-Power Pact, that country reopened the Burma route and has since been trying to transport goods by that route. Furthermore, Great Britain recently granted the Chiang regime a 10,000,000 pound sterling loan, while about the same time the United States, too, offered a loan of 100,000,000 dollars. The latter country is now endeavoring to extend assistance to Great Britain on a large scale by mobilizing her entire resources; while on the other hand, the Burma route is being frequently and seriously damaged by the successful activities of our loyal and gallant air forces. It seems highly doubtful, therefore, what aid Great Britain and the United States can actually afford the Chiang regime. In the light

[1] The Wang Ching-wei regime is referred to.

of such an international situation, the Japanese Government, in pursuance of their fixed policy, recognized the National Government at Nanking and on November 30 of last year concluded with the latter the Sino-Japanese Basic Treaty. This treaty embodies the three basic principles of good neighborliness, economic cooperation and joint defense against Communist activities. It stipulates that both Japan and China respect each other's sovereignty and territorial integrity, and undertake close economic cooperation on the basis of equality and reciprocity, and that Japanese forces be stationed in certain specified areas in Mengchiang [1] and North China. Not only does Japan demand no territorial cession and no indemnities, but she has willingly pledged to China a policy of abolishing extraterritoriality and also of restoring the "concessions" to China. This is an eloquent testimony of her sincere desire for the attainment of a moral union of the Asiatic peoples. Now that the Basic Treaty has been signed and the Joint Declaration by Japan, Manchoukuo and China issued, it is incumbent upon us to concentrate our efforts on assisting the Nanking Government to develop into the Government of China both in name and in fact. We have thus been taking an attitude of surmounting all obstacles for the purpose of establishing a sphere of co-prosperity throughout Greater East Asia with Japan, Manchoukuo and China as the nucleus and mainstay.

Let me now make a brief survey of our relations with the Netherlands East Indies, French Indo-China and Thailand, which lie within the aforementioned sphere of common prosperity.

The Netherlands East Indies and French Indo-China, if only for geographical reasons, should be in an intimate and inseparable relationship with our country. Therefore, the situation which has hitherto thwarted the development of this natural relationship must be thoroughly remedied, and relations of good neighborliness secured for the promotion of mutual prosperity. With this in view, early in September last, the Government dispatched Mr. Ichizo Kobayashi, Minister of Commerce and Industry, to the Netherlands East Indies as a special envoy. When a definite stage had been reached in his negotiations with the Netherlands East Indies authorities concerning the purchase of oil and other urgent questions, Mr. Kobayashi was obliged to return to Japan by circumstances preventing his prolonged stay there. As his successor, the Government have recently sent to the islands Mr. Kenkichi Yoshizawa, formerly Minister of Foreign Affairs. He has already resumed the negotiations with the Netherlands East Indies authorities.

[1] The Mongolian Federation; see U. S. Bureau of Foreign and Domestic Commerce, *Foreign Commerce Weekly*, III, p. 487.

As regards French Indo-China, it formed the most important route of supply for Chungking since the beginning of the China Affair. Consequent, however, upon the sudden change in the European situation last June, a change has occurred in the relations between Japan and French Indo-China, resulting in the closure of the border between that French colony and China itself, and in the entry, by agreement, of Japanese armed forces into the colony. Negotiations are now in progress in Tokyo in an amicable atmosphere on the basis of the Notes exchanged between the French Ambassador and myself in August last. It is my opinion that a realization, on the part of France, of the necessity for cooperation with Japan, in the light of the new situation in the world in general and in East Asia in particular, is responsible for this development.

In connection with the French Indo-China question, I should like to refer to the relations between our country and Thailand. It may be recalled that at the General Assembly of the League of Nations dealing with the Manchurian Affair, in 1933, the Thai delegate did not leave the Assembly Hall but remained in his seat, and boldly announced his abstention from voting. This is still fresh in the memory of our people.

In June last year, a treaty of amity and neutrality was concluded by Japan with Thailand. With the exchange of ratifications, completed on December 23 at Bangkok, the bonds of friendship between the two countries have been drawn closer. A movement is now stirring the Thai people for the recovery of the lost territories which are at present incorporated in French Indo-China. The Thai troops are confronting the French Indo-China forces across the border with frequent conflicts occurring between them. Japan as the leader in East Asia cannot afford to remain indifferent to such a dispute, which, she hopes, will be settled at an earliest possible date.

An exchange of diplomatic representatives has taken place between Japan and Australia. We hope that the two countries will make contributions toward the promotion of peace in the Pacific by furthering their cordial relations through friendly cooperation and the elimination of unnecessary misunderstandings.

The relations between Japan and Near Eastern Countries have recently increased in cordiality. Our ratification of the Treaty of Amity with Iran is only one of many proofs that illustrate this happy state of affairs.

Japan and Argentina have agreed to elevate the status of their Legations in each other's country to that of Embassies. With Brazil, a cultural agreement was signed in September last, and it has already been sanctioned by His Majesty the Emperor. Relations between

Japan and Brazil are thus growing more and more cordial. It is a matter for hearty congratulation that Japan and those Latin American countries have of recent years become increasingly closer in their political, economic and cultural relations.

While these diplomatic relations have taken such a favorable turn, the development of the European war has obliged us to suspend or temporarily withdraw some of our diplomatic establishments in that region. But Japan's diplomatic service abroad is being steadily strengthened on the principle of priority; in particular we are reinforcing our diplomatic machinery in Greater East Asia.

In establishing a sphere of common prosperity throughout Greater East Asia and ensuring the peace of the Orient, it is not desirable that the present diplomatic relations between Japan and the Soviet Union should be left as they are. The utmost efforts are being made, therefore, to remove mutual misunderstandings and, if possible, to bring about a fundamental and far-reaching adjustment of diplomatic relations. We are pursuing negotiations at this moment upon such questions as the frontier demarcation between Manchoukuo and Outer Mongolia, the fisheries, and the Japanese concessions in North Saghalien. Regarding the fisheries question in particular, an agreement of views has already been reached concerning the establishment of a mixed commission composed of Japanese and Soviet representatives for the purpose of revising the long-term treaty and also concerning the conclusion of a *modus vivendi* for the fishing industry for this year. On this point both Germany and Italy share Japan's desire. The provisions of Article 5 of the Three-Power Pact make it clear, in accordance with the aforementioned intentions of Japan, that the Pact is not directed against the Soviet Union. We earnestly hope that the Soviet Union will understand Japan's true intentions and that the two countries, actuated by the spirit of mutual concession and conciliation, will succeed in achieving the readjustment of their relations.

Japan's foreign trade, with the exception of that with Manchoukuo and China, is conducted mostly with Great Britain, the United States and their respective colonies and possessions. Since notifying Japan of the abrogation of the Treaty of Commerce and Navigation in July 1939 [1] the United States has been enforcing, in succession, embargoes or restrictions on the exports to Japan of aircraft, arms and ammunition, aviation gasoline, machine tools, scrap iron, iron and steel manufactures, copper, nickel, and other important war materials, while the British Dominions and colonies are in various ways interfering with Japan's

[1] See *Documents, II*, p. 242.

shipping. The Japanese Government have lodged protests against such actions on each occasion, and yet this tendency has recently been so greatly aggravated that Japan must meet the situation adequately prepared.[1] No other course is left to her but to go forward, perfecting herself as a State highly organized for national defense, not only in order to meet this pressure that I have referred to but also to ensure economic self-sufficiency within the region of Greater East Asia.[2]

In this connection, I should like to refer to our relations with the United States. The United States has evinced no adequate understanding of the fact that the establishment of a sphere of common prosperity throughout Greater East Asia is truly a matter of vital concern to Japan. She apparently entertains an idea that her own first line of national defense, on the east, lies along the mid-Atlantic and, on the west, not only along the eastern Pacific, but even as far as China and the South Seas. If the United States assumes such an attitude, it would be, to say the least, a very one-sided contention on her part, and would cast reflections on our position of superiority in the Western Pacific, thus intimating that it betokens ambitious designs on our part. I, for one, believe that such a position assumed by the United States would not contribute toward the promotion of world peace. Speaking frankly, I extremely regret such an attitude of the United States for the sake of Japanese-American friendship, for the sake of peace in the Pacific, and, also, for the sake of the peace of the world. It is my earnest hope that a great nation that is exerting such a tremendous influence in the world as the United States will realize her responsibility for the maintenance of peace, will reflect deeply on her attitude with fear of God, that is, true piety, will courageously liquidate the state of things created

---

[1] For a more detailed discussion with reference to the effect upon Japan's economy see the statement of the president of the Cabinet Planning Board to the Prefectural Governors' Conference at Tokyo October 8, 1940 (*Trans-Pacific*, October 17, 1940, p. 10).

[2] In a statement to a Japanese Diet committee the Minister for Foreign Affairs (Matsuoka) on February 24, 1941, said (United Press version, *New York Times*, February 25, 1941, p. 1):

"While it is difficult to conduct actual political affairs according to advocated ideals, I believe that the white race must cede Oceania to the Asiatics. It has always been my pet theory that Oceania, which is 1,200 miles north and south and 1,000 miles east and west, must be made a place for Asiatic peoples to migrate. This region has sufficient natural resources to support from 600,000,000 to 800,000,000 people. I believe we have a natural right to migrate there."

The statement was explained by its maker the next day as not referring to Australia, Hawaii or New Zealand and as expressing only a long-range ideal. An amplification was to the effect that Japan hoped to gain a migration region by an "understanding" with other countries.

by the force of past circumstances and put forth her utmost efforts toward overcoming the impending crisis of civilization.

The prevailing confusion of the international situation shows no sign of subsiding, but on the contrary, it tends to increase. Should the United States unfortunately become involved in the European war, and should Japan, too, be compelled to participate in the conflict, another great World War both in name and reality would ensue, precipitating a situation which would defy all attempts at saving it. Should the war take its furious course, unleashing formidable new weapons which have not hitherto been used, no one could guarantee that it would not develop into a war spelling the downfall of modern civilization. The Three-Power Pact has been concluded for the purpose not only of making sustained efforts for the establishment of a sphere of common prosperity throughout Greater East Asia, but of preventing, in the course of such efforts, any further aggravation of the present disturbances. We must endeavor to terminate the current war as speedily as possible and to put an end to the chaos in which the world is plunged. We must, meanwhile, study in advance to discover some formula avoiding the recurrence of any such disturbance in future.

With an unbroken line of the Emperors reigning since its foundation, our Empire constitutes a unique family-State unparalleled in the world for unity and solidarity, growing stronger with every national emergency. It is reassuring, moreover, to observe that the Japanese Empire is endowed with the most favorable geographical conditions, powerful enough to influence the course of world politics. With the conviction of our race that light radiates from the East and with the great ideal of *Hakkō Itiu*, we must put forth our highest efforts in the momentous task of establishing a new world order which is the object of the tripartite Pact. That we shall succeed in this regard I have not the slightest doubt. If we are fully prepared for this task under these circumstances, the future of our Empire, I firmly believe, is full of promise.

In concluding my address, I respectfully pay my tribute to the spirits of those loyal and valiant officers and men, our compatriots, who have fallen in action, and at the same time, I tender my warm thanks to our Fighting Services who are enduring many hardships and privations, and extend to them my most sincere wishes for every success in the field.

3. MANIFESTATIONS OF JAPANESE POLICY

A. Treaty between Japan and Thailand Concerning the Continuance of Friendly Relations and the Mutual Respect of Each Other's Territorial Integrity, June 12, 1940 [1]

In force from exchange of ratifications, December 23, 1940

ARTICLE 1. The High Contracting Parties shall mutually respect each other's territorial integrity and hereby reaffirm the constant peace and the perpetual friendship existing between them.

ARTICLE 2. The High Contracting Parties shall mutually maintain friendly contact in order to exchange information, and to consult one another, on any question of common interest that may arise.

ARTICLE 3. In the event of one of the High Contracting Parties suffering an attack from any third Power or Powers, the other Party undertakes not to give aid or assistance to the said Power or Powers against the Party attacked.

ARTICLE 4. The present Treaty shall be ratified and the ratifications thereof shall be exchanged at Bangkok, as soon as possible.

ARTICLE 5. The present Treaty shall come into effect on the date of the exchange of ratifications and shall remain in force for five years from that date.

In case neither of the High Contracting Parties shall have given notice to the other six months before the expiration of the said period of five years of its intention to terminate the Treaty, it shall continue operative until the expiration of one year from the date on which either Party shall have given such notice.

[Formal clauses and signatures not given.]

B. Communication with China. Temporary Closing of the Burma Road

The Japanese Government has attempted to shut off foreign supplies from the Chinese Government, a naval cordon called a "blockade" having been established along the coast as soon as occupation of Chinese ports had been accomplished. Three other routes were utilized by the Chinese in their trade with foreign countries. The route from the French Indo-China port of Haiphong over the Yunnan Railway to Kunming and thence to the interior carried most of the traffic and was used all through the year until its closing by the Japanese agreement of August 30, 1940, with French Indo-China (p. 275). The Burma Highway links the railhead at Lashio with Kunming. The northern route from the Soviet

---

[1] *Tokyo Gazette*, IV, p. 336. A concurrent comment of the spokesman of the Japanese Foreign Office stated that the negotiations were proposed by the Thailand Government, were conducted through the Japanese Minister at Bangkok and were carried on quite apart from the simultaneous negotiations of Thailand with France and the United Kingdom. See also "Japan and Thailand," *Tokyo Gazette*, IV, p. 48.

Union reaches Chungking by way of Suchow, Ningsia, Lanchow, Hsian and Chengtu. Japan moved to close these routes as opportunity offered and concentrated attention upon that objective after France sought and was granted an armistice by Germany in June 1940.

(1) Statement of the Spokesman of the Japanese Foreign Office, July 8, 1940 [1]

The British Ambassador, Sir Robert Craigie, under instructions from his Government called on the Foreign Minister, Mr. Hachiro Arita, at 2:30 o'clock this afternoon at the latter's official residence. At the interview the British Ambassador stated in reply to the Japanese representation of June 24 concerning the question of prohibiting the transportation of materials and goods through Burma and Hongkong in aid of the Chiang Kai-shek regime that, with regard to the export of military supplies through Hong Kong, the Hong Kong Government has hitherto strenuously prohibited such export and, therefore, the British Government believe that they are meeting the demand of the Japanese Government. The British Ambassador further stated that the question of prohibiting the transportation of military supplies through Burma has been considered, but since Burmese and Indian products are found among such goods it is naturally difficult to prohibit legal trade, and that moreover, judging from last year's record the rainy season begins at the end of June and consequently the amount of goods transported until September through that territory will not reach even a tenth of the normal quantity.

The Foreign Minister expressed the deep dissatisfaction of the Japanese Government with the British reply and emphatically stated the views and opinions of the Japanese Government regarding the question. He further told the British Ambassador that the Japanese Government cannot but urge the British Government to reconsider the matter. The British Ambassador replied that he would promptly transmit to his home Government the substance of what the Foreign Minister stated. The interview came to an end at 3:30 o'clock P.M.

(2) Press Release of the Department of State, July 16, 1940 [2]

The Secretary of State, in reply to inquiries by press correspondents for comment in regard to reports that, at the instance of the Japanese Government, the British Government would prohibit temporarily the movement of certain commodities through Burma into China over what is known as the Burma Route, said that this Government has a legitimate interest in the keeping open of arteries of commerce in every

[1] *Contemporary Japan*, IX, p. 1078.   [2] Department of State, *Bulletin*, III, p. 36.

part of the world and considers that action such as this, if taken, and such as was taken recently in relation to the Indo-China railway would constitute unwarranted interpositions of obstacles to world trade.

(3) Statement of the Spokesman of the Foreign Office (Suma), Tokyo, July 16, 1940 [1]

The steps taken by our Government toward the stoppage of transportation of goods to the Chiang Kai-shek Government over the Haiphong-Yunnan and the Burma-Yunnan routes were taken because they were necessary for stopping traffic in materials being shipped along these routes to the Chungking regime and so were absolutely necessary for diminishing the power of the Chungking regime from the military standpoint.

This problem concerns only Japan, Britain and France and is not meant to have been a step through which the general commerce of the world would be hindered. Stated simply, we asked the Governments of Britain and France to cease aiding the Chiang Kai-shek regime and they accepted our requests. Therefore there is no reason why the United States should offer any protest.

The stoppage of shipments of goods to the Chungking regime affects only certain specified materials and does not affect the shipment of the natural products of the territories concerned.

The American protest sounds as if the United States were asking Japan to stand by and allow it to aid the Chungking regime. It is needless to say that we could not possibly allow any such thing at a time when our nation is fighting the forces of Chiang Kai-shek.

If Secretary of State Cordell Hull made this kind of gesture in an attempt to bring pressure to bear against Japan in view of the current relations between the United States and Japan, it is most difficult for us to understand the spirit which led him to take such action. We may rightly say that there have been many gestures recently by the United States against Japan which are most trying and hard to understand.

(4) Agreement between Japan and the United Kingdom with Respect to Transit through Burma, July 17, 1940 [2]

[Paraphrase]

As a result of negotiations which have recently been conducted between the Japanese and British Governments regarding the trans-

---

[1] *The Trans-Pacific*, July 25, 1940, p. 8.

[2] Statement of the spokesman for the Japanese Foreign Office, *Tokyo Gazette*, IV, p. 81.

portation of war materials through British territories to China, agreement has now been reached as follows:

1. The export of arms and ammunition from Hong Kong has been prohibited since January 1939. None of the war materials to which the Japanese Government attach importance are neither being exported at present nor will be exported in the future. The export of those kinds of goods which are prohibited from being exported from Burma as mentioned below will of course be prohibited in Hong Kong.

2. The British Government are to prohibit for a period of three months from July 18 of this year the transit through Burma of arms and ammunition as well as petrol, trucks, and railway materials.

3. The Japanese consular officials in Hong Kong and Rangoon will maintain a close contact with the British authorities regarding the measures to be taken for the purpose of rendering this prohibition effective.

(5) *Statement of the Prime Minister of the United Kingdom (Churchill) to the House of Commons, July 18, 1940* [1]

On June 24 the Japanese Government requested His Majesty's Government to take measures to stop the transit to China via Burma of war material and certain other goods. A similar request was made in respect of Hong Kong. The continuance of the transit of these materials was represented as having a serious effect on Anglo-Japanese relations.

An agreement has now been reached with the Japanese Government as follows:

Hong Kong — The export of arms and ammunition from Hong Kong has been prohibited since January 1939, and none of the war materials to which the Japanese Government attach importance are in fact being exported.

Burma — The Government of Burma have agreed to suspend for a period of three months the transit to China of arms and ammunition as well as the following articles: Petrol, lorries and railway material.

The categories of goods prohibited in Burma will be prohibited in Hong Kong.

In considering the requests made by the Japanese Government and in reaching the agreement to which I have referred, His Majesty's Government were not unmindful of the various obligations accepted by this country, including their obligations to the National Government of China and to the British territories affected. His Majesty's Govern-

[1] Parliamentary Debates, 5th Series, House of Commons, p. 363, col. 399.

ment were, however, also bound to have regard to the present world situation, nor could they ignore the dominant fact that we ourselves are engaged in a life and death struggle.

The general policy of this country toward Far Eastern troubles has been repeatedly defined. We have persistently asserted our desire to see assured to China a free and independent future, and we have as frequently expressed our desire to improve our relations with Japan.

To achieve these objectives two things were essential — time and a relief of tension. On the one hand, it was clear that tension was rapidly growing owing to Japanese complaints about the passage of war material by the Burma Route. On the other, to agree to permanent closure of the route would be to default from our obligations as a neutral and friendly power to China. What we have therefore made is a temporary arrangement in the hope that the time so gained may lead to a solution just and equitable to both parties of the dispute, and freely accepted by them both.

We wish for no quarrel with any nation in the Far East. We desire to see China's status and integrity preserved, and as was indicated in our note of January 14, 1939,[1] we are ready to negotiate with the Chinese Government, after the conclusion of peace, the abolition of extraterritorial rights, the rendition of concessions and the revision of treaties on the basis of reciprocity and equality. We wish to see Japan attain that state of prosperity which will ensure to her population the welfare and economic security which every Japanese naturally desires. Toward the attainment of the aims of both these countries we are prepared to offer our collaboration and our contribution. But it must be clear that if they are to be attained, it must be by a process of peace and conciliation, not by war or threat of war.

(6) *Communiqué of the Japanese Foreign Office, October 8, 1940* [2]

Sir Robert Craigie, British Ambassador, called on Foreign Minister Yosuke Matsuoka on the morning of October 8. Sir Robert, as under instructions of his Government, informed Mr. Matsuoka to the effect that the British Government do not see their way to renew the British-Japanese Agreement concerning the closure of the Burma Route, when it expires on October 17.

(7) *Statement of the Japanese Minister for Foreign Affairs (Matsuoka), October 10, 1940* [2]

I am rather reluctant to make comment on Mr. Churchill's statement reported to have been made in the British Parliament in reference to

[1] *Documents, I, 1938–39,* p. 252; see also p. 241 above.
[2] *Contemporary Japan,* IX, p. 1496.

the British Government's decision to re-open the so-called Burma Route.[1] But since it might be of some use to clarify the situation about this problem and the conclusion of the tripartite Pact among Japan, Germany and Italy, I might make a few observations at this juncture.

In the first place, it was not understood that the closure of the Burma Route for three months was conditional on Japan's ability to conclude peace with China within that period. Japan of course then wished earnestly, as she does today, to bring about an all-around peace in China at the earliest possible date, and naturally said so to the British Ambassador at Tokyo. No one would deny the fact that no other people have been more eager than the Japanese to see peace restored between Japan and China. As a matter of fact, Japan has been and is actually bending every effort to that end. The conclusion of the very Pact with Germany and Italy, which Mr. Churchill seems to deplore, is in a way another attempt to achieve the same end.

In the second place, if the British Government really wish, as they profess, to see peace restored in East Asia as quickly as possible, I have to confess that it is past my comprehension how the British Government could hope to contribute to the realization of such wish by re-opening the Burma Route, thereby encouraging Chiang Kai-shek to persist in opposing and fighting Japan. The decision unfortunately taken will have, as anyone can see, the effect of encouraging Chiang Kai-shek whether it is intended or not. Mr. Churchill's statement on this point is, to say the least, self-contradictory.

Lastly, I might add that the tripartite Pact was not entered into with the intention of directing it "against" the United States, but it was, I should say, directed, if at all, "for" the United States. To state frankly, the parties to the Pact wished earnestly that such a powerful nation as the United States in particular and all other nations at present neutral would not be involved in the European War, or come by any chance into conflict with Japan because of the China affair or otherwise. Such an eventuality, with all the possibility of bringing an awful catastrophe upon humanity, is enough to make one shudder if one stops to imagine the consequences. In short, the Pact is a pact of peace.

---

[1] The Prime Minister of the United Kingdom on October 8, 1940 (Parl. Deb., 5th series, House of Commons, vol. 365, col. 301) told the House of Commons that the "just and equitable settlement" contemplated in his former statement (p. 271, above) had not been reached, and continued: "On the contrary, the protracted struggle of Japan to subjugate the Chinese race is still proceeding with all its attendant miseries. We much regret that the opportunity has been lost. In the circumstances His Majesty's Government propose to allow the agreement about closing the Burma Road to run its course until October 17, but they do not see their way to renew it after that."

C. Facilities in French Indo-China

After the collapse of France, Japan secured from the French Ambassador at Tokyo prohibition of exports from Indo-China to the Chinese Government, the measures to be under the supervision of Japanese officials (*Documents, II, 1939–40*, p. 271). The Japanese Government followed this penetration into Indo-Chinese economy with negotiations which resulted in an agreement by exchange of notes August 30, 1940 for "the closure of the border between French Indo-China itself and the entry, by agreement, of Japanese armed forces into the colony." The latter forces immediately engaged in incidents, of which the United States took note, and which were a prelude to an agreement between the Japanese and French military authorities on September 22. These developments were announced only on September 23 in a series of obscure communiqués. In the face of United States disapproval of any territorial change, this seemed to be the best the Japanese felt like doing for themselves at the time. Attention was thereafter diverted to the development of trouble between French Indo-China and Thailand, culminating in the exchange of notes of March 11, 1941 (p. 298).

(1) *Present and Future Foreign Trade of Indo-China: Memorandum of the Governor-General (Catroux), July 1940* [1]

[Excerpt]

Trade between France and French Indo-China had always been on the upward tendency, exports from French Indo-China to France in the years 1933–38 reaching 50 per cent of the total exports. However, since the autumn of 1939 this tendency had been reversed, for during the eight months since the outbreak of the European war the exports of French Indo-China to France decreased to 500,000 tons from the 940,000 ton level of the corresponding period of the preceding year. The export of such staple products as rice, onions and coal to France witnessed a noticeable decrease during this period.

Accordingly it is a matter of urgent necessity for French Indo-China to seek an outlet for her exports other than France, especially in the countries of the Pacific. Regarding staple products, fortunately Japan has replaced France as a large buyer of agricultural products, and it might be well said that Japan has saved French Indo-China from an economic crisis. America too has increased her purchase of French Indo-China rubber since the outbreak of the European war, but there is a limit to the export of other goods to the United States. Japan is a good customer for coal, iron ore, salt, etc., and there is a great prospect of increasing exports of rubber, tin and rock phosphate to Japan, while French Indo-China can buy Japanese cotton yarn, cotton textiles, rayon, porcelain-ware and chemical products.

The 1932 Trade Treaty with Japan imposed the lowest tariff rates

[1] Translation by *Japan Weekly Chronicle*, Com. Sup. July 25, 1940, p. 14.

on some Japanese goods, but French Indo-China should provide for better conditions for shipping. As goods from France are duty free, even if a lower tariff is now applied to Japanese goods the customs revenue will increase. Furthermore, in view of the fact that Japanese goods are reasonably priced, the import of Japanese goods will fall in line with the low price policy of French Indo-China, especially at a time when prices are on an upward tendency due to the decrease of imports from France.

(2) *Statement of the Secretary of State (Hull), September 4, 1940* [1]

I have noted the reports in the press regarding which inquiry is made to the effect that Japanese military authorities have delivered an ultimatum to the local authorities of French Indo-China in connection with demands for passage of Japanese troops across Indo-China and for use of bases in Indo-China for military operations against China. It will be remembered that during recent months this Government and several other governments, including the Japanese Government, have given expression to their desire that the principle of the *status quo* be respected and be preserved unimpaired in the Pacific, with special references to the Netherlands East Indies and French Indo-China. In the absence of official confirmation of the reports of a Japanese ultimatum to the authorities of French Indo-China, this Government is reluctant to give credence to the reports now under reference. The situation and the subject to which these reports relate is, however, a matter to which this Government attaches importance, and it stands to reason that, should events prove these reports to have been well-founded, the effect upon public opinion in the United States would be unfortunate.

(3) *Statements of Japanese Foreign Office, Tokyo, September 23, 1940* [2]

With a view to settling the China affair and thereby facilitate the establishment of a new order in East Asia, the Foreign Minister, Yosuke Matsuoka, held conversations in a friendly spirit with the French Ambassador, Charles Arsène-Henry, on basic matters regarding the question of French Indo-China at Tokyo during the month of August of this year.

As a result of these conversations, France agreed to afford in French Indo-China all such facilities of a military nature as are required by

[1] Department of State, *Bulletin*, III, p. 196. The statement was made in response to inquiries by press correspondents.　　[2] *Contemporary Japan*, IX, p. 1369.
[3] Agreement of August 30, 1940.

the Japanese Army and Navy for executing their campaign for the settlement of the China affair.

On the basis of this agreement, negotiations were conducted on the spot — at Hanoi — for the purpose of deciding upon concrete matters between the Japanese and French military authorities, which resulted in an agreement in the afternoon of September 22.

———

Despite the understanding reached between Japan and France with regard to French Indo-China after prolonged negotiations in which Japan manifested consistent patience and forbearance, a local skirmish has occurred in the border region of French Indo-China. This is entirely due to a misunderstanding on the part of French Indo-China. Therefore, it is expected that the agreement concluded between Japan and France will be smoothly and peacefully carried out with the French misunderstanding naturally dispelled.

Inasmuch as the present agreement between Japan and France has been based on peaceful talks between the two countries, there could be no objection to it from any other foreign country.

(4) *Announcement of Japanese Imperial Headquarters, Tokyo, September 23, 1940* [1]

On the basis of conversations which took place between the Japanese Government and the French Government between August 25 and 30, the Japanese and French Indo-Chinese military authorities on the spot have negotiated regarding military questions since the beginning of September, reaching an agreement at 4:30 o'clock (Tokyo time) Sunday afternoon [September 22.]

Accordingly, Japanese military and naval units, under terms of the agreement, started a peaceful advance toward the northern border of French Indo-China today (Monday). When the Japanese units passed the border, disputes arose in certain places, according to reports received thus far, but it is expected that the advance will be completed without much difficulty.

(a) *Dispatch of Domei, Japanese News Agency, September 23, 1940* [2]

Discussions have been in progress since last month between Foreign Minister Yosuke Matsuoka and the French Ambassador, Mr. Charles Arsène-Henry, with a view to finding a solution of the French Indo-China question which will facilitate the performance of the greatest task undertaken by Japan in its project for the construction of a new order in East Asia.

[1] *The Trans-Pacific*, September 26, 1940, p. 11.   [2] *Ibid.*, p. 11.

Paralleling the discussions, talks have been progressing on the spot between Major-General Issaku Nishihara, head of the delegation of inspectors supervising traffic between French Indo-China and the Chungking Government, and Vice-Admiral Jean Decoux, Governor-General of French Indo-China, regarding plans for a concrete settlement of the question.

The Franco-Japanese negotiations were brought to a satisfactory settlement through a compromise reached on Sunday afternoon. The happy conclusion of the negotiations may be attributed to the fact that the French Indo-China authorities appreciate the great ideal of the Japanese Empire for the construction of a new order in East Asia, and accordingly agreed to extend military facilities in the French colony, which are required by the Japanese army and navy.

In accordance with the agreement, Japanese military and naval forces started their advance into French Indo-China this morning. There is no doubt that the move will be a large factor in the ultimate collapse of the Chungking Government.

The Franco-Japanese agreement is the result of a complete identity of views between the two countries. Thus any third-Power interference in the settlement would be entirely unwarranted. There is a firm determination on the part of the Japanese Government to act with resolution in rejecting any third-Power attempt at interference or oppression.

(5) *Statement of the Secretary of State (Hull), September 23, 1940* [1]

Events are transpiring so rapidly in the Indo-China situation that it is impossible to get a clear picture of the minute-to-minute developments. It seems obvious, however, that the *status quo* is being upset and that this is being achieved under duress. The position of the United States in disapproval and in deprecation of such procedures has repeatedly been stated.

(6) *Release of the Department of State, September 23, 1940*

This Government has not at any time or in any way approved the French concessions to Japan. The attitude of this Government toward developments in French Indo-China is as expressed by the Secretary of State this morning and in previous public statements.

(7) *Joint Communiqué, September 27, 1940* [2]

The Japanese Government have given the French Government an assurance they will respect the rights and interests of France in East

---

[1] Department of State, *Bulletin*, III, p. 253; in response to inquiries at the press conference.

[2] *Ibid.*,

[3] *Contemporary Japan*, IX, p. 1492. The communiqué was presumably issued jointly by the Governments of Indo-China and of Japan, but this is not clear from the text.

Asia, especially the territorial integrity of French Indo-China and the French sovereignty over all parts of the Union of Indo-China, while the French have agreed to accord to the Japanese Army and Navy special facilities in Indo-China which are necessary for the execution of the latter's military operations.

In order to decide upon concrete matters pertaining to the above mentioned extension of military facilities, conversations were held at Hanoi between the Japanese and French military authorities. As a result of these conversations a satisfactory agreement was concluded on September 22.

D. The Three-Power Pact between Germany, Italy, and Japan, Signed at Berlin, September 27, 1940

For the text and other material see p. 304. Only Japanese papers are assembled here.

(1) *Rescript of the Emperor of Japan (Hirohito), September 27, 1940* [1]

To enhance justice and to make of the world one household is the great injunction bequeathed by Our Imperial Ancestors, and which We lay to Our heart day and night. In the stupendous crisis now confronting the world, it appears that endless will be the aggravation of war and confusion, and incalculable the disasters to be inflicted on all mankind. We fervently hope that the cessation of hostilities and the restoration of peace will be realized as quickly as possible. Accordingly We commanded Our Government to deliberate on the matter of mutual assistance and cooperation with Germany and Italy which share in the views and aspirations of Our Empire. We are deeply grateful that a Pact has been concluded between these three Powers.

The task of enabling each nation to find its proper place and all individuals to live in peace and security is indeed one of great magnitude unparalleled in history. The goal lies still far distant. Ye, Our subjects, clarify ever more the concept of national polity; think deeply and look far; unite in heart and strength, and surmount the present emergency, to assist thereby the promotion of the Imperial fortune coeval with heaven and earth.

[1] *The Japan Weekly Chronicle*, October 3, 1940, p. 401; *Tokyo Gazette*, IV, p. 173.
The rescript was accompanied by a message of the Premier reiterating its content and noting that "the goal lies far distant," with "numerous obstacles as we go on" (*Tokyo Gazette*, IV, p. 194; *Contemporary Japan*, IX, p. 1493).

(a) **Comments on the Treaty by the Spokesman of the Japanese Foreign Office (Suma), September 27, 1940** [1]

Q. Is the new treaty accompanied by any protocol or additional rules?

A. No.

Q. When were the negotiations for the conclusion of the present treaty opened?

A. They were opened early in September and ended, to be exact, today.

Q. Where are the Joint Technical Commissions provided for in Article 4 going to be established?

A. That is a matter yet to be fixed, but they will be established in more than one place.

Q. How will they be constituted and what are their functions?

A. I am not in a position to make any definite statement on those points.

Q. How does the new treaty bear on the Japan-German-Italian Anti-Comintern Agreement? [2]

A. There is no connection whatever between the two.

Q. Is it to be understood that the Anti-Comintern Agreement has been rendered null and void by the new treaty?

A. That is a very delicate question to answer. At the moment, all I can say is that there is no connection between the two pacts.

Q. It is mentioned in Article 5 that " . . . the aforesaid terms do not in any way affect the political status which exists at present as between each of the three Contracting Parties and Soviet Russia"; how is it that Soviet Russia is specifically mentioned in the treaty?

A. It is because Soviet Russia is actually in special relationship with Germany and also because she is Japan's neighbor.

Q. Referring to the phrase in Article 3, "They further undertake to assist one another with all political, economic and military means when one of the three Contracting Parties is attacked by a Power at present not involved in the European War or in the Sino-Japanese Conflict," what does the word "attacked" imply? Supposing that economic pressure, such as an embargo on exports, takes a very intensive form, is that to be regarded as an "attack"?

A. That is a matter of interpretation, but I think there exists an understanding in this regard among the Contracting Parties.

Q. Does "a Power," as mentioned in Article 3, refer to any specific country? Why was the phrase used in the singular form?

A. It does not refer to any specific Power. Although "a power" is the phrase, the Contracting Powers will also assist one another when one of them is attacked by two outside Powers or more in unison.

Q. Is the new treaty to be regarded as a military alliance or as a treaty of mutual aid?

A. The new treaty provides for a closer relationship among the Contracting Parties than is usually to be found in a treaty of mutual aid. On the other hand,

---

[1] *The Japan Weekly Chronicle*, October 3, 1940, p. 406.

[2] This agreement, signed at Berlin November 25, 1936, and in force for 5 years from that date, is printed in Martens, *Nouveau recueil général de traités*, 3ᵉ série, XXXIII, p. 376; XXXV, p. 3.

whereas a military alliance usually has a certain specific potential enemy in view, the new treaty has no potential enemy against which it is directed. A tripartite treaty may be a better nomenclature.

Q. What is the reason for fixing the term of the pact at ten years?

A. I think the term has been fixed at such a long period because the Three Contracting Powers intend to maintain cooperation in real earnest for the establishment of a new order.

Q. How will the new treaty be operated against America?

A. Japan's relations with America will remain the same as hitherto. We do not think that Japanese-American relations will particularly deteriorate on account of the new treaty. Japan is as eager to adjust relations with that country as heretofore. As a matter of fact, the treaty is not directed against any particular country. It is not intended to provoke war, but to bring peace to the world as early as possible.

Q. What will become of the non-involvement policy announced by the Abe Cabinet in September last year?

A. I hold that it remains in force.

Q. What does the recognition of leadership in Europe and in Asia mean?

A. It means leaving to the Contracting Parties concerned everything in their respective spheres.

(2) Statement of the Chinese Minister for Foreign Affairs (Wang Chung-hui), Chungking, September 30, 1940 [1]

The consistent policy of the Chinese Government has been to maintain international law and order, in which all the nations of the world can live on terms of equality and amity. Any attempt at aggression and violation of the legally constituted world order under the pretext of establishing a "new order" will be firmly opposed by the Chinese Government in accordance with its traditional policy.

The Chinese Government and people are firmly resolved to continue their struggle for the maintenance of world order. The Chinese Government will never recognize the so-called "New Order in Greater East Asia," especially Japan's so-called leadership in East Asia. It goes without saying that any pact or agreement signed between third Powers will not in any wise affect the legal position, rights and interests of China, or the attitude and policy of the Chinese Government.

(3) Statement of the Japanese Premier (Konoe), Kyoto, October 4, 1940 [2]

[Excerpt]

The aim of the tripartite pact among Japan, Germany and Italy is to bring about cooperation among the signatory powers in the establish-

[1] *China at War*, V, No. 4, p. 92.

[2] *The Trans-Pacific*, October 10, 1940, p. 8; the statement was reported as the substance of an interview.

ment of a new world order. Under the provisions of the agreement, if any signatory is attacked by a third Power, including the United States, it will be assisted by the other signatories.

But there is no thought of challenging third countries.

Under the treaty, Germany and Italy recognize Japan's position to lead others in the establishment of a new order in the Orient. Japan, on its part, recognizes the guiding positions of Germany and Italy in Europe.

If the United States recognizes the positions and stands of Japan, Germany and Italy, those countries will recognize the guiding position of the United States on the American continent. But there is no tangible intention to make overtures to the United States in that respect.

The fate of the Pacific area and the question of peace or war in the Pacific will be decided by whether Japan and the United States respect and understand the stand of each other.

I think the United States would do well to understand the real intentions of Japan and to cooperate in a positive manner in the task of establishing a new world order. I would like the United States to ponder and to understand Japan, Germany and Italy, which are proceeding with the construction of a new world order, and to adjust its course to this new world trend.

Should the United States refuse to understand the real intentions of Japan, Germany and Italy and persist in challenging them in the belief that the pact among them represents a hostile action, there will be no other course open to them than to go to war.[1] . . .

The question of settling the China incident must be approached from every possible angle. The conclusion of the tripartite agreement has as its standpoint the settlement of the incident. We are engaging in diplomatic maneuvers to induce not only the Soviet Union but also Great Britain and the United States to suspend operations for assistance to the China regime.

E. Denunciation of the Fur Seal Convention

(1) *Statement of the Japanese Foreign Office, Issued October 23, 1940* [2]

The Convention for the Protection of Fur Seals was first concluded in 1911 between Japan, the United States, Great Britain and Russia.

---

[1] The same day the Foreign Office spokesman in a broadcast declared that recent moves of the United States in the Far East "clearly indicate it is taking step after step in the wrong direction which might precipitate it into the vortex of armed conflict." (*New York Times*, October 5, 1940, p. 1.)

[2] *Tokyo Gazette*, IV, p. 245. Receipt of the Japanese notice was reported to the United States, October 25, 1940 (Department of State, *Bulletin*, III, p. 412).

In 1925, upon the expiration of its term of 15 years the Japanese Government, proposing the revision of the same, conducted negotiations with the other signatory Powers, but their efforts failed to bring about any concrete results and the Convention, unrevised, has continued in force for 14 years more up to the present.

In the meantime fur seals in the north Pacific have greatly multiplied, with the direct and indirect damages inflicted upon the fishing industry growing also with the years to such an extent that Japan with her important fishery industry can no longer tolerate the continuance of the said Convention which aims solely at the protection of the seals and provides nothing for safeguarding fishery interests. Accordingly the Japanese Government, acting under the stipulations of Article XVI of the Convention, have notified the three other Powers concerned today (October 23, 1940) of their abrogation of the Convention to be effective one year hence, submitting at the same time a proposal for the conclusion of a new convention concerning the protection of fur seals.

———

By Article XVI of the Convention of July 7, 1911 it entered into effect on December 15, 1911 and continued in force for a period of 15 years from that date and thereafter until terminated by 12 months' written notice given by one of the parties to all of the others. At any time prior to the termination of the Convention, a conference may be held upon the request of any of the parties to consider and if possible agree upon a further extension of the convention, with such additions and modifications, if any, as may be found desirable.

The countries which are parties to the Convention are the United States of America, Great Britain, Canada, Japan, and the Union of Soviet Socialist Republics.

F. The Wang Ching-wei Regime at Nanking

[See *Documents, II, 1939–40*, p. 298.]

The Wang Ching-wei "puppet government" was finally set up at Nanking on March 30, 1940 and a Japanese embassy accredited to it shortly afterward began negotiations for a "basic" treaty which were completed by August 31.[1] The signing of the treaty and the accompanying joint declaration including "Manchoukuo" was postponed until November 30.

(1) *Treaty Concerning Basic Relations Signed at Nanking, November 30, 1940* [2]

The Imperial Government of Japan and

The National Government of the Republic of China:

[1] See statements of the Japanese Ambassador and Wang, *Japan Weekly Chronicle*, September 5, 1940, p. 280.

[2] *Tokyo Gazette*, IV, p. 272. The instrument is stated to be "between Japan and China"; it was signed by a Japanese of ambassadorial rank, Nobuyuki Abe, and Wang Ching-wei acting as president of the Executive Yuan instead of president of the "national government," which was said to represent a consolidation of former Peiping and Nanking regimes.

Being desirous that these two countries should respect their inherent characteristics and closely cooperate with each other as good neighbors under their common ideal of establishing a new order in East Asia on an ethical basis, establishing thereby a permanent peace in East Asia, and with this as a nucleus contributing toward the peace of the world in general, and

Desiring for this purpose to establish fundamental principles to regulate the relations between the two countries, have agreed as follows:

ARTICLE 1. The Governments of the two countries shall, in order to maintain permanently good neighborly and amicable relations between the two countries, mutually respect their sovereignty and territories and at the same time take mutually helpful and friendly measures, political, economic, cultural and otherwise.

The Governments of the two countries agree to eliminate, and to prohibit in the future, such measures and causes as are destructive of amity between the two countries in politics, diplomacy, education, propaganda, trade and commerce, and other spheres.

ARTICLE 2. The Governments of the two countries shall closely cooperate for cultural harmony, creation and development.

ARTICLE 3. The Governments of the two countries agree to engage in joint defense against all destructive operations of communistic nature that jeopardize the peace and welfare of their countries.

The Governments of the two countries shall, in order to accomplish the purpose mentioned in the preceding paragraph, eliminate communistic elements and organizations in their respective territories, and at the same time cooperate closely concerning information and propaganda with reference to the defense against communistic activities.

Japan shall, in order to carry out the defense against communistic activities through collaboration of the two countries, station required forces in specified areas of Mengchiang [1] and of North China for the necessary duration, in accordance with the terms to be agreed upon separately.

ARTICLE 4. The Governments of the two countries undertake to cooperate closely for the maintenance of common peace and order until the Japanese forces sent to China complete their evacuation in accordance with the terms as provided for separately.

The areas for stationing Japanese forces for the period requiring the maintenance of common peace and order and other matters pertaining thereto shall be determined as agreed separately between the two countries.

[1] "The Mongolian Federation."

ARTICLE 5. The Government of the Republic of China shall recognize that Japan may, in accordance with previous practices or in order to preserve the common interests of the two countries, station for a required duration its naval units and vessels in specified areas within the territory of the Republic of China, in accordance with the terms to be agreed upon separately between the two countries.

ARTICLE 6. The Governments of the two countries shall effect close economic cooperation between the two countries in conformance with the spirit of complementing each other and ministering to each other's needs, as well as in accordance with the principles of equality and reciprocity.

With reference to specific resources in North China and Mengchiang, especially mineral resources required for national defense, the Government of the Republic of China undertake that they shall be developed through close cooperation of the two countries. With reference to the development of specific resources in other areas which are required for national defense, the Government of the Republic of China shall afford necessary facilities to Japan and Japanese subjects.

With regard to the utilization of the resources referred to in the preceding paragraph, while considering the requirements of China, the Government of the Republic of China, shall afford positive and full facilities to Japan and Japanese subjects.

The Governments of the two countries shall take all the necessary measures to promote trade in general and to facilitate and rationalize the demand and supply of goods between the two countries. The Governments of the two countries shall extend specially close cooperation with respect to the promotion of trade and commerce in the lower basin of the Yangtze River and the rationalization of the demand and supply of goods between Japan on the one hand and North China and Mengchiang on the other.

The Government of Japan shall, with respect to the rehabilitation and development of industries, finance, transportation and communication in China, extend necessary assistance and cooperation to China through consultation between the two countries.

ARTICLE 7. According to the development of the new relations between Japan and China under the present Treaty, the Government of Japan shall abolish extraterritorial rights possessed by Japan in China and render to the latter its concessions; and the Government of China shall open its territory for domicile and business of Japanese subjects.

ARTICLE 8. The Governments of the two countries shall conclude separate agreements regarding specific items which are necessary to accomplish the object of the present Treaty.

ARTICLE 9. The present Treaty shall come into effect from the date of its signature.

IN WITNESS WHEREOF the undersigned, duly authorized by their respective Governments, have signed the present Treaty and have affixed thereto their seals.

DONE in duplicate, in the Japanese and Chinese languages, at Nanking the 30th day of the 11th month of the 15th year of Syōwa, corresponding to the 30th day of the 11th month of the 29th year of the Republic of China.

[Signatures not given in source.]

ANNEXED PROTOCOL

In proceeding this day to the signature of the Treaty Concerning the Basic Relations between Japan and China, the Plenipotentiaries of the two countries have agreed as follows:

ARTICLE 1. The Government of the Republic of China, understanding that, during the period in which Japan continues the warlike operations it is at present carrying on in the territory of China, there exists a special state of affairs attendant upon such warlike operations, and that Japan must take such measures as are required for the attainment of the object of such operations, shall accordingly take the necessary measures.

Even during the continuation of the said warlike operations, the special state of affairs referred to in the preceding paragraph shall, in so far as there is no obstacle to the attainment of the object of the operations, be adjusted in accordance with the changing circumstances and in conformity with the Treaty and its annexed documents.

ARTICLE 2. While the affairs previously administered by the Provisional Government of the Republic of China, the Reformed Government of the Republic of China and others have been taken over and temporarily maintained as they are by the Government of the Republic of China, those which require adjustment but are not yet adjusted shall be adjusted in conformity with the purpose of the Treaty and its annexed documents through consultation between the two countries, as promptly as circumstances may permit.

ARTICLE 3. When general peace is restored between the two countries and the state of war ceases to exist, the Japanese forces shall commence evacuation with the exception of those which are stationed in accordance with the Treaty Concerning the Basic Relations between Japan and China signed today and the existing agreements between the two countries, and shall complete it within two years with the firm establishment of peace and order; and the Government of the Republic of China shall guarantee the firm establishment of peace and order during this period.

ARTICLE 4. The Government of the Republic of China shall compensate the damages to rights and interests suffered by Japanese subjects in China on account of the China Affair since its outbreak.

The Government of Japan shall, with respect to the relief of the Chinese rendered destitute by the China Affair, cooperate with the Government of the Republic of China.

ARTICLE 5. The present Protocol shall come into effect simultaneously with the Treaty.

IN WITNESS WHEREOF the Plenipotentiaries of the two countries have signed this Protocol and have affixed thereto their seals.

DONE in duplicate, in the Japanese and Chinese languages, at Nanking the 30th day of the 11th month of the 15th year of Syōwa, corresponding to the 30th day of the 11th month of the 29th year of the Republic of China.

AGREED TERMS OF UNDERSTANDING BETWEEN THE PLENIPOTENTIARIES OF JAPAN AND CHINA CONCERNING THE ANNEXED PROTOCOL

In proceeding this day to the signature of the Treaty Concerning the Basic Relations between Japan and China, the following understanding has been reached between the Plenipotentiaries of the two countries in connection with the stipulations of Articles 1 and 2 of the Annexed Protocol of the Treaty.

1. With regard to those various organs for collecting taxes in China which are at present in a special condition owing to military necessity, an adjustment shall be made promptly in accordance with the spirit of respecting the financial independence of China.

2. With regard to those industrial, mining and commercial establishments under governmental or private management which are at present controlled by Japanese forces, the necessary measures shall be taken for their prompt transfer to Chinese management in a rational manner, with the exception of those which are of enemy character or under special circumstances of unavoidable character including military necessity.

3. In case any Sino-Japanese joint enterprise requires modification in the evaluation of original assets, the proportion of capital investments and other matters, measures for their rectification shall be taken in accordance with the terms to be agreed upon separately through consultation between the two countries.

4. The Government of the Republic of China shall, in case they find it necessary to institute control on foreign trade, effect such control

autonomously. They may not, however, infringe upon the principle of Sino-Japanese economic cooperation mentioned in Article 6 of the Treaty; and they shall consult with Japan with regard to such control during the continuation of the China Affair.

5. With regard to matters pertaining to transportation and communication in China which require adjustment, they shall be adjusted, as promptly as circumstance may permit, in accordance with the terms to be agreed upon separately through consultation between the two countries.

DONE in duplicate, in the Japanese and Chinese languages, at Nanking the 30th day of the 11th month of the 15th year of Syōwa, corresponding to the 30th day of the 11th month of the 29th year of the Republic of China.

JOINT DECLARATION BY THE GOVERNMENTS OF JAPAN, MANCHOUKUO AND CHINA

The Imperial Government of Japan;

The Imperial Government of Manchoukuo; and

The National Government of the Republic of China:

Being desirous that the three countries should respect one another's inherent characteristics and closely cooperate with one another as good neighbors under their common ideal of establishing a new order in East Asia on an ethical basis, constituting thereby the mainstay of a permanent peace in East Asia, and with this as a nucleus contributing toward the peace of the world in general, declare as follows:

1. Japan, Manchoukuo and China will respect mutually their sovereignty and territories.

2. Japan, Manchoukuo and China will bring about general cooperation on a reciprocal basis among the three countries, especially a good neighborly friendship, common defense against communistic activities and economic cooperation, and for that purpose will take all the necessary measures in every direction.

3. Japan, Manchoukuo and China will promptly conclude agreements in accordance with the present Declaration.

DONE at Nanking on this the 30th day of the 11th month of the 15th year of Syōwa, corresponding to the 30th day of the 11th month of the 7th year of Kangte, and to the 30th day of the 11th month of the 29th year of the Republic of China.

———

Wang Ching-wei was ceremoniously taken to Tokyo where on June 18, 1941 he had an audience with the Japanese Emperor. The Vice Minister of Imperial

Household Affairs issued the following statement (*New York Times*, June 19, 1941, p. 9):

"Wang Ching-wei was deeply moved by the overwhelming honor done to him by the Imperial House. He was meticulous in regard to correct behavior at court and was greatly relieved after his return that he had made no blunder."

In the course of that visit the Wang Ching-wei regime was "recognized" by Germany, Italy and the adherents to the treaty of September 27, 1940.

(2) *Statement of the Minister for Foreign Affairs of the Republic of China (Wang Chung-hui)* [1]

The conclusion by Japan with the puppet organization at Nanking of what purports to be a treaty is but the culmination of a series of aggressive acts on her part designed to overthrow law and order not only in China, but in the whole Pacific. Having set up a regime to suit their own purposes, the Japanese have now signed with it the so-called treaty to facilitate the execution of their policy of domination and expansion in the Far East. Such a regime is in reality a part of the Government at Tokyo planted on Chinese soil, to be used by the Japanese militarists as an instrument for the realization of their scheme.

The National Government of the Republic of China has repeatedly declared, and desires to reiterate most emphatically, that Wang Ching-wei is the arch-traitor of the Republic and that the puppet regime at Nanking is an illegal organization whose acts of whatever character are null and void in respect of all Chinese citizens and all foreign countries. The so-called treaty just signed at Nanking is totally devoid of legality and has no binding force whatever.

Should any foreign country choose to accord recognition to the puppet organization, the Government and people of China would consider it a most unfriendly act and would be constrained to discontinue their normal relations with such a country.

Whatever Japan may attempt or conspire to do in China or in the Pacific, China is determined to fight on till victory is won, and she is confident of victory because to freedom and right and justice victory inevitably belongs.

G. Japanese Tender of Mediation

February 1941 was an uncertain month in Japanese foreign affairs. The Italian partner in the treaty of September 27, 1940 was losing in Greece, in Libya and in the Mediterranean, to British Empire forces; Singapore and Malaya were being reinforced by Australian and other troops; the Netherlands East Indies

---

[1] China Information Committee, *News Release*, December 2, 1940, p. 768; *China at War*, VI, No. 1, p. 93.

were not amenable to the Japanese demands; the Lend-Lease Act reached a stage which foretold its passage by the United States Congress, which had, moreover, decided to fortify the Pacific islands; the new Japanese Ambassador to the United States Admiral Kichisaburo Nomura on landing had thought that war in the Pacific was "unthinkable"; the President on February 11 told his press conference it was "unlikely" but, if it involved the United States, aid to Britain would not be curtailed; on February 14 the acceptance of the Ambassador's credentials at Washington was purely formal [1] and on the same day strategic areas were set up in the United States Pacific islands.[2] Both the United Kingdom and the United States were apprehensive that Japan's mediation of the Indo-China and Thailand dispute might be the occasion for a Japanese advance southward toward Malaysia and the Netherlands East Indies. On February 17 the Japanese Ambassador at London visited the Foreign Office and the next day it became known through a communiqué in Tokyo that the Japanese Minister for Foreign Affairs was the author of an offer to mediate anywhere in the world. The Minister had sent such a message to the British Secretary of State for Foreign Affairs. The British Prime Minister replied to the démarche.

(1) *Statement of the Spokesman (Ishii) of the Japanese Board of Information, February 18, 1941* [3]

Various alarming reports have reached Japan purporting to give an impression that the situation in East Asia has become radically tense. We are surprised to learn that some foreign countries felt undue concern regarding the alleged tension in the situation in East Asia, and want to emphasize that so far as we can see there is no ground for entertaining alarming views on the East Asiatic situation.

We want to repeat that the purpose of the Tripartite Pact is peaceful. We cannot help feeling, therefore, a certain amount of anxiety, if not misgivings, as to the warlike preparations of the British and American Governments to meet the supposed contingencies in the Pacific and the South Seas. The press reports, concerning these movements on the part of Britain and the United States originating from British and American sources and elsewhere, are causing increasing misgivings, resulting in the contention advanced in some quarters in Japan that Japan should lose no time to take necessary steps to meet the worst eventuality in those regions. If the American Government could only be persuaded to restrict their activities in this respect to the Western Hemisphere and avoid causing anxiety unnecessarily in the mind of the Japanese people, the situation would indeed be greatly mitigated.

[1] Department of State, *Bulletin*, IV, p. 183.
[2] See p. 708.
[3] *Tokyo Gazette*, IV, p. 386. As a result of the reorganization of the government under Premier Konoe, the Foreign Office ceased to maintain a "spokesman" and the function of speaking for publication was placed under the control of the inner cabinet and assigned to its Board of Information.

We are utterly unable to see any good purpose to be served by prolonging war, whatever the motive may be. The present situation demands statesmanship of a high order. Such a statesmanship, we trust, will not be wanting in the British Empire or elsewhere.

In concluding, we want to make it clear that Japan is fully prepared to act as a mediator or to take whatever action calculated to recover normal conditions, not only in Greater East Asia but anywhere in the world. Leading Powers have great responsibility of restoring world peace and civilization; and such responsibility can only be fulfilled by a wise and generous statesmanship willing to listen to other's claims and contentions.

(2) Comment by the Under Secretary of State (Welles), February 18, 1941 [1]

In response to questions of newspaper correspondents at his press conference February 18, regarding reported remarks of spokesmen of foreign governments, including statements attributed to Japanese officials that Japan had no intention of attacking British and Dutch interests in the South Pacific; minimizing reports of anxiety on the part of Great Britain, the United States, and other countries; and declaring, among other things, that everything would be all right if the United States would withdraw to the Western Hemisphere, the Under Secretary of State, Summer Welles, made the following general statement:

"In the very critical world condition which exists today, the Government of the United States is far more interested in the deeds of other nations than the statements which some of their spokesmen may make."

(3) Statement of Foreign Office to the House of Commons, February 25, 1941 [2]

In a recent communication to the Foreign Secretary [Anthony Eden] the Japanese Minister for Foreign Affairs [Yosuke Matsuoka], after referring generally to the European War, observed that Japan was fully prepared to act as mediator or to take whatever action was calculated to restore peace and normal conditions not only in Greater East Asia but anywhere in the world. The Japanese Minister for Foreign Affairs in subsequent public statements (made, he has said, after consulting Germany), has indicated that his words were not to be regarded as an offer of mediation in the European war. In any case, the Japanese Minister for Foreign Affairs has been informed by the Prime Minister

---

[1] Release of the Department of State, *Bulletin*, IV, p. 211.
[2] Parliamentary Debates, 5th Series, House of Commons, vol. 369, col. 370.

that in a cause of the kind for which we are fighting — a cause in no way concerned with territory, trade or material gains, but affecting the whole future of humanity — there can be no question of compromise or parley.

H. Neutrality Pact between Japan and the Soviet Union

Yosuke Matsuoka, Minister for Foreign Affairs of Japan, arrived in Moscow March 24, 1941, en route to a visit to the members of the German and Italian Governments. On his return he stopped off at Moscow again and the signing of the neutrality pact was accomplished just before he left for home.

(1) *Neutrality Pact, Moscow, April 13, 1941* [1]

The Presidium of the Supreme Soviet of the Union of Soviet Socialist Republics and His Majesty the Emperor of Japan, guided by a desire to strengthen peaceful and friendly relations between the two countries, decided to conclude a pact on neutrality, for the purpose of which they appointed as their representatives:

For the Presidium of the Supreme Soviet of the Union of Soviet Social-ist Republics, Vyacheslav Molotov, Chairman of the Council of People's Commissars and People's Commissar for Foreign Affairs.

For His Majesty the Emperor of Japan, Yosuke Matsuoka, Minister of Foreign Affairs, Ju San Min, Cavalier of the Order of the Sacred Treasure, First Class; and Yoshitsugu Tatekawa, Ambassador Extraor-dinary and Plenipotentiary in the Union of Soviet Socialist Republics, Lieut. Gen., Ju San Min, Cavalier of the Order of the Rising Sun, First Class, and the Order of the Golden Kite, Fourth Class.

Who, after the exchange of their credentials, which were found in due and proper form, agreed on the following:

ARTICLE I. Both Contracting Parties undertake to maintain peaceful and friendly relations between them and mutually respect the territorial integrity and inviolability of the other Contracting Party.

ARTICLE II. Should one of the Contracting Parties become the object of hostilities on the part of one or several third Powers, the other Contract-ing Party will observe neutrality throughout the duration of the conflict.

[1] English version as released by Tass news agency, *New York Times*, April 14, 1941, p. 8. A French version, released through the Deutsches Nachrichtenbüro, Berlin, to France differs in phrasing. In that version, notably, Art. 2 reads:
"Art. 2. — Au cas où l'une des parties contractantes serait engagée dans une action militaire du fait d'une ou plusieurs autres puissances, l'autre partie contractante observerait une attitude de neutralité pendant toute la durée du conflit."
A third version, in English, corresponding in sense with the Tass version is given in *Tokyo Gazette*, IV, p. 487.

ARTICLE III. The present Pact comes into force from the day of its ratification by both Contracting Parties and remains valid for five years. In case neither of the Contracting Parties denounces the Pact one year before expiration of the term, it will be considered automatically prolonged for the next five years.

ARTICLE IV. The present Pact is subject to ratification as soon as possible. Instruments of ratification shall be exchanged in Tokyo also as soon as possible.

In confirmation whereof the above-named representatives signed the present Pact in two copies, drawn up in the Russian and Japanese languages, and affixed thereto their seals.

DONE in Moscow April 13, 1941, which corresponds to the 13th day of the 4th month of the 16th year of Showa.

Signed by:

> MOLOTOV,
> YOSUKE MATSUOKA,
> YOSHITSUGU TATEKAWA.

FRONTIER DECLARATION

In conformity with the spirit of the Neutrality Pact concluded April 13, 1941, between the Union of Soviet Socialist Republics and Japan, the Governments of the Union of Soviet Socialist Republics and Japan, in the interests of ensuring peaceful and friendly relations between the two countries, solemnly declare that the Union of Soviet Socialist Republics pledges to respect the territorial integrity and inviolability of Manchoukuo, and Japan pledges to respect the territorial integrity and inviolability of the Mongolian People's Republic.

Moscow, April 13, 1941.

Signed on behalf of the Government of the Union of Soviet Socialist Republics by:

> MOLOTOV

On behalf of the Government of Japan by:

> YOSUKE MATSUOKA,
> YOSHITSUGU TATEKAWA.

(2) *Statement of the Japanese Prime Minister (Konoe), April 14, 1941* [1]

The Japanese Government some time ago made public both at home and abroad their unalterable determination, by concluding the Tripartite Pact between Japan, Germany and Italy, to prevent the world-wide spread of the war and to secure the peace of Greater East Asia with that

[1] *Tokyo Gazette*, IV, p. 488.

Pact as the axis of the country's foreign policy. It goes without saying that, in order to realize such a purpose, it is essential that Japan and the Soviet Union, which are neighbors in the Far East, should strengthen their peaceful and friendly relations on a lasting basis, reinforcing thereby the spirit of the said Pact of alliance. With this conviction, the Government have for some time been conducting negotiations with the Soviet Government with a view to bringing about a fundamental adjustment of Japan's relations with the Soviet Union. With the present visit to Moscow of the Foreign Minister, Mr. Yosuke Matsuoka, as a turning point, the conversations between the two Governments have made rapid progress, resulting in the signature today, April 13, of the Pact of Neutrality between the Foreign Minister, Mr. Yosuke Matsuoka, and Ambassador Lieutenant-General Yoshitsugu Tatekawa, and the Soviet Commissar for Foreign Affairs, M. Viacheslav Molotov, which has just been announced. At the same time the Joint Declaration by the two countries has been issued, through which Japan respects the territorial integrity and inviolability of the People's Republic of Mongolia and the Soviet Union respects the territorial integrity and inviolability of the Empire of Manchoukuo, thereby expecting to bring tranquillity to the Manchoukuo-Soviet and Manchoukuo-Outer Mongolian borders.

It is my belief that the present Pact has an epoch-making significance in the relations between Japan and the Soviet Union and that it will greatly contribute toward the promotion of world peace. I have no doubt that the Pact will serve as a basis for the rapid solution in a concrete manner of various pending questions between the two countries.

(3) *Statement of the Secretary of State (Hull), April 14, 1941* [1]

The significance of the Pact between the Soviet Union and Japan relating to neutrality, as reported in the press today, could be overestimated. The agreement would seem to be descriptive of a situation which has in effect existed between the two countries for some time past. It therefore comes as no surprise, although there has existed doubt whether the two Governments would or would not agree to say it in writing. The policy of this Government, of course, remains unchanged.

I. Japanese Mediation between French Indo-China and Thailand

Following the limited occupation of French Indo-China by Japanese troops under the agreement of August 30, 1940, hostilities over border territories broke out between French Indo-China and Thailand. In December 1940 the Japanese

---

[1] Department of State, *Bulletin*, IV, p. 472.

Government informally proposed mediation to France, but the hostilities became extended. A formal proposal of mediation, conditioned upon an immediate cessation of hostilities, was made by the Japanese Government on January 20, 1941. It was accepted. A two-weeks' armistice was signed February 1 aboard a Japanese warship on the high seas off Saigon. The Mediation Conference began at Tokyo February 7, 1941, being the first experience of Japan in adjusting disputes in "Greater East Asia." Japan presented a mediation plan on February 24 after arduous *pourparlers* and, after two extensions of the armistice, agreement was reached on March 11. As between France and Thailand the settlement was said by the Japanese Foreign Office to be "just and fair." The advantage of the mediation to Japan appears in the exchange of notes between Japan and the individual parties.

The settlement was effected in May. On May 6 at Tokyo the Japanese Minister for Foreign Affairs and the Ambassador to French Indo-China signed with the French Ambassador to Japan and the Governor of French Indo-China a Convention of Establishment and Navigation and an Agreement concerning the Customs Tariff, Trade and Method of Payment, the latter being in 30 articles.[1]

On May 9 the Treaty of Peace between France and Thailand was formally signed at Tokyo by their delegates. A first protocol between the parties concerned evacuation and delivery of the territories affected; second and third protocols, also signed by Japan, concerned the delimitation commission and fulfillment of the terms concerning the demilitarized zones.[2]

Protocols concerning guaranty and political understanding, subject to ratification within two months, "in conformity with the purpose of the documents exchanged" on March 11, were signed on May 9 by the Japanese representatives and the French and Thai plenipotentiaries.[3]

(1) *Joint Communiqué by Japan, France and Thailand, Tokyo, March 11, 1941* [4]

Since the Mediation Conference for the settlement of the Thai-French Indo-China border dispute was opened in Tokyo with its first formal session held on February 7, three informal meetings have been held besides daily individual conversations in which the mediators have steadily exercised their good offices to bring about an agreement of views of the two countries concerned. As the result of these endeavors it became clear that an agreement could in all probability be reached. The mediators, therefore, presented a plan of mediation at the fourth informal meeting, held on the 24th of the same month, following which they have continued to persuade the two parties concerned to accept that plan. The Governments of France and Thailand have accepted it with some modifications and have initialled the terms of mediation at 4 : 00 o'clock this afternoon (March 11).

[1] Summarized in *Tokyo Gazette*, IV, p. 539.
[2] *Ibid.*, p. 542.   [3] *Ibid.*, p. 544.
[4] *Tokyo Gazette*, IV, p. 417; see also *Contemporary Japan*, X, p. 568.

The essential points of the mediation terms are as follows:

1. France cedes to Thailand the district of Paklay, which is mentioned in Article II of the Convention between France and Siam of February 13, 1904,[1] and the region lying to the north of the boundary line between the Provinces of Battambang and Pursat and the region lying on the right bank of the Mekong River bounded in south by the line running northward along the Longitude from the point touching Grand Lac and the southernmost end of the boundary line between the Provinces of Siem Reap and Battambang to the crossing point of that Longitude and the line of the 15th degree G of the Latitude and then eastward along that line of the Latitude to the Mekong River. However, a small area lying opposite to Stung Treng is reserved to French Indo-China.

2. All of the above-mentioned ceded territories are to be made demilitarized zones, and French nationals and the people of French Indo-China are to enjoy an absolutely equal treatment with nationals of Thailand throughout these areas with respect to entry, domicile and occupations and their pursuit.

3. The Government of Thailand will respect the mausolea of the Luang Prabang Royal House situated in the triangular zone lying opposite to Luang Prabang, and afford facilities for its preservation and worship, etc.

4. The Mekong frontier will be fixed in accordance with the principle of the deep-water channel, but the two islands, namely, Khong and Khone, will, under the sovereignty of Thailand, be jointly administered by France and Thailand, and the existing French establishments on the islands shall belong to France.

In signing the above-mentioned terms of mediation, letters were exchanged between Japan and France and between Japan and Thailand which have clarified to the effect that Japan guarantees the definitive nature of the settlement of the dispute by the aforementioned terms of mediation and that agreements will subsequently be made with respect to the maintenance of peace in Greater East Asia and the establishment and promotion of the specially closer relations between Japan and Thailand and between Japan and French Indo-China.

The friendly and peaceful relations between France and Thailand will thereby be restored and the bond of friendship that binds Japan, France and Thailand will further be strengthened.

[1] 97 *British and Foreign State Papers*, p. 961.

(a) *Disavowal of Cooperation with Other Powers Aimed Against Japan. Exchange of Notes between France and Japan, Tokyo, March 11, 1941* [1]

(i) *The Japanese Minister for Foreign Affairs (Matsuoka) to the French Ambassador (Arsène-Henry)*

TOKYO, *March 11, 1941.*

YOUR EXCELLENCY,

I have the honor to state that the Japanese Government, in view of the greatest importance which they attach to the maintenance of peace in Greater East Asia, have been watching with concern the development of the dispute to which French Indo-China, whose special relations with Japan have grown still closer as a result of the agreement of the 30th August, 1940,[2] is a party against Thailand.

The Japanese Government, from the standpoint of the maintenance of peace in Greater East Asia and recalling the peaceful and friendly spirit which prompted the conclusion of the aforementioned agreement between Japan and France, have offered their mediation to the Governments of France and Thailand with a view to bringing to an end the dispute between French Indo-China and Thailand. They, therefore, propose to the Government of France their plan of mediation which is presented on separate sheet with confidence that it will be unconditionally accepted by the latter Government. The Japanese Government are prepared, upon its acceptance by the French Government, to guarantee to the Government of France that the settlement of the said dispute through the mediation plan submitted by them will be definitive and irrevocable.

The Japanese Government, on the other hand, entertain no doubt that the Government of France, on their part, will endeavor for the maintenance of peace in Greater East Asia and especially for the establishment of good neighborly and amicable relations between Japan and French Indo-China, as well as for the promotion of closer economic relations between Japan and French Indo-China, and that they will declare to the Japanese Government that they will not enter into any agreement or understanding with a third Power or Powers regarding French Indo-China envisaging political, economic or military cooperation aimed either directly or indirectly against Japan.

[1] *Tokyo Gazette,* IV, p. 422; see also *Contemporary Japan,* X, p. 569. The protocol concerning guaranty and political understanding "in conformity" with this exchange was not available June 30, 1941.

[2] See p. 275-6.

It is understood that the aforementioned guarantee by the Japanese Government and the declaration of the French Government shall by formal documents be confirmed simultaneously with the conclusion of a treaty for the settlement of the dispute between France and Thailand.

I avail myself of this opportunity to renew to Your Excellency the assurance of my highest consideration.

YOSUKE MATSUOKA

(*ii*) *The French Ambassador* (*Arsène-Henry*) *to the Japanese Minister for Foreign Affairs* (*Matsuoka*)

TOKYO, *the 11th March, 1941.*

MONSIEUR LE MINISTRE,

By the letter under today's date, Your Excellency was good enough to inform me as follows:

[Text of the Japanese letter, see p. 296.]

I have the honor to acknowledge the receipt of the above letter and to inform Your Excellency that the Government of France are disposed, under the present situation, to accede to the instance of the Japanese Government, although they are not obliged to renounce the benefits of their treaties freely negotiated and concluded with the Government of Thailand, either from the standpoint of the local situation or from that of the fortune of arms. The Government of France, being constantly solicitous of the maintenance of peace of Greater East Asia, have never taken initiative of such a nature as of disturbing that peace, but testify to their fidelity to the basic spirit which inspired the agreement of August 30, 1940, by accepting the Mediation Plan presented on separate sheet. On the basis of that spirit and being desirous of avoiding all kinds of engagement which will involve their possessions in the Far East in a conflict between third Powers, the Government of France hereby declare that they have no intention of entering into any agreement or understanding with a third Power or Powers regarding French Indo-China envisaging political, economic or military cooperation aimed either directly or indirectly against Japan. Moreover, it is expected by the Government of France that the Government of Japan will assure the strict observance of the agreement of the 30th of August, 1940, and the subsequent military arrangements.

I avail myself of this opportunity to renew to Your Excellency the assurance of my highest consideration.

CHARLES ARSÈNE-HENRY

(b) *Exchange of Notes between Japan and Thailand, March 11, 1941*

(i) *The Japanese Minister for Foreign Affairs (Matsuoka) to the Thai Plenipotentiary (Varavarn)*

TOKYO, *March 11, 1941.*

YOUR HIGHNESS,

I have the honor to state that the Japanese Government, in view of the greatest importance which they attach to the maintenance of peace in Greater East Asia, have been watching with concern the development of the dispute to which Thailand, whose special relations with Japan have grown still closer as a result of the treaty of the 12th June, 1940, is a party against French Indo-China.

The Japanese Government, from the standpoint of the maintenance of peace in Greater East Asia and recalling the peaceful and friendly spirit which prompted the conclusion of the aforementioned treaty between Japan and Thailand, have offered their mediation to the Governments of Thailand and France with a view to bringing to an end the dispute between Thailand and French Indo-China. They, therefore, propose to the Government of Thailand their plan of mediation which is presented on separate sheet with confidence that it will be unconditionally accepted by the latter Government. The Japanese Government are prepared, upon its acceptance by the Thai Government, to guarantee to the Government of Thailand that the settlement of the said dispute through the mediation plan submitted by them will be definitive and irrevocable.

The Japanese Government, on the other hand, entertain no doubt that the Government of Thailand, on their part, will endeavor for the maintenance of peace in Greater East Asia and especially for the establishment of good neighborly and amicable relations between Japan and Thailand, as well as for the promotion of closer economic relations between Japan and Thailand, and that they will declare to the Japanese Government that they will not enter into any agreement or understanding with a third Power or Powers envisaging political, economic or military cooperation aimed either directly or indirectly against Japan.

It is understood that the aforementioned guarantee by the Japanese Government and the declaration of the Thai Government shall by formal documents be confirmed simultaneously with the conclusion of a treaty for the settlement of the dispute between Thailand and France.

I avail myself of this opportunity to renew to Your Highness the assurance of my highest consideration.

YOSUKE MATSUOKA

(*ii*) *The Thai Plenipotentiary (Varavarn) to the Japanese Minister for
Foreign Affairs (Matsuoka)*

TOKYO, *the 11th March, 1941.*

MONSIEUR LE MINISTRE,

By the letter under today's date, Your Excellency was good enough
to inform me as follows:

[Text of the Japanese letter, see p. 296.]

I have the honor to acknowledge the receipt of the above letter and
to inform Your Excellency that the Government of Thailand are disposed, under the present situation, to accede to the instance of the
Japanese Government, although they are not obliged to do so either
from the standpoint of the local situation or from that of the fortune
of arms. The Government of Thailand, being constantly solicitous of
the maintenance of peace of Greater East Asia, have never taken initiative of such a nature as of disturbing that peace, but testify to their
fidelity to the basic spirit which inspired the treaty of June 12, 1940,
by accepting the Mediation Plan presented on separate sheet. On the
basis of that spirit and being desirous of avoiding all kinds of engagement
which will involve their country in a conflict between third Powers, the
Government of Thailand hereby declare that they have no intention of
entering into any agreement or understanding with a third Power or
Powers envisaging political, economic or military cooperation aimed
either directly or indirectly against Japan. Moreover, it is expected by
the Government of Thailand that the Government of Japan will assure
the strict observance of the Treaty of the 12th of June, 1940.

I avail myself of this opportunity to renew to Your Excellency the
assurance of my highest consideration.

VANVAIDYAKARA VARAVARN

J. Trade with Netherlands East Indies

[See also p. 263.]

On the German invasion of the Netherlands, the authorities in the Netherlands East Indies arrested the German conspirators there and so prevented
trouble.[1] The authorities, after efficiently organizing the defense of the islands,
considered on their merits the proposals the Japanese Minister of Commerce and
Industry brought to Batavia in September 1940. The twenty-two demands of
Japan in general asked for a privileged position in the Netherlands East Indies
and included demands for more oil, tin and rubber, an increased immigration
quota, an increased import quota for Japanese products, mining and prospecting
facilities and the opening of direct air and cable services between Tokyo and

[1] *New York Times*, July 13, 1941, p. 31.

Batavia.[1] An agreement between the oil companies of Japan and the Netherlands East Indies producing companies for export to Japan of an additional 1,800,000 tons of products was initialed November 12, 1940 and extended in May 1941. Late in December 1940 a new Japanese economic mission arrived at Batavia and negotiations continued for months. The Ministers for Foreign Affairs and Colonies of the Netherlands visited the islands during the course of the conversations. In addition to the character of the Japanese demands the island authorities were determined not to assent to any agreement which would permit Netherlands East Indian products reaching Germany. The "final" Japanese note, on which Japan expected "nothing less than acceptance as a reply,"[2] was rejected. "Normal relations" were not changed as a result.

(1) *Oil Agreement between Japanese Importers and Netherlands Indies Companies, November 12, 1940*[3]

Consul Walter A. Foote at Batavia, Java, Netherlands Indies, has informed the Department that an agreement was initialed in Batavia on November 12 by representatives of Japanese oil importers and representatives of the local oil companies. The agreement provides for the export of 1,800,000 tons of petroleum products per annum to Japan from the Netherlands Indies. These exports will be composed of 250,000 tons of motor gasoline, 73,000 tons of fuel oil, 57,000 tons of kerosene, 100,000 tons of crude for lubricants, 540,000 tons of other crude, 120,000 tons of aviation crude, 50,000 tons of gas oil, and 116,000 tons of Diesel oil, in addition to the normal import quota of 494,000 tons of petroleum products.

(2) *Joint Japanese-Netherland East Indian Communiqué, Batavia, June 17, 1941*[4]

Both the Netherland and Japanese delegations greatly regret that economic negotiations between them have unfortunately come to no satisfactory result. It is needless, however, to add that discontinuing the present negotiations will lead to no change in normal relations between the Netherlands Indies and Japan.

(3) *Statement of the Japanese Cabinet Information Bureau, June 18, 1941*[5]

As early as November 1939, the Japanese Government proposed to the Netherlands Government to open economic negotiations between

---

[1] *The Times* (London), June 19, 20, 1941, p. 3.
[2] *New York Times*, June 1, 1941, p. 25.
[3] Release of Department of State, *Bulletin*, III, p. 432.
[4] Associated Press dispatch, *New York Times*, June 18, 1941, p. 13.
[5] *New York Times*, June 19, 1941, p. 8.

Japan and the Netherlands Indies. Having received the latter's acceptance of our proposals in principle, we informally showed them an outline of our proposals. Meanwhile we carried on negotiations with Netherlands authorities in Tokyo, The Hague and Batavia with respect to opening negotiations in a concrete manner.

However, the European War spread to the Netherlands in May 1940, and the Netherlands Indies came to feel its effects, with the result that the situation developed in such a manner that Japan could not remain indifferent. The Japanese Government, therefore, made a request to the Netherlands Government that negotiations be speedily opened with a view to establishing economic cooperation between Japan and the Netherlands Indies.

The situation at that time was such, since the Netherlands Government had moved to London and decided to carry on the war in alliance with England and the economy of the Netherlands Indies was mobilized for war purposes, that economic relations between Japan and the Netherlands Indies were bound to be gravely affected.

Due to the necessity of establishing a relationship of common prosperity through close cooperation among the people of East Asia, the Japanese Government cannot, of course, remain indifferent to the spread of the European war to the South Seas.

Moreover, it was clear that her [Japan's] demand for the resources of the Netherlands Indies would steadily increase in the course of the establishment of a high-degree defense State.

Under these circumstances it was necessary for Japan to be assured, as soon as possible, of a supply of essential resources and to establish economically cooperative relations between Japan and the Netherlands Indies, thereby bringing about the stabilization of East Asia. The Japanese Government accordingly requested of the Netherlands Government in May of last year an assurance of the supply to Japan of those important materials and goods which Japan expected of the Netherlands Indies under the prevailing situation.

In response the Netherlands Government expressed the intention of actively cooperating with Japan by assuring that the economic relations of the Netherlands Indies with Japan would continue as smoothly as before and confirming that such relations would be in harmony with the vital interests of the Netherlands Indies and would contribute toward the peace and stability of East Asia. On the basis of this agreement of views between Japan and the Netherlands Indies the Japanese Government has conducted economic negotiations in Batavia since September of last year, exerting the utmost efforts for their amicable conclusion.

The negotiations between Japan and the Netherlands Indies were so varied as to include not only the question of acquiring materials and goods, but the question of promoting general trade relations, and the entry of Japanese into the Netherlands Indies in pursuit of occupations and investment in enterprise of shipping, aviation service and communications.

As regards the aforementioned matters, especially aviation connections, they had already been carried on between third Powers and the Netherlands Indies, and regarding investment in enterprises such as the oil industry, Anglo-American capital has shown remarkable activities. Third powers are thus very liberally permitted to engage in all these enterprises.

In the light of these facts the requests of the Japanese Government are very reasonable.

If such Japanese requests — for the participation of Japanese in the development of the abundant natural resources of the Netherlands Indies, the entry of Japanese there accompanying such a development in pursuit of their occupations, the calling of Japanese ships at closed ports for the purpose of transporting materials produced by such a development, the partial opening of coastwise navigation to Japanese ships, and the development of the fishing industry by Japanese who are there — were dealt with on a basis of promoting economic cooperation between Japan and the Netherlands Indies, the solution of these questions would be very simple.

Regarding these requests, the Netherlands Indies Government stressed that the basis of their policy lies in the progress, prosperity and emancipation of the inhabitants of the Netherlands Indies. It is clear, however, that the proposals of the Japanese Government do not in any respect run counter to such a policy in the Netherlands Indies.

It is needless to say that the progress, prosperity and emancipation of the inhabitants would be promoted on the part of the Netherlands Indies through the establishment of economic cooperation between Japan and the Netherlands Indies and would thereby contribute toward the peace and stability of East Asia.

However, along with the intensification of economic warfare the situation surrounding the Netherlands Indies made the smooth progress of negotiations difficult. The reply of the Netherlands of June 6 is not only very unsatisfactory but asserts in connection with the question of the acquisition of essential materials and goods, to which Japan attaches importance, that their quantities may be decreased at any time to suit their own convenience.

In view of the fact that in respect to this question the Netherlands Government as well as the Netherlands Indies on many occasions in the past made promises or declarations to Japan, the Japanese Government, deeming such contents as embodied in the Netherlands reply hardly worth being incorporated in an international agreement, has decided to discontinue the negotiations.

CHAPTER IV

EUROPEAN RELATIONS

(INCLUDING THE NEAR AND MIDDLE EAST)

1. THREE–POWER PACT

(1) *The Three-Power Pact between Germany, Italy and Japan, Signed at Berlin, September 27, 1940* [1]

In force September 27, 1940

[Translation]

The Governments of Germany, Italy and Japan consider it the prerequisite of a lasting peace that every nation in the world shall receive the space to which it is entitled. They have, therefore, decided to stand by and cooperate with one another in their efforts in Greater East Asia and the regions of Europe respectively. In doing this it is their prime purpose to establish and maintain a new order of things, calculated to promote the mutual prosperity and welfare of the peoples concerned.

It is, furthermore, the desire of the three Governments to extend cooperation to nations in other spheres of the world who are inclined to direct their efforts along lines similar to their own for the purpose of realizing their ultimate object, world peace.

Accordingly, the Governments of Germany, Italy and Japan have agreed as follows:

ARTICLE 1. Japan recognizes and respects the leadership of Germany and Italy in the establishment of a new order in Europe.

ARTICLE 2. Germany and Italy recognize and respect the leadership of Japan in the establishment of a new order in Greater East Asia.

ARTICLE 3. Germany, Italy and Japan agree to cooperate in their efforts on aforesaid lines. They further undertake to assist one another with all political, economic and military means if one of the three Con-

---

[1] German Library of Information, *Facts in Review*, II, p. 486. The instrument has been officially called a treaty and a pact. German, Italian and Japanese texts exist in the *alternat*, but it is not stated which of them is controlling; the authorized English translation here given, which differs from other English translations in the grammatical construction of the preamble, is from the German text.

tracting Powers is attacked by a Power at present not involved in the European War or in the Chinese-Japanese conflict.

ARTICLE 4. With the view to implementing the present pact, joint technical commissions, to be appointed by the respective Governments of Germany, Italy and Japan, will meet without delay.[1]

ARTICLE 5. Germany, Italy and Japan affirm that the above agreement affects in no way the political status existing at present between each of the three Contracting Parties and Soviet Russia.

ARTICLE 6. The present pact shall become valid immediately upon signature and shall remain in force ten years from the date on which it becomes effective.

In due time, before the expiration of said term, the High Contracting Parties shall, at the request of any one of them, enter into negotiations for its renewal.

In recognition thereof, the undersigned, duly authorized by their respective governments, have signed this pact and have affixed their seals thereto.

DONE in triplicate at Berlin, the 27th day of September, 1940, in the eighteenth year of the Fascist era, corresponding to the 27th day of the ninth month of the fifteenth year of Showa.

[Here follow signatures.]

(a) Statements at the Signing Ceremony, September 27, 1940 [2]

(i) The German Minister for Foreign Affairs, Joachim von Ribbentrop

Since the National and Socialist Revolution of 1933 it has been the aim of the German Government to bring about by peaceful ways and means, based on mutual agreements, those revisions which would not only remove the injustices of the Versailles Treaty, but would insure a cooperative way of living along new and permanent lines for the nations of Europe.

[1] The following announcement was issued by the Cabinet Information Bureau at Tokyo, December 20, 1940 (*Japan Weekly Chronicle*, December 26, 1941, p. 810):

"With regard to the organization of joint technical commissions charged with the task of executing the provisions stipulated by the Three-Power Pact concluded among Japan, Germany and Italy on September 27, 1940, an agreement of views has been reached among the Japanese, German and Italian Governments for the setting up of a General Commission, a Military Commission and an Economic Commission at the capitals of the three countries concerned.

"The Commissions will start work upon the completion of necessary preparations."

The mixed committees consist of the foreign ministers and the ambassadors of the three states at Berlin, Rome and Tokyo, with subordinate military and economic committees at each capital (*Japan Weekly Chronicle*, February 20, 1941, p. 201).

[2] German Library of Information (New York City), *Facts in Review*, II, p. 487–8.

The German people had a right, like the other great nations, to participate in the riches of the earth and, especially, to administer themselves that share of it which once belonged to them.

The struggle of the nations for social justice and for equitable conditions and opportunities at home presupposes the achievement of similar conditions in international relations.

The endeavor of the German people for a free hand in the living space to which they are entitled by their geographical situation, their history and their national greatness, as well as by their economic position, involved no invasion of foreign vital interests, but respresented, on the contrary, an extraordinary self-restraint.

In an age in which other, smaller nations have claimed for centuries their right to entire continents, the National Socialist Government was, however, determined to safeguard under all circumstances the right of the German people to exist within their own appropriate living-space. Its efforts coincided with those of other nations against whom, as in the case of the German people, attempts had been made to restrict their means of existence and to deny them the space they need to live.

After years of labor had succeeded in removing, by peaceful agreements, a large part of the injustices inflicted upon Germany, the organized warmongers of the Jewish capitalist democracies finally succeeded in throwing Europe into a new struggle, undesired by Germany.

However, far from impeding the rectification of those conditions in Europe which could no longer be borne, the conflict is actually accelerating it. A state of world affairs that was no longer tolerable is collapsing under the military blows of the nations attacked.

Great nations which have hitherto been denied participation in the wealth of the earth as equal members of human society, will achieve their final equality in combat, by virtue of the most inalienable of earthly rights. This fight, therefore, is not directed against other people, but against the existence of an international conspiracy which once before succeeded in plunging mankind into a bloody war.

The Three-Power Pact which I have just signed by order of the Führer with the plenipotentiaries of Italy and Japan, solemnly proclaims the union of Germany, Italy and Japan in one bloc, representing their highest common interest in the midst of a new world order that is now evolving. Its aim is to secure the new order in the sections of Europe which are at war, under the joint leadership of Germany and Italy, and to achieve the same object in the Greater Asiatic realm under Japanese leadership. Its foundation rests not only upon friendship, but above all upon the identity of interests existing between three young peoples, striving onward and serving the same social ends.

This pact, accordingly, is not directed against any other people. It is aimed exclusively against those warmongers and irresponsible elements in the rest of the world who, contrary to the real intersts of all nations, strive to prolong and extend the present conflict.

In view of this objective, the three Powers were able to note to their great satisfaction, both in the course of their negotiations and in the conclusion of their agreement, that these new arrangements in nowise affect the relations now existing or in process of formation, between themselves and Soviet Russia.

The pact now signed is a military alliance between three of the most powerful States on earth. It proposes to bring about a just order, both in the European sphere and in the Greater Asiatic realm. Above all, it proposes to bring peace to the world as soon as possible.

Any State, therefore, which meets this bloc with the intention of contributing to the restoration of peaceful relations between peoples will be welcomed sincerely and gratefully and will be invited to cooperate in the political and economic organization of the new order.

But any State which might harbor the intention of interfering in the final phase of the solution of these problems in Europe or Eastern Asia, and of attacking any signatory of the Three-Power Pact, will have to reckon with the entire, massed energy of the three nations, embracing 250 million people. This means that this pact will, in any event, serve the restoration of peace.

In the name of the Reich Government, I salute on this historic day the Emperor, King of Italy; the great Duce, Benito Mussolini, and his Fascist Revolution.

In the name of the Reich, I salute the Emperor of Japan, his Government and his Foreign Minister, who has done so much to bring about this pact.

Above all, I salute the Italian and the Japanese people who are bound to us by an irrevocable decision to struggle jointly for their freedom and their future, a new world order and, ultimately, a durable peace.

(ii) *The Italian Minister for Foreign Affairs, Count Galeazzo Ciano*

The Treaty which today joins Italy, Germany and Japan, seals and confirms in a solemn pledge of political, economic and military cooperation the mutuality of interests and aims which has existed between the three countries in these years during which a new history of the world was being forged.

Italy, Germany and Japan were the agents responsible for shaping these events; they represented their active and creative forces and knew how to enlist from their glorious traditions in war and peace those virtues and energies with which they have given form to a new culture within their own countries, even as they are doing now in the world at large.

In this magnificent work for regeneration, our three nations have constantly encountered the same sinister and stubborn resistance, the same unwillingness to understand and the same hostility.

All three needed air to breathe in order to live. They all three needed work for their sons and space for their peoples. This breath, this space and this work were refused them by those mighty empires which, having monopolized the resources of the world, intended to deny to us the elementary and vital requirements which were our imperative need.

The solidarity that developed during these years between Italy and Japan, and that today unites our three countries in a pact, found its origin and strength in the struggle which, now as in the past, we are forced to carry on.

It is not the outcome of some provisional diplomatic calculation, but the expression of a historical position. In this situation it finds its causes and its aims — causes and aims which, because they correspond with the innermost needs of the three nations, impart to their alliance a quality of indissoluble unity which unites their possessions, their forces and their intentions.

The terms of this Treaty which we have this day concluded, are unequivocal in their simplicity and clarity:

Germany and Italy recognize and respect the leading part to be played by Japan in the creation of a new order in Greater East Asia, just as Japan recognizes and respects the leading part to be played by Italy and Germany in the creation of a new order in Europe.

The three Powers have no wish to threaten or to challenge anyone. Their alliance, confirmed by today's Treaty aimed at preventing any unnecessary extension of the present conflict, and the bloc ensuing from the union of the military and civil forces of our three empires represents an insurmountable rampart that will shatter every attempt to spread the conflict beyond its present confines.

But the significance and the effectiveness of this Treaty extend beyond the present solidarity upon which our three peoples have today agreed; a solidarity existing not merely for the present, but whose inherent creative force affects the future as well.

We are fighting today to create foundations and premises for a new order, which shall promote and ensure the prosperity and welfare of nations. The final victory, for which we are striving with unbending resolution and which, under the guidance of the great leaders of our peoples, will unquestionably be ours is the surest guarantee for all nations of the earth, of a future based on justice and peace.

(iii) *The Japanese Ambassador to Germany, Saburo Kurusu*

It is a sincere pleasure to me that on this day the Three-Power Pact, which is of truly historic importance, has been signed with Germany and Italy, two nations with whom we are friends.

In view of the circumstance that our three nations reveal many similar traits in tradition and national character, and because each one of us is at present actively engaged in the establishment of a new order in Greater East Asia and in Europe respectively, a reciprocal feeling of deep understanding and sympathy has already manifested itself and the firm tie of friendship links us together.

That this friendship now takes concrete shape and leads to the formation of the Three-Power Pact, that these nations should unite their forces with common aims and have resolved to advance toward their ideal — that is truly a great and epoch-making event.

Therefore, on behalf of the Imperial Japanese Government, I desire to express my best wishes for the promising future of the collaboration of our three countries.

The final aim of this Pact is the establishment of general and lasting world peace based on right and justice. It is, therefore, self-evident that we cannot deny our collaboration to those countries who share our views and endeavors; nor does this Pact in any way affect the present political situation existing between Japan, Germany and Italy on the one hand, and the Soviet Union on the other.

The chivalrous spirit of the Japanese Bushido was originally symbolized by the sword. Yet the fundamental principle of the proper handling of the sword does not consist in wanton killing but in protecting human beings.

I feel impelled to express the hope that this Pact, in the hands of the champions of justice in these countries, Japan, Germany and Italy, may become a sword in the hand of the proper judge and will thus contribute toward the establishment of universal peace.

(2) *Statement of the Secretary of State (Hull), September 27, 1940* [1]

The reported agreement of alliance does not, in the view of the Government of the United States, substantially alter a situation which has existed for several years. Announcement of the alliance merely makes clear to all a relationship which has long existed in effect and to which this Government has repeatedly called attention. That such an agreement has been in process of conclusion has been well known for some time, and that fact has been fully taken into account by the Government of the United States in the determining of this country's policies.

(3) *Protocol of Adhesion by Hungary, Vienna, November 20, 1940* [2]

The Governments of Germany, Italy and Japan on one hand and the Government of Hungary on the other hand acknowledge the following through the undersigned plenipotentiaries:

ARTICLE 1. Hungary adheres to the Three-Power Pact signed in Berlin September 27, 1940, between Germany, Italy and Japan.

ARTICLE 2. In so far as joint technical commissions provided for in Aticle 4 of the Three-Power Pact deal with questions touching upon Hungary's interests, representatives of Hungary will also be called in for commission conferences.

ARTICLE 3. The text of the Three-Power Pact is added to this protocol as an annex. The present protocol is drawn up in German, Italian, Japanese and Hungarian languages, of which each text is authentic. The protocol is effective on the day of signing.

[Here follow signatures]

(a) *Attitude of the Soviet Union. Statement of Tass News Agency, November 22, 1940* [3]

The American United Press agency reports that, according to the assertion of the German newspaper *Hamburger Fremdenblatt*, Hungary's adherence to the Three-Power Pact allegedly was reached "with the cooperation and full approval of the Soviet Union." Tass is authorized to state that this report does not correspond with the facts in any extent.

[1] Department of State, *Bulletin*, III, p. 251; issued at the press conference in response to inquiries.

[2] *New York Times*, November 21, 1940. The technical language of the protocols of adhesion has been revised for conformity, since the English versions are of various origins.

[3] United Press, night report, November 22, 1940; printed *New York Times*, November 23, 1940, p. 1.

(4) *Protocol of Adhesion by Rumania, Berlin, November 23, 1940* [1]

The Governments of Germany, Italy and Japan on the one hand and the Government of Rumania on the other acknowledge the following through their undersigned plenipotentiaries:

ARTICLE 1. Rumania adheres to the Three-Power Pact between Germany, Italy and Japan, signed at Berlin, September 27, 1940.

ARTICLE 2. In so far as joint technical commissions provided for in Article 4 of the Three-Power Pact deal with questions affecting Rumania's interests, representatives of Rumania will also be called in for commission conferences.

ARTICLE 3. The text of the Three-Power Pact is added to this protocol as an annex. The present protocol is drawn up in the German, Italian, Japanese and Rumanian languages of which each text is authentic. The present protocol is effective on the day of signing.

[Here follow signatures]

(a) *Withdrawal of British Diplomatic Mission from Rumania. Ministry of Information Release, London, February 10, 1941* [2]

It has been learned in official circles in London that His Majesty's Government has decided to withdraw His Majesty's Minister, his staff and other British officials from Rumania.

It will be recalled that some months ago German troops began to arrive in Rumania in small numbers. At this time the head of the Rumanian Government informed His Majesty's Minister that these German troops had come to Rumania in order to instruct the Rumanian Army in modern methods of warfare.

Some instruction has, no doubt, been imparted, but the essential development is that the German High Command is building up in Rumania all the elements of an expeditionary force and has concentrated at various points large supplies of munitions and oil fuel.

Rumanian territory is thus being used by Germany as a military base in furtherance of her plans for prosecuting the war. These measures are being taken without a word of dissent from the Rumanian Government.

In these circumstances, the position of His Majesty's Legation has become impossible and Sir Reginald Hoare has been instructed to withdraw his mission and the consular officers under his control. This withdrawal will take place in the course of the next few days.

[1] The protocol was signed by Joachim von Ribbentrop, German Minister for Foreign Affairs, Gino Buti, Director of the Political Department, Italian Foreign Office, and Saburo Kurusu, Japanese Ambassador to Germany, on the one side and Ion Antonescu, Prime Minister of Rumania, on the other. See p. 309, note 2.

[2] *New York Times*, February 11, 1941, p. 4.

(5) *Other Adhesions*

Germany, as part of its diplomatic offensive and following visits of officials of the smaller states to that country, secured the subsequent adhesion of the following to the instrument by protocols of like tenor:

Slovakia, Berlin, November 24, 1941
Bulgaria, Vienna, March 1, 1941
Yugoslavia, Vienna, March 25, 1941 (see p. 324)

The "Kingdom of Croatia" became an adherent at Venice on June 15, 1941.

2. WAR AND DIPLOMACY IN EASTERN EUROPE AND THE NEAR AND MIDDLE EAST

A. Italian Invasion of Greece

(1) *The Italian Minister to Greece (Grazzi) to the Greek Government, Athens, October 28, 1940* [1]

The Italian attack on Greece, which took place in the early morning of October 28, after delivery in Athens at 3 A.M. of an ultimatum expiring at 6 A.M., was not entirely unexpected, though the moment was not foreseen. The Greek Government regarded the ultimatum as a declaration of war, and chose the path of resistance. Previously Greece had repeatedly affirmed a policy of neutrality in the European War. On May 1, 1940 General Metaxas, the Greek Prime Minister, declared that Greece would not fight "except to defend her independence and neutrality," and the declaration was repeated in substance on many occasions.

The Italian Government has repeatedly noted how, in the course of the present conflict, the Greek Government assumed and maintained an attitude which was contrary not only with that of formal, peaceful, good neighborly relations between two nations but also with the precise duties which were incumbent on the Greek Government in view of its status as a neutral country.

On various occasions the Italian Government has found it necessary to urge the Greek Government to observe these duties and to protest against their systematic violation, particularly serious since the Greek Government permitted its territorial waters, its coasts and its ports to be used by the British fleet in the course of its war operations, aided in supplying the British air forces and permitted organization of a military information service in the Greek archipelago to Italy's damage.

---

[1] Associated Press version, *New York Times*, October 29, 1940, p. 4. The Italian Premier in an address to the Chamber of Fasces and Corporations on June 10, 1941 said: "On October 15 it was unanimously decided to break hesitancies and take to the field at the end of the month." The time was chosen because the long nights would permit safe convoying and the winter would eliminate malaria (*New York Times*, June 11, 1941, p. 9).

The Greek Government was perfectly aware of these facts, which several times formed the basis of diplomatic representations on the part of Italy to which the Greek Government, which should have taken consideration of the grave consequences of its attitude, failed to respond with any measure for the protection of its own neutrality, but, instead, intensified its activities favoring the British armed forces and its cooperation with Italy's enemies.

The Italian Government has proof that this cooperation was foreseen by the Greek Government and was regulated by understandings of a military, naval and aeronautical character. The Italian Government does not refer only to the British guarantee accepted by Greece as a part of the program of action against Italy's security but also to explicit, precise engagements undertaken by the Greek Government to put at the disposal of powers at war with Italy important strategic positions on Greek territory, including air bases in Tessaglia and Macedonia designed for attack on Albanian territory.

In this connection the Italian Government must remind the Greek Government of the provocative activities carried out against the Albanian nation, together with the terroristic policy it has adopted toward the people of Ciamuria and the persistent efforts to create disorders beyond its frontiers.

For these reasons, also, the Italian Government has accepted the necessity, even though futilely, of calling the attention of the Greek Government to the inevitable consequences of its policy toward Italy. This no longer can be tolerated by Italy.

Greek neutrality has been tending continuously toward a mere shadow. Responsibility for this situation lies primarily on the shoulders of Great Britain and its aim to involve ever more countries in war.

But now it is obvious that the policy of the Greek Government has been and is directed toward transforming Greek territory, or at least permitting Greek territory to be transformed, into a base for war operations against Italy.

This could only lead to armed conflict between Italy and Greece, which the Italian Government has every intention of avoiding.

The Italian Government, therefore, has reached the decision to ask the Greek Government, as a guarantee of Greek neutrality and as a guarantee of Italian security, for permission to occupy with its own armed forces several strategic points in Greek territory for the duration of the present conflict with Great Britain.[1]

[1] On May 6, 1941 the British Secretary of State for Foreign Affairs (Eden) said to the House of Commons:

The Italian Government asks the Greek Government not to oppose this occupation and not to obstruct the free passage of the troops carrying it out.

These troops do not come as enemies of the Greek people and the Italian Government does not in any way intend that the temporary occupation of several strategic points, dictated by special necessities of a purely defensive character, should compromise Greek sovereignty and independence.

The Italian Government asks that the Greek Government give immediate orders to military authorities that this occupation may take place in a peaceful manner. Wherever the Italian troops may meet resistance this resistance will be broken by armed force, and the Greek Government would have the responsibility for the resulting consequences.

(2) *The British Prime Minister (Churchill) to the Greek Prime Minister (Metaxas), London, October 28, 1940* [1]

Italy has found threats and intimidation of no avail against your calm courage. She has therefore resorted to unprovoked aggression against your country, seeking justification for wanton attack in baseless accusations.

The way in which the Greek people under your trusted leadership have faced dangers and provocations of recent months has gained for Greece the admiration of the British people; the same qualities will uphold them in their present hour of trial.

We will give you all the help in our power. We fight a common foe and we will share a united victory.

(3) *His Britannic Majesty (George VI) to the King of Greece (George II), London, October 28, 1940* [1]

In this hour of Greece's need I wish to say to the heroic Greek nation and to my cousin George, King of the Hellenes, this:

"We are with you in this struggle — your cause is our cause — we shall be fighting against a common foe."

There are doubtless hard trials to be borne, but we shall both meet

" . . . In the early morning, at 3 : 00 o'clock, the Italian Minister called on General Metaxas and presented him with an ultimatum, which, he said, would come into force at 6 : 00. The ultimatum contained this clause: — that Italy demanded certain bases in Greece. General Metaxas said, 'What bases?' The Italian Minister said that he did not know. Those were the cynical conditions in which the first attack on Greece was made, before even the ultimatum expired, and those were the conditions in which our guarantee first came into effect." (Parliamentary Debates, House of Commons, 5th series, vol. 371, col. 733.)

[1] *New York Times*, October 29, 1940, p. 7.

them in the firm faith that ultimate victory is assured by the ever-increasing strength of the free peoples.

We may hope indeed that we are already near the turn of the tide, when the power of the aggressor will begin to ebb and our growing might to prevail.

Long live Greece and her leaders. Long live the King of the Hellenes.

(4) *Proclamation of the Prime Minister (Metaxas), November 22, 1940* [1]

Twenty-five days ago we were attacked with the only aim of stealing from us those qualities that the enemy did not possess — our liberty and our national independence and our honor. All Greece took up arms and the desperate struggle began immediately.

Our success soon began and it has been followed by one victory after another. Our army, navy and air force have rivalled each other in glorifying the name of Greece. We must thank our brave ally the British for their wholehearted help, and for the incomparable exploits of their fleet and their famous aviators.

During the past ten days the struggle became most intense in the west, where a continuous heavy battle resulted in the fall of the Merova bastion and the capture today of Koritza, as well as an advance on all fronts.

When Mussolini decided to subjugate Greece we took the decision not to be exterminated. We will live, and with our ally Britain we will conquer. Our path will not be strewn with flowers, but we will face all dangers and we will conquer the enemy.

We fight not only for our existence but for the other Balkan peoples and the liberation of Albania. We are struggling for ideals whose importance transcends our boundaries and the boundaries of the Balkans, and extends to all humanity. We should thank God, whose providence has once more designated Greece as a champion in such a supreme struggle.

(5) *The King of Greece (George II) to the President (Roosevelt), December 3, 1940* [2]

ROYAL GREEK LEGATION,
WASHINGTON, *December 3, 1940.*

TO THE PRESIDENT OF THE UNITED STATES:

In this hour in which my country is engaged in a hard and unequal struggle, forced upon it by an enemy whose actions are motivated by

---

[1] *New York Times*, November 23, 1940, p. 2. Greek troops on November 22 occupied the Albanian town of Koritza, which had been the base of the Italian forces that invaded Greece at the beginning of the Italian aggression.

[2] Department of State, *Bulletin*, III, p. 503.

cruelty and violence, I am deeply moved by the warm sympathy and the keen interest manifested by the great Nation whose destinies you guide.

The noble American people have often in the past rendered assistance to my country in all critical moments of its history, and the recent organization of the Greek War Relief Association is further proof that philhellenism continues to inspire Americans of today in their lofty aims.

Guardians across the seas of the ideals for which throughout the centuries Greeks have lived and died, Americans today are aware that the Greek nation is again fighting for the principles of justice, truth and liberty, without which life for us is inconceivable.

I wish to assure you that with the help of the Almighty, we will march forward until our sacred struggle is crowned with success. All moral and material assistance will strengthen the heroic Greek army and will bring it nearer to victory.

GEORGE II
R

(6) *The President (Roosevelt) to the King of Greece (George II),
December 5, 1940* [1]

DECEMBER 5, 1940.

His Majesty GEORGE II,
    King of Greece.

I thank Your Majesty for your friendly message which comes at a time when all free peoples are deeply impressed by the courage and steadfastness of the Greek nation.

The American Red Cross has already sent substantial amounts of funds and supplies for the relief of suffering in your country and I am sure that my countrymen will give generously to the new organizations which are being established for the same purpose.

As Your Majesty knows, it is the settled policy of the United States Government to extend aid to those governments and peoples who defend themselves against aggression. I assure Your Majesty that steps are being taken to extend such aid to Greece which is defending itself so valiantly.

FRANKLIN D. ROOSEVELT

(7) *The King of Greece (George II) to the President (Roosevelt),
March 17, 1941* [2]

In his speech of March 15, 1941, the President of the United States made several references to Greece. He mentioned it as one of the nations actuated

---

[1] Department of State, *Bulletin*, III, p. 503.   [2] *Ibid.*, p. 374.

by loyalty without coercion; he included it as one of the countries to receive "all-out aid" under the "Lend-Lease Act," and specifically said Greece would get ships, planes, food, tanks, guns, ammunition and supplies of all kinds.

ATHENS, *March 17, 1941.*

Your noble words [1] have been deeply felt in Greece whose gratitude toward the United States of America and its illustrious President is infinite. In the name of the Hellenic people I thank you for the confidence in it which you are good enough to express. In the name of the Greek Army I wish to assure you that every cannon, every shell placed in its hands will be a gain for the ideas to which the Union devotes in so lofty a spirit its immense resources. The soldiers of Greece also are resolved to win the right that free nations worthy of liberty may be able to repeat in the days of posterity your moving words blessed be our ancestors.

GEORGE II

(8) *The President (Roosevelt) to the King of Greece (George II), March 24, 1941* [2]

WASHINGTON, *March 24, 1941.*

I deeply appreciate Your Majesty's cordial message. Greece has abundantly proved herself a free nation worthy of the liberty she is so brilliantly maintaining. I have every certainty that the resources which the United States is making available to free peoples will make it possible for these peoples to create a nobler world. I am very sure that the will to victory of the soldiers of Greece will be rewarded by success.

FRANKLIN D. ROOSEVELT

B. German Invasion of Greece

(1) *The German Foreign Office to the Greek Minister at Berlin, April 6, 1941* [3]

The German note of April 6, 1941 which launched the attack on Greece was full of concern for the Greek people. The extent to which the Greek Government had sided with the enemies of Germany was dilated upon from documents of the French General Staff found by the Germans at La Charité, which were said to be published but have not become available. In face of the "irresponsible policy" of the Greek Government in permitting "British troops to set foot again on European soil," Germany could "no longer remain inactive." And so:

[1] See address of the President, March 15, 1941, p. 38–40.

[2] Department of State, *Bulletin,* IV, p. 374.

[3] German Library of Information, *Facts in Review,* April 21, 1941, p. 207. The Germans crossed the Bulgaro-Greek frontier at 5:45 A.M. April 6 without ultimatum or warning.

[Excerpt]

The German Government has therefore given orders to its forces to drive the British from Greek territory. Any opposition which may be offered to the German forces will be ruthlessly crushed. In notifying the Greek Government of this, the Reich Government emphasizes that the German troops are not coming as enemies of the Greek people, and that the German people have no desire to fight and destroy the Greek people.

The blow which Germany is forced to deal on Greek soil is intended for Britain. The Reich Government is convinced that in rapidly expelling the British intruders from Greece it will be rendering an important service to the people of Greece and to the European community.

(2) The British Secretary of State for Foreign Affairs (Eden) to the House of Commons, May 6, 1941 [1]

[Excerpt]

We [the Secretary of State for Foreign Affairs, the Chief of the Imperial General Staff, the Commander-in-Chief of the Middle East Army, a representative of the Commander-in-Chief in the Mediterranean and the Air Officer Commanding] went to Athens to see the representatives of the Greek Government. That, I think, probably would be about February 22. The moment we landed at the aerodrome I received a message saying that the King and the Prime Minister wished to see me alone before the actual meeting began. When I saw them they told me this: They made it once more abundantly clear that Greece was determined to resist German aggression as she had resisted Italian aggression. The Prime Minister added that, whatever the hope of repulsing the enemy, Greece would defend her national territory, even if she could count only on her own forces. . . .

At these discussions we told the Greek Government our views of the German plans, and we told them what forces could be made available by our Commanders-in-Chief in the Middle East. Then the Chiefs of Staff and the Commanders-in-Chief of the two armies considered what were the possibilities of holding a line, with our forces and with such forces as the Greeks could make available.

[1] Parliamentary Debates, House of Commons, 5th series, vol. 371, col. 732.

(3) *The Order of the Day to the Greek Army, April 6, 1941* [1]

Once more Greek arms are called upon to defend the national territory. One more invader, one more opponent, belonging unfortunately to a group of self-styled civilized countries, is attempting to trod on our sacred things. We shall resist and win as we defeated other numerous enemies, as we resisted his words and his despised demands.

We shall win because we shall fight under the standard of supreme justice, and because at our side stands a determined ally, the armed might of the British Empire.

We shall fight, opposing our arms and breasts to the force of the invader, teaching our new opponent that the Greece from whom one invader learned so many valuable lessons is not dishonored.

Fighters of the Italian front, go on in glorious and unexcelled effort, keeping always under your feet and under your will your opponent.

Fighters of the German front, show that you are worthy of your fellow-fighters on the Italian front. Make it your ambition to add new laurels to the pages of the history of our nation.

Officers, non-commissioned officers and soldiers, the God of Greece is with us. The Virgin Mary will follow us up with devotion in our new struggles. The immortal fate of the nation which preserved and maintained the liberties and high manifestations of the human spirit and of the morality and good through the ages is at our side today.

With our British brothers at arms — because they are now our brothers and the two countries follow united the same path which leads to a difficult trial — we shall preserve the honor of the fatherland.

We look forward, drawing superhuman courage from our souls which feel fully that we always will fight for our hearths and homes with arms in hand and under God's cover we shall walk to victory.

A final most brilliant, most sacred Greek victory — there are no Greek doubts — will be ours.

(4) *The King of Greece (George II) to His People, April 6, 1941* [2]

Hellenes! A new enemy has this morning attacked the honor of our country. At the same moment that the German Government was handing the Greek Government a document informing it of its action, German troops, without warning, struck at our frontier. Our valorous army,

---

[1] *New York Times*, April 7, 1941, p. 3; issued by Field Marshal Alexander Papagos, the Commander-in-Chief.

[2] Recorded from broadcast, *New York Times*, April 7, 1941, p. 3.

the vigilant guardian of our sacred soil, is already defending it with its blood.

Hellenes! The Greek people who have already proved to the world that they valued their honor above all else, will now defend it to the very last against a new foe.

Another empire has today attacked this country of ours which is small in size but at the same time is so great in spirit as to allow no one to outrage us.

Our trouble will be harsh, difficult and ruthless. We shall not cry before any pain nor stop at any sacrifice. We know that victory is at the journey's end and will once more and this time definitely crown our efforts. At our side stand our powerful allies, the nations of the British Commonwealth, with their indomitable will as well as the United States of America, with their inexhaustible resources.

On the field of battle we fight shoulder to shoulder with our brothers, the Yugoslavs, who, together with us, are shedding their blood for the salvation of the Balkans and humanity. We shall win with the help of God, and the blessing of the Holy Virgin we shall surely win. History will once more record that the country glorified by Marathon and Ptolemy has not bowed down, will not bend, will never surrender.

Altogether, men, women, children of Hellenes, rise up, clench your fists, stand at my side to defend the country, the Greece of yesterday, of today and of tomorrow and prove yourselves worthy of your forefathers and examples for the generations to come, soldiers in the vanguard of that freedom, which has sprung from the sacred bones of the Greeks.

Forward! Sons of Hellas in the fight for body and soul.

(5) *Terms of Surrender between the Greek Army of Epirus and the German and Italian High Commands, Salonika, April 23, 1941* [1]

The High Command of the Greek Army in Epirus and Macedonia represented by General Tsolakoglou turns to the Italian High Command of Armed Forces in Albania and the High Command of German Forces in Greece to ask that unconditional surrender of the Greek Army in Epirus and Macedonia be accepted.

ARTICLE I. The Italian High Command in Albania and the High Command of German troops in Greece accept this surrender without condition.

[1] Associated Press version, *New York Times*, April 24, 1941, p. 4. The text was telegraphed from Rome.

ARTICLE II. Men of the Greek Army of Epirus and Macedonia are prisoners of war. In consideration of the courage shown by Greek troops on the battlefield and the fact that in this way they saved their military honor, Greek officers may keep their sidearms and uniform distinctions.

All Italian prisoners of war in territory of the Greek Army of Epirus and Macedonia must be handed over to Italian troops immediately.

Greek prisoners of war meanwhile will be assembled in concentration camps.

After conclusion of military operations in Continental Greece and the Ionian Islands, liberation of all officers, subofficers and soldiers will be taken into consideration.

ARTICLE III. The Greek High Command will see that Greek detachments remain under the commands of their officers and will take all measures to carry out the surrender.

The provisioning and sanitary service of Greek prisoners will in the beginning be handled by the Greek High Command.

ARTICLE IV. Arms, all war material and provisions of the Army of Epirus and Macedonia, including aviation material and its ground works, constitute spoils of war.

ARTICLE V. The High Command of the Greek troops will, with all its means, see that hostilities cease immediately and that all damage as well as destruction of war materials and supplies and also roads in the army's territory, be immediately prohibited.

ARTICLE VI. The departure of ships of all kinds from ports and all air traffic in the territory of the Army of Epirus and Macedonia must be suspended.

ARTICLE VII. The Greek High Command guarantees that shipping in ports and port works remain under guard of Greek troops until a definite decision is taken in the matter.

ARTICLE VIII. The High Command of the Greek troops will name commissions furnished with full power to carry out details of the surrender with Italian and German organs that will be named later.

The above commission will report on the situation of force, arms and war formations of the surrendered Army of Epirus and Macedonia.

ARTICLE IX. Cessation of hostilities for German troops and Greek troops of Epirus and Macedonia stands as agreed upon in surrender terms of April 21.

Cessation of hostilities between Italian troops and the Greek Army of Epirus and Macedonia will go into effect today, April 23, at 6 P.M., except for Greek detachments on the Italian front who already have laid down their arms.

ARTICLE X. With the conclusion of the present convention of surrender, the convention concluded April 21 between the German High Command in Greece and the Commander of the Greek Army in Epirus and Macedonia ceases to be effective.

Salonika, April 23, 1941.

For the German High Command: JODL
For the Italian High Command: FERRERO
For the Greek High Command: TSOLAKOGLOU

(6) *Manifesto of the King of Greece (George II), Athens, April 23, 1941* [1]

The hard destinies of war compel us to get away from Athens, together with the Crown Prince and lawful government of the country, and to transfer the capital of the country to Crete, whence we shall be able to continue the fight which is the will of the nation and the duty of safeguarding the independence and integrity imposed upon us and undertaken after unprovoked aggressions of which we have been the object by two empires.

Our will, the will of the Government and of the Greek people, having been manifested in various ways so far, means resistance to the end on the part of Greek troops which, despite the unequal fight, particularly after the German invasion, have stubbornly fought beside the English allies who rushed help to us and are still fighting on Greek territory for the sake of the right cause.

Our troops, exhausted from the hard and victorious war which they had been waging for six months against a much stronger enemy and having written the most glorious pages of our military history, continued the fight against the Germans with inconceivable heroism.

We do not yet know in what conditions exactly our army of Epirus has been found and signed an armistice with the enemy without our knowing it.

This act in no way binds the free will of the nation, the King and the Government, which consists of a continuation of the struggle with all remaining forces with a view to securing the supreme national interests.

Being compelled to proceed to Crete, I do it only in order that freely and from Greek territory we may be able to continue to fight against the invaders until the final victory which will crown in full the great sacrifices of the nation.

Do not lose your courage, Greeks, even during this painful moment of our history. We shall always be among you.

[1] Associated Press version, *New York Times*, April 24, 1941, p. 3.

The right of our struggle and God will help us to secure by all means final victory, in spite of the trials, pains and dangers which we shall go through in the meantime.

Remain faithful to the idea of a united and undivided free country. Intensify your will, oppose Greek pride to enemy force and enemy temptations. Have courage — good days will come again. Long live the nation!

GEORGE II

ATHENS, *April 23, 1941*.

(7) *Proclamation of the Greek Prime Minister* (*Tsouderos*), *Athens, April 23, 1941* [1]

In this so hard but so great moment, at which we are leaving for Crete with the heroic King of our country, worthy counselor and premier adviser in the struggle that his country is continuing, I feel obliged to say that I am really proud of this national political unity, which symbolizes in the best way the inflexible Greek mold and manifests the steadfast will of all of us not to surrender to the invader.

We are defending ourselves against an unfair aggression, but also against the unprecedented infamy on the part of an empire of 100,000,000 that struck us from the back in order to save its cowardly colleague and partner, whom we had defeated.

From the endurances of this hard struggle against our race, which is disapproved by all those who are morally superior and by free peoples of the world, who have expressed their disgust, we shall come out victorious, glorious and great. The moral power of our country has never reached such a height before.

The armistice that has been signed with the Germans without authority appears to have been precipitated by exhaustion from an unequalled victorious struggle of six months and more. It is the result of crushing pressure exerted on our gallant army.

The struggle is full of material calamities and cowardly blows against civilians. But losses do not daunt the brave. These will be replaced and compensated for. All Greeks will share the losses, and we shall restrict compensation to those who will suffer them. This is a sacred and invaluable obligation.

Have endurance. In this way you will increase the moral benefits to the country, whereby very soon a new and great Greece will be reborn. Nations that keep their honor and respect their friendly obligations obtain title deeds serving their interests.

[1] Associated Press version, *New York Times*, April 24, 1941, p. 3.

These titles are written in blood and describe sacrifices and supreme heroisms. We are bound to respect and safeguard them.

Be sure that soon a brilliant national day will break, a greater day for Hellenism.

TSOUDEROS

ATHENS, *April 23, 1941*.

The surrender of the Greek army in Epirus and Macedonia by its commanding general without authority strategically forced the Greek and British forces farther east to withdraw. The Greek Government transferred the capital to Crete on April 23. German forces entered Athens April 27. On the 29th General Tsolakoglou, who had surrendered in Epirus, charged that the King had forfeited his right to represent the nation, and followed up this statement by heading a puppet government. The Allied forces in Crete were placed under a single command May 5. German attacks on Crete, with increasing use of parachute troops, began on May 11, its occupation being completed June 2. The Greek Government removed to Cairo on May 25.

(8) *Statement of the President* (*Roosevelt*), *April 25, 1941* [1]

The heroic struggle of the Hellenic people to defend their liberties and their homes against the aggression of Germany after they had so signally defeated the Italian attempt at invasion has stirred the hearts and aroused the sympathy of the whole American people.

During the Hellenic War of Independence more than a century ago, our young Nation, prizing its own lately won independence, expressed its ardent sympathy for the Greeks and hoped for Hellenic victory. That victory was achieved.

Today, at a far more perilous period in the history of Hellas, we intend to give full effect to our settled policy of extending all available material aid to free peoples defending themselves against aggression. Such aid has been and will continue to be extended to Greece.

Whatever may be the temporary outcome of the present phase of the war in Greece, I believe that the Greek people will once more ultimately achieve their victory and regain their political independence and the territorial integrity of their country. In that high objective, the people of Greece and their Government can count on the help and support of the Government and the people of the United States.

[1] Text from the Office of the Secretary to the President; Department of State, *Bulletin*, IV, p. 497.

C. Invasion of Yugoslavia

The recurrent defeats of Italy in Albania by Greece, in Africa and the Mediterranean by the British Commonwealth between October 1940 and February 1941 impelled Germany to enter Italy in force in an effort to bolster up the Fascist regime. Since September 1940 Germany and Italy (with Japan) added to the façade of their Three-Power Pact by the adherence of Hungary on November 20, 1940, of Rumania on November 23, and of Bulgaria on March 1, 1941. With the exception of Greece, all the States bordering on Yugoslavia were bound to the German regime.

Germany thereupon began to undermine Yugoslav independence by the customary method of undesired visits by the Regent, the Premier and the Minister for Foreign Affairs to Hitler and other German officials. Opposition within the country delayed signing of the protocol of adherence by Yugoslavia to the treaty of September 27, 1940. It was signed at Vienna, March 25, 1941, by the representatives of Germany, Italy and Japan and by a Yugoslav delegation. The instrument stipulated that it was in force from signing, though ratification by Yugoslavia was provided for.

This act of subordination was badly received in Yugoslavia. On March 26–27 Premier Dragisha Cvetkovitch, Foreign Minister Aleksandr Cincar-Markovitch and the rest of the cabinet were arrested by army officers, and Regent Prince Paul was sent out of the country. At 2 : 00 A.M., March 27, King Peter II, in whose name the overthrow of the cabinet occurred and who was six months short of his legal majority, assumed the headship of the state with General Dusan Simovitch as Premier. The Vienna protocol to the Three-Power Pact was neither repudiated nor denounced.

These events took place at Belgrade, the capital and the center of the Serbian portion of Yugoslavia. The revolution was carried off by Serbians. Vladimir Matchek, the leader of the Croats, as vice-premier typified the governmental collaboration between the Serbs, Croats, and Slovenes which the regency had secured. Whether the Croats and Slovenes, whose part of the country is low and lay next to Germany, were susceptible of defection was not long in doubt.

(1) *Protocol of Adhesion of Yugoslavia to the Three-Power Pact, Vienna, March 25, 1941* [1]

[For the Pact and other Protocols of Adhesion, see p. 304, 309, 310, 311.]

The Governments of Germany, Italy and Japan on the one hand and the Government of Yugoslavia on the other hand, through their plenipotentiaries, acknowledge the following:

ARTICLE I. Yugoslavia adheres to the Three-Power Pact, which was signed September 27, 1940, at Berlin, between Germany, Italy and Japan.

ARTICLE II. Representatives of Yugoslavia will be present at conferences of commissions for common technical questions created under

---

[1] United Press version, *New York Times*, March 26, 1941, p. 3. The preamble and other formal clauses were not telegraphed.

Article IV of the Three-Power Pact so far as the commission deals with matters touching Yugoslavia's interests.

ARTICLE III. The text of the Three-Power Pact is added as an annex to this protocol. This protocol is drawn up in the German, Italian, Japanese and Yugoslav languages, each of which is authentic. The present protocol comes into effect on the day of signing.

[Here follow signatures.]

(a) The German Secretary of State for Foreign Affairs (Ribbentrop) to the Yugoslav Prime Minister (Cvetkovitch), Vienna, March 25, 1941 [1]

MR. PRIME MINISTER:

In the name of the German Government and at its behest I have the honor to inform Your Excellency of the following:

On the occasion of the Yugoslav adherence today to the Three-Power Pact the German Government confirms its decision to respect the sovereignty and territorial integrity of Yugoslavia at all times.

(b) The German Secretary of State for Foreign Affairs (Ribbentrop) to the Yugoslav Prime Minister (Cvetkovitch), Vienna, March 25, 1941 [1]

MR. PRIME MINISTER:

With reference to the conversations that occurred in connection with Yugoslav adherence to the Three-Power Pact I have the honor to confirm to Your Excellency herewith in the name of the Reich Government that in the agreement between the Governments of the Axis powers and the Royal Yugoslav Government the Axis power governments during this war will not demand of Yugoslavia to permit the march or transportation of troops through the Yugoslav State or territory.

Permit me, Mr. Prime Minister, to express the assurance of my highest respects.

JOACHIM VON RIBBENTROP

(2) Proclamations of the King (Peter II) on Assuming Royal Powers, March 27, 1941 [2]

FIRST PROCLAMATION

Serbs, Croats, Slovenes!

In this moment so grave for our people I have decided to take the royal power into my hands.

[1] United Press version, New York Times, March 26, 1941, p. 3. Identic notes were addressed to the Yugoslav plenipotentiaries by the representatives of Italy and Japan.

[2] Version circulated by the British Broadcasting Corporation, transcribed by the Columbia Broadcasting System, New York Times, March 28, 1941, p. 2.

The members of the Regency Council have appreciated the correctness of the reasons for my action and immediately resigned at their own accord.

My royal army and the navy have at once placed themselves at my disposal and are already carrying out my orders.

I appeal to all Serbs, Croats, and Slovenes to rally round the Throne.

Under the present grave circumstances this is the surest way of preserving internal order and external peace.

I have charged General Simovitch with the formation of a new government.

With trust in God and the future of Yugoslavia I appeal to all citizens and all authorities of the country to fulfill their duties to King and country.   PETER II

SECOND PROCLAMATION

In these moments so grave for our nation I am taking over the discharge of my functions as King.

The Regents have resigned. I have already begun to exercise my royal functions.

My army and the navy are at my orders, which is the best means of maintaining order and peace.

I appeal to all Serbs, Croats and Slovenes to go on with their normal work.   PETER II

(3) *The President* (*Roosevelt*) *to the King of Yugoslavia* (*Peter II*), *March 28, 1941* [1]

MARCH 28, 1941.

At this moment when Your Majesty has assumed the full exercise of your royal rights and powers and the leadership of a brave and independent people, I wish to share with the people of the United States in the expression of our sincere and genuine wishes for the health and well being of Your Majesty and for the freedom and independence of Yugoslavia. Furthermore, I extend the hope that the relations between your Government and the Government of the United States may be mutually beneficial in the support of those principles of liberty and tolerance so cherished by the Yugoslav and American peoples.

FRANKLIN D. ROOSEVELT

[1] Department of State, *Bulletin*, IV, p. 350.

(4) Reports of the American Minister to Yugoslavia (Lane) [1]

[This release is printed to present the facts of the *coup d'état* and to indicate the type of information on which the Department of State has to act in critical situations.]

The American Minister to Yugoslavia, Mr. Arthur Bliss Lane, reported to the Department of State under date of March 27 that a successful military *coup d'état* took place at approximately 2 : 15 o'clock that morning under the leadership of General Simovitch, Chief of Aviation. A manifesto made public early that morning and signed by King Peter II stated that he had assumed power, that the Regents had resigned, that Yugoslavia hoped for external and internal peace and appealed to the population to support the Throne.

The Constitution of the new Government under General Simovitch as Prime Minister was announced at about 9 : 30 A.M., March 27. It included Matchek as Vice President and Nincic as Foreign Minister. All major parties are represented. Mr. Lane reported, "There was wild enthusiasm in Belgrade this morning with continuous demonstrations, including two in front of this Legation." It was announced from radio cars that the *coup d'état* had been acclaimed in cities throughout the country including Zagreb.

Mr. Lane reported at midnight on March 27 that during the evening he had made an official call on the newly appointed Minister for Foreign Affairs. He had requested audiences with King Peter and General Simovitch.

Again on March 27, Mr. Lane reported that all Americans in Belgrade were safe and well. He said that communications with the rest of the country were difficult but that reports indicated that there were no disorders.

On March 28, Mr. Lane reported that he had addressed a note to the Minister for Foreign Affairs embodying the message which he had been instructed to deliver to the Yugoslav Government.[2]

On March 28, Mr. Lane reported that after a Cabinet meeting which began at 9 o'clock on the night of March 27, the following statement was given to the press by the new President of the Council, General Simovitch:

"In these serious days the people of Yugoslavia felt concern at the manner in which public affairs were being handled. This lack of confidence in the state of affairs created during the last few days was manifested with such vigor that public order was endangered. The present changes came about under the pressure of this public anxiety. There are no other reasons for the change since the accession to power of King Peter II who at once formed a Government of national union representing the views of the Serb, Croat and Slovene peoples.

[1] Press release of March 29, 1941; Department of State, *Bulletin*, IV, p. 349.
[2] Mr. Lane had been instructed to state more or less the following to the new Government of Yugoslavia: That the information which has been received has been widely welcomed in the United States as a matter for self-congratulation to every liberty-loving man and woman; and that in accordance with the terms of the Lease-Lend Act the President is, of course, enabled in the interest of the national defense of the United States to render effective material assistance to nations which are seeking to preserve their independence and integrity against aggression.

"In the name of the Government at the head of which I stand, I today as my first duty address an appeal to the citizens as well as to the authorities to assist the Royal Government in the carrying out of its duties, the first of which at this moment is to preserve internal order and external peace.

"I call on the patriotic citizens of Yugoslavia to desist from any manifestations which might make more difficult our relations with our neighbors, with whom we wish to remain in peace and friendship.

"I appeal to the people not to give way to any rash acts nor to be influenced by any side. We continue to watch over our own interests — independent and honorable. Strict order and correct attitude are the first conditions for the successful carrying out of the task which lies before us."

At the same time the Belgrade prefecture forbade public meetings or demonstrations, decreed a closing time for cafés and prohibited the sale of alcohol in any form.

On the evening of March 28, Mr. Lane reported that a *Te Deum* was held in the Orthodox cathedral at which the King, the Government, and the Diplomatic Corps were present. The King received a tremendous ovation from the crowd, which spontaneously demonstrated in favor of the United States. Mr. Lane's car, which carried the American flag, was surrounded by a cheering crowd from the cathedral to the Legation. Persons there told him that the enthusiasm over the accession of the King is the most intense and spontaneous since the demonstration against the occupation of Bosnia and Herzegovina by Austria-Hungary in 1908.

Mr. Lane said, "I was greatly impressed by the change in appearance of the King. His bearing was dignified and indicated that he fully appreciates the responsibility with which he is faced. He has greatly matured in appearance since I last saw him some months ago."

All diplomatic missions were represented at the ceremony.

Early in the morning of March 28, the Government at Belgrade issued the following statement: "His Royal Highness the Prince with his family left Belgrade last night at 23 : 50 at his own wish, for Athens."

Mr. Lane reported on the night of March 28 that Belgrade was calm during the day. All normal activities of the city had been resumed. The section of the city which was blocked off by tanks and troops on March 27 had been opened and communications had been re-established. The censorship had been relaxed.

(5) *The German Government to the Yugoslav Minister, Berlin, April 6, 1941* [1]

The note of April 6 in which the German Government announced its attack upon Yugoslavia, which began at dawn that day, is a long, tendentious document typically distorting known facts. It was based partly on documents of the French General Staff found by the Germans at La Charité which are not available in published form. Germany had pursued a policy of conciliation "with unparalleled magnanimity and patience" in the hope of leading Yugoslavia "back onto the path of common sense, that of an understanding with the Axis." All this and more having failed:

[1] German Library of Information, *Facts in Review*, April 21, 1941, p. 205.

[Excerpt]

The German Government is not willing to look on while the machinations of a criminal clique in Belgrade continue, nor to tolerate Yugoslavia's being turned into the happy hunting ground of British mercenaries who have no business on the Continent. Therefore orders have now been given to the German army to re-establish law and order in this part of Europe also, by all available military means.

(6) Statement of the Yugoslav Government issued at Vichy, April 6, 1941 [1]

The real reason for the German aggression is that Germany wanted Yugoslavia to depart from the position of neutrality she adopted in the European conflict since the beginning of the war.

Unjustly attacked, Yugoslavia in defending herself against an aggressor is faithful to her history and national traditions and firmly resolved to defend her national independence, territorial integrity and national honor.

In answer to German allegations regarding the causes of this aggression, it is replied in authorized Yugoslav quarters that Germany is the aggressor State and Yugoslavia has done nothing against Germany.

Even in signing the Three-Power Pact Yugoslavia affixed her signature with a profound conviction she could preserve her neutrality.

(7) Statement of the Secretary of State (Hull), April 6, 1941 [2]

The barbaric invasion of Yugoslavia and the attempt to annihilate that country by brute force is but another chapter in the present planned movement of attempted world conquest and domination. Another small nation has been assaulted by the forces of aggression and is further proof that there are no geographical limitations or bounds of any kind to their movement for world conquest.

The American people have the greatest sympathy for the nation which has been thus so outrageously attacked, and we follow closely the valiant struggle the Yugoslav people are making to protect their homes and preserve their liberty.

This Government with its policy of helping those who are defending themselves against would-be conquerors is now proceeding as speedily as possible to send military and other supplies to Yugoslavia.

[1] Associated Press version, *New York Times*, April 7, 1941, p. 5.
[2] Department of State, *Bulletin*, IV, p. 448. The statement was issued after consultation with the President.

(8) *The President (Roosevelt) to the King of Yugoslavia (Peter II), April 8, 1941* [1]

APRIL 8, 1941.

The people of the United States have been profoundly shocked by the unprovoked and ruthless aggression upon the people of Yugoslavia. The Government and people of the United States are witnessing with admiration the courageous self-defense of the Yugoslav people, which constitutes one more shining example of their traditional bravery.

As I have assured Your Majesty's Government, the United States will speedily furnish all material assistance possible in accordance with its existing statutes.

I send Your Majesty my most earnest hopes for a successful resistance to this criminal assault upon the independence and integrity of your country.

FRANKLIN D. ROOSEVELT

(9) *The Government of the United Kingdom to the Government of Yugoslavia, April 6, 1941* [2]

The savage outrage committed by Germany against Yugoslavia without the slightest provocation and the valiant resistance of the Serbs, Croats and Slovenes ranges the British Empire on the side of the southern Slavs. We welcome them as a resolute and powerful ally.

We renew the comradeship which in the Great War carried us through tribulations to victory. We will conduct the war in common and make peace only when right has been vindicated and law and justice are again enthroned.

(10) *Hungarian Occupation of Yugoslav Territory*

Hungary maintained irredentist sentiments toward sections of Yugoslavia as established in 1919 and had permitted on its soil a seat of Ustasha, a Croatian terrorist revolutionary society, which promoted the assassination of King Alexander at Marseilles October 9, 1934. Ante Pavelitch, the head of Ustasha, was given refuge from French law on Italian soil. On April 10, 1941, Pavelitch was proclaimed at Zagreb as the head of a Croat state with the approval of the German Führer. Hungarian troops thereupon occupied the Banat of Batchka and Baranya in the Serbian part of Yugoslavia.

[1] Department of State, *Bulletin*, IV, p. 449.
[2] Recorded by National Broadcasting Company, *New York Times*, April 7, 1941, p. 5.

(a) *Statement of Hungarian Telegraph Agency, Budapest, April 15,*
    1941 [1]

It would appear that the Soviet Government [2] is ill-informed of the
true state of affairs that preceded the entry of Hungarian troops into
Yugoslavia.

The Belgrade *coup d'état* overthrew the legitimate Yugoslav Government which had sought to improve relations between that country and
the Axis powers.

Not satisfied with that, the Yugoslav Air Force bombed and machine-
gunned Hungarian soil from the air, without any hostile act having been
committed by Hungary previously. When Hungarian citizens were
killed and Hungarian property was damaged, it was considered that
by this action the Simovitch government had cancelled the amity pact.

With the proclamation of independent Croatia, Yugoslavia ceased
to exist as such and it became the duty of Hungary to protect Magyar
citizens living there.

A treaty of friendship between Hungary and Yugoslavia, signed at Belgrade,
December 12, 1940, read (English version of articles, *New York Times*, December 13, 1940, p. 5):

Article I. There will be constant peace and perpetual friendship between
the Kingdom of Yugoslavia and the Kingdom of Hungary.

Article II. The High Contracting Parties agree to consult each other on all
questions which they believe could affect their mutual relationship.

Article III. The present treaty shall take effect on the exchange of articles
of ratification in Budapest as soon as possible.

The preamble to the treaty mentions the neighborly feelings of Yugoslavia
and Hungary and their mutual esteem and confidence and expresses a desire
to place these sentiments on a solid and durable basis that will serve the interests
of the two countries and Danubian peace and prosperity.

(11) *United States Continued Recognition of Yugoslavia*

The defection of Croatia on April 10, 1940, the invasion by Hungarian forces on
April 12 and the entry of Bulgaria into the conflict April 15 were followed by a
semi-official statement at Berlin on April 18 that Yugoslavia had forfeited a place
in the "new order" by its lack of cooperation. The German and Italian forces
in Yugoslavia had by April 19 made organized resistance futile, and the people
resorted to guerrilla tactics. A Slovene area was annexed by Italy on May 3 as

---

[1] *New York Times*, April 15, 1941, p. 8.
[2] The Soviet Foreign Commissariat, on being informed April 12 of the invasion,
commented that "it could easily be understood in what a position Hungary might
find itself if it, while in misfortune, should be subjected in its turn to an attack of
this kind — since in Hungary there are also substantial national minorities."

the "province of Ljubljana." The Throne of Croatia was restored on May 14 and the crown of Zvonimir [1] was put on the head of Aimone of Savoy-Aosta, Duke of Spoleto, at Rome May 18. On the same day a territorial agreement, a military accord and a treaty of guaranty and collaboration were signed. The following correspondence defines the attitude of the United States toward these occurrences.

(a) **The Minister of Yugoslavia (Fotitch) to the Secretary of State (Hull), May 12, 1941** [2]

MAY 12, 1941.

SIR:

I have the honor to convey to Your Excellency the following statement which I have been instructed to make by my Government:

In the course of the first few days following the unprovoked attack on Yugoslavia the German army occupied a part of the territory of the Banovine of Croatia including its capital city Zagreb. Acting under the protection of the army of occupation the notorious conspirator, Ante Pavelitch, who had been sentenced to death by French courts for the assassination of the late King Alexander, proclaimed, with the support of a small group of partisans having no following whatever among the Croat people, a so-called "Independent State of Croatia." The legitimate representatives of the Croat people in the Yugoslav Government as well as those of the autonomous authorities of the Banovine of Croatia have been forced to withdraw under the onslaught of enemy armies.

It is, of course, a cardinal principle of International Law that military occupation of territory in the course of hostilities does not change the juridical status of the territory thus occupied and that occupation by enemy armies provides no legal basis for the establishment of a new juridical status within such territory. In consequence, the establishment of so-called "Independent Croatia" imposed by, or at the instigation of the authorities of occupation is devoid of any basis in law and constitutes a patent violation of the Law of Nations to which the Yugoslav Government continues to adhere.

The Royal Yugoslav Government desires to register its most emphatic protest against this unlawful action of the German Reich and considers null and void all acts relating to the creation of the so-called "Independent State of Croatia," the sole object of which is to dismember the national territory of the Kingdom of Yugoslavia.

Accept [etc.]   CONSTANTIN FOTITCH

[1] The crown was the symbol of the feudal Croatian independence which existed between the years 924 and 1089.

[2] Department of State, *Bulletin*, IV, p. 682.

(b) **The Minister of Yugoslavia (Fotitch) to the Secretary of State (Hull), May 24, 1941** [1]

MAY 24, 1941.

MR. SECRETARY:

I have the honor to refer to my note of May 12, 1941 and, acting under the instructions of my Government, to convey to Your Excellency the following communication:

In the course of ceremonies staged in Rome on May 18 last purported agreements were signed ceding to Italy integral parts of the national territory of the Kingdom of Yugoslavia. By virtue of further agreements entered into with representatives of the so-called "Independent State of Croatia" that "state," previously established on Yugoslav territory by the military authorities of occupation, has been declared by the Italian Government to be a hereditary monarchy under Italian protection, thus establishing in effect if not in name an annexation of these territories by the Italian Government.

These agreements were entered into with the same persons who, instigated and aided by the military authorities of occupation, had usurped power in Croatia without consultation with or participation of its people, in direct violation of their essential rights and in total disregard of their vital interests.

The Royal Yugoslav Government protests against this new violation of the integrity of its national territory and against the separation of the Croat people who, through their legitimate representatives within the Royal Government continue the struggle for the liberation of Yugoslavia, which includes all Croat territory, and recognize His Majesty King Peter the Second as their only legitimate Sovereign.

Accept [etc.]

CONSTANTIN FOTITCH

(c) **The Under Secretary of State (Welles) to the Minister of Yugoslavia (Fotitch), May 28, 1941** [1]

MAY 28, 1941.

SIR:

I have the honor to acknowledge the receipt of your note of May 12, 1941 concerning the creation of the so-called "Independent State of Croatia." I observe that the Royal Yugoslav Government desires to register its most emphatic protest against this unlawful action of the German Reich and considers null and void all acts relating to the creation

[1] Department of State, *Bulletin*, IV, p. 683.

of the so-called "Independent State of Croatia," the sole object of which is to dismember the national territory of the Kingdom of Yugoslavia.

I also wish to refer to your note of May 24, 1941 concerning the purported agreements said to have been signed in Rome on May 18 last providing for the cession to Italy of integral parts of the national territory of the Kingdom of Yugoslavia. I note that the Royal Yugoslav Government protests against this new violation of its integrity and against the separation of the Croat people who, through their legitimate representatives within the Royal Government continue the struggle for the liberation of Yugoslavia, which includes all Croat territory, and recognize His Majesty King Peter the Second as their only legitimate Sovereign.

I desire to thank you for your courtesy in furnishing me with this expression of your views and to reiterate the indignation of this Government and the American people at the invasion and mutilation of Yugoslavia by various member states of the Tripartite Pact.

Accept [etc.]

For the Secretary of State:
SUMNER WELLES

D. Hostilities in Syria and Lebanon

(1) Declaration of United Kingdom Government Respecting Status of Syria and Lebanon, July 1, 1940 [1]

His Majesty's Government understand that General Eugene Mittelhauser, Commander in Chief of the French forces in the Levant, stated (in his original declaration) that hostilities have ceased in Syria. His Majesty's Government assume this does not mean that if Germany and Italy sought to occupy Syria and Lebanon, and were to try such in the face of the British command of the sea, no attempt would be made by the French forces to oppose them.

In order, however, to set at rest doubts which may be felt in any quarters, His Majesty's Government declare that they could not allow Syria and Lebanon to be occupied by any hostile power or used as a base for attacks on countries in the Middle East which they have pledged to defend, or to become the scene of disorders constituting danger to those countries.

They therefore hold themselves free to take whatever measures they may in the circumstances consider necessary to their own interests. Any action which they may be obliged to take in fulfilling this declaration will be without prejudice to the future status of territories now under French mandate.

[1] United Press dispatch, New York Times, June 9, 1941, p. 4.

(2) *Broadcast of the French High Commissioner for Syria and Lebanon (Dentz), Beirut, May 18, 1941* [1]

A *coup d'état* incited by German agents began in Iraq April 3, followed by the German attack on Greece and Yugoslavia April 6 and completion of the German attack on Crete beginning May 11. As a result of the arrival of about 30 German aircraft with Iraqi markings, the British bombed several Syrian airfields on May 15. Syria and Lebanon are "A" mandates under the League of Nations Covenant which are to be independent eventually by virtue of treaties concluded in 1936, but not yet in force.

British, British Imperial and Allied troops, consisting of Free French, Belgian and some other contingents, entered Syria on June 8 and the hostilities ceased as the result of an armistice granted to the Vichy French forces at Acre, Palestine, on July 12, 1941.

French Lebanese and Syrians, you have heard the appeal of Marshal Pétain; [2] you have heard his moving words, replete with firmness and wisdom, words inspired with an ardent desire for peace and order.

At the same moment in which he was speaking, English airplanes attacked our airdromes without warning. Once more, after Mers el Kebir and Dakar, England has spilled French blood and has attacked French soil.

The British Government, in order to justify these aggressions against France, has accused it of not having forcibly repelled German airplanes flying over Syria, some of which were forced to make landings. Nothing can justify this accusation. Marshal Pétain has confirmed that France has no aggressive intentions against England. The privileged move by our former enemy was strictly within the terms of the armistice.

This is the truth. All the accusations of Britain against France are only calumnies and criminal pretext. But we will act accordingly with calm and dignity.

Certainly we French, Syrians and Lebanese are in an unprecedentedly close association and will collaborate in brotherly fashion against any act of hostility of which the victims are innocent populations.

I have received the mission of defending the soil of Syria and Lebanon. I shall fulfill this mission inflexibly. The army is ready to reply to force with force.

(3) *Declaration of United Kingdom Government Respecting Occupation of Syria and Lebanon, June 8, 1941* [3]

In their declaration of July 1, 1940, His Majesty's Government stated they would not allow Syria and Lebanon to be occupied by any hostile

---

[1] *New York Times*, May 19, 1941, p. 7.
[2] Broadcast of May 15, see p. 397.
[3] Associated Press dispatch, *New York Times*, June 9, 1941, p. 4.

power or be used as a base for attacks upon those countries in the Middle East which they are pledged to defend.

In spite of this clear warning, the Vichy Government, in pursuance of their policy of collaboration with the Axis powers, have placed air bases in Syria and Lebanon at the disposal of Germany and Italy and have supplied war material to the rebel forces in Iraq.

German infiltration into Syria has begun and the Vichy Government are continuing to take measures whose effect must be to bring Syria and Lebanon under full German control.

His Majesty's Government could not be expected to tolerate such actions, which go far beyond anything laid down in the terms of the French armistice and are in flagrant conflict with the recent declaration of Marshal Pétain that honor forbade France to undertake anything against her former allies.

The Free French [1] troops have therefore, with the support of Imperial forces, entered Syria and Lebanon at an early hour this morning. At the same time a declaration has been issued by General Georges Catroux on behalf of General Charles de Gaulle guaranteeing the liberty and independence of Syria and Lebanon, and undertaking to negotiate a treaty to insure these objects. His Majesty's Government support and associate themselves with this promise of independence.

(4) *Declaration for Independence by the Commander of the Free French Forces in the Middle East (Catroux), June 8, 1941* [2]

Inhabitants of Syria and Lebanon!

At the moment when forces of Free France united to the forces of the British Empire, her ally, are entering your territory, I declare that I assume the powers, responsibilities and duties of the representative of France in the Levant.

I do this in the name of Free France, who identifies herself with the traditional and real France, and in the name of her chief, General Charles de Gaulle.

In this capacity I come to put an end to the mandatory regime and proclaim you free and independent.

You will therefore be from henceforward sovereign and independent peoples and you will be able either to form yourselves into separate states or unite into a single state. In either event, your independent and sovereign status will be guaranteed by a treaty in which our mutual relations will be defined. This treaty will be negotiated as soon as pos-

[1] See p. 433.
[2] Associated Press dispatch, *New York Times*, June 9, 1941, p. 4.

sible between your representatives and myself. Pending its conclusion our mutual position will be one of close unity in the pursuit of a common ideal and common aims.

Inhabitants of Syria and Lebanon, you will see from this declaration that if Free French and British forces cross your frontier it is not to take away your liberty. It is to insure it. It is to drive out of Syria the forces of Hitler. It is to prevent the Levant from becoming an enemy base directed against the British and against ourselves.

We who are fighting for the liberty of the people cannot allow the enemy to submerge your country step by step, obtain control of your persons and your belongings and turn you into slaves. We cannot allow the populations which France has promised to defend to be thrown into the hands of the most wanton and pitiless master history has known. We cannot allow the age-long interests of France in the Levant to be handed over to the enemy.

Inhabitants of Syria and Lebanon, if in answer to our appeal you rally to us you should know that the British Government, in agreement with Free France, has promised to grant you all the advantages enjoyed by free countries who are associated with them. Thus the blockade will be lifted and you will enter into immediate relations with the sterling bloc, which will open the widest possibilities to your imports and exports. You will be able to buy and sell freely with all the free countries.

Inhabitants of Syria and Lebanon, the great hour in your history has sounded for you. France declares you independent by the voice of her sons who are fighting for her life and for the liberty of the world.

(5) *Declaration of Support by the British Ambassador to Egypt (Lampson), Cairo, June 8, 1941* [1]

General Georges Catroux on behalf of General Charles de Gaulle, chief of the Free French, has issued a declaration to the inhabitants of Syria and Lebanon before advancing with the object of expelling the Germans. In this he declares the liberty and independence of Syria and Lebanon. He undertakes to negotiate a treaty to insure these objects.

I am authorized by His Majesty's Government in the United Kingdom to declare that they support and associate themselves with the assurance of independence given by General Catroux on behalf of General de Gaulle to Syria and Lebanon.

[1] Associated Press dispatch, *New York Times*, June 9, 1941, p. 4.

I am also authorized to give you the assurance that should you support and join the Allies His Majesty's Government in the United Kingdom offer you all the advantages enjoyed by free countries who are associated with them.

The blockade will be lifted and you may enter into immediate relations with the sterling bloc, which will give you enormous, besides immediate, advantages from the point of view of your exports and imports. You will be able to sell your products and buy freely in all free countries.

(6) *The French Ambassador to Spain (Piétri) to the British Ambassador to Spain (Hoare), June 8, 1941* [1]

On instructions from his Government the French Ambassador has the honor to communicate to His Majesty's Ambassador the following text of a note handed this morning by Admiral Darlan, Minister for Foreign Affairs, to the United States Ambassador at Vichy:

The French Government have just learned by a telegram received from the French High Commissioner at Beirut that Syrian territory has been attacked this morning near Mer Jayoun, south of Jebel Druz, and that enemy reconnaissance elements, armored cars, and infantry have come into contact with our posts. Fighting is in progress. The Ministry for Foreign Affairs again draws the attention of the United States Embassy to the fact that there has been no collaboration between the French and Germans in Syria, and that all German air material and personnel which might have been there during events in Iraq have been withdrawn, with the exception of two or three damaged machines and about 10 men.

The Ministry for Foreign Affairs wishes most particularly to draw the United States Embassy's attention to the fact that any British attack, which nothing in the present situation in Syria can explain, risks producing the gravest consequences. As the Embassy are already aware the French Government are determined to defend their territory and possessions wherever they may be attacked and with all the means at their disposal. Every measure is being taken accordingly to this effect in Syria. Aware of the danger of the present situation, the French Government will for their part avoid, pending further information, taking any action which might aggravate or spread the conflict. If the trouble is in fact extended, the French Government will find themselves

---

[1] Associated Press text, *New York Times*, June 14, 1941, p. 4, the main text checked to the Foreign Office release, *The Times* (London), June 14, 1941, p. 4. The notes were given out by the Foreign Office in London. For the message addressed June 8 by the French Chief of State to the French forces in the Near East see *New York Times*, June 9, 1941, p. 4.

obliged to assure, by necessary measures, the defense of territories under French sovereignty.

(7) *The British Ambassador to Spain (Hoare) to the French Ambassador to Spain (Piétri), June 8, 1941* [1]

His Majesty's Government in the United Kingdom have had the honor to receive the communication which the French Ambassador at Madrid handed to His Majesty's Ambassador on June 8.

His Majesty's Government will not be expected to enter into an argument with Marshal Pétain's Government on the subject of the meaning of the word "collaboration," more especially since it has not been clearly defined in the communication under reference. His Majesty's Government have based their action in Syria on the facts of the case as known to them and not on theoretical considerations, and this has been made clear in their public statement on the subject, issued on June 8.

His Majesty's Government would recall that His Majesty's Principal Secretary of State for Foreign Affairs stated in the House of Commons on May 22 that if the Vichy Government, in pursuance of their declared policy of collaboration with the enemy, took action or permitted action detrimental to His Majesty's Government's conduct of the war or designed to assist the enemy's war effort, His Majesty's Government would naturally hold themselves free to attack the enemy wherever he might be found.[2] The responsibility for the consequences of the assistance which the French authorities in Syria were instructed to render to the enemies of His Majesty must therefore rest with Marshal Pétain's Government.

His Majesty's Government are happy to note that Marshal Pétain's Government will avoid taking any action which might aggravate or spread the conflict. They have no desire that French blood should be shed, and should consequently suggest that it would be in the interest of both countries if Marshal Pétain's Government saw their way to instruct their forces in Syria to offer no opposition to the measures which

---

[1] Associated Press text, *New York Times*, June 14, 1941, p. 4; *The Times* (London) *ibid*.

[2] The statement of the note is a third-person transcript of the original declaration which, however, closed as follows: "We shall naturally hold ourselves free to attack the enemy wherever he may be found, and in so doing we shall no longer feel bound to draw any distinction between occupied and unoccupied territories in the execution of our military plans." The statement also reiterated the assurance of August 7, 1940 (p. 433) to General de Gaulle.

the Allied forces are taking in order to prevent the enemy from using
Syria as a base of operations against them.

His Majesty's Government take this opportunity to repeat that
they have no territorial designs on Syria or anywhere in French oversea
possessions, and that it is their intention, when victory is won, to restore
the independence and greatness of France.

E. Other Developments in the Near and Middle East

(1) Mutual Pledges of the Soviet Union and Turkey. Identic Communiqué, Ankara and Moscow, March 25, 1941 [1]

To the treaty of mutual assistance October 19, 1939, between France, Turkey
and the United Kingdom [2] was attached a protocol which provided that Turkey
was not obligated "to take action having as its effect or involving as its consequence entry into armed conflict with the Union of Soviet Socialist Republics."
The declarations of March 25, 1941, gave Turkey the counter assurance that the
Soviet Union would respect Turkey's undertakings to other States.

The Soviet and Turkish Governments have exchanged declarations
because statements have been published in parts of the foreign press
to the effect that Russia might take advantage of difficulties in which
Turkey might find herself in case of its being obliged to enter the war,
and might attack Turkey. The Soviet Government has made the following declarations to the Turkish Government:

First, such rumors do not in any way correspond to the intentions of
the Soviet Government.

Second, if Turkey be attacked and be obliged to enter the war for
the purposes of defending her territory, it can rely upon the complete
neutrality and understanding of the Soviet Union, based on the existing
treaty of friendship between the two countries.

The Turkish Government has thanked the Soviet Government very
sincerely for this declaration and has declared, on its part, that if the
Soviet Union should be attacked and obliged to take similar action, it
may also rely on Turkey's full neutrality and understanding.

(2) Iraqi-Soviet Relations. Statements of Tass News Agency, May 12 and 17, 1941 [3]

Iraq, in alliance with the United Kingdom by the treaty of June 30, 1930,[4]
has a child king in Feisal II, whose regent, Emir Abdul Illah, was thrown out of

[1] *New York Times*, March 25, 1941, p. 5. It will be noted that the communiqué does
not purport to give the actual text of the declarations.

[2] Department of State, *Bulletin*, I, p. 544, 604. The instrument continued in force
between Turkey and the United Kingdom after the collapse of France.

[3] *New York Times*, May 13, 1941, p. 1; *ibid.*, May 18, p. 1.

[4] League of Nations, *Treaty Series*, CXXXII, p. 363.

office by Rashid Ali el Gailani, a pro-German politician, on April 4, 1941. By the alliance British troops are quartered at certain centers in Iraq. On May 2, with equipment secured from German sources and with the encouragement of the former Mufti of Jerusalem, the disaffected Haj Amin el Husseini, Rashid Ali attacked the British. The hoped-for support of the Iraqi and the peninsular Arabs did not materialize and on May 30 Rashid Ali had to flee the country with his German advisers after an armistice had restored the authority to the constitutional government.

The belated recognition of Iraq by the Soviet Union in the midst of this *coup* is explained by the Soviet Union as due to the retirement of the condition respecting Arabian countries; at the time it was ascribed in some quarters to German influence.

At the end of 1940 the Iraqi Government, through the medium of its Minister in Turkey, repeatedly proposed to the Government of the Union of Soviet Socialist Republics the establishment of diplomatic relations between the Union of Soviet Socialist Republics and Iraq. In so doing the Iraqi Government expressed the wish that simultaneously with the establishment of diplomatic relations the Soviet Government should publish a declaration on the recognition of independence of the Arabian countries, including Iraq.

The Government of the Union of Soviet Socialist Republics, entertaining a positive attitude toward the proposal on the establishment of diplomatic relations between the Union of Soviet Socialist Republics and Iraq, did not consider it possible, however, to make this conditional on the publication of any declaration.

A reply in this sense was given at that time to the Iraqi Government, in consequence of which negotiations were interrupted.

On May 3, 1941, the Iraqi Government, through the medium of the Soviet Ambassador in Ankara, again proposed the establishment of diplomatic relations between the Union of Soviet Socialist Republics and Iraq, without making this time the establishment of diplomatic relations dependent on any condition such as a declaration regarding Arabian countries.

The Government of the Union of Soviet Socialist Republics withdrew its objections and accepted the proposal of the Iraqi Government on the establishment of diplomatic relations.

May 16th in Ankara, the Ambassador of the Union of Soviet Socialist Republics [Sergei A.] Vinogradov, and the Iraq Minister, Gailani, exchanged notes on the establishment of diplomatic, trade and consular relations between the Union of Soviet Socialist Republics and Iraq.

(3) *Treaty of Friendship between Germany and Turkey, Ankara, June 18, 1941* [1]

In force June 18, 1941

[Translation]

The German Government and the Turkish Republic, inspired by a desire to place relations between the two countries on a basis of mutual confidence and sincere friendship, have agreed, without prejudice to present obligations of both countries, to conclude a treaty.

For this purpose the German Reich Chancellor appointed Ambassador Franz von Papen and the President of the Turkish Republic appointed Foreign Minister Shukru Saracoglu as plenipotentiaries, who, on the basis of full powers accorded them, have agreed on the following declaration:

ARTICLE 1. Germany and Turkey bind themselves mutually to respect the integrity and inviolability of their national territory and not to resort to any measures, direct or indirect, aimed at their Treaty partner.

ARTICLE 2. Germany and Turkey bind themselves in future in all questions touching their common interests to meet in friendly contact in order to reach an understanding on the treatment of such questions.

ARTICLE 3. The above Treaty will be ratified and the instruments of ratification will be duly exchanged in Berlin. The Treaty comes into force from the day of signature and will be valid for a period of 10 years. The Parties concluding the Treaty will at the time specified come to an understanding on the prolongation of the Treaty.

Drawn up in duplicate in one original, in the German and Turkish languages, in Ankara on June 18, 1941.

(a) *Economic Relations. Exchange of Notes, Ankara, June 18, 1941* [2]

In view of the auspicious conclusion of today's Treaty, I have the honor to notify your Excellency that my Government is prepared to promote as far as possible economic relations between Germany and Turkey, bearing in mind the openings presented by the economic structure of the two countries, and using as a basis the experience that each country has had of the other in this war. The two countries will forthwith enter into negotiations to establish a Treaty basis for the carrying out of this agreement.

[1] The text is a composite of the preamble from the Berlin version transmitted by the United Press, *New York Times*, June 19, 1941, p. 4, and the articles from the version of *The Times* (London), June 19, 1941, p. 4, which was couched in language more usual in treaties. Ratification procedure by the Turkish Assembly took place June 25, 1941.

[2] *The Times* (London), June 19, 1941, p. 4. The Turkish counterpart has not been seen.

(b) Joint Declaration to the Press, Ankara, June 18, 1941 [1]

In view of the auspicious conclusion of this Treaty, the two plenipotentiaries express the wish that the press and wireless in both countries shall always bear in mind in all they publish or broadcast the spirit of friendship and mutual trust animating their nations.

(4) Status of French Somaliland. The French Ambassador to Spain (Piétri) to the British Ambassador to Spain (Hoare); the French Ambassador to the United States (Henry-Haye) to the Secretary of State (Hull), June 21, 1941 [2]

First, on June 9 General Wavell, acting as the British Government's representative, officially notified French Somaliland by letter and tracts of a real ultimatum demanding that the colony rally to the de Gaulle movement under pain of condemnation to famine through the application of a brutal and rigorous blockade.

Wavell clarified his intentions by declaring that reinforcement of the blockade of French Somaliland would be ordered immediately if the colony refused to join the war alongside Britain. On the contrary, all measures would be taken for feeding the colony and insuring it economic advantages if it joined the British.

Second, this ultimatum is unprecedented in history and is the same as condemning the population, living on a soil which cannot be cultivated, to a slow death by famine, with the aim of forcing the population to revolt against their homeland.

French Somaliland, however, has unanimously manifested the loyalty of its civil and military population to the Pétain Government. Any allegation attempting to cast doubt on the colony's loyalty can come only from false or incorrect information.

In the past two months French Somaliland has been virtually encircled by British and de Gaullist troops, but only five out of 2,000 Frenchmen living in the colony have crossed the frontier, and they were persons of doubtful character who had good reason to quit the colony.

Third, measures taken by the British authorities to tighten the rigorous blockade to which French Somaliland has been submitted since September 1940, already have borne fruit. In March and April deaths caused by insufficient food occurred among children.

The population of French Somaliland is sadly tired by the inhuman measures, for which the British people bear a heavy responsibility.

[1] *The Times* (London), June 19, 1941, p. 4.
[2] United Press version, *New York Times*, June 22, 1941, p. 6.

An appeal has been addressed to the local representative of the British Government and to the International Red Cross at Geneva.

Fourth, the attitude of the British Government contrasts with that which the French Government decided to adopt authorizing traffic via Jibuti under control of the International Red Cross for foodstuffs destined for the sick and wounded and children in Ethiopia.

By that offer, which does not favor any belligerent, France sought to demonstrate that even in this painful epoch through which she is passing she preserves the traditional sentiments of disinterestedness and humanity.

_____

The United States by proclamation No. 2474 of April 10, 1941 (see p. 654) opened the Red Sea to American shipping.

F. German-Soviet Diplomatic Relations, 1941

(1) *Communiqué on the Economic Agreement between Germany and the Union of Soviet Socialist Republics, Moscow, January 10, 1941* [1]

The Soviet-German economic negotiations that have been held in Moscow since the end of October of last year were concluded January 10, 1941, by the signature of an enlarged economic agreement. This agreement was signed on behalf of the Union of Soviet Socialist Republics by the People's Commissar of Foreign Trade of the Union of Soviet Socialist Republics [Anasthasius I.] Mikoyan, and on behalf of Germany by a minister of the Ministry for Foreign Affairs, Dr. [Kurt] Schnurre.

The new agreement is based on the Soviet-German economic agreement of February 11, 1940, and constitutes a further step in execution of the economic program outlined by the two governments in 1939. The agreement regulates the trade turnover between the Union of Soviet Socialist Republics and Germany until August 1, 1942. It provides for an amount of mutual deliveries considerably exceeding the level of the first year of operation of the agreement.

The Union of Soviet Socialist Republics delivers to Germany industrial raw materials, oil products and foodstuffs, especially cereals; Germany delivers to the Union of Soviet Socialist Republics industrial equipment.

[1] *New York Times,* January 11, 1941, p. 8. The Tass Agency report was transmitted by the United Press.

The negotiations passed in a spirit of mutual understanding and confidence conforming to the friendly relations existing between the Union of Soviet Socialist Republics and Germany. All economic problems, including those that arose in connection with the incorporation of new territories into the Union of Soviet Socialist Republics, were solved in conformity with the interests of both countries.

(2) *Communiqué Concerning the German-Soviet Agreement Respecting Property and Migration with Reference to the Estonian, Latvian and Lithuanian Soviet Socialist Republics, Moscow, January 10, 1941* [1]

In recent weeks negotiations were conducted in Riga and Kaunas between German and Soviet delegations on the migration of German citizens and persons of German nationality from the Lithuanian, Latvian and Estonian Soviet Socialist Republics to Germany, and Lithuanian citizens and persons of Lithuanian, Russian and Byelo-Russian nationalities from Germany [the former Memel and Suwalki regions] to the Union of Soviet Socialist Republics.

On January 10, 1941, these negotiations ended in the signature in Riga and Kaunas of agreements settling all problems connected with migration.

On the strength of these agreements the above-mentioned persons, who state their desire to migrate, may effect migration within two and one-half months after signature of the agreements in conformity with procedure laid down in these agreements.

The agreement on migration from Latvia and Estonia was signed by the chairman of the Soviet delegation, [Vladimir] Bochkarev, and the chairman of the German Government delegation, Bentsler.

The agreement on migration for Lithuania was signed by the chairman of the Soviet Government delegation, [N. G.] Pozdnyakov, and the chairman of the German Government delegation, Neldecke.

The agreement between the Union of Soviet Socialist Republics and Germany on settlement of mutual property claims connected with this migration was signed simultaneously in Moscow, on authorization of the Government of the Union of Soviet Socialist Republics by the vice chairman of the Council of People's Commissars [Andrey Y.] Vishinsky, and, on the authorization of the German Government, by a minister for the Ministry for Foreign Affairs, Dr. Schnurre.

[1] *New York Times*, January 11, 1941, p. 8. The Tass Agency report was transmitted by the United Press.

(3) *Boundary Treaty between Germany and the Union of Soviet Socialist Republics, Moscow, January 10, 1941* [1]

The Government of the Union of Soviet Socialist Republics in the person of the chairman of the Council of People's Commissars of the Union of Soviet Socialist Republics [Vyacheslav M.] Molotov, on the one hand and the Government of Germany through [its Ambassador] Count [Friedrich Werner] von der Schulenburg, on the other hand, have concluded this treaty on the State frontier of the Union of Soviet Socialist Republics and Germany in the sector from the River Igorka to the Baltic Sea in connection with the admission of the Lithuanian Soviet Socialist Republic into the Union of the Soviet Socialist Republics, which took place August 3, 1940.

ARTICLE I. The State frontier of the Union of Soviet Socialist Republics and Germany in the above sector passes from a point on the River Igorka, with frontier Post No. 1–1, installed in 1940 in course of the demarcation of the State frontier of the Union of Soviet Socialist Republics and the State frontier of Germany, in approximately a northwestern direction to the coast of the Baltic Sea. This frontier passes:

(A) In the sector from Post No. 1–1 on the River Igorka to the point of junction of the former frontiers of Germany, Lithuania and the former Poland, along the line of the former factual State frontier between Lithuania and Poland described in the decision of the Conference of Ambassadors of March 15, 1923;

(B) In the sector from the junction of the State frontiers mentioned in Paragraph (A) to the frontier of the former Memel region — along the former State frontier between Lithuania and Germany described in the treaty between the Lithuanian Republic and Germany of January 29, 1938;

(C) In the sector from the southern point frontier of the former Memel region to the Baltic Sea along the former State frontier between Lithuania and Germany established by Article I of the treaty between Lithuania and Germany of March 22, 1939.

ARTICLE II. The provisions of the Soviet-German treaty of frontier of August 31, 1940, shall be respectively applied to juridical frontier relations along the frontier established by Article I.

ARTICLE III. The two Contracting Parties have agreed to consider the problem of a juridical regime of waters in the frontier zone in the course of subsequent negotiations.

[1] *New York Times*, January 11, 1941, p. 8. The Tass Agency report was transmitted by the United Press.

ARTICLE IV. The present treaty is subject to ratification. An exchange of ratification instruments shall take place in Berlin within a possibly short space of time. This treaty comes into force from the moment of its signature. Made in two originals, each in the Russian and the German languages, both originals being equally valid.

Moscow, January 10, 1941.

Signed: On the authorization of the Government of the Union of Soviet Socialist Republics by

MOLOTOV.

On behalf of the German Government by

SCHULENBURG.

(4) *Statement of the Soviet People's Commissariat of Foreign Affairs Concerning Dispatch of German Troops to Bulgaria, Moscow, March 3, 1941* [1]

On March 1, 1941, the Prime Minister of Bulgaria signed a protocol of adhesion to the Three-Power Pact at a ceremony in Vienna. Prof. Filoff stated that Bulgaria owed its recovery of the Dobruja " to the Axis Powers and to their great leaders." He also said that Bulgaria was determined to continue and further develop the traditional friendly relations with the Soviet Union.

On March 1, a representative of the Ministry of Foreign Affairs of Bulgaria, Altynoff, made a statement to the Union of Soviet Socialist Republics Minister in Bulgaria, Alexander Lavridev, that the Bulgarian Government had given its consent to the dispatch of German troops to Bulgaria, having in view the preservation of peace in the Balkans.

On March 3, Deputy People's Commissar for Foreign Affairs A. Y. Vishinksy conveyed to the Bulgarian Minister, Ivan Sramenoff, the following reply:

"In reply to the communication the Bulgarian Government conveyed March 1 of this year through the Union of Soviet Socialist Republics Minister in Bulgaria, Lavridev, by the representative of the Ministry of Foreign Affairs of Bulgaria, Altynoff, to the effect that the Bulgarian Government had agreed to the dispatch of German troops to Bulgaria and that this action pursues peace aims in the Balkans, the Soviet Government deems it necessary to state that:

"First, the Soviet Government cannot share the opinion of the Bulgarian Government as to the correctness of the latter's position in this matter, since the position, irrespective of the desire of the Bulgarian

[1] As announced by Tass and carried by the United Press, *New York Times*, March 4, 1941, p. 1.

Government, does not lead to consolidation of peace but to the extension of the sphere of the war and to Bulgaria's being involved in it.

"Second, in view of this the Soviet Government, true to its policy of peace, cannot render any support to the Bulgarian Government in application of its present policy. The Soviet Government is compelled to make the present statement, especially in view of the fact that the Bulgarian press freely circulates rumors fundamentally misrepresenting the real position of the Union of Soviet Socialist Republics."

G. German Invasion of the Soviet Union

(1) *Soviet Disclaimer of War Rumors. Statement Broadcast for the Soviet Union, Moscow, June 13, 1941* [1]

This broadcast was issued in reply to rumors that an *impasse* was developing between the Soviet Union and Germany. It was subsequently stated that the intention of the broadcast was to put on record that Soviet policy and action were neither aggressive nor provocative.

Even before arrival of the British Ambassador in the Union of Soviet Socialist Republics [Sir Stafford] Cripps in London, and particularly after his arrival,[2] the British and in general the foreign press began an intense dissemination of rumors on the "proximity of war between the Union of Soviet Socialist Republics and Germany."

According to these rumors:

First. Germany allegedly presented to the Union of Soviet Socialist Republics claims of a territorial and economic nature and negotiations are now under way between Germany and the Union of Soviet Socialist Republics concerning conclusion of a new, closer agreement between them.

Second. The Union of Soviet Socialist Republics allegedly declined these claims, in consequence of which Germany began concentrating her troops at the borders of the Union of Soviet Socialist Republics for the purpose of attacking the Union of Soviet Socialist Republics.

Third. The Soviet Union on its part allegedly began intense preparations for war with Germany and concentrating troops at the latter's borders.

Despite the obviously nonsensical character of these rumors, responsible Moscow quarters still found it necessary, in view of persistent intense dissemination of these rumors, to authorize Tass to state that these rumors constitute clumsily concocted propaganda of forces hostile

[1] Associated Press version, *New York Times*, June 14, 1941, p. 6.
[2] Sir Stafford Cripps left Moscow June 6 and arrived in London June 11.

to the Union of Soviet Socialist Republics and to Germany and interested in further extension and unleashing of war.

Tass declares that:

First. Germany did not present any claims to the Union of Soviet Socialist Republics and does not propose any new, clear agreement, in view of which no negotiations on this subject could have taken place.

Second. According to information at the disposal of the Union of Soviet Socialist Republics, Germany abides by the provisions of the Soviet-German Pact of Nonagression as unswervingly as the Soviet Union, in view of which, in the opinion of Soviet quarters, rumors on Germany's intention to disrupt the pact and undertake attack on the Union of Soviet Socialist Republics are devoid of any ground, whereas the dispatching of German troops relieved from operations in the Balkans to eastern and northeastern districts of Germany which now is taking place is connected, it should be assumed, with other motives having no bearing on Soviet-German relations.

Third. The Union of Soviet Socialist Republics, as follows from its peace policy, abided and intends to abide by the provisions of the Soviet-German Nonaggression Pact, in view of which rumors to the effect that the Union of Soviet Socialist Republics is preparing for war with Germany are false and provocational.

Fourth. Summer camp drills of Red Army reservists held at present and forthcoming maneuvers have no other purpose than the training of reservists and the checking of the work of railroad organization, carried out, as it is known, every year, in view of which to present these measures of the Red Army as inimical to Germany is, at least to say, absurd.

(2) *Proclamation of the German Führer (Hitler), June 22, 1941* [1]

German people!

National Socialists!

Weighted down with heavy cares, condemned to months-long silence, the hour has now come when at last I can speak frankly.

When on September 3, 1939, the German Reich received the English declaration of war there was repeated anew a British attempt to render impossible every beginning of a consolidation and thereby of Europe's

[1] Associated Press version, *New York Times*, June 23, 1941, p. 6. A variant English version was given out by Reuter's, *The Times* (London), June 23, 1941, p. 3. A note of the German Foreign Office, a narrative of 10,000 words dated June 21, was handed to the Soviet Ambassador at Berlin early on June 22 and made public with the proclamation. The text in the Associated Press version is in *New York Times*, June 23, 1941, p. 4.

rise, by fighting whatever power on the Continent was strongest at any given time.

That is how of yore England ruined Spain in many wars. That is how she conducted her wars against Holland. That is how later she fought France with the aid of all Europe and that is how at the turn of the century she began the encirclement of the then German Reich and in 1914 the World War. Only on account of its internal dissension was Germany defeated in 1918. The consequences were terrible.

After hypocritical declarations that the fight was solely against the Kaiser and his regime, the annihilation of the German Reich began according to plan after the German Army had laid down its arms.

While the prophecies of the French statesman that there were 20,000,000 Germans too many; in other words, that this number would have to be exterminated by hunger, disease or emigration, were apparently being fulfilled to the letter, the National Socialist movement began its work of unifying the German people and thereby initiating resurgence of the Reich. This rise of our people from distress, misery and shameful disregard bore all the signs of a purely internal renaissance. Britain especially was not in any way affected or threatened thereby.

Nevertheless, a new policy of encirclement against Germany, born as it was of hatred, recommenced immediately. Internally and externally there resulted that plot familiar to us all between Jews and democrats, Bolshevists and reactionaries, with the sole aim of inhibiting the establishment of the new German people's State, and of plunging the Reich anew into impotence and misery.

Apart from us the hatred of this international world conspiracy was directed against those peoples which like ourselves were neglected by fortune and were obliged to earn their daily bread in the hardest struggle for existence.

Above all the right of Italy and Japan to share in the goods of this world was contested just as much as that of Germany and in fact was formally denied.

The coalition of these nations was, therefore, only an act of self-protection in the face of the egoistic world combination of wealth and power threatening them.

As early as 1936 Prime Minister Churchill, according to statements by the American General Wood [1] before a committee of the American House of Representatives, declared Germany was once again becoming too powerful and must therefore be destroyed.

[1] Robert E. Wood, chairman of the "America First Committee," an organization opposing the trend of the Government's policies.

In the Summer of 1939 the time seemed to have come for England to begin to realize its intended annihilation by repetition of a comprehensive policy of encirclement of Germany.

The plan of the campaign of lies staged for this purpose consisted in declaring that other people were threatened, in tricking them with British promises of guarantees and assistance, and of making them march against Germany just as it did preceding the great war.

Thus Britain from May to August 1939, succeeded in broadcasting to the world that Lithuania, Estonia, Latvia, Finland and Bessarabia as well as the Ukraine were being directly threatened by Germany.

A number of these States allowed themselves to be misled into accepting the promise of guaranty proffered with these assertions, thus joining the new encirclement front against Germany. Under these circumstances I considered myself entitled to assume responsibility before my own conscience and before the history of the German people not only of assuring these countries or their Governments of the falseness of British assertions, but also of setting the strongest Power in the east, by especially solemn declarations, at rest concerning the limits of our interests.

National Socialists! At that time you probably all felt that this step [1] was bitter and difficult for me. Never did the German people harbor hostile feeling against the peoples of Russia. However, for over ten years Jewish Bolshevist rulers had been endeavoring from Moscow to set not only Germany but all Europe aflame. At no time ever did Germany attempt to carry her National Socialist *Weltanschauung* into Russia, but on the contrary Jewish Bolshevist rulers in Moscow unswervingly endeavored to foist their domination upon us and other European peoples, not only by ideological means but above all with military force.

The consequences of the activity of this regime were nothing but chaos, misery and starvation in all countries. I, on the other hand, have been striving for twenty years with a minimum of intervention and without destroying our production, to arrive at a new Socialist order in Germany which not only eliminates unemployment but also permits the worker to receive an ever greater share of the fruits of his labor.

The success of this policy of economic and social reconstruction of our people, which by systematically eliminating differences of rank and class, has a true peoples' community as the final aim of the world.

It was therefore only with extreme difficulty that I brought myself in August 1939, to send my Foreign Minister to Moscow in an endeavor there to oppose the British encirclement policy against Germany.

I did this not only from a sense of all responsibility toward the German

[1] See the Treaty of Nonaggression, *Documents, II, 1939-40*, p. 334.

people, but above all in the hope after all of achieving permanent relief of tension and of being able to reduce sacrifices which might otherwise have been demanded of us.

While Germany solemnly affirmed in Moscow that the territories and countries enumerated — with the exception of Lithuania — lay outside all German political interests, a special agreement was concluded in case Britain were to succeed in inciting Poland actually into war with Germany.

In this case, too, German claims were subject to limitations entirely out of proportion to the achievement of German forces.

National Socialists! The consequences of this treaty which I myself desired and which was concluded in the interest of the German nation were very severe, particularly for Germans living in the countries concerned.

Far more than 500,000 German men and women, all small farmers, artisans and workmen, were forced to leave their former homeland practically overnight in order to escape from a new regime which at first threatened them with boundless misery and sooner or later with complete extermination.

Nevertheless, thousands of Germans disappeared. It was impossible ever to determine their fate, let alone their whereabouts. Among them were no fewer than 160 men of German citizenship. To all this I remained silent because I had to. For, after all, it was my one desire to achieve final relief of tension and, if possible, a permanent settlement with this State.

However, already during our advance in Poland, Soviet rulers suddenly, contrary to the treaty, also claimed Lithuania.

The German Reich never had any intention of occupying Lithuania and not only failed to present any such demand to the Lithuanian Government, but on the contrary refused the request of the then Lithuania to send German troops to Lithuania for that purpose as inconsistent with the aims of German policy.

Despite all this I complied also with this fresh Russian demand. However, this was only the beginning of continually renewed extortions which kept on repeating ever since.

Victory in Poland which was won by German troops exclusively caused me to address yet another peace offer to the Western Powers. It was refused owing to efforts of international and Jewish warmongers.

At that time already the reason for such refusal lay in the fact that Britain still had hopes of being able to mobilize a European coalition against Germany which was to include the Balkans and Soviet Russia.

It was therefore decided in London to send Mr. Cripps [Sir Stafford

Cripps] as Ambassador to Moscow. He received clear instructions under all circumstances to resume relations between the English and Soviet Russia and develop them in a pro-British direction. The British press reported on the progress of this mission as long as tactical reasons did not impose silence.

In the Autumn of 1939 and Spring of 1940 the first results actually made themselves felt. As Russia undertook to subjugate by armed force not only Finland but also the Baltic States she suddenly motivated this action by the assertion, as ridiculous as it was false, that she must protect these countries from an outside menace or forestall it.

This could only be meant to apply to Germany, for no other Power could even gain entrance into the Baltic area, let alone go to war there. Still I had to be silent. However, those in power in the Kremlin immediately went further.

Whereas in the Spring of 1940 Germany, in accordance with the so-called pact of friendship, withdrew her forces from the far eastern frontier and, in fact, for the most part cleared these areas entirely of German troops, a concentration of Russian forces at that time was already beginning in a measure which could only be regarded as a deliberate threat to Germany.

According to a statement that [Premier] Molotov personally made at that time, there were twenty-two Russian divisions in the Baltic States alone already in the Spring of 1940.

Since the Russian Government itself always claimed it was called in by the local population, the purpose of their presence there could only be a demonstration against Germany.

While our soldiers from May 5, 1940 on had been breaking Franco-British power in the west, Russian military deployment on our eastern frontier was being continued to a more and more menacing extent.

From August 1940 on I therefore considered it to be in the interest of the Reich no longer to permit our eastern provinces, which moreover had already been laid waste so often, to remain unprotected in the face of this tremendous concentration of Bolshevist divisions.

Thus there resulted British-Soviet Russian cooperation intended mainly at the tying up of such powerful forces in the east that radical conclusion of the war in the west, particularly as regards aircraft, could no longer be vouched for by the German High Command.

This, however, was in line with the objects not only of the British but also of the Soviet Russian policy, for both England and Soviet Russia intend to let this war go on for as long as possible in order to weaken all Europe and render it progressively more impotent.

Russia's threatened attack on Rumania was in the last analysis equally intended to gain possession of an important base, not only of Germany's but also of Europe's economic life, or at least destroy it. The Reich, especially since 1933, sought with unending patience to gain States in Southeast Europe as trading partners. We therefore also had the greatest interest in their internal constitutional consolidation and organization. Russia's advance into Rumania and Greece's tie-up with England threatened to turn these regions, too, within a short time into a general theatre of war.

Contrary to our principles and customs, and at the urgent request of the then Rumanian Government, which was itself responsible for this development, I advised acquiescence to the Soviet Russian demands for the sake of peace and the cession of Bessarabia.

The Rumanian Government believed, however, that it could answer for this before its own people only if Germany and Italy in compensation would at least guarantee the integrity of what still remained of Rumania.

I did so with heavy heart, principally because when the German Reich gives a guaranty that means it also abides by it. We are neither Englishmen nor Jews.

I still believe at this late hour to have served the cause of peace in that region, albeit by assuming serious personal obligation. In order, however, finally to solve these problems and achieve clarity concerning the Russian attitude toward Germany, as well as under pressure of continually increasing mobilization on our eastern frontier, I invited Mr. Molotov to come to Berlin.

The Soviet Minister for Foreign Affairs then demanded Germany's clarification of, or agreement to, the following four questions:

Point One was Molotov's question: Was the German guaranty for Rumania also directed against Soviet Russia in case of attack by Soviet Russia on Rumania?

My answer: The German guaranty is a general one and is unconditionally binding upon us. Russia, however, never declared to us that she had other interests in Rumania beyond Bessarabia. The occupation of Northern Bukovina had already been a violation of this assurance. I did not therefore think that Russia could now suddenly have more far-reaching intentions against Rumania.

Molotov's second question: That Russia again felt menaced by Finland. Russia was determined not to tolerate this. Was Germany ready not to give any aid to Finland and above all immediately to withdraw German relief troops marching through to Kirkenes?

My answer: Germany continued to have absolutely no political interests in Finland. A fresh war by Russia against the small Finnish people could not, however, be regarded any longer by the German Government as tolerable, all the more so as we could never believe Russia to be threatened by Finland. Under no circumstances did we want another theatre of war to arise in the Baltic.

Molotov's third question: Was Germany prepared to agree that Russia give a guaranty to Bulgaria and send Soviet Russian troops to Bulgaria for this purpose in connection with which he — Molotov — was prepared to state that the Soviets did not intend on that account, for example, to depose the King?

My answer: Bulgaria was a sovereign State and I had no knowledge that Bulgaria had ever asked Soviet Russia for any kind of guaranty such as Rumania had requested from Germany. Moreover, I would have to discuss the matter with my allies.

Molotov's fourth question: Soviet Russia required free passage through the Dardanelles under all circumstances and for her protection also demanded occupation of a number of important bases on the Dardanelles and Bosphorus. Was Germany in agreement with this or not?

My answer: Germany was prepared at all times to agree to alteration of the Statute of Montreux [1] in favor of the Black Sea States. Germany was not prepared to agree to Russia's taking possession of bases on the Straits.

National Socialists! Here I adopted the only attitude that I could adopt as the responsible leader of the German Reich but also as the representative of European culture and civilization and conscious of my responsibility.

The consequence was to increase in Soviet Russia the activity directed against the Reich, above all, however, the immediate commencement of undermining the new Rumanian State from within and an attempt to remove the Bulgarian Government by propaganda.

With the help of the confused and immature leaders of the Rumanian Legion (Iron Guard) a *coup d'état* was staged in Rumania whose aim was to overthrow Chief of State General Antonescu and produce chaos in the country so as to remove all legal power of the Government and thus the precondition for an implementation of the German guaranty.

---

[1] The Convention relating to the Regime of the Straits, signed at Montreux. Switzerland, July 20, 1936, League of Nations, *Treaty Series*, CLXXIII, p. 213, Germany was not a contracting party. The convention abolished the Straits Commission established by the convention of July 24, 1923, and intrusted the regime of the Straits to Turkey in accordance with the regulations laid down in it.

I nevertheless still believed it best to remain silent.

Immediately after the failure of this undertaking, renewed reinforcement of concentrations of Russian troops on Germany's eastern frontier took place. Panzer detachments and parachutists were transferred in continually increasing numbers to dangerous proximity to the German frontier. German fighting forces and the German nation know that until a few weeks ago not a single tank or mechanized division was stationed on our eastern frontier.

If any final proof was required for the coalition meanwhile formed between England and Soviet Russia despite all diversion and camouflage, the Yugoslav conflict provided it.

While I made every effort to undertake a final attempt to pacify the Balkans and in sympathetic cooperation with Il Duce invited Yugoslavia to join the Tripartite Pact, England and Soviet Russia in a joint conspiracy organized that *coup d'état* which in one night removed the then Government which had been ready to come to agreement.

For we can today inform the German nation that the Serb *putsch* against Germany did not take place merely under the British, but primarily under Soviet Russian auspices. As we remained silent on this matter also, the Soviet leaders now went still one step further. They not only organized the *putsch*, but a few days later also concluded that well-known friendship pact with the Serbs in their will to resist pacification of the Balkans and incite them against Germany.

And this was no platonic intention: Moscow demanded mobilization of the Serb Army.

Since even now I still believed it better not to speak, those in power in the Kremlin went still further: The Government of the German Reich today possesses documentary evidence which proves that Russia, in order finally to bring Serbia into the war, gave her a promise to supply her via Salonika with arms, aircraft, munitions and other war materials against Germany.

And this happened almost at the very moment when I myself advised Japanese Foreign Minister Matsuoka that eased tension with Russia always was in hope, thereby to serve the cause of peace.

Only the rapid advance of our incomparable divisions to Skoplje as well as the capture of Salonika itself frustrated the aims of this Soviet Russian-Anglo-Saxon plot. Officers of the Serb air force, however, fled to Russia and were there immediately received as allies.

The victory of the Axis Powers in the Balkans in the first instance thwarted the plan to involve Germany this Summer in months-long battles in Southeastern Europe while meantime steadily completing the alignment of Soviet Russian armies and increasing their readiness for war in order, finally, together with England and supported by American supplies anticipated, to crush the German Reich and Italy.

Thus Moscow not only broke but miserably betrayed the stipulations of our friendly agreement, all this was done while the rulers in the Kremlin, exactly as in the case of Finland and Rumania, up to the last moment pretended peace and friendship and drew up an ostensibly innocent *démenti*.

Although until now I was forced by circumstances to keep silent again and again, the moment has now come when to continue as a mere observer would not only be a sin of omission but a crime against the German people — yes, even against the whole of Europe.

Today something like 160 Russian divisions are standing at our frontiers. For weeks constant violations of this frontier have taken place, not only affecting us but from the far north down to Rumania.

Russian airmen consider it sport nonchalantly to overlook these frontiers, presumably to prove to us that they already feel themselves masters of these territories.

During the night of June 17 to June 18 Russian patrols again penetrated into the Reich's territory and could only be driven back after prolonged firing. This has brought us to the hour when it is necessary for us to take steps against this plot devised by the Jewish Anglo-Saxon warmongers and equally the Jewish rulers of the Bolshevist center in Moscow.

German people! At this moment a march is taking place that, as regards extent, compares with the greatest the world hitherto has seen. United with their Finnish comrades, the fighters of the victory of Narvik are standing in the Northern Arctic. German divisions commanded by the conqueror of Norway, in cooperation with the heroes of Finnish freedom, under their marshal, are protecting Finnish soil.

Formations of the German Eastern Front extend from East Prussia to the Carpathians. German and Rumanian soldiers are united under Chief of State Antonescu from the banks of the Pruth along the lower reaches of the Danube to the shores of the Black Sea. The task of this front, therefore, no longer is the protection of single countries, but the safeguarding of Europe and thereby the salvation of all.

I therefore decided today again to lay the fate and future of the German Reich and our people in the hands of our soldiers.

May God help us especially in this fight!

(3) *Broadcast of the Soviet People's Commissar of Foreign Affairs (Molotov), Moscow, June 22, 1941* [1]

Citizens of the Soviet Union:

The Soviet Government and its head, Comrade Stalin, have authorized me to make the following statement:

Today at 4 : 00 o'clock A.M., without any claims having been presented to the Soviet Union, without a declaration of war, German troops attacked our country, attacked our borders at many points and bombed from their airplanes our cities Zhitomir, Kiev, Sebastopol, Kaunas and some others, killing and wounding over 200 persons.

There were also enemy air raids and artillery shelling from Rumanian and Finnish territory.

This unheard of attack upon our country is perfidy unparalleled in the history of civilized nations. The attack on our country was perpetrated despite the fact that a Treaty of Nonaggression had been signed between the Union of Soviet Socialist Republics and Germany and that the Soviet Government most faithfully abided by all provisions of this treaty.

The attack upon our country was perpetrated despite the fact that during the entire period of operation of this treaty the German Government could not find grounds for a single complaint against the Union of Soviet Socialist Republics as regards observance of this treaty.

Entire responsibility for this predatory attack upon the Soviet Union falls fully and completely upon the German Fascist rulers.

At 5 : 30 A.M. — that is, after the attack had already been perpetrated, Von der Schulenburg, the German Ambassador in Moscow, on behalf of his Government made the statement to me as People's Commissar of Foreign Affairs to the effect that the German Government had decided to launch war against the Union of Soviet Socialist Republics in connection with the concentration of Red Army units near the eastern German frontier.

In reply to this I stated on behalf of the Soviet Government that, until the very last moment, the German Government had not presented any claims to the Soviet Government, that Germany attacked the Union of Soviet Socialist Republics despite the peaceable position of the Soviet Union, and that for this reason Fascist Germany is the aggressor.

On instruction of the Government of the Soviet Union I also stated that at no point had our troops or our air force committed a violation

[1] Tass version by Associated Press, *New York Times*, June 23, 1941, p. 10.

of the frontier and therefore the statement made this morning by the Rumanian radio to the effect that Soviet aircraft allegedly had fired on Rumanian airdromes is a sheer lie and provocation.

Likewise a lie and provocation is the whole declaration made today by Hitler, who is trying belatedly to concoct accusations charging the Soviet Union with failure to observe the Soviet-German pact.

Now that the attack on the Soviet Union has already been committed, the Soviet Government has ordered our troops to repulse the predatory assault and to drive German troops from the territory of our country.

This war has been forced upon us, not by the German people, not by German workers, peasants and intellectuals, whose sufferings we well understand, but by the clique of bloodthirsty Fascist rulers of Germany who have enslaved Frenchmen, Czechs, Poles, Serbians, Norway, Belgium, Denmark, Holland, Greece and other nations.

The Government of the Soviet Union expresses its unshakable confidence that our valiant army and navy and brave falcons of the Soviet Air Force will acquit themselves with honor in performing their duty to the fatherland and to the Soviet people, and will inflict a crushing blow upon the aggressor.

This is not the first time that our people have had to deal with an attack of an arrogant foe. At the time of Napoleon's invasion of Russia our people's reply was war for the fatherland, and Napoleon suffered defeat and met his doom.

It will be the same with Hitler, who in his arrogance has proclaimed a new crusade against our country. The Red Army and our whole people will again wage victorious war for the fatherland, for our country, for honor, for liberty.

The Government of the Soviet Union expresses the firm conviction that the whole population of our country, all workers, peasants and intellectuals, men and women, will conscientiously perform their duties and do their work. Our entire people must now stand solid and united as never before.

Each one of us must demand of himself and of others discipline, organization and self-denial worthy of real Soviet patriots, in order to provide for all the needs of the Red Army, Navy and Air Force, to insure victory over the enemy.

The Government calls upon you, citizens of the Soviet Union, to rally still more closely around our glorious Bolshevist party, around our Soviet Government, around our great leader and comrade, Stalin. Ours is a righteous cause. The enemy shall be defeated. Victory will be ours.

(4) Broadcast of the Prime Minister of the United Kingdom (Churchill), London, June 22, 1941 [1]

I have taken occasion to speak to you tonight because we have reached one of the climacterics of the war. In the first of these intense turning points, a year ago, France fell prostrate under the German hammer and we had to face the storm alone.

The second was when the Royal Air Force beat the Hun raiders out of the daylight air and thus warded off the Nazi invasion of our islands while we were still ill-armed and ill-prepared.

The third turning point was when the President and Congress of the United States passed the lease and lend enactment,[2] devoting nearly 2,000,000,000 sterling of the wealth of the New World to help us defend our liberties and their own.

Those were the three climacterics.

The fourth is now upon us.

At 4 : 00 o'clock this morning Hitler attacked and invaded Russia. All his usual formalities of perfidy were observed with scrupulous technique. A nonaggression treaty had been solemnly signed and was in force between the two countries. No complaint had been made by Germany of its non-fulfillment. Under its cloak of false confidence the German armies drew up in immense strength along a line which stretched from the White Sea to the Black Sea and their air fleets and armored divisions slowly and methodically took up their stations.

Then, suddenly, without declaration of war, without even an ultimatum, the German bombs rained down from the sky upon the Russian cities; the German troops violated the Russian frontiers and an hour later the German Ambassador, who till the night before was lavishing his assurances of friendship, almost of alliance, upon the Russians, called upon the Russian Foreign Minister to tell him that a state of war existed between Germany and Russia.

Thus was repeated on a far larger scale the same kind of outrage against every form of signed compact and international faith which we have witnessed in Norway, in Denmark, in Holland, in Belgium and which Hitler's accomplice and jackal, Mussolini, so faithfully imitated in the case of Greece.

All this was no surprise to me. In fact I gave clear and precise warnings to Stalin of what was coming. I gave him warnings as I have given warnings to others before. I can only hope that these warnings did not fall unheeded.

---

[1] As transcribed by the *New York Times*, June 23, 1941, p. 8.   [2] See p. 711.

All we know at present is that the Russian people are defending their native soil and that their leaders have called upon them to resist to the utmost.

Hitler is a monster of wickedness, insatiable in his lust for blood and plunder. Not content with having all Europe under his heel or else terrorized into various forms of abject submission, he must now carry his work of butchery and desolation among the vast multitudes of Russia and of Asia. The terrible military machine which we and the rest of the civilized world so foolishly, so supinely, so insensately allowed the Nazi gangsters to build up year by year from almost nothing; this machine cannot stand idle, lest it rust or fall to pieces. It must be in continual motion, grinding up human lives and trampling down the homes and the rights of hundreds of millions of men.

Moreover, it must be fed not only with flesh but with oil. So now this bloodthirsty guttersnipe must launch his mechanized armies upon new fields of slaughter, pillage and devastation. Poor as are the Russian peasants, workmen and soldiers, he must steal from them their daily bread. He must devour their harvests. He must rob them of the oil which drives their plows and thus produce a famine without example in human history.

And even the carnage and ruin which his victory, should he gain it — though he's not gained it yet — will bring upon the Russian people, will itself be only a stepping stone to the attempt to plunge the four or five hundred millions who live in China and the 350,000,000 who live in India into that bottomless pit of human degradation over which the diabolic emblem of the swastika flaunts itself.

It is not too much to say here this pleasant Summer evening that the lives and happiness of a thousand million additional human beings are now menaced with brutal Nazi violence. That is enough to make us hold our breath.

But presently I shall show you something else that lies behind and something that touches very nearly the life of Britain and of the United States.

The Nazi regime is indistinguishable from the worst features of Communism. It is devoid of all theme and principle except appetite and racial domination. It excels in all forms of human wickedness, in the efficiency of its cruelty and ferocious aggression. No one has been a more consistent opponent of Communism than I have for the last twenty-five years. I will unsay no words that I've spoken about it. But all this fades away before the spectacle which is now unfolding.

The past, with its crimes, its follies and its tragedies, flashes away.

I see the Russian soldiers standing on the threshold of their native land, guarding the fields which their fathers have tilled from time immemorial. I see them guarding their homes, their mothers and wives pray, ah, yes, for there are times when all pray for the safety of their loved ones, for the return of the breadwinner, of the champion, of their protectors.

I see the 10,000 villages of Russia, where the means of existence was wrung so hardly from the soil, but where there are still primordial human joys, where maidens laugh and children play. I see advancing upon all this, in hideous onslaught, the Nazi war machine, with its clanking, heel-clicking, dandified Prussian officers, its crafty expert agents, fresh from the cowing and tying down of a dozen countries. I see also the dull, drilled, docile, brutish masses of the Hun soldiery, plodding on like a swarm of crawling locusts. I see the German bombers and fighters in the sky, still smarting from many a British whipping, so delightful to find what they believe is an easier and a safer prey. And behind all this glare, behind all this storm, I see that small group of villainous men who planned, organized and launched this cataract of horrors upon mankind.

And then my mind goes back across the years to the days when the Russian armies were our allies against the same deadly foe, when they fought with so much valor and constancy and helped to gain a victory, from all share in which, alas, they were, through no fault of ours, utterly cut off.

I have lived through all this and you will pardon me if I express my feelings and the stir of old memories. But now I have to declare the decision of His Majesty's Government, and I feel sure it is a decision in which the great Dominions will, in due course, concur. And that we must speak of now, at once, without a day's delay. I have to make the declaration but, can you doubt what our policy will be?

We have but one aim and one single irrevocable purpose. We are resolved to destroy Hitler and every vestige of the Nazi regime. From this nothing will turn us. Nothing. We will never parley; we will never negotiate with Hitler or any of his gang. We shall fight him by land; we shall fight him by sea; we shall fight him in the air, until, with God's help we have rid the earth of his shadow and liberated its people from his yoke.

Any man or State who fights against Nazism will have our aid. Any man or State who marches with Hitler is our foe. This applies not only to organized States but to all representatives of that vile race of Quislings who make themselves the tools and agents of the Nazi regime against their fellow-countrymen and against the lands of their births. These

Quislings, like the Nazi leaders themselves, if not disposed of by their fellow-countrymen, which would save trouble, will be delivered by us on the morrow of victory to the justice of the Allied tribunals. That is our policy and that is our declaration.

It follows, therefore, that we shall give whatever help we can to Russia and to the Russian people. We shall appeal to all our friends and Allies in every part of the world to take the same course and pursue it as we shall, faithfully and steadfastly to the end.

We have offered to the Government of Soviet Russia any technical or economic assistance which is in our power and which is likely to be of service to them. We shall bomb Germany by day as well as by night in ever-increasing measure, casting upon them month by month a heavier discharge of bombs and making the German people taste and gulp each month a sharper dose of the miseries they have showered upon mankind.

It is noteworthy that only yesterday the Royal Air Force, striking inland over France, cut down with very small loss to themselves twenty-eight of the Hun fighting machines in the air above the French soil they have invaded, defiled and profess to hold.

But this is only a beginning. From now henceforward the main expansion of our air force proceeds with gathering speed. In another six months the weight of the help we are receiving from the United States in war materials of all kinds, especially in heavy bombers, will begin to tell. This is no class war. It is a war in which the whole British Empire and Commonwealth of Nations is engaged without distinction of race, creed or party.

It is not for me to speak of the action of the United States, but this I will say: If Hitler imagines that his attack on Soviet Russia will cause the slightest division of aims or slackening of effort in the great democracies, who are resolved upon his doom, he is woefully mistaken. On the contrary, we shall be fortified and encouraged in our efforts to rescue mankind from his tyranny. We shall be strengthened and not weakened in our determination and in our resources.

This is no time to moralize upon the follies of countries and governments which have allowed themselves to be struck down one by one when by united action they could so easily have saved themselves and saved the world from this catastrophe.

But, when I spoke a few minutes ago of Hitler's bloodlust and the hateful appetites which have impelled or lured him on his Russian adventure, I said there was one deeper motive behind his outrage. He wishes to destroy the Russian power because he hopes that if he succeeds in this he will be able to bring back the main strength of his army and air force from the east and hurl it upon this island, which he knows he must conquer or suffer the penalty of his crimes.

His invasion of Russia is no more than a prelude to an attempted invasion of the British Isles. He hopes, no doubt, that all this may be accomplished before the Winter comes and that he can overwhelm Great Britain before the fleets and air power of the United States will intervene. He hopes that he may once again repeat upon a greater scale than ever before that process of destroying his enemies one by one, by which he has so long thrived and prospered, and that then the scene will be clear for the final act, without which all his conquests would be in vain, namely, the subjugation of the Western Hemisphere to his will and to his system.

The Russian danger is therefore our danger and the danger of the United States just as the cause of any Russian fighting for his hearth and home is the cause of free men and free peoples in every quarter of the globe.

Let us learn the lessons already taught by such cruel experience. Let us redouble our exertions and strike with united strength while life and power remain.

(5) *Statement of the Acting Secretary of State* (*Welles*), *June 23, 1941* [1]

If any further proof could conceivably be required of the real purposes and projects of the present leaders of Germany for world-domination, it is now furnished by Hitler's treacherous attack upon Soviet Russia.

We see once more, beyond peradventure of doubt, with what intent the present Government of Germany negotiates "nonaggression pacts." To the leaders of the German Reich sworn engagements to refrain from hostile acts against other countries — engagements regarded in a happier and in a civilized world as contracts to the faithful observance of which the honor of nations themselves was pledged — are but a symbol of deceit and constitute a dire warning on the part of Germany of hostile and murderous intent. To the present German Government the very meaning of the word "honor" is unknown.

This Government has often stated, and in many of his public statements the President has declared, that the United States maintains that freedom to worship God as their consciences dictate is the great and fundamental right of all peoples. This right has been denied to their peoples by both the Nazi and the Soviet Governments. To the people

---

[1] Department of State, *Bulletin*, IV, p. 755.

of the United States this and other principles and doctrines of communistic dictatorship are as intolerable and as alien to their own beliefs as are the principles and doctrines of Nazi dictatorship. Neither kind of imposed overlordship can have or will have any support or any sway in the mode of life or in the system of government of the American people.

But the immediate issue that presents itself to the people of the United States is whether the plan for universal conquest, for the cruel and brutal enslavement of all peoples, and for the ultimate destruction of the remaining free democracies, which Hitler is now desperately trying to carry out, is to be successfully halted and defeated.

That is the present issue which faces a realistic America. It is the issue at this moment which most directly involves our own national defense and the security of the New World in which we live.

In the opinion of this Government, consequently, any defense against Hitlerism, any rallying of the forces opposing Hitlerism, from whatever source these forces may spring, will hasten the eventual downfall of the present German leaders, and will therefore redound to the benefit of our own defense and security.

Hitler's armies are today the chief dangers of the Americas.

H. Relations Between Finland and the Soviet Union

(1) *Soviet Broadcast Berating Finland, Moscow, June 26, 1941* [1]

On June 23 German planes flying from Finnish territory attempted to bomb the vicinity of Kronstadt. The following day four German planes tried to bomb the vicinity of Kandalaksha and in the region of Kuolajaervi enemy units attempted to cross the border.

The Finnish militarists have flagrantly violated the Soviet-Finnish peace treaty. The rulers of Finland have begun military operations against our country.

The peace treaty concluded between the Soviet Union and Finland on March 12, 1940,[2] provides that the two parties to the treaty agree to mutually refrain from any attack upon each other, and not to conclude any alliances or take part in coalitions directed against the one or the other country.

The Soviet Union has fulfilled the peace treaty conscientiously. But the rulers of Finland, under orders from Hitler, have plunged the long-suffering Finnish people into a war against the Soviet Union.

[1] Reported without further identification by Columbia Broadcasting System, *New York Times*, June 27, 1941, p. 4.   [2] *Documents, II, 1939–40*, p. 392.

The Soviet Government concluded the peace treaty with Finland in the interests of the peoples of both countries. In speaking on the negotiations preceding the conclusion of the peace treaty, Comrade Kalinin, the Chairman of the Presidium of the Supreme Soviet of the Union of Soviet Socialist Republics, said in March last year:

Despite the biased version spread by circles that are obviously not interested in having peace in Europe, the only purpose of these negotiations is to improve relations between the Soviet Union and Finland and to consolidate the friendly collaboration of the two countries and to insure the safety of the Soviet Union and of Finland.

Scorning the most elementary of international laws and the vital interests of their own people, the Finnish warmongers have again launched a campaign against the Soviet Union. The unbelievable provocations perpetrated by the Finnish militarists have aroused profound indignation on the part of all Soviet citizens.

The ignoble rulers of Finland have not learned any lessons from the campaign of the Winter of 1939 and 1940. They are asking for another, a final, lesson, and that lesson the Finnish perpetrators of Fascism will get.

Our valiant Red Army and Navy will make short work of the Finnish military provocateurs.

(2) *Announcement by Finland, June 25, 1941* [1]

Violations of Finnish territory from the side of the Union of Soviet Socialist Republics, which have taken place in the last few days, have since this morning become systematic and have developed into an attack of large scale.

More than ten towns and villages have today been bombed several times, causing fatal casualties among the civilian population and material damage.

The Finnish Government has previously asked the Soviet Government for explanations as to the reasons for the violations, but has not received a reply. This and the fact that the Union of Soviet Socialist Republics has thus opened hostilities against Finland compel her from now on to defend herself with every means in her power.

(a) *Statement of the Finnish Legation, Washington, June 28, 1941* [2]

Analysis of the Russian-Finnish situation in mid-June, 1941, reveals the following factors, further expanded in this text:

[1] Issued by the Finnish Legation, London; *New York Times*, June 26, 1941, p. 2.
[2] Release of the Legation.

1. Not content with the terms of the March 12, 1940, peace treaty with Finland, Russia has continuously made new demands on Finland.

2. Russia has engaged in subversive Fifth Column activities in Finland stemming from her consular agent.

3. Russia already before the present crisis made 109 registered cases of violation of Finnish territory and 804 instances of Russian planes flying over Finnish territory.

4. Nevertheless, Finland has continued her efforts toward collaboration with her totalitarian giant neighbor of the east, Russia.

5. Finland is in the midst of the international turmoil, cut off from the Western democracies, but nevertheless striving to maintain her freedom, and defending herself against the ruthless Russian aggression.

The peace treaty concluded in Moscow on the 12th of March, 1940, should have fully satisfied Russia. Finland, left alone in her fight against the aggressor, was forced to make concessions that went far beyond the Russian demands, during the negotiations in the Fall of 1939.

Hardly a month after the conclusion of the peace, Russia made a demand that Finland should compensate for or return machinery and other property removed from the ceded territory during the war, a matter that was not mentioned in the peace treaty or raised during the peace negotiations. For Finland this demand was, from the economic point of view, a very heavy one, actually a war levy, which, especially with regard to Hanko, had no legal basis whatever. Russia thus sought by economic pressure to impoverish Finland and reduce the war-exhausted country to distress. By political claims that soon followed on the trail of the economic ones, Russia aimed to establish rights that would give her a dominating influence — as for instance a control of Finnish foreign policy. These had not even been mentioned in the negotiations preceding the peace treaty, and no reference is to be found in the treaty itself. Finland adopted a conciliatory attitude, as far as was possible without giving up her status as an independent nation. Thus she, for instance, assented to transit of Russian troops over Southern Finland to Hanko in spite of the dangerous character of such a concession.

In June 1940, Russia presented a series of far-reaching claims. Demilitarization and control of the Aaland Islands was requested and Russia also demanded that the nickel mines of Petsamo be ceded to her.

These new demands were presented as conditions for a trade treaty in spite of the fact that the conclusion of such a treaty was clearly agreed upon in the treaty of peace.

It was pointed out in the ensuing negotiations that the treaty of Moscow contained no stipulations concerning the Aaland Islands. Mr. Molotov, the Russian Prime Minister, in his reply stated bluntly that the Soviet Government did not want to raise the question at the time of peace negotiations, as this problem might have rendered the conclusion of peace more difficult.

The International Convention of 1921, concerning the demilitarization of the Aaland Islands, was disregarded and belittled by Russia. Being reminded of the convention, the Russian Government asked for a privileged position over the signatory powers. The Finnish Government wanted the signatories to be informed about the matter, but the Russians flatly rejected this suggestion.

Russia preferred to omit from the new agreement a statement to the effect that the International Convention of 1921 [1] is still in force.

The demilitarization of the Aaland Islands actually amounted to their abandonment to the mercy of an aggressor.

Russia was, in this connection, granted the right to maintain a consulate on the Aaland Islands. This right has been abused by Russia; the personnel of the consulate has been increased excessively and the consular officers and the employes of the consulate have carried on subversive and incendiary propaganda among the people of the islands.

The demand concerning the nickel mines of Petsamo disregarded altogether the fact that a concession for the exploiting of the mines had been granted to a British-American company, the Mond Nickel Company. In the negotiations concerning this demand, as in other matters, Russia has repeatedly taken a most threatening attitude, alluding to the use of force and pressing Finland to cancel illegally the concession. The Russian negotiators did not conceal that territorial acquisition was in their mind and that the economic interests came only in second place.

An attempt to wrench from Finland without adequate compensation the energy of the important Vallinkoski waterfalls has also been made by Russia. In this connection she has *ad absurdum* referred to the peace treaty, being however, unwilling to recompense for the power to be delivered by the Finnish power station.

The diplomatic and consular representatives of Russia have been engaged in flagrant espionage. They have also in an arrogant and offensive manner urged for themselves privileges which it has been impossible to grant as they would have endangered public order.

Russia has, moreover, by her malicious radio and newspaper propaganda in a disturbing way intervened in the domestic affairs of Finland. She has supported a subversive society working under the misleading name of "The Association of Peace and Friendship With Union of Soviet Socialist Republics," by the help of which she has tried to weaken Finland internally. These subversive methods are well known and contributed to the total destruction of the independence of the Baltic States.

Russia even has made official attempts to interfere with the domestic affairs of Finland. She has, moreover, striven to chain the Finnish foreign policy to her own, and, referring irrelevantly to the Moscow treaty, she prevented the conclusion of a defensive alliance by the Northern countries, planned in the Spring of 1940. Negotiations for such an alliance were under way after the conclusion of the peace in Moscow, and did certainly in no way constitute a threat directed against Russia.

The hidden purpose of Russia was to destroy once for all Finland's possibilities to defend herself against a new aggression.

While adopting, when presenting her new claims, a menacing and imperative attitude, Russia in no way showed willingness to develop the Russo-Finnish relations in a positive direction. Finland, on the other hand, has over and over again in word and deed proved her readiness for collaboration. A special committee was appointed to draft a program for reciprocal cultural intercourse.

[1] *Convention relating to the Nonfortification and Neutralization of the Aaland Islands*, Geneva, October 20, 1921, League of Nations, *Treaty Series*, IX, p. 211.

The Russian Government ignored all the efforts of this committee. All Finnish attempts to establish a fruitful collaboration in the economic, cultural and other fields have been repulsed by Russian indifference. Russia has been interested in getting contact only with the subversive elements in Finland. It is an established fact that the Russians have tried to convert into their agents all Finns, including prisoners of war, who have fallen into their hands.

Before the outbreak of the war between Russia and Germany, there were 109 registered cases of violation of Finnish frontiers by Russians and 804 cases of Russian airplanes flying over Finnish territory.

Even if the change that has taken place in the balance of power in Eastern Europe has had a restraining effect on Russia in her politics toward Finland, she has not abandoned her claims and designs, as some recent incidents show. As late as June 17 the Russian Commissariat of Foreign Affairs, in an evident effort to create complications, asserted that Finland is not fulfilling the stipulations of the Hanko transit agreement. The same day the Commissariat insolently demanded the release of an offender sentenced to prison for espionage.

Since the Moscow treaty and up to the new aggression launched against Finland in June 1941, the attitude of Russia toward Finland made it fully clear that the Russian policy tends to the enslaving of Finland. The final aim of Russian policy has always been the destruction of Finland's independence.

Finland still stands as a bulwark of freedom and democracy against the murderous aggression of a totalitarian giant which has enslaved nearly 200,000,000 people and is not willing to let a small nation of 4,000,000 live in peace and freedom.

3. UNITED STATES RELATIONS WITH INDIVIDUAL STATES

A. The British Commonwealth of Nations

[See also Chapters I, II, V, VI, etc.]

1. FLEET OF THE BRITISH COMMONWEALTH

(1) *The Secretary of State (Hull) to the British Ambassador to the United States (Lothian), Washington, August 29, 1940* [1]

The Prime Minister of Great Britain is reported to have stated on June 4, 1940, to Parliament in effect that if during the course of the present war in which Great Britain and the British Commonwealth are engaged the waters surrounding the British Isles should become untenable for British ships of war, the British Fleet would in no event be surrendered or sunk but would be sent overseas for the defense of other parts of the Empire.

The Government of the United States would respectfully inquire

[1] Department of State, *Bulletin*, III, p. 195.

whether the foregoing statement represents the settled policy of the British Government.

C. H.

DEPARTMENT OF STATE, *
   Washington, August 29, 1940.

(2) *The British Ambassador to the United States (Lothian) to the Secretary of State (Hull), Washington, September 2, 1940* [1]

In his *Aide-Mémoire* of August 29, 1940, the Secretary of State enquired whether the Prime Minister's statement in Parliament on June 4, 1940, regarding the intention of His Majesty's Government in the United Kingdom never to surrender or sink the British Fleet in the event of the waters surrounding the British Isles becoming untenable for His Majesty's Ships "represents the settled policy of His Majesty's Government."

His Majesty's Ambassador is instructed by the Prime Minister to inform Mr. Secretary Hull that this statement certainly does represent the settled policy of His Majesty's Government. Mr. Churchill must however observe that these hypothetical contingencies seem more likely to concern the German fleet or what is left of it than the British Fleet.

L.

BRITISH EMBASSY,
   WASHINGTON, D. C.,
     September 2, 1940.

2. BRITISH OUTLOOK ON THE WAR AND FUTURE PEACE

(1) *Address of the British Ambassador to the United States (Lothian), Baltimore, Md., December 11, 1940* [2]

[Excerpt]

It is now nearly five months since I made a public speech in the United States. Since then I have been home to consult with my Government and to find out for myself how things were going in Britain. I want tonight to give you some of the conclusions I have formed.

In these last five months there have been tremendous changes. When last I spoke we had just experienced the terrific shock of the overthrow of France. Hitler seemed irresistible. First Poland had been over-

---

[1] Department of State, *Bulletin*, III, p. 195.

[2] From print of the British Library of Information. The address was read at the annual dinner of the Farm Bureau Federation by the Ambassador's representative. The Marquess of Lothian, who had returned to the United States from London in December, died at the Embassy December 12 and his ashes temporarily repose in Arlington National Cemetery.

whelmed, then Norway, then Holland, then Belgium. Finally came the destruction in less than a month's fighting of what had been rated as the finest army for its size in Europe, and the disarmament and division of France.

If you recall those dismal days you will remember that there was something like despair in many diplomatic and business circles in Washington, New York and other cities in the United States. What could be the future of civilization if France, that beautiful child of liberty, had erased the rights of man established at the Revolution and defined in three immortal words *Liberté, Egalité, Fraternité*, from her escutcheon. Further, Hitler had announced that he would dictate peace in London in August, or at latest by the middle of September. And had not he always been right about his military dates? Britain had saved her soldiers, it is true by a miracle, at Dunkerque. But they had lost all their equipment, guns, tanks, motor vehicles, machine guns and rifles. The German Air Force, too, was known to be far superior in numbers to the Royal Air Force, and its dive bombers had just crushed the resistance of the French Army. Was it not certain that England was going to be conquered and that with Hitler's crossing of the Channel the end of the British Commonwealth would come?

If these were the gloomy prophecies in circulation about us, there were hardly less gloomy speculations about the future of the United States. If Hitler conquered Britain the British fleet would be sunk or surrendered or scattered among the British nations overseas. Yet was it not clear that American security required two fleets, the British fleet, based on Britain blocking the entry of hostile European fleets into the Eastern Atlantic, and the United States fleet predominant in the Pacific? It was this dual system which protected the Monroe Doctrine and which alone could keep war distant from American shores. That, too, was the time of the gloomy revelation in Congress that the United States was as unprepared for modern war as all the other Democracies had been. It was said that she had full modern equipment only for 75,000 to 100,000 soldiers, an air force which was very good in quality but terribly small and with none of the reserves and organized manufacturing capacity of the nation behind it, and an excellent navy, but a one-ocean navy facing the possibility of a two-ocean war. The prospect, therefore, before the United States if the British fleet was sunk or surrendered or sailed away to the outer parts of the British Empire was not rosy. With Hitler's and Mussolini's navies and the remains of the French fleet based on the Eastern rim of the Atlantic and on strategic islands well out in the Atlantic, Iceland and the Faroes, the Azores and

Teneriffe, would not the whole American fleet have to come back to the Atlantic, leaving the Pacific, both North and South, at the mercy of Japan? Moreover, even if some part of the British fleet passed across to North American ports it would not have a quarter as much value to North America. If Gibraltar and the West African ports fell into Axis hands how could the United States defend the Monroe Doctrine, especially if some thousands of planes were assembled at Dakar with Fifth Columns in the Americas, elated and arrogant at the downfall of Britain? Finally, what would happen to the rearmament program of the United States, if Hitler and his allies, with Britain conquered, in possession of nearly all the strategic positions and the industrial resources of the globe, were able to hold three battleships or tanks or aeroplanes for one against the United States?

[Here follows an account of events from July to September 1940.]

Thus if Hitler won the first round of the great battle which began in Norway in April, we have won the second. For without the conquest of Britain Hitler cannot win the war.

But the war is not yet won. Do not think that Hitler and Nazidom is going to be easily overthrown. Hitler is certainly going to make another attempt next year — and earlier rather than later — to beat down our resistance by new methods and still greater violence, and so open the way to world domination for the Nazis.

I do not think that even now we realize the true nature of National Socialism. The triumph of Hitler no doubt grew out of the despair which settled on Central Europe in the long years of war, defeat, inflation, revolutionary propaganda, and which grew out of the unemployment and frustration which followed from the absence of any real unity in Europe, the sudden restriction of immigration overseas and the attempt to combine the collections of reparations and war debts by the Allies with the imposition of unjust tariffs after the war. That was what gave Hitler his chance. But modern National Socialism is the reassertion of the strongest tradition in German and Prussian history, the belief in the all-powerful military state, creating order and discipline at home by ruthless Gestapo methods and expanding its wealth and power by ruthless conquest abroad. Hitler has created a movement in Germany which is so unfamiliar to the Western Democracies as to be almost incomprehensible to us. The central purpose of the democratic movement in the West of the last few centuries has been to enlarge the liberty and responsibility of the individual citizen. War and despotism have been anathema to the democratic mind just because they are both inherently destructive of individual liberty. We have almost lost the capacity to understand that war and conquest can be regarded and preached as heroic and legitimate ends in themselves.

Yet that is precisely what National Socialism under the leadership of Hitler does. Nazism is the application of the principle of army organization, obedience and discipline to a whole nation, to men, women and children alike, partly as the basis of order at home, and partly so that it can be used in war, total war, war without limit and without mercy, with its concomitants, propaganda and fraud, as the means of the total subjugation of other nations to serve the Nazi will. I repeat that it is almost impossible for us to believe that such a program can be made the central purpose of a modern nation. Yet it is beyond question that this is what Hitler's Germany stands for. Hitler and his party are not concerned to bring about juster frontiers in Europe between free peoples or a fairer distribution of colonial raw materials between the leading nations of the world. Their object is to subjugate others so that they and their resources can be organized on totalitarian lines for the benefit of the German military state. And they believe that, provided they use that power with efficient ruthlessness, modern science and modern psychology have given them the means with which to create the greatest military empire the world has known. First they demoralize and disintegrate their neighbors by the propaganda of fear, appeasement, pacifism and internal division. Then they knock them out by total war.

Hitler first used those methods to conquer the old Germany and to destroy all opposing forces within it. He then set out to organize Germany as a military state and propaganda machine of tremendous power. He then turned this terrific instrument on Europe to overthrow and enslave the peace-loving nations, one by one, first Austria, then Czechoslovakia, then Poland, then Norway, Denmark, Holland and Belgium until Europe, save for Britain and Russia, now lies prostrate before him. But that is not going to satisfy Hitler and the National Socialists. If they are allowed to do so they will now go on to organize Europe itself for war and propaganda in order to use it for further expansion later on.

Under Hitler the free nations of Europe are never going to reappear. They are going to be reduced permanently to political, economic and military impotence, so that they can act as the suppliers and serfs of the ruling German race. You can see the process beginning in the annexation of Lorraine and the transplantation of its people, and in the hideous treatment of the Poles. You can see it in the transportation of machine-tools into Germany, so that Berlin will control all economic power and the rest of Europe has to toil for its masters. Hitlerism cannot stop and become peaceful. Nazi Germany is organized for war and totalitarian economics and for nothing else. Its economic system, like everything else, is built on fraud. War and preparation for war is its only real remedy for unemployment.

This war, therefore, is not a war between nations like the last war. It is more of a revolution than a war — a revolutionary war waged by Hitler and his military totalitarian machine against all other nations and the free world in which we have lived, so as to make them military, political and economic satellites of a totalitarian world empire. Then Hitler will have given the world peace — the peace of death — and employment, the employment of a slave.

It is quite obvious that the only way of stopping the expansion of the Hitler Europe is to confront it somewhere with a power possessed of superior armaments and an impregnable strategic position. As we have found through bitter experience it will never be stopped by appeasement or concessions. It is equally obvious that there will be no freedom for the conquered peoples of Europe until the authority of the Nazi group and its brutal philosophy have been overthrown in Germany itself.

Today, however, we have still to build up the peace which will certainly be able to stop Hitler. Hitler, as we have seen, has lost the second round of the war. But we think that he certainly is going to renew the attack on Britain with all his might this winter and spring. Everything else is for him a side-show. But if he can destroy Britain he and his friends will have won the basis of world domination. But this time he is going to concentrate on the sea. He has failed to overwhelm us in the air and we are sure that he will continue to fail, while with your help our power to hit back with our bombers will steadily increase. But he is building submarines and long-distance planes with all his might and main with which to bomb the convoys and to announce their location to the submarines. He will base them on all the ports and aerodromes along that line which runs like a vast semi-circle around Britain, from Narvik down the Northern and Western coasts of France to Spain. He will have two new 35,000-ton battleships, the *Tirpitz* and the *Bismarck*, and other vessels in the North Sea early next year. With these he will try to deliver a knock-out blow at our communications so as to prevent us getting the food, the raw materials and aeroplanes necessary to enable us to continue the war at full strength. The danger, of course, springs ultimately from the fact that in the last war we had the support of the Japanese, the Italian, the French, and, after April 1917, of your navy, whereas today, since the disappearance of the powerful French Navy, we are fighting alone. Our navy, therefore, with the tremendous tasks which rest upon it, no one of which has it shirked or evaded, is strung out terribly thin.

We think that this is a situation which concerns you almost as much as it concerns us. It has long been clear that your security no less than ours depends upon our holding the Atlantic impregnably and you the Pacific. So long as this is so, the way of life to which we are attached can continue and our free economic system can resist totalitarian attack. But if one of those two navies fails the unity of the British Commonwealth begins to disappear, control of the trade routes begins to pass to the Axis powers and those controlling bastions of sea power which now keep war away from America, become the jumping-off points from which it can be menaced.

Moreover the Axis-Japanese Pact of September last [1] makes nakedly clear the ultimate objective of totalitarian strategy. As soon as an Italian or German army or fleet can occupy Gibraltar or northwest Africa or Great Britain's control of the Atlantic has been sufficiently weakened to cause doubt where the American fleet should be stationed the two-ocean attack on us both in the Atlantic and the Pacific, will be simultaneously launched. The more secure is our control of the Atlantic the less likely is the two-ocean war to break out.

We have both, therefore, a vital interest in decisively defeating the now rapidly maturing naval attack on the communications of the British Isles. It is the best way of preventing the spread of the war. And it is an essential step to that victory which will eventually follow the failure of Hitler to destroy Great Britain, both by air and by sea, and the uninterrupted flow of American munitions to the British Isles.

We have no illusions, therefore, about 1941. It is going to be a hard and a dangerous year. Our shipping losses have recently been formidable. In one week British, Allied and Neutral losses were nearly 200,000 tons. Only one of the two passages to Britain around Ireland is open to us, which enables Germany to concentrate its submarines on the other. We are suffering, on the average of October, 200 civilian deaths and 300 civilians mutilated every night from enemy bombardment and our food supplies are gradually being more strictly rationed.

But we are not in the least dismayed. With help from you we are confident that we can win, and win decisively in 1942, if not before. We are confident, first of all, for spiritual reasons. The core of Hitlerism is moral rottenness, the belief that the use of utter brutality and ruthless power in the prosecution of domination is the road to greatness both in individuals and nations. Hitlerism is the tragedy of Germany. Its

[1] See p. 304.

doctrine is not true. All history proves it wrong. The Sermon on the Mount in the long run is much stronger than all Hitler's propaganda or Goering's guns and bombs. The core of the Allied creed, for all our mistakes of omission and commission, is liberty, justice, and truth, and that we believe will infallibly prevail, if we have the resolution and the courage to resist to the end.

But on the side of armaments, also, we have great and growing assets. The curve of our munition and aeroplane production is steadily rising — despite the bombing. The number of our divisions, of our aeroplanes, of our pilots is also steadily going up.

What is more important, the young nations of the Commonwealth, Canada, Australia, South Africa, New Zealand, are fast getting into their stride. The number of their divisions is increasing. You will soon hear of their prowess on more than one front, as you have heard of the New Zealand *Achilles* in the *Graf Spee* battle and the Australian *Sydney* in the Mediterranean. The Canadian training scheme is rapidly coming into output. You will be staggered at what will come out of Canada shortly in the shape of trained pilots and men. And Canada produced perhaps the best airmen in our forces in the Great War. Australia and New Zealand are producing pilots also in great numbers. South Africa is actively engaged both in the air and on land in Abyssinia, Kenya and in the Sudan. Indian troops and Indian munitions are now coming into the battle fronts, and ever-increasing resources are coming from the colonies and territories, loyal to a man and proud of their membership of the Commonwealth.

The whole of this growing aggregation of power is now being mobilized. Its first task is to defend that great ring of defensive positions which lie around you, Britain itself, Gibraltar, Cape Town, Egypt and the Suez Canal, Singapore, Australia and New Zealand. If Hitler and his friends could smash through these great positions his power could begin to spread over Africa and the Pacific, and it would make the problem both of security and of bringing the war to a victorious end immeasurably more difficult.

But as long as we can hold these positions, we and the democratic world beyond them are safe. Napoleon saw that all war is a struggle for position. Our second task is to enable us to deliver increasingly formidable blows at Germany itself, at her allies, one of whom is already beginning to crack, and to bring assistance to the subjugated peoples now once more beginning to show signs of a resistance to Hitler's will. The heroic Greeks now striking a mortal blow at the prestige of Mussolini and his system are showing how much the position has already improved since the legend of totalitarian invulnerability was broken last September.

But that result is not yet secure. It will be put to the test in 1941. If we can now stave off the attack on Britain, if we can last out next year still holding all the positions I have mentioned, Hitlerism in the end must go down unless Admiral Mahan is all wrong. By ourselves we cannot be sure of this result — though we will try our best. Not only is there the situation in the North Atlantic I have described, but no one can yet tell what the constant pressure of Hitler both on the Vichy Government to give him control of the French fleet and bases in the Mediterranean, and on Japan to extend the war in the Pacific, may lead to.

But with your help in aeroplanes, munitions, in ships and on the sea, and in the field of finance now being discussed between your Treasury and ours, we are sure of victory — sure that the gangster menace to human freedom, the greatest the world has ever seen, will go down to the oblivion it deserves.

It is not for me to try to tell you what you ought to do. That is entirely for you to decide for yourselves. But it is my business to see that you are informed of the essential facts, because unless you are so informed you cannot form a judgment and I and not you would be responsible for the consequences; hence this speech tonight. You have already declared your interest in the survival of Britain. It is for you to decide whether it is to your interest to give us whatever assistance may be necessary in order to make certain that Britain shall not fall.

There are only two more things I want to say in conclusion. The first is that nobody who, like myself, has seen what the steady and constant bombardment of great cities from the air means, could wish any friendly country like the United States of America to undergo any similar experience. Hitler has let loose this kind of warfare on mankind and will have to take the consequences. And we for geographical reasons are in the firing line. But you and Canada and Australia and New Zealand and probably South Africa have the chance, if you take it, of saving yourselves from being the theatre of total war. You are the center of that great ring of fortresses, Britain, Gibraltar, Cape Town, Suez, Singapore and Australia, I have mentioned, to which I should add Hawaii and Panama. So long as these fortresses stand, the war, with its aerial bombardment, cannot in any real sense of the word roll up to your shores or devastate your towns and cities. I do not believe that a liberal civilization can develop under conditions of constant bombardment and war. Modern individual freedom developed first in England precisely because the Channel protected Britain from constant war, and later in America because the Atlantic did the same. Almost alone among the nations you still have the chance of making your country immune from the devastation of war, not by pacifism or attempted appeasement of the dictators, but by helping to maintain the frontiers I have described, all occupied by liberal democracies like yourselves and prepared to fight for their independence and yours and with your help able collectively to generate more power than the totalitarian alliance can bring against them.

But if ramparts fall the war will inevitably cross the oceans and roll up against your shores. If Britain and the eastern shores of the Atlantic and the islands which lie off its shores, Iceland, the Azores or bases like Dakar, fall into the dictators' hands, or if you are unable to defend the island fortresses in the Pacific, then the jumping-off grounds go against you, the oceans become a passageway, and your power to strike back at an enemy disappears because you have no bases from which to do so.

The last thing I want to say concerns the future. There were two things which I found the ordinary citizen in Britain thinking about. The first was that all his and her suffering and sacrifice should, if possible, end, not all war, for human nature is probably not yet ready for that, but the kind of total war Hitler is waging, with its hideous mutilation and destruction from the air and its brutal persecution of conquered peoples. The second was that after this war no one who had done his duty should be thrown on the scrap heap of unemployment, with nothing but a bonus or a dole. Somehow or other employment must be found for everybody.

Some people are spreading the legend that democracy is disappearing from Britain and that she will come out at the end of the war a Fascist or a Communist state. Nothing could be further from the truth. I have never known Britain more truly democratic. The British are not going to change their essential character. It has shown itself in this war. They will move forward, of course, with the times, but without revolutionary violence.

But the more people think about the future the more they are drawn to the conclusion that all real hope depends upon some form of cooperation between the United States and the British Commonwealth of Nations. Even if we win a total victory there will be no chance of immediately creating an effective new League of Nations. There will be nothing in Europe out of which to make it. A majority of the younger generation consist of people who have been educated in such brutish doctrines as blood and earth, that might is right, that Jews are social poison or that business men are hyenas only fit for destruction. No man can even say what the France of tomorrow will be like.

The plain truth is that peace and order always depend not upon disarming the police but upon there being overwhelming power behind just law. The only place where that power can be found behind the laws of a liberal and democratic world is in the United States and in Great Britain supported by the Dominions and in some other free nations. The only nucleus round which a stable and peaceful and democratic world can be built after this war is if the United States and Great Britain possess between them more aeroplanes and ships of war and the key positions of world power, such as I have described, than any possible totalitarian rival. Then and then only will political and industrial freedom be secure, and will it be possible for a free economic system to prevail against the economics of totalitarianism. If we are to set the world going again, not only must we have strength, but we must not adopt the fatal policies we all pursued after the last war, the establishment of prohibitive tariffs, trying to collect fantastic reparations and war debts across these tariffs, and then hoping to dodge the inevitable consequences of these follies by a policy of reckless lending. Markets and employment for all should be the main purpose of post-war economic policy.

I have done. I have endeavored to give you some idea of our present position, of the dangers and problems of 1941, of our hopes for the future. It is for you to decide whether you share our hopes and what support you will give us in realizing them. We are, I believe, doing all we can. Since May there is no challenge we have evaded, no challenge refused. If you back us you will not be backing a quitter. The issue now depends largely on what you decide to do. Nobody can share that responsibility with you. It is the great strength of democracy that it brings responsibility down squarely to every citizen and every nation. And before the Judgment Seat of God each must answer for his own actions.

(2) *British Post-War Reconstruction. Statement of the Government, London, January 6, 1941* [1]

[Excerpt]

The Prime Minister has made the following changes in the machinery of the government for dealing with . . . post-war reconstruction policy:

1. The Minister Without Portfolio has undertaken responsibility for the study of reconstruction and post-war problems, and later on,

[1] *New York Times*, January 7, 1941, p. 5. The remainder of this statement describes British governmental reorganization for better prosecution of the war, see p. 661.

when the end of the war can be more clearly foreseen, a Ministry will be formed for this purpose.

Meanwhile Mr. Arthur Greenwood will be chairman of the group of Ministers. The object will be to find practical solutions for the immediate problem of a transition from war to peace and also to outline and presently to amplify a policy for the years immediately following the war which will command the support of the nation as a whole and enable united action to proceed in peace as in war.

(3) *Reconstruction. Address by the British Principal Secretary of State for Foreign Affairs (Eden), Mansion House, London, May 29, 1941* [1]

[Excerpt]

This statement was partially in response to much popular discussion of the shape of the post-war world. After references to events then current, Mr. Eden quoted President Roosevelt's four freedoms [2] and devoted a large section of his address to "our own conception" of practical ways of applying the freedom from want to Europe. This passage is given.

We have declared that social security must be the first object of our domestic policy after the war. And social security will be our policy abroad not less than at home. It will be our wish to work with others to prevent starvation in the post-armistice period, currency disorders throughout Europe and wide fluctuations of employment markets and prices which were the cause of so much misery in the 20 years between the two wars. We shall seek to achieve this in ways which will interfere as little as possible with the proper liberty of each country over its own economic fortunes.

Countries of the British Empire and their Allies, with the United States and South America, are alone in a position to carry out such a policy. For, irrespective of the nature of the political settlement, Continental Europe will end this war starved and bankrupt of all foods and raw materials which she was accustomed to obtain from the rest of the world. She will have no means, unaided, of breaking the vicious circle. She can export few goods until she has first received the necessary raw materials. Wasteful wartime cultivations in many lands will leave agriculture almost as weak as industry. Thus Europe will face vast problems of general demobilization with a general lack of the necessary means to put men to work.

It is right to think of these things now.

[1] Edited from the Associated Press dispatch, *New York Times*, May 30, 1941, p. 4, and the report of *The Times* (London), May 30, 1941, p. 2.
[2] See p. 33, 38.

Let no one suppose that we, for our part, intend to return to the chaos of the old world. To do so would bankrupt us no less than others. When peace comes we shall make such relaxations of our wartime financial arrangements as will permit the revival of international trade on the widest possible basis. We should hope to see development of a system of international exchange in which the trading of goods and services will be the central feature.

I echo Mr. [Secretary] Hull's admirable summing up in his recent declaration when he said:

Institutions and arrangements of international finance must be so set up that they lend aid to essential enterprises and continuous development of all countries and permit payment through the processes of trade consonant with the welfare of all countries.

However, to meet problems of the immediate post-war period, action in other directions will also be required. Liberated countries, and maybe others too, will require initial pool resources to carry them through the transitional period.

To organize the transition to peaceful activities we will need the collaboration of the United States, of ourselves and of all other free countries which have not themselves suffered the ravages of war. The Dominions and ourselves can make our contribution to this because the British Empire will actually possess overseas enormous stocks of food and materials which we are accumulating so as to ease the problems of overseas producers during the war and of a reconstructed Europe after war. The Prime Minister has already made clear the importance he attaches to this. What has Germany to offer on her side? Absolutely nothing.

No one can suppose that economic reorganization of Europe after the Allied victory will be an easy task. But we shall not shirk our opportunity, and our responsibility will be to bear our share of these burdens. The peaceful brotherhood of nations, with due liberty to each to develop its own balanced economic life and its characteristic culture, will be the common object of us all. But it is the transition to this end which presents the problem. It is the establishment of an international economic system capable of translating the technical possibilities of production into actual plenty and maintaining the whole population in continuous fruitful activity. It is that which is difficult.

The world cannot expect to solve the economic riddle easily or completely. But the free nations, America, the Dominions and ourselves alone possess a command of the material means, — and what is more important, these nations clearly have the will and intention to evolve a post-war order which seeks no selfish national advantage; an order where each member of the family shall realize its own character and perfect its own gifts in liberty of conscience and person. We have learned a lesson in the interregnum between the two wars. We know that no escape can be found from the curse which has been lying on Europe except by creating and preserving economic health in every country.

Under a system of free economic cooperation Germany must play a part. But here I draw a firm distinction. We must never forget that Germany is the worst master Europe has yet known. Five times in the last century she has violated the peace. She must never be in a position to play that role again. Our political and military terms for peace will be designed to prevent repetition of Germany's misdeeds. . . .

The right economic outcome after the war requires on our part no exceptional unselfishness, but will require constructive imagination. It is obvious that we have no motive of self-interest prompting us to economic exploitation either of Germany or the rest of Europe. This is not what we want nor what we could perform. The lasting settlement and internal peace of the Continent as a whole is our only aim. The fact that at the bottom of his heart every combatant knows this is the ultimate source of our strength. To every neutral, satellite, or conquered country, it is obvious that our victory is, for the most fundamental and unalterable reasons, to their plain advantage. But that victory stands also for something greater still. Only our victory can restore, both to Europe and to the world, that freedom which is our heritage from centuries of Christian civilization, and that security which alone can make possible the betterment of man's lot upon the earth.

In the tasks that lie ahead may there be given to our statesmen the vision to see, the faith to act, and the courage to persevere.

3. REPRESENTATION OF HIS BRITANNIC MAJESTY GEORGE VI

(1) *Death of the British Ambassador to the United States, the Marquess of Lothian, December 12, 1940*

(a) *Statement of the President (Roosevelt)* [1]

I am deeply shocked and grieved at the news of the death of Lord Lothian, the British Ambassador. It was my good fortune to count him as a personal friend over a period of many years. As Philip Kerr and

[1] Department of State, *Bulletin*, III, p. 547. For the exchange of telegrams between His Britannic Majesty and the President, see *ibid.*, p. 547, 548.

the private secretary of the wartime British Prime Minister he displayed an understanding of and friendship for the United States that continued throughout his long and distinguished career. As the Marquess of Lothian he continued his many contacts and friendships with this country and made a real contribution toward understanding between our peoples.

His appointment as British Ambassador last year was a fitting and natural recognition by his Government of the lifelong efforts of a great figure toward good relations between our two countries.

Lord Lothian's tragic death deprives his country of a tried and true public servant at the peak of his usefulness. All of the people of this country who were privileged to know him will join with me in mourning his untimely passing.

(b) Statement of the Secretary of State (Hull) [1]

The death of Lord Lothian has brought me deep and profound sorrow. Not only has the British Empire lost a great and faithful servant in him, but the United States has lost a real friend, a true interpreter to us of his country at a time when it was exceptionally important that both nations should have a knowledge and understanding of their mutual problems and interests.

The British Ambassador has an important role to play in this country. Lord Lothian, who remained always a devoted Englishman, brought distinction to his mighty task. His deep-seated knowledge of the British Empire, derived from many years of service to his country in Europe and throughout the Empire gave great weight to his counsels at this time.

It is not only the people of this country that knew him in these last months as British Ambassador, but the American friends of a lifetime as well, who will mourn him.

(c) Funeral and Interment at Arlington, December 15, 16, 1940 [2]

Services for His Excellency the Right Honorable the Marquess of Lothian, K. T., C. H., late Ambassador Extraordinary and Plenipotentiary of Great Britain, will be held in the Washington Cathedral, Massachusetts and Wisconsin Avenues, on Sunday, December 15, at 2 : 30 o'clock.

[1] Department of State, *Bulletin*, III, p. 547. An exchange of telegrams was also made between the Secretary of State and the Prime Minister (*ibid.*, p. 547, 562).

[2] Press release, Department of State, *Bulletin*, III, p. 548.

A caisson bearing the remains of the late Ambassador will leave the Embassy at 2 P.M., escorted by a squadron of cavalry and will arrive at the Cathedral at 2 : 30 P.M. Seats will be reserved for American and British officials and for the members of the Diplomatic Corps and the personal friends of the late Ambassador.

Following the services at the Cathedral, a private cremation service will be held in the Church of Fort Lincoln, Bladensburg Road, at the District Line.

On Monday, December 16, at 12 o'clock noon the ashes of the late Ambassador will be received at Arlington National Cemetery and placed with full military honors in the vault under the mast of the U. S. S. *Maine* near the Amphitheatre, to remain for an indefinite period until arrangements can be made for final disposition.

(2) *Arrival of the British Ambassador to the United States (Halifax). Statement to the Press, Annapolis, January 24, 1941* [1]

Viscount Halifax, His Britannic Majesty's Principal Secretary of State for Foreign Affairs and a member of the War Cabinet, was designated to succeed the Marquess of Lothian, the British Ambassador at Washington, who died at his post December 12, 1940. Following the announcement of the assignment and a public dinner to Viscount Halifax, who retained his membership in the War Cabinet, silence shrouded his movements. At 1 : 30 P.M., January 24, 1941, the President of the United States and a party left the White House and proceeded to Annapolis, where the Chief Executive boarded the yacht *Potomac*. Six miles outside the yacht met the battleship *H.M.S. King George V* and took the British Ambassador designate aboard. The President as host at the unprecedented ceremony of welcome on Chesapeake Bay entertained the official British party on the *Potomac* and conferred with the Ambassador designate.

Lady Halifax and I are very glad to be here, and we have had a voyage which we shall always remember. It has been something of a rest for me, for this is almost the first time I have been out of daily and nightly touch with the War Cabinet in London since the war began a year and a half ago.

The Prime Minister and Mrs. Churchill came to the port from which we sailed to say good-bye to us and now the President has done my country the greatest honor of coming to greet us on arrival.

His action in meeting His Majesty's ship *King George V* has been tremendously appreciated by the whole ship's company from the captain to the last-joined member of the crew, as it most certainly will be in Great Britain and every part of the British Empire.

I expect you know more of the latest news of what is going on in the world than I do, for I have been rather cut off from news for the past

[1] *New York Times*, January 25, 1941, p. 3.

week or so, and I have therefore nothing much to say to you on that score.

I have come here, as a member of the War Cabinet serving as His Majesty's Ambassador, to make known to the Government and people of the United States from time to time in what way, if they are willing, they can best give us the help we need.

The more quickly your generous help can be made effective, the sooner shall we be able to break this Nazi power that is trying to enslave Europe and the world.

I shall thus be continuing the work begun by my predecessor, Lord Lothian, whose death has been such a loss to his country, and who I know is mourned by the many friends he made in the United States.

We have assuredly a rough, difficult and perhaps a very long road before us; but the British people are united as never before in history, and I have no doubt that with your help we can win through and so save those causes on which your civilization and ours depend.

(3) *Remarks of Viscount Halifax upon Presentation of Credentials as Ambassador, January 24, 1941* [1]

MR. PRESIDENT:

In handing you today the Royal letter accrediting me as His Majesty's Ambassador to the United States, I am instructed by the King, my August Sovereign and Master, to convey to you his friendly greetings and to express his earnest hope for the happiness and prosperity of the United States.

The sudden death of my distinguished predecessor, the Marquess of Lothian, deprived Great Britain of a representative who knew and loved the United States of America and who had labored unceasingly to draw still more close the ties which unite our two countries. His Majesty's Government are gratified to know that his labors were not unfruitful.

In these heroic and tragic days, when it is the privilege of my country to be the champion against brutal wrong-doing of all that the American and British Nations hold most dear, my Sovereign has deemed it expedient to entrust to me, as a member of his War Cabinet, the task which the late Ambassador had so worthily discharged.

Following his example, and in accordance with my instructions, I shall do all in my power to maintain and strengthen the close relations which now for many years have so happily existed between Great Britain and the United States. I know that in this important task I shall receive your support, Mr. President, and that of your administration.

[1] Department of State, *Bulletin*, IV, p. 135.

I take up my office at a time when the help which the people of the United States are giving to the people of Great Britain assumes an ever-increasing importance. That assistance has already been invaluable, and its continuance as your nation speedily develops its unrivalled industrial strength, will assuredly secure the triumph of the cause on which you, no less than we, are resolved.

In conclusion I would say how deeply I appreciate the honor of representing His Majesty in the United States. I have been a visitor here before, and I welcome the opportunity thus afforded to me of acquiring a more intimate knowledge of this great people whose qualities and achievements I have already learnt to respect.

(4) *Reply of the President (Roosevelt), January 24, 1941* [1]

MR. AMBASSADOR:

I am delighted, Mr. Ambassador, to welcome you to Washington and to receive from your hands the letters which accredit you, a member of the British War Cabinet, as His Britannic Majesty's Ambassador Extraordinary and Plenipotentiary to the United States.

I greatly appreciate the friendly personal greeting and the expression of good wishes for the United States which you have just conveyed to me from His Britannic Majesty, and I take this occasion to reaffirm the warm friendly feeling of myself and of the American people for the Government and people of Great Britain and of the whole British Commonwealth of Nations.

The tragic and untimely death of your distinguished predecessor, Lord Lothian, came as a profound shock to all of us who had been privileged to know him. He had deeply impressed us all with his sincere friendship for the United States and with his untiring efforts toward closer understanding between English-speaking peoples.

Great Britain and the United States have long been linked by intimate bonds of blood and friendship. I feel confident, Mr. Ambassador, that your presence in the United States will increasingly strengthen these strong ties between our two countries.

Let me assure you that in all your work here you may always count upon my full cooperation and the cooperation of the various agencies of this Government. I want to assure you further of our firm determination to continue on an ever-increasing scale our assistance to Great Britain and to make available munitions and supplies now flowing from the rapidly expanding industrial facilities of the United States.

[1] Department of State, *Bulletin,* IV, p. 135.

4. CONCILIATION TREATIES WITH THE BRITISH COMMONWEALTH OF NATIONS

In the Treaty for the Advancement of Peace signed September 15, 1914, with Great Britain it was provided that the commission established for the consideration of disputes not submitted to arbitration should include a commissioner appointed by any Dominion, in lieu of a commissioner appointed by Great Britain, for any dispute to which that Dominion was a party. In time several places in the commission and the panel of Dominion alternates became vacant. In the interval since the entry of the treaty into force the British Dominions have acquired the right to make treaties on their own behalf and have become equal members in the British Commonwealth of Nations. As they were not primary parties to the 1914 treaty the filling of the commission, as stipulated in the treaty, by appointments to the panel was incompatible with the status of Members of the Commonwealth.

It was therefore represented to the Department of State in October 1938 that the treaty of 1914 should be revised so as to permit of the appointment of commissions by each member of the British Commonwealth of Nations. Identic treaties, *mutatis mutandis*, were signed with them as follows:

> Union of South Africa, April 2, 1940;
> Canada, September 6, 1940;
> Australia, September 6, 1940;
> New Zealand, September 6, 1940.

(1) *Advancement of Peace. Treaty between the United States of America and the Union of South Africa Amending in Their Application to the Union of South Africa Certain Provisions of the Treaty for the Advancement of Peace between the United States of America and Great Britain signed September 15, 1914, Signed at Washington April 2, 1940* [1]

In force March 11, 1941

The President of the United States of America and His Majesty the King of Great Britain, Ireland, and the British Dominions beyond the Seas, Emperor of India, acting for the Union of South Africa, being desirous, in view of the present constitutional position and international status of the Union of South Africa as an independent State, to amend in their application to the Union of South Africa certain provisions of the Treaty for the Advancement of Peace between the President of the United States of America and His Majesty the King of the United Kingdom of Great Britain and Ireland and of the British Dominions beyond the Seas, Emperor of India, signed at Washington, September 15, 1914,[2] have for that purpose appointed as their plenipotentiaries:

The President of the United States of America:

Mr. Cordell Hull, Secretary of State of the United States of America; and

[1] United States *Treaty Series* No. 966.
[2] *Ibid.*, No. 602; 38 Stat. 1853; *Treaties, Conventions*, etc., 1910–1923, III, p. 2642.

His Majesty the King of Great Britain, Ireland, and the British Dominions beyond the Seas, Emperor of India, for the Union of South Africa:

Mr. Ralph William Close, Envoy Extraordinary and Minister Plenipotentiary of the Union of South Africa at Washington;

Who, having communicated to each other their respective full powers, found to be in due and proper form, have agreed upon and concluded the following articles:

ARTICLE I. Article II of the Treaty for the Advancement of Peace between the President of the United States of America and His Majesty the King of the United Kingdom of Great Britain and Ireland and of the British Dominions beyond the Seas, Emperor of India, signed at Washington, September 15, 1914, is hereby superseded in respect of the Union of South Africa by the following:

Insofar as concerns disputes arising in the relations between the United States of America and the Union of South Africa, the International Commission shall be composed of five members to be appointed as follows: One member shall be chosen from the United States of America by the Government thereof; one member shall be chosen from the Union of South Africa by the Government thereof; one member shall be chosen by each Government from some third country; the fifth member shall be chosen by agreement between the Government of the United States of America and the Government of the Union of South Africa, it being understood that he shall be a citizen of some third country of which no other member of the Commission is a citizen. The expression "third country" means a country not under the sovereignty or authority of the United States of America nor under the sovereignty, suzerainty, protection or mandate of His Majesty the King of Great Britain, Ireland, and the British Dominions beyond the Seas, Emperor of India. The expenses of the Commission shall be paid by the United States of America and the Union of South Africa in equal proportions.

The International Commission shall be appointed within six months after the exchange of the ratifications of the present Treaty; and vacancies shall be filled according to the manner of the original appointment.

ARTICLE II. The second paragraph of Article III of the said Treaty of September 15, 1914, is hereby abrogated so far as concerns its application to the Union of South Africa.

ARTICLE III. Except as provided in Articles I, II and IV of the present Treaty the stipulations of the said Treaty of September 15, 1914, shall be considered as an integral part of the present Treaty and shall be observed and fulfilled by the United States of America and the Union of South Africa as if all such stipulations were literally herein embodied.

ARTICLE IV. The present Treaty shall be ratified by the President of the United States of America by and with the advice and consent of the Senate thereof and by His Majesty in respect of the Union of South Africa. It shall take effect on the date of the exchange of the ratifications which shall take place at Washington as soon as possible. It shall continue in force for a period of five years; and it shall thereafter remain in force until twelve months after one of the High Contracting Parties has given notice to the other of an intention to terminate it.

On the termination of the present Treaty the said Treaty of September 15, 1914, shall in respect of the Union of South Africa cease to have effect.

IN WITNESS WHEREOF the respective plenipotentiaries have signed the present Treaty and have affixed their seals thereto.

DONE in duplicate at the City of Washington this second day of April, one thousand nine hundred and forty.

CORDELL HULL [SEAL]

RALPH W. CLOSE [SEAL]

B. France

1. OUTLOOK OF THE FRENCH GOVERNMENT FOLLOWING THE ARMISTICE WITH GERMANY

(1) *Speech of the Premier* (*Pétain*) *to the French National Assembly, Vichy, July 10, 1940* [1]

Gentlemen, we must make a lesson of the lost battles.

We must revise our common errors and point out responsibilities and discover the reason for our weaknesses. This task will be accomplished.

Accomplishing this would be insufficient unless it would be the first condition for our revival, for we must first rebuild France. Having calculated the importance of her defeat, a country such as ours, whatever may be her pains, will not lose herself in vain regrets.

She will not rely on the past and the task will not be to reconstruct the country as she was. It is in military defeat and interior troubles that other countries found strength to discover themselves and transform.

In the cruelest moments of our history France must accept the necessity

[1] United Press version, *New York Times*, July 11, 1941, p. 4. The speech introduced to the National Assembly (the Senate and Chamber of Deputies sitting as a constituent body) the resolution whereby the premier became Chief of State and the parliamentary system was suspended.

of a national revolution, which is necessary for her future. This reconstruction requires the total effort of all Frenchmen — more than resigned to acceptance or disciplined acceptance — because of love for the fatherland. It is collective understanding and support that gives all the necessary strength and meaning to individual life.

Because of this task, the Government has asked the National Assembly to render the most immense effort possible by the sudden act in order to establish its legality. You Deputies and Senators know better by your own experience what are the weaknesses of our legal institutions. Many among you have ample reason to request sweeping reforms of our legal and political habits.

Recent declarations coming from all the ancient parties serve as testimonies to the sharp realization of the great duties which must be solved nationally. France recognizes herself in the midst of an immense brotherhood movement. Parliament will reorganize itself, opening the doors of the future and thus win the appreciation of the entire nation.

The Government must have all the power to decide, undertake, negotiate and save what can be saved, destroy what must be destroyed, reconstruct what must be reconstructed.

The Government consequently asks Parliament, meeting in National Assembly, to give its full confidence to Marshal Henri Philippe Pétain, President of the Council, to promulgate under his signature the responsibility and fundamental laws of a French State.

The first necessity is to restore the sovereignty of the Government and the independence of the Government. The Government will direct the country's future with dignity and manage all activities for the common good of all Frenchmen.

The Government will respect the rights of labor. It is in this spirit that modern, simple institutions and administration of courts, which were disorganized by the invasion, will be reconstructed.

Controlling the interests of all Frenchmen, the Government will try by a fixed economy to reduce the weight of public expenditures rendered by a heavier account of the war.

National education and formation of the youth will be among the first objectives.

Conscious of the fatal danger of the spread of intellectual and moral perversity throughout the country at a critical hour, the Government will support with all its power all institutions likely to prevent the corruption of morals and likely to protect real happiness.

Besides, the Government knows that families, common professions and religion existed before the State. The State is only a political machine for the national gathering of units and must not prevent or harm the duties of these groups. The Government, however, will control them in the interests of common good.

It is true that the common life of our nation must now have a new orientation and must be integrated within the continental system of production and exchange. Furthermore, France must return to her agricultural and peasant character primarily, and her industry must refind its traditional quality. It is therefore necessary to put an end to the current economic disorders by rational organization, production and corporative institutions.

The transformation in professional ranks thus will be left to the Government to establish equal order in justice and find a means in the enterprise it directs, assuring all Frenchmen of their livelihoods and those of their families.

The professional organization achieved under control of the State and according to its plans for collaboration will assure better distribution of profits, abolishing on one hand dictatorship of money and plutocracy and on the other hand misery and unemployment. Restoration of order and value will remain a most pressing task in all fields.

Each Frenchman in France or the Empire must be placed where best he can serve the nation and the only aristocracy that will be recognized is that of intelligence and the only merit that of labor. They will guide the nation toward a new destiny and France will continue the age-old sacred task of France. Thus our nation, instead of letting herself be floored by trials, will refind herself by her efforts in her traditions and the pride of our race.

(2) Broadcast of the French Chief of State (Pétain), Vichy, August 13, 1940 [1]

[Excerpts]

Among the trials that weigh upon us some bear the character of fatality; they come from war and peace; we are not in a position to attenuate their rigor. Others spring from the very causes that led the country to disaster in the midst of demoralization and disorganization which, like gangrene had invaded the body of the State, by introducing thereinto idleness and incompetence, even, sometimes, systematic sabotage, in order to breed social disorder or international revolution. These causes have not disappeared with the change of institutions; they will disappear only with a change of men.

[1] Summary of extracts, version of *New York Times*, August 14, 1940, p. 4.

In many circumstances I have been able to note with real pain that the Government's intentions were disguised and denatured by perfidious propaganda and that fully matured measures were prevented from bearing fruit by the inertia, incapacity or treason of too great a number of executive agents.

These weaknesses and treasons will be sought out and punished.

New France needs servants animated with a new spirit; she will have them.

Paris, the heart and brain of the nation, the crucible in which, at all times, the destinies of the country have been elaborated, remains in the eyes of all Frenchmen the natural seat of governmental authority. I learn without surprise that the population of Paris, so sensitive and so proud, wonders at the absence of its leaders and, above all, of that of the head of the State. I know that all the population of the occupied zone considers, and not without reason, that if the Government resided in Paris it would be better placed to care for it more efficaciously. I share these sentiments.

Immediately the armistice entered into force my Government strove to obtain from the German Government the possibility of its return to Paris and Versailles.

On August 7 the German Government informed me that while maintaining its acceptance of the principle already written into the armistice convention, it could not authorize such a transfer for reasons of a technical nature and so long as certain material conditions had not been realized.

We must, therefore, wait still longer, but I think I can assure you that it is now only a matter of delay. I may add that I hope for my return as ardently as you do. But for all of us today patience, perhaps, is the most necessary form of courage.

Now that France is a prey there is no longer room for lies and illusions. All Frenchmen must bear the inevitable firmly and patiently. It is the Government's part to aid them therein by constant action inspired solely by a passion for public good.

I would fail in my duty if I did not seize this occasion to express my heartfelt thanks for American generosity.[1] Thanks thereto, in a few weeks more than 1,000 carloads of various foodstuffs and clothing have been distributed among refugee populations in the free zone, while a considerable number of other carloads went to the needy population of Paris. This help, infinitely precious in itself, is even more precious by the token it brings us of the fidelity of America for our country.

[1] See p. 590.

We have drafted, with the help of the National Aid Organization and the French Red Cross, in cooperation with the American Committee for Aid to the Refugees, a vast plan of relief and reconstruction.

(3) Statement of the French Chief of State (Pétain) Prepared for the American Press, Vichy, August 20, 1940 [1]

In the interview with the 17 correspondents from North and South America, M. Pétain said: "I do not pretend that this Government is free. We are bound absolutely by the clauses of the armistice. The Germans hold the rope and twist it whenever they consider the accord is not being carried out."

It is a real pleasure for me to receive representatives of the American press and bid them welcome. I am happy to seize this occasion to tell them of the sincere friendship that France holds for America, for both Americas, Anglo-Saxon and Latin.

We piously preserve the memory of the brotherhood in arms of our Lafayettes and our Rochambeaus with the heroes of your War of Independence. The friendship linked at that time has enjoyed the rare privilege of remaining unchanged through all the vicissitudes of fortune. Recently again you have given us a new token of your magnificent generosity toward our refugees and évacués. Precious in itself, this aid was even more precious for the testimony it brought of the fidelity of your sentiments toward us.

With Argentina and with Brazil we feel united by the community of our Latin culture. Therein lies a bond of which I was able to test the strength during my embassy in Spain. We know the extent to which Latin America shares our trials, and her fidelity, too, touches us deeply.

You have manifested, gentlemen, a great and cordial interest in what France will be tomorrow. I am no prophet, yet there are certain things that I may say, if not with certainty, at least with absolute conviction.

First, I have faith in France rising anew, and that with a rapidity that once again will astonish the world. France has ever been a land of "luminous and surprising awakenings," to cite our great Bossuet. Her past is a pledge for her future.

The France of tomorrow will be at once very new and very ancient. She will become again what she never should have ceased to be — essentially an agricultural nation. Like the giant in the fable, she will recover all her strength by renewed contact with the earth.

She will restore those old traditions of craftsmanship that in the past made her fortune and glory. A classic land of quality, she will know how to impart again to all her production that finish, that delicacy

[1] *New York Times*, August 21, 1940, p. 6.

and that elegance in which for long she was without a rival. It goes without saying that she will remain a land of arts, of high culture, of disinterested research.

She will cultivate the virtues that make strong peoples; she will know how to temper by vigorous discipline an individualism that at times may become excessive; she will honor anew those great truths of Christian morality that form the solid basis of our civilization.

She will remain firmly attached to the ideal that she professes in common with the great American democracies, an ideal founded on respect for the human individual, on the cult of family, community and country, on love of justice and humanity; she will strive more than ever to develop between the old world and the new those relations and those exchanges, cultural as well as economic, that create between peoples the very atmosphere of comprehension and amity.

2. ARRIVAL OF A NEW FRENCH AMBASSADOR

(1) *Remarks of the Ambassador of the French Republic (Henry-Haye) upon Presentation of His Letters of Credence, September 13, 1940* [1]

[Translation]

MR. PRESIDENT:

The Marshal of France, Philippe Henri Pétain, Chief of the French State, has entrusted to me the great honor of handing to Your Excellency the letters accrediting me near you as Ambassador Extraordinary and Plenipotentiary of the French Republic.

The Government of France has likewise directed me to hand to you the letters of recall of my eminent predecessor, Mr. Doynel de Saint-Quentin, who has been called to another diplomatic post.

I have, Mr. President, the privilege of knowing and loving the great country over whose destinies you preside with such high authority. I have made frequent journeys and long visits here and I know the generosity of heart and spirit of the citizens of the United States. This experience encouraged me to accept the mission of representing my country in yours in hours the tragedy of which it is needless to emphasize.

Never, in the course of the history of our two nations, has a French Ambassador assumed a task like that for which I today take the responsibility.

My unhappy country has just suffered the most cruel reverses which it has ever had to record in the course of the vicissitudes of its long and glorious past. Having entered into this war for the sake of European

[1] Department of State, *Bulletin*, III, p. 215.

solidarity and to fulfill obligations which it had contracted, France has been terribly wounded thereby and must now submit to the implacable law of the victor. But, Mr. President, I can say to you that even if my country cannot free itself from the hard obligations which are the result of its defeat, the ideal, for the defense of which my countrymen courageously took up arms again only 20 years after the most bloody of victories, still remains alive in the heart of Frenchmen.

Despite appearances, the war is not over for us. Cruel sufferings, both material and spiritual, will still for long be felt in innumerable homes. The majority of French families are scattered. Our women and children will await for a long time yet the return of men who, at the present moment, are enduring a hard captivity. Other women will await, in vain, alas, the return of their husbands, their sons, or their brothers, who will never return again.

In spite of these new misfortunes, let me assure you, Mr. President, that there is a force which no power can crush, it is that force which, despite apparent and transitory differences, will proudly maintain that French unity consecrated by so many sacrifices.

Allow me, Mr. President, to compare the mission with which I am entrusted by the French Republic with that which, in 1776, was confided to the great Benjamin Franklin by the thirteen United States of America. I shall certainly not have the presumption to claim to possess the incomparable attributes of the American Ambassador Extraordinary. But I may doubtless hope, in attempting to solve the difficult problems before me, to have the benefit of your personal good will and the generous understanding of your countrymen.

The ardent patriotic faith which I express to Your Excellency will inspire and guide all my undertakings and all my actions in the accomplishment of my mission.

Such, Mr. President, simply but sincerely expressed, is the spirit in which I shall endeavor worthily to represent my country in yours.

May Providence aid me in the accomplishment of the task which the Government of France has entrusted to me near you.

(2) Reply of the President (Roosevelt) to the Ambassador of the French Republic (Henry-Haye), September 13, 1940 [1]

MR. AMBASSADOR:

I am happy to welcome you on your return to this country as Ambassador Extraordinary and Plenipotentiary of the Republic of France

[1] Department of State, *Bulletin*, III, p. 216.

near the Government of the United States of America and to receive from your hands the letters accrediting you near the Government of the United States in that capacity. I likewise accept the letters of recall of your predecessor, Count Doynel de Saint-Quentin, who has so ably represented your country here during the recent eventful years. I wish him success in his new mission.

I have been particularly pleased to hear from you that France in its travail bears still in its heart the ideals for which it took up arms. Frenchmen have my sympathy and the sympathy of the people of the United States, and I hope with you that despite all, French unity, which has been consecrated by so many sacrifices, will continue to subsist.

I wish to assure you, Mr. Ambassador, of a cordial welcome to Washington. You may count upon my cooperation, as well as that of the officials of this Government, in your efforts to solve the problems which will confront you, and to develop the understanding and friendly relations which have so happily existed between our two nations.

3. FRENCH COLLABORATION WITH GERMANY

(1) *The Montoire Interview*

(a) *Communiqué of the French Government, Vichy, October 24, 1940* [1]

Marshal Pétain, accompanied by Pierre Laval, crossed the interzone boundary line toward 8 : 00 A.M. Military honors were rendered him and he talked for a minute with an officer who came to salute him.

Late in the afternoon he had a long conversation with Chancellor Hitler in an impressive setting.

The situation of France and its future depend to a large degree on this historical meeting.

(b) *Communiqué of the Chief of the French State (Pétain), October 26, 1940* [2]

The conversation on October 24 between Chancellor Hitler and Marshal Pétain, in the presence of Foreign Minister Joachim von Ribbentrop and Vice Premier Pierre Laval, occurred [at Montoire] in an atmosphere of high courtesy. The Marshal was received with honors due to his rank. The conversation that followed between the two leaders gave rise to a general examination of the situation, and particularly

[1] United Press version, *New York Times*, October 25, 1940, p. 4. A semi-official commentary on the interview is in *Le Temps*, October 28, 1940.

[2] *New York Times*, October 27, 1940, sec. 1, p. 32. See further the allocution of the Chief of State, *Le Temps*, November 1, 1940.

of means of reconstructing peace in Europe. The two interlocutors came to agreement on the principle of collaboration. Methods of application are to be examined later.

(2) *American Reference to the Traditional Republicanism of France*

(a) *The Chief of the French State (Pétain) to the President (Roosevelt), January 2, 1941* [1]

VICHY, *January 2, 1941.*

In this New Year which is beginning I wish to extend to you the personal good wishes I feel for you and your family, as well as for the prosperity of the United States.

PHILIPPE PÉTAIN

(b) *The President (Roosevelt) to the Chief of the French State (Pétain), January 8, 1941* [1]

JANUARY 8, 1941.

Your very kind message of good will for me and for my family, and for the prosperity of the United States was delayed in transmission and has just reached me. I hasten to convey to you my deep appreciation.

My heart goes out to France in these days of her travail and I pray that the French people may soon once again enjoy the blessings of peace with Liberty, Equality and Fraternity.

Please accept my most cordial personal wishes for the coming year.

FRANKLIN D. ROOSEVELT

(3) *Broadcast Message of the French Chief of State (Pétain), Vichy, May 15, 1941* [2]

Frenchmen:

You have learned that Admiral Darlan recently conferred with Chancellor Hitler.[3] I had approved this meeting in principle. The new interview permits us to light up the road into the future and to continue the conversations that had been begun with the German Government.

It is no longer a question today of public opinion, often uneasy and badly informed, being able to estimate the chances we are taking or measure the risks we take or judge our acts.

For you, the French people, it is simply a question of following me without mental reservation along the path of honor and national interest.

[1] Department of State, *Bulletin,* IV, p. 59.
[2] *New York Times,* May 16, 1941, p. 1.
[3] On May 12, François Darlan, vice president of the French Ministerial Council, was received by the Führer, in the presence of the Reichsminister of Foreign Affairs at Berchtesgaden (*New York Times,* May 13, 1941, p. 1).

If through our close discipline and our public spirit we can conduct the negotiations in progress, France will surmount her defeat and preserve in the world her rank as a European and colonial power.

That, my dear friends, is all that I have to say to you today.

(4) *Statement of the President (Roosevelt), May 15, 1941* [1]

The President's statement was issued after a long conference with the Secretary and Under-Secretary of State. It coincided in time with orders to the Coast Guard to put guards on French ships in United States ports, and with speculation as to the status of Martinique and Dakar.

The policy of this Government in its relations with the French Republic has been based upon the terms of the armistice between Germany and France and upon recognition of certain clear limitations imposed upon the French Government by this armistice. Furthermore, we have had assurances given by the head of the French State on behalf of his Government that it did not intend to agree to any collaboration with Germany which went beyond the requirements of that armistice agreement. This was the least that could be expected of a France which demanded respect for its integrity.

The people of France, who cherish still the ideals of liberty and free institutions and guard that love of these priceless possessions in their minds and hearts, can be counted on to hold out for these principles until the moment comes for their reestablishment. It is inconceivable they will willingly accept any agreement for so-called "collaboration" which will in reality imply their alliance with a military power whose central and fundamental policy calls for the utter destruction of liberty, freedom, and popular institutions everywhere.

The people of the United States can hardly believe that the present Government of France could be brought to lend itself to a plan of voluntary alliance implied or otherwise which would apparently deliver up France and its Colonial Empire, including French African colonies and their Atlantic coasts, with the menace which that involves to the peace and safety of the Western Hemisphere.

(a) *Statement of the Office Française d'Information, May 16, 1941* [2]

Surprise is manifested in government circles at the declarations which Mr. Roosevelt is reported to have made in Washington, according to which he inter-

[1] Department of State, *Bulletin*, IV, p. 584.
[2] *New York Times*, May 17, 1941, p. 1. This text is a translation of the original French.

prets Marshal Pétain's broadcast as placing French colonies at the disposal of Germany.

This interpretation seems all the more astonishing since it is accompanied by semi-official declarations looking to the occupation of French Guiana and Martinique.

Moreover, the occupation by an armed guard of ten French ships, including the *Normandie*, in American ports constitutes an act whose nature cannot be explained solely by the ideological reasons with which it is sought to cover it on the other side of the ocean.

In May 1940, when France was left in the lurch by Britain, America did not see fit to answer her appeal. Today France, anxious to preserve her position as a great power as well as the integrity of her territory and of her empire, has certainly the right to envisage with her victory the conditions of a common reorganization of Continental Europe.

This in no way means that she has the intention of attacking Britain, much less the United States.

Mr. Eden's [British Foreign Secretary Anthony Eden] threats against Syria and the bombing of Syrian airfields have added themselves to what France still refuses to consider as an Anglo-Saxon aggressive desire.

Moreover, the declarations made to the American press in Washington by M. Henry-Haye,[1] French Ambassador, express on this matter the viewpoint of the French people, "enemy of all dissidence and confident in the wisdom and lofty patriotism of Marshal Pétain."

(5) Statement of the British Principal Secretary of State for Foreign Affairs (Eden), London, May 22, 1941 [2]

It was announced by Vichy on May 14 that [Vice Premier François] Darlan's report [3] of his visit to Hitler had been unanimously approved by the Vichy Government and that the effect of those deliberations would shortly be felt.

On the following day Pétain broadcast a short statement to the French people appealing for their unquestioning acceptance of whatever results might issue from the negotiations between the Darlan government and the German Government.

These negotiations had been described in Vichy as opening up a new phase of Franco-German collaboration, of which, no doubt, the action of the Vichy Government in allowing Syrian airdromes to be used by German aircraft is an example.

President Roosevelt stated clearly his view of this new and sinister development of Vichy policy, and the United States Government has already taken certain preventive action regarding French shipping in United States ports.

[1] See statement of Marshal Pétain prepared for American Press, p. 393.
[2] United Press dispatch, *New York Times*, May 23, 1941, p. 4.
[3] Not published.

In a confused and uneasy explanation put out in Vichy it has been suggested that the policy of collaboration between the Vichy Government and Germany is political and economic only, and it was stated that the Vichy Government had no intention of attacking Britain and still less the United States. This explanation cannot conceal that the Vichy Government has embarked on a course which must place the resources and territory of France and her empire increasingly at the disposal of a power which is the enemy not only of France's former ally but of France herself.

The French people will, His Majesty's Government is sure, regard this policy as incompatible with the honor of France.

Nor will they believe that the future of France and her Empire will better be served by surrendering them to Hitler's so-called new order than by resolutely maintaining and defending independence until such time as the victorious Allies complete their liberation.

The British Government must, however, take account of the acts of the Vichy Government. If the Vichy Government, in pursuance of their declared policy of collaboration with the enemy, take action or permit action detrimental to our conduct of the war or designed to assist the enemy's war effort, we shall naturally hold ourselves free to attack the enemy wherever he may be found, and in so doing we shall no longer feel bound to draw any distinction between occupied and unoccupied territory in the execution of our military plans.

On August 7 the Government assured [1] de Gaulle of its determination, when victory was won, to secure the full restoration of the independence and greatness of France.

It rests with the people of France to determine whether they will play a part in assisting those who continue to fight for the liberation of France or whether France henceforward will serve in the ranks of Germany's satellites.

(6) Broadcast of the French Vice Premier (Darlan), Vichy, May 23, 1941 [2]

Frenchmen:

You have already heard our Chief, Marshal Pétain, tell you that it was with his approval that I went at the invitation of Chancellor Hitler and that conversations between the Chief of the German Reich and myself had been approved by him and by the Government.

[1] See p. 433.
[2] Associated Press version, New York Times, May 24, 1941, p. 4.

The Marshal, having given me the undoubted honor of designating me as his second in his heavy task, I have come to bring you details which you have been impatiently awaiting.

The Chancellor did not ask me to hand over our fleet to him. Every one knows — and the English better than any one — that I will never hand it over.

The Chancellor did not ask me for any colonial territory. He did not ask me to declare war on England.

Why has he acted so?

Germany began the war alone and judges herself able to end it alone against no matter what coalition.

At no moment in the conversations was there any question of France abandoning in any way her sovereignty.

France freely is choosing the road she is taking. On her depends her present and her future. She will have the peace which she makes herself. She will have the place in the organization of Europe which she will have made for herself.

Remember — some seem to have forgotten — that France has suffered the gravest defeat in her history, that three-fifths of her continental territory has been occupied, that we have a million and a half prisoners.

This defeat was due to our past errors. From 1919 to 1939 our governments and our legislative assemblies stored up errors and let themselves be led to defend interests which were not our own to the detriment of our own.

Domestically, they permitted sabotage of morale of the nation; they legalized laziness and disorder.

Abroad they carried out an incoherent policy; they made us the protectors of small European powers without having been capable of forging the indispensable arms for carrying out that mission.

They decided to give aid to every one, which made necessary a powerful offensive army. Our governments and our assemblies, however, only gave the country a defensive army.

Not having known how to prepare for war, either morally or materially, our Government nevertheless declared it. We lost it because of the mistakes and weakness of those who led us into it.

And it is as a result of the indescribable *débâcle* of which many of you have horrible memories, it is as a result of the defection of our former allies, it is as a result of the default of the Government which declared it was ready to continue the fight without having the means, but which in reality only thought of flight, that the Marshal was called to take the destiny of the country in his hands and ask an honorable armistice.

In June 1940, the victor could have refused us an armistice, beaten us and wiped France off the map of the world. They did not do it. In May 1941, the victor has agreed to negotiate with the French Government.

Since the Montoire interview,[1] during which the principle of collaboration was decided, France has shown by acts her desire to continue that policy.

These are acts which determined Chancellor Hitler to grant us ameliorations of the consequences of defeat and of the conditions of the armistice which you just learned.

Listen well to my words.

On the result of the negotiations in course directly depends the future of France. It is necessary for her to choose between life and death. The Marshal and the Government have chosen life.

Your duty is clearly traced: follow the Marshal, aid him with all your force, as I am doing in his work of national restoration.

Like him and like me, in your thoughts and in your acts, be inspired only by the interests of France.

(7) Relations with the French Government at Vichy. Statement of the Secretary of State (Hull), June 5, 1941 [2]

We have received some preliminary reports from Ambassador Leahy. Frankly we are very much concerned about the situation which seems to be growing up. As you know, we have throughout our history been sympathetic to the true aspirations of France. We have fought beside her. Her cause has been our cause. The principles of free, representative government by the people have been the bases of the democratic institutions of both of our countries.

In her present difficult situation we have given concrete evidence of our sympathetic friendship and thought for the well-being of the French people and the French Empire.

We have continued to maintain full and friendly diplomatic relations with the French Government at Vichy and have received its emissaries freely in this country. We have given the fullest and most sympathetic consideration to financial problems connected with the maintenance of French establishments, not only in this hemisphere but in the Far East, both diplomatic and semi-official services.

[1] See p. 396.
[2] Department of State, *Bulletin*, IV, p. 681.

We have, through Admiral Leahy, the American Ambassador at Vichy, consistently conveyed to the French Government our understanding of the difficulties of their position and our determination to be of every assistance we could in solving their problems for the ultimate benefit of the French people. We have made clear to the French Government that a basic policy of this Government was to aid Great Britain in her defense against those same forces of conquest which had invaded and are subjugating France.

We have aided in the furnishing of foodstuffs for unoccupied France, and children's supplies are now being distributed through the American Red Cross, and we had planned the continuation of these services.

We have facilitated the passage of ships from this hemisphere to France's African colonies.

We have collaborated with the other American Republics as well as with the French Government in safeguarding the welfare and maintaining the integrity of the French possessions in the Western Hemisphere.[1]

In collaboration with the French Government we have arranged for the maintenance of the economic stability of the French North African territories by providing facilities for increasing trade and the purchase from us of commodities urgently needed by the people of North Africa with a view to maintaining their previous status as an integral part of the French Empire.

Happily, whenever such action was necessary, Ambassador Leahy has been able to assure the Vichy Government that this Nation had no other interest in any territories of the French Empire than their preservation for the French people.

We have given the most sympathetic consideration to the financial problems arising out of the freezing of French funds.

It has been the determined policy of this Government to continue friendly and helpful cooperation with France in the present difficult situation, in which its action is restricted and limited by the terms of its armistice with Germany and Italy. This policy has been based upon assurances by the French Government that there was no intention on its part to exceed the strict limitations imposed by those terms.

It would seem scarcely believable that the French Government at Vichy should adopt the policy of collaboration with other powers for the purpose of aggression and oppression, despite indications appearing in our preliminary reports. Such action would not only be yielding priceless rights and interests beyond the requirements of a harsh armistice but it would at once place France in substantial political and military

[1] See p. 95.

subservience and would also make her, in part, the instrument of aggression against many other peoples and nations. This could only be utterly inimical to the just rights of other countries, to say nothing of its ultimate effects on the liberties, the true interests, and the welfare of the people of France.

We are therefore undertaking as speedily as possible to assemble every material fact and circumstance calculated to shed light on this alleged course of the French Government.

(a) Official Commentary of the Vichy Government, June 6, 1941 [1]

[The Secretary of State's statement of June 5 was not published in France, but the following observations on it were issued to the press.]

Mr. Cordell Hull made a statement to the press conference on Franco-American relations in which he said that "if the French Government should adopt a policy of collaboration with other powers for the purpose of aggression and oppression this policy would be considered unfriendly to the United States."

Authorized French circles are surprised to have the American Secretary of State describe as a policy of aggression and oppression a policy which is not directed against any one and damages the interests of no other power and which is inspired by the strict desire of establishing better relations in Europe and of maintaining against any attack the freedom of the French Empire and its lines of communications.

It is pointed out that the French Government, for its part, is anxious to preserve friendly relations but that the Federal Government cannot but understand that the foremost task of the French Government, in the particularly difficult situation in which it is placed, is to safeguard the vital interests of France and her Empire.

(b) Press Statement of the French Ambassador (Henry-Haye), Washington, June 6, 1941 [2]

After perusing the statement issued by Secretary of State Cordell Hull, I am myself very much concerned about a situation which is steadily growing more complicated, mostly through false rumors or intentionally exaggerated reports.

All the news pretending that German troops were at Dakar, Casablanca or French Mediterranean ports have been emphatically denied, and the official representatives of the United States in those places can assert that these informations are contrary to the truth.

Untrue also is the statement that German forces landed at Lataquie [Latakia], Syria.[3]

Furthermore, I am able to deny formally today that any air-borne Axis troops ever landed in the French possessions of the Near East.

But true is the statement of the leaders of France that they will defend French territories against any attack.

Incontestable is also the declaration that French forces will never, by air, sea, or land, take the initiative of any operation against the British.

[1] *New York Times*, June 7, 1941, p. 3.   [2] *Ibid.*
[3] See "Hostilities in Syria and Lebanon," p. 404.

Therefore, it is difficult for the French Government to understand the reasons for the accusations made against its policy.

I beg to remind you that all those made against the government of Marshal Pétain during the last year have been proved totally unjustified.

Is it necessary to recall that the French soldiers and the French people, who fought and resisted almost alone last May and June, have made sacrifices comparable to none others, and after the defeat of our armies the French people in the occupied and unoccupied zones went proudly through the most cruel Winter with starving rations?

We are deeply grateful to the American Government for the four shipments of food sent to France, through the good care of the American Red Cross, but may I be permitted to recall that our most urgent needs were estimated at roughly 170 shiploads to be purchased in the United States with the frozen funds, accumulated through the thrift of our forefathers.

It is most painful to recall that even a request to use $2,000,000 from our funds to buy meat for our war prisoners was rejected.

Frenchmen have the greatest difficulty to understand why, in these financial matters, they are much more severely treated than the Japanese, the Italians or the Germans.

Despite the most cruel and unjustified attacks at Oran and Dakar, where hundreds of French lives were lost amongst the sailors, who fought gallantly to protect the British Isles, we refused to take arms against our former ally.

Every day the populations of the cities of the French coast are stoically enduring British bombardments and never a complaint is made about that.

It is perfectly clear that the United States Government's policy is based on aiding Great Britain, but is it because we Frenchmen, who have been the first to aid England by declaring a war at her suggestion, by mobilizing all the men of France between 20 and 50, by putting all our resources, blood, money, material, land to aid Great Britain in this struggle; is it because we have made such tremendous sacrifices that we should be denied the right to defend French sovereignty?

I want to emphasize that, far from attacking and oppressing other nations, France always gave a helpful hand to other countries.

Before this war and after the Armistice, France has been the land where millions of people of all races and religions found refuge and are now, according to American observers on the spot, receiving the best possible treatment in view of the terribly precarious situation in France.

It has been our privilege, since the days of Rochambeau, de Grasse and Lafayette, to have the most cordial relations with the United States of America. We intend to keep this friendly collaboration as far as it is possible. Never did we commit any unfriendly gesture against the United States. On the contrary, we have given to the American Government all conceivable assurances and guarantees about the French possessions of this hemisphere.

The government of Marshal Pétain, namely, the government of all the Frenchmen heartily united behind this great soldier, with the exception of a few thousands of refugees residing abroad, claims for our nation the right to live and asserts its will to maintain the sovereignty of France.

It is impossible to conceive that such action might interfere with the interests or ideals of the Americans.

No propaganda, no false rumors, can prevent the French nation, which has such a long and glorious past, from following the road of her destiny.

I can assure, solemnly and most sincerely, that, in the French conception, the destiny of France can never be opposed to that of America.

(8) Statement of the Secretary of State (Hull) on Franco-German Collaboration, June 13, 1941 [1]

From the standpoint of the French people and others who have a love for freedom and have freedom, the attitude of the present Government of Vichy is a matter of the deepest disappointment and sorrow.

The original scheme of the Darlan-Laval group to deliver France politically, economically, socially, and militarily to Hitler seems now to have been brought out into the open by a succession of public statements by French authorities and especially those by Messrs. Laval [2] and Darlan.

[1] Department of State, *Bulletin*, IV, p. 715.

[2] Pierre Laval, who was succeeded as Vice Premier of France on December 13, 1940, by Admiral François Darlan, divulged his views in conversation at Paris with the United Press on May 24, 1941 (*New York Times*, May 26, 1941, p. 4). In this interview he disclosed the text of a "diplomatic note" said to have been in reply to a letter of the President to the French Chief of State. As the paper was actually a message sent through the Chargé d'Affaires at Paris November 13, 1940, and not a formal note of the French Government, it is not available in an official version. In the published version it reads:

"The Chief of the French State has received the message President Roosevelt sent him through the United States Chargé d'Affaires. Animated by a desire to preserve the friendship which, since the foundation of the American Republic, has bound America to the French people, he abstains from referring to that portion of the Roosevelt message which might lead him to doubt the fair intentions of the American Government.

"To reply to the preoccupations of Mr. Roosevelt he desires to affirm that the French Government always kept its liberty of action and can only be astonished by any judgment as inexact as it is unjust that France would have sacrificed her freedom of action. The French Government has declared that the French fleet never will be handed over and nothing can authorize the American Government to doubt today that solemn engagement. Mr. Roosevelt has spoken of operations against the British fleet. He has forgotten, undoubtedly, that in fact naval operations have occurred, but they were engaged by the British fleet in a most unexpected manner. Furthermore, England has adopted an anti-French position which the French people cannot tolerate.

"His Majesty's Government supports Frenchmen in rebellion against their country, whose activities, thanks to the support of the British fleet and air force, have affected the unity of the French Empire. France and its government can give assurance never to participate in any unjustified attack against England but, conscious of her duties, France knows how to honorably respect its essential interests.

"The French Government continues to be attached to the maintenance of the traditional friendship which binds our two countries and will in all circumstances endeavor to avoid misunderstandings or wrong interpretations such as those which doubtless led Mr. Roosevelt to send us his message."

When Germany recently desired to make use of Syria to attack British forces in Iraq no objection, much less resistance, to this action was made by France, although the terms of the armistice between France and Germany did not require that France permit territory under French control outside occupied France to be used as a base for German military operations, and Marshal Pétain declared as recently as a few weeks ago that he would not permit such use. The use of Syria is a vitally important part of the general plan of Hitler's to invade Iraq, Egypt, the Canal area, and Africa. When the French authorities in Syria, acting under the Vichy Government, made no effort to prevent German use of Syria as a military base, and when they permitted even the shipment from Syria of military supplies of French manufacture to be used by the Germans against France's former ally, they permitted Germany to extend the theatre of war into French mandated territory. To resist this further expansion of German aggression the British forces in the Near East entered Syria to prevent German actions there which the French, under the direction of the Vichy Government, were permitting if not abetting. Yet the French authorities in Syria have considered it necessary to contest bitterly this British effort to prevent Syria from being used as a German base. These facts unmistakably demonstrate that the German military effort is making use of France and that the German initiative in Syria is resulting in a conflict, not only of France against Britain but of Frenchmen against Frenchmen. Germany seems to have prevailed on the Vichy Government to do Germany's fighting in the Syria area of the general German advance.

But aside from the situation in Syria and considering the broader aspects of Franco-German collaboration, the public statements of the Darlan-Laval element demonstrate that the people of France are expected not only to surrender permanently and unconditionally their loyalty to all French traditions, institutions, liberties, interests, culture, and the entire way of life which made France great, but actually to transfer all of these loyalties — all hope of the future — to Hitler in the hope of securing his personal favor. The general adoption of Hitlerism would set the world back five to ten centuries.

In a statement on June 10, Admiral Darlan,[1] Vice Premier of France, urged the French people to conquer their illusions and consent to sacrifices and indicated that France would be utterly destroyed unless the French people should take this unprecedented and revolutionary action.

---

[1] For the United Press version of the broadcast to the French people by Vice Premier François Darlan, which is here summarized, see *New York Times*, June 11, 941, p. 10.

Unless a military invader is devoid of all human attributes he extends to the conquered all of those considerations and recognitions contemplated by the rules and principles of civilized society. An armistice signifies a temporary cessation of hostilities between the parties to it. It does not contemplate that the successful belligerent shall make inhuman demands upon the country and people of the defeated belligerent nor does it contemplate that they shall be bludgeoned into becoming allies of their enemy. If, therefore, Hitler cannot be depended upon, as implied by Darlan's statement, to observe such rules and laws in dealing with the conquered, how much less can he be depended upon to show the least consideration in these vital respects should the conquered peoples prostrate themselves before him and bestow upon him unrestrained license to deal as he may see fit with their lives, their liberties, and their entire future welfare.

It remains to be seen whether the French people accept this preposterous status and thus pave the way for them to find themselves assisting Hitler as his co-belligerents in his desperate effort to conquer Great Britain and secure control of the high seas.

In the prevention of such a possibility, both the French people and the people of the United States have a common interest of tremendous importance to the future.

(a) *Press Statement of the French Ambassador (Henry-Haye), Washington, June 13, 1941* [1]

I can only express my surprised disappointment at the new interpretation given by the Secretary of State of the events now taking place in the French mandated territory of the Near East.

From the official communiqués issued by the British forces which have invaded Syria and Lebanon, it appears clearly that no land, naval or air forces belonging to the Axis powers have been encountered.

Moreover the French Government has reaffirmed, over and over again, that our armies were alone to assure the defense of the territories placed under French protection.

French, Lebanese, Syrian and Empire soldiers, who are fighting with heroic abnegation, are fighting for a France they love all the more since their ever-proud country is now, in spite of her distress, facing a new attack.

It is precisely in order to keep up French traditions and all that they stand for in the world that our soldiers are once more generously shedding their blood after so many sacrifices already consented. Furthermore, they defend countries where, ever since the remote times of the Crusades, French language and culture have been closely associated with the life of their inhabitants.

[1] *New York Times*, June 14, 1941, p. 4.

The leaders who are now devoting themselves to the task — unprecedented in our history — to bring about the resurrection of the French nation and to protect the populations of her Empire, know better than any one else where their duty lies. Many times they have pledged themselves to accomplish it with honor.

It is quite unnecessary to wait any longer to see that the people of France are following the course decided upon by the government of Marshal Pétain. Frenchmen stand united behind the leader whom they worship because his long life is a life of righteousness which has always been inspired by the purest patriotism.

C. Germany

1. GERMANY'S WAY OF DOING BUSINESS

(1) *Address by the Führer (Hitler) to the National Socialist Party, February 24, 1941* [1]

[Excerpt]

After thirteen years we finally came into power. We did not ask anything of the world. We went about our business and always said that we did not want anything that the others did not have. I was ready to disarm, if the others were ready.

But there were certain things of which Germany stood in dire need. Those things were vital to her national interests. Their aims and ours are radically different. They are fighting for the maintenance of their gold bags. But we are not fighting for things like that. I am not going to buy money bags for the German people. I am going to buy goods for them. It is a simple fact that nations today can no longer be built and exist on the capitalistic basis.

And it is absolutely useless for any nation to say whether or not they like that fact. Germany is an immensely powerful factor in world economics. We must be reckoned with, and whether we deal on an exchange basis or not, that is no business of any New York or London international bankers. We are going to do business solely on the basis of German advantage. If it's good for Germany, we shall trade. And no American or British interests are going to put a stop to our way of doing business.

As soon as I found that our present-day enemies were unwilling to come to peaceful agreement, I began to prepare our national defense mechanism.

[1] English version of National Broadcasting Company, *New York Times*, February 25, 1941, p. 4.

2. THE COURSE OF THE UNITED STATES ARMY TRANSPORT
AMERICAN LEGION

(1) *German Disclaimer of Responsibility, Berlin, August 17, 1940* [1]

The United States Government informed the Reich Government in Berlin August 9 through a verbal note that the United States Army troop transport, the *American Legion,* was leaving Petsamo for New York August 16 in order to transport United States and other citizens to the United States.

The verbal note stated that the ship would be marked and illuminated day and night in a particular manner and would furthermore hold to a certain course. That course led between Rona Island and Cape Wrath on the northeast coast of England.

The United States Government in its verbal note expressed the expectation that the ship be not halted or molested. The United States Embassy further asked acquiescence to the free passage of the ship.

The Reich Government thereupon answered the United States that this case does not require acquiescence by the Reich Government, since it is self-evident that the German armed forces would not attack a neutral military vessel.

The Reich Government, however, declared itself willing to informatively acquaint the responsible German quarters of the departure of the ship from Petsamo and the prospective course it intended to follow.

On August 14 the Reich Government informed the United States Embassy in Berlin that the responsible German quarters, after learning the prospective course, pointed out that this course passes very close to the military operations area around England and that extraordinary dangers are connected with such a voyage. Urgent advice was therefore given that the *American Legion* on its return voyage follow a less dangerous course.

This warning was also discussed in conferences with the United States Embassy and it was pointed out that the sea area around Britain was completely infested with mines.

On August 16 the United States Embassy, in a verbal note, informed the Reich Government that the *American Legion* was departing from Petsamo on the same day. The Embassy further stated, despite the German warning, that the ship would follow the originally intended course.

The Foreign Office thereupon, in a verbal note to the United States

[1] United Press dispatch, *New York Times,* August 18, 1940, p. 25. See also Repatriation, p. 580.

Embassy, stated that the ship was voyaging to an area of operations despite warnings and in full consciousness of the dangers.

The Reich Government must therefore disclaim responsibility should any damages be incurred by the ship. The responsibility must be borne solely by the United States Government.

The Reich Government further points to the circumstance that final notice of the departure of the *American Legion* was given to the Foreign Office only on August 16 at midday, despite the fact that the United States Embassy previously had expressly named August 15 as the latest date for the notification about the finally chosen course.

(2) *The Chargé d'Affaires of the American Embassy at Berlin (Kirk) to the German Foreign Office, August 17, 1940* [1]

The Government of the United States desires first to point out that the course on which it was proposed that the *American Legion* should sail from Petsamo to New York was indicated to the German Government through the American Embassy at Berlin on August 9, together with a statement of the distinguishing characteristics of the ship for her ready identification and a statement that she was scheduled to sail from Petsamo on August 16, in sufficient time for the German Government to notify the appropriate German authorities so as to assure the vessel against attack by the German fighting forces. The United States Government was informed on August 13 that the German Foreign Office had stated that the appropriate German authorities had been informed of the date of departure, course and description of the *American Legion,* the understanding being that the vessel would depart on August 16 and, if she should depart at a later date, then the Foreign Office would again have to be notified three days before the actual departure since otherwise it would not be possible to give informatory instructions to the appropriate German authorities. The German Foreign Office called attention to its previous communications to the American Embassy on the subject of the *American Legion,* in which the Foreign Office had stated that instructions to the German combatant forces with respect to possible action against neutral ships were, in accordance with international rules, and the German Prize Law Codes, limited to merchant ships. The Foreign Office had further stated that it was, therefore, out of the question that German forces should stop neutral vessels of war or take any other measures against them and that in view of those facts there was no occasion, in the opinion of the German Government, to give any special assurances with regard to a neutral war vessel. The

[1] Department of State, *Bulletin,* III, p. 152.

German Government was, however, prepared to notify the German forces for their information in order to avoid confusion with enemy warships that an American war vessel (namely, the *American Legion*) would travel on a specified course at a specified time.

Subsequently, and not until the late afternoon of August 14, as reported to the American Government that same day, the Foreign Office stated that the German Air Force had pointed out that the proposed course of the *American Legion*, passing between N. Rona and Cape Wrath, would bring the vessel into the field of dangerous air operations, and that the German authorities, therefore, recommended a more northern route. Upon inquiry of the Foreign Office as to how much advance notice of the change of course of the vessel would be required by the Foreign Office in order that it might effect complete notification of all German combat units the vessel might encounter, the answer was made that if such notice were received by noon, Berlin time, August 15 there would be time to effect proper notification and the vessel could leave Petsamo August 16 as scheduled.

Under instructions of the United States Government, on August 14, the attention of the Foreign Office was invited to the assurances which it had given that the appropriate German authorities had been duly informed of the date of departure, course and description of the *American Legion*, and it was asked to stand by its original acceptance of the course of the *American Legion*. In reply, Dr. Ritter of the Foreign Office stated that if the American Government insisted on the ship following the proposed course, then the German Government had nothing to do but accept the decision, pointing out again the great danger involved. Dr. Ritter also stated that the Foreign Office had merely agreed to notify the appropriate German authorities for their information of the course and description of the vessel, and that it had never guaranteed the safe conduct of the vessel for assurances of safe conduct could only be given in the cases of merchant vessels and not in the cases of naval vessels, in which category the *American Legion* falls. The United States Government considers in that connection, that Dr. Ritter's statement was hardly in line with the previous communication of the Foreign Office, referred to above, when the Foreign Office stated that there was no occasion, in the opinion of the German Government, to give any special assurances with regard to a neutral war vessel since it was out of the question that German forces should stop neutral vessels of war or take any other measures against them, and that the German forces would be notified in order to avoid confusion of the *American Legion* with enemy warships.

Following the United States Government's learning of Dr. Ritter's conversation, and of the American Chargé d'Affaires' communication of the Foreign Office's note in confirmation of the conversation, the subject of the course to be followed by the *American Legion* had the serious and protracted consideration of the United States Government. However, it was determined that no other practical course existed for the vessel to follow than that proposed, the vessel to sail on August 16 as scheduled and already notified to all the belligerent governments. As instructed by his Government, the American Chargé d'Affaires informed the German Foreign Office on August 15 accordingly, and stated that the Government of the United States consequently reverted to its original communication to the German Government on the subject and took note of the fact that the German Government had brought the voyage of the vessel to the attention of its appropriate agencies.

The United States Government is of the opinion, therefore, that the German Government received sufficient advance notice of the sailing of the *American Legion* from Petsamo on the date scheduled and the course to be followed, to take every precaution against attack on the vessel by the German combat forces. The German Government acknowledged the receipt of this notification prior to the vessel's departure and stated that the appropriate German authorities had been informed of the date of departure, course, and description of the vessel. The German Government did not give assurance of safe conduct for the vessel but explained that there was no occasion to give any such assurance with regard to the vessel as it was out of the question that German forces should stop the vessel or take any other measures against her. All the other belligerent governments have given assurance of safe conduct for the vessel for her sailing on the date scheduled and on the course indicated.

The German Government now points out that it did not receive final notification of the ship's departure from Petsamo on August 16 until noon of that day and that the American Embassy at Berlin had been informed that August 15 was the latest date for such notification of the intended route. However, the stipulation of the German Foreign Office that it be notified by noon, Berlin time, August 15, with respect to the vessel's course was in reply to the Embassy's inquiry as to how much advance notice of the change of course of the vessel would be required by the Foreign Office. Since no change was made in the course of the vessel, further advance notice became entirely unnecessary.

Stated briefly, the German Government has on several occasions during the conversations about the voyage of the *American Legion* stated that the vessel in question as a public vessel of the United States, actually being a transport of the United States Army, needed no safe conduct from the German Government because safe conducts were reserved only for merchant vessels. The German Government having repeatedly made that statement and having stated also that they would notify their armed forces of the route on which it was informed the vessel would proceed and of the date of her departure from Petsamo and of the description of the vessel, and having assured the Government of the United States that it had actually notified its armed forces of the route, date of sailing and description of the *American Legion*, and in continuing reliance upon the original statements of the German Government, the American Chargé d'Affaires is instructed to inform the German Government that under the circumstances above related the Government of the United States expects that the vessel will not suffer molestation by any action undertaken by the German armed forces.

3. GERMAN REPRESENTATION IN THE UNITED STATES

(1) *The Secretary of State (Hull) to Congressman John Z. Anderson (California), December 10, 1940* [1]

DECEMBER 10, 1940.

My dear Mr. ANDERSON:

I acknowledge receipt of your letter of November 28, 1940,[2] in which you call this Department's attention to a recent magazine article dealing with German representation in this country.

With respect to the questions treated therein, I feel you might wish to have the following information: The relations between the United States and most countries are generally established by treaty, and in the case of Germany and the United States the pertinent treaty is the Treaty of Friendship, Commerce, and Consular Rights, signed at Washington, December 8, 1923, a copy of which is enclosed.[3] This treaty still remains in effect with the exception of certain paragraphs of article VII, which were abrogated by a special agreement signed at Washington on June 3, 1935,[4] a statement concerning which is enclosed with a copy of the treaty.

This treaty determines the status of German consular representatives

[1] Department of State, *Bulletin*, III, p. 549.
[2] Not printed.
[3] *Treaties, Conventions*, etc. *1923–1937*, IV, p. 4191.
[4] *Ibid.*, p. 4221.

in this country, and upon a reciprocal basis, of our consular representatives in Germany. I may observe that the privileges which are accorded the respective consular officers in articles XVII, XVIII, XIX, and XX of the treaty, and which were so accorded them for the appropriate exercise of their official functions, conform with general international practice, and do not constitute diplomatic immunity. I may also mention that treaties of a similar nature were subsequent to 1923 negotiated with several other governments.

The Department publishes each month, in the form of a diplomatic list, the names of all those diplomatic officers accredited to this Government, together with their immediate families. The regulations of the Department of State also require a record of the names of the members of the households of these diplomatic officers. The Department of State, furthermore, keeps a record of all foreign consular officers serving in the United States and United States territory; and a record is likewise maintained of all employees, both foreign and American, of foreign diplomatic and consular establishments. These lists are open to inspection by any Member of Congress.

Apart from the groups mentioned above, a record is kept of another category of persons who are associated with foreign agencies. This includes those persons, both foreign and American, who are required to register with the Department of State under the terms of the act of June 8, 1938, as amended August 7, 1939,[1] to require the registration of certain persons employed by agencies to disseminate propaganda in the United States, and for other purposes. This list is open to inspection by the general public.

It may be mentioned that although there has been an increase in the staffs of the German consulates in the United States, these have not been out of proportion to increases in the staffs of other foreign government establishments in this country. In view of press assertions made with specific regard to the German Consulate General at New York, I might mention that the records of the Department indicate that as of October 1, 1939, there were 9 officers and 40 employees in that consulate, and that as of October 1, 1940, there were 8 officers and 40 employees.

This Department has not been unmindful of its responsibility to be informed of the activities of foreign consular representatives in this country, and of determining whether such activities conform with their official status and duties in the United States. In this connection I enclose for your information the Department's statement to the press

[1] See *Documents, I, 1938–39*, p. 559; *II, 1939–40*, p. 821.

dated July 5, 1940,[1] regarding the German consul general in New Orleans.

I have endeavored herein to give you all possible information from the Department of State and other authorized sources, in the light of which you may be able to appraise any assertions alleging that the competent agencies of this Government are not closely following such activities within the United States as may be inimical to American interests.

Sincerely yours,

CORDELL HULL

(2) *Closing of the German Consulates, etc. The Under Secretary of State (Welles) to the German Chargé d'Affaires (Thomsen), June 16, 1941* [2]

JUNE 16, 1941.

SIR:

It has come to the knowledge of this Government that agencies of the German Reich in this country, including German consular establishments, have been engaged in activities wholly outside the scope of their legitimate duties. These activities have been of an improper and unwarranted character. They render the continued presence in the United States of those agencies and consular establishments inimical to the welfare of this country.

I am directed by the President to request that the German Government remove from United States territory all German nationals in anywise connected with the German Library of Information in New York, the German Railway and Tourists Agencies, and the Trans-Ocean News Service, and that each of these organizations and their affiliates shall be promptly closed.

I am also directed to request that all German consular officers, agents, clerks, and employees thereof of German nationality shall be removed from American territory and that the consular establishments likewise be promptly closed.

It is contemplated that all such withdrawals and closures shall be effected before July 10.[3]

Accept [etc.]

For the Secretary of State:

SUMNER WELLES

[1] See Department of State, *Bulletin*, III, p. 4.

[2] *Ibid.*, IV, p. 743.

[3] Officials and employees of German nationality in the United States, other than those in the Embassy in Washington, total 171.

(3) Announcement of the German Government on Removal of American Officials, June 19, 1941 [1]

To the American Chargé d'Affaires was handed a note today in the Foreign Ministry in which the Reich Government pointed out that the conduct of American consular authorities and the American Travel Agency, the American Express Company, for a long time has occasioned heavy objections and that the Reich Government for that reason is forced to petition the American Government to remove, not later than July 15 of this year, American officials and American employes of consular authorities of the United States in Germany, as well as in Norway, Holland, Belgium, Luxemburg, the occupied part of France, in Serbia, and in all parts of Greece occupied by German troops, and to close the consulates.

At the same time the note requested the closing of the establishments of the American Express Company in the above-named territories and the removal of all American employes of this company not later than July 15 of this year, because the American Express Company and its employes conducted themselves in a manner contrary to the interests of the German Reich.

4. SINKING OF THE S.S. *ROBIN MOOR* BY GERMAN SUBMARINE

The American Ambassador to Brazil, Jefferson Caffery, reported to the Department of State by telegram on June 9, 1941 that word had been received by port authorities at Fortaleza, Brazil, that a 5,000-ton American vessel, the S.S. *Robin Moor*, had been sunk in the south Atlantic on May 21 while navigating on latitude 6.10 north and longitude 25.40 west. The report further stated that the Brazilian S.S. *Osorio* had picked up on June 8 at 9 P.M. 11 survivors who were drifting in a lifeboat belonging to the *Robin Moor*. Three other lifeboats, aboard which there were reported to be 27 crew members and 8 passengers, including 3 women and 1 child, had not been found, despite all efforts of the *Osorio*. Brazilian authorities ordered all Brazilian vessels in the vicinity to join in the search.

The 35 other persons were picked up June 4 by a British vessel and were landed at Cape Town, on June 16. Twenty-two arrived at Boston July 17 by the *Robin Locksley* and six July 21 by the *Exilona*. The passengers landed in Brazil reached New Orleans June 26.

For Message of the President to Congress, June 20, 1941, see p. 58.

[1] Associated Press version, *New York Times*, June 20, 1941, p. 6. The announcement is that of the Deutsches Nachrichtenbüro. News dispatches referred to several American consular officers by name as having participated in acts objectionable to the German Reich, including those expelled from Paris in December 1940 (Department of State, *Bulletin*, III, p. 586). About 70 persons were affected.

On the same day Italy took similar action alleging that "the attitude and activities of American officers in Italy had given rise to grave developments."

(1) *Reports of United States Consul at Pernambuco, Brazil (Linthicum), June 12, 1941* [1]

Robin Moor undoubtedly sunk by a German submarine at six Greenwich time on the morning of May 21 at latitude 6.10 north and longitude 25.40 west. The commander of the submarine was fully aware that the vessel was American. All survivors in good health.

Depositions of the survivors have been taken and comprehensive summary will be telegraphed as soon as coded.

I boarded the *Osorio* before it docked in Pernambuco last night and with full cooperation of the local authorities privately took the individual depositions of the American survivors; a comprehensive summary of their testimony follows:

"At 6 o'clock Greenwich time May 21 last the *Robin Moor* was ordered to stop by the use of a blinking light signal and to 'send a boat with papers'; upon inquiry what ship, the reply was just submarine. The *Robin Moor* then lowered a lifeboat in charge of the Chief Officer which proceeded about a mile and a half. No ship's papers taken. Submarine commander asked as to identity of ship and was told that 'American *Robin Moor* New York to Capetown.' The First Mate was then ordered into the submarine reappearing about 10 minutes later when the submarine commander was heard by the men manning the lifeboat to give the command to abandon ship within 20 minutes which upon request was extended to one-half hour from the time the lifeboat returned to her vessel. Upon the return three other lifeboats were lowered, one containing eleven seamen; another with twelve seamen; another with ten seamen and one passenger; and fourth contained three married couples, a child and five seamen.

"After abandonment of the ship the submarine fired a torpedo amidships then some thirty odd shells until the *Robin Moor* sank sternmost in about 23 minutes. Her position at this time was latitude 6.10 north, longitude 25.40 west and the hour was 8:05 Greenwich time. Afterwards floating wreckage was destroyed by gunfire.

"After the sinking of the *Robin Moor* the submarine circled by the lifeboat carrying the survivors interviewed and its commander remarked 'I have given some food to your captain' and then left the scene of the sinking remaining on the surface until out of sight. There is no doubt in the minds of the survivors that the commander and submarine were German although the latter had no visible markings other than the name *Lorricke* or *Lorickke* and a figure described as a laughing cow both painted on the conning tower. The commander spoke to the men in poor English.

"The lifeboats remained together at the scene of the sinking for about 24 hours because the commander of the submarine had said that he would wireless their position to expedite their rescue. Finding that this was useless the captain instructed all boats to proceed to Saint Paul's Rock or the Brazilian coast. They all remained together until May 26 when the survivors interviewed were given permission to proceed on their own which they did in the direction of the Brazilian coast. Survivors were picked up by the *Osorio* at latitude 0.46 north longitude 37.37 west.

[1] Department of State, *Bulletin*, IV, p. 716.

"The evidence also reveals that the *Robin Moor* had the American ensign and 'U.S.A.' painted on either side and an illuminated flag flying from her stern at the time she was sunk and when stopped she was instructed not to use her radio."

(2) *Press Conference Statement of the Under Secretary of State (Welles), June 12, 1941* [1]

The Under Secretary of State, Mr. Sumner Welles, informed newspaper correspondents at the press conference on June 12 that he thought it would be helpful to them and to the American people if he made a brief statement with regard to the *Robin Moor* and its cargo. The Under Secretary then said that the destinations of the cargo were to Lourenço Marques, Port Elizabeth, Capetown, Port Natal, and East London and added that none of these ports, of course, were included in the combat area. The cargo, he remarked, was entirely general in character. The Under Secretary went on to say that an examination of the ship's manifest [2] revealed no ammunition, explosives, military equipment, or any material of a military character nor had the examination shown anything on board the ship that was inconsistent with the President's proclamation of May 1, 1937 under the so-called Neutrality Act. The Under Secretary, in describing the type of cargo that was carried by the *Robin Moor*, said that it consisted of hundreds of items of a general character ranging all the way from steel rails to ladies' brassières and hosiery, interspersed with chemicals, paints, and considerable quantities of canned goods and packaged foods, automobiles and automobile parts, radio receiving sets, etc. These were the facts, he said, so far as the Department had them up to the present time.

(3) *The Under Secretary of State (Welles) to the Chargé d'Affaires (Thomsen), June 20, 1941* [3]

JUNE 20, 1941.

SIR:

I am directed by the President of the United States to transmit to you herewith, for the information of your Government, a copy of a message addressed today by the President to the Congress of the United States.

Accept [etc.]

For the Secretary of State:

SUMNER WELLES

[Enclosure: Message, see text, p. 58.]

[1] Department of State, *Bulletin*, IV, p. 717.

[2] The Seas Shipping Company gave out the complete manifest, which was printed in *New York Times*, June 14, 1941, p. 31.

[3] Department of State, *Bulletin*, IV, p. 741.

5. FLAG INCIDENT

(1) *The German Chargé d'Affaires (Thomsen) to the Secretary of State (Hull), January 18, 1941* [1]

[Translation]

THE GERMAN EMBASSY, II S. F.,
Washington, D. C., January 18, 1941.

MR. SECRETARY OF STATE:

I have the honor to inform you of the following occurrence:

As the day of the founding of the German Reich in the year 1871, January 18 was declared a German national holiday which is to be observed by the display of the German Reich flag by all German Reich offices in Germany as well as abroad. In conformity with the pertinent instructions issued by the German Reich Government the German Consul General in San Francisco today displayed the prescribed German Reich flag from his office.

The German Consul General in San Francisco has just informed me that the German Reich flag placed by him on his office was today at noon forcibly taken down from its staff by unknown persons in the presence of a large shouting throng of people and was torn to pieces by the throng. The perpetrator or perpetrators appear to have climbed by the fire-escape up to the ninth floor of the office building housing the Consulate General, without being prevented from doing so by the local police.

In the name of the German Reich Government I make the most emphatic protest against this act which represents a serious violation of the right, prescribed by treaty and recognized in international law, of the German Consul General in San Francisco to raise the German Reich flag over his office. I am permitted to express the expectation that the Government of the United States will adopt all appropriate measures to bring the perpetrators to responsibility and to submit them to merited punishment and that the Government of the United States will also take all appropriate steps in order to prevent a repetition of occurrences of this nature.

I request your Excellency to make it possible for me immediately to furnish my Government with a report in this regard.

Accept [etc.]   THOMSEN

[1] Department of State, *Bulletin*, IV, p. 108.

(2) *The Secretary of State (Hull) to the German Chargé d'Affaires (Thomsen), January 19, 1941* [1]

JANUARY 19, 1941.

MY DEAR MR. CHARGÉ D'AFFAIRES:

I have received your note of January 18, 1941 regarding a report reaching you from the German Consul General in San Francisco that the German Reich flag was forcibly taken down by unknown persons from the ninth floor of the office building housing the Consulate General.

I hasten to express the regret of the Government of the United States at such an incident and have requested that the appropriate agencies of this Government should make an immediate investigation, after which I shall communicate with you again.

I remain, Mr. Chargé d'Affaires,

Very sincerely yours,

CORDELL HULL

D. Italy

(1) *Exchange of Notes Concerning an Italian Air Attack on Americans in Anglo-Egyptian Sudan*

(a) *The American Chargé d'Affaires at Rome (Kirk) to the Italian Government, November 1, 1940* [2]

On August 23, 1940, shortly after nine o'clock in the morning, two Italian aircraft attacked the compound of the Sudan Interior Mission at Doro in the Anglo-Egyptian Sudan, resulting in the killing of Dr. and Mrs. Robert C. Grieve and the wounding of the Reverend and Mrs. C. K. Oglesby, all American citizens.

As soon as my Government learned of the occurrence, the American Legation at Cairo was instructed to make a most thorough investigation of all the facts and circumstances concerning the incident so far as might be possible, based in particular on eye-witness sources. That investigation has now been completed and, under instructions of my Government, I have been directed to acquaint the Royal Italian Government with what follows.

[Here follows a detailed account.]

From the above facts it is clear that:

The airplanes making the attack were Italian, in accordance with the sworn statements of two eye-witnesses.

[1] Department of State, *Bulletin*, IV, p. 109.   [2] *Ibid.*, p. 148.

The Italian military authorities at Kurmuk had knowledge prior to the attack on Doro of the presence there of American missionaries and of their non-combatant character.

Doro is an open undefended village with no military or police posts or any military works of any character.

The attack on Doro by Italian airplanes was consequently a deliberate and wanton assault on a non-military objective and on non-combatant civilians, including four American citizens.

My Government is confident that the Royal Italian Government will promptly condemn the acts of those responsible for the brutal unprovoked attack against the four American citizens concerned and that prompt steps will be taken to punish those guilty of an outrage shocking to all those who continue to preserve any respect for the principles of civilized behavior. My Government must of course make full reservations concerning the subsequent entering of claims for compensation for the killing of Dr. and Mrs. Grieve, the wounding of the Reverend and Mrs. Oglesby and for any property damage suffered by American interests.

(b) The Italian Foreign Office to the American Embassy at Rome, November 6, 1940 [1]

Detailed information in the premises has been requested of the competent military authorities.

However, as it relates to facts supposed to have occurred more than two months ago in a distant locality it is very probable that a report on the matter cannot be received for some time.

Much more expeditious procedure on the part of North America [sic] would have been to have requested information concerning the bombardments in question simultaneously from Cairo and from Rome.

That among other things would probably have resulted in a composition different from your note of November 1 which in its concluding portion contains criticisms of the Italian armed forces which cannot but be rejected in toto.

(c) Note Verbale of the Italian Foreign Office, January 31, 1941 [2]

With reference to the Embassy's letter of November 1, 1940, the Ministry of Foreign Affairs has the honor to enclose a copy of the report from the competent Italian military authorities regarding the alleged bombardment of Doro. The said authorities after careful investigation state that it is to be excluded that the air action in question was carried

[1] Department of State, Bulletin, IV, p. 151.   [2] Ibid., p. 184.

out by Italian airplanes and emphasize the point that the Government of the Province concerned had in fact given orders that the two missions whose presence at Doro and Chali was perfectly well known should be left undisturbed where they were.

[The enclosed report is omitted.]

(2) *Prophecy of the Italian Premier (Mussolini) to the Chamber of Fasces and Corporations, Rome, June 10, 1941* [1]

[Excerpt]

Although Spain and Turkey are outside the fighting, there is a State across the ocean which expects to enter. It is well to make it known that American intervention does not disturb us excessively. An explicit declaration of war would not modify the present situation, which is one of war *de facto* if not *de jure*. American intervention even if it becomes complete would be too late, and even if it were not late it would not alter the terms of the problem.

American intervention will not give victory to Great Britain, but will prolong the war. American intervention will not limit the war in space, but will extend it to other oceans. American intervention will transmute the United States regime into an authoritarian and totalitarian regime, which will very much surpass and perfect its European precursors — Fascist and Nazi. . . .

(3) *Closing of Two Italian Consulates. The Secretary of State (Hull), to the Italian Ambassador (Colonna), March 5, 1941* [2]

Consuls, who are agents of their Governments for the facilitation of commercial relations, enjoy the privileges requisite for fulfilling their duties at the posts in the country to which they are assigned. Consular districts are delimited in accordance with the commercial, demographic and other interests of the consul's country with the acquiescence of the country of residence. The consul's status in his district is established by the formal permission known as an exequatur issued to him by the country of residence. The Treaty of Commerce and Navigation between Italy and the United States signed February 26, 1871, as amended February 25, 1913,[3] ceased to be in force on December 15, 1937.[4] Since then commercial relations between the two countries have been based on the comity of nations and the most-favored-nation agreement of December 16, 1937,[5] which is denunciable on 30-days' notice.

In February 1941 the Italian Government wished to remove American consuls from Mediterranean coasts which were within visual range of waters where the Italian Navy was being defeated by the British Navy. Certain manufacturing

---

[1] *New York Times*, June 11, 1941, p. 9.
[2] Department of State, *Bulletin*, IV, p. 249.
[3] *Treaties, Conventions, etc.*, 1910–1923, III, p. 2699.
[4] Department of State, *Treaty Information*, Bulletin No. 87, p. 13.
[5] Executive Agreement Series No. 116.

centers in the United States were the seat of Italian consuls. On March 6, 1941, the Department of State made this announcement: [1]

"For reasons of national policy it has been decided that foreign consulates in certain areas should be closed. At the present time the Italian Government has been requested to close its consulates at Detroit, Michigan, and Newark, New Jersey, and to withdraw the personnel."

The Secretary of State presents his compliments to His Excellency the Royal Italian Ambassador and has the honor to refer to his oral communication of February 12, 1941, with respect to the Italian Government's request that the Consulates now established at Palermo and Naples should be moved to a place as far north as Rome or farther north, and to a place which was not on the sea coast.

Instructions to these offices of the American Government have been issued in accordance with this request and the supervisory consulate general of the United States in Italy is being established in Rome.

The Secretary of State avails himself of this opportunity to make request of the Italian Ambassador that all officials of his Government within the territory of the United States will confine their movements to those areas in which they exercise the recognized duties of their respective offices. This request does not include the personnel of the Italian Embassy in Washington whose names appear on the Diplomatic List. It would be appreciated, however, if the Italian Ambassador would keep the Department of State currently informed of the movements outside of Washington of the military and naval personnel attached to the Italian Embassy.

As regards the Italian consular offices at Newark, New Jersey, and Detroit, Michigan, the Italian Ambassador is informed that the American Ambassador in Rome has been requested to convey orally to the appropriate Italian authorities the desire of the United States Government that these offices should be closed and that the Italian personnel be withdrawn from these places. Should they remain within the jurisdiction of the United States the Department of State should be kept fully informed of their place of residence.

(4) *Withdrawal of Italian Naval and Military Attachés*

(a) *The Secretary of State (Hull) to the Royal Italian Ambassador (Colonna), April 2, 1941* [2]

APRIL 2, 1941.

EXCELLENCY:

I have the honor to state that various facts and circumstances have come to the attention of the Government of the United States con-

---

[1] Department of State, *Bulletin*, IV, p. 249.   [2] *Ibid.*, p. 420.

necting Admiral Alberto Lais, Naval Attaché of the Royal Italian Embassy, with the commission by certain persons of acts in violation of the laws of the United States.[1]

The President has reached the conclusion that the continued presence of Admiral Lais as Naval Attaché of the Embassy would no longer be agreeable to this Government.

The President has directed me, therefore, to notify Your Excellency that Admiral Lais is persona non grata to this Government as Naval Attaché of the Royal Italian Embassy at Washington, and to request that Your Excellency's Government withdraw him immediately from the United States.

The Royal Italian Government will no doubt realize that the Government of the United States has, in view of all the circumstances, no alternative course.

Accept [etc.]   CORDELL HULL

(b) Request by Italian Government for Withdrawal of American Military Attaché, April 8, 1941 [2]

By note of April 2, 1941, the Secretary of State notified the Royal Italian Ambassador that Admiral Alberto Lais, Naval Attaché of the Royal Italian Embassy, was persona non grata to this Government and requested that the Royal Italian Government withdraw him immediately from the United States.

The Secretary of State has now been informed by the Royal Italian Ambassador in a note dated April 8 that Admiral Lais has ceased from his functions and will leave this country without delay.

In the same note, the Royal Italian Ambassador stated that Capt. William C. Bentley, Jr., Assistant Military Attaché and Assistant Military Attaché for Air of the United States Embassy in Rome, is persona non grata to the Royal Italian Government, and requested that he be withdrawn immediately from Italy.

(5) Closing of All Italian Consulates, etc. The Under Secretary of State (Welles) to the Italian Ambassador (Colonna), June 20, 1941 [3]

                                              JUNE 20, 1941.
EXCELLENCY:

I have the honor to inform Your Excellency that the President has directed me to request that the Italian Government promptly close all

---

[1] Relates to the sabotage on Italian ships in United States ports, March 30, 1941; see p. 621.
[2] Release of the Department of State, Bulletin, IV, p. 453.
[3] Ibid., p. 743.

Italian consular establishments within United States territory and remove therefrom all Italian consular officers, agents, clerks and employees of Italian nationality. In the opinion of the Government of the United States it is obvious that the continued functioning of Italian consular establishments in territory of the United States would serve no desirable purpose.

I am likewise directed to request the closing of all agencies in this country connected with the Italian Government, together with the cessation of their activities, and, furthermore, the removal of all Italian nationals in any way connected with organizations of the Italian Government in the United States, with the exception of its duly accredited representation in Washington.

It is contemplated that all such withdrawals and closures shall be effected before July 15, 1941.

Accept [etc.]

For the Secretary of State:

SUMNER WELLES

———

The Italian Government matched the move of the United States, but gave out no note or communiqué concerning its action. On the other hand, on June 24, 1941, it retaliated to the United States fund-control ruling with respect to departing Italians by a measure prohibiting Americans from leaving Italian territory without special authorization. By July 15, when consular officers left the two countries, Americans were receiving exit visas from the Italian authorities.

E. Portugal

(1) *The Portuguese Minister* (*Bianchi*) *to the Secretary of State* (*Hull*) *May 30, 1941* [1]

The Portuguese Government would not feel justified in addressing itself to the Government of the United States to refer to an address made by the Chief Executive of the great American nation to its citizens, were it not for the fact that it contains direct references [2] to Portuguese territories which, coupled with some of the thesis set forth by President Roosevelt, and unaccompanied by any express mention of respect for the complete and centuries-old sovereignty of Portugal over those territories, are open to diverse interpretations and, therefore, could not fail to surprise the Portuguese people.

[1] *New York Times*, June 13, 1941, p. 8.
[2] Address of the President of May 27, 1941, see p. 51, 53, 54.

Portugal has maintained during the present war a neutral position which does not imply the breach of any of its international undertakings. This neutrality has been unimpeachably observed and has provided Europe and the two Americas with their last direct contact.

In order to ensure it and to assert their sovereignty in an unmistakable way in the present conjuncture or any other with which they may be confronted, the Portuguese Government have endeavored to set up a state of efficient defense, with all the means at their disposal, in the territories which it is said are more exposed to attack, precisely those very same ones to which His Excellency President Roosevelt made direct and repeated references: the islands of Cape Verde and the Azores.

The sending of troops to the said possessions together with other defense measures already accomplished and in progress were not kept secret, and the Government of the United States are certainly aware of them.

The Portuguese territories have not, therefore, presented any harm, hindrance or menace to any of the belligerents or their allies, in the first place owing to the irreproachable attitude maintained; secondly, because the Portuguese Government declare and manifest their disposition to defend such an attitude against whoever may be; and, in the third place, due to the fact that such territories have not been the object of any threat by any of the belligerents or third powers.

It is therefore not possible to understand the specific reference by name to those Portuguese possessions, which by itself could not fail to surprise the Portuguese people and Government.

Furthermore, those references are involved with the expounding of the thesis that it devolves on the United States to define and decide whether, and when and where they are threatened and how their forces are to be used to defend themselves or others. And in expounding such a thesis there is not the slightest reference to the fundamental principle of respect for the sovereignty of others exercised and maintained without prejudice to anybody.

Regarding such a thesis, in so far as it may involve their territories, the Portuguese Government deem it their imperative duty to request a clarification, otherwise it might be interpreted as conducting to the admission that, in order to defend other countries or for its own defense, a great nation would be at liberty to commit a violation similar to those the threat of which is said to exist from third States.

The Portuguese Government, having recently received, with satisfaction and gratitude, from the United States Government through the words of the Secretary of State assurances of the respect for their sovereignty, would now appreciate being placed in a position to assure that in the references made by His Excellency President Roosevelt and in the thesis that he expounded nothing exists that is contrary to the former declaration or which may be interpreted as derogatory of the sovereign rights of Portugal.

For their own part, the Portuguese Government reassert their indefectible determination to defend to the limit of their forces their neutrality and their sovereign rights against all and any attack to which they may be exposed, though continuing to state they do not anticipate any such event.

(2) *The Secretary of State (Hull) to the Minister of Portugal (Bianchi), June 10, 1941* [1]

SIR:

I have the honor to acknowledge your communication of May 30, 1941, transmitting the observations of the Government of Portugal with respect to the references to the Portuguese Islands in the Atlantic made by the President in his address of May 27, 1941. [2]

I have carefully studied the observations of the Portuguese Government, and have noted the declarations reaffirming its position of neutrality and its determination to defend its neutrality and sovereign rights against any attack.

For its part, the Government of the United States can state categorically that it harbors no aggressive intentions against the sovereignty or territorial integrity of any other country. The Government and people of the United States have sought to live in peace and friendship with all other nations, and have consistently supported the principle of nonaggression and non-intervention in the relations between states. This Government time and again has reiterated its support of this principle.

Our policy today is based upon the inalienable right of self-defense. The Government of the United States cannot but view with increasing anxiety the constantly expanding acts of aggression on the part of a certain belligerent power, which now threaten the peace and safety of the countries of this hemisphere.

In referring to the Islands in the Atlantic it was the intention of the President to point out the dangers to this hemisphere which would result if these Islands were to come under the control or occupation of forces pursuing a policy of world conquest and domination. The strategic

[1] Department of State, *Bulletin*, IV, p. 718.
[2] See p. 51, 53, 54.

importance of these Islands, because of their geographical location, was stressed by the President solely in terms of their potential value from the point of view of attack against this hemisphere.

Accept [etc.]

CORDELL HULL

F. Soviet Union

(1) *Statement respecting the Baltic Republics by the Acting Secretary of State (Welles), July 23, 1940* [1]

The Soviet Union pressed upon Estonia, Latvia and Lithuania the signing on September 28, October 5 and 10, 1939, of "treaties of nonaggression," [2] the salient feature of which was the acquisition by the Soviet Union of the control of strategic points in those countries. In mid-June 1940 the Soviet Government, on various allegations against governments in succession, demanded that each form a government which should enjoy the confidence of Moscow. Such governments were formed under the hand of an official of the Soviet People's Commissariat of Foreign Affairs. Elections held on July 14 gave majorities in each state which formed governments that applied for admission into the Soviet Union. The United States blocked the funds of the three Baltic states on July 15, 1940.[3]

During these past few days the devious processes whereunder the political independence and territorial integrity of the three small Baltic republics — Estonia, Latvia, and Lithuania — were to be deliberately annihilated by one of their more powerful neighbors, have been rapidly drawing to their conclusion.

From the day when the peoples of these republics first gained their independent and democratic form of government the people of the United States have watched their admirable progress in self-government with deep and sympathetic interest.

The policy of this Government is universally known. The people of the United States are opposed to predatory activities no matter whether they are carried on by the use of force or by the threat of force. They are likewise opposed to any form of intervention on the part of one state, however powerful, in the domestic concerns of any other sovereign state, however weak.

These principles constitute the very foundations upon which the existing relationship between the 21 sovereign republics of the New World rests.

The United States will continue to stand by these principles, because

[1] Department of State, *Bulletin*, III, p. 48.
[2] *Ibid.*, I, p. 542, 543, 705.
[3] *Documents, II, 1939–40*, p. 548.

of the conviction of the American people that unless the doctrine in which these principles are inherent once again governs the relations between nations, the rule of reason, of justice, and of law — in other words, the basis of modern civilization itself — cannot be preserved.

(2) Lifting of "Moral Embargo" on Exports to the Soviet Union. The Under Secretary of State (Welles) to the Soviet Ambassador to the United States (Oumansky), January 21, 1941 [1]

DEPARTMENT OF STATE,
Washington, January 21, 1941.

MY DEAR MR. AMBASSADOR:

Following our recent conversations, I am happy to inform you that the Government of the United States of America has decided that the policies set forth in the statement issued to the press by the President on December 2, 1939,[2] and generally referred to as the "moral embargo," are no longer applicable to the Union of Soviet Socialist Republics.

This decision is being communicated to interested American manufacturers and exporters.

I am, my dear Mr. Oumansky,

Very sincerely yours,

SUMNER WELLES

(a) Recapitulation by the Department of State [1]

In the statement issued to the press by the President on December 2, 1939, the hope was expressed that American manufacturers and exporters of airplanes, aeronautical equipment, and materials essential to airplane manufacture, would bear in mind before negotiating contracts for the exportation of these articles that the American Government and the American people had for some time pursued the policy of wholeheartedly condemning the unprovoked bombing and machine-gunning of civilian populations from the air.

In a statement issued to the press on December 15, 1939,[3] the Department of State took the position that molybdenum and aluminum were included among "materials essential to airplane manufacture." On December 20, 1939, [3] the Department of State issued a statement to the press to the effect that after consultation with the War and Navy Departments it had decided, as an extension of the announced policy of this Government in regard to the sale to certain countries of airplanes, aeronautical equipment, and materials essential to airplane manufacture that the national interest suggested that for the time being there should be no further delivery to these countries of plans, plants, manufacturing rights, or technical information required for the production of high quality aviation gasoline.

[1] Department of State, *Bulletin*, IV, p. 107.
[2] *Documents, II, 1939–40*, p. 725.
[3] *Ibid.*, p. 727.

The President's statement of December 2, 1939, and the Department's supplementary statements of December 15, 1939, and December 20, 1939, referred to above, are no longer applicable to the Union of Soviet Socialist Republics.

All of the articles and materials covered by what has generally been referred to as the "moral embargo" are included in the list of articles and materials now subject to the export-license system.

Arms, ammunition, and implements of war have been subject to the export-license system since November 29, 1935.[1] The definition of arms, ammunition, and implements of war now in effect is contained in the President's proclamation of May 1, 1937.[2] In that proclamation are listed aircraft of all types, aircraft armament, and all major aircraft parts. On July 2, 1940,[3] the President, by proclamation, added to the list of articles and materials, subject to the export-license system, aluminum, molybdenum, and aircraft parts other than those listed in his proclamation of May 1, 1937. In his proclamation of September 12, 1940,[4] the President added to the list of articles and materials, subject to the export-license system, equipment which can be used, or adapted to use, for the production of aviation motor fuel from petroleum, petroleum products, hydrocarbons, or hydrocarbon mixtures; and equipment which can be used, or adapted to use, for the production of tetraethyl lead; and any plans, specifications, or other documents containing descriptive or technical information relating to either of the above.

G. Spain — Concerning the International Zone of Tangier

The United States is concerned with the international status of Tangier through its being a party to the treaty signed at Algeciras April 7, 1906,[5] from which that status developed. The organization of the statute by the convention of December 18, 1923,[6] by France, Spain and the United Kingdom, with the Netherlands adhering, formally revised a system of international administration that had been in operation for many years. The representative of the United States in the Tangier Zone was a member of the Commission of Control, the legislative Assembly and other organs of the autonomous administration. The revision of the convention of July 25, 1928,[7] admitted Italy to participation in the administration.

The German Consulate at Tangier was reopened March 17, 1941 in the building occupied in 1914.

(1) Statement of the British Under Secretary of State for Foreign Affairs (Butler), House of Commons, November 13, 1940 [8]

On November 3 the Officer Commanding the Spanish troops in Tangier published a notice stating that by reason of the present situation

[1] Department of State, Press Releases, XIII, p. 221, 492.
[2] Documents, II, 1939–40, p. 694.   [3] Ibid., p. 796.
[4] See p. 477.
[5] Treaties, Conventions, etc. 1776–1909, II, p. 2157.
[6] League of Nations, Treaty Series, XXVIII, p. 542; XXXIX, p. 198.
[7] Ibid., CXXXVII, p. 211.
[8] Parliamentary Debates, 5th series, House of Commons, vol. 365, col. 1678 p. 1957.
For further discussion see ibid. House of Commons, January 22, 1941.

the Committee of Control, the Legislative Assembly, and the Mixed Bureau of Information would cease to function and that he himself would take charge of the Zone of Tangier under the title of Governor and as delegate of the Spanish High Commissioner in Morocco.

On November 5 his Majesty's Ambassador at Madrid was instructed to record a formal protest in regard to this Spanish action undertaken without any consultation with the other Governments interested in the International Regime, and to reserve all the rights of his Majesty's Government under the international instruments of 1923 and 1928, which govern the international administration and provide for the neutrality of the Tangier Zone. It is understood that the majority of the other Governments concerned in the International Regime at Tangier have also lodged protests with the Spanish Government.

His Majesty's Government appreciate the importance of Spanish interests at Tangier, as was shown by their attitude in regard to the occupation of the Zone by Spanish military forces last June. His Majesty's Ambassador has been instructed to make it clear to the Spanish Government that his Majesty's Government attach great importance to the maintenance of the neutrality of the Zone, and to the avoidance of any action which might be harmful to British interests.

I understand that the component parts of the Tangier administration, apart from the International Gendarmerie, have continued to function as usual under the direct supervision of the Officer Commanding the Spanish troops.

(2) *Treaty Rights in Tangier. Statement of the Department of State, November 15, 1940* [1]

Upon instructions of the Department of State, the American Ambassador to Spain has made certain representations to the Spanish Government concerning the recent action of the Spanish military authorities at Tangier, Morocco. Although the United States has not adhered to the convention of December 18, 1923, revised on July 25, 1928, regarding the organization of the Statute of the Tangier Zone, it possesses certain treaty rights in Morocco, including the International Zone of Tangier, on which the representations of this Government have been based.

[1] Department of State, *Bulletin*, III, p. 430.

4. OCCUPIED STATES IN EUROPE AND AFRICA

(1) *Agreement by Exchange of Letters Concerning the Organization, Employment and Conditions of Service of the French Volunteer Force, London, August 7, 1940* [1]

(a) *The Prime Minister of the United Kingdom (Churchill) to General Charles de Gaulle*

10 DOWNING STREET, LONDON, S. W. 1,
August 7, 1940.

DEAR GENERAL DE GAULLE:

You were good enough to give me your ideas as to the organization, employment and conditions of service of the French volunteer force now being assembled under your command, in your capacity, in which you are recognized by his Majesty's Government in the United Kingdom, of leader of all Free Frenchmen, wherever they may be, who rally to you in support of the Allied Cause.

I now send you a memorandum which, if you concur, will be agreed between us as governing the organization, employment and conditions of service of your force.

I would take this opportunity of stating that it is the determination of his Majesty's Government, when victory has been gained by the Allied arms, to secure the full restoration of the independence and greatness of France.

Yours sincerely,

WINSTON S. CHURCHILL

GENERAL C. DE GAULLE,
&C., &C., &C.

MEMORANDUM OF AGREEMENT

I.

(1) General de Gaulle is engaged in raising a French force composed of volunteers. This force, which includes naval, land and air units and scientific and technical personnel, will be organized and employed against the common enemies.

(2) This force will never be required to take up arms against France.

[1] United Kingdom, Parliamentary Papers, France No. 2 (1940), Cmd. 6220. The French text is equally authentic with the English.

II.

(1) This force will, as far as possible, retain the character of a French force in respect of personnel, particularly as regards discipline, language, promotion and duties.

(2) So far as may be necessary for their equipment, this force will have priority of allocation as regards property in and the use of material (particularly weapons, aircraft, vehicles, ammunition, machinery and supplies) which has already been brought by French armed forces from any quarter, or which may so be brought in the future by such French forces, into territory under the authority of his Majesty's Government in the United Kingdom or into territory where the British High Command exercises authority. In the case of French forces, the command of which has been delegated by agreement between General de Gaulle and the British High Command, no transfer, exchange, or reallocation of equipment, property and material in possession of these forces will be made by order of General de Gaulle without prior consultation and agreement with the British High Command.

(3) His Majesty's Government will, as soon as practicable, supply the French force with the additional equipment which may be essential to equip its units on a scale equivalent to that of British units of the same type.

(4) Naval vessels from the French Fleet will be allocated as follows: —

(a) The French force will commission and operate as many vessels as it is able to man.

(b) The allocation of the vessels to be commissioned and operated by the French force under (a) will be a matter for agreement from time to time between General de Gaulle and the British Admiralty.

(c) Vessels not allocated under (b) to the French force will be available for commissioning and operating under the direction of the British Admiralty.

(d) Of the vessels mentioned under (c) some may be operated under direct British control and some may be operated by other allied naval forces.

(e) Vessels operated under British control will when possible include in their complement a proportion of French officers and men.

(f) All vessels concerned will remain French property.

(5) The possible use of French merchant ships and of their crews, in so far as this is for the purpose of military operations by General de Gaulle's force, will be the subject of arrangements between General de Gaulle and the British Departments concerned. Regular contact will be maintained between the Ministry of Shipping and General de Gaulle as regards the use of the rest of the ships and the employment of the merchant seamen.

(6) General de Gaulle, who is in supreme command of the French force, hereby declares that he accepts the general direction of the British High Command. When necessary he will delegate, in agreement with the British High Command, the immediate command of any part of his force to one or more British officers of appropriate rank, subject to what is stated at the end of Article I above.

III.

The status of French volunteers will be established in the following manner: —

(1) Volunteers will enroll for the duration of the war for the purpose of fighting against the common enemies.

(2) They will receive pay on a basis to be settled separately by agreement between General de Gaulle and the Departments concerned. The period of time during which such rates will apply will be a matter for settlement between General de Gaulle and his Majesty's Government in the United Kingdom.

(3) The volunteers and their dependents will be granted pensions and other benefits in respect of the disablement or death of the volunteers on a basis to be settled by separate agreement between General de Gaulle and the Departments concerned.

(4) General de Gaulle will be entitled to form a civil establishment containing the administrative services required for the organization of his force, the numbers and emoluments of the members of this establishment being settled in consultation with the British Treasury.

(5) The General will also be entitled to recruit technical and scientific staff for war work. The numbers, manner of remuneration, and method of employment of this staff will be settled in consultation with the Departments of his Majesty's Government concerned.

(6) His Majesty's Government in the United Kingdom will use their best endeavors, at the time of the conclusion of peace, to help the French volunteers to regain any rights, including national status, of which they may have been deprived as a result of their participation in the struggle against the common enemies. His Majesty's Government are willing to afford special facilities to such volunteers to acquire British nationality, and will seek any necessary powers.

IV.

(1) Any expenditure incurred for the purpose of the constitution and maintenance of the French force under the provisions of this agreement will be met in the first instance by the appropriate Departments of his Majesty's Government in the United Kingdom, which will be entitled to exercise any necessary examination and audit.

(2) The sums required will be regarded as advances and specially recorded; all questions relating to the ultimate settlement of these advances, including any credits which may be set off by agreement, will be a matter for subsequent arrangement.

V.

This agreement shall be regarded as having come into force on July 1, 1940.

(b) *General de Gaulle to the Prime Minister of the United Kingdom* (*Churchill*)

4 CARLTON GARDENS, LONDON, S. W. 1,
August 7, 1940.

MY DEAR PRIME MINISTER:

You have been good enough to send me a memorandum dealing with the organization, employment and conditions of service of the force of French volunteers which is at present being constituted under my command.

In the capacity in which I have been recognized by his Majesty's Government in the United Kingdom as leader of all Free Frenchmen, wherever they may be, who rally to me in support of the Allied cause, I hereby inform you that I accept this memorandum. It will be considered as constituting an agreement concluded between us in regard to these questions.

I am glad that on this occasion his Majesty's Government have taken an opportunity to state that they are determined, when victory has been gained by the Allied arms, to secure the full restoration of the independence and greatness of France.

For my part, I confirm to you that the French force now in process of constitution is intended to take part in operations against the common enemies (Germany, Italy or any other hostile foreign power), including the defense of French territories and territories under French mandate, and the defense of British territories and communications, and territories under British mandate.

Yours sincerely,
C. DE GAULLE

THE RT. HON. WINSTON S. CHURCHILL,
   C. H., M. P., &c., &c., &c.

(2) *Broadcast of King Haakon VII of Norway, London, August 26, 1940* [1]

The fact that I am speaking to Norwegian listeners from London is an excellent proof that rumors should not be believed. I heard today, for instance, that I had left London and gone to America on account of differences of opinion with the British Government.

It appears that the correspondence between the Presidential Board of the Storting and myself concerning the question of my abdication has not been published by the Norwegian newspapers. This seems to have led to a misunderstanding of the whole political situation in Norway since April 9; but it must be borne in mind that the country unexpectedly and suddenly found itself in an extremely critical situation and that it was necessary to take the serious decision whether the country should surrender at once or defend itself.

The Storting and the Government had to be given time and tranquillity to come to a decision. As it became quite clear that in Oslo these conditions could not be reckoned with, the authorities which had to take the decision were forced to transfer their activities to a safer place. On their arrival at Hamar the same day the Government tendered

[1] The Times (London), August 27, 1940, p. 3.

their resignation, which was immediately submitted to the Storting. The Storting unanimously gave the Government a vote of confidence, asked them to continue, and advised them to include members of the minority parties. This was done. Later the Storting unanimously decided that the country was to be defended by force of arms as long as possible.

It appears also that the Government have been reproached with not having been sufficiently active during the first days of the war, with not having been able to wield power. It must be remembered that during the whole of the first period we were literally hunted from place to place, that during meetings of the Government air raid warnings were constantly sounded and that we had to carry on our discussions even when the aeroplanes were over our heads. It was only when we came to Northern Norway, about a month after the outbreak of the war, that we all, to a certain extent, were able to settle down to work.

During our stay in Northern Norway the reconstruction of the Government was under discussion. Being debarred from the rest of Norway, I did not find it possible to undertake a reconstruction of the Government. Besides, I thought it was very important to keep in office a Government in whom the Storting had confidence, and thus to abide by Parliamentary practice, the more so as Major Quisling had formed an unconstitutional government. My view was endorsed by the majority of the Government.

In certain circles it has been asserted that my departure from Norway and that of the Government has caused difficulties for the country and for those who remained behind. I think we did right. If we had stayed in Norway the present rulers of the country would have been able to force us to accept what they desired. It was in order to avoid this that we left the country, and we had the vote of the Storting to support us in doing so.

From the place where we are now staying we can still represent a free Norway. It was clear to me and to the Government that the only possibility of recreating a free Norway lay in the victory of those who uphold the right of small nations to lead their own lives.

I should like to seize this opportunity to express it as my conviction that the Council of Administration in Norway have surely carried out their task in an excellent manner and that they deserve well of the Fatherland in having assumed what must be a grievous task to every true Norwegian, to act as an intermediary between the present rulers and the people of Norway. I express my best thanks to the members of the Council of Administration for the unselfish and self-sacrificing work they have undertaken, not least because in doing so they have been able to keep order in circumstances where inconsiderate actions might have led to catastrophic results not only for individuals but for the whole nation.

At the same time I express my thanks and send my greetings to all Norwegian men and women — to those who are working and suffering in silence and to all those in official or other positions who must work in conditions which must involve an almost unbearable strain. Avoid everything which is inconsistent with our national dignity; remain Norwegian in your heart and in your thoughts, even if your thoughts in the present circumstances cannot be translated into speech, writing, or action. Only so shall we maintain the strong national feeling which characterizes our people and which ultimately will render impossible every attempt to destroy Norway as an independent kingdom.

God save the land and the people of Norway!

(3) *Remarks of Hugues Le Gallais upon Presentation of Credentials as Minister Plenipotentiary of the Grand Duchy of Luxemburg, November 8, 1940* [1]

The PRESIDENT:

I have the honor to place in Your Excellency's hands the letters which accredit me to you as Envoy Extraordinary and Minister Plenipotentiary of Her Royal Highness the Grand Duchess of Luxemburg.

It is a great honor for me to have been designated by My Gracious Sovereign to fulfill this high mission, the importance of which I fully realize.

No doubt you are aware, Mr. President, that the most friendly sentiments have always been manifested by the people of Luxemburg to the people of the United States. After the war of 1914–1918, to these sentiments was added one of deep gratitude when the United States and their Allies restored to the Grand Duchy of Luxemburg its independence and freedom.

At this tragic hour in my country's history, our eyes are again turned to the United States, which, under your enlightened leadership, have become the foremost guardian of the traditions of justice and right.

Your declaration, Mr. President, that the United States would never recognize territorial acquisition by violence inspires my countrymen while they await a happier future.

Mr. President, all my efforts will be directed toward strengthening the bonds existing between our two countries, and I am convinced that

[1] Department of State, *Bulletin*, III, p. 408.

in the future, as has been the case in the past, I can always rely on your kind support in the fulfilment of my task.

(a) Reply of the President (Roosevelt), November 8, 1940 [1]

MR. MINISTER:

It is a pleasure to receive from your hands the letters of Her Royal Highness the Grand Duchess of Luxemburg accrediting you near the Government of the United States of America as Envoy Extraordinary and Minister Plenipotentiary.

I am gratified to hear from you that the people of Luxemburg continue to hold toward the people of the United States the friendly sentiments you have expressed. The people of the United States cherish the friendship of the people of Luxemburg and reciprocate those sentiments to the fullest extent.

In this tragic hour in the history of your country the sympathy of the United States goes out to the people of Luxemburg, who may take comfort in the assurance that the people of the United States desire nothing more than to see them happy once more in full independence under their Gracious Sovereign.

You may count upon my full cooperation and that of the competent officers of the Government of the United States in your efforts to strengthen the bonds which exist between our two countries.

(4) Remarks of Jan Ciechanowski upon Presentation of His Credentials as Polish Ambassador, March 6, 1941 [2]

The Polish Government, having been forced out of Warsaw by the German attack in September 1939, was reconstituted by the constitutional transmission of the Presidency at Paris on September 30, 1939, and the Government reestablished itself at Angers, France. During the events leading to the collapse of France in May–June 1940, the Polish Government made its way to the United Kingdom and took up quarters in London. The United States continuously accredited its ambassador near that Government during its movements. Count Jerzy Potocki, who had been accredited Polish Ambassador to the United States since May 29, 1936, resigned to become an American citizen, and the acceptance of his successor under the circumstances of the time had an extrinsic significance.

MARCH 6, 1941.

MR. PRESIDENT:

I have the honor to hand to Your Excellency the letters by which the President of the Republic of Poland recalls Count George Potocki from his post of Ambassador of the Republic of Poland to the United States.

---

[1] Department of State, *Bulletin*, III, p. 409.   [2] *Ibid.*, IV, p. 249.

The President of the Republic of Poland desires me to express to Your Excellency his sincere thanks for the kindness, the understanding, and the support which Your Excellency and the Government of the United States have given to Ambassador Potocki throughout his mission in Washington.

The President of the Republic has instructed me to assure Your Excellency that he is following with concentrated attention and admiration your splendid activity for the preservation of freedom and civilization on which the whole future and happiness of humanity depend.

I have now the honor to present to Your Excellency the letters by which the President of the Republic of Poland accredits me to be Ambassador Extraordinary and Plenipotentiary of the Republic of Poland to the United States.

I beg leave to assure you, Mr. President, that I am deeply conscious of the honor of representing Poland in the United States at this exceptionally grave time, when the fate of my country and, indeed, that of human freedom and civilization are at stake. I am especially conscious of the responsibility placed upon me.

For nearly a year and a half Poland is suffering inhuman oppression at the hands of two ruthless invaders.

These two powerful neighbors of Poland have unprovokedly attacked and overrun her national territory in a concerted action of aggressive imperialism, with a view of repeating the crime of Poland's partitions of the end of the eighteenth century, and of renewing their previous unsuccessful attempt at total annihilation of the Polish Nation.

The Polish people, irrespective of party and creed, united in the sacred cause of Poland's independence, have never for one moment departed from their attitude of calm national dignity and determined opposition to political and physical pressure ruthlessly applied by the invaders with unprecedented cunning and brutality in order to break their spirit of resistance.

The Polish armed forces continue to be active. The Polish Army fought gallantly against overwhelming forces in Poland. After being overpowered, those of our soldiers who were able to thwart the vigilance of the enemy, surmounted countless dangers and hardships, and succeeded by heroic migration in single file in crossing the greater part of the European Continent, in order to join the Polish Government and to re-form the Allied National Polish Army on the friendly soil of France. After fighting bravely against the common enemy in Norway and on French territory, they refused to capitulate and migrated once more from that unfortunate allied country at the time of its surrender, in order to re-form their decimated forces on the friendly and hospitable soil of our British ally, there to carry on the fight against our enemy on land, on sea, and in the air.

The record of this Polish Army, of our Navy, and our Air Force is worthy of the heroic ages of history. It is, above all, the tangible proof of that undaunted spirit of patriotism and national consciousness which has always been and which, I firmly believe, will never cease to be one of Poland's recognized traditions.

The entire Polish Nation loyally supports its President and its Government, and is determined to carry on this mortal struggle in defense of freedom and democracy to a victorious end.

These are, Mr. President, for the time being, the principal assets of the Poland of today, which I can spread before you, but which, I venture to believe, in the pure primitive splendor of what they represent in terms of human endurance and sacrifice, of patriotism, of national consciousness and dignity, of faith and vitality, constitute intrinsic values bearing the indelible hallmarks of Poland's immortality.

If at this time of our history, unworthy though I feel, I have accepted to undertake the great mission entrusted to me, it is because I have had once before the privilege of representing my country in the United States, of interpreting its deep traditional friendship for the American people, of explaining its policies to the Government of this great democracy.

In the course of my previous mission, I gained a fervent faith in the unfaltering spirit of justice and respect for the freedom of others, which characterizes the American people, whose President and Government so greatly contributed to the restoration of Poland's independence after the World War.

I feel sure that this great and responsive Nation will not fail Poland in this hour of her struggle for her right to live in peace, in dignity, and democratic freedom, and that once more it will assist in her liberation from ruthless Germanic and Soviet tyranny.

To the Polish Nation, you are, Mr. President, the generally recognized personification of active and creative democratic statesmanship.

To us Poles the necessity of your personal influence on the establishment of the new order in the world after the war, has become a dogma of faith in the future stability of peace and, indeed, the very survival of civilization.

I venture to express the hope that Your Excellency will not refuse to grant me the invaluable support of your confidence which, on my part, I shall ever do my very utmost to deserve.

(a) Reply of the President (Roosevelt), March 6, 1941 [1]

MR. AMBASSADOR:

In receiving the letters of recall of your predecessor, Count George Potocki, and the letters accrediting you as Ambassador Extraordinary and Plenipotentiary of the Republic of Poland to the United States, I wish to welcome you back to Washington. I have noted the expression of thanks of the President of Poland for the understanding and support shown your distinguished predecessor and wish to assure you of the same measure of support and cooperation.

The friendly mention made by the President of Poland of our efforts in behalf of the preservation of freedom is appreciated. It is with sympathetic interest that the valiant efforts which are being made by the Government of Poland toward this same end are being followed. The loyal support given these efforts by the Polish people is, I am sure, a matter of deep satisfaction to the President and Government of Poland.

That spirit of justice and respect for freedom of the people of the United States, which you observed on your previous mission to this country, I can assure you, still lives and can be relied upon by you in your efforts to fulfill your present mission.

(5) Radio Address of Her Majesty Queen Wilhelmina on the Occasion of the Commemoration of the Invasion of The Netherlands, London, May 10, 1941 [2]

A year ago the German armies invaded my country. For a year The Netherlands people have maintained resistance against the invader. For a year The Netherlands Empire, under the direction of the Government in London, has maintained the effort to overthrow the aggressor and to give freedom back to the Mother Country. Today, therefore, I would like to express to all English-speaking peoples, in the name of The Netherlands people, my confidence in final victory.

From Curaçao to New Guinea, The Netherlands Empire stands fast. Daily, Netherlands ships leave ports laden with war materials for the Allied cause. These are but one manifestation of the way in which The Netherlands Empire is participating in the effort of civilized peoples to check the aggressor. My people in The Netherlands have found other ways to hamper the invader, which I cannot tell here, but of which I daily have fresh evidence. While Hitler has succeeded in invading Dutch

[1] Department of State, Bulletin, IV, p. 251.
[2] From the Netherlands Legation, Washington.

territory, he has never succeeded in invading the Dutch spirit. The occupied and unoccupied territories know but one conviction — our resistance must be resolute. It must be absolute because negotiation or compromise is impossible with an enemy who introduced the lie and the myth as main instruments of policy, and whose false rule depends on the machinations of secret state police.

That you British share our conviction is shown not only by the words of your Prime Minister, but also by the conduct of every member of the British Empire. I have been deeply moved in England by the heroism which, since September, has become almost commonplace. Every civilian now is in the front line and considers it a privilege to be there. I have been touched too, if I may add a personal note, by the infinite sympathy which I and my family have received from the British people. At a time when your own safety and existence was so nearly threatened, you did not hesitate to extend to me your understanding and hospitality which neither I nor my people will ever forget.

Throughout the year spent among you I have been encouraged by the steady development of the war effort of the British dominions and colonies. The presence in England of Imperial troops is tangible proof of the unity which binds the British Empire. These troops called forth world admiration, too, by their fight at the side of the Greeks and the Yugoslavs against overwhelming odds. The tragic defeat of the Yugoslav and Greek armies saddened all, and the sympathy of my people is, I know, with the Greek people who are now suffering German occupation after long and heroic resistance.

But in this moment of grievous events in the East we are given fresh courage from the West where the great American people are laboring to equip us for the fight. The Netherlands people of Europe can only offer active resistance with those forces that escaped from the aggressor's power: cruisers, destroyers, submarines, mine sweepers, merchant ships, soldiers and pilots. The Netherlands East Indies can continue freely to strengthen the army, the navy, and the air forces.

I want to express gratitude to the great people of the United States of America and their noble president, for they show a deep understanding of the world situation by supplying all the needs of the people already fighting against aggression.

Mr. Stimson's speech encouraged us all by showing how clearly the United States understood its opportunity. The American people understand too well the principles of freedom for which we fight not to give all the help needed.

American citizens of Dutch origin, are, of course, primarily good

American citizens, but at the same time I am proud that they feel a kinship with the country of their ancestors and I know this feeling deepens the affection existing between the two peoples.

The ties already binding the two nations have been further strengthened by the fact that my daughter, now living in the vast and beautiful part of the British Empire — Canada— has been able to express to President Roosevelt the principles we both share.

We are grateful for the sympathy they — the Americans — already have shown us in so many ways, particularly for help in the production and transport of war materials, and I am confident their help in our struggle against the aggressor will steadily increase for they understand the aggressor's "new order" can only be based on slavery.

They understand, too, that we shall need their help even more after victory and that our two countries need to cooperate in world reconstruction that we may together promote the common weal.

(6) *Resolution of the Governments Engaged in the Fight Against Aggression, London, June 12, 1941* [1]

The Governments of the United Kingdom of Great Britain and Northern Ireland, Canada, Australia, New Zealand and South Africa, the Government of Belgium, the Provisional Czecho-Slovak Government, the Governments of Greece, Luxemburg, The Netherlands, Norway, Poland, and Yugoslavia, and the representatives of General de Gaulle, leader of Free Frenchmen,

Engaged together in the fight against aggression,

Are resolved:

(1) That they will continue the struggle against German or Italian aggression until victory is won, and will mutually assist each other in this struggle to the utmost of their respective capacities;

(2) That there can be no settled peace and prosperity so long as free peoples are coerced by violence into submission to domination by Germany or her associates, or live under the threat of such coercion;

(3) That the only true basis of enduring peace is the willing cooperation of free peoples in a world in which, relieved of the menace of aggression, all may enjoy economic and social security; and that it is their intention to work together, and with other free peoples, both in war and peace to this end.

[1] *The Times* (London), June 13, 1941, p. 4.

(7) *Address by the Prime Minister of the United Kingdom (Churchill) at the Meeting of the Allied Governments, London, June 12, 1941* [1]

In the twenty-second month of the war against Nazism we meet here in this old Palace of St. James's, itself not unscarred by the fire of the enemy, in order to proclaim the high purposes and resolves of the lawful constitutional Governments of Europe whose countries have been over-run; and we meet here also to cheer the hope of free men and free peoples throughout the world. Here before us on the table lie the title-deeds of ten nations or States whose soil has been invaded and polluted and whose men, women, and children lie prostrate or writhing under the Hitler yoke. But here also, duly authorized by the Parliament and democracy of Britain, are gathered the servants of the ancient British Monarchy and the accredited representatives of the British Dominions beyond the seas, of Canada, Australia, New Zealand, and South Africa, of the Empire of India, of Burma, and of our Colonies in every quarter of the globe. They have drawn their swords in this cause. They will never let them fall till life is gone or victory is won.

Here we meet, while from across the Atlantic Ocean the hammers and lathes of the United States signal in a rising hum their message of encouragement and their promise of swift and evergrowing aid.

What tragedies, what horrors, what crimes have Hitler and all that Hitler stands for brought upon Europe and the world. The ruins of Warsaw, of Rotterdam, of Belgrade are monuments which will long recall to the future generations the outrage of the unopposed air-bombing applied with calculated scientific cruelty to helpless populations. Here in London and throughout the cities of our island, and in Ireland, there may also be seen the marks of devastation. They are being repaid, and presently they will be more than repaid.

But far worse than these visible injuries is the misery of the conquered peoples. We see them hounded, terrorized, exploited. Their manhood by the million is forced to work under conditions indistinguishable in many cases from actual slavery. Their goods and chattels are pillaged or filched for worthless money. Their homes, their daily life, are pried into and spied upon by the all-pervading system of secret political police which, having reduced the Germans themselves to abject docility, now stalks the streets and byways of a dozen lands. Their religious faiths are affronted, persecuted, or oppressed in the interests of a fantastic paganism devised to perpetuate the worship and sustain the tyranny of one abominable creature. Their traditions, their culture, their

[1] *The Times* (London), June 13, 1941, p. 4.

laws, their institutions, social and political alike, are suppressed by force or undermined by subtle, coldly planned intrigue.

The prisons of the Continent no longer suffice. The concentration camps are overcrowded. Every dawn the German volleys crack. Czechs, Poles, Dutchmen, Norwegians, Yugoslavs and Greeks, Frenchmen, Belgians, Luxemburgers, make the great sacrifice for faith and country. A vile race of Quislings — to use the new word which will carry the scorn of mankind down the centuries — is hired to fawn upon the conqueror, to collaborate in his designs, and to enforce his rule upon their fellow-countrymen, while grovelling low themselves.

Such is the plight of once glorious Europe, and such are the atrocities against which we are in arms.

It is upon this foundation that Hitler, with his tattered lackey, Mussolini, at his tail and Admiral Darlan frisking by his side, pretends to build out of hatred, appetite and racial assertion a new order for Europe. Never did so mocking a fantasy obsess the mind of mortal man.

We cannot tell what the course of this fell war will be as it spreads remorseless through ever-wider regions.

We know it will be hard, we expect it will be long; we cannot predict or measure its episodes or its tribulations. But one thing is certain, one thing is sure, one thing stands out stark and undeniable, massive and unassailable, for all the world to see.

It will not be by German hands that the structure of Europe will be rebuilt or the union of the European family achieved. In every country into which the German armies and the Nazi police have broken there has sprung up from the soil a hatred of the German name and a contempt for the Nazi creed which the passage of hundreds of years will not efface from human memory. We cannot yet see how deliverance will come, or when it will come, but nothing is more certain than that every trace of Hitler's footsteps, every stain of his infected and corroding fingers will be sponged and purged and, if need be, blasted from the surface of the earth.

We are here to affirm and fortify our union in that ceaseless and unwearying effort which must be made if the captive peoples are to be set free. A year ago His Majesty's Government was left alone to face the storm, and to many of our friends and enemies alike it may have seemed that our days too were numbered, and that Britain and its institutions would sink forever beneath the verge. But I may with some pride remind Your Excellencies that, even in that dark hour when our Army was disorganized and almost weaponless, when scarcely a gun or a tank remained in Britain, when almost all our stores and ammunition had been lost in France, never for one moment did the British people dream of making peace with the conqueror, and never for a moment did they despair of the common cause. On the contrary, we proclaimed at that very time to all men, not only to ourselves, our determination not to make peace until every one of the ravaged and enslaved countries was liberated and until the Nazi domination was broken and destroyed.

See how far we have traveled since those breathless days of June a year ago. Our solid, stubborn strength has stood the awful test. We are masters of our own air and now reach out in ever-growing retribution upon the enemy. The Royal Navy holds the seas. The Italian fleet cowers diminished in harbor, the German Navy is largely crippled or sunk. The murderous raids upon our ports, cities, and factories have been powerless to quench the spirit of the British nation, to stop our national life, or check the immense expansion of our war industry. The food and arms from across the oceans are coming safely in. Full provision to replace all sunken tonnage is being made here, and still more by our friends in the United States. We are becoming an armed community. Our land forces are being perfected in equipment and training.

Hitler may turn and trample this way and that through tortured Europe. He may spread his course far and wide, and carry his curse with him: he may break into Africa or into Asia. But it is here, in this island fortress, that he will have to reckon in the end. We shall strive to resist by land and sea. We shall be on his track wherever he goes. Our air power will continue to teach the German homeland that war is not all loot and triumph.

We shall aid and stir the people of every conquered country to resistance and revolt. We shall break up and derange every effort which Hitler makes to systematize and consolidate his subjugations. He will find no peace, no rest, no halting place, no parley. And if, driven to desperate hazards, he attempts the invasion of the British Isles, as well he may, we shall not flinch from the supreme trial. With the help of God, of which we must all feel daily conscious, we shall continue steadfast in faith and duty till our task is done.

This, then is the message which we send forth to-day to all the States and nations, bound or free, to all the men in all the lands who care for freedom's cause. To our Allies and well-wishers in Europe, to our American friends and helpers drawing ever closer in their might across the ocean this is the message — Lift up your hearts. All will come right. Out of the depths of sorrow and sacrifice will be born again the glory of mankind.

(8) *Resumption of Ethiopian Government. The President (Roosevelt) to the Emperor of Ethiopia (Haile Selassie), May 20, 1941* [1]

The Emperor of Ethiopia was driven out of Addis Ababa, his capital, by the Italian invaders in May 1936 and, after some wandering, made his residence in England. In December 1940 the Middle East Command of the British Common-wealth, consisting of Australian, British, Indian, South African and Sudanese troops, began a campaign against the enemy in "Italian East Africa," in which the Ethiopians took an increasing part. The Emperor joined his own forces and on May 5, 1941, entered the capital, from which the Italians had been expelled. The United States took positive notice of this event on the day when the main Italian army under the Duke of Aosta surrendered.

MAY 20, 1941.

I have received Your Majesty's message [2] informing me of your return to Addis Ababa, and I assure you of the satisfaction with which I have received these tidings. On behalf of the people and Government of the United States I have great pleasure in extending to Your Majesty my most sincere felicitations on this notable occasion and my best wishes for Your Majesty's health and happiness.

FRANKLIN D. ROOSEVELT

(9) *Costs of Occupation by German Authorities. Statement to the House of Commons by the British Under Secretary of State for Foreign Affairs (Butler), March 19, 1941* [3]

The burden imposed on the occupied territories can be reckoned only partly in terms of money paid by the Governments of the occupied countries to the German Government. The greater part of the burden consists essentially of various obligations exacted in kind.

In the first place, the territories have to contribute directly to the cost of the army of occupation; this charge includes generous pay for the troops. The following are the estimated annual costs of occupation in the Western occupied territories, the sterling equivalents being based on the rates of exchange prior to the occupation. The figures must be treated with reserve in the case of Holland.

[1] Department of State, *Bulletin*, IV, p. 635.
[2] Not printed herein.
[3] *The Times* (London), March 20, 1941, p. 3; Parliamentary Debates, 5th Series House of Commons, vol. 370, col. 138.

	TOTAL (in millions)	TOTAL	PER HEAD OF POPULATION
Norway	1,200 crowns	£68,000,000	£25
Denmark	540 crowns	£26,000,000	£8
Belgium	9,000 francs	£75,000,000	£8
Holland	405 guilders	£54,000,000	£6
France	14,600 francs	£827,000,000	£20

It will thus be seen that the German occupation is estimated to be costing the Western occupied territories annually a sum in the neighborhood of £1,050,000,000. In addition Germany receives certain amounts, estimates of which are not yet available, from Poland, Czechoslovakia, Rumania and Bulgaria. Relatively, Norway suffers the heaviest burden per head of population, which amounts to over one-third of her prewar national income. It may also be noted that the maximum annual demand from Germany ever contemplated under the Young Plan was £125,000,000, which, even taking into account the change in the sterling price of gold since that date, amounts to less than one-third of the present French payment.

The second form of burden arising out of the German occupation is that the occupied territories are obliged to send to Germany more goods than they receive from her in return. This surplus of exports is paid for in blocked marks from which no benefit is, or is likely to be, derived. Under this heading may be reckoned the value of goods requisitioned in the country by the German authorities and sent to Germany, including articles belonging to individuals, such as gold and jewelry. This second type of burden is considerably less now than it was in 1940 owing to the fact that the territories have to a large extent been denuded of readily exportable surpluses. Even so, the total annual loss to the Western occupied territories may still be estimated at about £100,000,000 a year.

The estimated total burden is thus in the neighborhood of £1,150,000,000 a year, and this does not take into account the many indirect losses caused to the territories concerned by the German occupation for which no estimates are available.

CHAPTER V

TRADE

1. BASIC POLICY OF THE UNITED STATES

(1) *Radio Address by the Secretary of State (Hull), May 18, 1941* [1]

[Excerpt]

Tonight we inaugurate another annual National Foreign-Trade Week. Again, as a year ago, it comes in the midst of war. You know as well as I that now there is little use in our talking about and planning for foreign trade unless the outcome of the war is favorable to the free peoples of the world. For trade means free bargaining to mutual advantage. To us it does not mean exploitation by military cliques backed by cannon. And so, for the present, our foreign trade consists more and more, and will consist more and more, of making and placing in the hands of nations which are resisting unlawful attack the tools of self-defense. This trade, like all trade, is futile if the goods produced do not reach those for whom they are intended.

We are a practical people. When we set ourselves to a task we finish it. We have set ourselves to the task of arming and supplying those whose successful defense is vital to our security. I have said before, and I repeat: we will not permit this purpose to be frustrated. We will find a way to insure that the weapons pouring in ever greater volume from our factories will reach the hands which eagerly await them. Only as we stand strong and united in this purpose, can we look forward to a brighter day.

. . . .

These are obvious dangers that lie immediately ahead. But they are not the only dangers. To get a more complete picture of what they involve, it is necessary to envisage the kind of an economic world that would exist if the would-be conquerors were to win. Their current pronouncements and practices provide an ample warning on that score.

[1] Department of State, *Bulletin*, IV, p. 573. A statement by the President was made public on May 17, *ibid.* See Department of Commerce, Bureau of Foreign and Domestic Commerce, *Impact of the War upon the Trade Policies of Foreign Countries*, by Henry Chalmers (International Reference Service, I, No. 6, March 1941).

The key to their economic program is contained in one simple word — conquest. Every territory that they conquer is reduced forthwith to an economic master-and-slave relationship. The economic structure of the enslaved country is forcibly reshaped and systematically subordinated to the economy of the ruling country. Within the entire tributary area, autarchy or economic self-sufficiency is set up as the central feature of economic policy. At the center of this widely dispersed web of captive nations, the master country wields its vastly enlarged powers in an unceasing effort to ensnare, overwhelm, and enslave every remaining free nation in the world.

The tragic experience of the conquered countries of Europe provides unassailable evidence of how this system is applied in the field of trade. Under it, trade is reduced essentially to enforced barter. The would-be conqueror forces delivery to him, at his own price, of the goods he wants; and enforces this arrangement by every device of discrimination and arbitrary control. There is not the slightest pretense of promoting mutually profitable trade with other countries upon the basis of equality and fair-dealing. It is a system based upon the principle, not of economic cooperation, but of economic spoliation.

In the face of these facts, no one need be in doubt as to the situation that would confront this Nation, in the realm of trade as elsewhere, in the event of an Axis victory. For the past seven years our Government has taken the leadership in an effort to re-open the channels of international trade and thus to assist in world economic restoration, with resulting political stability, from which all countries, great and small, would benefit. It has proceeded throughout upon broad principles of cooperation and fair-dealing, and has recognized that only mutually profitable trade can be truly beneficial and enduring. These principles are broad enough to include every country willing to cooperate in a program of economic peace. By the same token they stand at the opposite pole from the predatory policies and methods of the totalitarians. Between the two systems there can be no workable adjustment.

After the first World War an attempt was made to reorganize the world on a sound basis. New institutions were created, and new methods of cooperation were established. All peoples shared the hope that a new era in international relations had begun.

Unhappily, shortly after the close of the World War, power fell into the hands of groups which advocated political and economic nationalism in their most extreme forms. The inevitable effects, politically, economically, and socially, during the years that followed were utterly disastrous. The outcome was division and weakening, and final break-down, of the necessary international foundation on which peace is based.

Knowing these facts as we do, it is none too early to lay down at least some of the principles by which policies must be guided at the conclusion of the war, to press for a broad program of world economic reconstruction and to consider tentative plans for the application of those policies.

The main principles, as proven by experience, are few and simple:

1. Extreme nationalism must not again be permitted to express itself in excessive trade restrictions.

2. Non-discrimination in international commercial relations must be the rule, so that international trade may grow and prosper.

3. Raw-material supplies must be available to all nations without discrimination.

4. International agreements regulating the supply of commodities must be so handled as to protect fully the interest of the consuming countries and their people.

5. The institutions and arrangements of international finance must be so set up that they lend aid to the essential enterprises and the continuous development of all countries, and permit the payment through processes of trade consonant with the welfare of all countries.

Measures taken to give effect to these principles must be freely open to every nation which desires a peaceful life in a world at peace and is willing to cooperate in maintaining that peace.

Such a program has strength and endurance. It will stand long after the war-built arrangements forced on disheartened or imprisoned peoples by military conquest have fallen to pieces and have vanished utterly.

There still are people who do not see that if, when the present conflict ends, we do not have a system of open trade, they will not be able either to buy or to sell except on terms really laid down by the military forces and political authorities of the countries with which they have to deal.

Unless a system of open trade becomes firmly established, there will be chronic political instability and recurrent economic collapse. There will never be peace in any real sense of the term.

In the final reckoning, the problem becomes one of establishing the foundations of an international order in which independent nations cooperate freely with each other for their mutual gain — of a world order, not new but renewed, which liberates rather than enslaves.

We shall not be able to do this until we have a world free from imminent military danger and clear of malign political intrigue. At present the world is scourged by both. We can expect no healthy development until the menace of conquest has been brought to an end. Only then will the time have arrived when steel is valued, not in terms of the bombs that can be made of it, but in terms of the instruments of peaceful life into which it can be forged; and when foreign trade has reverted again from cargoes of weapons and explosives to commodities that nourish and heal and enrich their consumers.

This Nation is resolved to evade no issues and to face harsh facts. We believe that there can be created a safer and more prosperous world. We have the tools — the resources, the brains, the hands — with which to help make it such. But first the tide of force must be turned back. Once that is done, we and other nations can reestablish an open, cooperative, economic life in which trade may increase, economic welfare may grow, civilization may advance, and the peaceful and benevolent instincts of masses of now prostrate people may once more flourish in the really worthwhile ways of life.

2. TREATIES AND AGREEMENTS OF THE UNITED STATES CONTAINING THE MOST–FAVORED–NATION CLAUSE [1]

The following countries are those with which there were in force on July 31, 1940, treaties and other agreements of the United States containing the most-favored-nation clause governing customs duties, regulations, and facilities and other charges affecting commerce.

The instruments listed are reciprocal, that is, the most-favored-nation clause applies equally to each party to the contract, except in the two cases of Morocco and Muscat, in which the clause is obligatory on the other party but not on the United States. Under the most-favored-nation clause in a bilateral treaty or agreement concerning commerce, each of the parties undertakes to extend to the goods of the country of the other party treatment no less favorable than the treatment which it accords to like goods originating in any third country. The unconditional form of the most-favored-nation clause provides that any advantage, favor, privilege, or immunity which one of the parties may accord to the goods of any third country shall be extended immediately and unconditionally to the like goods originating in the country of the other party. In this form only does the clause provide for complete and continuous nondiscriminatory treatment. Under the conditional form of the clause, neither party is obligated to extend immediately and unconditionally to the like products of the other party the advantages which it may accord to products of third countries in return for reciprocal concessions; it is obligated to extend such advantages only if and when the other party grants concessions "equivalent" to the concessions made by such third countries. When one part of a treaty may be terminated in a different manner from other parts, the reference is to the part containing the most-favored-nation clause. Where such a clause is contained in more than one treaty or agreement with a country, the reference is to the later in date.

Instruments are classified as treaties when they are ratified with the consent of the Senate; as Executive agreements when they are acts of the Executive without reference to the Senate.

The treaties of the United States relating to A and B mandates, with countries mandatories under the League of Nations, provide that the commerce of the

[1] Department of State, *Bulletin*, III, p. 96.

United States shall receive in the mandated areas the treatment accorded to the commerce of countries members of the League of Nations. This is essentially most-favored-nation treatment. These treaties are with Belgium, for Ruanda-Urundi; France, for Syria and the Lebanon, the Cameroun, and Togoland; and Great Britain, for Palestine and Trans-Jordan, the Cameroons, Tanganyika, and Togoland. The United States has not entered into treaties relating to C-mandated territories except with Japan, which provides for the same treatment in the mandated area that is accorded in Japan under existing treaties.

(1) *Reciprocal Trade Agreements Signed under the Trade Agreements Act of 1934* [1]

COUNTRY	DATE IN FORCE	WHEN AND HOW TERMINABLE
Belgo-Luxemburg Economic Union. (E. A. S. 75)	May 1, 1935	Six months' notice, or in special circumstances on shorter notice.
Brazil . . . . . (E. A. S. 82)	Jan. 1, 1936	Six months' notice, or in special circumstances on shorter notice.
Canada . . . . (E. A. S. 149)	Jan. 1, 1939 (provisionally) June 17, 1939 (definitively)	Six months' notice, or in special circumstances on shorter notice. Initial period until Dec. 31, 1941.
Canada [2]	Jan. 1, 1940 (provisionally)	
Colombia . . . . (E. A. S. 89)	May 20, 1936	Six months' notice, or in special circumstances on shorter notice.
Costa Rica . . . (E. A. S. 102)	Aug. 2, 1937	Six months' notice, or in special circumstances on shorter notice. Initial period three years.
Czechoslovakia [3] . . (E. A. S. 147)	Apr. 16, 1938 (provisionally)	Six months' notice, or in special circumstances on shorter notice. Initial period one year.
Ecuador [4] . . . . . (E. A. S. 133)	Oct. 23, 1938	Six months' notice.
El Salvador . . . . (E. A. S. 101)	May 31, 1937	Six months' notice, or in special circumstances on shorter notice. Initial period three years.
Finland . . . . . (E. A. S. 97)	Nov. 2, 1936	Six months' notice, or in special circumstances on shorter notice. Initial period three years.
France [5] and its colonies, dependencies, and protectorates other than Morocco. (E. A. S. 146)	June 15, 1936 (provisionally)	Six months' notice, or in special circumstances on shorter notice.

[1] The trade agreement with Cuba (E. A. S. 67), effective Sept. 3, 1934, does not contain a most-favored-nation clause. It is the only agreement in force for the United States which provides for preferential treatment. A supplementary trade agreement entered into force Dec. 23, 1939 (E. A. S. 165).

Country	Date in Force	When and How Terminable
Guatemala . . . . (E. A. S. 92)	June 15, 1936	Six months' notice, or in special circumstance on shorter notice. Initial period three years.
Haiti . . . . . . (E. A. S. 78)	June 3, 1935	Six months' notice.
Honduras . . . . . (E. A. S. 86)	Mar. 2, 1936	Six months' notice, or in special circumstances on shorter notice.
Netherlands, including Netherlands Indies, Netherlands Guiana, and Netherlands West Indian Islands. (E. A. S. 100)	Feb. 1, 1936 (arts. I–XVI) May 8, 1937 (entire agreement)	Six months' notice, or in special circumstances on shorter notice.
Nicaragua [6] . . . . (E. A. S. 95)	Oct. 1, 1936	Six months' notice, or in special circumstances on shorter notice. Initial period three years.
Sweden . . . . . . (E. A. S. 79)	Aug. 5, 1935	Six months' notice, or in special circumstances on shorter notice. Initial period three years.
Switzerland . . . . (E. A. S. 90)	Feb. 15, 1936 (arts. I–XVII) June 6, 1936 (entire agreement)	Six months' notice, or in special circumstances on shorter notice.
Turkey . . . . . . (E. A. S. 163)	May 5, 1939 (provisionally) Nov. 20, 1939 (definitively)	Two months' notice on Dec. 31, 1939, Dec. 31, 1940, or Dec. 31, 1941. Six months' notice, or in special circumstances on shorter notice.
United Kingdom . . (E. A. S. 164)	Jan. 1, 1939 (provisionally) Dec. 24, 1939 (definitively)	Six months' notice, or in special circumstances on shorter notice. Initial period until Dec. 31, 1941.
Venezuela . . . . . (E. A. S. 180)	Dec. 16, 1939 (provisionally) Dec. 14, 1940 (definitively)	Six months' notice, or in special circumstances on shorter notice. Initial period one year.

[2] Supplementary trade agreement re: certain foxes, fox furs, and fox-fur articles.

[3] The rates of duty proclaimed in connection with this agreement have been terminated effective Apr. 22, 1939, by Presidential proclamation of Mar. 23, 1939. The agreement remains in effect but its operation has been suspended.

[4] Under the provisions of art. VII Ecuador imposed quantitative restrictions on certain articles as a temporary measure.

[5] This agreement supersedes the agreement on quotas of May 31, 1932, modified Jan. 21, 1935.

[6] On Mar. 10, 1938, reciprocal tariff concessions ceased to be effective; remainder of agreement in force.

(2) *Treaties in Force Containing Unconditional Most-Favored-Nation Clause* [1]

Country	Date in Force	When and How Terminable
China . . . . . . (T. S. 773)	June 20, 1929	Contains no provision regarding termination.
Danzig, Free City of . (T. S. 865)	Mar. 24, 1934	Six months after notice by either party.
El Salvador . . . (T. S. 827)	Sept. 5, 1930	One year after notice by either party, but not before Sept. 5, 1940.
Estonia . . . . . (T. S. 736)	May 22, 1926	One year after notice by either party.
Finland . . . . . (T. S. 868)	Aug. 10, 1934	Six months after notice by either party.
Honduras . . . . (T. S. 764)	July 19, 1928	One year after notice by either party.
Hungary . . . . (T. S. 748)	Oct. 4, 1926	One year after notice by either party.
Iraq . . . . . . (T. S. 960)	June 19, 1940	One year after notice by either party but not before June 19, 1943.
Latvia . . . . . (T. S. 765)	July 25, 1928	One year after notice by either party.
Liberia . . . . . (T. S. 956)	Nov. 21, 1939	One year after notice by either party but not before Nov. 21, 1944.
Morocco . . . . (T. S. 244–2)	Jan. 28, 1837 [2]	Twelve months after notice by either party.
Muscat . . . . . . (In force also with Zanzibar [4]) (T. S. 247)	Sept. 30, 1835 [3]	Contains no provision regarding termination.
Norway . . . . (T. S. 852)	Sept. 13, 1932	One year after notice by either party.
Poland . . . . . (T. S. 862)	July 9, 1933	Six months after notice by either party.
Thailand (Siam) . . . (T. S. 940)	Oct. 1, 1938	One year after notice by either party. Initial period five years.
Turkey . . . . . (T. S. 813)	Apr. 22, 1930	One year after notice by either party.
Yugoslavia . . . . (T. S. 319)	Nov. 15, 1882	One year after notice by either party.
Zanzibar . . . . (See Muscat)	. . . . . .	.

[1] The numbers in parentheses in this and the following tables refer to United States Treaty Series and Executive Agreement Series.

[2] Date of ratification by the President of the United States; no date is specified in treaty for its entry into force and no ratification by Morocco was necessary.

[3] Date of exchange of ratifications; the treaty does not specify the date of its entry into force.

[4] Accepted by Zanzibar after separation from Muscat, Oct. 20, 1879.

(3) *Executive Agreements in Force Containing Unconditional Most-Favored-Nation Clause*

COUNTRY	DATE IN FORCE	WHEN AND HOW TERMINABLE
Albania . . . . . (not printed)	July 28, 1922 [1]	Contains no provision regarding termination.
Bulgaria . . . . (E. A. S. 41)	Aug. 18, 1932	Three months' notice by either party or by legislative action of either party.
Chile [2] . . . . . . (E. A. S. 119)	Feb. 1, 1938 (provisionally) Jan. 5, 1940 (definitively)	Until superseded by a more comprehensive commercial agreement or by a definitive treaty of friendship, commerce, and navigation, or 30 days' notice by either party.
Dominican Republic . (T. S. 700)	Sept. 25, 1924	Thirty days after notice by either party, or by legislative action of either party.
Egypt . . . . . . (E. A. S. 5)	May 24, 1930	Ninety days after notice by either party, or by legislative action of either party.
Greece . . . . . . (E. A. S. 137)	Jan. 1, 1939	Until superseded by a more comprehensive commercial agreement or by a definitive treaty of commerce and navigation, or 30 days' notice by either party.
Iran . . . . (E. A. S. 19)	May 10, 1928 [3]	Thirty days after notice by either party, or by legislative action of either party.
Italy (E. A. S. 116) .	Dec. 16, 1937	Thirty days' notice by either party.
Lithuania . . . . (T. S. 742)	July 10, 1926	Thirty days after notice by either party, or by legislative action of either party.
Rumania . . . . . (E. A. S. 8)	Sept. 1, 1930	Thirty days after notice by either party, or by legislative action of either party.
Saudi Arabia . . . (E. A. S. 53)	Nov. 7, 1933	Upon entry into force of a definitive treaty of commerce and navigation, or by legislative action of the United States.
Spain [4] (T. S. 758–A) .	Nov. 27, 1927	Three months' notice by either party.
Soviet Union . . . (E. A. S. 105 and 151)	Aug. 6, 1939	Effective for 12 months.
Venezuela . . . . . (E. A. S. 180) . .	Dec. 16, 1939	Until supplanted by the entry into force of the reciprocal trade agreement signed Nov. 6, 1939.

[1] Date of official recognition by the United States.

[2] This agreement was continued provisionally in effect by an exchange of notes signed Feb. 20 and 24, 1939 (Executive Agreement Series 144). By legislative action of the Chilean Government it was brought into definitive force as of Jan. 5, 1940.

[3] Retroactively.   [4] Extending previous regime.

457

(4) *Treaties in Force Containing Conditional Most-Favored-Nation Clause* [1]

COUNTRY	DATE IN FORCE	WHEN AND HOW TERMINABLE
Argentina . . . . . (T. S. 4)	Dec. 20, 1854 [2]	Contains no provision regarding termination.
Belgium . . . . . (T. S. 28)	June 11, 1875	Twelve months after notice by either party.
Bolivia . . . . . . (T. S. 32)	Nov. 9, 1862	One year after notice by either party.
Borneo . . . . . . (T. S. 33)	July 11, 1853 [2]	Contains no provision regarding termination.
Colombia . . . . . (T. S. 54)	June 10, 1848 [2]	Twelve months after notice by either party.
Costa Rica . . . . (T. S. 62)	May 26, 1852 [2]	Contains no provision regarding termination of covering most-favored-nation clause; 12 months after notice by either party, *vis-à-vis* other equality-of-treatment provisions.
Denmark [3] . . . . (T. S. 65)	Apr. 26, 1826 [4]	One year after notice by either party.
Ethiopia . . . . . (T. S. 647)	Sept. 19, 1914	One year after notice by either party, but not before Sept. 19, 1948.
Great Britain [5] . . . (Ireland also) (T. S. 110) Ireland (See Great Britain)	July 3, 1815 [4]	Twelve months after notice by either party.
Paraguay . . . . . (T. S. 272)	Mar. 7, 1860	Twelve months after notice by either party.

(5) *Executive Agreement in Force Containing Conditional Most-Favored-Nation Clause* [1]

COUNTRY	DATE IN FORCE	WHEN AND HOW TERMINABLE
Portugal . . . . . (T. S. 514½)	June 28, 1910	Contains no provision regarding termination.

[1] In accordance with a provision of the Trade Agreements Act of 1934, which gives effect to the unconditional most-favored-nation principle, the United States extends the benefits of concessions granted in trade agreements to all countries which do not discriminate against the trade of the United States, regardless of the nature or existence of obligations to extend most-favored-nation treatment to them.

[2] Date of exchange of ratifications.

[3] Abrogated by notice, Apr. 15, 1856; renewed by convention of which ratifications were exchanged Jan. 12, 1858.

[4] The date given is that of signature. Though subject to ratification, the treaty provides that it shall be in force from its signature.

[5] Extended by conventions of Oct. 20, 1818 (T. S. 112), and Aug. 6, 1827 (T. S. 117).

3. RECIPROCAL TRADE AGREEMENTS PROGRAM

A. Proposed Negotiations with the Argentine and Uruguayan Republics

See *Documents, II, 1939–40*, p. 471, for the previous negotiations, begun August 23, 1939 and discontinued January 8, 1940.

Notices of intention to negotiate trade agreements with the Argentine and Uruguayan Republics were issued on May 13, 1941, when the list of products to come under consideration for the possible granting of concessions by the United States was announced. The lists were more extensive than in the previous negotiations. The Committee for Reciprocity Information received briefs relating to articles on the lists until June 12 and opened hearings June 23.

(1) *Trade Agreement Negotiations with Argentina. Public Notice Given by the Department of State, May 13, 1941* [1]

Pursuant to section 4 of an act of Congress approved June 12, 1934, entitled "An Act to Amend the Tariff Act of 1930," as extended by Public Resolution 61, approved April 12, 1940, and to Executive Order 6750, of June 27, 1934, I hereby give notice of intention to negotiate a trade agreement with the Government of Argentina.

All presentations of information and views in writing and applications for supplemental oral presentation of views with respect to the negotiation of such agreement should be submitted to the Committee for Reciprocity Information in accordance with the announcement of this date issued by that Committee concerning the manner and dates for the submission of briefs and applications, and the time set for public hearings.

CORDELL HULL
Secretary of State

WASHINGTON, D. C.,
May 13, 1941.

B. Modification of Existing Agreements

(1) *Importations of Silver and Black Foxes and Fox Furs from Canada, December 18, 1940* [2]

On December 18, 1940 the President issued his proclamation of the Supplementary Trade Agreement between the United States and Canada concerning silver or black foxes and silver- or black-fox furs and skins

---

[1] Department of State, *Bulletin*, IV, p. 680.
[2] *Ibid.*, III, p. 575; also see *ibid.*, p. 553, 591; Executive Agreement Series 184.

and related articles which was signed by the Secretary of State and the Minister of Canada on December 13, 1940.

The agreement proclaimed on December 18, 1940 will enter provisionally into force on December 20, 1940 and from the latter date will take the place of the supplementary trade agreement relating to silver- or black-fox furs and skins which was signed and proclaimed on December 30, 1939. The new agreement will enter definitively into force on the day following the date of the exchange of the President's proclamation and the ratification of His Britannic Majesty.[1]

(2) *Importation of Oranges into Canada. The Secretary of State (Hull) to the Canadian Chargé d'Affaires ad interim (Mahoney), March 15, 1941* [2]

Adjustment of commerce through a trade agreement was illustrated by an agreement through exchange of notes with Canada whereby the Canadian tariff was changed to admit oranges free of duty during the months January to July instead of December through April as formerly. A Canadian Order-in-Council of April 1, 1941 made the change effective.

DEPARTMENT OF STATE,
Washington, March 15, 1941.

SIR:

Acknowledgment is made of the receipt of your note No. 102 of March 3, 1941, informing me that the Canadian Government has decided to exercise the right provided for in Schedule I of the new trade agreement between the United States and Canada, signed at Washington on November 17, 1938, to substitute for Tariff Item No. 101, as it stands in that agreement, the following:

Oranges, n.o.p.: —
January to July, inclusive . . . . Free
August to December, inclusive, per cubic foot 35 cts.

In reply you are informed that this Government has no objection to the exercise by the Canadian Government of this right of substitution at this time.

Accept [etc.]

For the Secretary of State:

DEAN ACHESON

[1] The letter of the President to the Secretary of the Treasury relating to the duties and other import restrictions proclaimed in connection with the trade agreement is printed in 5 *Fed. Reg.*, p. 5215 (December 21, 1940).

[2] Department of State, *Bulletin*, IV, p. 426. The proposing note of March 3, 1941, omitted here, is given at that place.

(3) *Termination of Concession on Handkerchiefs Imported from Switzerland, January 1, 1941* [1]

The President on November 28, 1940 signed a proclamation terminating in part, as of January 1, 1941, the concession on handkerchiefs contained in item 1529 (*b*) of schedule II of the reciprocal trade agreement between the United States and Switzerland signed January 9, 1936. The effect of the proclamation will be to exclude from the benefit of the reduced rates of duty provided for in this item handkerchiefs appliquéd by hand or having drawn work made by hand.

The action taken by the President was based on article XVI of the agreement, by which each country has reserved the right, after consultation with the Government of the other country, to withdraw or to modify the concession granted on any article, if, as a result of the extension of the concession to third countries, such countries obtain the major benefit of the concession and in consequence thereof an unduly large increase in imports takes place.

It has been ascertained that imports into the United States of handkerchiefs included in item 1529 (*b*) of schedule II of the agreement have been in major part from countries other than Switzerland and that imports of these handkerchiefs have increased very considerably over the levels obtaining before the entry into effect of the reduced duties established pursuant to the agreement. . . .

C. Allocation of Tariff Quotas

1. CRUDE PETROLEUM AND FUEL OIL

A supplementary proclamation was issued by the President on November 27, 1940 declaring that the definitive trade agreement with Venezuela signed November 6, 1939 would enter into full force on December 14, 1940.[2]

The conditions under which this quota became operative under the trade agreement with Venezuela are set forth in *Documents, II, 1939–40*, p. 483–6.

(1) *Summary of the Department of State Issued January 4, 1941* [3]

The President signed a proclamation on December 28, 1940, allocating for the period from January 1 to December 31, 1941, inclusive, among countries of supply, the quantity of crude petroleum and fuel oil entitled to a reduction in the rate of import tax under the trade agreement with Venezuela, signed on November 6, 1939. The agreement

---

[1] Department of State, *Bulletin*, III (November 30, 1940), p. 480. Executive Agreement Series No. 90.

[2] *Ibid.*, p. 481; Executive Agreement Series No. 810.   [3] *Ibid.*, IV, p. 31.

provides for a reduction in the import tax on crude petroleum, topped crude petroleum, and fuel oil derived from petroleum, including fuel oil known as gas oil, from ½¢ to ¼¢ per gallon on an annual quota of imports not in excess of 5 per cent of the total quantity of crude petroleum processed in refineries in the continental United States during the preceding calendar year. Imports above these amounts are taxable at ½¢ per gallon.

Under the terms of the proclamation, the shares of the total imports of such petroleum and fuel oil entitled to a reduction in the rate of import tax are allocated among countries of supply on the basis of the proportions of the total imports for consumption in the United States supplied during the calendar year 1939. The following allocations of the tariff quota are set forth in the proclamation:

United States of Venezuela	70.4 per cent
Kingdom of the Netherlands (its overseas territory)	21.3 per cent
Republic of Colombia	3.2 per cent
Other foreign countries	5.1 per cent

2. WHEAT AND WHEAT FLOUR

Wheat is the most important food crop, of which the United States produces approximately a fifth of the world's supply. The United States always has an export surplus and annually imports small percentages of its total distribution. Canada is also an exporter and the two adjacent markets react on each other. In the United States wheat is subject to the Agricultural Adjustment Act, sec. 22 of which [1] provides for limitations on importation under certain conditions. A report of the United States Tariff Commission to the President under that section on May 17, 1941 fixed quotas for import.[2] The report was based upon findings that, with annual production of 750,000,000 bushels for 1939 and 817,-000,000 bushels for 1940, the carry-over stock was rising and was estimated at 381,000,000 bushels for 1941 as compared with 295,000,000 for 1940. Over 90% of United States wheat imports come from Canada. The total quantity imported averaged 5,196,000 bushels for the period 1929–40.

(1) *Imposing Quotas on Imports of Wheat and Wheat Flour. Proclamation by the President (Roosevelt), May 28, 1941* [3]

BY THE PRESIDENT OF THE UNITED STATES OF AMERICA
A Proclamation [No. 2489]

WHEREAS pursuant to section 22 of the Agricultural Adjustment Act of 1933 as amended by section 31 of the act of August 24, 1935 (49 Stat.

[1] 49 Stat. 773, § 31; 49 Stat. 1152, § 5; 50 Stat. 246, § 1; 54 Stat. 17.
[2] United States Tariff Commission, Wheat and Wheat Flour; report to the President under Section 22 of the Agricultural Adjustment Act of 1933 as amended.
[3] Department of State, *Bulletin*, IV, p. 663; 6 *Fed. Reg.*, p. 2673.

730, 773), as amended by section 5 of the act of February 29, 1936 (49 Stat. 1148, 1152), as reenacted by section 1 of the act of June 3, 1937 (50 Stat. 246), and as further amended by the act of January 25, 1940 (54 Stat. 17), I caused the United States Tariff Commission to make an investigation to determine whether wheat or wheat products are being or are practically certain to be imported into the United States under such conditions and in sufficient quantities as to render or tend to render ineffective or materially interfere with the program undertaken with respect to wheat under the Soil Conservation and Domestic Allotment Act, as amended, or to reduce substantially the amount of any product processed in the United States from wheat; and

WHEREAS, in the course of the investigation, after due notice, hearings were held, at which parties interested were given opportunity to be present, to produce evidence, and to be heard, and, in addition to the hearings, the Commission made such investigation as it deemed necessary for a full disclosure and presentation of the facts; and

WHEREAS the Commission has made findings of fact and has transmitted to me a report of such findings and its recommendations based thereon, together with a transcript of the evidence submitted at the hearings, and has also transmitted a copy of such report to the Secretary of Agriculture:

NOW, THEREFORE, I, FRANKLIN D. ROOSEVELT, PRESIDENT OF THE UNITED STATES OF AMERICA, do hereby find, on the basis of such investigation and report, that wheat and wheat flour are practically certain to be imported into the United States under such conditions and in sufficient quantities as to tend to render ineffective and materially interfere with the program undertaken with respect to wheat under the Soil Conservation and Domestic Allotment Act, as amended, and to reduce substantially the amount of flour processed in the United States from wheat produced in the United States. Accordingly, I hereby proclaim that the total quantities of wheat and wheat flour originating in any of the countries named in the following table which may be entered, or withdrawn from warehouse, for consumption in any period of 12 months, commencing May twenty-ninth, shall not exceed the quantities shown opposite each of said countries, which quantities I hereby find and declare shown by the investigation to be necessary to prescribe in order that the entry of wheat and wheat flour will not render or tend to render ineffective or materially interfere with the program undertaken with respect to wheat under the Soil Conservation and Domestic Allotment Act, as amended, or reduce substantially the amount of any product processed in the United States from wheat produced in the United States:

| COUNTRY | IMPORT QUOTAS | |
	Wheat	Wheat Flour, Semolina, Crushed or Cracked Wheat, and Similar Wheat Products
	Bushels	*Pounds*
Canada	795,000	3,815,000
China	——	24,000
Hungary	——	13,000
Hong Kong	——	13,000
Japan	——	8,000
United Kingdom	100	75,000
Australia	——	1,000
Germany	100	5,000
Syria	100	5,000
New Zealand	——	1,000
Chile	——	1,000
Netherlands	100	1,000
Argentina	2,000	14,000
Italy	100	2,000
Cuba	——	12,000
France	1,000	1,000
Greece	——	1,000
Mexico	100	1,000
Panama	——	1,000
Uruguay	——	1,000
Poland and Danzig	——	1,000
Sweden	——	1,000
Yugoslavia	——	1,000
Norway	———	1,000
Canary Islands	——	1,000
Rumania	1,000	——
Guatemala	100	——
Brazil	100	——
Union of Soviet Socialist Republics	100	——
Belgium	100	——
Total	800,000	4,000,000

I find and declare that the total quantity of wheat or wheat flour which may be entered hereunder with respect to each of the countries named herein is not less than 50 per centum of the average annual quantity of wheat or wheat flour, respectively, which was imported from each of such countries during the period from January 1, 1929, to December 31, 1933, both dates inclusive, and that during the period named no wheat or wheat flour originating in any foreign countries other than those enumerated in the foregoing table was imported into the United States. No wheat or wheat flour originating in any other foreign country shall be permitted to be entered, or withdrawn from warehouse, for consumption during the effectiveness of this proclamation.

As used in this proclamation, "wheat flour" includes semolina, crushed or cracked wheat, and similar wheat products. Except as used in the first paragraph, "wheat" and "wheat flour" do not include wheat or wheat flour unfit for human consumption.

This proclamation shall become effective on the twenty-ninth day of May 1941.

IN WITNESS WHEREOF, I have hereunto set my hand and caused the Seal of the United States to be affixed.

DONE at the City of Washington this twenty-eighth day of May, in the year of our Lord nineteen hundred and forty-one, and of [SEAL] the Independence of the United States of America the one hundred and sixty-fifth.

FRANKLIN D. ROOSEVELT

By the President:
    CORDELL HULL
        Secretary of State.

(2) The American Minister to Canada (Moffat) to the Secretary of State for External Affairs of Canada, May 28, 1941 [1]

SIR:

I have been instructed to call to your attention the fact that, due to legislative action looking toward an increase in the income of American wheat producers there has been a substantial rise in the price of wheat in the United States. As a result of this development the spread between the price of wheat in the United States and the price of wheat in Canada has materially widened, thus making practicable an abnormal importation of Canadian wheat into the United States for consumption.

In view of the prospects of a record carry-over of wheat in the United States, prospects for a better than average wheat production this year and extremely limited possibilities for export, it is obvious that the United States is faced with a surplus problem of its own. Furthermore, the importation of appreciable quantities of wheat from Canada would materially interfere with the purposes of the wheat program of the United States set forth in the preceding paragraph.

In view of this situation, the Government of the United States regret-

[1] Department of State, *Bulletin*, IV, p. 665.

fully finds it necessary on the basis of the findings of the United States Tariff Commission to place a limitation on the importation of Canadian wheat. Such action, however, will not apply to the movement of Canadian wheat into the United States for milling in bond and export, or to Canadian wheat moving through the United States for export. In the latter connection, moreover, the Government of the United States is anxious to collaborate closely with Canadian wheat authorities in making the most effective use of the available storage facilities in the United States.

In taking the action referred to above, the Government of the United States recognizes that the wheat problem is, in fact, an international problem and one in which the Governments of Canada and the United States have mutual interests. It is for this reason that the Government of the United States welcomes the recent indication of the Canadian Government of its willingness to resume discussions on an international basis of the whole wheat surplus problem. The Government of the United States accordingly proposes to extend invitations for such discussions in Washington in the near future.

In addition to such discussions, however, the Government of the United States feels that there is a need for continuing consultation between appropriate authorities of our two Governments with a view to preventing to the fullest possible extent divergencies in our respective wheat programs and policies. It is believed such collaboration would be in accord with the purposes of the two Governments to work toward a closer integration of the economies of both countries. The Government of the United States would accordingly welcome an expression of the views of the Canadian Government on this subject.

Accept [etc.]   PIERREPONT MOFFAT

(3) The Acting Under Secretary of State for External Affairs of Canada (Robertson) to the American Minister to Canada (Moffat), May 28, 1941 [1]

SIR:

I have the honor to acknowledge receipt of your note of May 28, 1941, and in reply to inform you that the Canadian Government appreciates fully the nature of the wheat program now being undertaken in the United States. In view of the circumstances described in your Note I am glad to be able to assure you that Canada is prepared to cooperate by avoiding, so far as may be possible, any action which would be likely

[1] Department of State, *Bulletin*, IV, p. 666.

to embarrass your Government in the execution of measures designed to improve the domestic position of wheat producers in the United States.

2. The Canadian Government is gratified to note that nothing will be done to impede the movement through the United States of Canadian wheat destined for export from American seaboard ports, or for milling in bond for export. As you are aware this movement through the United States is important in order to maintain the regular and continuous shipment of Canadian wheat overseas.

3. In view of the problem of surplus wheat with which the governments of almost all the major exporting countries are now confronted, and having in mind the altered conditions and prospects for trade resulting from the war, the Canadian Government welcomes the proposal that the discussions of this problem with the United States Government and other interested governments should be resumed.

4. Apart from discussion of the international problem, the Canadian Government recognizes the value of, and is willing to participate in, continuing consultations on this subject as it affects the United States and Canada. It is assumed that these consultations will embrace such aspects of the problem as the mutually advantageous use of storage facilities in the United States and Canada, as well as all decisions in the field of wheat policy which, although taken by one Government, may have a bearing on the interest of the other.

Accept [etc.]   NORMAN ROBERTSON

(4) *Commodities Imported by the United States under Quota Provisions* [1]

COMMODITY AND COUNTRY	QUOTA PERIOD	UNIT OF QUANTITY	ESTABLISHED QUOTA
Cattle weighing under 200 lbs. each	Calendar year	Head	100,000
Cattle weighing 700 lbs. or more each, other than dairy cows:			
Canada	Quarter year from Apr. 1, 1941	Head	51,720
Other countries	Quarter year from Apr. 1, 1941	Head	8,280

[1] Adapted from *Bulletin of the Treasury Department*, June 1941, p. 46. The monthly reprint of the table shows the quantities imported.

Commodity and Country	Quota Period	Unit of Quantity	Established Quota
Whole milk, fresh or sour . .	Calendar year	Gallon	3,000,000
Cream, fresh or sour . . .	Calendar year	Gallon	1,500,000
Fish, fresh or frozen, filleted, etc., cod, haddock, hake, pollock, cusk and rosefish	Calendar year	Pound	15,000,000
White or Irish potatoes:			
Certified seed	12 months from Sept. 15, 1940	Pound	90,000,000
Other	12 months from Sept. 15, 1940	Pound	60,000,000
Silver or black foxes, furs and articles:			
Foxes valued under $250 each and whole furs and skins:			
Canada	12 months from Dec. 1, 1940	Number	70,000
Other than Canada . .	12 months from Dec. 1, 1940	Number	30,000
Tails	12 months from Dec. 1, 1940	Piece	5,000
Paws, heads or other separated parts	12 months from Dec. 1, 1940	Pound	500
Piece plates	12 months from Dec. 1, 1940	Pound	550
Articles, other than piece plates	12 months from Dec. 1, 1940	Unit	500
Cuban filler tobacco, unstemmed or stemmed (other than cigarette leaf tobacco), and scrap tobacco	Calendar year	Pound (unstemmed equivalent)	22,000,000
Red cedar shingles	Calendar year	Square	2,488,359
Molasses and sugar sirups, containing soluble non-sugar solids equal to more than 6% of total soluble solids	Calendar year	Gallon	1,500,000
Crude petroleum, topped crude petroleum and fuel oil:			
Venezuela	Calendar year	Gallon	1,913,049,600
Netherlands and Netherlands Indies	Calendar year	Gallon	578,806,200
Colombia	Calendar year	Gallon	86,956,800
Other countries	Calendar year	Gallon	138,587,400

Commodity and Country	Quota Period	Unit of Quantity	Established Quota
Products of Philippine Islands:			
Coconut oil	Calendar year	Pound	425,600,000
Refined sugars	Calendar year	Pound	112,000,000 [1]
Sugars other than refined .	Calendar year	Pound	1,792,000,000 [1]
Cordage	May 1 to Dec. 31, 1941	Pound	4,000,000
Buttons of pearl of shell .	Calendar year	Gross	807,500
Cigars	Calendar year	Number	190,000,000
Scrap tobacco and stemmed and unstemmed filler tobacco	Calendar year	Pound	4,275,000
Cotton:			
Under $1\frac{1}{8}$ inches	12 months from Sept. 20, 1940	Pound	14,516,882
$1\frac{1}{8}$ to $1\frac{11}{16}$ inches	12 months from Sept. 20, 1940	Pound	45,656,420
Cotton waste	12 months from Sept. 20, 1940	Pound	5,482,509

4. AGREEMENT WITH THE SOVIET UNION

(1) *Exchange of Notes between the American Chargé d'Affaires (Thursston) and the People's Commissar for Foreign Trade of the Union of Soviet Socialist Republics (Mikoyan), Renewing for One Year the Commercial Agreement (August 6, 1937), Moscow, August 6, 1940* [2]

[The text is identic with that given in *Documents II, 1939–40*, p. 492.]

(2) *Statement Concerning the Commercial Agreement, Department of State, August 6, 1940* [3]

The commercial agreement between the United States of America and the Union of Soviet Socialist Republics which was proclaimed and became effective on August 6, 1937, and which was renewed for successive periods of one year on August 5, 1938, and August 2, 1939, was continued in force for another year, that is until August 6, 1941, by an exchange of identic notes at Moscow on August 6, 1940, between the American Chargé d'Affaires ad interim, Mr. Walter C. Thurston, and

[1] The duty-free quota on Philippine sugars applies to 850,000 long tons, of which not more than 50,000 long tons may be refined sugars.
[2] Department of State, *Bulletin*, III, p. 106; see also *Documents, I, 1938–39*, p. 383.
[3] Department of State, *Bulletin*, III, p. 105.

the People's Commissar for Foreign Trade of the Soviet Union, Mr. A. I. Mikoyan.

As in the previous three agreements, the Soviet Government has informed the American Government that the Soviet economic organizations intend to purchase during the next 12 months American goods to the value of at least $40,000,000. The agreement takes into account the possibility that various export restrictions imposed by the United States in carrying out its national-defense program may make it impossible for these organizations to carry out their intentions.[1]

The Government of the United States undertakes in the agreement to continue to accord to the commerce of the Soviet Union unconditional most-favored-nation treatment, with a reservation in respect of coal, deemed necessary because of the nature of the coal-tax provisions of the Revenue Act of 1932. Under this agreement, therefore, the Soviet Union will continue to receive the benefits of concessions granted by the United States in trade agreements with countries other than Cuba entered into under the authority of the Trade Agreements Act.

The Soviet Government has renewed in a note accompanying the agreement its commitment to export to the United States in the next 12 months not more than 400,000 tons of Soviet coal which was approximately the quantity of Soviet coal exported to the United States in the calendar year 1936. While there were imports of coal during each of the first three agreement years, such imports did not in any such year amount to as much as one half the 400,000-ton limitation. Since October 1939 there have been no imports of Soviet coal.

The following table gives the value in dollars of United States exports to and imports from the Soviet Union in the agreement years:

Agreement Year (Aug.–July)	U. S. Domestic Exports to U. S. S. R. (Thousands of U. S. Dollars)	U. S. Imports for Consumption from U. S. S. R. (Thousands of U. S. Dollars)
1935–36	33,286	21,200
1936–37	31,018	23,240
1937–38	64,224	22,874
1938–39	50,255	24,761
1939–40 [2] (first 11 months) . . .	67,779	23,916

[1] Communications Exchanged between the American Chargé d'Affaires (Thurston) and the People's Commissar for Foreign Trade (Mikoyan) concerning Purchases of U. S. S. R. under the Commercial Agreement (of August 6, 1937), August 6, 1940 (*Ibid.*, p. 107).

[2] Preliminary.

(3) *Exports to the Union of Soviet Socialist Republics. Statement by the Soviet Ambassador (Oumansky), March 1, 1941* [1]

In the course of his current discussions with Mr. Sumner Welles, Under Secretary of State, Mr. Constantine A. Oumansky, Soviet Ambassador, made the statement March 1 on behalf of his Government that goods which have been and are being purchased in the United States by the Union of Soviet Socialist Republics, and including oil products and industrial equipment of all categories, are destined exclusively for the domestic needs of the Union of Soviet Socialist Republics.

5. SUSPENSION OF TONNAGE DUTIES

(1) *Canada. Proclamation by the President (Roosevelt), August 8, 1940* [2]

[See also *Documents, II, 1939–40*, p. 490.]

BY THE PRESIDENT OF THE UNITED STATES OF AMERICA
A Proclamation [No. 2419]

WHEREAS section 4228 of the Revised Statutes of the United States, as amended by act of July 24, 1897, c. 13, 30 Stat. 214 (U. S. C., title 46, sec. 141), provides, in part, as follows:

Upon satisfactory proof being given to the President by the government of any foreign nation, that no discriminating duties of tonnage or imposts are imposed or levied in the ports of such nation upon vessels wholly belonging to citizens of the United States, or upon the produce, manufacture, or merchandise imported in the same from the United States or from any foreign country, the President may issue his proclamation, declaring that the foreign discriminating duties of tonnage and impost within the United States are suspended and discontinued, so far as respects the vessels of such foreign nation, and the produce, manufactures, or merchandise imported into the United States from such foreign nation, or from any other foreign country; the suspension to take effect from the time of such notification being given to the President, and to continue so long as the reciprocal exemption of vessels, belonging to citizens of the United States, and their cargoes, shall be continued, and no longer . . .

WHEREAS satisfactory proof was received by me from the Government of Canada that no discriminating duties of tonnage or imposts are imposed or levied in the ports of Canada upon vessels wholly belonging to citizens of the United States, or upon the produce, manufactures, or merchandise imported in such vessels, from the United States, or from any foreign country:

---

[1] Department of State, *Bulletin*, IV, p. 227. See Department of Commerce, Bureau of Foreign and Domestic Commerce, *Economic Conditions in the Union of Soviet Socialist Republics in 1940* (International Reference Service, I, No. 22, May 1941).
[2] 5 *Fed. Reg.*, p. 2813.

Now, THEREFORE, I, FRANKLIN D. ROOSEVELT, President of the United States of America, by virtue of the authority vested in me by the above-quoted statutory provisions, do hereby declare and proclaim that the foreign discriminating duties of tonnage and imposts within the United States are suspended and discontinued so far as respects the vessels of Canada and the produce, manufactures, or merchandise imported in said vessels into the United States from Canada or from any other foreign country; the suspension to take effect from the date of this proclamation, and to continue so long as the reciprocal exemption of vessels belonging to citizens of the United States and their cargoes shall be continued, and no longer.

IN TESTIMONY WHEREOF, I have hereunto set my hand and caused the seal of the United States of America to be affixed.

DONE at the City of Washington this 8th day of August in the year of our Lord nineteen hundred and forty, and of the Independ-
[SEAL]   ence of the United States of America the one hundred and sixty-fifth.

FRANKLIN D. ROOSEVELT

By the President:
SUMNER WELLES
    Acting Secretary of State.

(2) *Other Suspensions*

Suspension of tonnage duties has also been proclaimed with respect to the following areas:

	EFFECTIVE	PROCLAMATION	*Federal Register*
Iceland . . .	Sept. 13, 1940	No. 2429, Sept. 30, 1940	5 Fed. Reg., p. 3887
Peru	Oct 1, 1940	No. 2432, Oct. 17, 1940	5 Fed. Reg., p. 4163
Greenland . .	Oct. 9, 1940	No. 2434, Oct. 29, 1940	5 Fed. Reg., p. 4329
Egypt . . .	Oct. 3, 1940	No. 2435, Nov. 7, 1940	5 Fed. Reg., p. 4441
Guatemala .	Oct. 19, 1940	No. 2436, Nov. 7, 1940	5 Fed. Reg., p. 4441
Dominican Republic	Oct. 19, 1940	No. 2437, Nov. 7, 1940	5 Fed. Reg., p. 4442
Haiti . . .	Oct. 19, 1940	No. 2438, Nov. 7, 1940	5 Fed. Reg., p. 4443
Venezuela . .	Oct. 23, 1940	No. 2440, Nov. 8, 1940	5 Fed. Reg., p. 4444
Uruguay . .	Dec. 10, 1940	No. 2452, Dec. 28, 1940	6 Fed. Reg., p. 1
New Zealand .	Jan. 17, 1941	No. 2455, Jan. 31, 1941	6 Fed. Reg., p. 727
India . . .	Jan. 17, 1941	No. 2457, Feb. 6, 1941	6 Fed. Reg., p. 849
Iran	Feb. 5, 1941	No. 2462, Feb. 27, 1941	6 Fed. Reg., p. 1229
Switzerland .	May 20, 1941	No. 2491, June 7, 1941	6 Fed. Reg., p. 2811

6. EXPORT CONTROL

A long series of proclamations has successively added commodities to the list of articles and materials for which export licenses are required under sec. 6 of "An Act to Expedite the Strengthening of the National Defense," which provided a new and more effective method for procurement and supply of war materials than methods theretofore utilized.[1] The act was approved July 2, 1940 at 10:55 A.M., and at 11:00 A.M. E. S. T.; the first proclamation of the series was issued to cover arms, ammunition and implements of war, strategic and critical materials and a few related categories.

As the program of national defense progressed and the ramifications of its requirements appeared, fresh proclamations placed new commodities under export control. The office of the Administrator of Export Control, which from the outset had charge of the matter under a military order of the President as Commander-in-Chief, became the center of this development. The successive proclamations designated principal articles and materials subject to export control, and each was accompanied by an executive order of the President enumerating the forms, conversions and derivatives to which the proclamation was applicable. In this way several hundred items had been brought under control for the purposes of national defense and of directing their exportation so that they might contribute to the role of the United States as "the arsenal of democracy."

Each proclamation determining the principal articles subject to control came as the conclusion of an extensive examination of its uses in warfare either by belligerents or by the United States. The forms, conversions and derivatives of the principal articles which were to be controlled were designated in regulations or executive orders accompanying the proclamations and each such item was identified for the purposes of customs administration by the classifications applicable to domestic exports and to re-exports, the latter facilitating control of in-transit trade. For working purposes Executive Order No. 8712 of March 15, 1941 [2] authorized the Administrator of Export Control himself to determine forms, conversions and derivatives and thereafter, effective April 15, 1941, the detailed items affected were announced in Export Schedule No. 1 and subsequent issues.

The Division of Controls, Department of State, issues the licenses for the export of controlled articles. The increase of applications for licenses made their issuance for individual shipments unwieldy and on January 15, 1941 Executive Order No. 8640 authorized the issuance of general licenses for specific articles to specific countries. This system of general licenses applies to the Western Hemisphere and all portions of the British Commonwealth of Nations and several British colonial possessions.

A. Designation of an Administrator of Export Control

(1) *Military Order, July 2, 1940* [3]

The Materials and Production Divisions of the National Defense Advisory Commission collaborated with the Administrator of Export Control in the determination of the items to be controlled and the extent and character of the con-

---

[1] *Documents, II, 1939–40*, p. 786–801.
[2] 6 *Fed. Reg.*, p. 1501.
[3] Department of State, *Bulletin*, III, p. 12; 5 *Fed. Reg.*, p. 2491.

trols to be exercised. The Department of State provides the machinery for the actual issue of licenses under which any controlled items are released for export.

The administration of section 6 of the act of Congress entitled "An Act to Expedite the Strengthening of the National Defense," approved July 2, 1940, is essentially a military function, and by virtue of the authority vested in me as President of the United States and as Commander-in-Chief of the Army and Navy of the United States, I hereby designate Lieutenant Colonel Russell L. Maxwell, U. S. Army, Administrator of Export Control to administer the provisions of the said section under the direction and supervision of the President as Commander-in-Chief of the Army and Navy of the United States.

FRANKLIN D. ROOSEVELT
Commander-in-Chief.

THE WHITE HOUSE,
July 2, 1940.

B. Proclamations Controlling Articles and Materials

(1) *Administration of the "Export Control Act" (Section 6 of An Act to Expedite the Strengthening of the National Defense), Approved July 2, 1940* [1]

BY THE PRESIDENT OF THE UNITED STATES OF AMERICA
A Proclamation [No. 2413]

WHEREAS section 6 of the act of Congress entitled "An Act to Expedite the Strengthening of the National Defense," approved July 2, 1940, provides as follows:

Whenever the President determines that it is necessary in the interest of national defense to prohibit or curtail the exportation of any military equipment or munitions, or component parts thereof, or machinery, tools, or material or supplies necessary for the manufacture, servicing or operation thereof, he may by proclamation prohibit or curtail such exportation, except under such rules and regulations as he shall prescribe. Any such proclamation shall describe the articles or materials included in the prohibition or curtailment contained therein. In case of the violation of any provision of any proclamation, or of any rule or regulation, issued hereunder, such violator or violators, upon conviction, shall be punished by a fine of not more than $10,000, or by imprisonment for not more than two years or by both such fine and imprisonment. The authority granted in this Act shall terminate June 30, 1942, unless the Congress shall otherwise provide.

NOW, THEREFORE, I, FRANKLIN D. ROOSEVELT, President of the United States of America, acting under and by virtue of the authority

[1] Department of State, *Bulletin,* IV, p. 12; 5 *Fed. Reg.,* p. 2467; *Documents, II, 1939–40,* p. 796, being reprinted to complete the record. The regulations are at 5 *Fed. Reg.,* p. 2469.

vested in me by the said act of Congress, do hereby proclaim that the administration of the provisions of section 6 of that act is vested in the Administrator of Export Control, who shall administer such provisions under such rules and regulations as I shall from time to time prescribe in the interest of the national defense.

AND I do hereby further proclaim that upon the recommendation of the aforesaid Administrator of Export Control, I have determined that it is necessary in the interest of the national defense that on and after July 5, 1940, the articles and materials hereinafter listed shall not be exported from the United States except when authorized in each case by a license as hereinafter provided:

1. Arms, ammunition, and implements of war as defined in my Proclamation No. 2237, of May 1, 1937.[1]
2. The following basic materials and products containing the same:

a. Aluminum	n. Mica
b. Antimony	o. Molybdenum
c. Asbestos	p. Optical glass
d. Chromium	q. Platinum group metals
e. Cotton linters	r. Quartz crystals
f. Flax	s. Quinine
g. Graphite	t. Rubber
h. Hides	u. Silk
i. Industrial diamonds	v. Tin
j. Manganese	w. Toluol
k. Magnesium	x. Tungsten
l. Manila fiber	y. Vanadium
m. Mercury	z. Wool

3. Chemicals as follows:

a. Ammonia and ammonium compounds	g. Nitrocellulose, having a nitrogen content of less than 12 per cent
b. Chlorine	h. Soda lime
c. Dimethylaniline	i. Sodium acetate, anhydrous
d. Diphenylamine	j. Strontium chemicals
e. Nitric acid	k. Sulphuric acid, fuming
f. Nitrates	

4. Products as follows:

a. Aircraft parts, equipment, and accessories other than those listed in my proclamation of May 1, 1937.	c. Glass, nonshatterable or bullet proof.
	d. Plastics, optically clear.
b. Armor plate, other than that listed in my proclamation of May 1, 1937.	e. Optical elements for fire control instruments, aircraft instruments, etc.

[1] *Documents, II, 1939–40*, p. 693.

5. Machine tools [1] as follows:

Metal-working machinery for —	
(1) Melting or casting	(3) Cutting or grinding, power driven
(2) Pressing into forms	(4) Welding

AND I do hereby empower the Secretary of State to issue licenses authorizing the exportation of any of the said articles and materials the exportation of which is not already subjected to the requirement that a license be obtained from the Secretary of State authorizing their exportation and I do hereby authorize and enjoin him to issue or refuse to issue licenses authorizing the exportation of any of the articles or materials listed above in accordance with the aforesaid rules and regulations or such specific directives as may be, from time to time, communicated to him by the Administrator of Export Control.

AND I do hereby admonish all citizens of the United States and every person to abstain from every violation of the provisions of section 6 of the act above set forth, of the provisions of this proclamation, and of the provisions of such regulations as may be issued thereunder, and I do hereby warn them that all violations of such provisions will be rigorously prosecuted.

AND I do hereby enjoin upon all officers of the United States, charged with the execution of the laws thereof, the utmost diligence in preventing violations of the said act, of this my proclamation, and of any regulations which may be issued pursuant hereto, and in bringing to trial and punishment any offenders against the same.

IN WITNESS WHEREOF, I have hereunto set my hand and caused the Seal of the United States of America to be affixed.

[1] The circular telegram to all collectors of customs, January 17, 1941 (Department of State, *Bulletin*, IV, p. 93) specified as follows:

No. GDG 1 for the export of the following specifically enumerated machine tools and allied products:

"Pipe threading machines; metal cutting band saws; power driven hack saws; keyseating machines; disc grinding machines; car wheel and locomotive wheel presses; burring machines — gear; chamfering machines — gear; burnishing machines — gear; planers — crank; bench power presses; saw sharpening machines; filing machines; pipe bending machines; thread chaser grinders; burnishing machines; riveting machines; grinding machines — portable with flexible shaft; centering machines; arbor presses (hand, air and hydraulic); nibbling machines; grinders — lathe tool; gear lapping machines; gear shaving machines; polishing machines; heat treating furnaces; foundry machines; cold saws up to a capacity of 10-inch round stock; twist and other drills; reamers; milling cutters; hobs; taps; dies; die heads; shear knives; abrasives and abrasive products containing emery, corundum, or garnet, as well as abrasive paper and cloth; plastic moulding machines and presses; measuring machines; gauges; testing machines; balancing machines; hydraulic pumps; tools incorporating industrial diamonds."

DONE at the City of Washington this 2nd day of July, in the year of our Lord nineteen hundred and forty, and of the Independence [SEAL] of the United States of America the one hundred and sixty-fourth, at 11 A.M., E. S. T.

FRANKLIN D. ROOSEVELT

By the President:
CORDELL HULL,
    Secretary of State.

(2) Subsequent Proclamations of Equivalent Character

Proclamation No. 2417,[1] *July 26, 1940; effective August 1, 1940:*

    1. Petroleum products [2]
    2. Tetraethyl lead
    3. Iron and steel scrap [3]

Proclamation No. 2423,[4] *September 12, 1940; effective September 26, 1940:*

1. Equipment (excluding minor component parts) which can be used, or adapted to use, for the production of aviation motor fuel from petroleum, petroleum products, hydrocarbons, or hydrocarbon mixtures, by processes involving chemical change; and any plans,[5] specifications, or other documents containing descriptive or technical information of any kind (other than that appearing in any form available to the general public) useful in the design, construction, or operation of any such equipment, or in connection with any such processes. Aviation motor fuel shall mean such fuel as is defined in the regulations issued pursuant to Proclamation No. 2417 [6] of July 26, 1940, as may from time to time be amended.

2. Equipment (excluding minor component parts) which can be used, or adapted to use, for the production of tetraethyl lead; and any plans,[2] specifications, or other documents containing descriptive or technical information of any

---

[1] Department of State, *Bulletin*, III, p. 49; 5 *Fed. Reg.*, p. 2677; *Documents, II, 1939–40*, p. 800. The regulations are at 5 *Fed. Reg.*, p. 2682.

[2] By definition in the regulations includes only: "(a) Aviation Motor Fuel, *i.e.*, high octane gasolines, hydrocarbons, and hydrocarbon mixtures (including crude oils) boiling between 75° and 350° F. which with the addition of tetraethyl lead up to a total content of 3 c.c. per gallon will exceed 87 octane number by the A. S. T. M. Knock Test Method; or any material from which by commercial distillation there can be separated more than 3% of such gasoline, hydrocarbon or hydrocarbon mixture. (b) Aviation Lubricating Oil, *i.e.*, any lubricating oil of 95 or more seconds Saybolt Universal Viscosity at 210° F. with a viscosity index of 85 or more."

[3] By definition in the regulations includes: "Number 1 heavy melting scrap." Added by regulations issued September 30, 1940, effective October 16: "All iron and steel scrap of every kind and description, classified or unclassified."

[4] Department of State, *Bulletin*, III, p. 213; 5 *Fed. Reg.*, p. 3651.

[5] See Proclamation No. 2465, at p. 486.

[6] See next above, and *Documents, II, 1939–40*, p. 800.

kind (other than that appearing in any form available to the general public) useful in the design, construction, or operation of any such equipment, or in connection with any such processes. Tetraethyl lead shall mean such tetraethyl lead as is defined in the regulations issued pursuant to Proclamation No. 2417 of July 26, 1940, as may from time to time be amended.

3. Plans,[1] specifications, and other documents containing descriptive or technical information of any kind (other than that appearing in any form available to the general public) setting forth the design or construction of aircraft or aircraft engines.

Proclamation No. 2428,[2] September 30, 1940; effective October 15, 1940:

> Fire Control Instruments
> Military Searchlights
> Aerial Cameras and other types of
> Military Equipment containing optical elements

Proclamation No. 2449,[3] December 10, 1940; effective December 30, 1940:

> Iron and Steel [4]

Proclamation No. 2451,[5] December 20, 1940; effective June 6, 1941:

1. Bromine.
2. Ethylene.
3. Ethylene dibromide.
4. Methylamine.
5. Strontium Metals and Ores.
6. Cobalt.
7. Abrasives and abrasive products containing emery, corundum, or garnet, as well as abrasive paper and cloth.
8. Plastic molding machines and presses.
9. Measuring Machines.
10. Gauges.
11. Testing Machines.
12. Balancing Machines.
13. Hydraulic Pumps.
14. Tools incorporating industrial diamonds.
15. Equipment and plans [1] for the production of aviation lubricating oil.

Proclamation No. 2453,[6] January 10, 1941; effective February 3, 1941:

1. Copper
2. Brass and Bronze
3. Zinc
4. Nickel
5. Potash

---

[1] See Proclamation 2465, p. 486.

[2] Department of State, *Bulletin,* III, p. 279; 5 *Fed. Reg.,* p. 3869.

[3] *Ibid.,* p. 529; 5 *Fed. Reg.,* p. 4903.

[4] Defined by Executive Order No. 8607, December 10, 1940 (Department of State, *Bulletin,* III, p. 530) and redefined by Executive Order No. 8669, February 4, 1941 (*Ibid.,* IV, p. 158; 5 *Fed. Reg.,* p. 782).

[5] Department of State, *Bulletin,* III, p. 559; 5 *Fed. Reg.,* p. 5229. Original definitions in Executive Order No. 8617 (*Ibid.,* p. 560; 5 *Fed. Reg.,* p. 5230). Definitions hereafter are identified by the commodity number set out in Schedule B "Statistical Classification of Domestic Commodities Exported from the United States."

[6] Department of State, *Bulletin,* IV, p. 52. Original definitions in Executive Order No. 8631 (*Ibid.,* p. 53).

Proclamation No. 2456,[1] *February 4, 1941; effective February 10, 1941:*

(1) Well and refining machinery
(2) Radium
(3) Uranium
(4) Calf and kip skins

Proclamation No. 2460,[2] *February 25, 1941; effective March 10, 1941:*

(1) Belladonna
(2) Atropine
(3) Sole Leather
(4) Belting Leather

Proclamation No. 2461,[3] *February 25, 1941; effective February 25, 1941:*

(1) Beryllium
(2) Graphite electrodes
(3) Aircraft pilot trainers

Proclamation No. 2463,[4] *March 4, 1941; effective March 10, 1941:*

(1) Cadmium
(2) Carbon Black
(3) Coconut Oil
(4) Copra
(5) Cresylic Acid and Cresols
[(6) Fatty Acids produced from vegetable oils under export control][5]
(7) Glycerin
(8) Palm-Kernel Oil and Palm Kernels
(9) Pine Oil
(10) Petroleum Coke
(11) Shellac
(12) Titanium

Proclamation No. 2464,[6] *March 4, 1941; effective March 24, 1941:*

(1) Jute
(2) Lead
(3) Borax
(4) Phosphates

Proclamation No. 2468,[7] *March 27, 1941; effective April 15, 1941:*

1. Animal, fish and marine mammal oils, fats and greases, edible and inedible.
2. Vegetable oils and fats, edible and inedible.
3. Vegetable oilseeds, and vegetable and other oil-bearing raw materials.
4. Fatty acids.[8]
5. Bristles.
6. Nux vomica.
7. Nylon.
8. Kapok.
9. Purified wood pulp containing 80% or more alphacellulose.
10. Cork.

---

[1] Department of State, *Bulletin*, IV, p. 157; 6 *Fed. Reg.*, p. 781. Definitions in Executive Order No. 8668, February 4, 1941 (*ibid.*). Commodity numbers applicable to re-exports added in this and subsequent orders.

[2] *Ibid.*, p. 219; 6 *Fed. Reg.*, p. 1155. Original definitions in Executive Order No. 8693 (Department of State, *Bulletin*, IV, p. 220; 6 *Fed. Reg.*, p. 1156).

[3] *Ibid.*, p. 220, 6 *Fed. Reg.*, p. 1155. Original definitions in Executive Order No. 8694 (Department of State, *Bulletin*, IV, p. 221; 6 *Fed. Reg.*, p. 1157).

[4] *Ibid.*, p. 243; 6 *Fed. Reg.*, p. 1299. Definitions in Executive Order No. 8702, March 4, 1941 (Department of State, *Bulletin*, IV, p. 246; 6 *Fed. Reg.*, p. 1301).

[5] See Proclamation No. 2468, item 4.

[6] Department of State, *Bulletin*, IV, p. 244; 6 *Fed. Reg.*, p. 1299. Definitions in Executive Order No. 8703, March 4, 1941 (Department of State, *Bulletin*, IV, p. 247; 6 *Fed. Reg.*, p. 1301).

[7] *Ibid.*, p. 378; 6 *Fed. Reg.*, p. 1703.

[8] Item (6) of Proclamation 2463 of March 4, 1941, is superseded by item 4 of this proclamation.

11. Carbon electrodes.
12. Petrolatum.
13. Alkyd resins.
14. Explosives, in addition to those listed in Proclamation 2237 of May 1, 1937.
15. Detonators and blasting caps.
16. Naphthalene.
17. Phenol.
18. Aniline.
19. Phthalic anhydride.
20. Dibutyl phthalate.
21. Diethyl phthalate.
22. Dipropylphthalate.
23. Omega Chloroacetophenone.
24. Styrene.
25. Nitroderivatives of benzene, toluene, xylene, naphthalene, and phenols in addition to those specified in the proclamation of May 1, 1937.
26. Strychnine and salts thereof.
27. Polymers and copolymers of butadiene, acrylonitrile, butylene, chloroprene, styrene, vinylidene, chloride, and synthetic rubber-like compounds, fabricated or unfabricated.
28. Chloropicrin.
29. Tartaric acid.
30. Rochelle salts.
31. Cuprous oxide.
32. Acetic aldehyde.
33. Pentaerythrite.
34. Formaldehyde.
35. Nitroguanidine.
36. Guanidine nitrate.
37. Dicyanodiamide.
38. Monochloroacetic acid.
39. Chloroacetyl chloride.
40. Thiodiglycol.
41. Ethylene chlorhydrine.
42. Hexamethylene tetramine.
43. Acrylonitrile.
44. Butadiene.
45. Butylene.
46. Chloroprene.
47. Sodium chlorate.
48. Sulphur chlorides.
49. Arsenic trichloride.
50. Vinylidene chloride.
51. Iodine.

Proclamation No. 2475,[1] April 14, 1941; effective April 15, 1941:

Machinery

Proclamation No. 2476,[2] April 14, 1941; effective May 6, 1941:

(1) Vegetable fibers and manufactures
(2) Theobromine
(3) Caffein
(4) Sodium cyanide
(5) Calcium cyanide
(6) Casein

Proclamation No. 2482,[3] issued May 10, 1941; effective June 3, 1941:

Hyoscyamus (henbane)
Stramonium
Columbium
Tantalum
Cryolite
Fluorspar
Chemical wood pulps
Digitalis seeds

[1] Department of State, *Bulletin*, IV, p. 475; 6 *Fed. Reg.*, p. 1983.
Definitions of articles and materials included in this and subsequent proclamations are in the Export Control Schedules.
[2] *Ibid.*, p. 475; 6 *Fed. Reg.*, p. 1983.   [3] *Ibid.*, p. 561; 6 *Fed. Reg.*, p. 2373.

Proclamation No. 2492,[1] *issued June 10, 1941; effective July 2, 1941:*

1. Bismuth
2. Natural gums and resins

3. Zirconium

C. Determination of Forms, Conversions and Derivatives of Articles and Materials Subject to Export Control

(1) *Executive Order No. 8712, March 15, 1941, Giving Authority to the Administrator of Export Control* [2]

By virtue of and pursuant to the authority vested in me by section 6 of the act of Congress approved July 2, 1940, entitled "An Act to Expedite the Strengthening of the National Defense" (54 Stat. 712, 714), I hereby prescribe the following regulations governing the exportation of articles and materials designated in proclamations issued, or which may hereafter be issued, pursuant to the said section 6; except that these regulations shall not apply to the articles and materials designated in Proclamation No. 2465 of March 4, 1941, or proclamations amendatory thereof:

1. The Administrator of Export Control shall, under my direction, determine the forms, conversions, and derivatives of the articles and materials the exportation of which has been prohibited or curtailed pursuant to section 6 of the act of July 2, 1940; and the Administrator may from time to time make such additions to or deletions from the lists of forms, conversions, and derivatives as may be necessary in the interest of national defense.

2. The Administrator of Export Control shall cause such lists of forms, conversions, and derivatives to be published in the *Federal Register*. Such publication shall constitute notice to the public that, after the effective date therein stated, none of the forms, conversions, and derivatives listed shall be exported unless and until a license authorizing such exportation shall have been issued by the Secretary of State.

3. The forms for application for export licenses shall be prescribed by the Secretary of State: *Provided,* That such applications shall be required to contain adequate descriptions of the articles and materials to be exported, including type and model descriptions, if applicable.

4. The Secretary of State shall issue export licenses to authorize proposed shipments of the said articles and materials, and forms, conversions, and derivatives thereof, to applicants who shall have made applica-

[1] Department of State, *Bulletin*, IV, p. 728; 6 *Fed. Reg.*, p. 2811.
[2] *Ibid.*, p. 284; 6 *Fed. Reg.*, p. 1501.

tion on the prescribed form, unless the Administrator of Export Control, under my direction, shall have determined that the proposed exportation would be detrimental to the interests of the national defense.

5. Regulations contained in the document entitled *International Traffic in Arms* (7th ed., 1939), Department of State publication 1407, shall continue to govern the exportation of arms, ammunition, and implements of war, and tin-plate scrap, except that export licenses shall not be issued when in any case it shall have been determined by the Administrator of Export Control, under my direction, that the proposed shipment would be contrary to the interest of the national defense.

6. The country designated on the application for licenses as the country of destination shall in each case be the country of ultimate destination. If the goods to be exported are consigned to one country with the knowledge that they are intended for transshipment thence to another country, the latter country shall be named as the country of destination.

7. Export licenses are not transferable and are subject to revocation without notice. If not revoked, licenses are valid for one year from the date of issuance.

8. The original license must be presented, prior to exportation, to the collector of customs at the port through which the shipment authorized to be exported is being made. If shipment is made by parcel post, the license must be presented to the postmaster at the post office at which the parcel is mailed.

9. No alterations may be made in export licenses which have been issued by the Secretary of State except by the Department of State or by collectors of customs or postmasters acting under the specific instructions of the Department of State.

10. Export licenses which have been revoked or which have expired must be returned immediately to the Secretary of State.

[[1] 11. Articles and materials entering or leaving a port of the United States in transit through the territory of the United States to a foreign country shall not be considered as imported or exported for the purpose of these regulations.]

12. Except as may be prohibited by the Neutrality Act of 1939 (54 Stat. 4), the Secretary of State may issue general licenses authorizing the exportation to all or certain areas or destinations of any of the articles and materials named in proclamations issued pursuant to section 6 of the act of July 2, 1940, and any of the forms, conversions,

---

[1] Revoked by Executive Order No. 8752, May 6, 1941, Department of State, *Bulletin*, IV, p. 560; 6 *Fed. Reg.*, p. 2333.

and derivatives thereof, in accordance with the rules and regulations prescribed by the President and such specific directives as may from time to time be communicated to the Secretary of State through the Administrator of Export Control.

13. Paragraphs 3 and 8 shall not apply to the general licenses herein authorized.

14. These regulations shall be effective April 15, 1941, and shall on the effective date supersede the regulations heretofore prescribed by the President governing the exportation of the articles and materials named in proclamations issued pursuant to section 6 of the act of July 2, 1940; except that they shall not supersede the regulations governing the exportation of articles and materials designated in Proclamation 2465 of March 4, 1941.

FRANKLIN D. ROOSEVELT

THE WHITE HOUSE,
March 15, 1941.

(a) Export Control Schedule No. 1 [1]

By virtue of the Military Order of July 2, 1940,[2] and Executive Order of March 15, 1941,[3] I, Russell L. Maxwell, Administrator of Export Control, have determined that effective April 15, 1941, the articles and materials designated in the Proclamations issued pursuant to Section 6 of the Act of July 2, 1940, shall include the forms, conversions and derivatives hereinafter designated.

The numbers appearing in the columns designated B and F refer to the numbers in Schedule B "Statistical Classification of Domestic Commodities exported from the United States," and Schedule F "Foreign Exports (re-exports, *i.e.*, merchandise exported from the United States in the same condition as imported)," respectively, both effective January 1, 1941, issued by the United States Department of Commerce. The words are controlling and the numbers are included solely for the purpose of statistical classification. An asterisk (*) indicates that the classification herein is not coextensive with that in said Schedules B and F.

[Here follows table of the 430 articles and materials included in the export control established by the proclamations issued between July 2, 1940 and March 15, 1941, consolidating and revising the itemized lists contained in the regulations or executive orders accompanying proclamations, the whole arranged in categories as follows:

Animal Products — 6	Metals and Manufactures — 91
Vegetable Products — 29	Machinery — 56
Textile Fibers and Manufactures — 26	Chemicals — 142
	Miscellaneous — 38]
Nonmetallic Minerals — 42	

---

[1] Code of Federal Regulations, Title 32 — National Defense, Chap. VIII — Administrator of Export Control, 6 *Fed. Reg.*, p. 1536.
[2] 5 *Fed. Reg.*, p. 2491; see p. 473.　　　　[3] *Ibid.*, p. 1501; see p. 481.

The forms, conversions and derivatives above listed shall not include any of the articles named when exported in individual shipments not exceeding $25 in value; provided, that licenses may be required for any such exportation when the Administrator determines that it is necessary in the interest of the national defense.

By direction of the President.

RUSSELL L. MAXWELL,
Brigadier General, U. S. Army,
Administrator of Export Control.

March 15, 1941.

___

Additional Export Control Schedules, defining the articles and materials covered by proclamations issued subsequently to April 15, 1941, and also adding forms of items previously included, were issued and printed as follows:

Export Control Schedule No. 1, March 15, 1941, effective April 15, 1941, 6 *Fed. Reg.*, p. 1536;

No. 2, April 1, 1941, effective April 15, 1941, 6 *Fed. Reg.*, p. 1814;

No. 3, issued and effective April 15, 1941, 6 *Fed. Reg.*, p. 2004;

No. 4, April 17, 1941, effective May 6, 1941, 6 *Fed. Reg.*, p. 2033;

No. 5, issued and effective April 24, 1941, 6 *Fed. Reg.*, p. 2171;

No. 6, May 1, 1941, effective May 6, 1941, 6 *Fed. Reg.*, p. 2279;

No. 7, revoked before publication;

No. 8, May 12, 1941, effective June 3, 1941, 6 *Fed. Reg.*, p. 2431;

No. 9, June 10, 1941, effective July 2, 1941, 6 *Fed. Reg.*, p. 2852;

No. 10, issued and effective June 20, 1941, 6 *Fed. Reg.*, p. 3059;

No. 11, June 26, 1941, effective June 30, 1941, 6 *Fed. Reg.*, p. 3152.

No. 12, effective July 23, 1941, 6 *Fed. Reg.*, p. 3283;

No. 13, issued and effective, July 12, 1941, 6 *Fed. Reg.*, p. 3477.

The Administrator has published the Schedules with other information in pamphlet form.

A numbered series of "U. S. Export Control Act Announcements" of practical interest to shippers began in *Foreign Commerce Weekly*, October 5, 1940, p. 5, 42.

(2) *Licenses for Small Shipments. Circular Letter to Collectors of Customs, June 6, 1941* [1]

The complexities of supplying industry with the articles and materials needed for the national defense program are indicated in the whole extent of the list of forms, conversions and derivatives placed under export control. A closer view of the shift in demand of the developing program is indicated by the articles and materials on which, from time to time, restriction is placed upon small commercial quantities of articles and materials.

Collectors of customs are reminded that licenses are not required for exportation of individual shipments not exceeding $25 in value, but licenses may be required for any such exportation when considered necessary in the interest of national defense.

[1] Department of State, *Bulletin*, IV, p. 733. For previous list see *ibid.*, p. 478.

In accordance with the foregoing ruling, it has been determined that licenses will henceforth be required for all exportations of the articles and materials listed below, even when exported in individual shipments not exceeding $25 in value, including all forms, conversions, and derivatives named in the several Export Control Schedules, except as otherwise noted:

Aircraft parts, equipment and accessories other than those listed in the President's proclamation of May 1, 1937

Atropine

Belladonna

Bromine (not including conversions and derivatives)

Caffein

Cork

Digitalis seeds (not including conversions and derivatives)

Equipment and parts which can be used or adapted to use, for the production of aircraft motor fuel or tetraethyl of lead

Equipment for the production of aviation lubricating oil

Fire-control instruments, military searchlights, aerial cameras, and other types of military equipment containing optical elements

Gauges

Hyoscyamus (henbane)

Industrial diamonds

Mercury (not including conversions and derivatives)

Mica

Optical elements for fire-control instruments, aircraft instruments, etc.

Optical glass

Plastics, optically clear

Platinum group metals

Quartz crystals

Radium

Theobromine

Theophylline

Tools incorporating industrial diamonds

Uranium

Well and refining machinery

Quinine — except nonproprietary and proprietary preparations containing Quinine

(3) *Control of Petroleum Products. Directive of the President (Roosevelt), June 20, 1941* [1]

The President announced on June 20 that to meet a threatened shortage of petroleum products in the eastern United States he had directed the Administrator of Export Control to place all petroleum products under control and to permit exports from the eastern seaboard only to the British Empire, Egypt, and the Western Hemisphere, since supplies to these destinations are dependent in part on shipment from eastern ports. Meanwhile a plan will be prepared for the most effective use of tanker facilities available to supply petroleum to the eastern seaboard and the other American Republics. Further restriction of shipments of petroleum from the Gulf or Pacific ports of the United States is not contemplated.

[1] From the Office of the Secretary to the President; Department of State, *Bulletin*, IV, p. 750.

The execution of this directive of the President illustrates the repercussions of control. The domestic conditions which caused it, due to insufficient pipeline capacity and diversion of tankers, are well known. It resulted in the issuance of Export Control Schedule No. 10, which revised the forms, conversions and derivatives of petroleum products. All outstanding licenses for exportation of petroleum products from Atlantic coast ports were canceled except those granted for shipments to countries in groups A and B. General license No. GEG, valid till July 31, 1941, was issued for exports from Atlantic coast ports to countries in group B not previously subject to license requirements. General license No. GEH authorized exports from other United States ports "to any foreign destination" of the petroleum products not previously subject to the license requirement. Two series of general licenses authorized exportation of various petroleum products to Canada and Great Britain. Unlimited licenses to the British Purchasing Commission for exportation from Atlantic coast ports to Egypt and all other parts of the British Empire were issued for the products newly included in Export Control Schedule No. 10: Kerosene, gas oil and distillate fuel oil, residual fuel oil, liquefied petroleum gases, paraffin wax (refined and unrefined), petroleum asphalt, petroleum coke, petroleum products n.e.s., and all crude oils, gasoline, and lubricating oils.

D. Export Control of Models, Designs, Photographs, Plans, Specifications, etc.

(1) *Proclamation No. 2465,*[1] *March 4, 1941*

[Excerpt]

Now, THEREFORE, I, FRANKLIN D. ROOSEVELT, President of the United States of America, acting under and by virtue of the authority vested in me by the aforesaid act of Congress, do hereby proclaim that upon the recommendation of the Administrator of Export Control I have determined that it is necessary in the interest of the national defense that on and after April 15, 1941, the following-described articles and materials shall not be exported from the United States except when authorized in each case by a license as hereinafter provided:

Any model, design, photograph, photographic negative, document, or other article or material, containing a plan, specification, or descriptive or technical information of any kind (other than that appearing generally in a form available to the public) which can be used or adapted for use in connection with any process, synthesis, or operation in the production, manufacture, or reconstruction of any of the articles or materials the exportation of which is prohibited or curtailed in accordance with the provisions of section 6 of the act of Congress approved July 2, 1940, or of any basic or intermediary constituent of any such articles or materials.

[1] Department of State, *Bulletin*, IV, p. 245; 6 *Fed. Reg.*, p. 1300.

AND I do hereby empower the Administrator of Export Control to issue licenses authorizing the exportation of any of the above-named articles and materials in accordance with rules and regulations prescribed by the President.

Proclamation No. 2423,[1] of September 12, 1940, is hereby superseded except so far as and to the extent that it relates to (1) equipment (excluding minor component parts) which can be used, or adapted to use, for the production of aviation motor fuel (as is defined in the regulations issued pursuant to Proclamation No. 2417,[2] of July 26, 1940, as may from time to time be amended) from petroleum, petroleum products, hydrocarbon, or hydrocarbon mixtures, by processes involving chemical change; and (2) equipment (excluding minor component parts) which can be used, or adapted to use, for the production of tetraethyl lead (as is defined in the regulations issued pursuant to Proclamation No. 2417, of July 26, 1940, as may from time to time be amended).

Proclamation No. 2451,[3] of December 20, 1940, is hereby superseded so far as and to the extent that it relates to plans for the production of aviation lubricating oil.

(a) Authority to Determine Forms of Such Articles and Materials Subject to Export Control. Executive Order No. 8713, March 15, 1941 [4]

By virtue of and pursuant to the authority vested in me by section 6 of the act of Congress approved July 2, 1940, entitled "An Act to Expedite the Strengthening of the National Defense" (54 Stat. 712, 714), I hereby prescribe the following regulations governing the exportation of articles and materials designated in Proclamation No. 2465 of March 4, 1941, issued pursuant to the said section 6:

1. The Administrator of Export Control shall, under my direction, determine the forms of the articles and materials designated in the above-mentioned proclamation; and the Administrator may from time to time make such additions to or deletions from the lists of forms as may be necessary in the interest of national defense.

2. The Administrator of Export Control shall cause such lists of forms to be published in the *Federal Register*. Such publication shall constitute notice to the public that, after the effective date therein stated, none of the forms listed shall be exported unless and until a license authorizing such exportation shall have been issued by the Administrator of Export Control.

3. The forms for application for export licenses shall be prescribed by the Administrator of Export Control: *Provided*, That such applications shall be required to contain adequate descriptions of the articles and materials to be exported, including type and model descriptions, if applicable.

4. The Administrator of Export Control shall issue export licenses to authorize proposed shipments of the said articles and materials to applicants who shall

[1] See p. 477.   [2] See p. 477.   [3] See p. 478.
[4] Department of State, *Bulletin*, IV, p. 283; 6 *Fed. Reg.*, p. 1502.

have made application on the prescribed form, unless the Administrator of Export Control, under my direction, shall have determined that the proposed exportation would be detrimental to the interests of the national defense.

5. The country designated on the application for license as the country of destination shall in each case be the country of ultimate destination. If the articles and materials to be exported are consigned to one country with the knowledge that they are intended for transshipment thence to another country, the latter country shall be named as the country of destination.

6. Export licenses are not transferable and are subject to revocation without notice. If not revoked, licenses are valid for one year from the date of issuance.

7. The original license must be presented, prior to exportation, to the collector of customs at the port through which the shipment authorized to be exported is being made. If shipment is made by mail, the license must be presented to the postmaster at the post office at which the parcel is mailed, except that the Administrator of Export Control may authorize the mailing of the parcel without formal presentation of the license.

8. No alterations may be made in export licenses which have been issued by the Administrator of Export Control except by the Administrator or by collectors of customs or postmasters acting under the specific instructions of the Administrator.

9. Export licenses which have been revoked or which have expired must be returned immediately to the Administrator of Export Control.

10. Except as may be prohibited by law, the Administrator of Export Control may issue general licenses authorizing the exportation to all or certain areas or destinations of any of the above-mentioned articles and materials, and any of the forms thereof, in accordance with the rules and regulations prescribed by the President.

11. Paragraphs 3 and 7 shall not apply to the general licenses herein authorized.

12. These regulations shall be effective April 15, 1941.

FRANKLIN D. ROOSEVELT

THE WHITE HOUSE,
   March 15, 1941.

Export Control Schedules were issued under Executive Order No. 8713 as follows: A, April 1, 1941; effective, April 15, 1941, 6 *Fed. Reg.*, p. 1814, 2392.

E. General Licenses for Export

Applications for licenses for exports greatly increased as the proclamations placing additional commodity groups under license followed one another. Following application of the system to iron and steel products, approximately 10,000 licenses were issued during the period December 16, 1940 and January

16, 1941,[1] and 800 licenses were then being issued daily. Executive Order No. 8640 of January 15 was designed to avoid the congestion due to the increase of applications and to simplify the 'procedure. "General licenses for the export to Canada of articles and materials named in proclamations and regulations issued pursuant to sec. 6 of the Export Control Act of July 2, 1940" were made available by a circular telegram on January 17. General licenses for export to Canada of the 103 articles or categories of materials specified in seven proclamations and the relevant regulations and executive orders were designated by three letter symbols from GAA 1 to GQT 1.

General licenses for 84 articles and materials destined to the United Kingdom followed on February 28, and on April 12 [2] general licenses of specified commodities began to be issued for a list of 62 separate territorial destinations, component parts of the British Empire and the countries and territories of the Western Hemisphere, except French Guiana and other French possessions. On May 9 the Secretary of State reissued the list of countries in two groups and announced a system of general licenses for direct and indirect trade between the territories of the groups. This system was made possible by the revocation on May 6 of par. 11 of Executive Order No. 8712 (see p. 482) which read:

11. Articles and materials entering or leaving a port of the United States in transit through the territory of the United States to a foreign country shall not be considered as imported or exported for the purpose of these regulations.

The change and the installation of the inter-group general licenses at once created machinery for controlling leaks by transshipment and for maintaining at its maximum the freedom of legitimate trade.

The issuance of general licenses is conditioned upon an assurance that the exports involved contribute to the national defense either by immediate utilization for prosecuting the war or by utilization at destination to purposes consistent with the policy of hemispheric defense or aid to the Allies. Whether or not general licenses are issued for the American Republics depends, among other considerations, upon a finding by the United States that the Government in question has placed legal prohibitions upon re-exportations from its territory. For example, general licenses for certain items were issued to Cuba on March 26, 1941, and to Argentina and Brazil on May 29.[3]

The exhibits that follow illustrate various types of general licenses.

---

[1] Department of State, *Bulletin*, IV, p. 92. The number of applications for export licenses handled by the Division of Arms Control, Department of State, from October 14, 1940–January 20, 1941 follows:

Week beginning —		Week beginning —	
October 14, 1940	1,588	December 9, 1940	3,288
October 21, 1940	2,048	December 16, 1940	5,921
October 28, 1940	1,604	December 23, 1940	5,350
November 4, 1940	1,379	December 30, 1940	6,636
November 11, 1940	1,505	January 6, 1941	7,935
November 18, 1940	1,316	January 13, 1941	7,588
November 25, 1940	1,753	January 20, 1941	7,176
December 2, 1940	2,041		

U. S. Congress, House of Representatives, Committee on Appropriations, *Department of State Appropriation Bill for 1942: Hearings* . . . 77th Cong., 1st sess., p. 122.

[2] Department of State, *Bulletin*, IV, p. 454.

[3] *Ibid.*, p. 379, 658–60. For other notices of general licenses, see IV, p. 730, 749; V, p. 6.

(1) *Additional Regulations Governing the Exportation of Articles and Materials Described in Certain Proclamations of the President (Roosevelt) — Executive Order No. 8640, January 15, 1941* [1]

Pursuant to the authority vested in me by section 6 of the act of Congress, approved July 2, 1940, entitled "An Act to Expedite the Strengthening of the National Defense," I hereby prescribe the following additional regulations governing the exportation of the articles and materials named in Proclamations No. 2413 of July 2, 1940, No. 2417 of July 26, 1940, No. 2423 of September 12, 1940, No. 2428 of September 30, 1940, No. 2449 of December 10, 1940, No. 2451 of December 20, 1940, and No. 2453 of January 10, 1941: [2]

1. Except as may be prohibited by the Neutrality Act of 1939 (54 Stat. 4), the Secretary of State may issue general licenses authorizing the exportation to all or certain areas or destinations of any of the above-designated articles and materials, and forms, conversions, and derivatives thereof, in accordance with rules and regulations prescribed by the President or such specific directives as may from time to time be communicated to the Secretary of State through the Administrator of Export Control.

2. Paragraphs 5, 10, and 11 of the regulations prescribed by the President July 2, 1940, governing the exportation of articles and materials designated in Proclamation No. 2413 of that date, shall be inapplicable to the general licenses herein authorized.

FRANKLIN D. ROOSEVELT

THE WHITE HOUSE,
    January 15, 1941.

(2) *Scope of General Licenses for Exports to Canada, January 17, 1941* [3]

It will be observed that these general licenses cover all the articles and materials for which export licenses are required except arms, ammunition, and implements of war as listed in the President's proclamation of May 1, 1937; tinplate scrap; graphite; plans, specifications, and other documents containing descriptive or technical information within the purview of the President's proclamations of September 12, 1940, and

[1] Department of State, *Bulletin,* IV, p. 91; 6 *Fed. Reg.,* p. 455. The President issued a statement concerning the purpose of the executive order.

[2] The executive orders issued until April 15, 1941 each provided for amending Executive Order No. 8640 "to include within its provisions the articles and materials designated in" those proclamations.

[3] Excerpt from circular telegram to all collectors of customs, January 17, 1941, Department of State, *Bulletin,* IV, p. 93.

December 20, 1940; and all machine tools other than those specifically enumerated under license No. GDG 1.[1]

All other articles and materials for which a license is required may be permitted to proceed freely to Canada under the appropriate general license listed above and without an individual license covering the particular shipment. Statistics concerning these exportations should be reported in the customary manner under the general license numbers listed above.

(3) Unlimited Licenses for Certain Exports to the British Empire. Statement of the Division of Controls, Department of State, February 15, 1941 [2]

In an effort to expedite exports to the British Empire of the iron and steel products subject to the requirement of export licenses in accordance with the President's proclamation of December 10, 1940,[3] the British Iron & Steel Corporation has made arrangements to coordinate such shipments to the countries of the Empire. The British Iron & Steel Corporation has already obtained blanket licenses authorizing the exportation to those destinations of all the iron and steel products as defined in the President's Executive order of December 10, 1940.

In order to obtain a clearance of shipments for exportation of these particular steel products, it is necessary for the shipper to communicate with the British Iron & Steel Corporation, 43 Exchange Place, New York, New York, attention of Mr. R. W. Finlayson.

It will also be necessary for every company exporting such iron and steel products to the British Empire in connection with these blanket licenses to supply statistics every 10 days regarding their actual exportations. These statistics should be forwarded to the British Iron & Steel Corporation, which in turn is required to present summaries to the interested branches of this Government.

Applications for license to export the articles and materials referred to in the blanket licenses which have been issued to the British Iron & Steel Corporation are being returned to the applicants with the suggestion that they communicate with the Corporation.

An unlimited license to the British Purchasing Commission for the export to the British Empire of copper, bronze, brass, and nickel under Proclamation

---

[1] See p. 476, note.
[2] Department of State, *Bulletin*, IV, p. 175.
[3] See p. 478.

2453 of January 10, 1941 and the regulations was announced in similar terms on February 15, 1941.

Unlimited licenses were issued as follows:
  Iron and steel products, February 15;
  Copper, bronze, brass and nickel products, February 15;
  Metal drums or containers for oil, gas or other liquids, February 11;
  Aviation lubricating and motor oil, March 12;
  General list, May 27, June 14, 20, 1941.

———

Similar treatment was accorded The Netherlands Purchasing Commission, (Department of State, *Bulletin*, IV, p. 380, 660, 731).

———

(4) *Metal Containers. Telegram to All Collectors of Customs, February 11, 1941* [1]

[Excerpt]

FEBRUARY 11, 1941.

Pending further instructions, no licenses will be required for the export of the following types of "metal drums and containers, filled or unfilled, for oil, gas, and other liquids," referred to in the Executive order of February 4, 1941,[2] governing the exportation of iron and steel:

"(1) Metal containers of less than five gallons' capacity.

"(2) Metal drums and containers with capacity of five or more gallons but less than thirty gallons except those containing or clearly intended to contain gasoline, lubricating oil, or crude oil.

"(3) Metal drums or containers, regardless of size, containing chemicals and related products as classified in Schedule B, 'Statistical Classification of Domestic Commodities Exported from the United States.'"

(5) *Grouping of Territories for Shipments under General Licenses, May 9 and 15, 1941* [3]

In accordance with the provisions of the Executive order of January 15, 1941 [4] the Secretary of State on May 9, 1941, issued general licenses for all articles and materials which require yellow export licenses, as follows:

[1] Department of State, *Bulletin*, IV, p. 176. For a list of articles not requiring license on March 10, 1941 see Circular Letter by the Secretary of State to all Collectors of Customs, *ibid.*, p. 285.

[2] See 6 *Fed. Reg.*, p. 781.

[3] Department of State, *Bulletin*, IV, p. 560, 601.

[4] See p. 490.

1. General License GIT–A/A for shipments passing through the
   United States from any country in Group A to any other country
   in Group A.
2. General License GIT–A/B for shipments passing through the
   United States from any country in Group A to any country in
   Group B.
3. General License GIT–B/A for shipments passing through the
   United States from any country in Group B to any country in
   Group A.
4. General License GIT–B/B for shipments passing through the
   United States from any country in Group B to any other country
   in Group B.

The two groups of countries to which these general licenses are applicable are set forth in the following lists.

Group A

ADEN
ANGLO-EGYPTIAN SUDAN
AUSTRALIA, including Nauru, man-
    dated territory
BAHAMAS
BARBADOS
BERMUDA ISLANDS
BRITISH EAST AFRICA, including:
    Kenya
    Uganda
    Tanganyika, mandated territory
BRITISH GUIANA
BRITISH HONDURAS
BRITISH MALAYA, including:
    British North Borneo
    Brunei
    Federated Malay States
    Sarawak
    Straits Settlements
    Unfederated Malay States
    Christmas Island (Indian Ocean)
    Cocos Islands
BRITISH NEW GUINEA, including:
    Papua, territory of Australia
    Territory of New Guinea, mandated
        territory
BRITISH WEST AFRICA, including:
    Nigeria
    British Cameroons

Gambia
Sierra Leone
Gold Coast
    Togoland
    Northern Territories
    Ashanti
BURMA
CANADA
CEYLON
CYPRUS
EGYPT
FALKLAND ISLANDS, including South
    Georgia
GIBRALTAR
GREAT BRITAIN, including Northern
    Ireland
HONG KONG
INDIA
IRELAND
JAMAICA
LEEWARD ISLANDS, including:
    Antigua (with Barbuda and
        Redonda)
    British Virgin Islands
    Anguilla Island
    Antigua Island
    Barbuda Island
    Dominica Island
    Jost van Dykes Island

Group A — Continued

St. Christopher Island
Nevis Island
MAURITIUS ISLAND, including:
  Rodrigues Island
  Diego Garcia Island
NEWFOUNDLAND
NEW ZEALAND
NORTHERN RHODESIA
OCEANIA, including:
  British Solomon Islands
  Fiji Islands
  Gilbert and Ellice Islands
  New Hebrides Islands
  Pitcairn Island
  Tonga
  Santa Cruz Islands
  Solomon Islands
  Cook Islands
  Western Samoa, mandated territory
PALESTINE
PAPUA [see under British New Guinea]
ST. HELENA ISLAND, including:
  Ascension Island
  Gough Island
  Inaccessible Island
  Nightingale Island

Tristan da Cunha Island
SEYCHELLES ISLANDS, including:
  Admirantes Islands
  Aldabra Islands
  Alphonse Island
  Assumption Island
  Astove Island
  Bijoutier Island
  Coetivy Island
  Cosmoledo Islands
  Farquhar Island
  Flat Island
  Providence Island
  St. François Island
  St. Pierre Island
SOUTHERN RHODESIA
TRINIDAD AND TOBAGO
UNION OF SOUTH AFRICA, including
  South-West Africa
WINDWARD ISLANDS, including:
  Grenada
  Grenadines
  St. Lucia
  St. Vincent
  Carriacou Island

Group B

ARGENTINA
BOLIVIA
BRAZIL
CHILE
COLOMBIA
COSTA RICA
CUBA
CURAÇAO, including:
  Aruba
  Bonaire
  St. Eustatius
  Saba
  St. Martin (Netherlands portion)
DOMINICAN REPUBLIC
EL SALVADOR

ECUADOR
GREENLAND
GUATEMALA
HAITI
HONDURAS
ICELAND
MEXICO
NICARAGUA
PANAMA
PARAGUAY
PERU
SURINAM
URUGUAY
VENEZUELA

(6) *Announcement of the Secretary of State (Hull), May 21, 1941* [1]

The Secretary of State announced on May 21 that, in addition to the general licenses issued on May 9 and May 15, further general license

[1] Department of State, *Bulletin*, IV, p. 616.

have been issued for shipments passing through the United States as follows:

1. General License GIT–Ph/A for shipments passing through the United States from the Philippine Islands to any country in Group A;
2. General License GIT–Ph/B for shipments passing through the United States from the Philippine Islands to any country in Group B;
3. General License GIT–F/B for shipments passing through the United States from Finland to any country in Group B;
4. General License GIT–P/B for shipments passing through the United States from Portugal to any country in Group B;
5. General License GIT–S/B for shipments passing through the United States from Spain to any country in Group B.

Collectors of customs have been instructed to refuse clearance to any exportation under general license GIT–F/B, GIT–P/B, or GIT–S/B unless evidence of the issuance of a Certificate of Origin and Interest for each shipment is presented to the collector at the port of exit.

Whenever an exportation is made under one of the general licenses which have been issued for shipments passing through the United States, the departing vessel will furnish to the collector of customs at the port of exit, in accordance with the usual procedure, an extra copy of its in-transit manifest.

(7) *Sweden and Switzerland. Announcement of the Secretary of State* (*Hull*), *June 5, 1941* [1]

Sweden and Switzerland are neutral countries hemmed in by territories overrun by Germany. Their trade was consequently subject in full measure to the blockade restrictions of both belligerent groups, and they were not eligible to benefit by the general conditions of the system of export control. In consideration of their situation and integrity special general licenses for their export trade in transit to the Western Hemisphere were announced June 5 and 7, 1941. These arrangements were supplemented by general financial licenses on June 20 (p. 542).

The Swedish Cargo Clearance Committee, 630 Fifth Avenue, New York City, and the Swiss Military Transport Board, Bern (Behrer Gehrig, New York City, agents) respectively represent the countries.

The Secretary of State announced on June 5 that, in accordance with the provisions of the Executive order of March 15, 1941 an additional general license GIT–Sw/B [and on June 7 an additional general license GIT–Sd/B] has been issued for shipments passing through the United States from Switzerland [and from Sweden] to any country in group B or

[1] Department of State, *Bulletin*, IV, p. 706.

to Bahamas, Barbados, Bermuda, British Guiana, British Honduras, Canada, Falkland Islands, Jamaica, Leeward Islands, Newfoundland, Trinidad and Tobago, and Windward Islands.

It was also announced that general licenses GIT–F/B, GIT–P/B, and GIT–S/B have been amended by including in the list of countries to which re-exportations may be made, not only the countries in group B, but also the countries named in the above list.

Collectors of customs have been instructed to refuse clearance to any exportation under general license GIT–Sw/B [GIT–Sd/B] unless evidence of the issuance of a Certificate of Origin and Interest for each shipment is presented to the collector at the port of exit.

Whenever an exportation is made under one of the general licenses which have been issued for shipments passing through the United States, the departing vessel will furnish to the collector of customs at the port of exit, in accordance with the usual procedure, an extra copy of its in-transit manifest.

F. Extension of Export Control to the Philippine Islands

(1) *Joint Resolution Extending the Application of the "Export Control Act" to All Territories, Dependencies, and Possessions of the United States, Including the Philippine Islands, the Canal Zone, and the District of Columbia, Approved May 28, 1941* [1]

The "Export Control Act" (Sec. 6 of the act of July 2, 1940) did not apply to the Philippine Islands, which are still a dependency of the United States (*Cincinnati Soap Co. v. U. S.*, 301 U. S. 308, 322 [1937]). The object of extending the act to the Philippine Islands by specific legislation as required by sec. 8 of the act of August 29, 1916 (39 Stat. 416), was stated in Senate Report No 308, 77th Cong., as follows:

"The amount of Manila hemp, for example, exported from the Philippines to Japan has increased over 35 per cent, from 280,000 bales in 1939 to 387,000 bales in 1940. Hemp is of great importance to our Navy and is being used in increasing quantities. Other materials, such as iron ore, coconut oil, copra and mahogany are being exported from the Philippines to Japan and to Russia The mining of a high grade ore for Japan has risen to about 1,200,000 tons a year, and the ore goes exclusively to Japan because of the freight rates Most of the lumber exported from the Philippines goes to Japan. Copra, o dried coconut, with a 40 per cent oil content, which may be used in making glycerin for explosives, is going to Japan and Russia in considerable amounts In 1940 Japan took 200 long tons of copra, and in the first 3 months of 194 she took 7,000 tons. Vladivostok recently took 5,600 tons of copra from the Philippines. Japan took 685 tons of coconut oil last year, and in Januar and February of this year she took 5,133 tons of coconut oil. These material are of great value to our national-defense program, and an adequate system for exercising control in this situation is essential."

[1] Public Law 75, 77th Cong.; originated as S. J. Res. 76; Senate Report No. 308

Resolved by the Senate and House of Representatives of the United States of America in Congress assembled, That the provisions of section 6 of the Act of Congress entitled "An Act to Expedite the Strengthening of the National Defense," approved July 2, 1940 (54 Stat. 714), shall be applicable to all territories, dependencies, and possessions of the United States, including the Philippine Islands, the Canal Zone, and the District of Columbia, and the several courts of first instance of the Commonwealth of the Philippine Islands shall have jurisdiction of offenses committed in the Philippine Islands in violation of the provisions of that section or of any proclamation, or of any rule or regulation, issued thereunder.

(2) *Proclamation No. 2488, Issued and Effective May 28, 1941* [1]

[Excerpt]

The passage of Public Law 75, approved May 28, 1941 and quoted in the proclamation, made possible a fuller control over exports to Japan. Proclamation No. 2488 covers all articles and materials placed under control by proclamations issued since July 2, 1940 and all models, designs, plans, specifications, etc. placed under control by proclamations issued since March 4, 1941.

Licenses are issued in the Philippine Islands by the High Commissioner acting on behalf of the Secretary of State. The general license list for the Philippine Islands (designated as country 63) is in Department of State, *Bulletin*, IV, p. 728.

WHEREAS section 6 of the act of Congress entitled "An Act to Expedite the Strengthening of the National Defense," approved July 2, 1940, provides as follows:

AND WHEREAS the joint resolution of Congress approved May 28, 1941 provides as follows:

[See preceding document]

NOW, THEREFORE, I, FRANKLIN D. ROOSEVELT, PRESIDENT of the UNITED STATES OF AMERICA, acting under and by virtue of the authority vested in me by the said act of Congress and the said joint resolution, do hereby proclaim that upon the recommendation of the Administrator of Export Control I have determined that it is necessary in the interests of the national defense that on and after this date the articles and materials described in the proclamations heretofore issued pursuant to the said section 6 shall not be exported from the Territories, dependencies, and possessions of the United States, including the Philippine Islands, the Canal Zone, and the District of Columbia, except when authorized in each case by license. For all Territories, dependencies,

[1] Department of State, *Bulletin*, IV, p. 657; 6 *Fed. Reg.*, p. 2641.

and possessions of the United States, including the Philippine Islands, the Canal Zone, and the District of Columbia, licenses shall be issued in accordance with Proclamations 2413 of July 2, 1940 and 2465 of March 4, 1941, and the rules and regulations prescribed by Executive Orders 8712 and 8713 of March 15, 1941, as they may be from time to time amended.

IN WITNESS WHEREOF, I have hereunto set my hand and caused the Seal of the United States of America to be affixed.

DONE at the city of Washington this 28th day of May, in the year of our Lord nineteen hundred and forty-one, and of the Inde-
[SEAL]　pendence of the United States of America the one hundred and sixty-fifth.

FRANKLIN D. ROOSEVELT

By the President:
　CORDELL HULL
　　Secretary of State

———

The Secretary of State announced on June 7 [1] that, in accordance with the President's Executive order of March 15, 1941 general licenses have been issued authorizing exportation to the Philippine Islands of all articles and materials designated by the President as necessary to the national defense, pursuant to section 6 of the Export Control Act approved July 2, 1940, with the exception of arms, ammunition, and implements of war, tin-plate scrap, helium, mercury, and industrial diamonds.

On June 10, the Secretary of State announced the numbers of the general licenses issued on June 6, 1941.[2] Two additional general licenses were issued June 25 authorizing the exportation of certain petroleum products.[3]

7. BELLIGERENT RESTRICTIONS ON TRADE

A. British Economic Warfare

(1) *Statement Given to Correspondents at Ministry of Economic Warfare, London, on September 4, 1940 at 3:00 P.M.*[4]

I

The purpose of our Economic War is to smash Germany's industrial machine. That purpose is being served most directly by the carefully

[1] Department of State, *Bulletin*, IV, p. 706.
[2] *Ibid.*, p. 728.
[3] *Ibid.*, p. 766.
[4] Text furnished by British Library of Information, New York City.

planned and brilliantly executed raids of the R. A. F. on Germany. The Ministry of Economic Warfare has been engaged on longer-term operations whose effect is not so immediate. But they are none the less beginning to tell heavily on Germany's war effort, and are bound to have an increasing effect.

The main objects of the Ministry of Economic Warfare have remained the same throughout the war. They are to cut off Germany from all overseas supplies which might help her war effort; to seize German exports (since 27th November, 1939) and thereby deprive Germany of foreign exchange; and to buy up goods in the markets still open to Germany.

The form of our economic campaign has of course changed considerably since the beginning of the war. The main effort of the first year has been directed towards stopping the neutral channels by which Germany tried to keep up her trade with overseas countries.

In this effort there have been three main phases: —

1. First of all, the machinery of Contraband Control was devised (and later of Enemy Export Control). Naval patrols diverted shipping to the bases where they were examined for contraband, and detained or released by order of the Contraband and Enemy Exports Committees in London. At the same time the Ministry of Economic Warfare was concerned to make our control as little inconvenient as possible to neutral traders and shipping companies. To speed up the procedure of control, agreements were reached with individual firms, and sufficient guarantees accepted from them that they would not engage in contraband trade.

2. The second phase was the extension of these agreements with individual firms, and the negotiation of War Trade Agreements with the governments of neutral countries. Agreements were concluded with most of the countries adjacent to Germany and many others. They had a wide scope and their main objects were: —

   i. To make our control effective while easing the strain on our naval patrols.
   ii. To limit re-exports to Germany by the neutral countries concerned of goods from overseas sources, and to limit their own exports of domestic and manufactured products.
   iii. To ensure our own supplies from these countries.
   iv. To allow them reasonable imports for their own needs, and stocks in case of need.

Meanwhile in the Balkans, pre-emptive purchases were being made of goods which would otherwise have gone to Germany; and in the Americas, the Navicert system was introduced, by which consignments were certified before shipment as not being destined to the enemy. Some of the burden of control was thereby transferred to the consignor countries.

3. The third phase is that in which we now find ourselves. Since the German invasions of April, May and June, the scope and methods of the economic campaign have been fundamentally changed. Germany has added to her stocks, but the countries which she invaded depend, as she herself depends, very largely on imports from overseas. There is now a total blockade of German-controlled territory, a blockade which can be operated, and is bound to be very effective.

But the machinery of Agreements is out of date, and the old style of Contraband Control impracticable. It is more than ever essential to ease the strain on our naval patrols. In consequence, the work of control has to be done as far as possible in the consignor countries. The blockade has been transferred "from the seas to the quays." The Navicert system has, therefore, been made compulsory, and extended to cover complete cargoes and the ships that carry them.

The cooperation of neutral shipping firms, the supremacy of our Navy, and the safeguards devised by the Ministry of Shipping in conjunction with the Ministry of Economic Warfare have combined to make the total blockade of enemy-controlled territory a powerful reality. Some indication of the success of the Navicert system is given by these facts. The total number of applications since the system was instituted is 63,525. In August, after it was made compulsory, there were nearly three times as many applications as in July.

The following figures do something to illustrate the activity of the Ministry of Economic Warfare and the effect of the blockade up to date.

II

During the first year of the war the Contraband Committee held 348 meetings and the Enemy Export Committee 210. The Contraband Committee has considered the cases of 3,979 ships, and ordered the seizure of 763,344 tons of cargo suspected of enemy destination. The main items of cargo seized in Prize are as follows: —

Base metals and manufactures	236,785 tons
Petroleum and allied products	182,820 tons
Food products and beverages	83,593 tons
Oilseeds	74,499 tons
Feeding stuffs	39,714 tons
Textiles	37,097 tons
Non-metallic minerals	34,348 tons

It should be remembered that the goods actually seized represent only a very small fraction of what Germany has lost owing to our Contraband Control. Below are the figures of Greater Germany's imports in 1938, of which far the greater part was carried by sea, and could not now reach her.

Petroleum products . .	5,940,200 tons	
Copper	340,000 tons	
Cotton	330,876 tons	
Chrome ore	175,600 tons	(50% metal content)
Wool	139,432 tons	
Rubber	100,490 tons	
Molybdenum ore . . .	60,700 tons	(80–90% metal content)
Nickel and nickel ore .	36,500 tons	(3,300 Nickel. Metal content of ore 3–5%)
Wolfram ore	10,300 tons	(60–70% metal content)

It is impossible for Germany to replace the greater part of her former seaborne trade. Her supplies of oil, ferro-alloys for hardening steel, rubber and copper are notably short, and she cannot live forever on the stocks which she accumulated and has plundered from the occupied territories. These countries are in the main liabilities to Germany once their stocks of her deficiency materials have been exhausted. They can themselves supply none of Germany's chief deficiencies, and will have to be maintained at Germany's expense, at however low a level. Italy, her ally, is notoriously weak in industries and raw materials, and the limited supplies available to Germany in the Balkans must now be shared between both ends of the Axis.

There is no doubt that the total blockade is operating well, and that Germany and Italy are extremely vulnerable in the long run to its effects. At the same time, the R. A. F., who have at their disposal the Intelligence of the Ministry of Economic Warfare, are raining blows on the vital stores and industrial plant of Italy and Germany. This is economic warfare in its most direct form, and in the hands of the R. A. F. it has been immensely effective.

(2) *Form of Application for Neutral Exporters Desiring Navicerts* [1]

[Excerpt]

I desire to obtain a navicert for the under-mentioned consignment on the conditions prescribed by the Government of the United Kingdom. I certify that the particulars given below are, to the best of my knowledge and belief, true and correct, and I undertake to pay on request the sum of two, or, if the consignment exceeds 1,000 tons, eight dollars

[1] In effect from June 17, 1940.

if a navicert is granted, as a contribution to the cost of telegraphic enquiries.

> [Here follow blank spaces for name and address of firm or company; precise nature, quantity, net weight and shipping marks of goods; names and addresses of consignor, consignee and ultimate consignee; ports of shipment and consignment; proposed date of shipment; name and nationality of vessel.]

Signature..

Date..

NOTE. — This document, when signed overleaf by or for the British Ambassador and duly sealed, constitutes a navicert and should be carried in the same ship as the goods to which it relates. Its distinguishing letter and number should be entered against the item in the ship's manifest to which it relates. It must be surrendered on demand to any duly authorized official, or, in any case, to the British consular officer at the port of destination.

(3) Notice of British Certificates for Mail Parcels, British Embassy, June 23, 1941 [1]

The object of the mailcert system is to enable United States senders of parcels, small packets, or letters containing merchandise, to certain neutral countries to ascertain in advance of posting whether facilities can be given for their passage through the British censorship stations.

Mail certificates will not be available for parcels and packets containing printed matter, documents, photographs, stamps, literature for the blind, commercial papers and the like.

Applications for mailcerts (a separate mailcert will be required for each parcel, small packet or letter package) may be lodged with any British consulate. If the application is granted, the mailcert will be issued to the applicant, who should affix it to the outside of the parcel or the packet or package before posting.

Initially the mailcert system will extend to parcels, packets and packages addressed from the Continental United States to Eire, Finland, French West Africa, Iran, Iraq, Liberia, Madagascar, Morocco, Portugal, Portuguese Guinea, Portuguese and Spanish Atlantic Islands, Reunion,

---

[1] New York Times, June 24, 1941, p. 7.

Spain, Sweden, Switzerland and Turkey. Parcels, packets and packages to these destinations and unaccompanied by valid mailcerts will be liable to detention and, possibly, to seizure.

Mailcerts for parcels, packets and packages of value less than $25 will be issued free. When the value is $25 or more the fee will be $1.

Form of application of mailcerts will be supplied by any British consulate.

B. Blockaded Areas

Until July 2, 1941 a total of 127 notices restrictive of maritime navigation had been issued by belligerent and other countries in consequence of the war which began September 3, 1939. All are published by the United States Hydrographic Office in the weekly *Notice to Mariners*, where they are collected as "Special Warnings." They are printed together from time to time on the reverse of pilot charts.[1] On August 21, 1940 the United Kingdom established a blockade of the Atlantic coast of Europe and redefined it November 5. Germany set up a counter "combat zone" around the British Isles on August 28 and issued a justificatory essay;[2] this zone — now called a "zone of operations" — on March 26, 1941 was extended to include Iceland, where German planes had shown themselves on February 10. Two days after the invasion of the Union of Soviet Socialist Republics Germany announced "areas of operations" around that country.

The notices in effect as of July 1, 1941 relative to the British Isles and the Soviet Union are given.

(1) *British Admiralty Notice, November 5, 1940*

November 5, 1940. — Special Warning No. 106. — The British Admiralty announces that the following areas are dangerous to shipping:

All waters in the English Channel and Bay of Biscay lying the eastward of a line joining the following positions:

Bishops Rock Light, lat. 49° 52′ N., lon. 6° 27′ W.; lat. 49° 52′ N., lon. 7° 00′ W.; lat. 46° 30′ N., lon. 7° 00′ W.; Le Socoa Light, lat. 43° 23′.7 N., lon. 1° 41′.2 W.

Masters of vessels bound to or from British ports in the English Channel should apply for routing instructions to Naval Control Service Officer if in a British port or to the British consul if in a foreign port.

Vessels disregarding the terms of this notice do so at their risk and peril.

This warning cancels Special Warning No. 100 of August 21, 1940.

---

[1] Nos. 1–100 on the North Atlantic Pilot Chart for October 1940 and Nos. 100–22 on the Pilot Chart of the Central American Waters for June 1941.

[2] See *New York Times*, August 18, 1940, p. 22.

(2) *German Government Notice of a Zone of Operations, March 26, 1941* [1]

March 26, 1941. — Special Warning No. 118. — The German Government has announced that the zone of operations around the British Isles has been extended to include Iceland. The zone is now bounded as follows:

From the intersection of longitude 3° 00′ E., with the Belgian coast due north to lat. 62° 00′ N.; thence to lat. 68° 00′ N., lon. 10° 00′ W.; thence westward along the 68th parallel to the 3-mile limit of Greenland; thence southward along the 3-mile limit to a position in lat. 65° 24′ N., lon. 38° 00′ W.; thence due south to lat. 58° 50′ N.; thence to lat. 45° 00′ N., lon. 20° 00′ W.; thence eastward along the 45th parallel to longitude 5° 00′ W.; thence to the French coast in lat. 47° 30′ N., lon. 2° 40′ W.

Vessels entering this zone expose themselves to the danger of destruction.

This warning supersedes Special Warning No. 103 of August 28, 1940.

(3) *German Government Notice of Blockade of the Soviet Union, June 24, 1941* [2]

June 24, 1941. — Special Warning No. 126. — The German Government announces that the following areas in the Arctic Ocean and Black Sea have become areas of operations and vessels entering these areas expose themselves to destruction by mines or other war implements:

1. The Arctic Ocean from the Finnish eastern frontier northward within Russian territorial water to Majakkaniemi (Nemetski) Cape, and from there the entire sea area east of longitude 32° E.

2. The entire sea area of the Black Sea with the exception of the following coastal strips:

From the Bosphorus eastward along the southern coast of the Black Sea for a distance of 10 nautical miles offshore to the Russian-Turkish frontier (near Batum) and from the Bosphorus westward and northward for a distance of 10 nautical miles to the Russian-Rumanian frontier.

In the Baltic Sea mines have been laid in the following areas except against the German coast and within the 3-mile limit along the Swedish coast:

1. The area between Öland and the German-Lithuanian coast bounded on the north by latitude 56° 22′ N., and on the south by a line connecting

[1] U. S. Hydrographic Office, *Notice to Mariners* No. 14 (830), 1941.
[2] *Ibid.*, No. 27 (1623) of 1941.

Utklippan Lighthouse and the intersection of the German coast with latitude 55° 30′ N.

2. The area between Bornholm and the Swedish coast bounded by lines connecting Simrishamn Lighthouse with Hammer Odde Lighthouse and Sandhannaren Lighthouse with Roenne Lighthouse.

3. The area between Bornholm and the German coast bounded by lines connecting San Kaas Odde Lighthouse with Ruegenwalde Lighthouse and Due Odde Lighthouse with Funkenhagen Lighthouse. Off the German coast there remains a passage for shipping 4 nautical miles in width from the shoreline.

All merchant vessels are warned against travel in these areas.

C. Export of Relief Supplies to Blockaded Areas

(1) *Statement of the British Ambassador (Lothian), Washington, December 10, 1940* [1]

When he was recently in England the British Ambassador reported fully to His Majesty's Government the proposals of Mr. Hoover and others for sending food to civil populations in certain of the German subjugated nations in Europe. These proposals received most sympathetic attention, all the more so because His Majesty's Government have had in mind the noble services rendered by Mr. Hoover to the people of Belgium and other countries during and after the last war.

After the most careful consideration, however, His Majesty's Government have been reluctantly forced to the conclusion that under present conditions any such scheme must be of material assistance to Germany's war effort and would thereby postpone the day of liberation of these peoples from German subjugation.

They are therefore not able to give permission for the passage of food through the blockade.

The British Government and public feel the deepest sympathy with the Allied peoples and their own people in the Channel Islands, who are now likely to endure privation in addition to the sufferings caused by German-Nazi domination, but the British Government feels that the primary objective must be to bring about the release of the subjugated peoples from this alien oppression at the earliest possible moment.

From the information at its disposal the risk of starvation has been greatly exaggerated. It would be of no service to these people to send in food if it means the prolongation of their slavery. Moreover, any

[1] *New York Times*, December 11, 1940, p. 20.

shortage of food from which they may suffer is solely due to German action. Until they were conquered by Germany they had ample food for their own needs. In conquering them and installing German control Germany has assumed responsibility for their welfare.

The Nazi authorities, who state that their reserves are untouched by the blockade, persistently claim that they have plenty of food for Europe, so that if there is hardship in these countries it is because the German Government has been depriving them of their own supplies and refusing to give them that share of European production to which they are entitled.

Now that Germany is in control of the food supplies of almost all the Continent west of Russia, the introduction of food from outside would add to the total amount of food available to Germany for whatever purposes she decides to allot it. Nor can it be forgotten that the German Government converts foodstuffs on a large scale into valuable war material.

Moreover, it must be remembered that the war against Great Britain is being actively and ruthlessly prosecuted from the countries under German occupation which border on the North Sea and the Atlantic. In these countries are air fields and ground organizations which enable German aircraft to take off day and night to bomb British women and children and to conduct indiscriminate attacks on English towns and villages.

All the resources of these territories are being relentlessly harnessed to the German war machine and it is certain that the Germans will not allow starvation to disorganize the social and economic structures upon which an important portion of their war effort depends. Equally, it is clear that any food which was allowed to pass the blockade would merely permit the diversion of yet more of the indigenous stocks to Germany or for the use of the German troops of occupation.

His Majesty's Government have been unable to discover any scheme of distribution by neutral authorities in these countries which, in the light of the Nazi record, could provide guarantees against the strengthening of the German war potential by the importation of foodstuffs.

They feel, therefore, that they have no option but to stand by the decision announced by the Prime Minister in the House of Commons on August 20 that they will not agree to any lifting of the blockade for any country under German domination or so long as that domination continues. Directly, however, Germany withdraws its troops and restores control of these countries to their own citizens, they will immediately arrange for ample supplies of food to reach their inhabitants.

At the same time, as they have already announced, His Majesty's Government are at all times prepared to facilitate the passage through their blockade of medical supplies destined for distribution in territories occupied by Germany and in unoccupied France by approved bodies.

Great Britain is risking starvation and undergoing every conceivable hardship in the fight for freedom not only for herself but for all freedom-loving peoples. We cannot in these circumstances endanger our existence and imperil our cause by weakening our blockade. The British people who are in the firing line have, through their representatives in Parliament, expressed their determination not to give assistance to Germany such as would result from the adoption of Mr. Hoover's proposal. We trust that all those who share our love for freedom and hope for our victory will sympathize with and support our attitude.

(2) *Broadcast of the Foreign Minister, Provisional Czecho-Slovak Government (Masaryk), London, December 7, 1940* [1]

The Czecho-Slovak nation is determined to withstand without complaint the combined effect of German oppression and the British blockade, which result in a serious food shortage in our country. From our point of view it is much better to get along without material necessities, such as food and clothing, than that our souls should be destroyed. I am convinced that other peoples whose territory is occupied by the Germans feel as we do.

Can any one believe that the Nazis would not rob the conquered peoples of any food sent them, as they have already robbed Czecho-Slovakia, Poland, Norway, France and the others of everything they wished?

The Germans are sinking British ships daily regardless of whether they carry food, munitions or children. A complete blockade is essential to victory. Half measures are not enough.

We on the front line of battle can see the splendid sacrifices the British people are making. Arguments for softening the blows of one of their arms of defense, the blockade, are unthinkable to us, even though they may occur to some persons thousands of miles behind the front, say in California.

It would be a great injustice to accuse the British of indifference to the needs of other peoples. Czecho-Slovak children will be pale after this war is won, but their spirits will be free. There will come a day when America can help feed the hungry and restore weary bodies, but that day has not yet come.

[1] *New York Times*, December 11, 1940, p. 20.

To all who offer food to Czecho-Slovakia at the cost of delaying our victory we say: "Thank you — not yet. Germany and her ally must be defeated first."

(3) *Statement of the National Committee on Food for the Five Small Democracies, December 11, 1940* [1]

This committee was formed to raise a voice in behalf of the people of the small democracies which have been overrun by the brute force of Russia and Germany. The people of those countries, under these oppressions, cannot speak in their own lands. Their refugee governments in England are obviously handicapped in presenting their case. So the people inside these countries and their committees in the United States have appealed to us to speak for them and to secure some arrangement, under adequate safeguards, to save them from inevitable famine and pestilence.

We are a great neutral nation; our people can speak in terms of equality with both belligerents concerned. This is a country of free speech and action, and perhaps the only country in the world where this voice could be raised and continue to be raised with any prospect of gaining a hearing.

There is indeed a great desire in America that humanitarian effort should not be brushed aside in this war.

The fact still remains that unless some solution be found millions of people in the small democracies will soon be plunged into great suffering and loss of life. The situation in Belgium is already acute.

It is well known from experience with similar conditions in the last war that ten million lives in Belgium and Northern France were saved without any sacrifice of military advantage. Precisely the same objections were raised at that time. That service was repeatedly praised by British and French Prime Ministers. We believe it can be done again.

We appreciate the importance of the blockade. We feel that the statement of the British Government overlooks the stipulations which we insisted should be accepted by Germany as a condition for safeguarding these food supplies, that is, that the native food, equally with imports, should be reserved wholly for the populations of these countries, and that if such a protection could not be enforced, then the operation would be ended.

We deeply sympathize with Great Britain, which with indomitable spirit and courage, is fighting for its life. This committee, of course,

[1] *New York Times*, December 12, 1940, p. 13. Former President Herbert C. Hoover was honorary chairman of this Committee.

recognizes that in view of Lord Lothian's statement a solution of the problem is deferred.

This Committee on Food for the Five Small Democracies was organized to search for a solution of the plight of these helpless men, women and children. We feel that the solicitude of the American people will continue, as the cause is so just and so appealing. This committee hopes that a plan may yet be found. It will continue to search for a solution that will be acceptable to the governments concerned.

(4) *Report of a Press Conference of the Secretary of State (Hull), December 11, 1940* [1]

The fact that the State Department does not intend to challenge British views concerning German-occupied territory was made plain by Secretary Hull at his press conference. His position was that the Germans had taken food from these regions and that, having occupied them, it was their responsibility to care for the populations.

The United States, Mr. Hull recalled, had a definite policy on the whole question of human suffering and human needs wherever it exists, whether in China or other countries. But as for German-occupied territories, he suggested that perhaps the next step might logically be for some of the United States relief organizations which have been active in the effort to provide essentials to the destitute to approach the German Government.

The implication was that some of them had approached Britain but had not done more. He suggested that the organizations might ascertain the attitude of Berlin, to what extent Germany had deprived populations in occupied territory of food and what they would be disposed to contribute in accordance with the immemorial custom of nations where one country conquers another.

This would help the organization to visualize the problem in its entirety, Mr. Hull said.

(5) *Statement of the British Embassy, Washington, Released March 10, 1941* [2]

The attitude of His Majesty's Government in the United Kingdom toward the problem of the relief of the civilian populations in the Ger-

---

[1] *New York Times*, December 12, 1940. The discussions at press conferences are not textually available, except in rare instances; unless they are covered by releases or formal statements, news dispatches reporting them are the only public record.

[2] Release 46 of the British Embassy; *New York Times*, March 10, 1941, p. 6.

man-occupied territories was first stated in detail by the Prime Minister in his speech to the House of Commons on August 20, 1940. It was amplified in the statement made public by the late Lord Lothian just before his death. Nothing has since occurred to alter the view of His Majesty's Government that it is the responsibility of the German Government to see to the material welfare of the countries they have overrun, nor to weaken their conviction that no form of relief can be devised which would not directly or indirectly assist the enemy's war effort.

Nevertheless, His Majesty's Government would not think it right to pass over in silence, the various proposals put forward by certain organizations and by Mr. Hoover. They recognize that there is a body of opinion in the United States and elsewhere which, with motives which cannot be impugned, would like to be able to play an effective part in the prevention or relief of distress. Although convinced that the vast majority of the American people are determined to do nothing which would impair the war effort of the British people and their Allies, His Majesty's Government nevertheless recognize that this great body of opinion feels itself unable entirely to dismiss the possibility of giving relief unless it can be satisfied that such action is, in fact, incompatible with its desire for a speedy British victory and the release of Europe from enemy domination.

For these reasons, His Majesty's Government have considered afresh the whole problem of relief, including the proposal for the institution of soup kitchens in Belgium. They consider it desirable to restate certain basic facts and principles on which their policy rests.

The blockade is not a food blockade nor an oil blockade but a blockade directed against the whole economic war-machine of the enemy. It is intended to deprive him of imported goods, to drive him into using in uneconomic ways goods which he possesses or produces, to aggravate his transport difficulties and to render as costly and burdensome as possible distribution of supplies within the areas which he controls and utilizes for his military operations and war potential. Every import of foodstuffs into an occupied territory conflicts directly with one or other of these objectives.

Just as the blockade extends over the whole range of supplies and transport, so it must extend over the whole range of countries overrun by the enemy. The Germans are attempting to organize these territories to form an integral part of their war-machine. Their factories and their agriculture are forced to work for the enemy; their laborers are attracted into Germany by promises of more food and better wages. Their surplus products are taken by the enemy and this helps to create the disparity which exists today between rations in Germany and those allowed to the civilian populations in the occupied territories. All these territories are used by the enemy as bases for his attacks on Britain by sea and air. Railways and roads which should be used to carry food from one part of the occupied area to another are devoted instead to the transport of troops and of fuel and bombs for the campaign against Britain. The rolling stock of the occupied countries has been looted, and as far afield as the Balkans, Belgian and French wagons are even at this moment carrying German troops and munitions.

As a result, surplus products of one district are prevented from moving freely to others where they are urgently required. The surplus production of Norwegian fisheries and of the farms of Denmark and the Netherlands is not equitably divided among the Norwegians, the Danes and the Dutch; it is the Germans who claim the right to profit by all local surpluses in each separate area under their control. They disclaim the obligation to make good any local deficiencies except those in Germany itself. Every arrival of foodstuffs into any one part of the occupied area thus constitutes a direct encouragement to the German technique of exploitation. Unfortunately, therefore, there can be no doubt that the admission of relief supplies would benefit the enemy. It is not simply a question of ensuring that any supplies admitted are consumed only by the subject peoples for whom they are intended, but a question of whether the German economy is thereby relieved in another direction.

The British Government have already promised full support for the relief of distress in these territories the moment they are freed of German occupation. Speaking in the House of Commons on August 20, the Prime Minister stated:

Meanwhile we can and will arrange in advance for the speedy entry of food into any part of the enslaved area when this part has been wholly cleared of German forces and has genuinely regained its freedom. We shall do our best to encourage the building up of reserves of food all over the world so that there will always be held up before the eyes of the people of Europe, including — I say it deliberately — the German and Austrian peoples, the certainty that the shattering of the Nazi power would bring to them all immediate food, freedom and peace.

It may be urged that even although it is not possible to devise acceptable conditions, the duty of feeding the hungry overrules all other considerations. This is an argument which the British Government must respect, although they cannot accept it. It presupposes firstly that there is and will be hunger on a serious scale; and secondly, that hunger is a greater evil and one more urgent to be remedied than the prolongation of the war, the continued subjection of many nations to German oppression and tyranny, and the wounding and killing by the most barbarous means of countless thousands of people. But there need be no scarcity amounting to famine and starvation if the enemy would distribute his supplies equitably, and devote to the welfare of his conquered peoples a tithe of the ingenuity which he devotes to his attack on the civilian population of Britain or of the solicitude shown to his own armies of occupation. Germany has in fact proclaimed on many occasions that the so-called new order can assure all food supplies in the countries under her domination. The existence of local shortages in certain districts of the occupied territories is not an admissible argument; for it was not to be expected that the enemy would make good his depredations or restore the supplies he has looted, while he is still hopeful that supplementary supplies from overseas may be forthcoming. Provided that we do not play into his hands by admitting such assistance, it can hardly be supposed that he will allow hunger to impair the efficiency or to increase the discontent of the vast subject population which is essential to the functioning of the German war-machine.

The British Government do not deny that the oppressed peoples are likely to suffer some degree of hardship and privation and they are deeply moved by the sufferings of their Allies. The civilian population of Great Britain itself is suffering and has suffered many thousands of casualties from the brutal attacks which the German Air Force has directed against it.

The British people are, moreover, now deliberately subjecting themselves to privations; they are lowering their own standard of living to a minimum so that more and more shipping space can be allotted to the implements of war. They are doing all this in the common cause and they are confident that their Allies in the enslaved countries will scorn to shirk their share of the distresses which must be borne by each and every one if the common victory is to be assured.

Even if it were admitted that immediate shortages of food were likely, the British Government would regard it as false humanitarianism to agree to the admission of foodstuffs to the areas concerned, knowing as they do that the result of this action would be to prolong the war and to add in the long run to the sum of human misery. They believe that the conquered peoples have now had sufficient experience of German domination to realize the justice of this view.

For these reasons the British Government are satisfied that relief of countries in enemy occupation would, whatever the conditions might

be, postpone the day of victory. They regard it as their primary duty
to rid Europe of Nazi tyranny and to restore the conquered peoples to
physical and spiritual freedom. They cannot allow themselves to be
deflected from this goal and, in full realization of their responsibility,
they therefore feel obliged to reaffirm their determination not to permit
the blockade to be weakened or undermined by the admission of supplies
from overseas into any territory under enemy control.

(6) *Statement for the Executive Committee, National Committee on Food for the Small Democracies, March 9, 1941* [1]

The British Ambassador has courteously furnished me with an advance
copy of the British statement. The American people have a right to
know the views upon it of myself and the Executive Committee on Food
for the Small Democracies. Before giving those views, we wish no misunderstanding of our sympathy with the British cause, or that we have
any doubt that the original plight of the people in the small democracies
is due to the German invasion.

We believe that the British statement was prepared before they were
fully informed upon the undertakings we have now secured. And, in
this light, our full proposals in no way impair the British war effort.
At the same time they uphold the ideals of democracy to the world and
these little nations. They would save the lives of multitudes of children
and others.

Our recent surveys show that the food situation in the occupied democracies is far worse than the British statement would seem to indicate.
The Belgian ration is already down to 960 calories, or less than half
necessary to maintain life. Supplies to maintain even that will be
exhausted this month. Reports show many children already so weak
that they cannot attend school.

We do not agree that there are enough supplies on the Continent to
care for these people or that the supplies will ever be evenly distributed.
Devastation by the German Army and the blockade combined have
caused considerable shortage of bread supplies everywhere, but more
acutely a shortage of fats. No people — American, Belgian or British
— can survive without fats, meaning meat, dairy products, vegetable
oils, etc.

British reports state that the fat supply of the Continent as a whole
has been reduced 40 per cent. Our reports show over 50 per cent. And,

[1] *New York Times*, March 10, 1941. The statement was given out by Herbert C.
Hoover.

as the Germans are not likely to reduce their fat supplies below fighting levels, the shortage falls even more violently upon the occupied democracies. And the Belgians are the first to be exhausted.

In order to check our own information again, I requested a committee of experts, comprising John Lee Coulter, former member of the Tariff Commission; Professor J. I. Falconer of Ohio State University, Professor Asher Hobson of the University of Wisconsin and Dr. E. V. McCollum of Johns Hopkins University, to review objectively all of the data, not only our own investigations on the ground in Europe but also the data of the Department of Agriculture, the Department of Commerce, British reports and actual rations on the Continent. They fully confirm our conclusions.

While the occupied democracies formerly secured a large part of their fat supplies directly by imports from overseas, or indirectly through import of feed, we make no contention that blockade is not a part of war measures. However, the stark fact is that millions of children, and the weak, are threatened with stunted bodies and death in the occupied lands — unless relief is brought to them.

Our original plan of relief was based on the successful methods of the last war. The British felt they could not accept that plan. In the meantime the British Government agreed that supplies to French children could be taken through the blockade by the American Red Cross, and thus admitted that the blockade could be opened. Also Secretary Hull on December 11 [1] in a public statement suggested that relief organizations ask Germany to contribute food.

In all those lights we proposed a new and limited experiment in Belgium, by which 1,000,000 destitute adults and 2,000,000 children should be fed by soup kitchens. This called for 1,000,000 bushels of bread grains per month from German sources, 20,000 tons of fats and soup materials, and special food for children through the blockade. If this experiment were successful, then it could be extended to other democracies when their inevitable food crises approached.

In January we submitted our plan to the Belgian Government in London, and on January 30 they urged it strongly upon the British Government. At the same time we began negotiations with the Germans, who responded on February 26, and their undertaking was transmitted to the Belgian Government.

On their part the Germans have already shipped 800,000 bushels of bread grains into Belgium. They are now initiating a shipment of 3,200,000 bushels. They also agree that there shall be no interference

[1] See p. 509.

with imports, no requisition or absorption of native food; that ships will be free of attack; that a neutral commission shall supervise relief on the ground and see that agreements are complied with. We do not believe that the effect of this undertaking has yet been fully considered by the British Government.

A further part of the plan is that only ships not available to the British shall be used, and that the cost of imports from overseas is to be paid by the exiled Belgian Government. Thus no burdens are imposed upon either America or Britain.

These arrangements answer British objections:

1. No food goes directly or indirectly to the Germans. If the Germans furnish their part of the supplies, it will amount to more food values sent into Belgium than they could possibly have taken from Belgium or fed to their own army. The effect is to reduce, not increase, German supplies.

2. It would, in fact, increase their transportation burdens by the amount of imports.

3. If the guarantees and contribution of food from the Germans are not carried out, then the whole operation would be at once withdrawn. If the guarantees are violated, then the time by which the war could possibly be extended can be measured. The maximum benefit Germany could obtain would be seizure of the imported stocks — and those on hand at any time in Belgium would not feed Germany for one whole day.

4. It would not be furnishing food to persons working for the Germans, since it is limited to the destitute (and thus necessarily the unemployed) and to children.

5. It would not be using ships otherwise available for the British.

6. The plan could result in no military loss to the British, or military gain to the Germans. General John J. Pershing said on February 16:

"There is no doubt millions are in jeopardy unless they are given aid from somewhere. From my own war experience and some knowledge of problems involved, I have every confidence that the salvation of these people can be worked out along the lines proposed by Mr. Hoover, without military loss or benefit to either side. The interest of this committee in maintaining American ideals and the friendship to America of those nations, by saving these millions, is worthy of every support."

Admiral William V. Pratt, who dealt with the blockade in the last war and long commanded the United States Fleet, also said:

"I have no hesitation in saying that this aid can be given under Mr. Hoover's proposals without any damage to Great Britain. Taking the long view of the future of constructive forces in the world, and

America's relation to it, it is of vital importance to America that Mr. Hoover's plans be carried through. . . . Only America will be able to meet this emergency."

This committee wishes to make it clear that none of its members seeks to administer any relief. The American Red Cross has been given permission by Britain to import supplies through the blockade for French children, and this committee would favor the extension of their fine service, or those of the Friends Service Committee, to the Belgians.

The purpose of this committee is to raise a voice for those millions of helpless among the little nations who have been our life-long national friends. We believe it is a duty of the American people to interest itself in prevention of such catastrophes. We have no hesitation in saying that such action will uphold democratic ideals in the world.

It is no false humanity which saves the lives of countless children, and the committee has every evidence that millions of Americans wish it to continue its efforts toward finding a solution by which the lives of these helpless people may be saved.

(7) *Food Relief for Unoccupied France. Statement of the Acting Secretary of State (Welles), March 22, 1941* [1]

On March 17,[1] I referred to the matter of shipments of food to France and the President's willingness that the gift of two shiploads to unoccupied France, under the auspices of the American Red Cross, should be given consideration.

The President has authorized the American Red Cross to use for this specific purpose an allocation from the funds appropriated by Congress for civilian relief abroad. Arrangements have now been completed by the American Red Cross for the forwarding of two shiploads of flour to unoccupied France in two French ships now at New York, the distribution to be by the American Red Cross, which already has a large organization operating in unoccupied France in connection with the distribution of milk and clothing for children. The French Government has given all the assurances required in order that the American Red Cross may have every facility for carrying out its responsibilities with regard to the distribution, and the French Government has further given assurances that:

[1] Department of State, *Bulletin*, IV, p. 333. The earlier statement is, in effect, repeated.

(1) These shipments will be sent solely to unoccupied ports.

(2) Every pound of food so sent will be distributed within unoccupied France to its ultimate destination under the direct supervision of the American Red Cross.

(3) Not a single pound of similar or equivalent foodstuffs will be permitted to pass from unoccupied France to occupied France.

(4) These ships will return immediately to the United States.

The British Government has agreed to the passage of the two shipments because it is satisfied that the assurances given are adequate.

The steamship *Cold Harbor* left Baltimore January 25, 1941 with a cargo of food and medical supplies valued at $1,000,000 for unoccupied France and Spain consigned by the American Red Cross to its own distributing agents (*New York Times*, January 10, 1941, p. 6).

(8) *British Embassy Statement on Finnish Supplies, Washington, January 9, 1941* [1]

[Excerpt]

The British Embassy have noted that some misapprehension seems to exist in regard to the policy of His Majesty's Government toward the passage through the blockade of relief supplies and other commodities destined for Finland.

During the past three months navicerts have been approved for the despatch of such goods to the value of rather more than $1,000,000. These supplies include clothing, blankets, shoes, flour, sugar, lard and dried fruits. In addition, navicerts have been issued to cover the shipment of 140 tons of foodstuffs sent to Finland by the various relief organizations in the United States. Furthermore, apart from supplies sent by relief organizations, facilities have been given during the past two months for the despatch, both from the United States and other sources, of any important commodities for use in Finland, including substantial quantities of sugar, lard, edible oils, wheat and rye. The British Government wish to assist in maintaining Finnish economy and in preventing the Finnish people from suffering privations. On the other hand, the British Government must direct their blockade policy in such a way that supplies allowed to reach Finland in no way benefit Germany. . . .

[1] *New York Times*, January 10, 1941, p. 6. In a statement to the American Red Cross the Finnish Minister stated that in normal years Finland's imports amounted in value to 30% of the national income.

In October the Finnish Government agreed to permit the regular passage of German troops through Finnish territory and thereby called so seriously in question Finland's status as a neutral that it seemed doubtful whether she could still be regarded as wholly independent and neutral. Nevertheless, the British Government decided, after careful consideration, to allow passage through the blockade of such supplies as may be necessary to meet Finland's requirements, provided that — and this is an essential condition — Finland refrains from any further unneutral act.

CHAPTER VI

FINANCE

1. THE BALANCE OF INTERNATIONAL PAYMENTS OF THE UNITED STATES IN 1940

(1) *Summary Prepared by the Finance Division, Department of Commerce, March 29, 1941* [1]

For a number of years the balance of payments of the United States has characteristically shown an excess of merchandise exports, net payments on service account, large gold imports, and a fairly regular inflow of capital from abroad. These features continued to be manifested in 1940 and, in general, on a greatly increased scale, reflecting the impact of the war on this country's commercial and financial relations with the rest of the world.

Merchandise exports rose above the $4,000,000,000 level for the first time since 1929, and the export surplus mounted to almost $1,400,000,000, the largest since 1921. This balance, however, appears small in comparison with net gold imports of almost $4,750,000,000. Even if the $645,000,000 increase in gold under earmark is deducted, the net gold inflow was actually larger than gross merchandise exports.

Available data on capital movements account for an inflow of slightly more than $1,400,000,000, but the $2,835,000,000 excess of net gold and silver imports (deducting earmarking) over trade and service items shows that there must have been a net capital inflow perhaps twice as large as that indicated by statistics at hand.

Service transactions, such as tourist expenditures and freight payments, were variously affected by the war. On balance they showed the usual excess of payments over receipts, but the net figure was smaller than in other recent years, being estimated at less than $100,000,000.

Merchandise Trade

The effect of the war on United States foreign trade is partly indicated by the rise in exports from $3,177,000,000 in 1939 to $4,021,000,000 in

[1] Prepared by Hal B. Lary and Paul D. Dickens, Finance Division, U. S. Department of Commerce, *Foreign Commerce Weekly*, March 29, 1941, p. 515.

1940, an increase of 27 per cent. The big rise following the outbreak of war, however, had already begun in the closing months of 1939, as shown in figure 1.[1] After January 1940 there was, as a matter of fact, a slight declining tendency, although the monthly rate remained on a much higher level than in other recent years.

During the course of 1940, moreover, there occurred vast shifts in the destination of the export trade which, because of their offsetting character, are only slightly reflected in the general trend. These changes came in the second quarter of the year following the German invasion of Denmark, Norway, the Lowlands, and France and the entrance of Italy into the war. Up to that time, United States exports to Continental Europe had increased, despite the virtual elimination of the German and Polish markets from the moment the conflict began. After the events mentioned, the greater part of Europe became subject to British blockade, and trade dwindled to a mere trickle. By contrast, these same military developments caused tremendous expansion in exports to the United Kingdom and other parts of the British Empire. Prior to that time this trade had shown only a moderate rise as a result of the war, but thereafter it soared quickly. Broadly speaking, the export trade has come to be increasingly concentrated in supplying the materials and weapons of war to the British Empire.

The extent of the shifts described above is clearly brought out by the half-yearly totals. Exports to Continental Europe fell, $457,100,000 from $540,700,000 in the first half of 1940 to only $83,600,000 in the second half. Exports to the British Empire, on the other hand, rose by $403,500,000, climbing from $844,600,000 in the first half to $1,248,100,000 in the second half.

Although less sharply affected than exports, the import trade also showed important shifts to the British Empire, largely reflecting heavier purchases of strategic commodities. At the same time, shutting off of sources of supply in Continental Europe resulted in lower imports of finished goods.

Service Transactions

Various items classified as service transactions have reacted to conditions of 1940, each according to its own peculiarities. With the heavier volume of trade and higher freight rates, freight and shipping payments have risen on both sides of the balance. The net difference is not greatly changed from 1939.

---

[1] Not reproduced.

Tourist Expenditures

American tourist expenditures abroad, normally one of the most important items in the United States balance of payments, have dropped throughout most of the world, precipitously in the case of Europe and less sharply in the Western Hemisphere. Outlays by foreign visitors in the United States also declined greatly in 1940. As indicated in the footnote to the accompanying table, however, the extent of the decline in both payments and receipts on tourist account is not accurately measured in the unrevised figures for 1939 and the preliminary estimates for 1940. The latter are based, insofar as the highly important tourist trade with Canada is concerned, on new methods of recording travel outlays instituted by the Canadian authorities last year. The data so obtained, being far more extensive and presumably more reliable than anything previously available from either country, suggest that past estimates of travel expenditure in both directions have been too high. Revision of earlier estimates has not yet been completed, and the 1939 and 1940 totals therefore are not comparable.

Volume-of-travel data, however, leave no doubt as to the general decline in tourist outlays in 1940. With respect to Canada, that country's immigration records show entries of only 13,592,429 visitors from the United States in 1940 against 16,578,119 in 1939, while Canadians returning from the United States totaled only 6,448,500 in 1940 as compared with 11,555,236 in 1939. Travel to and from Mexico showed little change in 1940, but departures of United States residents to oversea countries, including air and cruise travel, dropped from 384,000 to 205,000. Departures to European and Mediterranean destinations declined most sharply, falling from 135,000 to 16,000, but there was also a considerable decrease in travel to the West Indies and South America.

Interest and Dividends

Despite the widespread economic effects of the war, United States receipts of interest and dividends on foreign investments during 1940, estimated at $525,000,000, showed no appreciable changes from those of the preceding year. The reduction by sinking-fund purchases and by repatriations of the principal amount of foreign dollar bonds held in the United States largely accounted for the slight decline from the estimated receipts of $531,000,000 in 1939. Cessation of receipts from Poland and a drop in receipts from Chile were offset by the resumption of partial interest payments by Brazil and Colombia. Dividends and other income received from direct investments in foreign countries in 1940 were probably unchanged, although later detailed information may require revision of this estimate.

Income derived from such investments in Latin America in 1940 was probably somewhat above the previous year because of the continued high level of activity in the raw-material industries so important in that area, particularly mining, and because blocked earnings were released in some volume in Brazil during the year. Remittances of income from Canada, the United Kingdom and Africa were not greatly restricted, while receipts from Continental Europe and Japan, which had not been very large for several years, were negligible in 1940.

Estimated interest and dividend payments of $215,000,000 during 1940 to foreigners on investments in the United States were, on the other hand, slightly higher than in 1939. The increase arose chiefly from a gain of 14 per cent in average dividend payments on United States common and preferred shares. This gain was more than sufficient to offset the combined effects of the year's net liquidation of certain outstanding foreign-owned issues and the difficulties encountered in the transmittal of coupons payable to investors residing in countries affected by the Treasury freezing orders, especially Belgium, France, and the Netherlands. Foreign income from direct investments in the United States, it is safe to assume, rose in 1940 in accordance with the upward trend in corporate profits.

Remittances

Personal or "immigrant" remittances to foreign countries, also a characteristic feature of the United States balance of payments, appear to have declined somewhat in 1940. There was also a drop in such remittances received from abroad. Institutional contributions to foreign countries, on the other hand, rose by about $12,000,000, the increase being accounted for by remittances for relief purposes to the belligerent countries of Europe.

Among other service items, Government transactions show considerably heavier payments abroad. Heavier outlays for various purposes in the Canal Zone and the Philippines, both of which are outside the "balance of payments" area of the United States, account for the increase.

Gold and Silver Movements

For many years gold has moved into the United States with only occasional interruption. From the beginning of 1934 there have been only 3 months in which the net flow has been outward, and the net inward movement has exceeded a billion dollars each year. Since the Munich conference in September 1938 the inflow has been greatly accelerated, as may be seen in figure 2.[1] Net gold imports, totaling almost $2,000,000,000 in 1938, reached $3,574,000,000 in 1939 and rose further to $4,744,000,000 in 1940.

In each of these last two years net gold imports actually exceeded gross merchandise exports — a situation without precedent in the history of the United States. This comparison is valid only for illustrating the magnitude of the gold movement — not, of course, for indicating specifically how the proceeds were used. Considerable quantities were added, in fact, to gold held under earmark for foreign account, the increase in the amount so held being $534,000,000 in 1939 and $645,000,000 in 1940. If these amounts are deducted, the net gold inflow remains slightly larger than total merchandise exports for 1940 but is somewhat smaller for 1939.

As in other recent years, the major portion of this gold was shipped from British Empire countries, including gold belonging to nonempire countries. This portion in 1940 was $3,627,917,000, or 76 per cent of the total for the year. Despite this high degree of concentration, however, there were 14 countries outside the British Empire that sent more than $20,000,000 each and 6 additional countries that sent more than $10,000,000 each. By contrast, there was only one country to which gold shipments exceeded gold receipts; that country was Bolivia, to which there was a net export of $4,714,619.

Record Shipments in 1940

While predictions in the matter are necessarily hazardous, it appears clear that huge gold movements such as have occurred since the fall of 1938 must decline drastically. Shipments have been greatly in excess of production for several years. There is good reason to believe that many of the principal gold stocks have already been transferred for the most part to the United States, and in certain other cases it seems unlikely that circumstances would permit further shipments of importance.

Future imports, therefore, will probably be limited more and more to current production. Nor, on the other hand, can circumstances be readily envisaged that would lead to a gold movement away from the United States on a scale comparable to imports during 1940. It is thus

---

[1] Not reproduced.

probable that 1940 has set a record for international gold shipments that will last for a very long time.

Net silver imports during 1940 were $54,760,000, the lowest since the silver-purchase program of 1934 was started. The figure was, nevertheless, large enough to bring cumulative net silver imports since the beginning of 1934 to more than $1,000,000,000.

Capital Movements

As already indicated, net gold and silver imports in 1940 exceeded net receipts on trade and service account by more than $2,800,000,000. Assuming that the trade and service estimates are reasonably correct, this difference indicates that there must have been a net capital movement of approximately that amount into the United States during the year. This figure would, in principle, represent the net result of all kinds of capital transactions — for example, the net rise in bank balances in this country for the account of foreigners; withdrawals on balance by Americans of their banking funds abroad; net sales of securities, either domestic or foreign, by Americans to foreigners or vice versa; net reductions in commercial credits granted to foreigners; advance payment by foreign purchasers for American goods; and similar transactions.

On the basis of available statistics, however, it is not possible to account for more than about half of the net capital movement indicated on the above basis. Figures on long- and short-term capital transactions available in official reports (Monthly Bulletin of the Treasury Department) show a net inflow of banking and brokerage funds amounting to $820,000,000 (or, as shown in the table, a net inflow of $873,000,000 in short-term banking funds and a net outflow of $53,000,-000 on long-term account).

Additional data not covered in the Treasury reports bring the net inflow to $1,400,000,000. These additional data relate chiefly to the financial operations of belligerent countries in the United States. In connection with their purchases of war supplies in this country, the United Kingdom and France made some payments considerably in advance of the export of the goods and provided capital assistance to certain producers where new plant facilities were needed. (After the Franco-German Armistice, the United Kingdom took over many of the French commitments in this country.) Up to the end of 1940, advance payments by the British Government had amounted to $570,000,000 and capital assistance to $150,000,000, a total of

$720,000,000 of what might be called British nonbanking credits in the United States. Adjustments to take care of estimated French advances, together with various other transactions, are included in the miscellaneous capital items shown in the accompanying table.

Rise in Foreign Deposits Here

Foreign short-term funds in the United States, as reported by banks and brokers to the Treasury, amounted to $3,980,000,000 at the end of 1940, an increase of $690,000,000 during the year. Most of these additional funds came from France, Canada, Switzerland, and Sweden and represented primarily the proceeds of gold shipments on official account to the United States. The greater part of the movement occurred during the first 7 months of the year. Far Eastern and Latin American short-term accounts also increased, but part of the latter probably represented European capital. Of the major countries, only the United Kingdom showed a substantial reduction in its bank balances here.

In contrast to the general rise in foreign short-term funds in the United States, foreign holdings of United States securities showed a net decline. Net sales of domestic securities, as reported to the Treasury, were $137,000,000 in 1940. The principal sellers were the United Kingdom, Canada, and Japan.

The possibility of changes in foreign investments in the United States has been restricted to a considerable degree by the action of the United States Government in blocking the assets of certain countries under foreign occupation. This step was first taken following Germany's occupation of Denmark and Norway in April 1940, and other countries subsequently affected during the year were the Netherlands, Belgium, Luxemburg, France, Estonia, Latvia, Lithuania, and Rumania. By Executive order it was required that the assets of these countries in the United States should be registered with the Treasury Department and that transactions relating to such assets should be subject to license by that Department.

Much of the increase in foreign short-term funds in the United States may be explained by these so-called "freezing" orders, which, particularly in the case of France, immobilized balances that had accumulated during the first half of the year and were intended to cover future procurement needs in this country.

Reduction in United States Assets Abroad

Foreign balances of United States banks and brokers were further drastically reduced during 1940 by more than $160,000,000 to $410,000,000. This withdrawal of funds was quite general from all areas except Latin America, where there was a slight increase. Such a trend was only natural in view of the restricted field for the extension of trade credits and the conduct of foreign trade.

Net purchases of foreign securities by foreigners amounted to $84,000,-000 and served to reduce still further the gradually dwindling portfolio of such investments held in the United States. Most of the net purchases were made by Canada, Latin American countries, and Japan. They were largely connected with ordinary sinking-fund operations and redemptions at maturity of foreign dollar bonds previously sold in the United States.

Unrecorded Capital Movement

The difference between the $1,400,000,000 net inflow accounted for by available data on capital movements and the $2,800,000,000 indicated by the other balance-of-payments items cannot be explained in quantitative terms on the basis of information now at hand. As implied above, this difference (shown in the table as "Other transactions and residual") is believed to represent chiefly unrecorded capital transactions in view of the fact that it would not be greatly reduced by the most generous revisions possible in trade and service items.

There are various possibilities whereby international capital transfers may not be fully reflected in the statistics on short-term balances and security transactions reported by banks and security brokers and dealers. For one thing, funds actually owned by foreigners may be held in this country under domestic names for various purposes and would thus not be included in the reported totals for foreign balances here. Similarly, funds previously held by banks in this country for foreign account may be withdrawn in the form of currency, thus tending to reduce the reported totals for foreign-owned bank balances here without, however, any actual transfer abroad having occurred. Furthermore, refugee funds previously transferred to the United States may be shifted from foreign to domestic addresses with the arrival of the owners in this country. Here again such changes would tend to reduce the net recorded inward movement.

In all these and other similar cases, however, it is possible only to speculate as to their actual importance, since no statistical measure of the unrecorded movement is available.

(a) Balance of International Payments of the United States, 1939–1940

[In millions of dollars]

ITEM	1939 (UNREVISED)			1940 (PRELIMINARY)		
	Receipts from Foreigners for "Exports" (Credits)	Payments to Foreigners for "Imports" (Debits)	Net Credits (+) or Debits (−)	Receipts from Foreigners for "Exports" (Credits)	Payments to Foreigners for "Imports" (Debits)	Net Credits (+) or Debits (−)
Trade and service items:						
Merchandise	3,177	2,318	+ 859	4,021	2,625	+ 1,396
Freight and shipping . .	125	249	− 124	223	327	− 104
Travel expenditures [1] . .	170	469	− 299	81	223	− 142
Personal remittances . .	45	144	− 99	30	120	− 90
Institutional contributions	—	43	− 43	—	55	− 55
Interest and dividends .	531	211	+ 320	525	215	+ 310
Government transactions	32	96	− 64	28	122	− 94
Miscellaneous services and adjustments . . .	211	103	+ 108	164	66	+ 98
Total trade and service items	4,291	3,633	+ 658	5,072	3,753	+ 1,319
Gold and silver:						
Gold exports and imports	1	3,575	− 3,574	5	4,749	− 4,744
Gold earmarking operations (net)	—	—	+ 534	—	—	+ 645
Gold movements (net) .	—	—	− 3,040	—	—	− 4,099
Silver exports and imports	14	85	− 71	4	59	− 55
Total gold and silver movements (net) . .	—	—	− 3,111	—	—	− 4,154
Capital items (net):						
Long-term capital movements	—	—	+ 114	—	—	[2] − 53
Movement of short-term banking funds. . . .	—	—	+ 1,116	—	—	[2] + 873
Advance payments and capital assistance by British Government .	—	—	—	—	—	+ 720
Miscellaneous capital items	—	—	+ 69	—	—	− 170
Paper currency movements	—	—	+ 117	—	—	+ 33
Total capital items . .	—	—	+ 1,416	—	—	+ 1,403
Other transactions and residual	—	—	+ 1,037	—	—	+ 1,432

[1] Receipts and payments on travel account for 1940 are estimated in part on the basis of data not previously available and therefore are not comparable with the unrevised figures for 1939. See text.
[2] Source: Bulletin of the Treasury Department.

2. FINANCIAL TRANSACTIONS WITH FOREIGN COUNTRIES

[See Chapter II for Financial Relations with the American Republics, p. 120.]

A. United States-British Empire Relations

(1) Notice by the Treasury Department of Conferences with British Treasury Representative (Phillips), July 19, 1940 [1]

Conferences during the past week between Sir Frederick Phillips, Under Secretary of the British Treasury, and Secretary Morgenthau

[1] Treasury Department, Press Service No. 21–65.

have provided an opportunity for the discussion of questions of mutual interest to the British and American Treasuries.

The British Under Secretary was able to assure Secretary Morgenthau, that, while Great Britain is now obliged by the exigencies of war to resort to exchange control and other temporary measures affecting international transactions, his Government plans to return to liberal monetary and trade policies as soon as possible after hostilities cease. Such temporary measures include the arrangement between the financial centers of London and New York inaugurated on July 18 for a system of registered sterling accounts, which should tend toward stabilizing the sterling rate and help protect the American market.

Prospective British purchases in the United States were considered in detail and their effects on the balance of payments between the two countries during the next twelve months were carefully examined.

The controls by the two Governments, as they affect their respective nationals over assets of invaded countries held in Great Britain and the United States were given attention.

———

The Bank of England and the Foreign Exchange Committee, 146 Broadway, New York City, have inaugurated several arrangements for stabilizing the sterling rate with regard to the American market.

The Bank of England on July 18, 1940 put into force a system of registered sterling accounts convertible into dollars or Swiss francs at the official sterling rate of \$4.025 for repurchase and \$4.035 for sale. To such accounts, opened in the name of banks resident in the United States, the Philippine Islands, United States dependencies or Switzerland with the consent of the Bank of England, approved sterling payments by proper residents of the territories named, including payments for imports [1] invoiced in sterling, are made by transfer. A system of special accounts was also in force for the purpose of making payments between a number of other countries and the sterling area. (Foreign Exchange Committee, Reference No. 185.)

On July 18, 1940 the Bank of England put into force a system of "sterling area accounts" for meeting the needs of non-residents who maintain sterling accounts with banks of the United Kingdom for personal purposes. Lists of permitted credits and debits were established for these accounts, which may be maintained by residents in the United States and its dependencies, the Philippine Islands, Switzerland, Argentina, Brazil and Chile.[2] (Foreign Exchange Committee, Reference No. 185.)

Payment from "Canadian authorized accounts" for goods re-exported from

[1] Subsequently registered accounts were restricted to shipments on an "approved ship," defined as one under the flag or chartered by a member of the British Commonwealth of Nations (excluding Eire) or under the flag of Norway, Poland, the Netherlands, Belgium, Sweden or the United States (*New York Times*, November 13, 1941).

[2] Added by later notice, *New York Times*, November 13, 1940.

the United Kingdom may be made either in sterling or in Canadian or Newfoundland dollars (*New York Times*, November 28, 1940).

A regulation of the British Treasury effective November 23, 1940 made payment to a non-resident of the sterling proceeds of specified capital transactions conditional upon such payment being made into a blocked account (*New York Times*, November 24, 1940).

(2) British Estimates of United Kingdom Gold and Dollar Resources [1]

In a letter dated January 21, the Secretary of the Treasury presented to Mr. Bloom, chairman of the Foreign Affairs Committee of the House of Representatives,[2] official British estimates of the gold and dollar resources of the United Kingdom on August 31, 1939 and December 31, 1940. The estimates showed a decline of $2,316,000,000 in British gold and dollar resources in the first 16 months of the war. The Secretary's statement contained a balance of payments with a breakdown of the transactions which account for this decline. This statement was prepared by economists of the Treasury, the Department of Commerce, and the Board of Governors of the Federal Reserve System on the basis of data supplied by the British Government. Previously, on January 15, the Secretary had presented to the Committee the British estimates of their main gold and dollar transactions in 1941, excluding payments on new British Government orders during the year.[3]

The following table shows the change in the position of the United Kingdom during the war period on the basis of the British figures.

[In millions of dollars]

GOLD AND DOLLAR RESOURCES	AMOUNT HELD AUG. 31, 1939	ExPENDED SEPT. 1, 1939– DEC. 31, 1940	AMOUNT HELD DECEMBER 31, 1940		
			Total	Unavailable [4]	Net Available
Gold	2,038	1,746	292	51	241
Dollar balances	595	236	359	305	54
Market securities	950	[5] 334	616	—	616
Direct and miscellaneous investments	900	—	900	—	900
Total	4,483	2,316	2,167	356	1,811

[1] *Federal Reserve Bulletin*, February 1941, p. 99.

[2] *Lend-Lease Bill.* Hearings before the Committee on Foreign Affairs, House of Representatives, 77th Cong., 1 sess., on H. R. 1776, p. 81.   [3] *Ibid.*, p. 52.

[4] The British regard as unavailable $30 million of gold scattered in different parts of the world, $21 million of gold held against outstanding forward exchange contracts, and $305 million representing private dollar balances, which are considered to be at the minimum level necessary for the transaction of current business.

[5] Including direct sales of British-held securities not recorded in the weekly capital movement statistics of the United States Treasury since they were not effected through reporting banks, brokers, and dealers.

For lists of American securities and foreign dollar bonds held by United Kingdom residents which have been requisitioned by the British Treasury, see *Federal Reserve Bulletin*, 1940, p. 206, 408; 1941, p. 25, 101, 410.

(3) *Estimated Gold and Dollar Transactions of Sterling Area* [1]

[In millions of dollars]

GOLD AND DOLLAR EXPENDITURES	SEPT. 1, 1939–DEC. 31, 1940 (16 MONTHS)	1941 ESTIMATES
Payments to United States by United Kingdom:		
On British Government orders in the U. S.:		
Goods delivered . . . . 660 [2]		*
Advance payments — net . 570		*
Capital assistance — net . 150		*
Total	1,380	1,274 [3]
For other merchandise imports from U. S.	705	280
For services (shipping, interest and dividends, etc.) — net	57	—
Total	2,142	1,554
Payments to United States by Sterling Area (excluding U. K.):		
For merchandise imports from United States	435	333
For services — net	18	5
Total	453	338
Payments to Countries Other than U. S. by Sterling Area:		
Balance of Sterling Area with Canada and Newfoundland settled in gold .	225 [4]	620 [4]
Gold and dollar payments to other countries — net	500 [5]	247
Total	725	867
Withdrawal of Capital from Sterling Area (principally from U. K.):		
By Americans and others through sale of free sterling to American importers	300	—
By repayment of outstanding export credits required by cash-and-carry provision of Neutrality Act . . .	200	—
By liquidation of forward exchange position in dollars	235	—
Total	735	—
Miscellaneous Items and Errors of Estimation:	71	—
Grand total	4,126	2,759

* Not reported separately.

Gold and Dollar Receipts	Sept. 1, 1939–Dec. 31, 1940 (16 Months)	1941 Estimates
Receipts from United States by United Kingdom:		
From merchandise exports to United States	205	165
From services — net	—	15
Total	205	180
Receipts from United States by Sterling Area (excluding United Kingdom):		
From merchandise exports to United States	640	560
Receipts by Sterling Area from sale abroad of currently mined and dishoarded gold	965	555 [6]
Receipts from use of gold and dollar resources held by United Kingdom at beginning of period	2,316	1,464
Grand total	4,126	2,759

For the balance sheet of the Exchange Stabilization Fund, December 31, 1940, see *Bulletin of the Treasury Department*, April 1941, p. 1; as of June 30, 1940 and March 31, 1941 see *ibid.*, July 1941, p. 75.

Public Law 142, 77th Cong., approved June 30, 1941, extended the time within which the powers, originally conferred on the President by secs. 10(c) and 12 of the "Gold Reserve Act of 1934" approved January 30, 1934 relating to the Stabilization Fund and alteration of the weight of the dollar, may be exercised until June 30, 1943.

[1] *Federal Reserve Bulletin*, February 1941, p. 101.

The Sterling Area represents broadly the British Empire excluding Canada and Newfoundland; the latter description was used for the sake of simplicity in the figures released by the Treasury. More specifically, it represents the British Empire exclusive of Canada, Newfoundland, and Hong Kong, but with the addition of British mandated territories and of Egypt, Iraq, and the Anglo-Egyptian Sudan. Within the Sterling Area, the United Kingdom represents England, Scotland, Wales, and Northern Ireland.

[2] Includes goods awaiting export at the year end and goods exported to Canada or other countries for United Kingdom account.

[3] No provision is made in this figure for prepayments or deliveries on orders placed in 1941; the figure represents only payments during 1941 on British Government orders placed before the end of 1940. Because of partial prepayment of these orders in 1940, these 1941 payments will be considerably less than the value of the goods delivered for export during the year.

[4] For derivation of this balance see table, *Federal Reserve Bulletin*, February 1941, p. 100.

[5] Composed of gold and dollar expenditures of $550 million and dollar receipts of $50 million.

[6] South African and Australian gold exports.

(4) *Estimated Long-Term Foreign Investments of the United Kingdom Outside the United States* [1]

This formal statement on the financial position of Great Britain was presented to the House Foreign Affairs Committee on January 15, 1941, by Secretary of the Treasury Morgenthau during the hearings on the Lend-Lease Bill, on the basis of information supplied by the British Treasury.

The following estimates are based on a number of studies, most of which were made by British economists before the outbreak of war.

Most of the investments are in sterling securities; a large part of the Canadian investment is in Canadian dollars, and some of the other investments are in the respective domestic currencies. However, for convenience of presentation, the estimated nominal value of the investments has been converted into sterling.

The market values, where given, are calculated from current market quotations of the securities. Since market quotations are not available for a large part of the investment, no total market value can be calculated.

Even where estimates of market value have been made, they have only a limited significance, for the future market or collateral value will depend on the rapidity with which the securities are liquidated, on the general course of the war, and on many other unpredictable factors. Of course, the figures of nominal value are of even more limited significance.

IN BRITISH EMPIRE

[In millions of pounds]

		GOVERN-MENT	RAIL-WAYS	OTHER	TOTAL
Canada	Nominal	75	187	219	481
Canada	Market	(70)	—	—	—
Australia	Nominal	425	3	75	503
Australia	Market	(410)	—	—	—
New Zealand	Nominal	131	1	14	146
New Zealand	Market	(125)	—	—	—
India	Nominal	300	[2]	250	550
India	Market	(250)	—	—	—
British Africa	Nominal	188	[2]	250	438
Malaya	Nominal	6	—	78	84
Other	Nominal	—	—	—	31
Total in British Empire	—	1,125	191	886	2,233

IN ASIA

		GOVERN-MENT	RAIL-WAYS	OTHER	TOTAL
China	Nominal	—	—	—	200
Japan	Nominal	—	—	—	50
Netherlands East Indies .	Nominal	—	—	—	50
Philippines	Nominal	—	—	—	8
Total in Asia . . .	—	—	—	—	308

[1] *Lend-Lease Bill.* Hearings before the Committee on Foreign Affairs, House of Representatives, 77th Cong. on H. R. 1776, p. 53–4.   [2] Not shown separately.

In Latin America

Argentina	Nominal	45	236	83	390
Argentina	Market	(32)	(52)	—	—
Brazil.	Nominal	75	38	47	160
Brazil	Market	(14)	(5)	(22)	(41)
Chile	Nominal	20	20	65	105
Chile	Market	(2)	(5)	—	—
Uruguay	Nominal	18	14	10	42
Uruguay	Market	(8)	(1)	(12)	(21)
Mexico	Nominal	38	90	44	173
Mexico	Market	(1)	(1)	—	—
Peru	Nominal	6	[1]	23	28
Peru	Market	(2)	—	(4)	(5)
Cuba	Nominal	2	25	(2)	28
Cuba	Market	(2)	(1)	—	—
Venezuela	Nominal	Nil	3	18	20
Venezuela	Market	—	0.2	(17)	(17)
Colombia, Ecuador, Bolivia, Paraguay, Central America	Nominal	—	—	—	50
International	Nominal	—	—	—	6
Total in Latin America	Nominal	204	451	317	1,002

Other Areas

In Europe	Nominal	—	—	—	250
In other areas [2]	Nominal	—	—	—	75
Total United Kingdom investment outside United States . .	Nom. value	—	—	—	3,868

B. Financial Regulations Resulting from German Occupation of European Countries

Executive Order No. 6560, January 15, 1934, regulated transactions in foreign exchange, transfers of credit and the export of coin and currency. With the German invasions of Denmark and Norway, sections 9 to 12 were added to it by Executive Order No. 8389 of April 10, 1940, and they were amended to embrace the Netherlands, Belgium and Luxemburg by Executive Order No. 8405 of May

[1] Not shown separately.
[2] Mainly Iran, Egypt, Iraq and Portuguese East Africa.

10, 1940, which was extended to France by Executive Order No. 8446 of June 17, 1940, and to Latvia, Estonia and Lithuania by Executive Order No. 8484 of July 15, 1940. Executive Order No. 8493 adds new provisions.

For Public Resolution No. 69, 76th Cong., 3d sess., approved May 7, 1940; Executive Order No. 8405, May 10, 1940, amending earlier executive orders; and their application to Denmark, Norway, Belgium, Luxemburg, the Netherlands, France, Estonia, Latvia and Lithuania, see *Documents, II, 1939–40,* p. 540–9.

As of December 17, 1940 the freezing orders had immobilized $4,369,000,000, of which $2,387,000,000 was in cash and $1,596,000,000 was in securities. Of the total, $1,619,000,000 belonged to the Netherlands; $1,593,000,000 to France; $760,000,000 to Norway; $92,000,000 to Denmark; $53,000,000 to Rumania; $48,000,000 to Luxemburg and $29,000,000 to the Baltic republics.

(1) *Control over Transactions the Object of Which Is Not in the United States. Executive Order No. 8493, July 25, 1940* [1]

By virtue of the authority vested in me by section 5(*b*) of the Act of October 6, 1917 (40 Stat. 411), as amended, and by virtue of all other authority vested in me, I, FRANKLIN D. ROOSEVELT, PRESIDENT of the UNITED STATES OF AMERICA, do hereby amend Executive Order No. 8389 of April 10, 1940, as amended, amending Executive Order No. 6560 of January 15, 1934, by adding the following sections after section 12 thereof:

SECTION 13A. The following are prohibited except as specifically authorized by the Secretary of the Treasury by means of rulings, regulations, instructions, licenses, or otherwise:

(1) The acquisition, disposition or transfer of, or other dealing in, or with respect to, any security or evidence thereof on which there is stamped or imprinted, or to which there is affixed or otherwise attached, a tax stamp or other stamp of a foreign country designated in this Order, or a notarial or similar seal which by its contents indicates that it was stamped, imprinted, affixed or attached within such foreign country, or where the attendant circumstances disclose or indicate that such a stamp or seal may, at any time, have been stamped, imprinted, affixed or attached thereto.

(2) The acquisition by, or transfer to, any person within the United States of any interest in any security or evidence thereof if the attendant circumstances disclose or indicate that the security or evidence thereof is not physically situated within the United States.[2]

[1] 5 *Fed. Reg.*, p. 2667.

[2] General License No. 26, August 2, 1940 relates to American depository receipts or American shares admitted to dealings on a national securities exchange prior to July 25, 1940 (5 *Fed. Reg.*, p. 2754).

B. The Secretary of the Treasury may investigate, regulate, or prohibit under such rulings, regulations, or instructions as he may prescribe, by means of licenses or otherwise, the sending, mailing, importing or otherwise bringing, directly or indirectly,[1] into the United States, from any foreign country, of any securities or evidences thereof or the receiving or holding in the United States of any securities or evidences thereof so brought into the United States. The provisions of General Ruling No. 5 of June 6, 1940,[2] and all instructions issued pursuant thereto, are hereby continued in full force and effect, subject to amendment, modification or revocation pursuant to the provisions of this Order.

C. In the case of any transaction covered by this section, an application for license may be filed in the manner indicated in the Regulations of April 10, 1940, as amended, issued pursuant to this Order.

D. The Regulations of November 12, 1934, are hereby modified in so far as they are inconsistent with the provisions of this section.

SECTION 14. The Secretary of the Treasury may require any person to furnish under oath, complete information relative to any transaction referred to in this Order, or with respect to any property in which any foreign country designated in this Order, or any national thereof, has any interest, including the production of any books of account, contracts, letters, or other papers, in connection therewith, in the custody or control of such person, either before or after such transaction is completed.

THE WHITE HOUSE,   FRANKLIN D. ROOSEVELT
   July 25, 1940.

General License No. 30, August 14, 1940, related to transactions in the United States affecting trust funds, not undertaken at a request or instruction of a person who is a national of the foreign countries designated in the orders. No. 32, August 30, 1940, and February 1, 1941, permits continuance of monthly remittances to foreigners by certain individuals under conditions existing before April 8, 1940; No. 33, September 10, 1940, and February 1, 1941, permits re-

[1] General Ruling No. 8, September 18, 1940 (5 *Fed. Reg.*, p. 3747) construes the executive order provisions as prohibiting, except under license, complying with a request or authorization to make a payment or transfer of credit either directly or indirectly to a foreign country designated by executive order, or a national thereof, through a bank or other person in a third foreign country not designated by executive order.

[2] *Documents, II, 1939–40*, p. 548. General Ruling No. 5 concerned privately owned foreign securities or evidences thereof. General Ruling No. 7, September 18, 1940, extended it to them when "coming from the Philippine Islands and the Panama Canal Zone into any other part of the United States" (5 *Fed. Reg.*, p. 3747).

mittances to citizens of the United States abroad, with special provision for their return.[1]

General License No. 37, dated March 12, 1941 [2] applied to accounts in the name of citizens of the United States who were within foreign countries in the course of employment by the Government of the United States.

(2) *Extension to Rumania. Executive Order No. 8565, October 10, 1940* [3]

By virtue of the authority vested in me by section 5 (*b*) of the Act of October 6, 1917 (40 Stat. 411), as amended, and by virtue of all other authority vested in me, I, FRANKLIN D. ROOSEVELT, PRESIDENT of the UNITED STATES OF AMERICA, do hereby amend Executive Order No. 8389 of April 10, 1940, as amended,[4] so as to extend all the provisions thereof to, and with respect to, property in which Rumania or any national thereof has at any time on or since October 9, 1940, had any interest of any nature whatsoever, direct or indirect; except that, in defining "Rumania" and "national" of Rumania, the date "October 9, 1940" shall be substituted for the dates appearing in the definitions of countries and nationals thereof.

FRANKLIN D. ROOSEVELT

THE WHITE HOUSE,
October 10, 1940.

(a) *Extensions to Other States*

Extensions identic in form were issued between July 1, 1940 and June 30, 1941, as follows:

Estonia [5]	July 10, 1940	Executive Order No. 8484	5 *Fed. Reg.*, p. 138
Latvia [5]	July 10, 1940	Executive Order No. 8484	5 *Fed. Reg.*, p. 138
Lithuania [5]	July 10, 1940	Executive Order No. 8484	5 *Fed. Reg.*, p. 138
Bulgaria	March 4, 1941	Executive Order No. 8701	6 *Fed. Reg.*, p. 1285
Hungary	March 13, 1941	Executive Order No. 8711	6 *Fed. Reg.*, p. 1443
Yugoslavia	March 24, 1941	Executive Order No. 8721	6 *Fed. Reg.*, p. 1622
Greece	April 28, 1941	Executive Order No. 8746	6 *Fed. Reg.*, p. 2187

[1] 5 *Fed. Reg.*, p. 2863, 3531, 3534; 6 *ibid.*, p. 748.

[2] *Ibid.*, p. 1443.

[3] 5 *Fed. Reg.*, p. 4062.

[4] That is, by Executive Order No. 8405 (*Documents, II, 1939–40*, p. 543) and Executive Order No. 8493, above p. 534.

[5] Resulted from occupation by the Soviet Union; see *Documents, II, 1939–40*, p. 548.

C. Freezing of All Continental European Assets

(1) *Regulation of Transactions in Foreign Exchange and Foreign-Owned Property, and Provision for the Reporting of All Foreign-Owned Property, and Related Matters, Executive Order No. 8785, June 14, 1941* [1]

[Excerpt]

By virtue of and pursuant to the authority vested in me by Section 5 (*b*) of the Act of October 6, 1917 (40 Stat. 415), as amended,[2] by virtue of all other authority vested in me, and by virtue of the existence of a period of unlimited national emergency, and finding that this order is in the public interest and is necessary in the interest of national defense and security, I, FRANKLIN D. ROOSEVELT, PRESIDENT of the UNITED STATES OF AMERICA, do prescribe the following:

Executive Order No. 8389 of April 10, 1940, as amended, is amended to read as follows:

SEC. 1. All of the following transactions are prohibited, except as specifically authorized by the Secretary of the Treasury by means of regulations, rulings, instructions, licenses, or otherwise, if (1) such transactions are by, or on behalf of, or pursuant to the direction of, any foreign country designated in this order, or any national thereof, or (2) such transactions involve property in which any foreign country designated in this order, or any national thereof, has at any time on or since the effective date of this order had any interest of any nature whatsoever, direct or indirect:

A. All transfers of credit between any banking institution within the United States and all transfers of credit between any banking institution within the United States and any banking institution outside the United States (including any principal, agent, home office, branch, or correspondent outside the United States, or a banking institution within the United States);

B. All payments by or to any banking institution within the United States;

C. All transactions in foreign exchange by any person within the United States;

D. The export or withdrawal from the United States, or the earmarking of gold or silver coin or bullion or currency by any person within the United States;

---

[1] 6 *Fed. Reg.*, p. 2897.
[2] *Documents, II, 1939–40*, p. 541.

E. All transfers, withdrawals or exportations of, or dealings in, any evidences of indebtedness or evidences of ownership of property by any person within the United States; and

F. Any transaction for the purpose or which has the effect of evading or avoiding the foregoing prohibitions.

SEC. 2. A. All of the following transactions are prohibited, except as specifically authorized by the Secretary of the Treasury by means of regulations, rulings, instructions, licenses, or otherwise:

(1) The acquisition, disposition or transfer of, or other dealing in, or with respect to, any security or evidence thereof on which there is stamped or imprinted, or to which there is affixed or otherwise attached, a tax stamp or other stamp of a foreign country designated in this order or a notarial or similar seal which by its contents indicates that it was stamped, imprinted, affixed or attached within such foreign country, or where the attendant circumstances disclose or indicate that such stamp or seal may, at any time, have been stamped, imprinted, affixed or attached thereto; and

(2) The acquisition by, or transfer to, any person within the United States of any interest in any security or evidence thereof if the attendant circumstances disclose or indicate that the security or evidence thereof is not physically situated within the United States.

B. The Secretary of the Treasury may investigate, regulate, or prohibit under such regulations, rulings, or instructions as he may prescribe, by means of licenses or otherwise, the sending, mailing, importing or otherwise bringing, directly or indirectly, into the United States, from any foreign country, of any securities or evidences thereof or the receiving or holding in the United States of any securities or evidences thereof, so brought into the United States.

SEC. 3. The term "foreign country designated in this order" means a foreign country included in the following schedule, and the term "effective date of this Order" means with respect to any such foreign country, or any national thereof, the date specified in the following schedule:

(a) April 8, 1940 — Norway and Denmark;
(b) May 10, 1940 — The Netherlands, Belgium and Luxemburg;
(c) June 17, 1940 — France (including Monaco);
(d) July 10, 1940 — Latvia, Estonia and Lithuania;
(e) October 9, 1940 — Rumania;
(f) March 4, 1941 — Bulgaria;
(g) March 13, 1941 — Hungary;
(h) March 24, 1941 — Yugoslavia;
(i) April 28, 1941 — Greece; and

(*j*) June 14, 1941 — Albania, Andorra, Austria, Czechoslovakia, Danzig, Finland, Germany,[1] Italy, Liechtenstein, Poland, Portugal, San Marino, Spain, Sweden, Switzerland, and Union of Soviet Socialist Republics.

(*k*)[2] June 14, 1941 — China and Japan.

The "effective date of this Order" with respect to any foreign country not designated in this order shall be deemed to be June 14, 1941.

SEC. 4. A. The Secretary of the Treasury and/or the Attorney General may require, by means of regulations, rulings, instructions, or otherwise, any person to keep a full record of, and to furnish under oath, in the form of reports or otherwise, from time to time and at any time or times, complete information relative to any transaction referred to in Section 5 (*b*) of the Act of October 6, 1917 (40 Stat. 415), as amended, or relative to any property in which any foreign country or any national thereof has any interest . . .

SEC. 5. A. As used in the first paragraph of Section 1 of this Order "transactions [which] involve property in which any foreign country designated in this Order, or any national thereof, has . . . any interest of any nature whatsoever, direct or indirect," shall include, but not by way of limitation (1) any payment or transfer to any such foreign country or national thereof, (2) any export or withdrawal from the United States to such foreign country, and (3) any transfer of credit or payment of an obligation, expressed in terms of the currency of such foreign country.

B. The term "United States" means the United States and any place subject to the jurisdiction thereof; the term "Continental United States" means the States of the United States, the District of Columbia and the territory of Alaska.

C. The term "person" means an individual, partnership, association, corporation or other organization.

D. The term "foreign country" shall include, but not by way of limitation:

(*i*) The State and the government thereof on the effective date of this order as well as any political subdivision, agency, or instrumentality thereof or any territory, dependency, colony, protectorate, mandate, dominion, possession or place subject to the jurisdiction thereof,

(*ii*) Any other government (including any political subdivision, agency, or instrumentality thereof) to the extent and only to the extent that such government exercises or claims to exercise de jure or de facto sovereignty over the area which on such effective date constituted such foreign country, and

(*iii*) Any person to the extent that such person is, or has been, or to the extent that there is reasonable cause to believe that such person is, or has been, since such effective date, acting or purporting to act directly or indirectly for the benefit or on behalf of any of the foregoing.

---

[1] German sources estimated the amount of German funds in the United States at not above 120,000,000 marks, whereas United States assets in Germany proper were said to be 1,700,000,000 marks (*New York Times*, June 23, 1941, p. 25).

[2] Amendment by Executive Order No. 8832 of July 26, 1941 (6 *Fed. Reg.*, p. 3715).

E. The term "national" shall include,

(1) Any person who has been domiciled in, or a subject, citizen or resident of, a foreign country at any time on or since the effective date of this order,[1]

(2) Any partnership, association, corporation or other organization, organized under the laws of, or which on or since the effective date of this order had or has had its principal place of business in such foreign country, or which on or since such effective date was or has been controlled by, or a substantial part of the stock, shares, bonds, debentures, notes, drafts, or other securities or obligations of which, was or has been owned or controlled by, directly or indirectly, such foreign country and/or one or more nationals thereof as herein defined,

(3) Any person to the extent that such person is, or has been, since such effective date, acting or purporting to act directly or indirectly for the benefit or on behalf of any national of such foreign country, and

(4) Any other person who, there is reasonable cause to believe, is a "national" as herein defined.[2]

In any case in which by virtue of the foregoing definition a person is a national of more than one foreign country, such person shall be deemed to be a national of each such foreign country. In any case in which the combined interests of two or more foreign countries designated in this order and/or nationals thereof are sufficient in the aggregate to constitute, within the meaning of the foregoing, control or 25 per centum or more of the stock, shares, bonds, debentures, notes, drafts, or other securities or obligations of a partnership, association, corporation or other organization, but such control or a substantial part of such stock, shares, bonds, debentures, notes, drafts, or other securities or obligations is not held by any one such foreign country and/or national thereof, such partnership, association, corporation or other organization, shall be deemed to be a national of each of such foreign countries. . . .

F. The term "banking institution" as used in this order shall include any person engaged primarily or incidentally in the business of banking, of granting or transferring credits, or of purchasing or selling foreign exchange or procuring purchasers and sellers thereof, as principal or agent, or any person holding credits for others as a direct or incidental part of his business, or brokers; and, each principal, agent, home office, branch or correspondent of any person so engaged shall be regarded as a separate "banking institution."

G. The term "this Order," as used herein, shall mean Executive Order No. 8389 of April 10, 1940, as amended.[3]

Sec. 6. Executive Order No. 8389 of April 10, 1940, as amended, shall no longer be deemed to be an amendment to or a part of Executive Order No. 6560 of January 15, 1934.[4] Executive Order No. 6560 of January 15, 1934, and the regulations of November 12, 1934, are hereby modified in so far as they are consistent with the provisions of this order, and except as so modified, continue in full force and effect. Nothing herein shall be deemed to revoke any license, ruling, or instruction now in effect and issued pursuant to Executive Order No.

[1] General License No. 42 of June 14, 1941 (6 *Fed. Reg.*, p. 2907) applies to such individuals.

[2] The Roman Curia of the Vatican City State is a generally licensed national by General License No. 44 (6 *Fed. Reg.*, p. 2907).

[3] *Documents, II, 1939–40*, p. 543.

[4] Sec. 1, *Documents, II, 1939–40*, p. 543; full text U. S. Code, title 12, sec. 95, annex.

6560 of January 15, 1934, as amended, or pursuant to this Order; provided, however, that all such licenses, rulings, or instructions shall be subject to the provisions hereof. . . .

SEC. 7. Without limitation as to any other powers or authority of the Secretary of the Treasury or the Attorney General under any other provision of this Order, the Secretary of the Treasury is authorized and empowered to prescribe from time to time regulations, rulings, and instructions to carry out the purposes of this order and to provide therein or otherwise the conditions under which licenses may be granted by or through such officers or agencies as the Secretary of the Treasury may designate, and the decision of the Secretary with respect to the granting, denial or other disposition of an application or license shall be final.

SEC. 8. Section 5 (b) of the Act of October 6, 1917, as amended, provides in part:

". . . Whoever willfully violates any of the provisions of this subdivision or of any license, order, rule or regulation issued thereunder, shall, upon conviction, be fined not more than $10,000, or, if a natural person, may be imprisoned for not more than ten years, or both; and any officer, director, or agent of any corporation who knowingly participates in such violation may be punished by a like fine, imprisonment, or both."

SEC. 9. This Order and any regulations, rulings, licenses or instructions issued hereunder may be amended, modified or revoked at any time.

(2) *Exceptions to Control Made by General License*

(a) *Netherlands East and West Indies. General License No. 15, Amended June 7, 1941* [1]

[See *Documents, II, 1939–40*, p. 543 for the Executive Order No. 8389, April 10, 1940 freezing credits of the Netherlands (and other countries) and their nationals.]

(1) A general license is hereby granted authorizing all transactions ordinarily incident to the importing and exporting of goods, wares and merchandise between the United States and the Netherlands East Indies and between the United States and the Netherlands West Indies, provided the following terms and conditions are complied with:

(a) Imports and exports between the United States and such areas shall not be financed, directly or indirectly, from any blocked account in which any blocked country or any national thereof, other than the Netherlands or any national thereof, has an interest; and

[1] 6 *Fed. Reg.*, p. 2789; Code of Federal Regulations, Title 31, Part 145; — Sec. 5 (b), 40 Stat. 415 and 966; Sec. 2, 48 Stat. 1; Public Resolution No. 69, 76th Congress; 12 U. S. C. 95a; Ex. Order 6560, Jan. 15, 1934; Ex. Order 8389, April 10, 1940; Ex. Order 8405, May 10, 1940; Ex. Order 8446, June 17, 1940; Ex. Order 8484, July 15, 1940; Ex. Order 8493, July 25, 1940; Ex. Order 8565, October 10, 1940; Ex. Order 8701, March 4, 1941; Ex. Order 8711, March 13, 1941; Ex. Order 8721, March 24, 1941; Ex. Order 8746, April 28, 1941; Regulations, April 10, 1940, as amended May 10, 1940, June 17, 1940, July 15, 1940, October 10, 1940, March 4, 1941, March 13, 1941, March 24, 1941 and April 28, 1941.

(b) Imports and exports between the United States and such areas shall not involve, directly or indirectly, property in which any blocked country or any national thereof, other than the Netherlands or any national thereof, has an interest, or has had an interest since the effective date of the Order.

(2) Banking institutions within the United States engaging in any transactions authorized by this general license shall file promptly with the appropriate Federal Reserve Bank monthly reports setting forth the details of such transactions during such period, including appropriate identification of the accounts which are debited or credited in connection with any such transaction.

D. W. BELL,
Acting Secretary of the Treasury

(b) Sweden. General License No. 50, June 20, 1941 [1]
[Switzerland. General License No. 49]

[Sweden and Switzerland, being neutral and surrounded by German-occupied territory, found that their exchange position was especially complicated. To maintain their own financial relations with other countries, while protecting their financial systems from being the channel for unneutral operations, was a delicate task. In June 1941 both governments had given appropriate assurances to the United States in connection with Executive Order No. 8389 of April 10, 1940 (*Documents, II, 1939–40*, p. 543) and the scope of general licenses issued under its consolidated amendment, Executive Order No. 8785 of June 14, 1941. General License No. 49 relating to Switzerland (6 *Fed. Reg.*, p. 3057) varies from the Swedish text printed so as to conform to differences in the Swiss control of exchange.]

(1) A general license is hereby granted licensing any transaction referred to in Section 1 of the Order, if (i) such transaction is by, or on behalf of, or pursuant to the direction of Sweden, or any national thereof, or (ii) such transaction involves property in which Sweden, or any national thereof, has at any time on or since the effective date of the Order had any interest, *provided, that:*

(a) Such transaction is not by, or on behalf of, or pursuant to the direction of any blocked country or any national thereof, other than Sweden or any national of Sweden; and

(b) Such transaction does not involve property in which any blocked country or any national thereof, other than Sweden or any national of Sweden, has at any time on or since the effective date of the Order had any interest; and

(c) If such transaction is not by, or on behalf of, or pursuant to the direction of the Government of Sweden or the Sveriges Riksbank, such transaction shall not be effected until a representative in New York, New York, of the Swedish Legation, designated for such purpose by the Minister of Sweden to the United States, has certified in writing that the Government of Sweden has determined that such transaction complies with the conditions of paragraphs (a) and (b) above.

[1] Code of Federal Regulations, Title 31, Part 179; — Sec. 5 (b), 40 Stat. 415 and 966; Sec. 2, 48 Stat. 1; 54 Stat. 179; Ex. Order 8389, April 10, 1940, as amended by Ex. Order 8785, June 14, 1941; Regulations, April 10, 1940, as amended June 14, 1941.

(2) This license shall not be deemed to permit any payment, transfer or withdrawal from any blocked account other than blocked accounts in the name of the Government of Sweden or the Sveriges Riksbank, until the said representative in New York, New York, of the Swedish Legation has certified, with respect to the transaction, as provided in paragraph (1) (c) above.

(3) This general license shall not apply with respect to any national of Sweden who is also a national of any other blocked country.

(4) Banking institutions within the United States engaging in any transactions authorized by this general license shall file promptly with the appropriate Federal Reserve Bank weekly reports setting forth the details of transactions effected by them under this license.

(5) As used in this general license, the "Government of Sweden" shall include the government of any political subdivision (territories, dependencies, possessions, states, departments, provinces, counties, municipalities, districts or other places subject to the jurisdiction thereof), or any political agency or instrumentality of the government.

E. H. FOLEY, JR.
Acting Secretary of the Treasury

(c) Soviet Union. General License No. 51, June 24, 1941 [1]

(1) A general license is hereby granted licensing the Union of Soviet Socialist Republics as a generally licensed country.

(2) As used in this general license:

Any foreign country licensed as a "generally licensed country," and nationals thereof, shall be regarded for all purposes as if such foreign country were not a foreign country designated in the Order.

E. H. FOLEY, JR.
Acting Secretary of the Treasury

(3) Italian Reprisal Order, Rome, June 17, 1941 [2]

Acts of legitimate reprisal against measures adopted by the United States affecting Italian interests, entered into effect immediately:

1. It is forbidden for persons of Italian nationality who are debtors in any way of sums of money toward persons having United States nationality wherever they are or who are obliged to deliver bonds, negotiable papers or other goods to provide for above-mentioned payments and delivery.

[1] 6 *Fed. Reg.*, p. 3100. This license was issued at the request of the Department of State, with the approval of the Treasury Department and the Department of Justice, without requirement of the formal assurances that have been made the prior condition of issuing general licenses (Treasury Department, Press Service No. 26-9).

[2] Associated Press version, *New York Times*, June 18, 1941, p. 12. New rules became effective on July 13, which further extended the Italian Government's control over American business concerns (*New York Times*, July 14, 1941, p. 5).

The same prohibition applies to foreigners having their residence in Italy, or even if residing elsewhere, for bonds, negotiable papers or other goods held by them within the territory of the State (Italy).

The prohibition in the first paragraph does not apply to persons of Italian nationality residing in the United States.

2. Null in full legality is any act of disposal performed by persons having United States nationality with regard to credits, bonds, negotiable papers and goods mentioned in the preceding article as well as real estate existing in territory of the State and belonging to them.

3. Persons of Italian nationality, associations and recognized organizations having domiciled residence or main offices in the territory of the State must present to the nearest branch of the Bank of Italy — as cashier of the National Institute for Foreign Trade — a written report of debits, even if not yet liquid, and persons having American nationality as well as bonds, negotiable papers and other goods belonging to those persons and held by them.

The same reports, even when conditions foreseen in the preceding paragraph do not exist, are required of persons of any nationality for bonds, negotiable papers and other goods belonging to persons having United States nationality, held by them in territory of the State, and for debts toward said persons arising from commercial activities exercised by them here. The report referred to in the preceding paragraph must be made within twenty days of the date of entrance into effect of the present decree and for obligations coming up within that time from the date on which they arrived.

4. Provisions contained in Article 1 do not apply to citizens of the United States who have their residence in Italy on the date of the present decree.

5. In cases of proved necessity or for other special motives payments and operations contrary to the dispositions of the present decree can be authorized.

6. Whoever effects payments or deliveries of goods in contravention to provisions of the present decree is punishable with imprisonment up to three years and with fines equal to five times the sum paid or the value of goods delivered and in any case not less than 100,000 lire.

Whoever takes part or in any way gives execution to operations mentioned in Article 2 is punishable with imprisonment up to six months and with fines up to 300 lire unless the hypothesis foreseen in the preceding paragraph exists.

Whoever, being obliged to do so, fails to make a report as provided for in Article 3 within the terms fixed there is punishable with imprisonment up to three months and with a fine up to 3,000 lire. Punishment is imprisonment up to six months and a fine up to 6,000 lire when a report has been presented which contains false indications.

(a) *Departure of Italians. Treasury Release, June 23, 1941* [1]

The Treasury Department today ordered Customs officials to take all necessary steps to prevent any Italian national from departing from the United States pending further instructions. It is understood the Department of Justice has issued similar instructions to Immigration officers.

The action was taken to insure compliance with the Executive Order of the President of June 14, 1941, regulating transactions in foreign exchange and foreign-owned property.

The Executive Order and the regulations approved by the President prohibit Italian nationals from exporting or withdrawing from the United States any gold or silver coin or bullion or any currency and require reports with respect to any and all property situated in the United States in which such Italian nationals have any interest whatsoever.

The Treasury instructions require Customs officials to cover all possible means of departure, including vessels, trains, busses, airplanes and international border roads so that no Italians may leave this country without having fully complied with the Executive Order and the regulations.

(b) *Italian Communiqué, Rome, June 24, 1941* [2]

In relation to the measure adopted by the American Government, by which Italian citizens are forbidden to leave the territory of the United States without special authorization from the Federal authorities, the Italian Government has adopted an analogous measure with regard to American citizens residing in the kingdom and territories under Italian sovereignty or occupied by our troops.

D. Use of Foreign Government Accounts

Foreign governments and foreign central banks have large deposit accounts and large amounts of gold under earmark with the Federal Reserve Banks and some insured commercial banks. Especially for those countries which have been invaded or occupied it might not be clear who has authority to withdraw or otherwise deal with such deposits or earmarked gold. An amendment to the Federal Reserve Act to remove uncertainty that banks might encounter and to prevent embarrassment to the relations of the United States and other governments from litigation was enacted. Any question as to who has title to, or the right to dispose of, funds in this country belonging to foreign governments and their central banks depends upon the laws of such foreign countries, and representation by the diplomatic representatives of such countries is the best evidence as to such laws. The legislation provides, in effect, that the banks may safely

[1] Treasury Department, Press Service No. 26–3.
[2] English version from *New York Times*, June 25, 1941, p. 6.

rely upon representations by the Secretary of State as to who is the duly accredited representative of any foreign country and may rely upon representations made by such representatives and accepted and certified by the Secretary of State as to who is entitled to withdraw or otherwise deal with such funds.

(1) An Act Relating to Foreign Accounts in Federal Reserve Banks and Insured Banks, Approved April 7, 1941 [1]

[Excerpts]

Be it enacted by the Senate and House of Representatives of the United States of America in Congress assembled, That subsection (e) of section 14 of the Federal Reserve Act, as amended, is amended by inserting before the period at the end of the first sentence thereof the following: ", or for foreign banks or bankers, or for foreign states as defined in section 25 (b) of this Act."

SEC. 2. Section 25 (b) of the Federal Reserve Act, as amended, is amended by adding at the end thereof the following new paragraph:

"Whenever (1) any Federal Reserve bank has received any property [2] from or for the account of a foreign state [3] which is recognized by the Government of the United States, or from or for the account of a central bank of any such foreign state, and holds such property in the name of such foreign state or such central bank; (2) a representative of such foreign state who is recognized by the Secretary of State as being the accredited representative of such foreign state to the Government of the United States has certified to the Secretary of State the name of a person as having authority to receive, control, or dispose of such property; and (3) the authority of such person to act with respect to such property is accepted and recognized by the Secretary of State, and so certified by the Secretary of State to the Federal Reserve bank, the payment, transfer, delivery, or other disposal of such property by such Federal Reserve bank to or upon the order of such person shall be conclusively presumed to be lawful and shall constitute a complete discharge and release of any liability of the Federal Reserve bank for or with respect to such property."

[1] Public Law 31, 77th Cong.; originated as S. 390; Senate Report No. 133.

[2] "The term 'property' includes gold, silver, currency, credits, deposits, securities, choses in action, and any other form of property, the proceeds thereof, and any right, title, or interest therein."

[3] "The term 'foreign state' includes any foreign government or any department, district, province, county, possession, or other similar governmental organization or subdivision of a foreign government, and any agency or instrumentality of any such foreign government or of any such organization or subdivision."

3. PROTECTION OF AMERICAN HOLDINGS IN FOREIGN COUNTRIES

(1) *Statement of the Department of State, March 22, 1941* [1]

Information regarding protection of American holdings in foreign countries follows:

1. The United States Government does not undertake to guarantee American holdings or investments in foreign countries against depreciation or to obtain preferential treatment for them. When occasion arises, however, it does extend to the property and holdings of American citizens in foreign countries such protection as may be appropriate and feasible under existing conditions. It must be remembered that real and personal property within the jurisdiction of a foreign government are, generally speaking, subject to the laws of that government, and in the absence of a specific treaty provision to the contrary there is no way in which a private individual or concern may secure immunity from the law for property held within the jurisdiction of a particular state, especially if applied to its nationals and foreigners alike. Moreover, American diplomatic and consular officers are prohibited by law from acting as agents or attorneys in connection with private matters for American citizens. The officers abroad of the Department of State are prepared to supply, without responsibility, the names of persons believed to be qualified to act in behalf of American citizens, and such officers will afford appropriate assistance to the representatives of American citizens. American citizens having property or other interests in foreign countries should endeavor to keep themselves currently informed of the status of their holdings through the usual channels.

2. In order that the Department of State may be in a position to consider issuing instructions to its representatives abroad in regard to the protection of specific American interests, it should be in possession of documentary evidence that the holdings in question are American-owned.

[Here follow instructions for individuals, corporations and unincorporated companies.]

3. Documentary evidence of ownership of the holdings should be submitted in triplicate in the form of certified copies or photostats of the original documents. . . .

4. Attention is invited to the provisions of the President's Executive Order No. 8389 of April 10, 1940, as amended, which prohibits, except under licensing regulations issued by the Secretary of the Treasury, transactions in foreign exchange, transfers of credits, et cetera, if involv-

[1] Department of State, *Bulletin*, IV, p. 337.

ing Denmark, Norway, the Netherlands, Belgium, Luxemburg, Latvia, Lithuania, Estonia, France, Rumania, Bulgaria, or Hungary, nationals thereof, or persons domiciled therein. Inquiries regarding this Executive order may be addressed to the Federal Reserve Bank of the district in which the applicant resides or has his principal office or agency, or to the Federal Reserve Bank of New York, N. Y.

This Department is not aware of any Executive order or statute under which claims of American citizens against nationals of any of the countries mentioned may be offset against the assets of those countries in the United States covered by Executive Order No. 8389,[1] as amended.

4. EXPORT–IMPORT BANK OF WASHINGTON AND THE RECONSTRUCTION FINANCE CORPORATION

A policy of assistance to the countries of the Western Hemisphere by development of resources, stabilization of economies and orderly marketing of products was established by legislation approved September 26, 1940. In form this was an act to provide for increasing the lending authority of the Export-Import Bank of Washington and for other purposes, which amended sec. 5 d of the Reconstruction Finance Corporation Act as it was amended by the act of June 25, 1940. [2] The act carried out a recommendation of the President in a message of July 22, 1940.

The legislation is complex not only because it amends prior legislation but because the lending power of the Export-Import Bank of Washington is subordinate to the Reconstruction Finance Corporation's assets, which are derived from its borrowing authority. The act of September 26, 1940 increased the lending authority of the Bank from $200,000,000 to $700,000,000 and the borrowing authority of the corporation under sec. 5 d of the Reconstruction Finance Corporation Act to $1,500,000,000. The act also eliminated a restriction of $20,000,000 to the amount of loans which the Bank may have outstanding to any one foreign country, and extended the life of the Bank to January 22, 1947.

(1) *Message of the President (Roosevelt) Regarding Increase in Capital and Lending Power of Export–Import Bank, July 22, 1940* [3]

To the Congress of the United States:

As a result of the war in Europe, far-reaching changes in world affairs have occurred, which necessarily have repercussions on the economic life both of the United States and of the other American Republics. All American Republics in some degree make a practice of selling, and should sell, surplus products to other parts of the world, and we in the United States export many items that are also exported by other countries of the Western Hemisphere.

[1] See p. 533–41.

[2] Public No. 664, 76th Cong.; *Documents, II, 1939–40*, p. 781. The relevant part of the original is U. S. Code, title 15, sec. 606 *b*.

[3] Department of State, *Bulletin*, III, p. 41; House Doc. No. 881, 76th Cong., 3d sess.

The course of the war, the resultant blockades and counterblockades, and the inevitable disorganization is preventing the flow of these surplus products to their normal markets. Necessarily this has caused distress in various parts of the New World, and will continue to cause distress until foreign trade can be resumed on a normal basis and the seller of these surpluses is in a position to protect himself in disposing of his products. Until liberal commercial policies are restored and fair trading on a commercial plane is reopened, distress may be continued.

I therefore request that the Congress give prompt consideration to increasing the capital and lending power of the Export-Import Bank of Washington by $500,000,000, and removing some of the restrictions on its operations to the end that the Bank may be of greater assistance to our neighbors south of the Rio Grande, including financing the handling and orderly marketing of some part of their surpluses.

It is to be hoped that before another year world trade can be reestablished, but, pending this adjustment, we in the United States should join with the peoples of the other Republics of the Western Hemisphere in meeting their problems. I call the attention of Congress to the fact that by helping our neighbors we will be helping ourselves. It is in the interests of the producers of our country, as well as in the interests of producers of other American countries, that there shall not be a disorganized or cut-throat market in those commodities which we all export.

No sensible person would advocate an attempt to prevent the normal exchange of commodities between other continents and the Americas, but what can and should be done is to prevent excessive fluctuations caused by distressed selling resulting from temporary interruption in the flow of trade, or the fact that there has not yet been reestablished a system of free exchange. Unless exporting countries are able to assist their nationals, they will be forced to bargain as best they can.

As has heretofore been made clear to the Congress, the Export-Import Bank is operated by directors representing the Departments of State, Treasury, Agriculture, and Commerce, and the Reconstruction Finance Corporation, and is under the supervision of the Federal Loan Administrator, so that all interested branches of our Government participate in any loans that are authorized, and the directors of the Bank should have a free hand as to the purposes for which loans are authorized and the terms and conditions upon which they are made.

I therefore request passage of appropriate legislation to this end.

FRANKLIN D. ROOSEVELT

THE WHITE HOUSE,
   July 22, 1940.

(2) *Sec. 5 d, par. 4,*[1] *of the Reconstruction Finance Corporation Act, Amended by Act Approved September 26, 1940* [2]

In order to aid the Government of the United States in its national-defense program, the Corporation is authorized —

(1) [3] To assist in the development of the resources, the stabilization of the economies, and the orderly marketing of the products of the countries of the Western Hemisphere by supplying funds, not to exceed $500,000,000 outstanding at any one time, to the Export-Import Bank of Washington, through loans to, or by subscriptions to preferred stock of, such bank, to enable such bank, to make loans to any governments, their central banks, or any other acceptable banking institutions and, when guaranteed by any such government, a central bank, or any other acceptable banking institution, to a political subdivision, agency, or national of any such government, notwithstanding any other provisions of law insofar as they may restrict or prohibit loans or other extensions of credit to, or other transactions with, the governments of the countries of the Western Hemisphere or their agencies or nationals: *Provided,* That no such loans shall be made in violation of international law as interpreted by the Department of State, or of the Act of April 13, 1934 (48 Stat. 574), or of the Neutrality Act of 1939.[4] Upon the written request of the Federal Loan Administrator, with the approval of the President, the bank is authorized, subject to such conditions and limitations as may be set forth in such request or approval, to exercise the powers and perform the functions herein set forth. Such loans may be made and administered in such manner and upon such terms and conditions as the bank may determine.

---

[1] The Reconstruction Finance Corporation Act came into force January 22, 1932 (47 Stat. 5), but has been extensively amended. Sec. 5, which defines the scope of its authority, has been repeatedly revised. Forms of sec. 5 d, as enacted June 19, 1934 (48 Stat. 1108) and January 31, 1935 (49 Stat. 4), stand as pars. 1–3 as enacted April 13, 1938 (52 Stat. 212; U. S. Code, title 15, 606 b); par. 4 was enacted by sec. 5 of Public No. 664, 76th Cong., approved June 25, 1940 (*Documents, II, 1939–40,* p. 781) and is printed here as further amended. Subparagraphs (2)–(4) of sec. 5 d, par. 4, are at p. 751.

[2] An act to provide for increasing the lending authority of the Export-Import Bank of Washington, and for other purposes, Public No. 792, 76th Cong., 3d sess.; H. R. 10361 from House Committee on Banking and Currency, August 15, 1940, House Report No. 2855; S. 4204 from Senate Committee on Banking and Currency, August 6, 1940, Senate Report No. 2005; House (conference) Report No. 2943, September 13, 1940.

[3] This subparagraph inserted by Public Law 792, 76th Cong., 3d sess., approved September 26, 1940.

[4] *Documents II, 1939–40,* p. 542, 656.

(3) Export-Import Bank Loans,[1] December 31, 1935–March 31, 1941 [2]

[In thousands of dollars]

| | MARCH 31, 1941 | | LOANS OUTSTANDING AT END OF — | | | | | |
COUNTRY OF BORROWER	Commitments to Make Additional Loans	Loans Outstanding	1940	1939	1938	1937	1936	1935
Latin America:								
Argentina	62,420	105	105	—	—	—	—	—
Brazil	51,392	13,545	13,621	16,395	925	1,320	508	—
Chile	14,637	3,926	2,890	485	630	—	—	—
Colombia	2,100	7,678	5,825	38	—	—	—	—
Costa Rica	5,539	61	4	—	—	—	28	—
Cuba	15,300	—	—	—	1,493	—	1,064	4,062
Dominican Republic .	3,275	25	—	—	—	—	—	—
Ecuador	1,150	30	15	—	—	—	—	—
Haiti	1,610	3,890	3,435	1,905	165	—	—	—
Mexico	—	121	130	136	472	890	73	50
Nicaragua	2,875	1,625	1,080	50	—	—	—	—
Panama	3,300	1,140	965	—	—	—	—	—
Paraguay	2,405	1,485	1,206	125	—	—	—	—
Peru	10,000	—	—	—	—	—	—	—
Uruguay	7,500	—	—	—	—	—	—	—
Venezuela	3,417	183	130	—	12	24	—	—
Total (16 countries) .	186,922	33,815	29,406	19,134	3,697	2,234	1,673	4,112
Other countries:								
Canada	—	—	—	—	—	—	15	—
China	40,500	80,820	54,697	24,991	11,823	13,700	15,700	—
Czechoslovakia . . .	—	—	—	—	75	112	46	49
Denmark	10,000	—	—	—	—	—	—	—
Finland	11,954	23,005	18,219	—	—	—	—	—
Hungary	1,000	—	—	—	—	—	—	—
Iceland	410	560	564	—	—	—	—	—
Iran	—	—	—	143	—	—	—	—
Italy	—	—	—	3,185	466	1,176	—	—
Norway	9,773	206	215	—	—	—	—	—
Poland	—	3,307	3,307	3,348	9	31	13	—
Portugal	331	744	862	246	—	—	—	—
Spain	—	11,200	12,481	4,281	47	53	56	99
Total (13 countries) .	73,968	119,843	90,345	36,194	12,420	15,072	15,830	148
Unclassified loans to U. S. exporters	5,067	12,530	11,281	9,915	10,085	65	70	11
GRAND TOTAL	265,957	166,188	131,032	65,243	26,201	17,371	17,573	4,271

[1] Defined as loans made by Export-Import Bank from its own resources plus loans made by cooperating banks under "take-out" commitment by Export-Import Bank. Of $166,188,000 outstanding on March 31, 1941, direct loans constituted $111,-121,000, and other loans $55,066,000.

[2] Federal Reserve Bulletin, May 1941, p. 386.

5. GOLD STOCK OF UNITED STATES [1]

(In millions of dollars)

PERIOD	TOTAL AT END OF PERIOD	INCREASE IN TOTAL	NET GOLD IMPORT	NET GAIN OR LOSS (−) THROUGH EARMARKING TRANSACTIONS [2]	DOMESTIC GOLD PRODUCTION [3]
1934 [4]	8,238	4,202.5	1,133.9	82.6	92.9
1935	10,125	1,887.2	1,739.0	.2	110.7
1936	11,258	1,132.5	1,116.6	− 85.9	131.6
1937	12,760	1,502.5	1,585.5	− 200.4	143.9
1938	14,512	1,751.5	1,973.6	− 333.5	148.6
1939	17,644	3,132.0	3,574.2	− 534.4	161.7
1940	21,995	4,351.2	4,744.5	− 644.7	168.1
1940 July.	20,463	499.4	520.0	− 55.1	16.0
August	20,913	450.2	351.6	67.0	12.3
September . . .	21,244	331.6	334.1	36.6	13.3
October	21,506	261.1	326.0	− 117.9	19.0
November . . .	21,801	295.2	330.1	− 39.5	16.4
December . . .	21,995	194.0	137.2	7.4	16.1
1941 January	22,116	121.7	234.2	− 52.8	13.5
February	22,232	115.4	108.6	− 46.2	12.6
March	22,367	135.4	118.6	.2	12.0
April	22,506	138.5	172.0	− 10.5	12.8
May	22,575	69.1	34.8	− 3.8	12.6
June	22,624	49.2	30.7	4.0	14.4

6. INTERGOVERNMENTAL DEBTS

[See *Documents, I, 1938–39*, p. 412; *II, 1939–40*, p. 520.]

Semi-annual payments under the funding agreements between the United States Treasury Department and the governments which incurred debts to the Government of the United States for war loans, surplus supplies, relief and food during and as a consequence of the war of 1914–18 were in general due on June 15 and December 15 of each year. The indebtedness of Austria and Greece was

[1] *Federal Reserve Bulletin*, July 1941, p. 652, and August 1941, p. 760.

[2] Gold held under earmark at Federal Reserve Banks for foreign account, in millions of dollars: June 30.

[3] Figures for domestic production are adjusted to exclude Philippine Islands production received in the United States.

[4] Figures based on rate of $20.67 a fine ounce in January 1934 and $35 a fine ounce thereafter.

the subject of agreements of a different type. The debt agreement with Germany of June 23, 1930 dealt with the payment of mixed claims awards and reimbursement of army of occupation costs, which amounted to $1,255,023,750 principal on June 30, 1938. The stoppage of payments by the moratoria of 1932 and the failure of debtor governments to resume payment afterward were superseded in 1940 by inabilities to pay of quite a different character.

Service of the Austrian debt was unsuccessfully claimed in 1939 from Germany as the successor state.[1] No statements were rendered Czecho-Slovakia after March 15, 1939. No statements were rendered to Estonia, Latvia and Lithuania after their absorption by the Soviet Union. A statement was presented unavailingly to Germany with respect to its defaults accumulated up to September 1940. The Treasury Department prepared and the Department of State transmitted statements with respect to payments due December 15, 1940 to eight governments.

Negative replies to the Secretary of State's note covering the respective statements were received in the same form as on the two preceding occasions (*Documents, II, 1939–40*, p. 527) from the following six governments:

Belgium, December 13, 1940 (Department of State, *Bulletin*, III, p. 567);
France, December 10, 1940 (*Ibid.*, p. 567);
Great Britain, December 15, 1940 (*Ibid.*, p. 568);
Italy, December 10, 1940 (*Ibid.*, p. 570);
Poland, December 14, 1940 (*Ibid.*, p. 571);
Yugoslavia, December 9, 1940 (*Ibid.*, p. 573).

Of these six, only Poland's reply made reference to the war which was in progress, citing as before the invasion to which it had been subjected.

Greece also made no payment in 1940. No statement of correspondence with Greece is normally released by the State Department.

By the terms of the agreements, the United States Government is under no obligation to render statements to the debtor governments. By the time statements concerning the payments due June 15, 1941 might have been rendered, none of the debtor governments in default was outside of the orbit of war. No announcement was made of statements rendered with respect to payments due on that date.

The terms of the debt agreements were fixed by the Congress, and the President is therefore not at liberty to modify them. The Congress failed to act upon proposals of Hungary[2] and Rumania[3] to revise those agreements. Finland, which had not been in default, was only granted a moratorium on current payments for 1940 by Public Resolution 84, 76th Cong., approved June 15, 1940 and for 1941–42 by Public Law No. 110, 77th Cong., approved June 12, 1941.

Material respecting the moratorium to Finland, the Hungarian payment, the German defaulted payments and the Rumanian offer is given.

A. Moratoria Granted to Finland

[See *Documents, II, 1939–40*, p. 389, 522.]

The Congress desired to alleviate the burden of Finland's indebtedness in view of its record in fulfilling the agreement for payment for relief supplies and as a testimonial to its stand against the Soviet Union in 1939–40. An act of Congress

---

[1] *Documents, I, 1938–39*, p. 428.
[2] *Ibid.*, p. 419; *II, 1939–40*, p. 528.
[3] *Ibid., II*, p. 532.

approved June 15, 1940 authorized postponement of the payments due during the calendar year 1940 and an agreement with the Treasury Department signed on May 1, 1941 provided for the repayment of that amount. Finland's difficulties in providing for necessities continued. Proposals were therefore introduced in Congress for further alleviation, and a further 2-year moratorium was enacted. The Secretaries of State and of the Treasury both approved the legislation.

(1) *The Minister of Finland (Procopé) to the Secretary of State (Hull), November 20, 1940* [1]

NOVEMBER 20, 1940

His Excellency the Honorable CORDELL HULL,
 Secretary of State,
  Department of State,
   Washington, D. C.

EXCELLENCY:

Referring to Your Excellency's note of June 22, 1940 [2] regarding the Public Resolution No. 84 approved on June 15, 1940 [3] by the President of the United States to authorize the postponement of payment of amounts payable to the United States by the Republic of Finland during the period from January 1, 1940 to December 31, 1940 under the agreements dated May 1, 1923 and May 23, 1932, I have the honor to submit to Your Excellency the following.

In spite of the many difficulties confronting Finland at present and notwithstanding her limited resources that are badly needed in the rehabilitation of the country, it is the firm intention and desire of the Finnish Government to maintain her credit record and to keep all her obligations in the same way as she has always done in the past.

However, the Finnish Government has with sincere gratitude noted the above mentioned Resolution, which, having been passed by both Houses of the Congress, was enacted by the President of the United States on the 15th of June, 1940, and offers the Finnish Government the opportunity of the postponement of payments specified therein. My Government appreciates this renewed proof of understanding and sympathy, so much the more as They see in this Resolution itself and in the debates which preceded it a sign of willingness on the part of the United States Government for a more extensive consideration of the two debt agreements to which the Resolution refers.

Under these circumstances and taking into consideration the present difficulties confronting Finland, my Government most gratefully accepts the offer contained in the said Resolution.

In consequence of the aforesaid I have the honor, under instructions from my Government, most respectfully to inform Your Excellency

[1] Department of State, *Bulletin*, III, p. 502.   [2] *Ibid.*, p. 501.
[3] *Documents, II, 1939–40*, p. 527.

that my Government is ready to enter into an agreement for the postponement of the payment of amounts payable by Finland to the United States on December 15, 1940, as provided for in the Public Resolution No. 84.

Accept [etc.]   H. J. PROCOPÉ

(2) *The Secretary of State (Hull) to the Minister of Finland (Procopé), November 29, 1940* [1]

NOVEMBER 29, 1940

The Honorable HJALMAR J. PROCOPÉ,
    Minister of Finland.

SIR:

I have the honor to acknowledge the receipt of your note of November 20, 1940 in which you refer to Public Resolution No. 84, approved June 15, 1940, and inform me that your Government is ready to enter into an agreement for the postponement of the payment of amounts payable by Finland to the United States on December 15, 1940, as provided for in the said Public Resolution No. 84.

I have transmitted this information to the Secretary of the Treasury, and shall be glad to make a further reply to your communication in due course.

Accept [etc.]   CORDELL HULL

(3) *The Secretary of the Treasury (Morgenthau) to the Chairman of the Senate Committee on Foreign Relations (George), May 8, 1941* [2]

[Excerpt]

The amounts payable to the United States by Finland which would be subject to postponement under the proposed joint resolution are as follows:

DATE PAYABLE	FUNDING AGREEMENT MAY 1, 1923		MORATORIUM AGREEMENT MAY 23, 1932	POSTPONEMENT AGREEMENT MAY 1, 1941	TOTAL
	Principal	Interest			
June 15, 1941 . .	—	$139,037.50	$19,030.50	$13,695.06	$171,763.06
Dec. 15, 1941 . .	$79,000	139,037.50	19,030.50	13,695.06	250,763.06
June 15, 1942 . .	—	137,655.00	19,030.50	13,695.06	170,380.56
Dec. 15, 1942 . .	82,000	137,655.00	19,030.50	13,695.06	252,380.56
Total	161,000	553,385.00	76,122.00	54,780.24	845,287.24

[1] Department of State, *Bulletin*, III, p. 503.
[2] Senate Report No. 274, 77th Cong., 1st sess.

Finland's indebtedness for relief supplies aggregated $8,281,926.17 and was represented by obligations of $3,289,276.98 dated June 30, 1919, and $4,992,-649.19 dated July 1, 1920. As a result of the negotiations initiated in 1922 by the World War Foreign Debt Commission, the Congress by an act approved March 12, 1924, authorized a refunding agreement with Finland under which interest on the original indebtedness at the rate of $4\frac{1}{4}$ per cent per annum to December 15, 1922, amounting to $1,027,389.10 was added to the original debt, and after a cash payment of $309,315.27 by Finland, the balance of $9,000,000 with interest at 3 per cent per annum from December 15, 1922, to December 15, 1932, and thereafter at $3\frac{1}{2}$ per cent per annum, was to be repaid over a period of 62 years. Each semi-annual installment has been promptly paid by Finland except the installments due in the fiscal year 1932 which were postponed under the moratorium proposed by President Hoover, and authorized by the joint resolution of Congress approved December 23, 1931, and the installment due on December 15, 1940, which was postponed pursuant to the joint resolution approved June 15, 1940. The postponed installments due in 1932 are being repaid in 10 annuities with interest at 4 per cent per annum from July 1, 1933, and the postponed installment due on December 15, 1940 is to be repaid in 10 annuities with interest at 3 per cent per annum from January 1, 1941.

Since 1923 Finland has paid to the United States the sum of $6,050,689.77, of which $960,398.17 represented principal and $5,090,291.60 represented interest. This includes the payment of $159,398 by Finland on June 15, 1940. . . .

The proposal embodied in the joint resolution will assist Finland to maintain the enviable record of its credit relationship with the United States. The difficulties now confronting Finland recommend our helpful attitude toward that debtor.

(4) *Joint Resolution to Authorize the Postponement of Amounts Payable to the United States by the Republic of Finland on Its Indebtedness under Agreements between That Republic and the United States Dated May 1, 1923, May 23, 1932, and May 1, 1941; Approved June 12, 1941* [1]

Resolved by the Senate and House of Representatives of the United States of America in Congress assembled, That the Republic of Finland, at its option, may postpone the payment of amounts payable to the United States of America during the period from January 1, 1941, to December 31, 1942, inclusive, under the agreements between that Republic and the United States of America dated May 1, 1923, May 23, 1932, and May 1, 1941. In the event of the exercise of the option granted in this section the Secretary of the Treasury is authorized to make, on behalf of the United States of America, an agreement with the Republic of Finland for the payment of the postponed amounts in forty semi-annual installments, the first two such installments to be paid during the calendar

[1] Public No. 110, 77th Cong.; originated as S. J. Res. 74; Senate Report No. 274; House Report No. 696 on H. J. Res. 184.

year beginning January 1, 1945, and two to be paid during each of the nineteen calendar years following: *Provided*, That the amounts postponed shall not bear any interest beyond the dates when such amounts first become payable under the above mentioned agreements.

SEC. 2. The agreement authorized in the first section of this joint resolution shall be in such form that payments thereunder shall, unless otherwise provided in such agreement, be in accordance with, and subject to the same terms and conditions as payments under, the agreement with the Republic of Finland dated May 1, 1923.

B. Statement of the German Default

(1) *The Secretary of State (Hull) to the German Chargé d'Affaires (Thomsen), September 12, 1940* [1]

SEPTEMBER 12, 1940.

HERR HANS THOMSEN,
    German Chargé d'Affaires ad interim.
SIR:

I am requested by the Secretary of the Treasury to transmit to you the enclosed statement of amounts due and payable on September 30, 1933 to March 31, 1940, inclusive, and September 30, 1940, from the German Government pursuant to the terms of the Debt Agreement of June 23, 1930, and the Moratorium Agreement of May 26, 1933.

Accept [etc.]   CORDELL HULL

[Enclosure follows.]

[1] Department of State, *Bulletin*, III, p. 284. For details of this indebtedness and of the awards and payments on account of the mixed claims, see Secretary of the Treasury, *Annual Report . . . on the State of the Finances for fiscal year ended June 30, 1940,* p. 191–5.

(a) *Statement of Amounts Due from the Government of Germany, from September 30, 1933 to March 31, 1940, Inclusive, and September 30, 1940*

[In Reichsmarks *]

	MIXED CLAIMS	ARMY COSTS	ANNUITY UNDER MORATORIUM AGREEMENT
Amount due September 30, 1933 . (Deposited by the German Government in the Konversionskasse für Deutsche Auslandeschulden)	2,040,000.00	458,562.50	1,529,049.45
Amount due March 31, 1934 . .	122,400,000.00	———	1,529,049.45
Amount due September 30, 1934 .	23,460,000.00	795,687.50	1,529,049.45
Amount due March 31, 1935 . .	23,970,000.00	63,464,250.00	1,529,049.45
Amount due September 30, 1935 .	24,480,000.00	10,432,812.50	1,529,049.45
Amount due March 31, 1936 . .	24,990,000.00	10,601,375.00	1,529,049.45
Amount due September 30, 1936 .	25,500,000.00	10,769,937.50	1,529,049.45
Amount due March 31, 1937 . .	26,010,000.00	10,938,500.00	1,529,049.45
Amount due September 30, 1937 .	26,520,000.00	10,007,062.50	1,529,049.45
Amount due March 31, 1938 . .	27,030,000.00	10,155,687.50	1,529,049.45
Amount due September 30, 1938 .	27,540,000.00	10,304,312.50	1,529,049.45
Amount due March 31, 1939 . .	28,050,000.00	10,452,937.50	1,529,049.45
Amount due September 30, 1939 .	28,560,000.00	11,701,562.50	1,529,049.45
Amount due March 31, 1940 . .	29,070,000.00	11,870,125.00	1,529,049.45
Total	439,620,000.00	171,952,812.50	21,406,692.30

Amount due September 30, 1940

Mixed Claims —
Semi-annual interest due September 30, 1940 on bonds A-4 to A-21, inclusive, in the principal amount of 20,-400,000, reichsmarks each . . 9,180,000.00
Principal of Bond A-22 . . . . 20,400,000.00
Army Costs —
Semi-annual interest due September 30, 1940 on bonds B-6 to B-21, inclusive . 2,738,687.50
Principal of bond B-22. . . . . 9,300,000.00
Moratorium Agreement —
Semi-annual installment due September 30, 1940 on the annuity of 3,058,098.90 reichsmarks under moratorium agreement of May 26, 1932 . . 1,529,049.45

Amount due 43,147,736.95

* One reichsmark = $.4033.

C. Partial Payment by Hungary

(1) *The Chargé d'Affaires ad interim of Hungary (Rothkugel) to the Secretary of State (Hull), December 13, 1940* [1]

ROYAL HUNGARIAN LEGATION,
Washington, D. C., December 13, 1940.

SIR:

By order of my Government I have the honor to inform you that the amount of $9,828.16 has been paid today at the Federal Reserve Bank of New York on account of the relief indebtedness of Hungary to the Government of the United States.

May I again express the earnest hope of my Government that the Congress of the United States will give favorable consideration to the offer of my Government submitted in the Aide Mémoire of February 7, 1938,[2] seeking to regularize its debt payments by a new agreement on a permanent basis which would pay off completely the original relief debt without interest in equal installments in the lifetime of the present generation, that is in approximately thirty years.

Accept [etc.]   S. ROTHKUGEL

(2) *Statement of the Department of State, December 16, 1940* [3]

The Department notes with gratification that the Hungarian Government has again made a partial payment on its relief debt contracted in 1920 for the purchase of flour from the United States Grain Corporation through the American Relief Administration. In its communication of December 13 on this subject, the Hungarian Government has expressed the earnest hope that favorable consideration will be given to its offer to undertake a new agreement on a permanent basis whereby payment of the original relief debt, without interest, would be completed in about 30 equal annual installments. The President, in his message of March 28, 1938 [4] recommending these proposals to the consideration of the Congress, expressed the belief that they represented a noteworthy wish and effort of the Hungarian Government to meet its obligations to this Government.

[1] Department of State, *Bulletin*, III, p. 570.
[2] *Documents, I, 1938–39,* p. 416.
[3] Release of December 16, 1940, Department of State, *Bulletin*, III, p. 569.
[4] *Documents, I, 1938–39,* p. 419.

D. Rumania's Continued Offer to Negotiate

(1) *The Chargé d'Affaires ad interim of Rumania (Coste) to the Secretary of State (Hull), December 14, 1940* [1]

ROYAL LEGATION OF ROMANIA,
Washington, D. C., December 14, 1940.

SIR:

I have the honor to acknowledge receipt of your note of December 4, 1940, enclosing the statement showing the amounts due from the Romanian Government up to December 15, 1940,[2] pursuant to the terms of the Debt Agreement of December 4, 1925, and the Moratorium Agreement of June 11, 1932.

As stated in the Romanian Minister's note of June 15, 1940,[3] the Royal Government earnestly desires to fulfill its obligations toward the United States, but, because of circumstances and reasons beyond its control, which were only aggravated by the events which have occurred since June 15, finds it impossible to carry out the terms of the Agreements referred to above.

I have the honor, therefore, to inform you that the Royal Government deeply regrets that it is unable to effect payment of the installment falling due on December 15, 1940, and stresses once more its desire, as expressed in this Legation's notes of May 3, 1939,[4] December 14, 1939,[5] and June 15, 1940, to negotiate a new agreement.

Accept [etc.]   BRUTUS COSTE

[1] Department of State, *Bulletin*, III, p. 572.

[2] The statement showed an accrued total due as principal, interest and moratorium annuities of $14,128,181.17; $48,750.08 moratorium annuity due December 15, 1940; $907,559.81 interest due December 15, 1940 on outstanding bonds aggregating $51,860,560.43.

[3] *Documents, II, 1939–40*, p. 534.

[4] *Ibid., I*, p. 423.

[5] *Ibid., II*, p. 533.

CHAPTER VII

TREATMENT OF PERSONS

1. LEGAL STATUS OF PERSONS. NATIONALITY AND NATURALIZATION

The legal status of persons, whether native, naturalized or alien, is one of the most important and complex matters that concerns legislators and administrators. Historically United States nationality legislation has responded to several different conceptions. A systematic statement of the laws upon citizenship, naturalization and expatriation was embodied in the Revised Statutes of 1878 but subsequent modification of existing laws was frequent. The result was a body of legislation vast in extent and extremely difficult to apply and interpret.

The President by executive order of April 25, 1933 designated the Secretary of State, the Attorney General and the Secretary of Labor to review the nationality laws, to recommend revisions and to codify the laws into a code for submission to Congress. A committee of advisers from the three departments carried out the long-sought object. The report was completed August 13, 1935, but the material was not transmitted to Congress until June 13, 1938.[1] The House Committee on Immigration and Naturalization held extensive hearings and otherwise studied the matter thoroughly before reporting out H. R. 9980, which differed but slightly from the code submitted.

So much of the act as serves to define nationals and those eligible for naturalization is given. The omitted parts deal with the detailed procedures of naturalization.

[1] U. S., Committee to Review the Nationality Laws. *Nationality Laws of the United States.* Message from the President of the United States transmitting a report proposing a revision and codification of the nationality laws of the United States . . . Washington, 1939. 3 pts. (Printed for the use of the Committee on Immigration and Naturalization, 76th Cong., 1st sess.)

Pt. 1, Proposed code with explanatory comments; pt. 2, Comparative print of the proposed and present nationality laws; pt. 3, Existing constitutional, statutory and treaty provisions at present in force.

(1) *The Nationality Act of 1940, Approved October 14, 1940* [1]

Effective January 12, 1941

An Act to Revise and Codify the Nationality Laws of the United States into a Comprehensive Nationality Code.

[Excerpt]

TITLE I

SECTION 1. This Act may be cited as the Nationality Act of 1940.

CHAPTER I — DEFINITIONS

SEC. 101. For the purposes of this Act —

(a) The term "national" means a person owing permanent allegiance to a state.

(b) The term "national of the United States" means (1) a citizen of the United States, or (2) a person who, though not a citizen of the United States, owes permanent allegiance to the United States. It does not include an alien.

(c) The term "naturalization" means the conferring of nationality of a state upon a person after birth.

(d) The term "United States" when used in a geographical sense means the continental United States, Alaska, Hawaii, Puerto Rico, and the Virgin Islands of the United States.

(e) The term "outlying possessions" means all territory, other than as specified in subsection (d), over which the United States exercises rights of sovereignty, except the Canal Zone.

(f) The term "parent" includes in the case of a posthumous child a deceased parent.

· · · · · · ·

CHAPTER II — NATIONALITY AT BIRTH

SEC. 201. The following shall be nationals and citizens of the United States at birth:

(a) A person born in the United States, and subject to the jurisdiction thereof;

(b) A person born in the United States to a member of an Indian, Eskimo, Aleutian, or other aboriginal tribe: *Provided,* That the grant-

---

[1] 54 Stat. 1133; Public No. 853, 76th Cong.; originated as H. R. 9980; House Report No. 2396, from Committee on Immigration and Naturalization, June 5, 1940; Senate Report No. 2150, September 23, 1940; House (conference) Report No. 3019, October 4, 1940.

ing of citizenship under this subsection shall not in any manner impair or otherwise affect the right of such person to tribal or other property;

(c) A person born outside of the United States and its outlying possessions of parents both of whom are citizens of the United States and one of whom has resided in the United States or one of its outlying possessions, prior to the birth of such person;

(d) A person born outside of the United States and its outlying possessions of parents one of whom is a citizen of the United States who resided in the United States or one of its outlying possessions prior to the birth of such person, and the other of whom is a national, but not a citizen of the United States;

(e) A person born in an outlying possession of the United States of parents one of whom is a citizen of the United States who resided in the United States or one of its outlying possessions prior to the birth of such person;

(f) A child of unknown parentage found in the United States, until shown not to have been born in the United States;

(g) A person born outside the United States and its outlying possessions of parents one of whom is a citizen of the United States who, prior to the birth of such person, has had ten years' residence in the United States or one of its outlying possessions, at least five of which were after attaining the age of sixteen years, the other being an alien: *Provided*, That, in order to retain such citizenship, the child must reside in the United States or its outlying possessions for a period or periods totaling five years between the ages of thirteen and twenty-one years: *Provided further*, That, if the child has not taken up a residence in the United States or its outlying possessions by the time he reaches the age of sixteen years, or if he resides abroad for such a time that it becomes impossible for him to complete the five years' residence in the United States or its outlying possessions before reaching the age of twenty-one years, his American citizenship shall thereupon cease.

The preceding provisos shall not apply to a child born abroad whose American parent is at the time of the child's birth residing abroad solely or principally in the employment of the Government of the United States or a bona fide American, educational, scientific, philanthropic, religious, commercial, or financial organization, having its principal office or place of business in the United States, or an international agency of an official character in which the United States participates, for which he receives a substantial compensation;

(h) The foregoing provisions of subsection (g) concerning retention of citizenship shall apply to a child born abroad subsequent to May 24, 1934.

SEC. 202. All persons born in Puerto Rico on or after April 11, 1899, subject to the jurisdiction of the United States, residing on the effective date of this Act in Puerto Rico or other territory over which the United States exercises rights of sovereignty and not citizens of the United States under any other Act, are hereby declared to be citizens of the United States.

SEC. 203. (a) Any person born in the Canal Zone on or after February 26, 1904, and whether before or after the effective date of this Act, whose father or mother or both at the time of the birth of such person was or is a citizen of the United States, is declared to be a citizen of the United States.

(b) Any person born in the Republic of Panama on or after February 26, 1904, and whether before or after the effective date of this Act, whose father or mother or both at the time of the birth of such person was or is a citizen of the United States employed by the Government of the United States or by the Panama Railroad Company, is declared to be a citizen of the United States.

SEC. 204. Unless otherwise provided in section 201, the following shall be nationals, but not citizens, of the United States at birth:

(a) A person born in an outlying possession of the United States of parents one of whom is a national, but not a citizen, of the United States;

(b) A person born outside the United States and its outlying possessions of parents both of whom are nationals, but not citizens, of the United States, and have resided in the United States or one of its outlying possessions prior to the birth of such person;

(c) A child of unknown parentage found in an outlying possession of the United States, until shown not to have been born in such outlying possession.

SEC. 205. The provisions of section 201, subsections (c), (d), (e), and (g), and section 204, subsections (a) and (b), hereof apply, as of the date of birth, to a child born out of wedlock, provided the paternity is established during minority, by legitimation, or adjudication of a competent court.

In the absence of such legitimation or adjudication, the child, whether born before or after the effective date of this Act, if the mother had the nationality of the United States at the time of the child's birth, and had previously resided in the United States or one of its outlying possessions, shall be held to have acquired at birth her nationality status.

Chapter III — Nationality through Naturalization

General Provisions

JURISDICTION TO NATURALIZE

SEC. 301. (a) Exclusive jurisdiction to naturalize persons as citizens of the United States is hereby conferred upon the following specified courts: District Courts of the United States now existing, or which may hereafter be established by Congress in any State, District Courts of the United States for the Territories of Hawaii and Alaska, and for the District of Columbia and for Puerto Rico, and the District Court of the Virgin Islands of the United States; also all courts of record in any State or Territory now existing, or which may hereafter be created, having a seal, a clerk, and jurisdiction in actions at law or equity, or law and equity, in which the amount in controversy is unlimited. The jurisdiction of all the courts herein specified to naturalize persons shall extend only to such persons resident within the respective jurisdictions of such courts, except as otherwise specifically provided in this Act.

(b) A person who petitions for naturalization in any State court having naturalization jurisdiction, may petition within the State judicial district or State judicial circuit in which he resides, whether or not he resides within the county in which the petition for naturalization is filed.

(c) The courts herein specified, upon request of the clerks of such courts, shall be furnished from time to time by the Commissioner or a Deputy Commissioner [1] with such blank forms as may be required in naturalization proceedings.

(d) A person may be naturalized as a citizen of the United States in the manner and under the conditions prescribed in this Act, and not otherwise.

Substantive Provisions

ELIGIBILITY FOR NATURALIZATION

SEC. 302. The right of a person to become a naturalized citizen of the United States shall not be denied or abridged because of sex or because such person is married.

SEC. 303. The right to become a naturalized citizen under the provisions of this Act shall extend only to white persons, persons of African nativity or descent, and descendants of races indigenous to the Western

[1] Sec. 102 (d): "The terms 'Commissioner' and 'Deputy Commissioner' mean the Commissioner of Immigration and Naturalization and a Deputy Commissioner of Immigration and Naturalization, respectively."

Hemisphere: *Provided*, That nothing in this section shall prevent the naturalization of native-born Filipinos having the honorable service in the United States Army, Navy, Marine Corps, or Coast Guard as specified in section 324, nor of former citizens of the United States who are otherwise eligible to naturalization under the provisions of section 317.

SEC. 304. No person except as otherwise provided in this Act shall hereafter be naturalized as a citizen of the United States upon his own petition who cannot speak the English language. This requirement shall not apply to any person physically unable to comply therewith, if otherwise qualified to be naturalized.

SEC. 305. No person shall hereafter be naturalized as a citizen of the United States —

(*a*) Who advises, advocates, or teaches, or who is a member of or affiliated with any organization, association, society, or group that advises, advocates, or teaches opposition to all organized government; or

(*b*) Who believes in, advises, advocates, or teaches, or who is a member of or affiliated with any organization, association, society, or group that believes in, advises, advocates, or teaches —

(1) the overthrow by force or violence of the Government of the United States or of all forms of law; or

(2) the duty, necessity, or propriety of the unlawful assaulting or killing of any officer or officers (either of specific individuals or of officers generally) of the Government of the United States or any other organized government, because of his or their official character; or

(3) the unlawful damage, injury, or destruction of property; or

(4) sabotage.

(*c*) Who writes, publishes, or causes to be written or published, or who knowingly circulates, distributes, prints, or displays, or knowingly causes to be circulated, distributed, printed, published, or displayed, or who knowingly has in his possession for the purpose of circulation, distribution, publication, or display any written or printed matter advising, advocating, or teaching opposition to all organized government, or advising, advocating, or teaching —

(1) the overthrow by force or violence of the Government of the United States or of all forms of law; or

(2) the duty, necessity, or propriety of the unlawful assaulting or killing of any officer or officers (either of specific individuals or of officers generally) of the Government of the United States or of any other organized government; or

(3) the unlawful damage, injury, or destruction of property; or

(4) sabotage.

(*d*) Who is a member of or affiliated with any organization, association, society, or group that writes, circulates, distributes, prints, publishes, or displays, or causes to be written, circulated, distributed, printed, published, or displayed, or that has in its possession for the purpose of circulation, distribution, publication, issue, or display, any written or printed matter of the character described in subdivision (*c*).

For the purpose of this section —

(1) the giving, loaning, or promising of money or anything of value to be used for the advising, advocacy, or teaching of any doctrine above enumerated shall constitute the advising, advocacy, or teaching of such doctrine; and

(2) the giving, loaning, or promising of money or anything of value to any organization, association, society, or group of the character above described shall constitute affiliation therewith; but nothing in this paragraph shall be taken as an exclusive definition of advising, advocacy, teaching or affiliation.

The provisions of this section shall be applicable to any applicant for naturalization who at any time within a period of ten years immediately preceding the filing of the petition for naturalization is, or has been, found to be within any of the clauses enumerated in this section, notwithstanding that at the time petition is filed he may not be included in such classes.

[SEC. 306 deals with deserters from the military or naval forces of the United States; secs. 307 and 308 with continuity of residence; sec. 309 with "requirements as of proof."]

MARRIED PERSONS

SEC. 310. (*a*) Any alien who, after September 21, 1922, and prior to May 24, 1934, has married a citizen of the United States, or any alien who married prior to May 24, 1934, a spouse who was naturalized during such period and during the existence of the marital relation may, if eligible to naturalization, be naturalized upon full and complete compliance with all requirements of the naturalization laws, with the following exceptions:

(1) No declaration of intention shall be required;

(2) In lieu of the five-year period of residence within the United States, and the six months' period of residence in the State where the petitioner resided at the time of filing the petition, the petitioner shall have resided continuously in the United States for at least one year immediately preceding the filing of the petition.

(*b*) Any alien who, on or after May 24, 1934, has married or shall hereafter marry a citizen of the United States, or any alien whose husband or wife was naturalized on or after May 24, 1934, and during the existence of the marital relation or shall hereafter be so naturalized may, if eligible for naturalization, be naturalized upon full and complete compliance with all requirements of the naturalization laws, with the following exceptions:

(1) No declaration of intention shall be required;

(2) In lieu of the five-year period of residence within the United States, and the six months' period of residence in the State where the petitioner resided at the time of filing the petition, the petitioner shall have resided continuously in the United States for at least three years immediately preceding the filing of the petition.

(*c*) The naturalization of any woman on or after May 24, 1934, by any naturalization court of competent jurisdiction, upon proof of marriage to a citizen or the naturalization of her husband and proof of but one year's residence in the United States is hereby validated only so far as relates to the period of residence required to be proved by such person under the naturalization laws.

(*d*) The naturalization of any male person on or after May 24, 1934, by any naturalization court of competent jurisdiction, upon proof of marriage to a citizen of the United States after September 21, 1922, and prior to May 24, 1934, or of the naturalization during such period of his wife, and upon proof of three years' residence in the United States, is hereby validated only so far as relates to the period of residence required to be proved by such person under the naturalization laws and the omission by such person to make a declaration of intention.

Sec. 311. A person who upon the effective date of this section is married to or thereafter marries a citizen of the United States, or whose spouse is naturalized after the effective date of this section, if such person shall have resided in the United States in marital union with the United States citizen spouse for at least one year immediately preceding the filing of the petition for naturalization, may be naturalized after the effective date of this section upon compliance with all requirements of the naturalization laws with the following exceptions:

(*a*) No declaration of intention shall be required.

(*b*) The petitioner shall have resided continuously in the United States for at least two years immediately preceding the filing of the petition in lieu of the five-year period of residence within the United States and the six months' period of residence within the State where the naturalization court is held.

SEC. 312. An alien, whose spouse is (1) a citizen of the United States, (2) in the employment of the Government of the United States, or of an American institution of research recognized as such by the Attorney General, or an American firm or corporation engaged in whole or in part in the development of foreign trade and commerce of the United States, or a subsidiary thereof, and (3) regularly stationed abroad in such employment, and who is (1) in the United States at the time of naturalization, and (2) declares before the naturalization court in good faith an intention to take up residence within the United States immediately upon the termination of such employment abroad of the citizen spouse, may be naturalized upon compliance with all requirements of the naturalization laws, with the following exceptions:

(a) No declaration of intention shall be required; and

(b) No prior residence within the United States or within the jurisdiction of the naturalization court of proof thereof shall be required.

CHILDREN

SEC. 313. A child born outside of the United States, one of whose parents at the time of the child's birth was an alien and the other of whose parents then was and never thereafter ceased to be a citizen of the United States, shall, if such alien parent is naturalized, be deemed a citizen of the United States, when —

(a) Such naturalization takes place while such child is under the age of eighteen years; and

(b) Such child is residing in the United States at the time of naturalization or thereafter and begins to reside permanently in the United States while under the age of eighteen years.

SEC. 314. A child born outside of the United States of alien parents, or of an alien parent and a citizen parent who has subsequently lost citizenship of the United States, becomes a citizen of the United States upon fulfillment of the following conditions:

(a) The naturalization of both parents; or

(b) The naturalization of the surviving parent if one of the parents is deceased; or

(c) The naturalization of the parent having legal custody of the child when there has been a legal separation of the parents; and if —

(d) Such naturalization takes place while such child is under the age of eighteen years; and

(e) Such child is residing in the United States at the time of the naturalization of the parent last naturalized under subsection (a) of this section, or the parent naturalized under subsection (b) or (c) of this section, or thereafter begins to reside permanently in the United States while under the age of eighteen years.

SEC. 315. A child born outside of the United States, one of whose parents is at the time of petitioning for the naturalization of the child, a citizen of the United States, either by birth or naturalization, may be naturalized if under the age of eighteen years and not otherwise disqualified from becoming a citizen and is residing permanently in the United States with the citizen parent, on the petition of such citizen parent, without a declaration of intention, upon compliance with the applicable procedural provisions of the naturalization laws.

SEC. 316. An adopted child may, if not otherwise disqualified from becoming a citizen, be naturalized before reaching the age of eighteen years upon the petition of the adoptive parent or parents if the child has resided continuously in the United States for at least two years immediately preceding the date of filing such petition, upon compliance with all the applicable procedural provisions of the naturalization laws, if the adoptive parent or parents are citizens of the United States, and the child was:

(a) Lawfully admitted to the United States for permanent residence; and

(b) Adopted in the United States before reaching the age of sixteen years; and

(c) Adopted and in the legal custody of the adoptive parent or parents for at least two years prior to the filing of the petition for the child's naturalization.

FORMER CITIZENS OF THE UNITED STATES

SEC. 317. (a) A person who was a citizen of the United States and who prior to September 22, 1922, lost United States citizenship by marriage to an alien or by the spouse's loss of United States citizenship, and any person who lost United States citizenship on or after September 22, 1922, by marriage to an alien ineligible to citizenship, may, if no other nationality was acquired by affirmative act other than such marriage, be naturalized upon compliance with all requirements of the naturalization laws with the following exceptions:

(1) No declaration of intention and no certificate of arrival shall be required, and no period of residence within the United States or within the State where the petition is filed shall be required.

(2) The petition need not set forth that it is the intention of the petitioner to reside permanently within the United States.

(3) The petition may be filed in any court having naturalization jurisdiction, regardless of the residence of the petitioner.

(4) The petition may be heard at any time after filing if there is attached to the petition at the time of filing a certificate from a naturalization examiner stating that the petitioner has appeared before such examiner for examination.

Such person shall have, from and after the naturalization, the same citizenship status as that which existed immediately prior to its loss.

(b) (1) From and after the effective date of this Act, a woman, who was a citizen of the United States at birth, and who has or is believed to have lost her United States citizenship solely by reason of her marriage prior to September 22, 1922, to an alien, and whose marital status with such alien has or shall have terminated, if no other nationality was acquired by affirmative act other than such marriage, shall, from and after the taking of the oath of allegiance prescribed by subsection (b) of section 335 of this Act, be deemed to be a citizen of the United States to the same extent as though her marriage to said alien had taken place on or after September 22, 1922.

(2) Such oath of allegiance may be taken abroad before a diplomatic or consular officer of the United States, or in the United States before the judge or clerk of a naturalization court.

(3) Such oath of allegiance shall be entered in the records of the appropriate embassy or legation or consulate or naturalization court, and upon demand, a certified copy of the proceedings, including a copy of the oath administered, under the seal of the embassy or legation or consulate or naturalization court, shall be delivered to such woman at a cost not exceeding $1, which certified copy shall be evidence of the facts stated therein before any court of record or judicial tribunal and in any department of the United States.

(c) A person who shall have been a citizen of the United States and also a national of a foreign state, and who shall have lost his citizenship of the United States under the provisions of section 401 (c) of this Act, shall be entitled to the benefits of the provisions of subsection (a) of this section, except that contained in subdivision (2) thereof. Such person, if abroad, may enter the United States as a nonquota immigrant, for the purpose of recovering his citizenship, upon compliance with the provisions of the Immigration Acts of 1917 and 1924.

SEC. 318. (a) A former citizen of the United States expatriated through the expatriation of such person's parent or parents and who has not acquired the nationality of another country by any affirmative act other than the expatriation of his parent or parents may be naturalized upon filing a petition for naturalization before reaching the age of twenty-five years and upon compliance with all requirements of the naturalization laws with the following exceptions:

(1) No declaration of intention and no certificate of arrival and no period of residence within the United States or in a State shall be required;

(2) The petition may be filed in any court having naturalization jurisdiction, regardless of the residence of the petitioner;

(3) If there is attached to the petition at the time of filing, a certificate from a naturalization examiner stating that the petitioner has appeared before him for examination, the petition may be heard at any time after filing; and

(4) Proof that the petitioner was at the time his petition was filed and at the time of the final hearing thereon a person of good moral character, attached to the principles of the Constitution of the United States, and well disposed to the good order and happiness of the United States, and that he intends to reside permanently in the United States shall be made by any means satisfactory to the naturalization court.

(b) No former citizen of the United States, expatriated through the expatriation of such person's parent or parents, shall be obliged to comply with the requirements of the immigration laws, if he has not acquired the nationality of another country by any affirmative act other than the expatriation of his parent or parents, and if he has come or shall come to the United States before reaching the age of twenty-five years.

(c) After his naturalization such person shall have the same citizenship status as if he had not been expatriated.

SEC. 319. (a) A person who as a minor child lost citizenship of the United States through the cancellation of the parent's naturalization on grounds other than actual fraud or presumptive fraud as specified in the second paragraph of section 15 of the Act of June 29, 1906, as amended (34 Stat. 601; 40 Stat. 544, U. S. C., title 8, sec. 405), or who shall lose citizenship of the United States under subsection (c) of section 338 of this Act, may, if such person resided in the United States at the time of such cancellation and if, within two years after such cancellation or within two years after the effective date of this section, such person files a petition for naturalization or such a petition is filed on such person's behalf by a parent or guardian if such person is under the age of eighteen years, be naturalized upon compliance with all requirements of the naturalization laws with the exception that no declaration of intention shall be required and the required five-year period of residence in the United States need not be continuous.

(*b*) Citizenship acquired under this section shall begin as of the date of the person's naturalization, except that in those cases where the person has resided continuously in the United States from the date of the cancellation of the parent's naturalization to the date of the person's naturalization under this section, the citizenship of such person shall relate back to the date of the parent's naturalization which has been canceled or to the date of such person's arrival in the United States for permanent residence if such date was subsequent to the date of naturalization of said parent.

PERSONS MISINFORMED OF CITIZENSHIP STATUS

SEC. 320. A person not an alien enemy, who resided uninterruptedly within the United States during the period of five years next preceding July 1, 1920, and was on that date otherwise qualified to become a citizen of the United States, except that such person had not made a declaration of intention required by law and who during or prior to that time, because of misinformation regarding the citizenship status of such person, erroneously exercised the rights and performed the duties of a citizen of the United States in good faith, may file the petition for naturalization prescribed by law without making the preliminary declaration of intention, and upon satisfactory proof to the court that petitioner has so acted may be admitted as a citizen of the United States upon complying with the other requirements of the naturalization laws.

NATIONALS BUT NOT CITIZENS OF THE UNITED STATES

SEC. 321. A person not a citizen who owes permanent allegiance to the United States, and who is otherwise qualified may, if he becomes a resident of any State, be naturalized upon compliance with the requirements of this Act, except that in petitions for naturalization filed under the provisions of this section, residence within the United States within the meaning of this Act shall include residence within any of the outlying possessions of the United States.

PUERTO RICANS

SEC. 322. A person born in Puerto Rico of alien parents, referred to in the last paragraph of section 5, Act of March 2, 1917 (U. S. C., title 8, sec. 5), and in section 5 *a*, of the said Act, as amended by section 2 of the Act of March 4, 1927 (U. S. C., title 8, sec. 5 *a*), who did not exercise the privilege granted of becoming a citizen of the United States, may make the declaration provided in said paragraph at any time, and from and after the making of such declaration shall be a citizen of the United States.

PERSONS SERVING IN ARMED FORCES OR ON VESSELS

SEC. 323. A person who, while a citizen of the United States and during the World War in Europe, entered the military or naval service of any country at war with a country with which the United States was then at war, who has lost citizenship of the United States by reason of any oath or obligation taken for the purpose of entering such service, may be naturalized by taking before any naturalization court specified in subsection (a) of section 301 the oaths prescribed by section 335.

SEC. 324. (a) A person, including a native-born Filipino, who has served honorably at any time in the United States Army, Navy, Marine Corps, or Coast Guard for a period or periods aggregating three years and who, if separated from such service, was separated under honorable conditions, may be naturalized without having resided, continuously immediately preceding the date of filing such person's petition, in the United States for at least five years and in the State in which the petition for naturalization is filed for at least six months, if such petition is filed while the petitioner is still in the service or within six months after the termination of such service.

(b) A person filing a petition under subsection (a) of this section shall comply in all respects with the requirements of this chapter except that —

(1) No declaration of intention shall be required;

(2) No certificate of arrival shall be required;

(3) No residence within the jurisdiction of the court shall be required;

(4) Such petitioner may be naturalized immediately if the petitioner be then actually in any of the services prescribed in subsection (a) of this section, and if, before filing the petition for naturalization, such petitioner and at least two verifying witnesses to the petition, who shall be citizens of the United States and who shall identify petitioner as the person who rendered the service upon which the petition is based, have appeared before and been examined by a representative of the Service.

(c) In case such petitioner's service was not continuous, petitioner's residence in the United States and State, good moral character, attachment to the principles of the Constitution of the United States, and favorable disposition toward the good order and happiness of the United States, during any period within five years immediately preceding the date of filing said petition between the periods of petitioner's service in the United States Army, Navy, Marine Corps, or Coast Guard, shall be verified in the petition filed under the provisions of subsection (a) of this section, and proved at the final hearing thereon by witnesses, citizens of the United States, in the same manner as required by section 309. Such verification and proof shall also be made as to any period between the termination of petitioner's service and the filing of the petition for naturalization.

(d) The petitioner shall comply with the requirements of section 309 as to continuous residence in the United States for at least five years and in the State in which the petition is filed for at least six months, immediately preceding the date of filing the petition, if the termination of such service has been more than six months preceding the date of filing the petition for naturalization, except that such service shall be considered as residence within the United States or the State.

(e) Any such period or periods of service under honorable conditions, and good moral character, attachment to the principles of the Constitution of the United States, and favorable disposition toward the good order and happiness of the United States, during such service, shall be proved by duly authenticated copies of records of the executive departments having custody of the records of such service, and such authenticated copies of records shall be accepted in lieu of affidavits and testimony or depositions of witnesses.

SEC. 325. (a) A person who has served honorably or with good conduct for an aggregate period of at least five years (1) on board of any vessel of the United States Government other than in the United States Navy, Marine Corps, or Coast Guard, or (2) on board vessels of more than twenty tons burden, whether or not documented under the laws of the United States, and whether public or private, which are not foreign vessels, and whose home port is in the United States, may be naturalized without having resided, continuously immediately preceding the date of filing such person's petition, in the United States for at least five years, and in the State in which the petition for naturalization is filed for at least six months, if such petition is filed while the petitioner is still in the service on a reenlistment, reappointment, or reshipment, or within six months after an honorable discharge or separation therefrom.

(b) The provisions of subsections (b), (c), (d), and (e) of section 324 shall apply to petitions for naturalization filed under this section, except that service with good conduct on vessels described in subsection (a) (2) of this section may be proved by certificates from the masters of such vessels.

ALIEN ENEMIES

SEC. 326. (a) An alien who is a native, citizen, subject, or denizen of any country, state, or sovereignty with which the United States is at war may be naturalized as a citizen of the United States if such alien's declaration of intention was made not less than two years prior to the beginning of the state of war, or such alien was at the beginning of the state of war entitled to become a citizen of the United States without making a declaration of intention, or his petition for naturalization shall at the beginning of the state of war be pending and the petitioner is otherwise entitled to admission, notwithstanding such petitioner shall be an alien enemy at the time and in the manner prescribed by the laws passed upon that subject.

(b) An alien embraced within this section shall not have such alien's petition for naturalization called for a hearing, or heard, except after ninety days' notice given by the clerk of the court to the Commissioner to be represented at the hearing, and the Commissioner's objection to such final hearing shall cause the petition to be continued from time to time for so long as the Commissioner may require.

(c) Nothing herein contained shall be taken or construed to interfere with or prevent the apprehension and removal, agreeably to law, of any alien enemy at any time previous to the actual naturalization of such alien.

(d) The President of the United States may, in his discretion, upon investigation and report by the Department of Justice fully establishing the loyalty of any alien enemy not included in the foregoing exemption, except such alien enemy from the classification of alien enemy, and thereupon such alien shall have the privilege of applying for naturalization.

PROCEDURAL AND ADMINISTRATIVE PROVISIONS

[SEC. 327 prescribes Executive Functions.]

REGISTRY OF ALIENS

SEC. 328. (a) The Commissioner shall cause to be made, for use in complying with the requirements of this chapter, a registry of each person arriving in the United States after the effective date of this Act, of the name, age, occupation, personal description (including height, complexion, color of hair and eyes, and fingerprints), the date and place of birth, nationality, the last residence, the intended place of residence in the United States, the date and place of arrival of said person, and the name of vessel or other means of transportation, upon which said person arrived.

(b) Registry of aliens at ports of entry required by subsection (a) of this section may be made as to any alien not ineligible to citizenship in whose case there is no record of admission for permanent residence, if such alien shall make a satisfactory showing to the Commissioner, in accordance with regulations prescribed by the Commissioner, with the approval of the Attorney General, that such alien —

(1) Entered the United States prior to July 1, 1924;

(2) Has resided in the United States continuously since such entry;

(3) Is a person of good moral character; and

(4) Is not subject to deportation.

(c) For the purposes of the immigration laws and naturalization laws an alien, in respect of whom a record of registry has been made as authorized by this section, shall be deemed to have been lawfully admitted to the United States for permanent residence as of the date of such alien's entry.

[Secs. 329–347 omitted.]

Chapter IV — Loss of Nationality

Sec. 401. A person who is a national of the United States, whether by birth or naturalization, shall lose his nationality by:

(a) Obtaining naturalization in a foreign state, either upon his own application or through the naturalization of a parent having legal custody of such person: *Provided, however,* That nationality shall not be lost as the result of the naturalization of a parent unless and until the child shall have attained the age of twenty-three years without acquiring permanent residence in the United States: *Provided further,* That a person who has acquired foreign nationality through the naturalization of his parent or parents, and who at the same time is a citizen of the United States, shall, if abroad and he has not heretofore expatriated himself as an American citizen by his own voluntary act, be permitted within two years from the effective date of this Act to return to the United States and take up permanent residence therein, and it shall be thereafter deemed that he has elected to be an American citizen. Failure on the part of such person to so return and take up permanent residence in the United States during such period shall be deemed to be a determination on the part of such person to discontinue his status as an American citizen, and such person shall be forever estopped by such failure from thereafter claiming such American citizenship; or

(b) Taking an oath or making an affirmation or other formal declaration of allegiance to a foreign state; or

(c) Entering, or serving in, the armed forces of a foreign state unless expressly authorized by the laws of the United States, if he has or acquires the nationality of such foreign state; or (*d*) Accepting, or performing the duties of, any office, post, or employment under the government of a foreign state or political subdivision thereof for which only nationals of such state are eligible; or

(*e*) Voting in a political election in a foreign state or participating in an election or plebiscite to determine the sovereignty over foreign territory; or

(*f*) Making a formal renunciation of nationality[1] before a diplomatic or consular officer of the United States in a foreign state, in such form as may be prescribed by the Secretary of State; or

(*g*) Deserting the military or naval service of the United States in time of war, provided he is convicted thereof by a court martial; or

(*h*) Committing any act of treason against, or attempting by force to overthrow or bearing arms against the United States, provided he is convicted thereof by a court martial or by a court of competent jurisdiction.

SEC. 402. A national of the United States who was born in the United States or who was born in any place outside of the jurisdiction of the United States of a parent who was born in the United States, shall be presumed to have expatriated himself under subsection (*c*) or (*d*) of section 401, when he shall remain for six months or longer within any foreign state of which he or either of his parents shall have been a national according to the laws of such foreign state, or within any place under control of such foreign state, and such presumption shall exist until overcome whether or not the individual has returned to the United States. Such presumption may be overcome on the presentation of satisfactory evidence to a diplomatic or consular officer of the United States, or to an immigration officer of the United States, under such rules and regulations as the Department of State and the Department of Justice jointly prescribe. However, no such presumption shall arise with respect to any officer or employee of the United States while serving abroad as such officer or employee, nor to any accompanying member of his family.

SEC. 403. (*a*) Except as provided in subsections (*g*) and (*h*) of section 401, no national can expatriate himself, or be expatriated, under this section while within the United States or any of its outlying possessions, but expatriation shall result from the performance within the United States or any of its outlying possessions of any of the acts or the fulfillment of any of the conditions specified in this section if and when the national thereafter takes up a residence abroad.

---

[1] The form of oath was prescribed by the Secretary of State in Departmental Order 908, Cod e of Federal Regulations, title 22, Part 19. 1–2, dated January 2, 1941 (Department of State, *Bulletin*, IV, p. 9; 6 *Fed. Reg.*, p. 75).

(*b*) No national under eighteen years of age can expatriate himself under subsections (*b*) to (*g*), inclusive, of section 401.

SEC. 404. A person who has become a national by naturalization shall lose his nationality by:

(*a*) Residing for at least two years in the territory of a foreign state of which he was formerly a national or in which the place of his birth is situated, if he acquires through such residence the nationality of such foreign state by operation of the law thereof; or

(*b*) Residing continuously for three years in the territory of a foreign state of which he was formerly a national or in which the place of his birth is situated, except as provided in section 406 hereof.

(*c*) Residing continuously for five years in any other foreign state, except as provided in section 406 hereof.

SEC. 405. Section 404 shall have no application to a person:

(*a*) Who resides abroad in the employment and under the orders of the Government of the United States;

(*b*) Who is receiving compensation from the Government of the United States and residing abroad on account of disability incurred in its service.

SEC. 406. Subsections (*b*) and (*c*) of section 404 shall have no application to a person:

(*a*) Who shall have resided in the United States not less than twenty-five years subsequent to his naturalization and shall have attained the age of sixty-five years when the foreign residence is established;

(*b*) Who is residing abroad upon the date of the approval of this Act, or who is thereafter sent abroad, and resides abroad temporarily solely or principally to represent a bona fide American educational, scientific, philanthropic, religious, commercial, financial, or business organization, having its principal office or place of business in the United States, or an international agency of an official character in which the United States participates, for which he receives a substantial compensation;

(*c*) Who is residing abroad on account of ill health;

(*d*) Who is residing abroad for the purpose of pursuing studies of a specialized character or attending an institution of learning of a grade above that of a preparatory school, provided that such residence does not exceed five years;

(*e*) Who is the wife, husband, or child under twenty-one years of age of, and is residing abroad for the purpose of being with, an American citizen spouse or parent who is residing abroad for one of the objects or causes specified in section 405 or subsections (*a*), (*b*), (*c*), or (*d*) hereof;

(*f*) Who was born in the United States or one of its outlying possessions, who originally had American nationality, and who, after having lost such nationality through marriage to an alien, reacquired it.

SEC. 407. A person having American nationality, who is a minor and is residing in a foreign state with or under the legal custody of a parent who loses American nationality under section 404 of this Act, shall at the same time lose his American nationality if such minor has or acquires the nationality of such foreign state: *Provided*, That, in such case, American nationality shall not be lost as the result of loss of American nationality by the parent unless and until the child attains the age of twenty-three years without having acquired permanent residence in the United States.

SEC. 408. The loss of nationality under this Act shall result solely from the performance by a national of the acts or fulfillment of the conditions specified in this Act.

SEC. 409. Nationality shall not be lost under the provisions of section 404 or 407 of this Act until the expiration of one year following the date of the approval of this Act: *Provided, however,* That a naturalized person who shall have become subject to the presumption that he has ceased to be an American citizen as provided for in the second paragraph of section 2 of the Act of March 2, 1907 (34 Stat. 1228), and who shall not have overcome it under the rules in effect immediately preceding the date of the approval of this Act, shall continue to be subject to such presumption for the period of one year following the date of the approval of this Act unless it is overcome during such period.

SEC. 410. Nothing in this Act shall be applied in contravention of the provisions of any treaty or convention to which the United States is a party upon the date of the approval of this Act.

CHAPTER V — MISCELLANEOUS

[Omitted]

2. REPATRIATION OF AMERICAN CITIZENS

A. From Europe

(1) *The S.S.* Manhattan. *Release of Department of State, July 13, 1940* [1]

The American steamship *Manhattan* sailed from Lisbon, Portugal, for New York at 4 : 35 P.M., Lisbon time, July 12 and arrived at New York July 18, 1940. She embarked approximately 800 American citizens and members of their families at Lisbon.

[1] Department of State, *Bulletin*, III, p. 24.

All belligerent governments were informed of the date of sailing, the course of the vessel and that the vessel was returning to the United States with Americans evacuated from Europe. She carried no cargo taken aboard in Europe. She carried American flags prominently displayed, proceeding fully lighted at night, was unarmed, and moving without convoy. The belligerent governments were also informed that the Government of the United States expected the vessel to make its return voyage without interruption or molestation by the air, naval, or military forces of any belligerent.

(2) *U. S. Army Transport* American Legion. *Release of Department of State, July 29, 1940* [1]

The Acting Secretary of State announces that the United States Army transport *American Legion* has, by arrangement with the appropriate authorities of the United States Government, been commissioned to proceed into and through the combat area defined by the President in his proclamation, numbered 2410, of June 11, 1940,[2] in order to evacuate citizens of the United States who are in imminent danger to their lives as a result of combat operations incident to the present war.

The Acting Secretary of State on July 25, 1940, announced that the Army transport *American Legion* was being sent to the port of Petsamo, Finland, in order to evacuate as many American citizens as possible who were stranded in the Baltic and Scandinavian areas and who could not return in any other safe way.

The *American Legion* was directed to sail August 16 on her return voyage.[3] This ship is filled to capacity with a total of 897 passengers from the following countries: Finland, 138; Estonia, 22; Latvia, 18; Lithuania, 102; Sweden, 250; Norway, 182; Denmark, 84; Germany, 88; and the Netherlands, 13. The Crown Princess Martha of Norway and her three children are among the passengers.

(3) *Request for Safe Conduct. Release of Department of State, November 7, 1940* [4]

The Department of State announces that a request was made of the German Government and of the Italian Government to grant a safe-conduct for an American vessel to proceed to a port on the west coast of Ireland to bring home about 1,200 American citizens still in Great Britain. The Italian Government very promptly responded favorably. A copy of the Italian reply was furnished to the German Government

[1] Department of State, *Bulletin*, III, p. 80.
[2] *Ibid.*, II, p. 641; *Documents, II, 1939–40*, p. 682.
[3] Department of State, *Bulletin*, III, p. 115; released August 16, 1940.
[4] *Ibid.*, p. 408.

with the suggestion that the Government of the United States would be glad to receive similar assurances.

After a considerable delay the following note, dated November 6, 1940, has been received from the German Government:

The Foreign Office has the honor to acknowledge the receipt of the notes of October 27 and November 1 regarding the voyage of an American ship to repatriate American citizens from an Irish port.

On the basis of the previous statement of the German Government to the effect that the areas around England are areas of military operations the Reich Government is not in a position to furnish any sort of assurance of the nature requested.

B. From the Far East

(1) Release of the Department of State, October 23, 1940 [1]

[Excerpt]

Following the suggestion which has been made to Americans in certain areas of the Far East that in view of abnormal conditions in those areas they withdraw so far as is practicable therefrom to the United States, the Department of State and the United States Maritime Commission, in conjunction with other agencies of the Government and in cooperation with American shipping lines, arranged for the dispatch of the S.S. *Monterey*, the S.S. *Mariposa*, and the S.S. *Washington* to the Far East. This was necessary in as much as it was determined that available accommodations on ships regularly operating to the Far East were booked to capacity for some time to come and reports were received by the State Department from consular officials and steamship company booking offices that the demands of American citizens desiring to come to the United States would require the additional accommodations.

In order to make these ships available, it was necessary to divert them from their regular scheduled sailings, thus causing extraordinary expense to the operating companies. As was ascertained by the Department of State and the Maritime Commission, the ships would incur a financial loss even though they were booked to capacity on the return voyage. The operating companies, having cooperated in diverting their ships from their regular schedules and in making them available, could not be justly asked to stand the loss. Accordingly, the Government was obliged to guarantee the companies against financial loss and agreed to make up any deficit which might occur, as has been done before in the cases of special ships sent to evacuate Americans from Europe.

[1] Department of State, *Bulletin*, III, p. 339.

3. PASSPORTS

(1) Validation and Issuance of Passports During Existence of War. Additional Regulations. Department of State Order No. 888, October 11, 1940 [1]

§ 32.9 *Passport to contain name of each country citizen intends to visit and object of visit.* In view of the exigencies of international travel, particularly the spread of military operations, the increasing hazards and difficulties involved in foreign travel and residence, and the fact that after October 16, 1940, male citizens between the ages of twenty-one and thirty-five years will be required, before departing from the United States, to obtain a permit on Form 351 to leave this country, the Secretary of State has deemed it desirable to revert to the former policy of the Department of State of setting forth in each passport issued by it or under its authority the names of the countries which the citizen intends to visit and the object of the visit to each country named in the passport. This policy shall become effective at once and shall apply to passports heretofore issued and presently valid, as well as to passports which may hereafter be issued, with the exception of passports intended for use in countries of the Western Hemisphere. In consequence, no passport heretofore issued shall be valid for travel from the United States to any foreign country requiring such a document, except countries of the Western Hemisphere, unless it is first submitted to the Department of State for validation in the same manner as is provided for by §§ 32.1–32.8 issued September 4, 1939, for the validation of passports for use in traveling from the United States to any country in Europe. . . .

§ 32.10 *Previous regulations still effective.* However, nothing in §§ 32.9–32.10 shall be construed as rendering ineffective the provisions of the regulation of November 6, 1939, under which an American citizen may not travel on a vessel of a belligerent country on or over the North Atlantic Ocean north of 35 degrees north latitude and east of 66 degrees west longitude except when specifically authorized to do so. The authorization may be granted by the Passport Division of the Department of State. American consular officers in the Dominion of Canada and in Newfoundland are authorized to endorse passports for travel on a vessel of a belligerent state in any case where the vessel begins its journey in a port in the Dominion of Canada or in Newfoundland, including Labrador, and ends at a port in any such place or the United States, provided the vessel is not scheduled to travel, between the beginning

---

[1] Code of Federal Regulations, Title 22, Chap. I., Part 32; Department of State, *Bulletin*, III, p. 314.

and ending of any such journey, in the waters above mentioned, except in the Gulf of St. Lawrence, Hudson Strait and the coastal or contiguous waters of the Dominion of Canada or Newfoundland, including Labrador, which are customarily navigated between points on these coasts. (Sec. 1, 44 Stat. 887; 22 U. S. C. 211a; Proc. No. 7856, Mar. 31, 1938)

[SEAL]
CORDELL HULL,
Secretary of State.

OCTOBER 11, 1940.

(2) *Passport Requirements for British Possessions in the Western Hemisphere. Release of Department of State, February 17, 1941* [1]

American citizens proceeding to Newfoundland, Bermuda, Jamaica, Antigua, St. Lucia, Trinidad, and British Guiana should be in possession of valid passports. Army and Navy personnel proceeding to these points, who have been documented by the War or Navy Departments, are exempt from this requirement. Persons proceeding on a continuous voyage on vessels which touch at these places do not need passports provided they are remaining at the places mentioned only while the ships on which they are traveling are in port.

At least 10 days will be required after an application is submitted before a passport will be granted. It will also be necessary for persons bearing passports to obtain British visas.

4. REFUGEES

A. Admission of British Refugee Children

(1) *The American Ambassador to the United Kingdom (Kennedy) to the Department of State, July 10, 1940* [2]

"Officials of the Department of State have cooperated whole-heartedly and enthusiastically with other officials of this Government charged with the control of immigration and also with interested private organizations, including the United States Committee for the Care of European Children, which has its headquarters in New York City. The fact is that all the red tape has been cut and all of the non-essential requirements have been eliminated, and this has been effective to the extent that up to today no visa has been refused to any qualified child in England."

I note in the press and elsewhere a disposition to blame red tape for the small number of British children thus far sent to America. There

[1] Department of State, *Bulletin*, IV, p. 212.
[2] *Ibid.*, III, p. 23. The head note is quoted from the press release.

is nothing to this charge. I dislike red tape more than most people, but I must admit that in this instance children are being passed by the American Consulate General faster than the British are able to find shipping accommodations for them. As a matter of record, many applicants who have received appointments for visa interviews report that they have not yet been able to procure their British passports. Visas for 1,735 additional children are now in process of issuance. The number who have actually been able to secure shipping accommodations is estimated to be around 600. In view of this situation, any discussion about cutting the red tape is purely academic at the moment.

(2) *Order of the Commissioner of Immigration and Naturalization, July 13, 1940* [1]

[Excerpt]

By virtue of the authority conferred by Section 3 of the Immigration Act of 1917 and all other authority conferred by law upon the Commissioner of Immigration and Naturalization and the Attorney General, the following rule is issued governing the admission of alien children under sixteen years of age who seek to enter the United States to be safe from the dangers of war.

1. Such children, when presenting visitors' visas and when otherwise admissible under this rule and under other applicable provisions of the immigration laws and regulations, may be admitted for a period of two years subject, however, to the power of the Attorney General to shorten or extend the period of admission.

2. Such children, whether presenting visitors' visas or quota visas, shall not be excludable on the ground that, being under sixteen years of age, they are unaccompanied by or not coming to one or both of their parents, provided that they are admissible under the provisions of Paragraphs 4 or 5 of this rule.

3. Such children, when presenting visitors' visas, shall not be excludable on the ground that their ticket or passage has been paid for by any corporation, association, society, municipality, or foreign government, nor, when presenting quota visas, on the ground that their tickets or passage has been paid for by any corporation not for profit and not operated, directly or indirectly, for profit.

4. Such children, when presenting visitors' visas, shall not be excludable as likely to become a public charge, provided either that they would

[1] Department of State, *Bulletin*, III, p. 32.

be admissible independently of the provisions of this rule or that the following conditions have been satisfied:

That a corporation not for profit organized for the purpose of assuring the care and support of refugee children, and approved by the Attorney General for such purpose, has given the Attorney General, with such supporting evidence as he may require and in such form as he may require, the following assurances: first, that an identified child or a child for whom provision for identification has been or will be made will not become a public charge; second, that arrangements have been or will be made for the reception and placement of such child in accordance with the standards of the Children's Bureau of the Department of Labor; and third, that the sum of fifty dollars for each such child has been or, upon the initial placement of the child, will be deposited in a trust fund established by and to be used by the corporation to meet all contingencies, not otherwise met or provided for, arising after such initial placement respecting either the care of the child while in the United States or its departure therefrom. Every corporation approved by the Attorney General to act under the provisions of this rule shall furnish the Attorney General with an affidavit containing an undertaking that the children admitted under the provisions of this paragraph will be under continuous supervision, during the period of their stay in the country, assuring that they are in proper custody and are being cared for in conformity with the standards of the Children's Bureau of the Department of Labor, and a further undertaking to comply with such directions as the Attorney General shall make respecting the admission, care and support, and departure of the children.

5. Such children, when presenting quota visas, shall not be excludable, as likely to become a public charge, provided either that they would be admissible independently of the provisions of this rule or that the following conditions have been satisfied:

[The conditions are the same as in sec. 4.]

EDWARD J. SHAUGHNESSY,

Acting Commissioner of Immigration and Naturalization
Approved:

LEMUEL B. SCHOFIELD, *Special Assistant in Charge; Immigration and Naturalization Service,*

FRANCIS BIDDLE
Acting Attorney General
July 13, 1940.

B. Political Refugees

(1) *Policy as to Political Refugees.* *Press Release of the Department of State, December 18, 1940* [1]

The refugee problem is inextricably involved with the question of visas. Persons desiring to come to the United States under the immigration laws must first obtain a visa from a consul of the United States abroad.

Persons coming for permanent residence must, under this law, secure immigrant visas; those coming for a temporary stay, visitors' visas; those who desire to pass through the country *en route* to another country, transit visas. The granting of visas is under the jurisdiction of the Department of State.

Persons arriving on visitors' visas are, under the law, permitted to remain for a temporary period. Those arriving as transients are limited to 60 days. If the privilege is not extended, the person is supposed to leave the United States or be deported. The extension of privilege and the steps looking to departure or deportation are under the jurisdiction of the Department of Justice.

Refugees developed into a definite problem after the invasion of France. Many persons had previously arrived in France to find asylum from persecution at the hands of the totalitarian states. To these were added several millions who fled from Holland and Belgium. They all became migrants again and their numbers were doubled or trebled by residents of France — all in flight before the advancing German armies and the Gestapo, which followed in its wake. Most of these unfortunates, persons persecuted because of adherence to their political or religious beliefs, desired to come to the United States.

Obviously it was legally impossible to accept them all, since the laws of this country prescribe the number of persons to be admitted as immigrants. Applications far in excess of the legal limit had already been made by other persons and from only a few countries of Europe were immigrant visas available. That, however, did not prevent the demand, but it did add to the congestion.

The American Consulates in Southern France — at Bordeaux, Marseilles, and Nice — were swamped with applicants. The staffs were increased but, even as enlarged, were unable to deal with the crowding multitude of daily supplicants for admission to a haven of refuge. Branch offices of our consulates were opened closer to the Spanish border as the horde moved south, frenzied at the near approach of the hostile army and the agents of the Gestapo. Then Spain closed its border.

[1] Department of State, *Bulletin*, III, p. 563.

Portugal, apprehensive lest the food supply in Portugal and the accommodations available would be insufficient for the mass threatening to arrive, closed its own border. Conditions were imposed upon travel; transportation became disorganized; communications were interrupted: fear, hunger, privation, and overcrowding threatened disaster.

From Spain and the French Mediterranean ports many poor unfortunates escaped to North Africa and besieged our consulates there. Casablanca, in Africa, and Lisbon, in Portugal, became eventually the places from which it was hoped passage might be obtained for America and consequently developed into the centers of the largest groups of refugees, though many, many thousands were caught in France behind the closed borders; and many found themselves in Spain. Some reached Switzerland, and a comparatively few reached Sweden.

In this mass of people were many men and women of intellectual superiority, persons of education, of culture, of character — brave men and women who had stood by their convictions and had, by reason of determined action, antagonized the totalitarian states to the point where their lives were in danger.

Spontaneously there developed in this country movements to save to the world the brains, the character, and the spirit which motivated these distraught persons and to facilitate their departure for this country. The names of some were well known to the American public because of their literary, musical, or artistic achievements, their political doctrines, their scientific contributions, or their capacity for organization; but there were many others whose names were not known who had been leaders of thought and directors of movements in entire accord with American social and political philosophies. The sentiment to save these persons from becoming derelicts or from death developed into committees organized by sympathetic and understanding Americans.

There were various of these committees, among the members of which were persons well known to the public. They recommended lists of names to the Department of State with the view that visas of some kind be issued to the persons on them to come to this country and be safe.

At this point it becomes necessary to recall that the law prescribes how many immigrants shall be admitted and prohibits admission for certain specified reasons. The law also establishes standards prerequisite to the issuance of visitors' visas and transit visas.

Visitors' visas are granted, provided that the person can return to the country of his origin or can leave for a third country; provided further that the person intends to do so (for otherwise he would be an immigrant intending to live here) and that he will not become a public charge while here.

Consequently, the committees requesting visas for certain persons were required to give assurances to the Department of State that they would make every effort to arrange for the departure of the person if admitted and that he would not become a public charge while here.

Transit visas are granted to permit a leisurely stay in the United States while traveling to, or awaiting accommodations to travel to, another country and with similar conditions.

Consequently, the committees asking visas of that character were requested to give those assurances before the visas could be issued.

Those assurances were satisfactorily given in each case and the name and other essential data were telegraphed to the consuls abroad. The various committees recommended a total of about 2,000 names. Each name was checked against official Government information lists, and only about 12 of those names were found to be of persons whose presence here would be prejudicial to the best interests of the United States. For the rest, visas were authorized. About 1,000 have actually been issued abroad. Of the balance, some have been only recently dispatched, some applicants are in hiding or under assumed names for their own protection, some are inaccessible to the consuls, and some have removed from the consular district to another district and are still being sought.

The consul, under the law, is the official who must exercise the function of interviewing the applicant to determine his fitness to receive a visa, considering, among other things, whether that particular person's entrance into the United States would be detrimental to the best interests of the United States.

It was necessary for the Department of State to be satisfied about these persons, particularly about their intentions while in the United States and their ability to leave this country for another place, because if they could not leave the country they would be permanent residents and should come as immigrants, not as visitors, and the immigrant quotas were then full. And to admit them wholesale would be to set aside the immigration laws.

As soon as the necessity for such action arose, the procedure with regard to the immigrant quota lists was revised, and the quotas are not full, except as to Germany and Poland, and even they will be open in a comparatively short time (about two months).

This has been accomplished by "unblocking" the quotas as fixed by law. By "unblocking" is meant that when a person's name is reached on the quota list he is given his visa if he has travel documents and an exit permit to allow him to leave that country so he can use the visa. Otherwise his name is passed and the next name is reached of the person on the list who has travel documents and an exit permit so he can use the visa. The applicant gets a visa. Under former practice the name at the top of the list stayed there even though he could not use the visa, and the names below him on the list were "blocked."

However, quotas are now "unblocked." Refugees can now obtain immigrant visas if they want to come to America and if they are acceptable under the laws. In exceptional cicumstances visitors' visas may still be useful in saving persons of exceptional merit, those of superior intellectual attainment, of indomitable spirit, experienced in vigorous support of the principles of liberal government and who are in danger of persecution or death at the hands of autocracy.

During this whole period the Department of State has given sympathetic assistance to these unfortunate people, has been fully conscious of the limitations imposed by law, and has been careful and deliberate in its acts to prevent enemies without from becoming enemies within.

(2) The Secretary of State (Hull) to the Ambassador of the French Republic (Henry-Haye), December 27, 1940 [1]

The Secretary of State presents his compliments to His Excellency the Ambassador of the French Republic and has the honor to acknowledge the receipt of his note of November 25, 1940 [2] requesting the assistance of the Government of the United States of America in the solution of the problem of refugees, primarily those of German origin, now in unoccupied France.

1. The view of the French Government is noted that the recent forced migration to French unoccupied territory of thousands of refugees of German nationality and the Jewish religion has seriously aggravated the difficulties of the French Government. The French Government, in consequence, is obliged to care for and feed these persons in addition to the many hundreds of thousands of refugees of other nationalities who have sought asylum on the territory of France.

2. It is noted, however, that, in the opinion of the French Government, the refugee problem can be solved only through a more equitable distribution of refugees, particularly those of the Jewish religion, among the "different countries." Based on the information furnished to the Intergovernmental Committee on Political Refugees, the countries of

[1] Department of State, *Bulletin*, IV, p. 57.
[2] Not printed herein.

the American Hemisphere must be prepared to make a material contribution in this sense.

3. Finally it is noted that His Excellency the French Ambassador expresses the hope that, in view of the fact that it is not possible to hold a meeting of the Intergovernmental Committee in the present circumstances, this Government will be prepared to study with the French Government the ways and means of organizing immigration to the American Hemisphere of foreign nationals now on French territory, particularly Jews. It is hoped that this Government through the Pan American Union or otherwise will approach the other American Governments with a view to enlisting their support of this project.

4. It is stated in conclusion that the French Government has refrained for the present from making a direct approach to the other American Governments.

5. While this Government appreciates the serious predicament in which the French Government finds itself as a consequence of the forced migration in mass of German nationals to French territory and while it is disposed to assist in solving the refugee problem to the full extent of the existing laws and practices of this country it believes that, in order that there may be no misunderstanding of its position, it is desirable to reiterate on this occasion the basic principles underlying President Roosevelt's invitation of March 1938[1] to the American Governments and others to consult on ways and means of relieving the pressure brought to bear on all countries by the chaotic unregulated migration from Germany and the countries under its control of German citizens who for political, racial or religious reasons were regarded by the German Government as undesirable. The basic principles enunciated at that time and which were accepted as fundamental by the Intergovernmental Committee throughout its sessions and are controlling in the relations in respect to migration between this Government and the other American Governments are (a) that no distinctions shall be made between refugees on grounds of race, nationality or religion; (b) that no country shall be asked or expected to receive a greater number of immigrants than is permitted by prevailing practices and existing laws.

6. In other words the fundamental principles on which action looking to the orderly migration of numbers of people to the Western Hemisphere have been and continue to be founded are (a) equality of treatment in the resettlement of refugees from Europe of all races, nationalities and creeds; (b) full respect for the sovereign rights of the immigration states in regulating migration currents according to their individual interests and in strict accordance with their respective laws.

[1] *Documents, I 1938-39, p. 438.*

7. At no time in its deliberations has the Intergovernmental Committee admitted the possibility that a distinction can be drawn between one and another category of refugees.

8. It has been recognized throughout the intergovernmental discussions that the right of determining the type and extent of immigration into a given country cannot be delegated to any outside authority. Moreover, it has been made plain repeatedly that this Government would not wish to suggest or be party to any international action which might be interpreted as placing pressure on any Government or Governments to take action in the field of migration contrary to or irreconcilable with their practices and laws.

9. Subject to these considerations and the added fact that the laws of the United States regarding immigration are quite explicit and do not permit of any further liberalization this Government is prepared to make and is making every consistent effort to contribute effectively to relieve the pressure caused by the overconcentration of refugees in certain countries, including France. A maximum number of persons who can fulfill the requirements is being received in this country under the present quotas established by American law and in addition very many persons are being admitted permanently to the territory of the Philippine Commonwealth and temporarily to American territory as visitors or in transit to other countries.

10. It is noted in this connection that many persons who have fulfilled the requirements for admission to the United States and have received visas have not been able to leave French territory owing to the fact that the French Government has been unwilling or has failed to grant the required exit permits with the consequence that these persons have not been able to proceed to the United States and remain on French territory where they must be cared for and fed.

11. It is the impression of this Government, moreover, that the other American Governments are likewise receiving persons in substantial numbers who can qualify for admission to their respective territories under their laws and practices and that persons qualifying for admission to these other American countries have, too, encountered difficulties in receiving exit permits from the French Government and, as a consequence, remain to be cared for and fed on French territory.

Finally, reference should be made to the fact that in addition to the persons who are being received in various American countries by infiltration, settlers who can fulfill certain specified requirements are being admitted in increasing numbers to the settlement established upon the invitation of the Dominican Government, under the aegis of the Intergovernmental Committee and at the direction of an American association at Sosua, in the Dominican Republic. These persons who are carefully selected in Europe by an agent of the Dominican Republic Settlement Association have also in many instances failed to receive the necessary permission of the French authorities to leave and remain to be supported in France.

12. The basic aim of the action undertaken by this Government through the Intergovernmental Committee and otherwise has been to bring order out of chaos in the migration of persons driven from their countries or countries of origin who must be resettled elsewhere. In fulfilling this aim the American Government has made it clear from the outset that it could not support or be party to any measures which would encourage the spread from points outside the Western Hemisphere to the Western Hemisphere of forced migration in which people in great numbers are intended to be driven anarchically upon the receiving states with unhappy consequences to the economic and social equilibrium of all. To permit the spread of this condition to the Western Hemisphere would be to impede not promote the solution of a problem which ultimately must be settled in an orderly manner and in calm consultation by Governments of countries where there is said to be overpopulation, Governments of countries of temporary reception and Governments of countries of final settlement.

13. Accordingly, while this Government holds the view that the time will come when such conditions of order and peace will prevail in the world as will warrant a humane and orderly approach to the migration problem by the Governments collaborating in mutual confidence and mutual respect, it does not believe that any useful purpose can be served by discussing migration problems bilaterally with the French Government or multilaterally with the several Governments at this time. Present world conditions operate to cause governments in many instances to forego the free exercise of their authority, and the essential requirements for a constructive solution of the fundamental problems of migration and resettlement do not prevail.

DEPARTMENT OF STATE,
Washington, December 27, 1940.

(3) *Meeting of the Intergovernmental Committee on Refugees, January 30–February 3, 1941* [1]

Representatives of the 32 nations holding membership in the Intergovernmental Committee on Refugees have been notified of a meeting

[1] Department of State, *Bulletin,* IV, p. 15.

in the Dominican Republic from January 30 to February 3 to inspect the Sosua colony, "test tube" of refugee settlement in the Western Hemisphere, it was announced January 3 by Alfred Wagg, 3d, secretary of the Intergovernmental Committee.

The meeting will be held on the first anniversary of the signing of the agreement between the Dominican Government and the Dominican Republic Settlement Association, which provided for the settlement of European refugees in the Caribbean republic.

The meeting will open in the National Palace at Ciudad Trujillo, and His Excellency Dr. Troncoso de la Concha, President of the Dominican Republic, will preside. James N. Rosenberg, President of the Dominican Republic Settlement Association, will report on the work of the Association for the first year.

The meeting will be addressed by representatives of the governments holding membership in the Intergovernmental Committee on Refugees, including a representative of the Government of the United States, and Mr. George Warren, representing President Roosevelt's Advisory Committee on Political Refugees. Moreover, messages will be read from the leaders in the refugee field, such as the Honorable Lord Winterton, Chairman of the Intergovernmental Committee; Sir Herbert Emerson, Director of the Committee; and the Honorable Myron C. Taylor, American Vice Chairman.

When the representatives of the nations holding membership in the Intergovernmental Committee meet in Ciudad Trujillo it will be the first time they have gathered together since the meeting in Washington in October 1939, when President Roosevelt warned that between 10 and 20 million refugees would be thrown on the world's mercy by the present war.

At that meeting the officers of the Intergovernmental Committee adopted, as a first step in meeting this awesome problem, a program for a "test tube" settlement in the Dominican Republic, to be financed by private capital.

The Dominican Republic Settlement Association was organized, with a capital of $10,000,000. It was organized along the lines of the charter companies which in the seventeenth century first settled America.

The Dominican Republic agreed to allow 100,000 refugees to settle within its borders. Generalissimo Trujillo, who took an active interest in the settlement as a concrete humanitarian measure, personally contributed an estate of 65,000 acres, and buildings and equipment, at Sosua, for the colony.

In its first months the Dominican Settlement Association encountered its principal difficulty in transporting refugee colonists to their new homeland.

Prospective colonists were chosen for their adaptability in agriculture and were trained as agriculturists before leaving Europe.

In spite of difficulties, 500 families have successfully been transplanted to the Sosua colony. Already, they have placed 3,000 acres in agriculture and have established their own dairy industry.

The Falk Foundation of Pittsburgh contributed $50,000 to make a complete economic survey of the Dominican Republic with the view of ascertaining the proper business and agricultural pursuits to be followed by the colonists. This survey is being undertaken by Dr. Dana G. Munro, Director of the School of Government of Princeton University, and is supervised by the Brookings Institution.

The meeting in the Dominican Republic will not be a formal meeting of the Intergovernmental Committee on Refugees, but rather a "report meeting" at which progress will be shown.

The following are members of the Intergovernmental Committee: Argentina, Australia, Belgium, Bolivia, Brazil, Canada, Chile, Colombia, Costa Rica, Cuba, Denmark, Dominican Republic, Ecuador, France, Guatemala, Haiti, Honduras, Ireland, Mexico, Netherlands, New Zealand, Nicaragua, Norway, Panama, Paraguay, Peru, Sweden, Switzerland, United Kingdom, United States, Uruguay, and Venezuela.

5. CONTROL OF ALIENS

A. Entry of Aliens

The following executive order supersedes Executive Order No. 8430 of June 5, 1940 (*Documents, II, 1939–40*, p. 577), but does not supersede Executive Order No. 4049 of July 14, 1924, "Documents Required of Aliens Entering the United States on Airships" or Executive Order No. 8429 of June 5, 1940 relating to documents required of bona fide seamen (*Ibid.*, p. 581).

(1) *Waiver of Passport and Visa Requirements for Certain Aliens . . . [Citizens of Canada, Mexico, etc.], Department of State Orders Nos. 874 and 877, August 24, 1940* [1]

Under the emergency provisions of section 30 of the Alien Registration Act, 1940 and of Executive Order No. 8430 of June 5, 1940,[2] citizens of Canada, Newfoundland, or Mexico, domiciled therein, and British subjects domiciled in Canada or Newfoundland do not require passports,

[1] Department of State, *Bulletin*, III, p. 176, 198. Par. (*b*) was issued as Order No. 877, and is *Code of Federal Regulations*, title 22, § 61.101.

[2] *Documents, II, 1939–40*, p. 578.

visas, reentry permits, or border-crossing identification cards when passing from and to such country in continuous transit through the territory of the United States under arrangements satisfactory to the Immigration authorities; and aliens lawfully resident in the United States shall not require passports, visas, reentry permits, or border-crossing identification cards when reentering the United States after continuous transit through foreign contiguous territory under arrangements satisfactory to the Immigration authorities.

———

(b) Under the emergency provisions of section 30 of the Alien Registration Act, 1940,[1] and of Executive Order No. 8430, of June 5, 1940, citizens of Canada, Newfoundland, and Mexico domiciled therein, and British subjects domiciled in Canada or Newfoundland, desiring to enter the United States for a period of less than 30 days on any one visit, may present a passport, or document in the nature of a passport duly issued by the government of the country to which they owe allegiance, and a nonresident alien's border-crossing identification card, issued by either an American diplomatic or consular officer or by an immigrant inspector.

CORDELL HULL

DEPARTMENT OF STATE,
August 24, 1940.

(2) *Documents Required of Aliens Entering the United States, Executive Order No. 8766, June 3, 1941* [2]

[Excerpt]

By virtue of and pursuant to the authority vested in me by the act of May 22, 1918, 40 Stat. 559, as extended by the act of March 2, 1921, 41 Stat. 1205, 1217, and by section 1752 of the Revised Statutes of the United States, and in connection with the Alien Registration Act, 1940, approved June 28, 1940 (54 Stat. 670),[3] I hereby prescribe the following regulations pertaining to documents required of aliens entering the United States (which regulations shall be applicable to Chinese and to Philippine citizens who are not citizens of the United States, except as may be otherwise provided by special laws and regulations governing the entry of such persons):

PART I

1. Nonimmigrants must present unexpired passports or official documents in the nature of passports issued by the governments of the coun-

[1] *Documents, I, 1938–39,* p. 584.
[2] Department of State, *Bulletin,* IV, p. 702; 6 *Fed. Reg.,* p. 2741.
[3] *Documents, II, 1939–40,* p. 582.

tries to which they owe allegiance or other travel documents showing their origin and identity, as prescribed in regulations issued by the Secretary of State, and valid passport or other nonimmigrant visas.

2. A nonimmigrant alien who is passing in transit through the United States may present a transit certificate granted by an authorized officer of the United States.

3. A nonimmigrant alien who enters the United States for a period not exceeding ten days, landing temporarily while the vessel on which he is a passenger is in port, or crossing the border, entering and departing via the same port of entry, may present a limited entry certificate granted by an authorized officer of the United States.

4. A nonimmigrant alien who is a citizen of Canada, Newfoundland, or Mexico, or who is a British subject domiciled in Canada or Newfoundland, may present a nonresident alien's border-crossing identification card issued by an authorized officer of the United States, if he is entering the United States for a period of less than thirty days.

5. The Secretary of State is authorized to define cases of emergency in which the passport and visa requirements may be waived for a nonimmigrant alien.

6. No passport visa, transit certificate, limited entry certificate, or nonresident alien's border-crossing identification card shall be granted to an alien whose entry would be contrary to the public safety nor to an alien who is unable to establish a legitimate purpose or reasonable need for the proposed entry.

PART II

1. Immigrants must present unexpired passports, or official documents in the nature of passports, issued by the governments of the countries to which they owe allegiance, or other travel documents showing their origin and identity, prescribed in regulations issued by the Secretary of State, and valid immigration visas granted by the consular officers of the United States in accordance with the requirements of the Immigration Act of 1924 and the regulations issued thereunder.

2. An alien immigrant who has previously been legally admitted into the United States for permanent residence, has departed therefrom and has returned from a temporary visit abroad, may present, in lieu of an immigration visa, an unexpired permit to reenter, issued pursuant to section 10 of the Immigration Act of 1924. The bearer of such a permit to reenter is not required to present a passport.

3. An alien immigrant who has previously been legally admitted into the United States for permanent residence and who has frequent occasion

to cross the land borders of the United States may present, in lieu of an immigration visa or a permit to reenter, a resident alien's border-crossing identification card. The bearer of such a border-crossing identification card is not required to present a passport.

4. An immigrant Spanish national who on April 11, 1899 (whether adult or minor) was a bona fide resident of Puerto Rico or adjacent islands which comprised the Province of Puerto Rico, and who, in accordance with Article IX of the treaty between the United States and Spain of April 11, 1899, has preserved his allegiance to Spain, may present a passport visa, in lieu of an immigration visa, for entry into Puerto Rico. Such aliens may be admitted into Puerto Rico without regard to the provisions of the Immigration Act of 1924, except section 23. (Act of May 26, 1926, ch. 400, 44 Stat. 657.)

5. The Secretary of State is authorized to define cases of emergency in which the passport and immigration visa requirements may be waived for an immigrant alien.

PART III

The Executive Secretary of the Panama Canal is hereby authorized to issue passport visas, transit certificates, limited entry certificates, and immigration visas to aliens coming to the United States from the Canal Zone. The Governor of American Samoa is hereby authorized to issue passport visas, transit certificates, limited entry certificates, and immigration visas to aliens coming to the United States from American Samoa. The Governor of Guam is hereby authorized to issue passport visas, transit certificates, limited entry certificates, and immigration visas to aliens coming to the United States from Guam.

(3) Limitation of Visas. Announcement of Department of State, June 18, 1941 [1]

In view of the increasing number of instances known to the Department where persons leaving certain countries in Europe have been permitted to leave only after entering into an obligation to act as agent in the United States for the governments controlling the countries from which they desired to depart, the Department of State on June 5, 1941, telegraphing instructions to diplomatic and consular officers, directed the withholding of visas from aliens having close relatives still residing in certain countries and in territories controlled by these countries.

Although each individual application for a visa is to be determined on its own merits, it was deemed advisable to withhold visas in all cases

[1] Department of State, *Bulletin*, IV, p. 748.

in which the visa applicant has children, parents, spouse, brothers or sisters still remaining in such territory.

In cases in which, in the consul's opinion, a visa may be granted without endangering the public safety of the United States to an alien who has some close relative residing in territory controlled by governments which have demonstrated that they have developed practices inimical to our national security, the consul is instructed to report the facts to the Department for further consideration.

A substantial number of meritorious cases have been reported to the Department and have received favorable consideration after a review of all the factors involved in each individual case. Instructions point out that aliens having close relatives in certain territories may receive further consideration on their applications as soon as their relatives have departed from such areas.

(4) *Regulations for Issuing Immigrant Visas. Release of the Department of State, June 24, 1941* [1]

[Excerpt]

In view of the declared emergency and the necessity from the standpoint of the national defense for careful supervision over the entry of aliens into the United States, the following procedure, effective July 1, 1941, has been instituted to require the submission of the cases of applicants for immigration visas and for nonimmigrant visas to the Department of State for preliminary examination before they are given final consideration by the consuls.

The procedure applies to the cases of all aliens who have not received visas prior to July 1, 1941, seeking permanent residence, temporary entry, or transit to a foreign destination, except native-born citizens of countries of the Western Hemisphere, officials of foreign governments, and seamen, where cases are subject to a different procedure.

. . . .

The forms referred to are prescribed by regulation and will be furnished upon request addressed to the Visa Division, Department of State, Washington, D. C. The forms must be fully completed by typewriter and signed under oath before a notary public or other person authorized by law to administer oaths.

. . . .

The cases will be considered in proper turn by interdepartmental committees acting in an advisory capacity with reference to the national-defense program.

[1] Department of State, *Bulletin*, IV, p. 764.

After examination of each case in the Department an appropriate communication will be sent to the consul concerned for further consideration of the case.

. . . .

Various social-service organizations interested in immigrants have indicated a willingness to proffer their services free of charge for the assistance of interested persons in preparing the required documents for presenting the cases of visa applicants to the Department of State. The President's Advisory Committee on Political Refugees, 122 East Twenty-second Street, New York, N. Y., has volunteered to act in an advisory liaison capacity between the social-service organizations offering their services to sponsors and the Department of State.

———

Alien-Visa Control.[1] As a result of the national emergency which has been found to exist, the Visa Division is charged, within the scope of the authority of the Department of State, with the coordination of, and supervision over, all activities relating to alien-visa control.

The provisions of this Order cancel and supersede the provisions of Departmental Order No. 870 of August 9, 1940.

(5) *Rendition of Escaped Prisoners. The Attorney General (Jackson) to All Immigration Officers, April 22, 1941* [2]

Franz von Werra, a German aviator, escaped from a Canadian prison camp and on January 24, 1941 reached the United States, where he was arrested for illegal entry. He was released in the care of the German consul at New York on deposit of a $10,000 bond while a decision as to his deportation or internment was being considered. About April 4 he left for South America. As a result of his having thus "flagrantly abused the hospitality of the United States," the Department of Justice issued the following instructions.

[Excerpt]

1. Any escaping prisoner of war shall be turned back at the United States borders and shall not be received into the United States. Any force reasonably necessary to protect our border against such intrusion is authorized and directed.

2. Any such escaped prisoner of war entering the United States shall be apprehended and held for instruction from this office.

3. In no case shall the immigration authorities extend or United States attorneys acquiesce in the release of such an escaping prisoner of war in the custody of consular officers.

[1] Department of State Order No. 946, June 20, 1941, Department of State, *Bulletin*, IV, p. 765.
[2] *New York Times*, April 13, 1941, p. 3.

4. In fixing the amount of bond and any recommendation of amount of bail to courts, the amount fixed shall be determined in the light of this incident.

B. Registration of Aliens

For the "Alien Registration Act, 1940," approved June 28, 1940, see *Documents, II, 1939–40*, p. 582. For provision concerning registration of newly arrived aliens, see the "Nationality Act of 1940," sec. 328, p. 576.

Protection of American institutions against subversive alien activities was deemed to require a better definition of "government official" in the "Immigration Act" of May 26, 1924 and this was effected by Public No. 701, 76th Cong., 3d sess., approved July 1, 1940. The law as thus amended is printed below.

The Attorney General was made the registration agency of organizations subject to foreign control which were engaged in political, civilian, military or like activities, by an act approved October 17, 1940. The act extended the act of June 8, 1938 (*Documents, I, 1938–39*, p. 559; *II, 1939–40*, p. 821).

(1) *Immigrant Defined — Immigration Act of 1924, as Amended July 1, 1940* [1]

§ *203. Immigrant defined.* When used in this sub-chapter the term "immigrant" means any alien departing from any place outside the United States destined for the United States, except (1) an accredited official of a foreign government recognized by the Government of the United States, his family, attendants, servants, and employees,[2] (2) an alien visiting the United States temporarily as a tourist or temporarily for business or pleasure, (3) an alien in continuous transit through the United States, (4) an alien lawfully admitted to the United States who later goes in transit from one part of the United States to another through foreign contiguous territory, (5) a bona fide alien seaman serving as such on a vessel arriving at a port of the United States and seeking to enter temporarily the United States solely in the pursuit of his calling as a seaman, and (6) an alien entitled to enter the United States solely to carry on trade between the United States and the foreign state of which he is a national under and in pursuance of the provisions of a treaty of commerce and navigation, and his wife, and his unmarried children under twenty-one years of age, if accompanying or following to join him. (May 26, 1924, c. 190, § 3, 43 Stat. 154; July 6, 1932, c. 434, 47 Stat. 607; July 1, 1940, c. 502, § 1.)

§ *215. Admission of persons excepted from definition of immigrant and nonquota immigrants; maintenance of exempt status.* The admission to

---

[1] U. S. Code, title 8, secs. 203, 215. The amending act is Public No. 701, 76th Cong., approved July 1, 1940; originating as H. R. 10112; House Report, No. 2645.

[2] The former language read: "(1) a government official, his family, attendants, servants, and employees."

the United States of an alien excepted from the class of immigrants by clause (1), (2), (3), (4), (5), or (6) of section [203], or declared to be a nonquota immigrant by subdivision (e) of section 4, shall be for such time and under such conditions as may be by regulations prescribed (including, when deemed necessary for the classes mentioned in clause (2), (3), (4), or (6) of section [203] and subdivision (e) of section 4, the giving of bond with sufficient surety, in such sum and containing such conditions as may be by regulations prescribed) to insure that, at the expiration of such time or upon failure to maintain the status under which admitted, he will depart from the United States: *Provided*, That no alien who has been, or who may hereafter be, admitted into the United States under clause (1) of section [203], as an official of a foreign government, or as a member of the family of such official, shall be required to depart from the United States without the approval of the Secretary of State. (May 26, 1924, c. 190, § 15, 43 Stat. 162; July 1, 1932, c. 363, 47 Stat. 524; July 1, 1940, c. 502, § 2.)

(a) The Term "Foreign Government Official" — Immigration and Naturalization Service General Order No. C–21, as Amended November 14, and December 4, 1940 [1]

[Excerpt]

29. 1 *Persons required to register and be fingerprinted.*

. . . .

(h) No foreign government official, or member of his family, shall be required to register or to be fingerprinted.

(1) The term "foreign government official," as used in the Alien Registration Act, 1940, and in this part, shall be construed to mean:

(i) Foreign diplomatic officers eligible to appear in the Diplomatic List issued monthly by the Department of State;

(ii) Foreign consular officers of career:

(iii) Employees of diplomatic missions;

(iv) Employees of foreign consular offices;

(v) Other officials of foreign governments who are in the United States in an official capacity, including commissioned officers, on active duty, of the military, naval and air forces of foreign countries; and including official delegates to international conventions and official conferences and their staffs, attendants, and employees;

(vi) Foreign government officials who are in the United States as temporary visitors or in transit through the United States:

[1] Regulations issued pursuant to authority contained in secs. 37(a), 34(a) and 32(c) of Title III of the "Alien Registration Act, 1940," approved June 28, 1940 (Public No. 670; 54 Stat. 670), dated August 8, 1940 and published as Code of Federal Regulations, Title 8, Aliens and Citizenship; Part 29, as amended November 14 and December 4, 1940 (5 *Fed. Reg.*, p. 2836, 3503, 4560, 4813).

Provided, however, In all such cases, except those of ambassadors and ministers and members of their missions whose names appear on the blue Diplomatic List published monthly by the Department of State, that within thirty days after the arrival of any such foreign government official, or his employment as a foreign government official, in the United States the Department of State is notified by the appropriate diplomatic mission, on an official form supplied by the Department of State of the full name of such official, together with such other information as the Department of State deems appropriate, and that the Department of State accepts such notification as satisfactory and recognizes the status claimed: *And provided further,* That a claim of exemption as a foreign government official in behalf of any alien shall operate to terminate any status as a permanent resident theretofore acquired by such alien for immigration and naturalization purposes.

(2) The term "member of his family," as used in the Alien Registration Act, 1940, and in this part, shall be construed to include a relative by blood or marriage who is regularly residing in, or is a member of, the household of a foreign government official. It shall also be construed to include a servant or other domestic employee residing as an employee in the household of a foreign government official; provided that within thirty days after the arrival or employment in the United States of any such servant or employee the Department of State is notified by the appropriate diplomatic mission, on an official form supplied by the Department of State of the full name of such servant or employee, together with such other information as the Department of State deems appropriate, and that the Department of State accepts such notification as satisfactory and recognizes the status claimed; and provided further that a claim of exemption as a member of the family of a foreign government official in behalf of any alien shall operate to terminate any status as a permanent resident theretofore acquired by such alien for immigration and naturalization purposes.

(3) Any person who, having had the status in the United States of a foreign government official or member of his family, shall cease to maintain such status, shall within thirty days of such cessation apply for registration and to be fingerprinted. (Sections 37(a), 34(a) and 32(c), Act of June 28, 1940; 54 Stat. 670)

	HENRY M. HART, JR.,
Approved:	*Special Assistant to the Attorney General,*
ROBERT H. JACKSON,	*In Charge pro tem., Immigration and*
Attorney General.	*Naturalization Service.*

(2) An Act to Require the Registration of Certain Organizations Carrying on Activities within the United States, and for Other Purposes, Approved October 17, 1940 [1]

Be it enacted by the Senate and House of Representatives of the United States of America in Congress assembled, That for the purposes of this Act—

[1] Public Law No. 870, 76th Cong., 3d sess.; originating as H. R. 9849, reported from House Committee on Judiciary as H. R. 10094, June 17, 1940; House Report No. 2582; Senate Report No. 2172; House (conference) Report No. 3024.

(a) The term "Attorney General" means the Attorney General of the United States;

(b) The term "organization" means any group, club, league, society, committee, association, political party, or combination of individuals, whether incorporated or otherwise, but such term shall not include any corporation, association, community chest, fund or foundation, organized and operated exclusively for religious, charitable, scientific, literary, or educational purposes;

(c) The term "political activity" means any activity the purpose or aim of which, or one of the purposes or aims of which, is the control by force or overthrow of the Government of the United States or a political subdivision thereof, or any State or political subdivision thereof;

(d) An organization shall be deemed to be engaged in "civilian military activity" if (1) it gives instruction to, or prescribes instruction for, its members in the use of firearms or other weapons or any substitute therefor, or military or naval science, or (2) it receives from any other organization or from any individual instruction in military or naval science, or (3) it engages in any military or naval maneuvers or activities, or (4) it engages, either with or without arms, in drills or parades of a military or naval character, or (5) it engages in any other form of organized activity which in the opinion of the Attorney General constitutes preparation for military action; and

(e) An organization shall be deemed "subject to foreign control" if (1) it solicits or accepts financial contributions, loans, or support of any kind, directly or indirectly, from, or is affiliated directly or indirectly with, a foreign government or a political subdivision thereof, or an agent, agency, or instrumentality of a foreign government or political subdivision thereof, or a political party in a foreign country, or an international political organization, or (2) its policies, or any of them, are determined by or at the suggestion of, or in collaboration with, a foreign government or political subdivision thereof, or an agent, agency, or instrumentality of a foreign government or a political subdivision thereof, or a political party in a foreign country, or an international political organization.

SEC. 2. (a) The following organizations shall be required to register with the Attorney General as hereinafter provided:

(1) Every organization subject to foreign control which engages in political activity;

(2) Every organization which engages both in civilian military activity and in political activity;

(3) Every organization subject to foreign control which engages in civilian military activity; and

(4) Every organization, the purpose or aim of which, or one of the purposes or aims of which, is the establishment, control, conduct, seizure, or overthrow of a government or subdivision thereof by the use of force, violence, military measures, or threats of any one or more of the foregoing.

Every such organization shall register by filing with the Attorney General, on such forms and in such detail as the Attorney General may by rules and regulations prescribe, a registration statement containing the information and documents prescribed in subsection (c) and shall within thirty days after the expiration of each period of six months succeeding the filing of such registration statement, file with the Attorney General, on such forms and in such detail as the Attorney General may by rules and regulations prescribe, a supplemental statement containing such information and documents as may be necessary to make the information and documents previously filed under this section accurate and current with respect to such preceding six months' period. Every statement required to be filed by this section shall be subscribed, under oath, by all of the officers of the organization.

(b) Nothing in subsection (a) shall be deemed to require registration or the filing of any statement with the Attorney General by (1) the armed forces of the United States, or (2) the organized militia or National Guard of any State, Territory, District, or possession of the United States, or (3) any law-enforcement agency of the United States or of any Territory, District, or possession thereof, or of any State or political subdivision of a State, or of any agency or instrumentality of one or more States, or (4) any duly established diplomatic mission or consular office of a foreign government which is so recognized by the Department of State, or (5) any nationally recognized organization of persons who are veterans of the armed forces of the United States, or affiliates of such organizations.

(c) Every registration statement required by subsection (a) to be filed by any organization shall contain the following information and documents:

(1) The name and post-office address of the organization in the United States, and the names and addresses of all branches, chapters, and affiliates of such organization;

(2) The name, address, and nationality of each officer, and of each person who performs the functions of an officer, of the organization, and of each branch, chapter, and affiliate of the organization;

(3) The qualifications for membership in the organization;

(4) The existing and proposed aims and purposes of the organization, and

all the means by which these aims or purposes are being attained or are to be attained;

(5) The address or addresses of meeting places of the organization, and of each branch, chapter, or affiliate of the organization, and the times of meetings;

(6) The name and address of each person who has contributed any money, dues, property, or other thing of value to the organization or to any branch, chapter, or affiliate of the organization;

(7) A detailed statement of the assets of the organization, and of each branch, chapter, and affiliate of the organization, the manner in which such assets were acquired, and a detailed statement of the liabilities and income of the organization and of each branch, chapter, and affiliate of the organization;

(8) A detailed description of the activities of the organization, and of each chapter, branch, and affiliate of the organization;

(9) A description of the uniforms, badges, insignia, or other means of identification prescribed by the organization, and worn or carried by its officers or members, or any of such officers or members;

(10) A copy of each book, pamphlet, leaflet, or other publication or item of written, printed, or graphic matter issued or distributed directly or indirectly by the organization, or by any chapter, branch, or affiliate of the organization, or by any of the members of the organization under its authority or within its knowledge, together with the name of its author or authors and the name and address of the publisher;

(11) A description of all firearms or other weapons owned by the organization, or by any chapter, branch, or affiliate of the organization, identified by the manufacturer's number thereon;

(12) In case the organization is subject to foreign control, the manner in which it is so subject;

(13) A copy of the charter, articles of association, constitution, bylaws, rules, regulations, agreements, resolutions, and all other instruments relating to the organization, powers, and purposes of the organization and to the powers of the officers of the organization and of each chapter, branch, and affiliate of the organization; and

(14) Such other information and documents pertinent to the purposes of this Act as the Attorney General may from time to time require.

All statements filed under this section shall be public records and open to public examination and inspection at all reasonable hours under such rules and regulations as the Attorney General may prescribe.

SEC. 3. The Attorney General is authorized at any time to make, amend, and rescind such rules and regulations as may be necessary to carry out the provisions of this Act, including rules and regulations governing the statements required to be filed by this Act.

SEC. 4. Any violation of any of the provisions of this Act shall be punishable by a fine of not more than $10,000 or by imprisonment for not more than five years, or both. Whoever in a statement filed pursuant to section 2 willfully makes any false statement or willfully omits to state any fact which is required to be stated, or which is necessary to make the statements made not misleading, shall, upon conviction, be subject to a fine of not more than $2,000 or to imprisonment for not more than five years, or both.

SEC. 5. If any provision of this Act, or the application thereof to any person or circumstances, is held invalid, the remainder of the Act, and the application of such provisions to other persons or circumstances, shall not be affected thereby.

SEC. 6. This Act shall take effect on the ninetieth day after the date of its enactment, except that prior to such ninetieth day the Attorney General may make, amend, or rescind such rules and regulations as may be necessary to carry out the provisions of this Act.

C. Protection from Alien Activities

(1) An Act to Amend the Act of May 22, 1918 (40 Stat. 559), Approved June 21, 1941 [1]

The act of May 22, 1918 (U.S. Code, title 22, §§ 223–6) authorized the President to restrict and prohibit the departure and entry of aliens in time of war. Public Law 114, 77th Cong., approved June 21, 1941, extended this authority throughout the duration of the unlimited national emergency or during the existence of foreign war, by amendment so as not to affect any judicial proceedings under the original act. The amount of a maximum fine was reduced from $10,000 to $5,000. The act was also made applicable to the Commonwealth of the Philippines.

[Excerpt]

Be it enacted by the Senate and House of Representatives of the United States of America in Congress assembled, That the first paragraph of section 1 of the Act of May 22, 1918 (40 Stat. 559), is amended to read as follows:

"When the United States is at war or during the existence of the national emergency proclaimed by the President on May 27, 1941, or as to aliens whenever there exists a state of war between, or among, two or more states, and the President shall find that the interests of the United States require that restrictions and prohibitions in addition to those provided otherwise than by this Act be imposed upon the departure of persons from and their entry into the United States, and shall make public proclamation thereof, it shall, until otherwise ordered by the President or Congress, be unlawful — " [2]

(*a*) For any alien to depart from or enter or attempt to depart from or enter the United States except under such reasonable rules, regulations,

[1] Public Law 114, 77th Cong., originating as H. R. 4973; House Report No. 754; Senate Report No. 444.

[2] The list is added from the act of 1918 for information.

and orders, and subject to such limitations and exceptions as the President shall prescribe;

(b) For any person to transport or attempt to transport from or into the United States another person with knowledge or reasonable cause to believe that the departure or entry of such other person is forbidden by this section and the three following;

(c) For any person knowingly to make any false statement in an application for permission to depart from or enter the United States with intent to induce or secure the granting of such permission either for himself or for another;

(d) For any person knowingly to furnish or attempt to furnish or assist in furnishing to another a permit or evidence of permission to depart or enter not issued and designed for such other person's use;

(e) For any person knowingly to use or attempt to use any permit or evidence of permission to depart or enter not issued and designed for his use;

(f) For any person to forge, counterfeit, mutilate, or alter, or cause or procure to be forged, counterfeited, mutilated, or altered, any permit or evidence of permission to depart from or enter the United States;

(g) For any person knowingly to use or attempt to use or furnish to another for use any false, forged, counterfeited, mutilated, or altered permit, or evidence of permission, or any permit or evidence of permission which, though originally valid, has become or been made void or invalid.

(2) An Act to Authorize the Refusal of Visas to Aliens Whose Admission into the United States Would Endanger the Public Safety, Approved June 20, 1941 [1]

Be it enacted by the Senate and House of Representatives of the United States of America in Congress assembled, That whenever any American diplomatic or consular officer knows or has reason to believe that any alien seeks to enter the United States for the purpose of engaging in activities which will endanger the public safety of the United States, he shall refuse to issue to such alien any immigration visa, passport visa, transit certificate, or other document entitling such alien to present himself for admission into the United States; but in any case in which a diplomatic or consular officer denies a visa or other travel document under the provisions of this Act, he shall promptly refer the case to the

---

[1] Public Law 113, 77th Cong.; originating as S. 913; Senate Report No. 386; passed in lieu of H.R. 4817; House Report No. 762.

Secretary of State for such further action as the Secretary may deem appropriate.

SEC. 2. The President is hereby authorized to prescribe such rules and regulations as may be necessary to carry out the provisions of this Act.

6. COORDINATION OF RELIEF

Relief activities occupy a great deal of American attention. Huge campaigns for raising funds have long been typical methods for alleviation of foreign disasters. The solicitation and collection of contributions for relief in belligerent countries [1] was subjected to registration with the Department of State by sec. 8 of the act of November 4, 1939 [2] and 409 organizations had registered for that purpose on January 4, 1941.[3] Altogether they had collected $23,518,852.43 by January 31,[4] and many more organizations were collecting much more money for the benefit of nonbelligerents,[5] without any central record of their efforts since registration was not required of them. In addition, community chests and other similar activities for national or local causes are constant features of life in the United States. On the suggestion of the Secretary of State, the President invited Joseph E. Davies, former Ambassador to Belgium, Washington; Charles P. Taft, Assistant Coordinator of Health, Welfare and Related Defense Activities, Washington; and Frederick P. Keppel, President, Carnegie Corporation, New York City, to serve as a committee for the purpose of studying and recommending methods of dealing with the raising of funds in the United States by private relief activities.

(1) *The Secretary of State (Hull) to the President (Roosevelt), March 3, 1941* [6]

MY DEAR MR. PRESIDENT:

Problems have arisen with regard to the raising of funds for private relief activities which I should lay before you, together with a suggestion for procedure which may aid in their solution.

The human suffering which has been caused by the conflicts raging in other portions of the world has called forth the humanitarian efforts of the American people. At the same time needs at home have continued, as they have in the past, to inspire similar efforts to relieve human need in this country. It seems likely that these efforts will be increased by the natural concern of our people to provide in every way for the young men who have been called for military training.

---

[1] The act was applicable to Australia, Belgium, Canada, France, Germany, Greece, India, Italy, Luxemburg, the Netherlands, New Zealand, Norway, Poland, South Africa and the United Kingdom.

[2] *Documents, II, 1939–40*, p. 663.

[3] Department of State, *Bulletin*, IV, p. 60.

[4] *Ibid.*, p. 251.

[5] Principally China.

[6] *Ibid.*, p. 282.

In the field of foreign relief about three hundred organizations, most of them of a temporary nature, are now registered with the Department of State in order that they may solicit and collect contributions. Here at home local private welfare agencies are continuing their efforts and must continue to rely on public support. We are also informed that some of our people are planning to launch campaigns to finance activities in areas adjacent to military camps established under the Selective Service Act. All of these efforts are inspired by the finest human instincts, but there is growing danger that they may be frustrated if they are conducted without regard to one another and without proper coordination.

In the field of foreign relief many agencies are now raising funds without full knowledge of the relief resources already at hand, the needs which actually require relief, or the shipping available for the transportation of relief materials. American aid is being extended to Great Britain, China, Greece, Finland, Spain and many other countries affected by the conflict through the American Red Cross and also through other organizations. While the need for greater coordination exists with regard to all of these undertakings, it is particularly apparent in British relief where the problem of obtaining shipping space for the transportation of relief materials is already serious and requires discriminating knowledge as to the needs existing and as to the most effective method of meeting them. Here it is particularly important that funds should not be solicited for categories of relief which have not been requested, or approved, or for which shipping space is not available. Moreover, in other countries of Europe, economic and military controls as well as limitations upon transportation and communication facilities make effective relief operation impracticable at the present time.

In relief, both at home and abroad, it is advisable that the efforts of all the relief organizations be considered in their relation to the program of the American Red Cross, which, as you indicated in your statement of October 12, 1939,[1] holds both under the laws of the United States and under International Agreements an official status and bears definite responsibilities both in domestic and foreign relief and particularly in relation to our armed forces.

My suggestion, therefore, would be that you appoint a committee of three men who are well informed on matters of local welfare, and foreign relief, and the needs for national defense. This committee might very well examine the entire problem and make recommendations as to what steps might be taken to preserve local and essential welfare

[1] *Documents, II, 1939–40,* p. 588.

services, and to maintain a balance between the facilities and resources available for foreign war relief with particular regard to the financing of new welfare activities in connection with national defense measures.

Faithfully yours,

CORDELL HULL

(2) *The President (Roosevelt) to Messrs. Davies, Taft and Keppel, March 13, 1941* [1]

I am enclosing a copy of a letter I have received from the Secretary of State with regard to certain problems existing in the field of foreign relief.[2] I would be grateful if you would be good enough to serve on a committee of three I would like to appoint for the purpose of making a thorough canvass of this situation and making recommendations with regard to the best methods of dealing with the problems which have arisen therein.

It would be appreciated if the committee would arrange to meet in Washington at an early date, at which time I will be glad to put at its disposal such information on the subject as may be available.

Very sincerely yours,

FRANKLIN D. ROOSEVELT

(3) *Statement of the Committee on Coordination of Relief Activities, March 20, 1941* [3]

Conforming to the President's request, the Committee is acting promptly and energetically in this matter which is directed not only to the protection of the public interest but for the benefit of the relief organizations in the United States and their beneficiaries.

The field is a broad one. It covers not only some 300 war-relief agencies under the Neutrality Act but many other agencies outside of the Neutrality Act provisions, as well as private, secular, and religious welfare agencies, the American Red Cross, the Federal Security Agency, and the Committee for the Educational and Recreational Facilities of the Army and Navy. The purpose of the Committee is to be helpful and constructive.

The Committee has already had conferences with the Federal Security Administrator, Mr. Paul McNutt; Chairman of the Red Cross, Mr. Norman Davis; and officials of the State Department. The plans

[1] Department of State, *Bulletin*, IV, p. 281.
[2] See p. 609.
[3] Department of State, *Bulletin*, IV, p. 336. The statement was issued after the first meeting of the Committee.

of the Committee have been made to obtain as quickly as possible a basis of all facts available, upon which judgments may be predicated, as to what if any action may be required to secure greater effectiveness in the public interest.

Many communications have already been received from relief organizations proffering their assistance and support and expressing their gratification that the Secretary of State should have proposed a centralized agency for the gathering of information covering the whole field and which would be available to them for their information in making their plans.

In the field of foreign relief many agencies now raise funds without full knowledge of the relief resources already in hand, the needs which actually require relief, or the shipping facilities available for the transportation of relief materials. Obviously this situation requires correction which can only be secured through a knowledge of the facts covering the entire field.

It should be said, for the information of the public, that the 300-odd war-relief organizations providing aid to foreign countries and which under the Neutrality Act are under the supervision of the State Department, have raised, collected, and administered a total of $27,000,000, in most cases at an average cost which reflects great credit on the ability and character of these organizations.

With the cooperation of the various relief agencies, and with the aid of the Red Cross and the Government agencies, the Committee expects to be able to secure, within a reasonably short time, sufficient basis of fact to enable it to report to the President and to make recommendation as to what steps, if any, might be taken to maintain a balance between the facilities available for foreign war relief and the necessities arising under our national defense, so that public and private welfare services in connection therewith and essential to our own war services, shall be conserved; and so that the most enlightened and intelligent judgment shall be applied in the raising and disbursing of moneys generously contributed by the American public to these worthy causes.

CHAPTER VIII

SHIPPING AND COMMUNICATIONS

1. TABLES ON MERCHANT SHIPPING LOSSES AND TRANSFER OF VESSELS

(1) *Merchant Shipping Losses, September 1939–April 1941* [1]

	BRITISH		WORLD	
	Ships	Tonnage	Ships	Tonnage
1939 —				
Sept.	35	155,160	49	187,465
Oct.	23	105,525	44	194,439
Nov.	28	58,711	47	164,626
Dec.	32	104,909	71	195,084
1940 —				
Jan.	28	95,544	66	199,701
Feb.	23	117,467	54	219,075
March	14	39,467	37	97,604
April	21	75,258	42	135,372
May	31	75,151	64	248,650
June	65	269,783	128	533,902
July	60	200,270	105	405,853
Aug.	58	282,432	88	387,471
Sept.	60	307,427	92	435,553
Oct.	66	299,399	96	423,616
Nov.	65	299,816	85	368,806
Dec.	55	230,307	72	313,197
1941 —				
Jan.	41	205,473	58	306,002
Feb.	68	264,523	85	334,004
March	81	326,631	119	489,229
April	60	293,089	106	488,124
Grand Total	923	3,896,242	1,508	6,127,673

[1] Tabulation of the British Admiralty, *The Times* (London), May 14, 1941. The figures for world tonnage include about 50,000 tons of Italian and Japanese shipping sunk by Germany and neutral ships engaged in neutral trading, as well as shipping at British disposal.

(2) *Nationality of Vessels Approved by U. S. Maritime Commission for Transfer to Alien Ownership and/or Registry and Flag, September 1, 1939–June 10, 1941, Inclusive* [1]

	No.	GROSS TONNAGE
Bahamian	1	45
Belgian	9	68,677
Brazilian	21	94,609.29
British	185	648,476
Canadian	50	64,327
Chinese	1	1,764
Colombian	3	488
Costa Rican	1	22
Cuban	3	1,166
Estonian	1	2,437
French	19	49,229
Greek	10	42,112
Guatemalan	1	32
Honduran	10	20,979
Italian	3	9,275
Mexican	18	907
Newfoundland	3	311
Nicaraguan	1	95
Norwegian	1	2,647
Panamanian	83	404,931
Peruvian	3	1,380
Philippine	8	31,488
Portuguese	1	277
Spanish	2	25,191
Thailand (formerly Siamese)	4	11,292
Uruguayan	1	1,782
Venezuelan	7	11,453
Yugoslavian	1	6,348
Total Transferred	451	1,501,740.29
Sale Alien only (still under U. S. registry)	7	8,394
Total Affected	458	1,510,134.29

[1] From United States Maritime Commission. Approval was given by the United States Maritime Commission under sec. 9 of the shipping act, 1916, as amended (U. S. Code, title 46, Chap. 27). For a tabulation up to April 30, 1940, see *Documents II, 1939-40*, p. 595.

(3) *Type of Vessels Approved for Transfer to Alien Ownership and/or Registry and Flag, September 1, 1939–June 10, 1941* [1]

	No.	Gross Tonnage
1. Sailing vessels	14	15,578
2. Tugs and barges	23	13,899
3. Pleasure vessels (Yachts, etc.)	75	18,194
4. Tankers	41	261,720
5. Commercial vessels under 1,000 gross tons (fishing vessels, motorboats, etc.)	70	10,492
6. Commercial vessels over 1,000 gross tons (cargo, combination cargo/passenger)	235	1,190,251.29
Total	458	1,510,134.29

The average age of the groups of ships sold during the various periods was as follows :

Period	Average Age
Sept. 1, 1939 to Oct. 25, 1939	22.21
Oct. 26, 1939 to Oct. 25, 1940	21.25
Oct. 26, 1940 to Apr. 30, 1941	20.4
May 1, 1941 to June 10, 1941	14.

[1] From United States Maritime Commission.

2. CONSTRUCTION OF CARGO VESSELS

The losses of merchant shipping due to sinkings by German submarines, aircraft and raiding warships aggravated the problem of supplying the United Kingdom with requisite food and materials from the outbreak of war. After June 1940, when the Germans gained control of the eastern coast of the North Sea and the French littoral on the Atlantic Ocean, the Germans acquired more advantageous bases for this type of warfare. The invasions of Norway, the Netherlands and Belgium, however, had brought most of their merchant fleets of several million tons into the Allied pool of shipping. On the other hand, the building facilities of the European occupied regions were added to German capacity and the German bombing attacks on the United Kingdom interrupted, jeopardized and occasionally destroyed the shipbuilding and ship-repairing equipment of the United Kingdom. Still further, the loss of effective capacity due to repairs under hazardous circumstances and long hauls, coupled with the possibility that shifts of route for strategic reasons might slow up cargo deliveries, pointed to the advisability of the United States supplementing the replacement program under way in the British Commonwealth of Nations.

The President made recommendations to the Congress in special messages of January 16 and 24, 1941 and the Congress enacted his proposals into law in an act approved February 6, 1941.

(1) *Message of the President (Roosevelt) to the Congress, January 16, 1941* [1]

To the Congress of the United States:

I am convinced that the national interest demands that immediate steps be taken upon an emergency basis to provide against the effect upon the United States of a possible world shortage of cargo vessels.

Therefore, I feel that there should be undertaken with the least possible delay the construction of not less than two hundred steel cargo vessels, suitable for use in the present emergency and of such type and design as will permit of their most rapid construction.

Such a program of emergency shipbuilding should be entirely distinct from the long-range construction program with which the U. S. Maritime Commission is proceeding under the 1936 Merchant Marine Act, and interference with that program, as well as interference with the Naval construction program, must be avoided. Additional shipways and other necessary shipyard facilities for the building of these emergency cargo ships should therefore be provided, so far as necessary, specifically for that purpose, in the simplest possible manner and in the shortest possible time. Title to such special facilities should in most instances vest in the Government, but the managerial abilities of private contractors

[1] House Doc. No. 51, 77th Cong., 1st sess. The message of January 24 is House Doc. No. 60, 77th Cong., 1st sess., and recommended the authorization in sec. 3 of the act.

must be utilized to the utmost in the construction of facilities and ships. By making use of the experience and administrative facilities of the Maritime Commission and by clothing that agency with appropriate authority, the contemplated emergency program can be handled most effectively and expeditiously, and without the creation of any new or special governmental agency.

Because of the urgency of the situation, and after consultation with the Office of Production Management with respect both to the necessity for immediate action and to the coordination of this ship construction with other phases of the national defense program, I have already allocated to the Maritime Commission the sum of $500,000 from the Emergency Fund for the President contained in the Military Appropriation Act, 1941, and have authorized the Commission to enter into contracts for these purposes to the extent of $36,000,000 under the contractual authority contained in said appropriation. An immediate appropriation is necessary for the payment of such contracts, and the proposed resolution provides that the appropriation contained therein shall be available for their liquidation and other expenditures pursuant to this program.

The Commission estimates that the total cost of this program will be $350,000,000. The $313,500,000 provided in the attached joint resolution, together with the $500,000 allocated from the Emergency Fund for the President, and the $36,000,000 which will be available on July 1, 1941 for the payment of obligations incurred under authority already provided, will make up this amount.

In view of the emergency, I ask your immediate and favorable consideration of the attached draft of joint resolution.

FRANKLIN D. ROOSEVELT

THE WHITE HOUSE,
January 16, 1941.

(2) *Joint Resolution Making an Appropriation to the United States Maritime Commission for Emergency Cargo Ship Construction, and for Other Purposes, Approved February 6, 1941* [1]

Resolved by the Senate and House of Representatives of the United States of America in Congress assembled, That for the purpose of providing as rapidly as possible cargo ships essential to the commerce and defense of the United States there is hereby appropriated to the United States Maritime Commission, out of any money in the Treasury not otherwise

---

[1] Public Law 5, 77th Cong., 1st sess.; originated as H. J. Res. 77, from Committee on Appropriations, January 22, 1941; House Report No. 10; Senate Report No. 7.

appropriated, the sum of $313,500,000, to remain available until expended, which amount shall be additional to the $500,000 allocated from the Emergency Fund for the President in the Military Appropriation Act, 1941, and $36,000,000 to be allocated during the fiscal year 1942 from funds available for the payment of obligations incurred for the purposes hereof under the contract authorizations under such emergency fund for the President, the total of such sums, aggregating $350,000,000, to be known as the "Emergency Ship Construction Fund, United States Maritime Commission," which fund shall be available for the payment of said contract authorizations and for (1) the construction in the United States of ocean-going cargo vessels of such type, size, and speed as the Commission may determine to be useful in time of emergency for carrying on the commerce of the United States and to be capable of the most rapid construction; (2) the production and procurement of parts, equipment, material, and supplies for such ships; (3) the establishment, acquisition, construction, enlargement, or extension of plants or facilities, on land whether owned by the Government or otherwise owned (including the acquisition by purchase or condemnation of real property or any interest therein), to be used for the construction of ships or for the production of parts, equipment, supplies, or material therefor, and the maintenance, repair, operation (under lease or otherwise), and management of such plants and facilities; and (4) all administrative expenses in connection with the program provided herein including personal services at the seat of government and elsewhere: *Provided*, That the employment of personnel engaged in the maintenance, repair, operation, or management of plants or facilities shall be without regard to the civil service and classification laws: *Provided further*, That no part of this appropriation shall be used to pay the salary or wages of any person who advocates, or who is a member of an organization that advocates, the overthrow of the Government of the United States by force or violence: *Provided further*, That for the purposes hereof an affidavit shall be considered prima facie evidence that the person making the affidavit does not advocate, and is not a member of an organization that advocates, the overthrow of the Government of the United States by force or violence: *Provided further*, That any person who advocates, or who is a member of an organization that advocates, the overthrow of the Government of the United States by force or violence and accepts employment the salary or wages for which are paid from this appropriation shall be guilty of a felony and, upon conviction, shall be fined not more than $1,000 or imprisoned for not more than one year, or both: *Provided further*, That the above penalty clause shall be in addition to, and not in substitution for, any other provisions of existing law.

SEC. 2. The provisions of section 207 of the Merchant Marine Act, 1936, as amended (46 U. S. C. 1117), and the Act of October 10, 1940 (Public, Numbered 831), shall apply to all the activities and functions which the Commission is authorized to perform under section 1 of this joint resolution; and the Commission is authorized to carry on the objects, activities, and functions provided for in section 1 of this joint resolution, without regard to the provisions of sections 355, 3648, and 3709 of the Revised Statutes of the United States; section 7 of the Act of May 27, 1930 (46 Stat. 391), relating to the purchase of prison-made goods; the Act of August 24, 1935 (49 Stat. 793), requiring performance and other bonds on public works; section 321 of the Act of June 30, 1932 (47 Stat. 412), relating to the lease of Government property, and any provision of law relating to the disposal of surplus Government property.

SEC. 3. In addition to contract authorizations for carrying out the provisions of the Merchant Marine Act of 1936, as amended, contained in previous Acts, the United States Maritime Commission is authorized to enter into contract or contracts for the purpose of carrying out the provisions of said Act in an amount not to exceed $65,000,000.

SEC. 4. The Commission is authorized to construct, reconstruct, repair, equip, and outfit, by contract or otherwise, vessels or parts thereof, for any other department or agency of the Government, to the extent that such other department or agency is authorized by law to do so for its own account, and any obligations heretofore or hereafter incurred by the Commission for any of the aforesaid purposes shall not diminish or otherwise affect any contract authorization granted to the Commission: *Provided,* The obligations incurred or the expenditures made are charged against and, to the amount of such obligation or expenditure, diminish the existing appropriation or contract authorization of such department or agency.

(3) *Additional Appropriation to the United States Maritime Commission, Approved April 5, 1941* [1]

[Excerpt]

To increase the construction fund established by the "Merchant Marine Act, 1936," $160,000,000, of which not to exceed $5,270,000

[1] *Independent Offices Appropriation Act, 1942,* Public Law No. 28, 77th Cong., approved April 5, 1941; originated as H. R. 2788; hearings by Committee on Appropriations; House Report No. 15; Senate Report No. 69; House (conference) Report No. 335.

shall be available for administrative expenses of the United States Maritime Commission, including the following: . . .

In addition to the contract authorizations contained in previous Acts, the Commission is authorized to enter into contract for further carrying out the provisions of the Merchant Marine Act, 1936, as amended, in an amount not to exceed $180,000,000.

3. FURTHER DEVELOPMENT OF THE EMERGENCY PROGRAM OF THE MARITIME COMMISSION

(1) *The President (Roosevelt) to the Chairman of the United States Maritime Commission (Land), April 30, 1941* [1]

APRIL 30, 1941

MY DEAR ADMIRAL:

As part of the defense effort to which this country is committed I wish you at the earliest possible moment to secure the service of at least two million tons of merchant shipping which now exists and plan the operation thereof in such a manner as will make their cargo space immediately effective in accomplishing our objective of all-out aid to the Democracies. I realize fully that to get cargo and refrigerated ships and tankers diverted from their existing or proposed routes of travel will cause not only great inconvenience but the loss of trade and sacrifices by the consuming public. But vital war materials are piling up at the ports or delayed at the factories. We must supply those ships and at once. I am sure the owners of our ships will gladly cooperate in this essential enterprise.

This program falls naturally into two parts. First, to arrange for the utilization in routes to the combat zone of foreign ships or ships which are to be transferred to foreign registry and secondly, to reallocate our own flag ships, including those which will be completed in the next few months, in such a way as to make every cargo directly or indirectly useful to our defense efforts and the winning by the Democracies of the battle now being waged in the Atlantic. As I indicated to you, I believe that you should assign a special person who will give his full time to the carrying out of this directive.

I have been pleased to hear of the progress you have made with the shipbuilding program but I cannot stress too strongly the urgent necessity of keeping all of the existing shipyards in continuous operation. Every possible means should be immediately explored to increase the number of employees at work, to further develop the training program and to speed up the building of the additional shipbuilding ways already authorized.

[1] From the Office of the Secretary to the President.

I know from long experience of the great capacity of our shipbuilders and of the skill of the workers who build the ships, but our merchant fleet must be expanded faster than we had planned so that ships and more ships will be available to carry the food and the munitions of war to the Democracies of the world.

Very sincerely yours,
FRANKLIN D. ROOSEVELT

4. PROTECTIVE CUSTODY OF FOREIGN SHIPS, MARCH 30, 1941

United States Coast Guard patrols, acting under orders of the Treasury Department, on Sunday, March 30, 1941 took possession of 28 Italian and 2 German ships, totaling 178,030 tons, in 16 ports and took into custody their officers and crews under Title II, sec. 1, of the Espionage Act of 1917 (U. S. Code, Title 50, sec. 191). Of these 30 ships 25 had been damaged by their crews, who wrecked the machinery with sledge hammers, acetylene torches, saws and chisels.[1] Italian captains stated in two instances that they acted under orders from the Italian naval attaché. The sabotage on several ships was interrupted by the arrival of the Coast Guardsmen.

In 9 American ports 35 Danish ships, totaling 105,155 tons, were taken into custody. None of them was found injured and their officers and crews were detained only a matter of hours. Efforts had been made by German officials in Denmark and in the United States to exercise authority over Danish shipping. Reports that the ships were in danger of sabotage "from outside" were cited as justifying their precautionary seizure. The Danish captains and crews were not held under charges.

The epidemic of sabotage of German and Italian vessels extended in the same week to the other American Republics, where the machinery of ships in harbor was damaged, ships burned, sunk and scuttled in harbor or at sea. Outside of Argentina, where there was about 90,000 tons of Italian and German shipping, some 30 vessels, totaling over 150,000 tons, were affected in Brazil, Chile, Costa Rica, Cuba, Ecuador, Mexico, Peru, Uruguay and Venezuela.[2] Mexico confis-

[1] For a list of the damage done see Coast Guard report, *New York Times*, April 2, 1941, p. 11.

[2] From Callao, Peru, the German freighters *München*, 3,315 tons, and *Hermonthis*, 2,819 tons, left without clearance papers on March 31 and were found by a Peruvian warship burning at sea with no sign of the crews.

Brazilian authorities took over the Italian freighter *Teresa*, 6,131 tons, at Rio de Janeiro April 3.

The complement of the German vessel *Cerigo* was interned by Ecuador after they had set it afire at Guayaquil March 31.

A German freighter and three Italian tankers were burned and sunk by their crews at Puerto Cabello, Venezuela, where three other Italian tankers were taken over before they could be burned.

At Tampico, Mexico, the Italian tanker *Atlas*, 2,005 tons, was scuttled in the harbor. Nine other vessels whose crews had planned to destroy them were taken over. German seamen on the *Orinoco*, 9,660 tons, resisted arrest. Expropriation against indebtedness for petroleum was carried out.

At San José, Costa Rica, the captains of the German *Eisenach*, 4,323 tons, and the Italian *Fella*, 6,072 tons, assumed responsibility for the sabotage of the ships, for which they had express orders.

cated the ships in payment of petroleum delivered to Germany and Italy. Peru extended its action to the bank deposits of the shipping companies and the taking over of the *Lufthansa* installations for air bases.

On May 15, 1941, the United States Government took into protective custody every vessel of the French Merchant Marine in American harbors on the Atlantic, Gulf and Pacific coasts. The crews of the French ships were not taken into custody but allowed to remain on board. Ten or eleven ships were involved, including the *Normandie*, with a gross tonnage estimated at 175,000. Federal authorities in New York and Washington emphasized the "free" status of the ships under guard. They said no seizures had taken place and that the craft were still in the hands of their owners and agents.

(1) *United States Code, Title 50, War, Chapter 12*

SEC. 191. *Vessels in Territorial Waters of the United States.* Whenever the President, by proclamation or Executive order, declares a national emergency to exist by reason of actual or threatened war, insurrection or invasion or disturbance or threatened disturbance of the international relations of the United States the Secretary of the Treasury may make, subject to the approval of the President, rules and regulations governing the anchorage and movement of any vessel, foreign or domestic, in the territorial waters of the United States, may inspect such vessel at any time, place guards thereon and if necessary in his opinion, in order to secure such vessels from damage or injury or to prevent damage or injury to any harbor or waters of the United States or to secure the observance of the rights and obligations of the United States, may take, by and with the consent of the President, for such purposes, full possession and control of such vessel and remove therefrom the officers and crew thereof and all other persons not specially authorized by him to go or remain aboard thereof.

Within the territorial waters of the Canal Zone the Governor of the Panama Canal, with the approval of the President, shall exercise all the powers conferred by this section on the Secretary of the Treasury. (June 15, 1917, c. 30, Title II, § 1, 40 Stat. 220.)

———

On February 11, 1941, the President issued Executive Order No. 8677 [1] providing that "upon request of the Secretary of the Treasury or the Governor of the Panama Canal (or of such officers as are designated in regulations prescribed pursuant to section 1 of Title II of the said act of June 15, 1917) for assistance in the control of vessels in the territorial waters of the United States or in the territorial waters of the Canal Zone, respectively, those in command of the land and naval forces of the United States shall employ such part of the forces under their respective commands as may be necessary and available to render the assistance requested: *Provided*, that any such request by the Governor of the Panama Canal shall . . . be subject to the approval of the commanding officer designated therein."

[1] 6 *Fed. Reg.*, p. 935.

(2) *The German Chargé d'Affaires (Thomsen) to the Secretary of State (Hull), March 31, 1941* [1]

His Excellency,
  Mr. Cordell Hull,
    The Secretary of State of the United States,
      Washington, D. C.

Sir:

In the name of my Government I have the honor to advise Your Excellency as follows:

According to yesterday's and today's press dispatches, which are confirmed by statements of responsible government officials in Washington, agencies of the United States Government have occupied and taken into custody the German vessels lying in American harbors, namely, the tanker *Pauline Friedrich*, lying in the Port of Boston, and the motorship *Arauca*, lying in Port Everglades.

In both cases the crew aboard, including the captain and the officers, was forcibly removed from the ship and is being detained on land by the American Federal authorities.

According to a report of the German Consul in Boston the entire crew of the tanker *Pauline Friedrich* is held at the immigration station there under conditions to which the members of the crew cannot be expected to submit.

Regarding the whereabouts of the crew of the motor ship *Arauca*, a report of the competent German Consul in New Orleans is still outstanding; from dispatches of press bureaus it appears, however, that the crew of this vessel, including the captain and the officers, are being held at the Coast Guard station in Fort Lauderdale.

A photograph published in today's Baltimore Sun confirms an earlier press dispatch that on the motor ship *Arauca* the American flag has been hoisted in place of the German flag. In the name of my Government I protest most urgently against the aforesaid measures of the United States Government, for which there is no legal basis in international law and which represent in particular a clear violation of the Treaty of Friendship, Commerce and Consular Rights of December 8, 1923, existing between Germany and the United States.

Pending further instructions from my Government I ask Your Excellency, in fulfillment of the obligations stipulated in the aforementioned

---

[1] *New York Times*, April 3, 1941, p. 8. It was reported that the Danish Government instructed the Minister at Washington to protest against the seizure of the Danish ships, but that no protest was presented.

treaty and affirmed by the amended treaty of June 3, 1935, to take all necessary measures in order to:

(1) Place the tanker *Pauline Friedrich* and the motor ship *Arauca* again at the free and unrestricted disposal of the rightful owners, *i.e.*, to rescind the occupation and custody and restore the unrestricted authority of the captains over the ships;

(2) Immediately to release the crews of the two vessels and to make possible their return and stay on board their ships;

(3) To remove the American flag hoisted on the motor ship *Arauca* and unreservedly restore to the ships the right recognized under international law and affirmed by treaty to fly the flag of their country.

Accept, Excellency, the renewed assurance of my highest consideration.

Signed:

THOMSEN

(3) *The Secretary of State (Hull) to the German Chargé d'Affaires (Thomsen), April 3, 1941* [1]

APRIL 3, 1941.

SIR:

I am in receipt of your two notes dated March 31 and April 1, 1941,[2] respectively, regarding the taking of possession and control of the German tanker *Pauline Friedrich* in the port of Boston and the motorship *Arauca* at Port Everglades and the removal therefrom of the officers and crews.

I note your allegation that there is no legal basis in international law for the action taken and that it constitutes a violation of the existing Treaty of Friendship, Commerce and Consular Rights, signed by our two Governments on December 8, 1923. You even go so far as to request that these vessels be restored to the "unlimited authority of the captains" and that the members of the crews be placed at "liberty immediately" and allowed "to return to and stay on board their ships," etc.

I am surprised at these extreme assertions and demands. In the first place, you do not state upon what principle of international law or upon what provision of the treaty between our two countries you rely, and in the second place, you seem wholly to disregard the plain provisions of our statutes which make it a felony for the master or any other person

[1] Department of State, *Bulletin*, IV, p. 419.

[2] Not printed herein. Apparently no texts of the second German note of protest of April 1, nor of the Italian protests of March 31 and April 1 were made available either by the Department of State or by the respective Embassies in Washington.

in charge or command of a vessel, foreign or domestic, or for any member of the crew or other person, within the territorial waters of the United States, wilfully to cause or permit the destruction or injury of such a vessel or to tamper with its motive power or instrumentalities of navigation; and which authorize the authorities of this Government to take possession and control of any vessel and to remove therefrom the officers and crew when such action is deemed to be necessary to protect the vessel from damage or injury or to prevent damage or injury to any harbor or waters of the United States.

I know of no principle of international law which permits the masters or crews of vessels of a country which have sought refuge in or entered the ports of another country, to commit acts of destruction in disregard of local law and of the hospitality which they have been permitted to enjoy; nor is there any provision in the treaty between our two countries which lends even color of support to any such argument. It would indeed be unthinkable that any civilized nation would become a party to a treaty containing any such provision or that it would subscribe to any so-called principle of international law which would permit foreign vessels to be brought to its harbors and roadsteads and there wilfully damaged and wrecked in violation of law and to the detriment of navigation and even the safety of its harbors without restraint or hindrance by the local sovereign.

On one of the vessels here in question the auxiliary machinery was smashed and the main propelling machinery was deliberately wrecked; and if the scuttling and burning of ships in other harbors of this continent may be regarded as indicative of what might be expected in our ports, it is difficult to see how your Government could expect this Government to be oblivious to the situation presented.

An inquiry is being made concerning other features of your complaint and I shall communicate with you regarding them at a later date.

Accept [etc.]   CORDELL HULL

(4) *The Secretary of State (Hull) to the Royal Italian Ambassador (Colonna), April 3, 1941* [1]

The Secretary of State presents his compliments to His Excellency the Royal Italian Ambassador and has the honor to acknowledge the receipt of his two communications dated March 31 and April 1, 1941,[2] concerning the taking of possession and control of certain Italian mer-

[1] Department of State, *Bulletin*, IV, p. 420.
[2] Neither printed herein. See pp. 423–6.

chant vessels lying in ports of the United States and the removal therefrom of the officers and crews.

The law of the United States makes it a felony for the master or any person in charge or command of a vessel within the territorial waters of the United States, or for any member of the crew or other person, wilfully to cause or permit the destruction or injury of such vessel or to tamper with its motive power or instrumentalities of navigation. It also authorizes the authorities of the Government of the United States to take possession and control of any vessel and to remove therefrom the officers and crews when such action is deemed to be necessary to protect the vessel from damage or injury or to prevent damage or injury to any harbor or waters of the United States.

Of the twenty-seven Italian vessels in ports of continental United States, twenty-five of them were so badly damaged that extensive repairs in shipyards will be necessary to render possible their navigation. These concerted and widespread acts of destruction on the part of officers and crews in violation of specific provisions of the statutory laws of the United States, and at a time when the vessels were enjoying the hospitality and protection of our ports cannot be viewed with equanimity. The Italian Ambassador must have overlooked the gravity of the situation when in his communication of March 31 he registered a protest against the action on the part of the Federal authorities with respect to "Italian properties and nationals."

With respect to the Ambassador's specific inquiry as to the views and intentions of the Government of the United States regarding the ships and their crews, the Ambassador is informed that this matter is now receiving the attention of the appropriate authorities of the Government and will be determined in the light of the law and the pertinent facts.

The Secretary of State will communicate with the Ambassador concerning the other questions raised by him as soon as advices thereon shall have been received from the authorities directly concerned.

DEPARTMENT OF STATE,
    Washington, April 3, 1941.

(5) *The Royal Italian Ambassador (Colonna) to the Secretary of State (Hull), April 14, 1941* [1]

The Royal Italian Ambassador presents his compliments to the Honorable Secretary of State and has the honor to refer to the Department's note of April 3, 1941, concerning the taking of possession and control

---

[1] *New York Times*, April 15, 1941, p. 9.

of twenty-eight Italian merchant vessels lying in ports of the United States and the removal therefrom of the officers and crews.

In said note the Honorable Secretary of State stated such an action has been taken in force of specific provisions of the law of the United States which make it a felony for the master or any person in charge or command of a vessel within the territorial waters of the United States, or for any member of the crew, or other person, willfully to cause or permit the destruction or injury of such vessel or tamper with its motive power or instrumentalities of navigation and which authorize the authorities of the United States Government to take possession and control of any vessel and to remove therefrom the officers and their crews when such action is deemed to be necessary to protect the vessel from damage or injury or to prevent damage or injury to any harbor or waters of the United States.

In this regard and following the instructions received, the Royal Italian Ambassador has the honor to bring to the attention of the Honorable Secretary of State the following points:

1. Section 502, Title 18 of the Criminal Code of the United States, to which the Honorable Secretary of State seems, at least in part, to refer, could be applied only when the destruction or injury in question is intended "to injure or endanger the safety of the vessel, or of the cargo, or of persons on board."

But, as a matter of fact, according to information in possession of the embassy, none of the damage and injury allegedly found on board the Italian vessels could affect or was intended to affect in any way the safety of the vessel or of the cargo or of persons on board thereof, nor could it constitute a danger to citizens, properties or waters of the United States.

It would seem to have been intended to, and did, affect only certain equipment of the vessels and, therefore, was forbidden by no law of the United States.

In fact, the Italian merchant ships were all docked as ships laid up and with machinery out of commission.

Furthermore, it is to be observed that the section of the statute above referred to applies exclusively to vessels engaged in foreign commerce of the United States, and was intended to protect such commerce from acts of sabotage committed by third persons to the prejudice of such commerce and of the vessels, their owners and their crews.

The vessels here in question, however, were not and at no time during a period of approximately ten months had been engaged in such commerce but during the whole of said time had been lying idle and out of commission in various ports of the United States.

2. If, on the other hand, the law meant to be referred to by the Honorable Secretary of State as having been violated, should be, as certain language in his note would seem to imply, Section 193 of Title 50 of the United States Code (Section 3 of Title 2 of the Act of June 15, 1917), it is to be observed that the very wording thereof seems to negative the suggested violation.

For that Section of the Statute draws a clear distinction between a vessel as such and its equipment. It prohibits, in certain cases, destruction and injury to the vessel but not to equipment on board the vessel; yet, in respect to the forfeiture therein provided for in certain other cases, it specifies that not only the vessel but her "tackle, furniture, apparel and equipment," as well, shall be subject to forfeiture.

It would seem, therefore, to follow from every recognized canon of statutory construction, that the prohibition of destruction and injury to the vessel was never intended to cover the case of an owner's dismantling, destroying or removing engine machinery or other equipment carried aboard his vessel.

And no claim has been made, it seems, that the vessels here involved were themselves destroyed or injured; the only claim asserted would seem to be that the vessel's equipment was destroyed or injured. If so, it must follow that there can be no justifiable complaint that the said Section 193 of Title 50 of the Code has been violated in any respect whatever.

3. The acts upon which action is taken against the masters of the ships as well as against officers and members of the crews of the Italian merchant vessels could not be denounced as a crime because the master of a ship is the legitimate representative of the legitimate owner of the ship and acts in his behalf and, therefore, the acts which allegedly implicated the Italian seamen constituted a legitimate exercise of the right of property.

4. To incriminate masters, officers and members of the crew for such acts is in conflict with the principles of international law in force of which acts performed on board foreign merchant vessels do not come under the jurisdiction of the State in whose harbors or territorial waters the ships happen to be, if and when — as in the case under discussion — the acts involved do not disturb the peace, the tranquility or the order of said State.

Penal sanctions of internal law cannot, therefore, be applied to the acts involved because such an extension of United States laws would be entirely incompatible with the principles of international law above mentioned.

5. Action taken against officers and crews of the Italian merchant vessels for violation of the Immigration Laws seems also to be without legal ground because said officers and crews lived on board their ships and the vessels were compelled to take refuge in United States waters owing to the exigencies of war.

Paragraph 1 of Subdivision I of Rule 7 of the immigration rules and regulations of the United States, which would seem to be the provision of law relied upon, could have, therefore, no proper application to these seamen. That provision has regard only to the case of seamen who have deserted their ships.

Moreover, the Italian officers and crews were requested to and did register their presence here as aliens under the Alien Registration Act many months ago, and their presence here had been at all times since a notorious public fact to which not the slightest objection was taken by any one connected with the enforcement of the immigration laws of this country.

To give to the said paragraph of Rule 7 of the Immigration Rules and Regulations the force now contended for would seem to constitute, therefore, a novel and wholly unjustified construction, without support either in the law itself or in the practical construction to which that law has heretofore been subjected.

The Italian Ambassador must, therefore, reiterate in the name of the Royal Italian Government the most vigorous protest for the arbitrary action taken by the United States Government against Italian property and nationals.

5. ACQUISITION OF FOREIGN MERCHANT VESSELS

The Inter-American Financial and Economic Advisory Committee, representing the 21 American Republics, at a meeting at the Pan American Union on April 26, 1941, unanimously adopted a resolution recognizing the right of each of these republics to requisition foreign-flag vessels in their ports. For text of resolution, see p. 116.

Legislation approved June 6, 1941 authorizing acquisition of domestic and foreign merchant vessels is printed below. The Act expires by its own terms on June 30, 1942; extension beyond that date requires further action of the Congress.

About 230 foreign-flag vessels of about 1,275,000 gross tons, were immobilized in ports of the Western Hemisphere at the time when the President sent his Message of April 10, 1941 to the Congress. Of these 83, of about 450,000 tons, were in the ports of the United States, including the Danish, German and Italian ships taken into protective custody on March 31, 1941.

(1) *Message of the President* (*Roosevelt*) *to the Congress, April 10,*
1941 [1]

To the Congress of the United States:

There are now in our ports a large number of foreign merchant vessels
which have been here for considerable periods of time and which because
of war conditions have not seen fit to depart.

Section 902 of the Merchant Marine Act of 1936, as amended by the
act of August 7, 1939, authorizes the Maritime Commission, whenever
the President shall proclaim that the security of the national defense
makes it advisable or during any national emergency declared by proclamation, to requisition or purchase any vessel or other watercraft owned
by citizens of the United States, or under construction within the United
States, or to requisition or charter the use of any such property, and
provides that the owner thereof shall be paid just compensation for the
property taken or for its use. The same section provides a method by
which compensation shall be determined. There does not appear to be
any comparable provision with respect to foreign-owned vessels lying
idle in our ports.

In view of the growing shortage of available tonnage suited to our
national needs, I am satisfied, after consultation with the heads of the
interested departments and agencies of the Government, that we should
have statutory authority to take over any such vessels as our needs may
require, subject, of course, to the payment of just compensation.

It is obvious that our own ultimate defense will be rendered futile
if the growing shortage of shipping facilities is not arrested. It is also
obvious that inability to remove accumulating materials from our ports
can only result in stoppage of production with attendant unemployment
and suspension of production contracts. It is therefore essential, both
to our defense plans and to our domestic economy, that we shall not
permit the continuance of the immobilization in our harbors of shipping
facilities.

I attach as of possible assistance to the Congress a draft resolution
designed to accomplish the purposes above outlined.[2] It will be noted
that the draft contemplates the use of funds appropriated by the
"Defense Aid Supplemental Appropriation Act, 1941," approved
March 27, 1941.[3]

FRANKLIN D. ROOSEVELT

The White House,
April 10, 1941.

---

[1] Sen. Doc. No. 42, 77th Cong., 1 sess., from text issued by the Office of the Secretary to the President.　　　　[2] Not reprinted here.　　　　[3] See p. 727.

(2) *An Act to Authorize the Acquisition by the United States of Title to or the Use of Domestic or Foreign Merchant Vessels for Urgent Needs of Commerce and National Defense, and for Other Purposes, Approved June 6, 1941, 11 a.m., E.S.T.*[1]

[Excerpt]

Be it enacted by the Senate and House of Representatives of the United States of America in Congress assembled, That whereas Congress has power to provide for the common defense and general welfare and to regulate commerce with foreign nations and whereas for this purpose embargo Acts and nonintercourse Acts have from time to time been passed and whereas the commerce of the United States is at the present time interrupted and the general welfare of its citizens is threatened and an emergency has been declared, for the purposes of national defense, during the existence of the national emergency declared by the President on September 8, 1939, to exist, but not after June 30, 1942, the President is authorized and empowered, through such agency or officer as he shall designate, to purchase, requisition, for any period during such emergency, charter or requisition the use of, or take over the title to, or the possession of, for such use or disposition as he shall direct, any foreign merchant vessel which is lying idle in waters within the jurisdiction of the United States, including the Philippine Islands and the Canal Zone, and which is necessary to the national defense: *Provided,* That just compensation shall be determined and made to the owner or owners of any such vessel in accordance with the applicable provisions of section 902 of the Merchant Marine Act, 1936, as amended: *Provided further,* That such compensation hereunder shall be deposited with the Treasurer of the United States, and the fund so deposited shall be available for the payment of such compensation, . . .

SEC. 2. Funds appropriated by the Act of March 27, 1941[2] (Public Law 23, Seventy-seventh Congress), are hereby made available to carry out the provisions of section 1 hereof, including payment of the costs of repair, reconstruction, or reconditioning necessary or incidental to the use or disposition under this Act of vessels acquired, or the use or possession of which is acquired, under such section.

SEC. 3. (a) During the national emergency declared by the President on September 8, 1939, to exist, but not after June 30, 1942, the United States Maritime Commission, whenever it finds that vessels in addition

---

[1] Public Law 101, 77th Cong.; originated, after hearings, as H. R. 4466 from the Committee on Merchant Marine and Fisheries; House Report No. 440; Senate Report No. 277; House (conference) Report No. 620.

[2] See p. 727.

to those otherwise available are necessary for transportation of foreign commerce of the United States or of commodities essential to the national defense, is authorized, notwithstanding any other provision of law, (1) to charter any vessel, whether undocumented or documented under the laws of the United States or of a foreign country, deemed by the Commission to be suitable for such transportation, without regard to the provisions of section 3709 of the Revised Statutes,[1] on a time-charter or bare-boat basis, upon such terms and conditions, and for such period or periods, as the Commission may deem necessary or desirable in the public interest, and at such rate of hire as it may deem to be fair and reasonable in view of the attendant circumstances, and (2) to charter any vessel chartered by the Commission under clause (1) hereof to a private operator, a citizen of the United States (including a corporation, partnership, or association, only if it is a citizen of the United States within the meaning of section 2 of the Shipping Act, 1916, as amended), or to any department or agency of the United States Government, without regard to the provisions of title VII of the Merchant Marine Act, 1936, on time-charter or bare-boat basis, for use in any foreign trade or service or as otherwise hereinafter provided, upon such terms and conditions, for such period or periods, and subject to such restrictions as the Commission may deem necessary or desirable for the protection of the public interest, and at such rate of hire as it may deem to be fair and reasonable. Any department or agency of the United States Government is authorized to enter into such charters. All moneys received by the Commission under the provisions of this subsection shall be deposited in the construction fund of the Commission, and all disbursements made by the Commission in carrying out the provisions of this subsection shall be paid from such fund.

(b) The Commission is authorized to provide such insurance and reinsurance with respect to vessels (including any interest of the owner or charterer) chartered, purchased, requisitioned, or the title to which or the possession of which is taken over, under this Act, as it may deem necessary . . .

---

[1] This section (U. S. Code, Title 41, §5) reads: "Except as otherwise provided by law all purchases and contracts for supplies or services, in any of the departments of the government, and purchases of Indian supplies, except for personal services, shall be made by advertising a sufficient time previously for proposals respecting the same, when the public exigencies do not require the immediate delivery of the articles, or performance of the service. When immediate delivery or performance is required by the public exigency, the articles or service required may be procured by open purchase or contract, at the places and in the manner in which such articles are usually bought and sold, or such services engaged, between individuals."

(c) Nothing in this Act shall be construed to modify or affect any provision of the Neutrality Act of 1939, as amended.

SEC. 4. Whenever the United States Maritime Commission is authorized to charter vessels under section 3 hereof, it is further authorized, notwithstanding any other provision of law, to purchase any vessel, whether undocumented or documented under the laws of the United States or of a foreign country, deemed by the Commission to be suitable for transportation of foreign commerce of the United States or of commodities essential to the national defense, without regard to the provisions of section 3709 of the Revised Statutes, at such price and upon such terms and conditions as it may deem fair and reasonable and in the public interest. Such vessels and vessels otherwise acquired by or made available to the Commission may be chartered as provided in section 3 of this Act, or operated by the Commission upon such terms and conditions as it may deem desirable and in the public interest, giving primary consideration to the needs of national defense; but no vessel constructed under the provisions of the Merchant Marine Act, 1936, as amended, may be chartered to a private operator hereunder. . . .

SEC. 5. (a) Notwithstanding any other provision of law, during the effective period of section 3 of this Act, any vessel (except a vessel constructed under the provisions of the Merchant Marine Act, 1936, as amended), not documented under the laws of the United States, acquired by or made available to the Commission under this Act or otherwise, may (1) in the discretion of the Secretary of Commerce be documented as a vessel of the United States under such rules and regulations or orders, and with such limitations, as the Secretary of Commerce may prescribe or issue as necessary or appropriate to carry out the purposes and provisions of this Act; and (2) in accordance with the provisions of subsection (c) hereof engage in the coastwise trade when so documented. . . .

(b) Notwithstanding any other provisions of law, the President may, by rules and regulations or orders, waive compliance with any provision of law relating to masters, officers, members of the crew, or crew accommodations on any vessel documented under authority of this Act to such extent and upon such terms as he finds necessary because of the lack of physical facilities on said ships, and because of the need to employ aliens for their operation. No vessel shall cease to enjoy the benefits and privileges of a vessel of the United States by reason of the employment of any person in accordance with the provisions of this subsection. . . .

(h) When used in this Act, the term "documented" means "registered" and "enrolled and licensed."

(a) *Executive Order No. 8771 Authorizing the United States Maritime Commission to Take Over Certain Foreign Merchant Vessels, June 6, 1941* [1]

WHEREAS section 1 of the act of Congress entitled "An Act to authorize the acquisition by the United States of title to or the use of domestic or foreign merchant vessels for urgent needs of commerce and national defense, and for other purposes," approved June 6, 1941, provides in part:

. . . during the existence of the national emergency declared by the President on September 8, 1939, to exist, but not after June 30, 1942, the President is authorized and empowered, through such agency or officer as he shall designate, to purchase, requisition, for any period during such emergency charter or requisition the use of, or take over the title to, or the possession of, for such use or disposition as he shall direct, any foreign merchant vessel which is lying idle in waters within the jurisdiction of the United States, including the Philippine Islands and the Canal Zone, and which is necessary to the national defense. . . .

AND WHEREAS I find that the foreign merchant vessels now lying idle in waters within the jurisdiction of the United States, including the Philippine Islands and the Canal Zone, are necessary to the national defense:

Now, THEREFORE, by virtue of the authority vested in me by the aforesaid act, it is hereby ordered as follows:

1. The United States Maritime Commission (hereinafter called the "Commission") is hereby authorized and empowered, at such time or times and upon such terms and conditions as the Commission shall deem desirable and conducive to the national defense, to purchase, requisition, charter, requisition the use of, or take over the title to, or the possession of, any or all foreign merchant vessels which are lying idle in waters within the jurisdiction of the United States, including the Philippine Islands and the Canal Zone, including all tackle, apparel, furniture, spare parts and equipment, and all stores, including fuel, aboard such vessels or appertaining thereto, for the use and disposition hereinafter directed.

2. Without limiting the authority of the Commission under the provisions of sections 3, 4, and 5 of the said act of Congress or under any other provision of law, the Commission is authorized and directed, to such extent and upon such terms and conditions as the Commission shall deem desirable and conducive to the national defense:

(a) To operate any or all of such vessels, either directly or by agent, in any service of the United States, or in any commerce, foreign or coastwise.

(b) To charter or lease any or all of such vessels to any persons for operation in any service of the United States, or in any commerce, foreign or coastwise: *Provided,* that no vessel shall be transferred, chartered, or leased to any belligerent government without the approval of the President.

(c) To document any or all of such vessels under the laws of the United States or any neutral country of the Western Hemisphere.

(d) To make such other use or disposition of any or all of such vessels as the President may hereafter direct.

(e) To repair, equip, and man such vessels and to do whatever may be necessary to accomplish the purposes of the said act or this order.

[1] 6 *Fed. Reg.,* p. 2759.

3. The Commission is directed to determine and make to the owner or owners of any vessel taken in accordance with the provisions hereof, just compensation for such vessel, or the use thereof, in accordance with the provisions of the aforesaid act.

FRANKLIN D. ROOSEVELT

THE WHITE HOUSE,
June 6, 1941.

(b) Notice of Taking Over Danish Ships, June 16, 1941 [1]

Six Danish ships of approximately 11,482 tons were involved in this action of the Maritime Commission on June 16, 1941. On July 12 the Commission took over sixteen more Danish cargo vessels in four Atlantic seaports, thus adding about 95,000 tons of shipping to the tonnage available for the defense needs of the United States. The following notice was posted on each seized vessel.

To the owner or owners of the vessel (and all persons claiming an interest therein).
Sirs:
Pursuant to the provisions of the Act approved June 6, 1941 (Public Law 101, 77th Congress), and by the authority of the President, the United States Maritime Commission has taken over the title to and possession of the above-named vessel, including all tackle, apparel, furniture, spare parts, gear and equipment, and all stores and supplies, including fuel, aboard the vessel, effective on June 16, 1941, at 9:00 A.M., Eastern Standard Time, under and subject to the terms and conditions of the taking, use and disposition of the vessel, a copy of which will be promptly furnished. Compensation for such taking will be determined and made in accordance with the provisions of the aforesaid act.

W. C. PEET, JR.,
Secretary, United States Maritime Commission

On June 25, 1941 the new Rumanian motorship *Mangalia* was taken over by the United States Government under the above authority.

6. COMMUNICATIONS

(1) Establishment of Defense Communications Board, September 24, 1940 [2]

The purpose of the Defense Communications Board, created today by Executive order,[3] is to coordinate the relationship of all branches of communication to the national defense.

The Defense Communications Board was initiated jointly by the various Government departments and agencies having a vital interest in this phase of the preparedness program. The Board is basically a planning agency, without operating or procurement functions. As such

[1] *New York Times*, June 17, 1941, p. 1.
[2] Released to the press by the White House; Department of State, *Bulletin*, III, p. 253.
[3] No. 8546, 5 *Fed. Reg.*, p. 3817, 3827.

it is charged with the important duty of charting the utilization and control of our communication systems in the best interests of the national security.

The Board will have no power to censor radio or other communications or to take over any facilities.

This task of planning is not confined to radio broadcasting, but also embraces common carriers such as commercial radiotelephone and radiotelegraph, as well as other telephone, telegraph, and cable facilities.

The Board does not propose to interfere with the normal operation of broadcasting or other forms of communication any more than is necessary for the national protection. Through correlated planning, it will seek to gear the great and strategically valuable American communications system, in both the domestic and international fields, to meet any situation the national interest may require.

The various branches of the communications industry will cooperate in an advisory capacity with the Board, which will be composed of the Chairman of the Federal Communications Commission, the Chief Signal Officer of the Army, the Director of Naval Communications, an Assistant Secretary of State, and an Assistant Secretary of the Treasury. Where the activities of the Board impinge upon any functions of Government departments, representatives of such departments will be placed upon appropriate committees.

The Board has had the cooperation of the radio industry in the preparation of this order. With industry cooperation, the Board will appoint committees from every branch of communications — broadcast and other radio services, cable, telegraph, and telephone — as well as from labor groups. All plans involving the utilization of private facilities, or requiring industry cooperation, will be adopted only after consultation with such industry representatives, and the particular private companies whose properties may be involved.

(2) *North American Regional Broadcasting. Recommendations of the Engineering Conference, Washington, January 30, 1941* [1]

Delegates of Canada, Cuba, Dominican Republic, Haiti, Mexico and the United States convened in Washington January 14–30, 1941 in a North American Regional Radio-Engineering Meeting for the purpose of harmonizing the action of the radio administrations acting under the agreement of 1937.

1. The representatives of the Governments of Canada, Cuba, the Dominican Republic, Haiti, Mexico, and the United States of America, having met in Washington, D. C., United States of America, in an

[1] Department of State, *Bulletin*, IV, p. 236.

Engineering Conference from January 14 to 30, 1941, for the purpose of resolving, so far as possible, all conflicts arising as a result of the listings of standard broadcast stations by these Governments communicated to the interested Governments pursuant to the provisions of Part III, Section 1, Paragraph *d* of the North American Regional Broadcasting Agreement (Havana, 1937), having given appropriate recognition to the sovereign rights of all countries parties to the Agreement to the use of every channel in the standard broadcast band as provided for in Part I, Section 4 of the Agreement, and having reconciled, in their technical aspects, the conflicts which have arisen as a result of the aforementioned listings, recommend that the appropriate radio administrations of these Governments take such action as may be necessary to accomplish the following:

(*a*) To make effective prior to March 29, 1941, such licenses, permits or authorizations as may be necessary under the laws, regulations or practices of the respective countries to place in effect the listings of broadcast stations as set forth in the appendices hereto;

(*b*) To adopt immediately adequate measures so that the crystals and associated frequency control apparatus as well as circuit tuning elements necessary for the proper operation of the stations in accordance with the listings included in the appendices hereto shall be installed prior to March 29, 1941;

(*c*) To place in effect at 0800 Greenwich Mean Time (3 A.M., E.S.T.) March 29, 1941, the actual operation of broadcast stations on frequencies and at locations in accordance with the listings set forth in the appendices hereto. When a directional antenna as required has not been installed, the operating power will be restricted to a value which will not cause any objectionable interference to stations of other countries. Each administration will take the necessary measures to prevent the operation of any station not conforming with these requirements and the listings included in the appendices hereto;

(*d*) To make adequate arrangements immediately in the manner provided for in paragraph (*a*) for the erection and operation of the necessary antenna system or other special construction required by the listings of the broadcast stations as set forth in the appendices hereto;

(*e*) To refrain from making any new station assignments or changes in existing assignments as to location, power, frequency, or hours of operation, effective prior to March 29, 1941, which are not specifically for the purpose of complying with the listings of broadcast stations as set forth in the appendices hereto. This, however, does not preclude notification of additional assignments to be made effective after March 29, 1941.

2. In case the operation of any station in accordance with the listings of broadcast stations as set forth in the appendices hereto may, as a result of actual measurements, be found to cause objectionable interference in excess of the amount computed in accordance with the standards set forth in the Agreement, negotiations may be instituted to reduce the interference in accordance with the appropriate technical principles thereof.

3. The radio administrations shall communicate to each other as soon as possible through the medium of the Inter-American Radio Office (O.I.R.) complete description of the directional antennas required by the listings as set forth in the appendices hereto.

4. The original of these Recommendations and their Appendices [1] shall be deposited in the Ministry of State of the Republic of Cuba at Havana with the original of the North American Regional Broadcasting Agreement (Havana, 1937) to which it is supplemental, and certified copies of these Recommendations shall be transmitted to the Governments through their respective delegations.

5. The Governments shall communicate to each other as soon as possible by telegraph and mail through the medium of the Inter-American Radio Office (O.I.R.) their acceptance of these recommendations. In the absence of any notification to the Inter-American Radio Office (O.I.R.) prior to March 1, 1941, by any Government, it will be understood that the listings of broadcast stations set forth in the appendices hereto, together with all other recommendations contained in this instrument, are approved and accepted by such Government.

6. Prior to March 1, 1941, no Government shall make public the listings of broadcast stations of any other Government unless the latter shall have already made its own listings public.

IN WITNESS WHEREOF, the respective representatives sign these Recommendations, in triplicate, one copy in English, one copy in Spanish and one copy in French, each of which shall be deposited in the archives of the Government of Cuba through the Department of State of the United States of America.

DONE at Washington, D. C., January 30, 1941.

For Canada: J. W. L. BAIN, RONALD MACDONNELL

For Cuba: F. SUAREZ LOPETEQUI, G. MORALES, ALFONSO HERNANDEZ CATA

For the Dominican Republic: A. PASTORIZA

For Haiti: JACQUES C. ANTOINE

For Mexico: J. C. BUCHANAN, S. TAYABAS

For the United States of America: THOMAS BURKE, T. A. M. CRAVEN.

(3) *Radio Monitoring Service. Appropriation to the Federal Communications Commission, April 5, 1941* [2]

[Excerpt]

National defense activities: For all necessary expenses to enable the Federal Communications Commission, during the fiscal year 1942, to

[1] Owing to their extensive nature, the Appendices to these Recommendations are not printed herein. Copies may be obtained in mimeographed form from the Division of International Communications, Department of State.

[2] *Independent Offices Appropriation Act, 1942*, Public Law No. 28, 77th Cong., approved April 5, 1941; originated as H. R. 2788; hearings by Committee on Appropriations; House Report No. 15; Senate Report No. 69; House (conference) Report No. 335.

continue to perform the functions or activities [expansion, modernization and operation of radio monitoring and direction-finding equipment, and the investigation of subversive activities] [1] for the performance of which, during the fiscal year 1941, the Federal Communications Commission received an allocation of funds from the appropriation "Emergency Fund for the President" contained in the Military Appropriation Act, 1941, including the objects for which and subject to the conditions under which such allocation was expended during the fiscal year 1941, $1,920,000.

7. DISSEMINATION OF FOREIGN PROPAGANDA

(1) *The Secretary of State (Hull) to Senator James M. Mead, New York, June 14, 1941* [2]

May I thank you for your letter of May 27, 1941 with which you enclosed a number of papers and articles which deal with the exhibition of certain Nazi and Fascist films in the United States. You ask whether this Department is taking any action toward the banning of such films in this country.

The matter of the dissemination of propaganda of all kinds, including films, by agents and representatives of the Axis powers is one which has received careful consideration of this Department as well as other departments of the Government which are immediately concerned. Under the act of June 8, 1938, which is commonly known as the Foreign Agent Registration Act,[3] any agent of a foreign principal disseminating propaganda material is required to register with this Department. A careful watch over propaganda material has been kept by this Department in order to determine whether the provisions of this act are being complied with. Since it has been felt for some time that an elaboration and tightening of the statutory restrictions would be desirable, proposed amendatory legislation is now being drafted.

Furthermore, this Department, together with and in cooperation with the Department of Justice and the Treasury Department, is now giving active consideration to the question of whether the dissemination of Axis propaganda in this country cannot be prevented by other means, and it is my hope that a solution will soon be reached by which a proper control over the dissemination of propaganda material may be effected.

[1] House Report No. 15, p. 6.
[2] Department of State, *Bulletin*, IV, p. 766.
[3] See *Documents, I, 1938-39*, p. 559.

CHAPTER IX

RELATIONS WITH INTERNATIONAL ORGANIZATIONS

1. LEAGUE OF NATIONS SECRETARIAT ON MISSION

[See *Documents, I, 1938–39*, p. 462; *II, 1939–40*, p. 601.]

In 1941 the states members of the League of Nations number 48, but its work has been curtailed and the regular functioning of its organs has been interrupted by the war. Transfer of two branches of its technical work has been made to the United States.

The Economic, Financial and Transit Department — one of the three departments of the technical staff of the Secretariat — established itself at Princeton, N. J., in August and September 1940, on mission, by invitation of Princeton University, the Rockefeller Institute for Medical Research and the Institute for Advanced Study.

Early in 1941, through the help of the United States member of the Opium Advisory Committee, the late Stuart J. Fuller of the Department of State, and the United States Commissioner of Narcotics, Harry J. Anslinger, branch offices of the Permanent Central Opium Board and the Supervisory Body, which are charged with duties under the limitation convention of July 13, 1931, were opened in Washington.

Americans who have participated in the work of the League met at Princeton April 19–20, 1941, and reviewed the work accomplished and its future possibilities. A report of the proceedings is published by Princeton University, the Institute for Advanced Study and the Rockefeller Institute at Princeton in *World Organization, 1920–1940: The Technical and Non-Political Activities of the League of Nations, the Permanent Court of International Justice, and the International Labor Organization described with particular reference to the future by a group of American experts who have participated in them during the past twenty years.*

(1) *The Princeton Institutions to the Secretary General of the League of Nations (Avenol), June 11, 1940* [1]

[Cable from
PRINCETON, NEW JERSEY
June 11, 1940.]

MR. JOSEPH A. AVENOL
Secretary General, League of Nations
Geneva, Switzerland

MY DEAR MR. AVENOL:

During the past two decades we have watched with the greatest admiration the growth of the technical sections of the Secretariat of the

[1] Text from carbon copy.

League of Nations. They have provided leadership in the promotion of international collaboration between scholars, in the furthering of public health, in the control of opium, and in the international exploration of economic and financial problems. Recently we have become increasingly apprehensive that the war may do more than merely interrupt this work. With the involvement in hostilities of all countries surrounding Geneva, we are fearful that the trained personnel of these sections, so carefully built up, may be destroyed.

Under these circumstances we should like to suggest to you very strongly that you consider the possibility of removing the technical sections of the Secretariat, including both the personnel and the records, to Princeton, New Jersey, for such period as may prove to be advisable. At Princeton are located, as you doubtless know, Princeton University, a branch of the Rockefeller Institute for Medical Research, and the Institute for Advanced Study. It gives us great pleasure to inform you that the governing authorities of these three educational and scientific institutions hereby unite in extending a most cordial invitation to the technical sections of the Secretariat to move from Geneva to this place. Should you find it possible to accept this invitation you may rest assured that the members of the three institutions indicated will do everything in their power to assist the technical sections in finding suitable offices and living quarters and to make it possible for these sections to continue their work in the most effective manner. They would, of course, be as independent in their work in Princeton as they are in Geneva.

We are extending this invitation because of the great importance which we attach to the scientific and scholarly work of the technical sections of the League. We understand the difficulty of building up such an effective personnel as these sections now contain, and are most eager that they should not be dispersed and that the work of these sections may not be interrupted by the war.

Very truly yours,

PRINCETON UNIVERSITY
Harold W. Dodds, *President*
ROCKEFELLER INSTITUTE FOR MEDICAL
RESEARCH
Carl TenBroeck, *Director*
Department of Animal and Plant
Pathology
INSTITUTE FOR ADVANCED STUDY
Frank Aydelotte, *Director*

(2) *The Secretary General of the League of Nations (Avenol) to the President of Princeton University (Dodds), June 15, 1940* [1]

(NIGHT LETTER — JUNE 15, 1940 — 7.00 P.M.)

MR. HAROLD W. DODDS, PRESIDENT,
Princeton University
Princeton, N. J.

MY DEAR MR. PRESIDENT:

In reply to your cable of June twelfth I wish to express my own and my collaborators' profound gratitude for the generous invitation sent to me by you together with the director of the Rockefeller Institute for Medical Research and the director of the Institute for Advanced Study to whom I beg you to transmit this cable. We are deeply touched by your appreciation of the services rendered hitherto by the Secretariat's technical sections and by your anxiety to see those services continued. My own desire to secure this object, having due regard to the responsibilities of my position, has led me to maintain at the disposal of the States members of the League a staff embodying the experience and competence acquired during the last twenty years. The statutory seat of the League being established at Geneva, I am certain that you will understand it is not within my power (a) even provisionally to alter this arrangement unless compelled by *force majeure* or (b) to transfer all or part of the Secretariat unless the initiative were taken by one or more States. These then have to envisage all responsibilities attendant upon such initiative, the final decision remaining subject to the approval of the States members. Heartened and encouraged by American friends' sympathetic concern for which we are all grateful.

Yours very truly,
AVENOL, *Secretary General.*

(3) *The Princeton Institutions to the Secretary General of the League of Nations (Avenol), July 12, 1940* [1]

(RCA RADIO NIGHT LETTER, JULY 12, 1940)

TO THE SECRETARY GENERAL
LEAGUE OF NATIONS
Geneva, Switzerland

DEAR MR. AVENOL:

Such meager reports as we are able to obtain from the press seem to indicate that the progress of the war has forced a further curtailment

[1] Text from carbon copy.

of the work of the technical and scientific sections of the League of Nations, and a further dispersion of their personnel. Under these circumstances, we desire to raise again for your consideration the possibility of moving these activities to Princeton for the duration of the emergency. We fully appreciate the difficult problems that stand in the way of an acceptance of our invitation on your part. It is our hope, however, that they are not so insoluble as to necessitate a discontinuance of the brilliant scientific work that has been developed under the auspices of the League.

Most of the difficulties, we feel, are formal rather than real. They grow out of the fact that the League is an intergovernmental body of which the United States is not a member, that it is located by law in Geneva and that its officials possess special legal status there. These facts obviously make it difficult, if not impossible, for the League to accept an invitation that is frankly private to move the legal seat of certain of its operations to Princeton. In a real sense, however, Princeton offers a more favorable environment under present conditions for the scientific and technical activities of the League than Geneva. It offers first of all the three primary requisites for successful scientific endeavor, namely an atmosphere of free inquiry, accessibility to relevant data and materials, and contact with other scholars. The Government of the United States moreover, though not a Member of the League of Nations, has always fostered cooperation with the technical and scientific activities of the League. Considered from the point of view of the presence or absence of conditions necessary to prosecute effectively their work, it is clear that the scientific personnel of the League could continue to function during the emergency much more freely at Princeton than in Geneva.

With these considerations in mind, we do feel that it should not be impossible to find a formula that would meet the formal requirements of the situation. It is not necessary that the technical sections be separated from the League or that their legal seat of operations be transferred to Princeton. All that is required is that a significant portion of the personnel move to Princeton to conduct their work in a more favorable environment for the duration of the emergency. The legal seat of operations could remain in Geneva and it would be understood that the personnel, at the termination of the emergency, would move back to Geneva, and report again directly to the Council and the Assembly of the League. Surely the League has power to authorize part of its personnel to proceed to the United States on mission and thus to work physically out of Geneva. Would not the proposal we have in mind be thoroughly analogous to this situation?

We communicate with you so frankly and at such length, Monsieur Avenol, because of our genuine concern for the preservation of the scientific activities of the League. We are confident that this objective is also your concern, for it is you who have sponsored them, and furnished the support that has enabled them to rise to eminence. It is our desire to do all we can in this hour of emergency to help you salvage this great work.

Very sincerely yours,
[Signed as cable of June 11, 1940.]

(4) *The Secretary General of the League of Nations (Avenol) to the President of Princeton University (Dodds), July 26, 1940* [1]

[Cable from GENEVA,
July, 26, 1940.]

MR. HAROLD W. DODDS
President, Princeton University
Princeton, N. J.

MY DEAR MR. PRESIDENT:

I am very grateful to you and to the Directors of the Rockefeller Institute for Medical Research and of the Institute for Advanced Study for the unflagging interest and the understanding of the League Secretariat's special status and conditions of work shown by your cable of the twelfth July.

After careful consideration of the problems involved in consultation with the heads of departments concerned I am glad to respond to your generous invitation by authorizing Mr. Loveday, Director of the Economic and Financial Department, and those of his collaborators whom he considers essential for the prosecution of their work to proceed to the United States on mission. Eight officials accompanied by wives and children to a total of twenty-two persons will start United States as soon as formalities can be completed including United States appropriate visas. I should be greatly obliged to you if you could inform the State Department that applications for such visas are being made forthwith through the proper channels.

The question of the work of other departments on which I have also consulted the various responsible officials raises special problems to which I am giving careful consideration.

Yours very truly,
AVENOL, *Secretary General*

[1] Text from carbon copy.

PART III

NATIONAL ACTION

CHAPTER X

NEUTRALITY OF THE UNITED STATES

Following the German campaign in western Europe which began May 10, 1940, the Neutrality Act of 1939 assumed a declining importance as an expression of American policy toward the war. The active elaboration and prosecution of a policy of hemispheric defense (as indicated by the Havana Conference, the Ogdensburg Agreement, the destroyers-bases deal and the adoption of military conscription), together with America's determination to become the "arsenal of democracy" (as shown by the Lend-Lease Act), overshadowed neutrality and became the dominant policies.

No proclamation of neutrality under international law was issued after November 15, 1940 and none under the Neutrality Act of 1939 after April 24, 1941, although hostilities later spread to additional nations. The subsequent "Lend-Lease Act" of March 11, 1941 took precedence over some of the intentions of the earlier act, which remained in force and applicable to the situations on which it specifically legislates. Inasmuch as the Neutrality Act provides for restrictions on nationals and vessels of national registry, and not to the United States Government and public vessels, modification of policy by the Government was possible despite the Neutrality Act. The general situation was once more profoundly affected by the proclamation of an unlimited national emergency May 27, 1941 [1] which omits entirely any reference to neutrality.

The following pages supplement the presentation of material in the preceding volume (*Documents, II, 1939–40*, pp. 629–97) and are arranged in the same schematic order.

1. PROCLAMATIONS AND REGULATIONS ISSUED UNDER GENERAL LAWS

See *Documents, II, 1939–40*, p. 629, for Proclamation No. 2348, September 5, 1939 relating to the state of war existing between Germany and France, Poland, the United Kingdom, India, Australia and New Zealand; and the subsequent proclamations applying "equally in respect" to the Union of South Africa, Canada, Norway, Belgium, Luxemburg, the Netherlands and Italy. It should be noted that the war in which Italy was recognized to be engaged by Proclamation No. 2408, June 10, 1940, was only "between Italy, on the one hand, and France and the United Kingdom, on the other hand."

No proclamations under general laws — *i.e.*, laws concerning activities as a neutral under the rules and procedures of international law and of domestic statutes in harmony therewith — were issued with respect to the state of war between Germany and Italy and Yugoslavia, and between Hungary and Yugoslavia, nor to the state of war between Germany and Italy and the Soviet Union.

[1] See p. 754.

(1) *Proclamation of Neutrality of the United States in the War Between Italy, on the One Hand, and Greece, on the Other Hand, November 15, 1940* [1]

BY THE PRESIDENT OF THE UNITED STATES OF AMERICA
A Proclamation [No. 2444]

WHEREAS a state of war unhappily exists between Italy, on the one hand, and Greece, on the other hand;

NOW, THEREFORE, I, FRANKLIN D. ROOSEVELT, President of the United States of America, in order to preserve the neutrality of the United States and of its citizens and of persons within its territory and jurisdiction, and to enforce its laws and treaties, and in order that all persons, being warned of the general tenor of the laws and treaties of the United States in this behalf, and of the law of nations, may thus be prevented from any violation of the same, do hereby declare and proclaim that all of the provisions of my proclamation of September 5, 1939, [2] proclaiming the neutrality of the United States in a war between Germany and France; Poland; and the United Kingdom, India, Australia and New Zealand apply equally in respect to Greece.

IN WITNESS WHEREOF, I have hereunto set my hand and caused the seal of the United States to be affixed.

DONE at the city of Washington this fifteenth day of November in the year of our Lord nineteen hundred and forty, and of the Inde-
[SEAL]   pendence of the United States of America the one hundred and sixty-fifth.

FRANKLIN D. ROOSEVELT

By the President:
CORDELL HULL
Secretary of State.

————

Executive Order No. 8233, September 5, 1939, prescribing regulations governing the enforcement of the neutrality of the United States (Department of State, *Bulletin,* I, p. 212; 4 *Fed. Reg.,* p. 3822) was applied "equally in respect to Greece" by Executive Order No. 8593, November 15, 1940 (Department of State, *Bulletin,* III, p. 428).

2. NEUTRALITY ACT OF 1939—AMENDMENT

For the original text of sec. 4 and the circumstances attending its amendment into sec. 4 (*a*), see *Documents, II, 1939–40,* p. 661.

Sec. 4 (*b*) deals with refugee children, primarily English children who in 1940 were being brought to the United States for residence with American families

[1] Department of State, *Bulletin,* III, p. 427; 5 *Fed. Reg.,* p. 4523.
[2] *Documents, II, 1939–40,* p. 629.

under the auspices of efficient organizations. The lack of shipping for the purpose created a vociferous demand for relaxation of the legal restriction. Hearings were held by the House Committee on Foreign Affairs, which reported out the bill which amended the law [1] on August 27, 1940.

The enactment of that amendment seems to have met the objectives aimed at in other pending legislation in behalf of refugee children.[2]

(1) *American Red Cross and Child Refugees* [1]

SECTION 4. (*a*) The provisions of section 2 (*a*) shall not prohibit the transportation by vessels, unarmed and not under convoy, under charter or other direction and control of the American Red Cross, of officers and American Red Cross personnel, medical personnel, and medical supplies, food, and clothing, for the relief of human suffering: *Provided*, That where permission has not been given by the blockading power, no American Red Cross vessel shall enter a port where a blockade by aircraft, surface vessel, or submarine is being attempted through the destruction of vessels, or into a port of any country where such blockade of the whole country is being so attempted: *Provided further*, That such American Red Cross vessel shall be on a mission of mercy only and carrying only Red Cross materials and personnel.

(*b*) The provisions of sections 2 (*a*) and 3 shall not prohibit a vessel, in ballast, unarmed, and not under convoy, and transporting refugee children, under sixteen years of age, from war zones, or combat areas, and shall not prohibit such vessel entering into such war zones or combat areas for this purpose, together with such necessary American citizen adult personnel in charge as may be approved by the Secretary of State, subject to the provisions of the immigration laws, if such vessel is proceeding under safe conduct granted by all of the States named in the proclamations issued under the authority of section 1 (*a*), and if such vessel has painted on a large scale prominently, distinctly, and unmistakably on each side thereof and upon the superstructure thereof plainly visible from the air an American flag and a statement to the effect that such vessel is a refugee-child rescue ship of the United States or under United States registry: *Provided*, That every such child so brought into

[1] Public Law No. 776, 76th Cong., 3d sess., an act to permit American vessels to assist in the evacuation from the war zone of certain refugee children, approved August 27, 1940; originating as H. R. 10213, July 29, 1940; House Report No. 2805; Senate Report No. 2012.

[2] See *Admission of German Refugee Children. Joint hearings* . . . 76th Cong., 1st sess., on S. J. Res. 64 and H. J. Res. 168, and H. R. 10323, a bill to provide a temporary haven for European children under 16 years of age, which passed the House on September 23, 1940.

the United States shall, previous to departure from the port of embarkation, have been so sponsored by some responsible American person, natural or corporate, that he will not become a public charge.

3. PROCLAMATIONS, ORDERS AND REGULATIONS ISSUED UNDER THE NEUTRALITY ACT OF 1939

(1) *Proclamations of a State of War Between Foreign States (Sec. 1)*

(a) *Between Italy and Greece, November 15, 1940* [1]

BY THE PRESIDENT OF THE UNITED STATES OF AMERICA
A Proclamation [No. 2443]

WHEREAS section 1 of the joint resolution of Congress approved November 4, 1939, provides in part as follows:

That whenever the President, or the Congress by concurrent resolution, shall find that there exists a state of war between foreign states, and that it is necessary to promote the security or preserve the peace of the United States or to protect the lives of citizens of the United States, the President shall issue a proclamation naming the states involved: and he shall, from time to time, by proclamation, name other states as and when they may become involved in the war.

AND WHEREAS it is further provided by section 13 of the said joint resolution that

The President may, from time to time, promulgate such rules and regulations, not inconsistent with law as may be necessary and proper to carry out any of the provisions of this joint resolution; and he may exercise any power or authority conferred on him by this joint resolution through such officer or officers, or agency or agencies, as he shall direct.

NOW, THEREFORE, I, FRANKLIN D. ROOSEVELT, President of the United States of America, acting under and by virtue of the authority conferred on me by the said joint resolution, do hereby proclaim that a state of war unhappily exists between Italy and Greece, and that it is necessary to promote the security and preserve the peace of the United States and to protect the lives of citizens of the United States.

And I do hereby enjoin upon all officers of the United States, charged with the execution of the laws thereof, the utmost diligence in preventing

[1] Department of State, *Bulletin*, III, p. 426; 5 *Fed. Reg.*, p. 4523. For the prior proclamations of this type see *Documents, II, 1939–40*, p. 647–70.

violations of the said joint resolution and in bringing to trial and punishment any offenders against the same.

And I do hereby delegate to the Secretary of State the power to exercise any power or authority conferred on me by the said joint resolution, as made effective by this my proclamation issued thereunder, which is not specifically delegated by Executive order to some other officer or agency of this Government, and the power to promulgate such rules and regulations not inconsistent with laws as may be necessary and proper to carry out any of its provisions.

IN WITNESS WHEREOF, I have hereunto set my hand and caused the Seal of the United States of America to be affixed.

DONE at the City of Washington this fifteenth day of November, in the year of our Lord nineteen hundred and forty, and of the [SEAL] Independence of the United States of America the one hundred and sixty-fifth.

FRANKLIN D. ROOSEVELT

By the President:
   CORDELL HULL
     Secretary of State.

(b) Proclamation of a State of War Between Germany and Italy, on the One Hand, and Yugoslavia, on the Other Hand, April 10, 1941 [1]

[Excerpt]

BY THE PRESIDENT OF THE UNITED STATES OF AMERICA
A Proclamation [No. 2473]

.   .   .   .

Now, THEREFORE, I, FRANKLIN D. ROOSEVELT, President of the United States of America, acting under and by virtue of the authority conferred on me by the said joint resolution, do hereby proclaim that, Germany and Italy having wantonly attacked Yugoslavia, a state of war exists between Germany and Italy, on the one hand, and Yugoslavia, on the other hand, and that it is necessary to promote the security and preserve the peace of the United States and to protect the lives of citizens of the United States.

.   .   .   .

[1] Department of State, *Bulletin*, IV, p. 449; 6 *Fed. Reg.*, p. 1905.

IN WITNESS WHEREOF, I have hereunto set my hand and caused the Seal of the United States of America to be affixed.

DONE at the City of Washington this 10th day of April, in the year of our Lord nineteen hundred and forty-one, and of the Inde-
[SEAL]   pendence of the United States of America the one hundred and sixty-fifth.

FRANKLIN D. ROOSEVELT

By the President:
CORDELL HULL
Secretary of State.

(c) *Proclamation of a State of War Between Hungary and Yugoslavia, April 15, 1941* [1]

[Excerpt]

BY THE PRESIDENT OF THE UNITED STATES OF AMERICA

A Proclamation [No. 2477]

. . . .

NOW, THEREFORE, I, FRANKLIN D. ROOSEVELT, President of the United States of America, acting under and by virtue of the authority conferred on me by the said joint resolution, do hereby proclaim that, Hungary having without justification attacked Yugoslavia, a state of war exists between Hungary and Yugoslavia and that it is necessary to promote the security and preserve the peace of the United States and to protect the lives of citizens of the United States.

. . . .

IN WITNESS WHEREOF, I have hereunto set my hand and caused the Seal of the United States of America to be affixed.

DONE at the City of Washington this 15th day of April, in the year of our Lord nineteen hundred and forty-one, and of the Inde-
[SEAL]   pendence of the United States of America the one hundred and sixty-fifth.

FRANKLIN D. ROOSEVELT

By the President:
CORDELL HULL
Secretary of State.

[1] Department of State, *Bulletin*, IV, p. 472; 6 *Fed. Reg.*, p. 1995.

(d) Proclamation of a State of War Between Bulgaria, on the One Hand, and Yugoslavia and Greece, on the Other Hand, April 24, 1941 [1]

[Excerpt]

BY THE PRESIDENT OF THE UNITED STATES OF AMERICA
A Proclamation [No. 2479]

.   .   .   .

NOW, THEREFORE, I, FRANKLIN D. ROOSEVELT, President of the United States of America, acting under and by virtue of the authority conferred on me by the said joint resolution, do hereby proclaim that, Bulgaria having without justification attacked Yugoslavia and Greece, a state of war exists between Bulgaria, on the one hand, and Yugoslavia and Greece, on the other hand, and that it is necessary to promote the security and preserve the peace of the United States and to protect the lives of citizens of the United States.

.   .   .   .

IN WITNESS WHEREOF, I have hereunto set my hand and caused the Seal of the United States of America to be affixed.

DONE at the City of Washington this 24th day of April, in the year of our Lord nineteen hundred and forty-one, and of the Inde-
[SEAL]   pendence of the United States of America the one hundred and sixty-fifth.

FRANKLIN D. ROOSEVELT

By the President:
CORDELL HULL,
Secretary of State.

(2) Commerce with States Engaged in Armed Conflict (Sec. 2(c) and (i)) [2]

§ 149.1 *Exportation or transportation of articles or materials* . . .

(*j*) *Greece.* The regulations under section 2 (*c*) and (*i*) of the joint resolution of Congress approved November 4, 1939, which the Secretary of State promulgated on November 10 [3] and November 25,[3] 1939, hence-

---

[1] Department of State, *Bulletin*, IV, p. 495; 6 *Fed. Reg.*, p. 2133.

[2] Code of Federal Regulations, Title 22, Foreign Relations; Chapter 1, Department of State; Subchapter C, Neutrality; Part 149 (formerly Part 12), Commerce with States engaged in Armed Conflict.
Reprinted from Department of State, *Bulletin*, III, p. 429; 5 *Fed. Reg.*, p. 4532.

[3] For these regulations, redesignated 22 CFR 149.1 (*a*)–(*e*), see *Documents, II, 1939–40*, p. 676, where they bear the former designation 12.1 (*a*)–(*e*).

forth apply equally in respect to the export or transport of articles and materials to Greece. (54 Stat. 4, 6; 22 U. S. C., Supp. V, 245*j*–1; Proc. No. 2443, November 15, 1940)

(*k*) *Yugoslavia.* [Included in virtue of Proc. No. 2473, April 10, 1941.[1]]

(*l*) *Hungary.* [Included in virtue of Proc. No. 2477, April 15, 1941.[2]]

(*m*) *Bulgaria.* [Included in virtue of Proc. No. 2479, April 24. 1941.[3]]

(3) Combat Area (Sec. 3)

Proclamation No. 2410 of June 11, 1940 defined as two combat areas the Mediterranean and Red Seas. By April 1941 the British Commonwealth was well advanced in clearing the Italians out of the northeast African regions which they had renamed "Italian East Africa." Moreover, new developments in the Near East made it desirable to send American material for British forces. An Iraqi politician, influenced by the Germans, was attempting a rebellion at Baghdad, and a controversy had arisen with the Vichy Government of France as to the extent which Syria and Lebanon were being utilized as German bases. A German force had joined the Italian in Libya and had driven the British back from their foremost advance points. On April 6 Germany attacked Yugoslavia and Greece. This military encirclement of the Suez Canal, potential focus of attack, called for rapid deliveries of American matériel, possible with safety only through the Red Sea. The modification of combat areas on April 10 made this possible.

(a) Proclamation Regarding Modification of a Combat Area, April 10, 1941 [4]

[Excerpt]

BY THE PRESIDENT OF THE UNITED STATES OF AMERICA
A Proclamation [No. 2474]

.   .   .   .

AND WHEREAS on June 11, 1940, I issued a proclamation [5] in accordance with the provision of law quoted above defining a combat area.

Now, THEREFORE, I, FRANKLIN D. ROOSEVELT, President of the United States of America, acting under and by virtue of the authority conferred on me by section 3 (*c*) of the joint resolution of Congress approved November 4, 1939, do hereby modify my proclamation of June 11, 1940, defining combat areas into which it shall be unlawful, except under such rules and regulations as shall be prescribed, for any citizen of the United States or any American vessel, whether a surface vessel or an aircraft, to proceed, by eliminating from the scope of that

[1] Department of State, *Bulletin*, IV, p. 451; 6 *Fed. Reg.*, p. 1921.
[2] *Ibid.*, p. 473; 6 *Fed. Reg.*, p. 2001.   [3] *Ibid.*, p. 496; 6 *Fed. Reg.*, p. 2160.
[4] *Ibid.*, p. 450; 6 *Fed. Reg.*, p. 1905.
[5] See *Documents, II, 1939–40*, p. 682.

proclamation the combat area defined in the second numbered section thereof as:

Beginning at the intersection of the North Coast of Italian Somaliland with the meridian of 50° longitude east of Greenwich;
Thence due north to the mainland of Arabia;
Thence eastward along the coast of Arabia to the meridian of 51° east longitude;
Thence due south to the mainland of Italian Somaliland;
Thence westward along the coast of Italian Somaliland to the point of beginning.

And I do hereby proclaim that it shall no longer be unlawful for any citizen of the United States or any American vessel, whether a surface vessel or an aircraft, to proceed into or through the area defined above.

IN WITNESS WHEREOF, I have hereunto set my hand and caused the Seal of the United States of America to be affixed.

DONE at the City of Washington this 10th day of April, in the year of our Lord nineteen hundred and forty-one, and of the Independence of the United States of America the one hundred and sixty-fifth.

[SEAL]

FRANKLIN D. ROOSEVELT

By the President:
CORDELL HULL
     Secretary of State.

(4) *Travel on Vessels of Belligerent States* (*Sec. 5*)

PART 156 — TRAVEL [1]

Pursuant to the provisions of section 5 of the joint resolution of Congress, approved November 4, 1939, and of the President's proclamation of April 10, 1941 (6 F. R. 1905), the regulations in 22 CFR 156.1 and 156.2 of November 6, 1939,[2] as amended November 17, 1939, April 25, 1940, May 11, 1940, June 10, 1940, November 15, 1940, and April 11, 1941, are hereby amended to read as follows:

§ 156.1. *American diplomatic, consular, military, and naval officers.* American diplomatic and consular officers and their families, members of their staffs, and their families, and American military and naval

---

[1] Code of Federal Regulations, Title 22, Foreign Relations; Chapter 1, Department of State; Subchapter C, Neutrality; Part 156 (formerly Part 55C), Travel.

[2] For the regulations as cumulatively amended, see *Documents, II, 1939–40*, p. 683. The whole Part 55C as compiled there takes account of assimilations from other parts, redesignations, amendments, and additions.

officers and personnel and their families may travel pursuant to orders on vessels of France; Germany; Poland; or the United Kingdom, India, Australia, Canada, New Zealand, the Union of South Africa; Norway; Belgium; the Netherlands; Italy; Greece;[1] Yugoslavia;[2] and Hungary[3] if the public service requires.   (54 Stat. 7; 22 U. S. C., Supp. V, 245*j*-4; Proc. No. 2477, April 15, 1941)

§ 156.2 *Other American citizens.* Other American citizens may travel on vessels of France; Germany; Poland; or the United Kingdom, India, Australia, Canada, New Zealand, the Union of South Africa; Norway; Belgium; the Netherlands; Italy; Greece;[1] Yugoslavia;[2] and Hungary:[3] *Provided, however,* That travel on or over the north Atlantic Ocean, north of 35 degrees north latitude and east of 66 degrees west longitude or on or over other waters adjacent to Europe or over the continent of Europe or adjacent islands shall not be permitted except when specifically authorized by the Passport Division of the Department of State or an American diplomatic or consular officer abroad in each case. (54 Stat. 7; 22 U. S. C., Supp. V, 245*j*-4; Proc. No. 2477, April 15, 1941)

CORDELL HULL,
Secretary of State.

APRIL 16, 1941.

The Secretary of State announces that the regulations under section 5 of the joint resolution of Congress approved November 4, 1939, which he promulgated on November 6, and amended November 17, 1939, henceforth apply equally in respect to travel by citizens of the United States on vessels of Bulgaria.[4]

APRIL 25, 1941.

[§ 156.4]   § 55C.4[5] *American vessels in combat areas — (c) Vessels authorized to evacuate American citizens and those under direction of American Red Cross.* The provisions of the proclamation do not apply to any American vessel which, by arrangement with the appropriate authorities

---

[1] Department of State, *Bulletin,* III, p. 429; 5 *Fed. Reg.,* p. 4532.
[2] *Ibid.,* IV, p. 451; 6 *Fed. Reg.,* p. 1921.   [3] *Ibid.,* p. 473; 6 *Fed. Reg.,* p. 2001.
[4] *Ibid.,* p. 496; 6 *Fed. Reg.,* p. 2160.
[5] *Ibid.,* III, p. 24.   § 156.4, redesignated, is here assimilated to the new arrangement, which it antedates. Previous to the amendment of sec. 4 of the joint resolution of November 4, 1939 (*Documents, II, 1939–40,* p. 661) by Public Res. 87, 76th Cong., June 26, 1940, specific permissions were granted to particular vessels to enter the combat area.   This regulation in Part 156 supersedes there pars. (2)–(4) of regulations issued November 6, 1939, under sec. 3 of the joint resolution of November 4, 1939 (*Documents, II, 1939–40,* p. 680).

of the United States Government, is commissioned [1] to proceed into or through this combat area in order to evacuate citizens of the United States who are in imminent danger to their lives as a result of combat operations incident to the present war, or to any American vessels proceeding into or through this area, unarmed and not under convoy, under charter or other direction and control of the American Red Cross, on a mission of mercy only and carrying only Red Cross materials and personnel: *Provided*, That where permission has not been given by the blockading power, no American Red Cross vessel shall enter a port where a blockade by aircraft, surface vessel, or submarine is being attempted through the destruction of vessels, or into a port of any country where such blockade of the whole country is being so attempted. (Secs. 3, 4, Public Res. 54, 76th Cong., 2d sess., approved Nov. 4, 1939, as amended by Public Res. 87, 76th Cong., 3d sess., approved June 26, 1940; Proc. No. 2410, June 11, 1940)

[SEAL]   CORDELL HULL,
                                                  Secretary of State.

JULY 5, 1940.

§ 156.7 [2] *Airplanes belonging to Pan American Airways, Incorporated, etc.* Airplanes belonging to Pan American Airways, Incorporated, and American citizens, members of the crew or passengers, traveling thereon, when proceeding between Lisbon and African ports south of 30° north latitude, may henceforth proceed into and through that portion of the combat area defined by the President in his proclamation numbered 2410, of June 11, 1940,[3] which is bounded as follows:

Beginning at the intersection of the coast of Portugal with the meridian of 8° 55′ west longitude;
Thence due south to the parallel of 33° 10′ north latitude;
Thence due west to the meridian of 20° west longitude;
Thence due north to the parallel of 37° 05′ north latitude;
Thence due east to the coast of Portugal.

(54 Stat. 7; 22 U. S. C., Supp. V, 245*j*–2; Proc. No. 2410, June 11, 1940)

                                                CORDELL HULL,
                                                  Secretary of State.

OCTOBER 28, 1940.

---

[1] The S.S. *McKeesport* was commissioned to proceed into and through the combat area on July 5, 1940.
[2] Department of State, *Bulletin*, III, p. 381; 5 *Fed. Reg.*, p. 4317.
[3] *Documents, II, 1939–40,* p. 682.

(5) *Solicitation and Collection of Funds and Contributions (Sec. 8)*

§ 161.20 [1] *Contributions for use in Greece.* The rules and regulations (22 CFR 161.1–16) under section 8 of the joint resolution of Congress approved November 4, 1939, which the Secretary of State promulgated on November 6, 1939,[2] henceforth apply equally to the solicitation and collection of contributions for use in Greece. (54 Stat. 8; 22 U. S. C., Supp. V, 245j–7; Proc. No. 2443, November 15, 1940)

§ 161.21 [3] *Contributions for use in Yugosalvia.* (Proc. No. 2473, April 10, 1941)

. . . .

§ 161.22 [4] *Contributions for use in Hungary.* (Proc. No. 2477, April 15, 1941)

. . . .

———

The Secretary of State announces that the rules and regulations under section 8 of the joint resolution of Congress approved November 4, 1939, which he promulgated on November 6, 1939, henceforth apply equally to the solicitation and collection of contributions for use in Bulgaria.[5]

APRIL 25, 1941.

———

(a) *Revocation of Registration to Solicit Contributions. The Secretary of State (Hull) to an Organization, May 8, 1941* [6]

FEDERATION OF THE ITALIAN WORLD
  WAR VETERANS IN THE U.S.A., INC.,
    626 Fifth Avenue, New York, N. Y.
SIRS:

Reference is made to your registration pursuant to the rules and regulations promulgated under section 8 of the Neutrality Act of 1939 governing the solicitation and collection of contributions to be used for relief in belligerent countries. Section 8 (*b*) of the Neutrality Act permits such solicitation and collection of

---

[1] Code of Federal Regulations, Title 22, Foreign Relations; Chapter 1, Department of State; Subchapter C, Neutrality; Part 161 (formerly Part 40), Solicitation and Collection of Funds and Contributions.
Reprinted from Department of State, *Bulletin,* III, p. 429; 5 *Fed. Reg.,* p. 4532.
[2] For these regulations, see *Documents, II, 1939–40,* p. 687, where they bear the former designation 40.1–16.
[3] Department of State, *Bulletin,* IV, p. 451; 6 *Fed. Reg.,* p. 1922.
[4] *Ibid.,* p. 474; 6 *Fed. Reg.,* p. 2001.   [5] *Ibid.,* p. 496; 6 *Fed. Reg.,* p. 2160.
[6] *Ibid.,* p. 551. A similar letter was also sent to the Ladies Auxiliary of the Providence (R. I.) Branch of the Federation.

contributions only by persons and organizations who are not acting for or on behalf of a belligerent government or any agency or instrumentality thereof. In your application for registration you named the Community Welfare Fund of Torino, Naples, Palermo, Bari, Venezia, Roma, Catania, and Reggio Calabria as distributors in Italy of contributions collected by your organization. In that application an oath was taken to the effect that these organizations were not acting for or on behalf of a belligerent government and, in view of this sworn statement, the application was accepted. Subsequent investigation, however, has given this Department reason to believe that the distributors named in your application for registration are not qualified distributors and that they are so closely identified with the Italian Government that they must be regarded as organizations acting for or on behalf of that Government.

It would appear, therefore, that the solicitation and collection of contributions for distribution by the distributors named in your application for registration constitutes a violation of section 8 of the Neutrality Act and the rules and regulations promulgated thereunder, and it has been determined that pursuant to the authority vested in the Secretary of State by paragraph (7) of the rules and regulations, your registration shall be revoked as of May 10, 1941. After that date you will be without legal authority to engage in the solicitation and collection of contributions to be used for relief in belligerent countries. You are requested to submit a report concerning your activities during the period May 1 to May 10 at your earliest convenience for which purpose blank forms are enclosed. You are further requested to inform the Department in regard to the disposition of any funds remaining on hand at the time of the revocation of your registration.

It will be understood, of course, that the revocation of your registration does not preclude this Department or any other Department or agency of this Government from taking such other action in regard to this matter as may be deemed appropriate.

(6) Submarines and Armed Merchant Vessels (Sec. 11)

(a) Proclamation Regarding the Use of Ports or Territorial Waters of the United States by Submarines of Foreign Belligerent States, November 15, 1940 [1]

BY THE PRESIDENT OF THE UNITED STATES OF AMERICA

A Proclamation [*No. 2445*]

WHEREAS section 11 of the Joint Resolution approved November 4, 1939, provides:

Whenever, during any war in which the United States is neutral, the President shall find that special restrictions placed on the use of the ports and territorial waters of the United States by the submarines or armed merchant vessels of a

[1] Department of State, *Bulletin*, III, p. 427; 5 *Fed. Reg.*, p. 4524. For the prior proclamations see *Documents, II, 1939–40*, p. 690.

No proclamations were issued relative to Bulgaria, Yugoslavia and the Soviet Union.

foreign state, will serve to maintain peace between the United States and foreign states, or to protect the commercial interests of the United States and its citizens, or to promote the security of the United States, and shall make proclamation thereof, it shall thereafter be unlawful for any such submarine or armed merchant vessel to enter a port or the territorial waters of the United States or to depart therefrom, except under such conditions and subject to such limitations as the President may prescribe. Whenever, in his judgment, the conditions which have caused him to issue his proclamation have ceased to exist, he shall revoke his proclamation and the provisions of this section shall thereupon cease to apply, except as to offenses committed prior to such revocation.

WHEREAS there exists a state of war between Italy and Greece;

WHEREAS the United States of America is neutral in such war;

WHEREAS by my proclamation of November 4, 1939, issued pursuant to the provision of law quoted above, I placed special restrictions on the use of ports and territorial waters of the United States by the submarines of France; Germany; Poland; and the United Kingdom, India, Australia, Canada, New Zealand, and the Union of South Africa;

Now, THEREFORE, I, FRANKLIN D. ROOSEVELT, President of the United States of America, acting under and by virtue of the authority vested in me by the foregoing provision of section 11 of the joint resolution approved November 4, 1939, do by this proclamation declare and proclaim that the provisions of my proclamation of November 4, 1939, in regard to the use of the ports and territorial waters of the United States, exclusive of the Canal Zone, by the submarines of France; Germany; Poland; and the United Kingdom, India, Australia, Canada, New Zealand, and the Union of South Africa, shall also apply to the use of the ports and territorial waters of the United States, exclusive of the Canal Zone, by the submarines of Greece.

AND I do hereby enjoin upon all officers of the United States, charged with the execution of the laws thereof, the utmost diligence in preventing violations of the said joint resolution, and this my proclamation issued thereunder, and in bringing to trial and punishment any offenders against the same.

IN WITNESS WHEREOF, I have hereunto set my hand and caused the Seal of the United States of America to be affixed.

DONE at the City of Washington this fifteenth day of November, in the year of our Lord nineteen hundred and forty, and of the [SEAL] Independence of the United States of America the one hundred and sixty-fifth.

FRANKLIN D. ROOSEVELT

By the President:

CORDELL HULL
Secretary of State.

CHAPTER XI

NATIONAL DEFENSE

1. GOVERNMENTAL ORGANIZATION RESULTING FROM THE EMERGENCY

The United States embarked on a vastly expanded program of national defense in May 1940, when the Executive called upon the Congress to appropriate money and to adopt legislation enlarging the defense forces. The execution of programs remained with the President by virtue of office and as Commander-in-Chief of the armed forces. The Council of National Defense as created in 1916 was available to him in a task which was conducted in part under the specific powers accruing to the President from the proclamation of a national emergency on September 8, 1939.[1]

Organization for the purpose of carrying out the will of the people fell into the following pattern:

(1) Limited national emergency, September 8, 1939–May 25, 1940; functions performed by regular administrative or executive bodies;

(2) Emergency management, May 25, 1940–January 7, 1941; the Office for Emergency Management in the Executive Office of the President established, the Council of National Defense called into activity and an Advisory Commission to it created;

(3) National production, January 7–May 27, 1941;[2] the Office of Production Management in the Executive Office of the President created under co-directors general, being a reallocation of the Advisory Commission to the Council of National Defense;

(4) Unlimited national emergency, May 27, 1941 —

Only the fundamental documents showing the evolution of organization so far as it appears to relate to the external aspects of the emergency are presented.

For the evolution of the whole system see the weekly *Defense: Official Bulletin of National Defense Advisory Commission Office for Emergency Management,* Washington, 1940–. (75 cents for 52 issues.)

A. Council of National Defense

For the appropriation provisions in Public No. 667, 76th Cong., June 26, 1940, revising the Council of National Defense, see *Documents, II,* p. 784.

[1] Proclamation No. 2352, *Documents, II, 1939–40,* p. 645.

[2] For a British Government statement concerning the establishment of Import and Production Executives, see *New York Times,* January 7, 1941, p. 5.

(1) *Code of Laws of the United States, Title 50. — War, Chapter 1*

SECTION 1. *Creation, purpose, and composition of council.* A Council of National Defense is hereby established for the coordination of industries and resources for the national security and welfare, to consist of the Secretary of War, the Secretary of the Navy, the Secretary of the Interior, the Secretary of Agriculture, the Secretary of Commerce, and the Secretary of Labor. (Aug. 29, 1916, c. 418, § 2, 39 Stat. 649.)

§ 2. *Advisory commission.* The Council of National Defense shall nominate to the President, and the President shall appoint, an advisory commission, consisting of not more than seven persons, each of whom shall have special knowledge of some industry, public utility, or the development of some natural resource, or be otherwise specially qualified, in the opinion of the council, for the performance of the duties hereinafter provided. The members of the advisory commission shall serve without compensation, but shall be allowed actual expenses of travel and subsistence when attending meetings of the commission or engaged in investigations pertaining to its activities. The advisory commission shall hold such meetings as shall be called by the council or be provided by the rules and regulations adopted by the council for the conduct of its work. (Aug. 29, 1916, c. 418, § 2, 39 Stat. 649.)

§ 3. *Duties of council.* It shall be the duty of the Council of National Defense to supervise and direct investigations and make recommendations to the President and the heads of executive departments as to the location of railroads with reference to the frontier of the United States so as to render possible expeditious concentration of troops and supplies to points of defense; the coordination of military, industrial, and commercial purposes in the location of branch lines of railroad; the utilization of waterways; the mobilization of military and naval resources for defense; the increase of domestic production of articles and materials essential to the support of armies and of the people during the interruption of foreign commerce; the development of seagoing transportation; data as to amounts, location, method and means of production, and availability of military supplies; the giving of information to producers and manufacturers as to the class of supplies needed by the military and other services of the Government, the requirements relating thereto, and the creation of relations which will render possible in time of need the immediate concentration and utilization of the resources of the Nation. (Aug. 29, 1916, c. 418, § 2, 39 Stat. 649; Nov. 9, 1921, c. 119, § 3, 42 Stat. 212.)

§ 4. *Rules and regulations; subordinate bodies and committees.* The

Council of National Defense shall adopt rules and regulations for the conduct of its work, which rules and regulations shall be subject to the approval of the President, and shall provide for the work of the advisory commission to the end that the special knowledge of such commission may be developed by suitable investigation, research, and inquiry and made available in conference and report for the use of the council; and the council may organize subordinate bodies for its assistance in special investigations, either by the employment of experts or by the creation of committees of specially qualified persons to serve without compensation, but to direct the investigations of experts so employed. (Aug. 29, 1916, c. 418, § 2, 39 Stat. 650.)

§ 5. *Reports of activities and expenditures.* Reports shall be submitted by all subordinate bodies and by the advisory commission to the council, and from time to time the council shall report to the President or to the heads of executive departments upon special inquiries or subjects appropriate thereto, and an annual report to the Congress shall be submitted through the President, including as full a statement of the activities of the council and the agencies subordinate to it as is consistent with the public interest, including an itemized account of the expenditures made by the council or authorized by it, in as full detail as the public interest will permit: *Provided, however,* That when deemed proper the President may authorize, in amounts stipulated by him, unvouched expenditures and report the gross sums so authorized not itemized. (Aug. 29, 1916, c. 418, § 2, 39 Stat. 650.)

The Council of National Defense on June 27, 1940, issued an order establishing the Office for the Coordination of National Defense Purchases (5 *Fed. Reg.*, p. 2446). By a further order approved by the President January 7, 1941, the records of that Office were made available to the Executive Office of the President, in which the Office of Production Management was simultaneously established.

B. Priorities Board

(1) *Executive Order No. 8612, December 15, 1940; Amendment of Executive Order No. 8572 of October 21, 1940, Authorizing the Priorities Board and the Administrator of Priorities to Perform Certain Functions under Section 2(a) of the Act of June 28, 1940* [1]

The Council of National Defense established the Priorities Board by its order of October 18, 1940 (5 *Fed. Reg.*, p. 4199). In revoking that order January 7, 1941, it made the records of the Board available to the Executive Office of the President, in which the Office of Production Management was simultaneously established.

[1] 5 *Fed. Reg.*, p. 5143. Revoked by sec. 7 of Executive Order No. 8629 of January 7, 1941, below p. 668.

Executive Order No. 8572[1] of October 21, 1940, authorizing the Priorities Board and the Administrator of Priorities to perform certain functions under section 2(a) of the act of June 28, 1940, is hereby amended to read as follows:

"WHEREAS section 2(a) of the act of June 28, 1940, Public No. 671, 76th Congress,[2] provides that all naval contracts and orders and all Army contracts and orders shall in the discretion of the President take priority over all deliveries for private account or for export; and

"WHEREAS the public interest requires that provision be made to insure the prompt delivery of materials, articles, equipment, and supplies essential to the national defense; and

"WHEREAS the Council of National Defense has established a Priorities Board composed of the following members of the Advisory Commission to the Council of National Defense: The Advisor on Industrial Production, as Chairman, the Advisor on Industrial Materials, and the Advisor on Price Stabilization; and

"WHEREAS the Priorities Board has designated Mr. Donald M. Nelson as Administrator of Priorities:

"Now, THEREFORE, by virtue of the authority vested in me by section 2(a) of the said act of June 28, 1940, and as President of the United States, I hereby approve the establishment of the aforesaid Board and the designation of the said Administrator and authorize the said Board and the said Administrator, acting in the public interest and in the interest of national defense, under rules and regulations prescribed by the Board with the approval of the President, to[3] require that deliveries of material under all orders placed pursuant to the authority of the said section 2(a) and all other naval and Army contracts and orders shall take priority over all deliveries for private account or for export."

C. Office for Emergency Management

(1) *Administrative Order Establishing the Office for Emergency Management in the Executive Office of the President and Prescribing Regulations Governing Its Activities, May 25, 1940* [4]

WHEREAS, I find there is a threatened national emergency;

Now, THEREFORE, by virtue of the authority vested in me by the Constitution and the Statutes, and in pursuance of Part I of Ex-

[1] 5 *Fed. Reg.*, p. 4199.
[2] *Documents, II, 1939–40*, p. 802.
[3] Executive Order No. 8572 concluded as follows: "to grant priority for deliveries pursuant thereto over all deliveries for private account or for export."
[4] 5 *Fed. Reg.*, p. 2109.

ecutive Order No. 8248 of September 8, 1939,[1] it is hereby ordered as follows:

SECTION 1. There is established in the Executive Office of the President an office to be known as the Office for Emergency Management which shall be under the direction of one of the Administrative Assistants to the President, to be designated by the President.

SECTION 2. The Office for Emergency Management shall:

(a) Assist the President in the clearance of information with respect to measures necessitated by the threatened emergency;

(b) Maintain liaison between the President and the Council of National Defense and its Advisory Commission, and with such other agencies, public or private, as the President may direct, for the purpose of securing maximum utilization and coordination of agencies and facilities in meeting the threatened emergency;

(c) Perform such additional duties as the President may direct.

FRANKLIN D. ROOSEVELT

THE WHITE HOUSE,
May 25, 1940.

(2) *Administrative Order Further Defining the Status and Functions of the Office for Emergency Management, January 7, 1941* [2]

WHEREAS Executive Order No. 8248, dated September 8, 1939, provides, in part, as follows: [3]

"There shall be within the Executive Office of the President the following principal divisions, namely: (1) The White House Office, (2) the Bureau of the Budget, (3) the National Resources Planning Board, (4) the Liaison Office for Personnel Management, (5) the Office of Government Reports, and (6) in the event of a national emergency, or threat of a national emergency, such office for emergency management as the President shall determine";

AND WHEREAS the Office for Emergency Management was formally established by Administrative Order of May 25, 1940, and it is deemed advisable to modify the said order and further define the duties and functions of the said office;

[1] *4 Fed. Reg.*, p. 3864. Provision was made by the order for "such office for emergency management as the President shall determine."

[2] *6 Fed. Reg.*, p. 192.

[3] *4 Fed. Reg.*, p. 3864. The executive order established the Divisions of the Executive Office and was issued by the President "by virtue of the authority vested in me by the Constitution and Statutes and in order to effectuate the purposes of . . . Reorganization Plans Nos. I and II" (4 *Fed. Reg.*, p. 2727, 2733; U. S. Code, Title 5, sec. 133).

Now, THEREFORE, by virtue of the authority vested in me by the Constitution and the Statutes, and in pursuance of Part I of the aforesaid Executive Order of September 8, 1939, it is hereby ordered as follows:

1. The Office for Emergency Management shall have the following duties and functions:

(a) To advise and assist the President in the discharge of extraordinary responsibilities imposed upon him by any emergency arising out of war, the threat of war, imminence of war, flood, drought, or other condition threatening the public peace or safety.

(b) To serve as a division of the Executive Office of the President, with such subdivisions as may be required, through which the President, during any emergency, may coordinate and supervise and, in appropriate cases, direct the activities of agencies, public or private, in relation thereto.

(c) To serve as a channel of communication between such agencies and the President concerning emergency activities, to keep the President currently advised of their progress, to assemble and analyze information concerning additional measures that should be taken, and to assist in the preparation of recommendations for any necessary legislation.

(d) To provide and maintain liaison during any such emergency with other divisions of the Executive Office of the President and with other agencies, public or private, for the purpose of bringing about maximum utilization and coordination of their services and facilities.

(e) To advise and assist the President upon or before termination of any such emergency with respect to any measures that may be needful to facilitate a restoration of normal administrative relations and to ameliorate the consequences of the emergency.

(f) To perform such other duties and functions with respect to any such emergency as the President may from time to time direct.

2. The work and activities of the following-named agencies, and such other agencies as the President may from time to time designate, shall be coordinated in and through the Office for Emergency Management under the direction and supervision of the President:

(a) The Council of National Defense, the Advisory Commission to the Council of National Defense and all subordinate bodies and agents of the Council and Commission.

(b) Defense Communications Board.

(c) Office of Production Management (to be created immediately hereafter).

3. Provision may be made in the Office for Emergency Management for liaison facilities and for the maintenance of routine office services required in the conduct of the work and activities of the agencies coordinated through or established in the Office for Emergency Management.

4. Any provisions of the Administrative Order of May 25, 1940 establishing the Office for Emergency Management inconsistent with this order are hereby superseded by this order.

FRANKLIN D. ROOSEVELT

THE WHITE HOUSE
January 7, 1941.

(3) *Administrative Memorandum, March 14, 1941* [1]

[Excerpt]

In accordance with Executive Orders of January 7 and 11, 1941, and the Administrative Order, dated January 7, 1941, the following agencies are established in or coordinated through the Office for Emergency Management:

Office of Production Management
Division of Labor of the Advisory Commission
Division of Agriculture of the Advisory Commission
Division of Price Stabilization of the Advisory Commission
Division of Transportation of the Advisory Commission
Division of Consumer Protection of the Advisory Commission
Division of Defense Housing Coordination [2]
Division of State and Local Cooperation
Office for Coordination of Commercial and Cultural Relations Between the American Republics [3]
National Defense Research Committee
Defense Communications Board.

———

Subsequently, the following were created and placed in or coordinated through the Office for Emergency Management, each with a director appointed by the President and with duties prescribed by him:

[1] Office for Emergency Management, release PM 160.
[2] Established by Executive Order No. 8632, dated January 11, 1941 (6 *Fed. Reg.*, p. 295).
[3] See p. 109.

The National Defense Mediation Board, created by Executive Order No. 8716 of March 19, 1941, 6 *Fed. Reg.*, p. 1532;

The Office of Price Administration and Civilian Supply, created by Executive Order No. 8734 of April 11, 1941, 6 *Fed. Reg.*, p. 1917;

The Office of Civilian Defense, created by Executive Order No. 8757, dated May 20, 1941, 6 *Fed. Reg.*, p. 2517.

The Liaison Officer for Emergency Management was designated as Secretary to the Council of National Defense and to the Advisory Commission on April 23, 1941 (6 *Fed. Reg.*, p. 2325).

D. Office of Production Management

(1) *Executive Order No. 8629 Establishing the Office of Production Management in the Executive Office of the President and Defining Its Functions and Duties, January 7, 1941* [1]

By virtue of the authority vested in me by the Constitution and the statutes, and in order to define further the functions and duties of the Office for Emergency Management with respect to the national emergency as declared by the President to exist on September 8, 1939, and to increase production for the national defense through mobilization of material resources and the industrial facilities of the Nation, it is hereby ordered:

1. There shall be in the Office for Emergency Management of the Executive Office of the President, an Office of Production Management which shall consist of (1) a Director General, and (2) an Associate Director General, each to be appointed by the President, (3) the Secretary of War, and (4) the Secretary of the Navy. The members shall serve as such without compensation but shall be entitled to actual and necessary transportation, subsistence, and other expenses incidental to the performance of their duties.

2. With such advice and assistance as it may require from other departments and agencies of the Federal Government, and subject to such regulations or directions as the President may from time to time prescribe, and subject further to the general policy that the Departments of War and Navy and other departments and agencies of the Government will be utilized to the maximum extent compatible with efficiency, the Office of Production Management shall:

(a) Formulate and execute in the public interest all measures needful and appropriate in order (1) to increase, accelerate, and regulate the production and supply of materials, articles and equipment and the provision of emergency plant facilities and services

[1] 6 *Fed. Reg.*, p. 191.

required for the national defense, and (2) to insure effective coordination of those activities of the several departments, corporations, and other agencies of the Government which are directly concerned therewith.

(b) Survey, analyze, and summarize for purposes of coordination the stated requirements of the War and Navy and other departments and agencies of the Government, and of foreign governments for materials, articles, and equipment needed for defense.

(c) Advise with respect to the plans and schedules of the various departments and agencies for the purchase of materials, articles, and equipment required for defense, to coordinate the placement of major defense orders and contracts and to keep informed of the progress of the various programs of production and supply.

(d) Plan and take all lawful steps necessary to assure the provision of an adequate supply of raw materials essential to the production of finished products needed for defense.

(e) Formulate plans for the mobilization for defense of the production facilities of the Nation, and to take all lawful action necessary to carry out such plans.

(f) Determine the adequacy of existing production facilities and to assure their maximum use; and, when necessary, to stimulate and plan the creation of such additional facilities and sources of production and supply as may be essential to increase and expedite defense production.

(g) Determine when, to what extent, and in what manner priorities shall be accorded to deliveries of material as provided in Section 2(a) of the Act entitled "An Act to Expedite National Defense and for other Purposes," approved June 28, 1940.[1] Deliveries of material shall take priority, as provided in said Act, in accordance with such determinations and the orders issued in pursuance thereof by the Office of Production Management.

(h) Perform the functions and exercise the authorities vested in the President by Section 9 of the Selective Training and Service Act of 1940.[2]

(i) Serve as the liaison and channel of communication between the Advisory Commission to the Council of National Defense and the Departments of War and Navy with respect to the duties imposed upon the Commission by the following named acts, and with respect

[1] *Documents, II, 1939–40*, p. 802. For the extended authority to determine priorities see the act of May 31, 1941, p. 748.
[2] See p. 743.

to all other matters pertaining to defense purchasing and production: Public Nos. 667,[1] 781,[2] 800 [3] and 801 [4] and Public Resolution No. 95,[5] 76th Congress.

(*j*) Perform such other functions as the President may from time to time assign or delegate to it.

3. The Director General, in association with the Associate Director General, and serving under the direction and supervision of the President, shall discharge and perform the administrative responsibilities and duties required to carry out the functions specified in paragraph 2, subject to and in conformity with the policies and regulations (not inconsistent with such regulations as may be issued by the President) prescribed by the Office of Production Management.

4. There shall be within the Office of Production Management the following and such other operating divisions as the President may from time to time determine:

(*a*) A Division of Production

(*b*) A Division of Purchases

(*c*) A Division of Priorities

Each division of the Office of Production Management shall be in charge of a director appointed by the Office of Production Management with the approval of the President.

5. There shall be within the Office of Production Management a Priorities Board composed of six members. A chairman and three other members shall be appointed or designated by the President; the Director General and Associate Director General shall be members, *ex officio.* The Priorities Board shall serve as an advisory body and, from time to time as may be required by the Office of Production Management, shall make findings and submit recommendations with respect to the establishment of priorities, the placing of mandatory orders, the assignment of preference ratings, the allocation of deliveries, and other related matters. In making its findings and recommendations, the Priorities Board shall

[1] See *Documents, II, 1939–40*, p. 784.

[2] *Second Supplemental National Defense Appropriation Act, 1941*, Public No. 781, 76th Cong., approved September 9, 1940, in Title I ("Title III, Military Appropriation Act, 1941"); appropriates $162,500,000 to be expended by the Secretary of War for expediting production.

[3] *Third Supplemental National Appropriation Act, 1941*, Public No. 800, 76th Cong., approved October 8, 1940, in Title I ("Title III, Military Appropriation Act, 1941"); appropriates additional $88,000,000, and contract authorization of $90,-000,000.

[4] *Second Revenue Act of 1940*, approved October 8, 1940.

[5] Relates to utilization of Tennessee Valley Authority facilities.

take into account general social and economic considerations and the effect the proposed actions would have upon the civilian population.

6. Within the limits of such funds as may be allocated to it by the President on the recommendation of the Bureau of the Budget, the Office of Production Management may employ necessary personnel and make provision for the necessary supplies, facilities, and services. However, the Office of Production Management shall use insofar as practicable such statistical, informational, fiscal, personnel, and other general business services and facilities as may be made available through the Office for Emergency Management or other agencies of the Government.

7. Executive Order No. 8572 of October 21, 1940, as amended by Executive Order No. 8612 [1] of December 15, 1940, is revoked.

FRANKLIN D. ROOSEVELT

THE WHITE HOUSE,
January 7, 1941.

The Office of Production Management on March 11, 1941, issued regulations dated March 7 defining the status and describing the functions of four divisions to carry out the duties prescribed in Executive Order No. 8629, dated January 7, 1941. These were the Division of Production, the Division of Priorities, the Division of Purchases, and the Bureau of Research and Statistics, which was established by the regulations dated March 7. For the regulations governing the divisions see 6 *Fed. Reg.*, p. 1595-8.

E. Emergency Funds for the President

(1) *Appropriation, April 5, 1941* [2]

To enable the President, through appropriate agencies of the Government, to provide for emergencies affecting the national security and defense and for each and every purpose connected therewith, and to make all necessary expenditures incident thereto for any purpose for which the Congress has previously made appropriation or authorization and without regard to the provisions of law regulating the expenditure of Government funds or the employment of persons in the Government service, such as section 3709 of the Revised Statutes and the civil service and classification laws; and any waiver hereunder of the provisions of any law regulating such expenditure or such employment shall not be

------

[1] See p. 663.

[2] *Independent Offices Appropriation Act, 1942*, Public Law No. 28, 77th Cong., approved April 5, 1941; originated as H.R. 2788; hearings by Committee on Appropriations; House Report No. 15; Senate Report No. 69; House (conference) Report No. 335.

exercised by any agency unless the allocation to such agency or subsequent action of the President in connection therewith permits any such waiver to be availed of; $100,000,000; and, in addition, the President is authorized, through such agencies, to enter into contracts during the fiscal year 1942 for the same purposes to an amount not exceeding $25,000,000: *Provided*, That an account shall be kept of all expenditures made or authorized hereunder, and a report thereon shall be submitted to the Congress on June 30, 1942.

For the payment of obligations incurred under the contract authorization of $66,000,000 under this head in the Military Appropriation Act, 1941, $66,000,000.

For the payment of obligations incurred under the contract authorization of $34,000,000 under this head in the Act making appropriations for the Navy Department and the naval service for the fiscal year ending June 30, 1941, $34,000,000: *Provided*, That the unobligated portion of said contract authorization is hereby continued in effect until June 30, 1942, and the unobligated balance of the appropriation under this head for the fiscal year 1941 is hereby continued available until June 30, 1942.

2. COMPULSORY MILITARY SERVICE

(1) *"Selective Training and Service Act of 1940," An Act to Provide for the Common Defense by Increasing the Personnel of the Armed Forces of the United States and Providing for Its Training, Approved September 16, 1940, 3:08 P.M., E.S.T.*[1]

[Excerpt]

Be it enacted by the Senate and House of Representatives of the United States of America in Congress assembled, That (a) the Congress hereby

[1] Public No. 783, 76th Cong., Chapter 720, 3d sess.; originated as S. 4164, June 20, 1940; Sen. Report No. 2002, with amendments, from the Committee on Military Affairs, August 5, 1940; passed Senate August 28 and House, amended, September 7; House (conference) Report No. 2937, September 12, 1940, in the nature of a substitute; House (conference) Report No. 2947, September 14, 1940, in the nature of a substitute. Also H.R. 10132, June 21, 1940; House Report No. 2903, August 29, with amendments, from Committee on Military Affairs after hearings; passed House, proceedings vacated and bill laid on table September 7; S. 4164 passed in lieu.

U. S. Congress, Senate, Committee on Military Affairs. *Compulsory Military Training and Service, Hearings* . . . 76th Cong., 3d sess., on S. 4164. July 3–12, 1940. Washington, Government Printing Office, 1940. 400 p.

— — House, Committee on Military Affairs. *Selective Compulsory Military Training and Service, Hearings* . . . 76th Cong., 3d sess., on H.R. 10132. July 10–August 14, 1940. Washington, Government Printing Office, 1940. v, 655 p.

declares that it is imperative to increase and train the personnel of the armed forces of the United States.

(*b*) The Congress further declares that in a free society the obligations and privileges of military training and service should be shared generally in accordance with a fair and just system of selective compulsory military training and service.

(*c*) The Congress further declares, in accordance with our traditional military policy as expressed in the National Defense Act of 1916, as amended, that it is essential that the strength and organization of the National Guard, as an integral part of the first-line defenses of this Nation, be at all times maintained and assured. To this end, it is the intent of the Congress that whenever the Congress shall determine that troops are needed for the national security in excess of those of the Regular Army and those in active training and service under section 3 (*b*), the National Guard of the United States, or such part thereof as may be necessary, shall be ordered to active Federal service and continued therein so long as such necessity exists.

SEC. 2. Except as otherwise provided in this Act, it shall be the duty of every male citizen of the United States, and of every male alien residing in the United States, who, on the day or days fixed for the first or any subsequent registration, is between the ages of twenty-one and thirty-six, to present himself for and submit to registration at such time or times and place or places, and in such manner and in such age group or groups, as shall be determined by rules and regulations prescribed hereunder.

SEC. 3. (*a*) Except as otherwise provided in this Act, every male citizen of the United States, and every male alien residing in the United States who has declared his intention to become such a citizen, between the ages of twenty-one and thirty-six at the time fixed for his registration, shall be liable for training and service in the land or naval forces of the United States. The President is authorized from time to time, whether or not a state of war exists, to select and induct into the land and naval forces of the United States for training and service, in the manner provided in this Act, such number of men as in his judgment is required for such forces in the national interest: *Provided*, That within the limits of the quota determined under section 4 (*b*) for the subdivision in which he resides, any person, regardless of race or color, between the ages of eighteen and thirty-six, shall be afforded an opportunity to volunteer for induction into the land or naval forces of the United States for the training and service prescribed in subsection (*b*), but no person who so volunteers shall be inducted for such training and service so long as he is deferred after classification: *Provided further*, That no man shall be inducted for training and service under this Act unless and until he is acceptable to the land or naval forces for such training and service and his physical and mental fitness for such training and service has been satisfactorily determined: *Provided further*, That no men shall be inducted for such training and service until adequate provision shall have been made for such shelter, sanitary facilities, water supplies, heating and lighting arrangements, medical care, and hospital accommodations, for such men, as may be determined by the Secretary of War or the Secretary of the Navy, as the case may be, to be essential to public and personal health: *Provided further*, That except in time of war there shall not be in active training or service in the land forces of the United States at any one time under subsection (*b*) more than nine hundred thousand men inducted under the provisions of this Act. The men inducted into the land or naval forces for training and service under this Act shall be assigned to camps or units of such forces.

(*b*) Each man inducted under the provisions of subsection (*a*) shall serve for a training and service period of twelve consecutive months, unless sooner discharged, except that whenever the Congress has declared that the national interest is imperiled, such twelve-month period may be extended by the President to such time as may be necessary in the interests of national defense.

(*c*) Each such man, after the completion of his period of training and service under subsection (*b*), shall be transferred to a reserve component of the land or naval forces of the United States; and until he attains the age of forty-five, or until the expiration of a period of ten years after such transfer, or until he is discharged from such reserve component, whichever occurs first, he shall be deemed to be a member of such reserve component and shall be subject to such additional training and service as may now or hereafter be prescribed by law: *Provided*, That any man who completes at least twelve months' training and service in the land forces under subsection (*b*), and who thereafter serves satisfactorily in the Regular Army or in the active National Guard for a period of at least two years, shall, in time of peace, be relieved from any liability to serve in any reserve component of the land or Naval forces of the United States and from further liability for the training and service under subsection (*b*), but nothing in this subsection shall be construed to prevent any such man, while in a reserve component of such forces, from being ordered or called to active duty in such forces.

(*d*) With respect to the men inducted for training and service under this Act there shall be paid, allowed, and extended the same pay, allowances, pensions, disability and death compensation, and other benefits as are provided by law in the case of other enlisted men of like grades and length of service of that component of the land or naval forces to which they are assigned, and after transfer to a reserve component of the land or naval forces as provided in subsection (c) there shall be paid, allowed, and extended with respect to them the same benefits as are provided by law in like cases with respect to other members of such reserve component. Men in such training and service and men who have been so transferred to reserve components shall have an opportunity to qualify for promotion.

(e) Persons inducted into the land forces of the United States under this Act shall not be employed beyond the limits of the Western Hemisphere except in the Territories and possessions of the United States, including the Philippine Islands.

(f) Nothing contained in this or any other Act shall be construed as forbidding the payment of compensation by any person, firm, or corporation to persons inducted into the land or naval forces of the United States for training and service under this Act, or to members of the reserve components of such forces now or hereafter on any type of active duty, who, prior to their induction or commencement of active duty, were receiving compensation from such person, firm, or corporation.

SEC. 4. (a) The selection of men for training and service under section 3 (other than those who are voluntarily inducted pursuant to this Act) shall be made in an impartial manner, under such rules and regulations as the President may prescribe, from the men who are liable for such training and service and who at the time of selection are registered and classified but not deferred or exempted: *Provided*, That in the selection and training of men under this Act, and in the interpretation and execution of the provisions of this Act, there shall be no discrimination against any person on account of race or color.

(b) Quotas of men to be inducted for training and service under this Act shall be determined for each State, Territory, and the District of Columbia, and for subdivisions thereof, on the basis of the actual number of men in the several States, Territories, and the District of Columbia, and the subdivisions thereof, who are liable for such training and service but who are not deferred after classification, except that credits shall be given in fixing such quotas for residents of such subdivisions who are in the land and naval forces of the United States on the date fixed for determining such quotas. After such quotas are fixed, credits shall be given in filling such quotas for residents of such subdivisions who subsequently become members of such forces. Until the actual numbers necessary for determining the quotas are known, the quotas may be based on estimates, and subsequent adjustments therein shall be made when such actual numbers are known. All computations under this subsection shall be made in accordance with such rules and regulations as the President may prescribe.

SEC. 5. (*a*) [see p. 682.]

(*b*) In time of peace, the following persons shall be relieved from liability to serve in any reserve component of the land or naval forces of the United States and from liability for training and service under section 3 (*b*)—

(1) Any man who shall have satisfactorily served for at least three consecutive years in the Regular Army before or after or partially before and partially after the time fixed for registration under section 2.

(2) Any man who as a member of the active National Guard shall have satisfactorily served for at least one year in active Federal service in the Army of the United States, and subsequent thereto for at least two consecutive years in the Regular Army or in the active National Guard, before or after or partially before and partially after the time fixed for registration under section 2.

(3) Any man who is in the active National Guard at the time fixed for registration under section 2, and who shall have satisfactorily served therein for at least six consecutive years, before or after or partially before and partially after the time fixed for such registration.

(4) Any man who is in the Officers' Reserve Corps on the eligible list at the time fixed for registration under section 2, and who shall have satisfactorily served therein on the eligible list for at least six consecutive years, before or after or partially before and partially after the time fixed for such registration: *Provided*, That nothing in this subsection shall be construed to prevent the persons enumerated in this subsection, while in reserve components of the land or naval forces of the United States, from being ordered or called to active duty in such forces.

(*c*) (1) The Vice President of the United States, the Governors of the several States and Territories, members of the legislative bodies of the United States and of the several States and Territories, judges of the courts of record of the United States and of the several States and Territories and the District of Columbia, shall, while holding such offices, be deferred from training and service under this Act in the land and naval forces of the United States.

(2) The President is authorized, under such rules and regulations

as he may prescribe, to provide for the deferment from training and service under this Act in the land and naval forces of the United States, of any person holding an office (other than an office described in paragraph (1) of this subsection) under the United States or any State, Territory, or the District of Columbia, whose continued service in such office is found in accordance with section 10 (*a*) (2) to be necessary to the maintenance of the public health, safety, or interest.

(*d*) Regular or duly ordained ministers of religion, and students who are preparing for the ministry in theological or divinity schools recognized as such for more than one year prior to the date of enactment of this Act, shall be exempt from training and service (but not from registration) under this Act.

(*e*) The President is authorized, under such rules and regulations as he may prescribe, to provide for the deferment from training and service under this Act in the land and naval forces of the United States of those men whose employment in industry, agriculture, or other occupations or employment, or whose activity in other endeavors, is found in accordance with section 10 (*a*) (2) to be necessary to the maintenance of the national health, safety, or interest. The President is also authorized, under such rules and regulations as he may prescribe, to provide for the deferment from training and service under this Act in the land and naval forces of the United States (1) of those men in a status with respect to persons dependent upon them for support which renders their deferment advisable, and (2) of those men found to be physically, mentally, or morally deficient or defective. No deferment from such training and service shall be made in the case of any individual except upon the basis of the status of such individual, and no such deferment shall be made of individuals by occupational groups or of groups of individuals in any plant or institution.

(*f*) Any person who, during the year 1940, entered upon attendance for the academic year 1940–1941 —

(1) at any college or university which grants a degree in arts or science, to pursue a course of instruction satisfactory completion of which is prescribed by such college or university as a prerequisite to either of such degrees; or

(2) at any university described in paragraph (1), to pursue a course of instruction to the pursuit of which a degree in arts or science is prescribed by such university as a prerequisite;

and who, while pursuing such course of instruction at such college or university, is selected for training and service under this Act prior to the end of such academic year, or prior to July 1, 1941, whichever occurs first, shall, upon his request, be deferred from induction into the land or naval forces for such training and service until the end of such academic year, but in no event later than July 1, 1941.

(g) Nothing contained in this Act shall be construed to require any person to be subject to combatant training and service in the land or naval forces of the United States who, by reason of religious training and belief, is conscientiously opposed to participation in war in any form. Any such person claiming such exemption from combatant training and service because of such conscientious objections whose claim is sustained by the local board shall, if he is inducted into the land or naval forces under this Act, be assigned to noncombatant service as defined by the President, or shall, if he is found to be conscientiously opposed to participation in such noncombatant service, in lieu of such induction, be assigned to work of national importance under civilian direction. Any such person claiming such exemption from combatant training and service because of such conscientious objections shall, if such claim is not sustained by the local board, be entitled to an appeal to the appropriate appeal board provided for in section 10 (a) (2). Upon the filing of such appeal with the appeal board, the appeal board shall forthwith refer the matter to the Department of Justice for inquiry and hearing by the Department or the proper agency thereof. After appropriate inquiry by such agency, a hearing shall be held by the Department of Justice with respect to the character and good faith of the objections of the person concerned, and such person shall be notified of the time and place of such hearing. The Department shall, after such hearing, if the objections are found to be sustained, recommend to the appeal board (1) that if the objector is inducted into the land or naval forces under this Act, he shall be assigned to noncombatant service as defined by the President, or (2) that if the objector is found to be conscientiously opposed to participation in such noncombatant service, he shall in lieu of such induction be assigned to work of national importance under civilian direction. If after such hearing the Department finds that his objections are not sustained, it shall recommend to the appeal board that such objections be not sustained. The appeal board shall give consideration to but shall not be bound to follow the recommendation of the Department of Justice together with the record on appeal from the local board in making its decision. Each person whose claim for exemption from combatant training and service because of conscientious objections is sustained shall be listed by the local board on a register of conscientious objectors.

(*h*) No exception from registration, or exemption or deferment from training and service, under this Act, shall continue after the cause therefore ceases to exist.

SEC. 6. The President shall have authority to induct into the land and naval forces of the United States under this Act no greater number of men than the Congress shall hereafter make specific appropriation for from time to time.

[Sec. 7 and 8 (*a*) omitted.]

(*b*) In the case of any such person who, in order to perform such training and service, has left or leaves a position, other than a temporary position, in the employ of any employer and who (1) receives such certificate, (2) is still qualified to perform the duties of such position, and (3) makes application for reemployment within forty days after he is relieved from such training and service —

(A) if such position was in the employ of the United States Government, its Territories or possessions, or the District of Columbia, such person shall be restored to such position or to a position of like seniority, status, and pay;

(B) if such position was in the employ of a private employer, such employer shall restore such person to such position or to a position of like seniority, status, and pay unless the employer's circumstances have so changed as to make it impossible or unreasonable to do so;

(C) if such position was in the employ of any State or political subdivision thereof, it is hereby declared to be the sense of the Congress that such person should be restored to such position or to a position of like seniority, status, and pay.

(*c*) Any person who is restored to a position in accordance with the provisions of paragraph (A) or (B) of subsection (*b*) shall be considered as having been on furlough or leave of absence during his period of training and service in the land or naval forces, shall be so restored without loss of seniority.

. . . .

(*i*) It is the expressed policy of the Congress that whenever a vacancy is caused in the employment rolls of any business or industry by reason of induction into the service of the United States of an employee pursuant to the provisions of this Act such vacancy shall not be filled by any person who is a member of the Communist Party or the German-American Bund.

[Sec. 9 omitted here, see p. 743.]

Sec. 10. (a) The President is authorized —

(1) to prescribe the necessary rules and regulations to carry out the provisions of this Act;

(2) to create and establish a Selective Service System, and shall provide for the classification of registrants and of persons who volunteer for induction under this Act on the basis of availability for training and service, and shall establish within the Selective Service System civilian local boards and such other civilian agencies, including appeal boards and agencies of appeal, as may be necessary to carry out the provisions of this Act. There shall be created one or more local boards in each county or political subdivision corresponding thereto of each State, Territory, and the District of Columbia. Each local board shall consist of three or more members to be appointed by the President, from recommendations made by the respective Governors or comparable executive officials. No member of any such local board shall be a member of the land or naval forces of the United States, but each member of any such local board shall be a civilian who is a citizen of the United States residing in the county or political subdivision corresponding thereto in which such local board has jurisdiction under rules and regulations prescribed by the President. Such local boards, under rules and regulations prescribed by the President, shall have power within their respective jurisdictions to hear and determine, subject to the right of appeal to the appeal boards herein authorized, all questions or claims with respect to inclusion for, or exemption or deferment from, training and service under this Act of all individuals within the jurisdiction of such local boards. The decisions of such local boards shall be final except where an appeal is authorized in accordance with such rules and regulations as the President may prescribe. Appeal boards and agencies of appeal within the Selective Service System shall be composed of civilians who are citizens of the United States. No person who is an officer, member, agent, or employee of the Selective Service System, or of any such local or appeal board or other agency, shall be excepted from registration, or deferred from training and service, as provided for in this Act, by reason of his status as such officer, member, agent, or employee;

(3) to appoint by and with the advice and consent of the Senate, and fix the compensation at a rate not in excess of $10,000 per annum, of a Director of Selective Service who shall be directly responsible to him and to appoint and fix the compensation of such other officers,

agents, and employees as he may deem necessary to carry out the provisions of this Act: . . .

[SECS. 11, 12, 13, and 14 (*a*) and (*b*) omitted.]

[SEC. 14.]

(*c*) Nothing contained in this Act shall be construed to repeal, amend, or suspend the laws now in force authorizing voluntary enlistment or reenlistment in the land and naval forces of the United States, including the reserve components thereof.

SEC. 15. When used in this Act —

(*a*) The term "between the ages of twenty-one and thirty-six" shall refer to men who have attained the twenty-first anniversary of the day of their birth and who have not attained the thirty-sixth anniversary of the day of their birth; and other terms designating different age groups shall be construed in a similar manner.

(*b*) The term "United States," when used in a geographical sense, shall be deemed to mean the several States, the District of Columbia, Alaska, Hawaii, and Puerto Rico.

(*c*) The term "dependent" when used with respect to a person registered under the provisions of this Act includes only an individual (1) who is dependent in fact on such person for support in a reasonable manner, and (2) whose support in such a manner depends on income earned by such person in a business, occupation, or employment.

(*d*) The terms "land or naval forces" and "land and naval forces" shall be deemed to include aviation units of such forces.

(*e*) The term "district court of the United States" shall be deemed to include the courts of the United States for the Territories and the possessions of the United States.

SEC. 16. (*a*) Except as provided in this Act, all laws and parts of laws in conflict with the provisions of this Act are hereby suspended to the extent of such conflict for the period in which this Act shall be in force.

(*b*) All the provisions of this Act, except the provisions of sections 3 (*c*), 3 (*d*), 8 (*g*), and 12, shall become inoperative and cease to apply on and after May 15, 1945, except as to offenses committed prior to such date, unless this Act is continued in effect by the Congress.

(*c*) There are hereby authorized to be appropriated, out of any money in the Treasury not otherwise appropriated, such sums as may be necessary to carry out the provisions of this Act.

SEC. 17. This Act shall take effect immediately.

SEC. 18. This Act may be cited as the "Selective Training and Service Act of 1940."

(2) *Registration Day Set for October 16, 1940* [1]

BY THE PRESIDENT OF THE UNITED STATES OF AMERICA
A Proclamation [No. 2425]

WHEREAS the Congress has enacted and I have this day approved the Selective Training and Service Act of 1940,[2] which declares that it is imperative to increase and train the personnel of the armed forces of the United States and that in a free society the obligations and privileges of military training and service should be shared generally in accordance with a fair and just system of selective compulsory military training and service; and

WHEREAS the said Act contains, in part, the following provisions:

SEC. 2. Except as otherwise provided in this Act, it shall be the duty of every male citizen of the United States, and of every male alien residing in the United States, who, on the day or days fixed for the first or any subsequent registration, is between the ages of twenty-one and thirty-six, to present himself for and submit to registration at such time or times and place or places, and in such manner and in such age group or groups, as shall be determined by rules and regulations prescribed hereunder.

. . . .

SEC. 5. (*a*) Commissioned officers, warrant officers, pay clerks, and enlisted men of the Regular Army, the Navy, the Marine Corps, the Coast Guard, the Coast and Geodetic Survey, the Public Health Service, the federally recognized active National Guard, the Officers' Reserve Corps, the Regular Army Reserve, the Enlisted Reserve Corps, the Naval Reserve, and the Marine Corps Reserve; cadets, United States Military Academy; midshipmen, United States Naval Academy; cadets, United States Coast Guard Academy; men who have been accepted for admittance (commencing with the academic year next succeeding such acceptance) to the United States Military Academy as cadets, to the United States Naval Academy as midshipmen, or to the United States Coast Guard Academy as cadets, but only during the continuance of such acceptance; cadets of the advanced course, senior division, Reserve Officers' Training Corps or Naval Reserve Officers' Training Corps; and diplomatic representatives, technical attachés of foreign embassies and legations, consuls general, consuls, vice consuls, and consular agents of foreign countries, residing in the United States, who are not citizens of the United States, and who have not declared their intention to

---

[1] Department of State, *Bulletin*, III, p. 221.

[2] Public No. 783, 76th Cong., 3d sess., approved September 16, 1940; *An Act to Provide for the Common Defense by Increasing the Personnel of the Armed Forces of the United States and Providing for Its Training:* originated as S. 4164, reported from Committee on Military Affairs, August 5, 1940; Senate Report No. 2002; passed Senate, August 28; H. R. 10132, reported from Committee on Military Affairs, after hearings, August 29; House Report No. 2903; passed House, proceedings vacated and laid on table September 7; S. 4164, amended, passed in lieu, September 7; House (conference) Report Nos. 2937, September 12, and 2947, September 14.

become citizens of the United States, shall not be required to be registered under section 2 and shall be relieved from liability for training and service under section 3 (*b*).

SEC. 10 (*a*). The President is authorized —
(1) to prescribe the necessary rules and regulations[1] to carry out the provisions of this Act;

(4) to utilize the services of any or all departments and any and all officers or agents of the United States and to accept the services of all officers and agents of the several States, Territories, and the District of Columbia and subdivisions thereof in the execution of this Act;

SEC. 14 (*a*). Every person shall be deemed to have notice of the requirements of this Act upon publication by the President of a proclamation or other public notice fixing a time for any registration under section 2.

Now, THEREFORE, I, FRANKLIN D. ROOSEVELT, President of the United States of America, under and by virtue of the authority vested in me by the aforesaid Selective Training and Service Act of 1940, do proclaim the following:

1. The first registration under the Selective Training and Service Act of 1940 shall take place on Wednesday, the sixteenth day of October, 1940, between the hours of 7 A.M. and 9 P.M.

2. Every male person (other than persons excepted by Section 5 (*a*) of the aforesaid Act) who is a citizen of the United States or an alien residing in the United States and who, on the registration date fixed herein, has attained the twenty-first anniversary of the day of his birth and has not attained the thirty-sixth anniversary of the day of his birth, is required to present himself for and submit to registration. Every such person who is within the continental United States on the registration date fixed herein shall on that date present himself for and submit to registration at the duly designated place of registration within the precinct, district, or registration area in which he has his permanent home or in which he may happen to be on that date. Every such person who is not within the continental United States on the registration date fixed herein shall within five days after his return to the continental United States present himself for and submit to registration. Regulations will be prescribed hereafter providing for special registration

---

[1] On September 23, 1940, the President signed Executive Order No. 8545 prescribing selective service regulations governing the administration of the Selective Training and Service Act, approved September 16, 1940; text of the Executive order, 5 *Fed. Reg.*, p. 3779–91. (Department of State, *Bulletin*, III, p. 252.)

of those who on account of sickness or other causes beyond their control are unable to present themselves for registration at the designated places of registration on the registration date fixed herein.

3. Every person subject to registration is required to familiarize himself with the rules and regulations governing registration and to comply therewith.

4. The times and places for registration in Alaska, Hawaii, and Puerto Rico will be fixed in subsequent proclamations.

5. I call upon the Governors of the several States and the Board of Commissioners of the District of Columbia to provide suitable and sufficient places of registration within their respective jurisdictions and to provide suitable and necessary registration boards to effect such registration.

6. I further call upon all officers and agents of the United States and all officers and agents of the several States and the District of Columbia and subdivisions thereof to do and perform all acts and services necessary to accomplish effective and complete registration; and I especially call upon all local election officials and other patriotic citizens to offer their services as members of the boards of registration.

7. In order that there may be full cooperation in carrying into effect the purposes of said Act, I urge all employers, and government agencies of all kinds — Federal, State and Local — to give those under their charge sufficient time off in which to fulfill the obligation of registration incumbent on them under the said Act.

America stands at the crossroads of its destiny. Time and distance have been shortened. A few weeks have seen great nations fall. We cannot remain indifferent to the philosophy of force now rampant in the world. The terrible fate of nations whose weakness invited attack is too well known to us all.

We must and will marshal our great potential strength to fend off war from our shores. We must and will prevent our land from becoming a victim of aggression.

Our decision has been made.

It is in that spirit that the people of our country are assuming the burdens that now become necessary. Offers of service have flooded in from patriotic citizens in every part of the nation, who ask only what they can do to help. Now there is both the opportunity and the need for many thousands to assist in listing the names and addresses of the millions who will enroll on registration day at school houses, polling places, and town halls.

The Congress has debated without partisanship and has now enacted a law establishing a selective method of augmenting our armed forces. The method is fair, it is sure, it is democratic — it is the will of our people.

After thoughtful deliberation, and as the first step, our young men will come from the factories and the fields, the cities and the towns, to enroll their names on registration day.

On that eventful day my generation will salute their generation. May we all renew within our hearts that conception of liberty and that way of life which we have all inherited. May we all strengthen our resolve to hold high the torch of freedom in this darkening world so that our children and their children may not be robbed of their rightful inheritance.

IN WITNESS WHEREOF I have hereunto set my hand and caused the Seal of the United States to be affixed.

DONE at the City of Washington this sixteenth day of September in the year of our Lord nineteen hundred and forty, and of the [SEAL] Independence of the United States of America the one hundred and sixty-fifth.

FRANKLIN D. ROOSEVELT

By the President:
    CORDELL HULL,
        Secretary of State

3. BUDGET MESSAGE OF THE PRESIDENT, JANUARY 3, 1941 [1]

[Excerpt]

TO THE CONGRESS OF THE UNITED STATES:

The Budget of the United States Government for the fiscal year ending June 30, 1942, which I transmit herewith, is a reflection of a world at war. Carrying out the mandate of the people, the Government has embarked on a program for the total defense of our democracy. This means warships, freighters, tanks, planes, and guns to protect us against aggression; and jobs, health, and security to strengthen the bulwarks of democracy. Our problem in the coming year is to combine these two objectives so as to protect our democracy against external pressure and internal slackness.

The threatening world situation forces us to build up land, sea, and air forces able to meet and master any contingency. It is dangerous to prepare for a little defense. It is safe only to prepare for total defense.

[1] *Congressional Record,* vol. 87, p. 76 (daily edition); H. Doc. 28, 77th Cong.

Total defense means more than weapons. It means an industrial capacity stepped up to produce all the matériel for defense with the greatest possible speed. It means people of health and stamina, conscious of the democratic rights and responsibilities. It means an economic and social system functioning smoothly and geared to high-speed performance. The defense budget, therefore, must go beyond the needs of the Army and Navy.

It is not enough to defend our national existence. Democracy as a way of life is equally at stake. The ability of the democracies to employ their full resources of manpower and skill and plant has been challenged. We meet this challenge by maximum utilization of plant and manpower and by maintaining governmental services, social security, and aid to those suffering through no fault of their own. Only by maintaining all of these activities can we claim the effective use of resources which our democratic system is expected to yield, and thus justify the expenditures required for its defense.

The National Program

In this Budget I am presenting a program for 1942, carefully worked out to combine these objectives. This program, including defense and nondefense activities, will cost about 17.5 billions of dollars. For the same period, we expect the largest national income for the Nation as a whole and also the largest tax receipts.

In addition to, but essentially and rightly as a complement to this program, the time has come for immediate consideration of assuring the continuation of the flow of vitally necessary munitions to those nations which are defending themselves against attack and against the imposition of new forms of government upon them.

Such a complementary program would call for appropriations and contract authorizations over and above this Budget. The sum of all these defense efforts should be geared to the productive capacity of this Nation expanded to literally its utmost efforts.

The Defense Program and Defense Expenditures

Sixty-two per cent of the expenditures proposed in this Budget are for national defense. No one can predict the ultimate cost of a program that is still in development, for no one can define the future. When we recall the staggering changes in the world situation in the last six months, we realize how tentative all present estimates must be.

These expenditures must be seen as a part of a defense program stretching over several years. On the basis of the appropriations and authorizations enacted for national defense from June 1940 up to the present time, plus the recommendations for supplementary appropriations and authorizations for 1941 and the recommendations contained in this Budget for 1942, we have a program of 28 billion dollars.

This is a vast sum, difficult to visualize in terms of work actually to be done. If we can prove that we are able to organize and execute such a gigantic program in a democratic way, we shall have made a positive contribution in a world in which the workability of democracy is challenged.

This defense program is summarized below:

Appropriations, Authorizations, and Recommendations
(June 1940, 1941, 1942) [1]

[In millions of dollars]

Army	13,704
Navy	11,587
Expansion of industrial plant	1,902
Other defense activities	1,287
Total	28,480

The Army funds provide for the training and maintenance of a force of men increasing from 250,000 in June 1940 to 1,400,000 in 1942, equipped with the most modern devices of motorized and mechanical warfare. The Navy estimates continue the construction of our over-all Navy and contemplate the doubling of naval personnel. There is provision for a great increase in the number of Army and Navy planes and for training pilots, technicians, and ground crews.

Behind the lines a whole new defense industry is being built with the financial support of the Federal Government. One hundred and twenty-five new plants are under contract; more are planned.

In submitting these recommendations, I have not covered the full requirements of the civilian training program. At present, surveys are under way which will provide a basis for transmitting an estimate of funds needed for the extension of this essential defense activity. In the current fiscal year, over a million men and women are included in the various programs of apprentice training, vocational training in trade schools and engineering colleges, work-experience shops, and pilot training.

Expenditures under the defense program during the last six months amount to 1,750 million dollars. This is two and one-half times the

---

[1] For a more complete table, see p. 691.

amount spent for national defense in the same period of the fiscal year 1940. However, these expenditures understate the progress already made. In six months, contracts and orders for 10 billion dollars have been placed. This means that in addition to present defense production, all over the country more factories, large and small, are getting ready rapidly to increase production. Once these preparations have been completed actual deliveries and expenditures will be greatly accelerated.

I expect actual expenditures to be stepped up to four and three-quarters billion dollars in the six months ending June 1941 and to almost 11 billion in the fiscal year 1942. We shall actually expend more than 25 billion dollars for defense within a 3-year period. This can be accomplished, but only if management, labor, and consumers cooperate to the utmost.

Nondefense Expenditures

The increased military expenditures permit a substantial reduction in nondefense expenditures, particularly for those activities which are made less necessary by improved economic conditions. Obligations such as interest, pensions, and insurance benefits are fixed. Almost as fixed are the appropriations for which the Congress has already made legislative commitments — security grants to the States, Federal aid for highways, the 30 per cent of tariff revenue set aside for reducing agricultural surpluses, and similar items. Together, these fixed items make up nearly half of the nondefense expenditures I am proposing for the fiscal year 1942. For the items subject to administrative rather than legislative action, I have been able to reduce expenditures by 600 million dollars or 15 per cent. This reduction and its relation to total expenditures are shown below:

EXPENDITURES	ESTIMATED IN MIILLIONS OF DOLLARS		PER CENT CHANGE
	1942	1941	
Defense program	$10,811	$6,464	+ 67
Fixed commitments	3,196	2,984	+ 7
Other activities.	3,478	4,094	− 15
Total (excluding returns from Government corporations)	17,485	13,542	+ 29

Certain reductions are possible in carrying out the established policies relating to public works and relief, but little change can be made in the regular operating costs of government. As I indicated in my Budget Message last year, the operating costs of the regular departments are already down to the bedrock of the activities and functions ordered by the Congress. In spite of the defense pressure on many of these regular programs, expenditures will be kept below the level of the current year.

. . . .

FINANCING THE NATIONAL PROGRAM

Estimates of expenditures and revenue compared: The defense program dominates not only the expenditure side of the Budget, but influences also the expected revenue. Economic activities and national income are rising to record heights. From a higher national income a greater revenue will flow, although in the case of most taxes there is, of course, a time lag. The revenue for the fiscal year 1941 will reflect some of the increase in defense activities; the revenue for the fiscal year 1942 will be affected to a larger extent; but the full impact will not be felt before the fiscal year 1943.

The revenue for the fiscal year 1942 is expected to be 9 billion dollars. It will exceed the revenue collected in the fiscal year 1940 — the last year before the start of the present defense program — by 3 billion dollars. One-half of this increase will come from the defense taxes already enacted by the Congress, the other half from the increase in national income.

The revenue expected for 1942 will be 1.6 billions larger than the total of all nondefense expenditures. This 1.6 billions is greater than the annual expenditure on defense before the present program started, but less than will be necessary for maintaining the Army and Navy at the new level.

. . . .

The Debt Problem: For more than 25 years the world has been in a state of political turmoil and its economies have been out of balance. This world condition is reflected in unbalanced budgets in all countries. Here, the first World War, the war against the depression, the present defense program, all resulted in large additions to the Federal debt.

I understand the concern of those who are disturbed by the growth of the Federal debt. Yet the main fiscal problem is not the rise of the debt, but the rise of debt charges in relation to the development of our resources.

The fight for recovery raised national income by more than 30 billion dollars above the depression depth. In the same period the total annual

Federal interest charges increased by 400 million dollars. Even if these interest charges increase, they can scarcely present a serious fiscal problem so long as a high level of national income can be maintained.

Investors are fully aware of this fact. The bonds of the United States Government are the safest securities in the world because they are backed by the best asset in the world — the productive capacity of the American people. Our tax burden is still moderate compared to that of most other countries.

It should be borne in mind that our national debt results from wars and the economic upheavals following war. These conditions are not of our own making. They have been forced upon us. The national debt of almost all nations would be far lower today if competitive armaments had not existed during the past quarter of a century. If this war should be followed, as I hope it will, by peace in a world of good neighbors, then the complete elimination of competitive armaments will become possible. Only in such a world can economic stability be restored.

If a high level of economic activity can be maintained during the defense period and — what will be a more difficult task — maintained in the post-defense period, then the fiscal needs can be readily met.

———

The budget of the United States presents our national program. It is a preview of our work plan, a forecast of things to come. It charts the course of the Nation.

The necessity for loading the present Budget with armament expenditures is regretted by every American. A wry turn of fate places this burden of defense on the backs of a peace-loving people.

We can meet the demands of armament because we are a people with the will to defend and the means to defend. The boundaries of our productive capacity have never been set.

The whole program set forth in this Budget has been prepared at a time when no man could see all the signposts ahead. One marker alone stands out all down the road. That marker carries not so much an admonition as a command to defend our democratic way of life.

FRANKLIN D. ROOSEVELT

January 3, 1941.

4. STATISTICS ON NATIONAL DEFENSE

(1) *Appropriations and Contract Authorizations, by Appropriation Acts, for the Navy Department and War Department, Military Activities, for the Fiscal Years 1940, 1941 and 1942, as of June 30, 1941* [1]

NAVY DEPARTMENT

APPROPRIATING ACTS AND DATE APPROVED	BUREAU OF AERONAUTICS	OTHER	TOTAL
Fiscal Year 1940			
Pub. No. 90, May 25, 1939:			
Appropriations	$82,798,000	$690,173,105 [2]	$772,971,105 [2]
Contract authorizations . . .	20,000,000	36,221,050	56,221,050
Pub. No. 361, August 9, 1939:			
Appropriations	—	5,138,860	5,138,860
Contract authorizations . . .	—	24,338,500	24,338,500
Pub. No. 415, February 12, 1940:			
Appropriations	28,661,000	108,511,238	137,172,238
Contract authorizations . . .	—	2,450,000	2,450,000
Pub. No. 416, February 21, 1940:			
Appropriations	—	28,000,000	28,000,000
Pub. No. 447, April 6, 1940:			
Appropriations	—	439,149	439,149
Pub. No. 668, June 27, 1940:			
Appropriations	—	302,612	302,612
Pub. No. 812, October 9, 1940:			
Appropriations	—	174,898	174,898
Private Relief acts	—	31	31
Total, fiscal year 1940:			
Appropriations	111,459,000	832,739,893	944,198,893
Contract authorizations . .	20,000,000	63,009,550	83,009,550
Fiscal Year 1941			
Pub. No. 588, June 11, 1940:			
Appropriations	138,483,300	1,135,493,820 [3]	1,273,977,120 [3]
Contract authorizations . . .	125,000,000	23,741,612	148,741,612

[1] From the Executive Office of the President, Bureau of the Budget.

For a similar tabulation including recommendations for national defense see *Congressional Record*, Vol. 86, p. 6440 (daily edition), July 24, 1941 (remarks of Mr. Woodrum).

[2] Exclusive of $190,000 "State Marine Schools" transferred to U. S. Maritime Commission pursuant to the provisions of the Reorganization act of 1939 and Reorganization Plan No. IV, and includes $11,954 adjustment in permanent appropriations.

[3] Exclusive of $190,000 "State Marine Schools" transferred to U. S. Maritime Commission and $4,018 transferred to Post Office Department pursuant to the provisions of the Reorganization act of 1939 and Reorganization Plan No. IV. Also, $34,000,000 "Emergency Fund for the President."

NAVY DEPARTMENT — *Continued*

APPROPRIATING ACTS AND DATE APPROVED	BUREAU OF AERONAUTICS	OTHER	TOTAL
Pub. No. 667, June 26, 1940:			
Appropriations	$22,885,000	$536,388,170	$559,273,170
Contract authorizations . . .	——	129,014,000	129,014,000
Pub. No. 668, June 27, 1940:			
Appropriations	——	21,900	21,900
Pub. No. 781, September 9, 1940:			
Appropriations	180,000,000	423,643,860	603,643,860
Contract authorizations . . .	375,000,000	127,740,000	502,740,000
Pub. No. 800, October 8, 1940:			
Appropriations	15,000,000	60,401,000	75,401,000
Contract authorizations . . .	——	8,500,000	8,500,000
Pub. No. 9, March 1, 1941:			
Appropriations	——	522,775	522,775
Pub. No. 13, March 17, 1941:			
Appropriations	96,382,300	584,839,302	681,221,602
Contract authorizations . . .	30,000,000	127,102,500	157,102,500
Pub. No. 25, April 1, 1941:			
Appropriations	——	1,543,314	1,543,314
Pub. No. 29, April 5, 1941:			
Appropriations	——	295,416,820	295,416,820
Total fiscal year 1941:			
Appropriations	452,750,600	3,038,270,961	3,491,021,561
Contract authorizations . .	530,000,000	416,098,112	946,098,112
Fiscal Year 1942 [1]			
Pub. No. 48, May 6, 1941:			
Appropriations	434,980,000	2,980,685,522	3,415,665,522
Contract authorizations . . .	——	31,448,894	31,448,894

Public Law 1, 77th Cong., approved January 29, 1941, authorized expenditures up to $300,000,000 for improving anti-aircraft defenses of combatant and auxiliary naval vessels.

Public Law 4, 77th Cong., approved January 31, 1941, authorized additional naval shipbuilding and ordnance manufacturing facilities amounting to $509,-000,000 and the construction of 400 small craft not to exceed a cost of $400,000,000.

Public Law 72, 77th Cong., approved May 24, 1941, authorized acquisition, conversion or construction of 550,000 tons of auxiliary vessels.

[1] Indefinite contract authorizations for construction of the expanded navy, according to estimates of the Navy Department, will call for appropriations after the fiscal year 1942 amounting to more than $6,000,000,000.

WAR DEPARTMENT, MILITARY ACTIVITIES

APPROPRIATING ACTS AND DATE APPROVED	AIR CORPS	OTHER	TOTAL
Fiscal Year 1940			
Pub. No. 44, April 26, 1939:			
Appropriations	$94,995,681	$413,725,528 [1]	$508,721,209 [1]
Contract authorizations . . .	32,205,988	8,000,000	40,205,988
Pub. No. 164, July 1, 1939:			
Appropriations	89,779,808	133,618,239	223,398,047
Contract authorizations . . .	44,000,000	26,497,500	70,497,500
Pub. No. 361, August 9, 1939:			
Appropriations	——	9,937,300	9,937,300
Contract authorizations . . .	——	8,500,000	8,500,000
Pub. No. 415, February 12, 1940:			
Appropriations	1,787,358	107,629,331	109,416,689
Pub. No. 447, April 6, 1940:			
Appropriations	——	3,974	3,974
Pub. No. 668, June 27, 1940:			
Appropriations	——	78,200	78,200
Claims and judgments Pub. Nos. 447 and 668 above and 812 below:			
Appropriations	——	788,625	788,625
Total, fiscal year 1940:			
Appropriations	186,562,847	665,781,197	852,344,044
Contract authorizations . .	76,205,988	42,997,500	119,203,488
Fiscal Year 1941			
Pub. No. 611, June 13, 1940:			
Appropriations	266,278,418	1,167,025,297 [2]	1,433,303,715 [2]
Contract authorization	103,300,000	153,929,636	257,229,636
Pub. No. 667, June 26, 1940:			
Appropriations	293,456,282	527,545,765	821,002,047
Contract authorizations . . .	109,259,597	144,917,164	254,176,761
Pub. No. 668, June 27, 1940:			
Appropriations	——	135,000	135,000
Pub. No. 781, Sept. 9, 1940:			
Appropriations	520,802,304	1,272,570,228	1,793,372,532
Contract authorizations . . .	1,002,600,000	1,249,130,000	2,251,730,000
Pub. Res. No. 99, Sept. 24, 1940:			
Appropriations	——	338,263,902	338,263,902
Pub. No. 800, October 8, 1940:			
Appropriations	109,995,957	1,113,192,017 [3]	1,223,187,974 [3]
Contract authorizations . . .	60,000,000	90,000,000	150,000,000

[1] Exclusive of $66,480 "Bureau of Insular Affairs" and $2,135 representing parts of various appropriations transferred out of the War Department pursuant to provisions of the Reorganization act of 1939 and Reorganization Plan No. II.

[2] Exclusive of $66,000,000 "Emergency Fund for the President" and $19,607 transferred to Post Office Department pursuant to provisions of the Reorganization act of 1939 and Reorganization Plan No. IV.

[3] Exclusive of $24,825,108 "Selective Service system."

WAR DEPARTMENT, MILITARY ACTIVITIES — *Continued*

APPROPRIATING ACTS AND DATE APPROVED	AIR CORPS	OTHER	TOTAL
Pub. No. 812, October 9, 1940:			
Appropriations	—	3,400,000	3,400,000
Pub. No. 6, February 13, 1941:			
Appropriations	—	175,000,000	175,000,000
Pub. No. 13, March 17, 1941:			
Appropriations	—	695,118,000	695,118,000
Pub. No. 25, April 1, 1941:			
Appropriations	—	$2,800,452	$2,800,452
Pub. No. 29, April 5, 1941:			
Appropriations	982,236,000	1,015,575,100	1,997,811,100
Contract authorizations . . .	524,025,000	1,569,428,254	2,093,453,254
Total, fiscal year 1941:			
Appropriations	2,172,768,961	6,310,625,761	8,483,394,722
Contract authorizations . .	1,799,184,597	3,207,405,054	5,006,589.651
Fiscal Year 1942			
Pub. No. 139, June 30, 1941:			
Appropriations	4,341,735,322	6,043,086,302	10,384,821,624
Contract authorizations . . .	104,258,995	78,886,700	183,145,695

NOTE: Pub. No. 23, March 27, 1941, contains an appropriation of $7,000,-
000,000 for Defense Aid. The Navy Department and the War Department,
Military activities, will probably receive a large proportion of this appropriation by allocations.

(2) *Combatant Ships, Built and Building for the Seven Principal Naval
Powers, February 1941* [1]

TYPE	BUILT	BUILD-ING	TOTAL	TYPE	BUILT	BUILD-ING	TOTAL
UNITED STATES				BRITISH EMPIRE			
Battleships .	15	17	32	Battleships .	16	7	23
Aircraft				Aircraft			
Carriers .	6	12	18	Carriers .	8	4	12
Cruisers . .	37	54	91	Cruisers . .	66	18?	84?
Destroyers .	159	205	364	Destroyers .	233	3?	236?
Submarines .	106	79	185	Submarines .	45	?	45?
Total . .	323	367	690 [2]	Total . .	368	32?	400?

[1] From Office of Public Relations, Navy Department. Statistics on navies other
than the United States are not official United States Navy statistics.

[2] As of May 1, 1941, there were 165 destroyers and 109 submarines built, with 78
submarines building. The totals then were: Built, 332; building, 360; total, 692.

TYPE	BUILT	BUILD-ING	TOTAL	TYPE	BUILT	BUILD-ING	TOTAL
JAPAN				GERMANY			
Battleships .	10	8(e)	18(e)	Battleships .	4	2	6
Aircraft				Aircraft			
Carriers .	8	2	10	Carriers .	1	1	2
Cruisers . .	46	10	56	Cruisers . .	9	6	15
Destroyers .	125	11	136	Destroyers .	47(e)	?	47?
Submarines .	71	7	78	Submarines .	120(e)	180(e)	300(e)
Total . .	260	38	298	Total . .	181	189?	370?
FRANCE				RUSSIA			
Battleships .	1	4	5	Battleships .	3	3	6
Aircraft				Aircraft			
Carriers .	1	2	3	Carriers .	0	2	2
Cruisers . .	14	3	17	Cruisers . .	9	4	13
Destroyers .	50(e)	30(e)	80(e)	Destroyers .	64	34(e)	98(e)
Submarines .	60(e)	22	82(e)	Submarines .	171(e)	?	171?(e)
Total . .	126	61	187	Total . .	247	43?	290?
ITALY							
Battleships .	6	2	8				
Aircraft							
Carriers .	0	0	0				
Cruisers . .	20	14	34				
Destroyers .	115	12	127				
Submarines .	92(e)	16	108				
Total . .	233	44	277				

(e) Estimated.

(3) *United States Army Strength. Estimate by War Department, June 5, 1941* [1]

The strength of the Army of the United States today is estimated at 1,362,300 officers and enlisted men. The breakdown is as follows:

OFFICERS

Regular Army 14,000
National Guard 21,800
Reserve Officers 49,500
   Total 85,300

ENLISTED MEN

Regular Army, 3–year enlistments 470,000
Regular Army, Reserve and 1–year enlistments 18,000
National Guard in Federal Service 269,000
Selective Service Trainees 520,000
   Total 1,277,000

[1] Release of War Department, Bureau of Public Relations, June 5, 1941.

TOTAL COMBINED STRENGTH

Regular Army	502,000
National Guard	290,800
Reserve Officers	49,500
Selective Service Trainees	520,000
Total	1,362,300

5. NAVAL POLICY AND ESTABLISHMENT

A. Naval Policy, 1940

(1) Statement for Guidance of the Naval Service, Prepared by the General Board with Approval by the Secretary of the Navy, Issued September 15, 1940 [1]

The entrance into force on August 17, 1923 of the Treaty for the Limitation of Naval Armament between the United States, the British Empire, France, Italy and Japan, signed at Washington, February 6, 1922 [2] prompted the enunciation of a definitely stated naval policy, which was printed in the Annual Report of the Secretary of the Navy for the fiscal year 1922. This was revised, largely in response to international naval developments, in 1928, 1929, 1931, 1933, 1937 and 1940, when it was revised to include the "two ocean navy" policy.

U. S. NAVAL POLICY

Naval policy is the system of principles, and the general terms of their application, governing the development, organization, maintenance, training, and employment of a Navy. It is based on and is designed to support national policies and interests. It comprehends questions of character, number, and distribution of naval forces and shore activities; of the number and qualifications of personnel; and of the character of peace and war strategy and operations.

FUNDAMENTAL POLICY

To maintain the Navy in strength and readiness to uphold National policies and interests, and to guard the United States and its continental and overseas possessions.

GENERAL POLICIES

To develop the Navy to a maximum in fighting strength and ability to control the sea in defense of the Nation and its interests.

To make effectiveness in war the objective of all development and training.

To organize and maintain the Navy for major operations in both the Atlantic and Pacific Oceans.

---

[1] Navy Department release.
[2] *Treaties, Conventions*, etc., 1923–1937, IV, p. 4889.

To maintain and develop Naval Aviation as an integral part of the naval forces.

To maintain the Marine Corps in such strength as to provide the requisite Fleet Marine Force and detachments for other naval purposes.

To develop and maintain shore activities, including bases suitably located and defended, for the support of the mobile forces.

To locate shore activities in such geographical areas and construct them in such sites and in such manner as will promote security against air and other attack; and to apply this policy to existing activities as practicable.

To advance the art of naval warfare and to promote the development of naval matériel.

To maintain and train the officer and enlisted personnel requisite for the regular establishment and to provide for the procurement and training of the personnel required for the expanded war organization.

To plan the procurement of matériel to meet wartime needs and to foster civil industries and activities useful in war.

To exercise economy in expenditures as compatible with efficiency.

To make systematic inspections of naval activities and matériel.

To encourage the growth of the merchant marine and of commercial aviation.

To cooperate fully with other departments and agencies of the Government.

Fleet Building and Maintenance Policy

To keep the fleet at the required strength, balanced as to types of ships, by a continuing building program.

To make superiority in their types the end in view in the design and construction of all naval vessels and aircraft.

To keep characteristics and designs for ships and aircraft up to date.

To maintain all ships and aircraft at the maximum of material readiness and fighting efficiency consistent with their age and military value, incorporating such improvements as are duly warranted.

COMBATANT SHIPS

To build capital ships, carriers, cruisers, destroyers, mine layers, submarines, and other combatant types in numbers adequate to maintain a well-balanced fleet of the required strength in under-age vessels.

AIRCRAFT

To build and maintain aircraft in numbers and classes adequate for the fleet requirements and for all other essential naval purposes.

To build and maintain nonrigid airships for coastal patrol and for other naval uses.

To build and maintain rigid airships as necessary to explore and develop their usefulness for naval purposes; and to cooperate with other agencies in developing commercial airships.

AUXILIARY VESSELS

To build or acquire, and to maintain the minimum number of auxiliary vessels of the several types needed for the normal operation of the fleet, and for the maintenance, supply, and potential defense of outlying bases and stations.

To cooperate with other Government Departments and agencies in planning for and in designing new merchant and Government vessels which can be utilized as naval auxiliaries.

To maintain plans for rapid acquisition and effective conversion of merchant vessels for naval use in time of war.

MINOR WAR VESSELS AND SMALL CRAFT

To build or acquire and to maintain such minor war vessels and small craft as required for naval districts and special service, developing suitable types as necessary.

FLEET OPERATING POLICY

To keep in commission, fully manned and in active training, the number of ships necessary to provide a fleet of required strength in all types.

To organize the forces afloat to obtain maximum flexibility, mobility, and effectiveness in strategical and tactical operations.

To give full effect to established command principles, stressing unity of command and appropriate decentralization in both execution and administration.

To operate forces afloat under balanced schedules formulated to secure excellence in strategy and tactics, gunnery, engineering and other technical performance, and in material upkeep; and also to promote proficiency, contentment, and discipline of personnel.

To keep the United States Fleet strategically disposed and to assemble the Fleet for a period of not less than two months annually for advanced training.

To operate and maintain the Asiatic Fleet and other detached forces in readiness for incorporation into the United States Fleet.

To make foreign cruises for cultivation of friendly international relations and for varied training of personnel.

To operate a naval train and a supply service sufficient for the upkeep and mobility of the forces afloat and for the maintenance and supply of outlying bases and stations.

To assign suitable vessels and facilities for training Naval Reserves.

To operate vessels necessary for surveying strategical and commercial areas outside the coastal limits of the United States and its possessions.

SHORE ACTIVITIES POLICY

To develop two main bases on each coast and one in Hawaii.

To develop air and other essential bases, coastal and outlying, for the support of naval operations.

To maintain a system of naval districts and corresponding district forces for the control and security of district waters, coastwise sea lanes and adjacent sea areas; for cooperation with the fleet; and for the coordinated administration and protection of naval bases, navy yards, and other naval activities within the particular district.

To maintain all navy yards and naval industrial plants in such condition of readiness as to sustain the fleet in war.

To construct such naval vessels in navy yards as necessary to assure the continued availability of experienced technical personnel.

To encourage civil industries and activities useful in war.

To insure the effective availability of private shipbuilding and other private industrial plants for the national defense by a continuing program of naval construction therein.

To procure and maintain suitable facilities for the training of naval and Marine Corps personnel, including reserves.

To maintain and operate the facilities necessary for the collection and dissemination of hydrographic, astronomical, and aerological information essential to the Navy and useful to governmental and commercial interests.

PERSONNEL POLICY

To maintain the personnel at a high standard of efficiency and in sufficient numbers to meet the requirements of the naval service.

To develop and coordinate systematic courses of instruction and training for officer and enlisted personnel.

To assign officers to duty in foreign countries to broaden their professional education.

To maintain a reasonable excess of petty officers and noncommissioned officers over peacetime requirements in order to facilitate wartime expansion.

To restrict the transfer of personnel to that compatible with a high degree of training, morale, professional experience, and service efficiency.

To build up, train, and maintain Naval and Marine Corps Reserves to provide for mobilization.

To cultivate close relations of personnel of the Navy and Marine Corps with the Reserves.

Communications Policy

To provide and maintain a naval communication system based on war requirements.

To operate the communication facilities as required, primarily, by the current operating force plan and for direct communication with overseas possessions.

To continue the use of naval communication facilities to increase safety at sea and in the air, including adequate communication with the United States Merchant Marine and commercial aircraft flying overseas.

To cooperate with American commercial communication activities so as to enhance their military value in time of national emergency and to safeguard the communication interests of the United States.

Information Policy

To acquire accurate information concerning the political, military, naval, economic, and industrial policies and activities of all countries.

To analyze and preserve information for ready reference and for historical purposes.

To disseminate useful information systematically throughout the naval service and to other Government Departments and agencies.

To provide protection against espionage and sabotage in cooperation with other departments and agencies.

To keep the public informed of the activities of the Navy, as compatible with military security.

Matériel Policy

To plan, in cooperation with other Government Departments and agencies, and with industry, for timely procurement of supplies and munitions necessary to maintain and augment the mobilized Navy.

To procure and maintain reserves of supplies and munitions in quantities to cover essential requirements beyond the productive capacity initially available in an emergency.

To procure and maintain, in cooperation with other Government Departments and agencies, adequate stocks of strategic raw materials.

To cooperate with other Government Departments and agencies, and with private industry, in the development of standards and specifications and of inspection organizations, methods, and procedures.

To promote by continuous research and investigation the application of scientific discoveries and technical invention to the improvement of naval matériel.

(2) *Obligations of United States Navy Shipbuilding Program Incurred During 1941* [1]

	NUMBER OF VESSELS (EXCLUDES DISTRICT CRAFT)	TONNAGE	TOTAL ESTIMATED COST (CONSTRUCTION AND MAINTENANCE, ARMS, ARMAMENT, AND AMMUNITION)
Title I:			
20 per cent act [2]	19	129,300	$349,498,000
Replacement tonnage	5	50,900	114,291,000
Total	24	——	——
Title III:			
11 per cent act [3]	22	162,150	483,746,000
20 per cent act	10	35,200	148,580,000
Replacement tonnage	36	118,000	483,323,000
Act of Aug. 29, 1916	1	4,000	4,800,000
Total	69	——	——
Title IV:			
70 per cent act [4]	340	1,439,136	4,688,914,400
11 per cent act	29	73,700	203,700,000
20 per cent act	8	46,100	75,700,000
Total	377	——	——
Reserve naval vessels:			
Additional obligations, construction and maintenance, 1941:			
1. Facilities (statutory limit) .	——	——	185,000,000
2. Yard and district craft (159)	——	——	69,663,000
Additional obligations, Arms, Armament, and Ammunition, 1941:			
1. Facilities	——	——	115,000,000
Total	——	——	6,922,215,400

[1] U. S. Congress, House of Representatives, Committee on Appropriations, *Navy Department Appropriation Bill for 1942; Hearings before the Subcommittee* . . . 77th Cong., 1st sess., p. 60.

[2] Approved May 17, 1938, *Documents I, 1938–39*, p. 507.

[3] Approved June 14, 1940, *ibid., II, 1939–40*, p. 761.

[4] Approved July 19, 1940, *ibid., II*, p. 764.

B. Preparation of Outlying Naval Stations

(1) *Report of the Committee on Naval Affairs, House of Representatives, February 17, 1941* [1]

[Excerpt]

In general, the public works projects that would be authorized by this bill [Public Law 22] are made necessary by the rapid expansion of our naval forces during the emergency, and nearly all are carried as items in title VI of the national defense budget recently submitted to the Congress. The committee have seen fit to increase the budget figures by $61,297,500. It will be noted that of this amount $58,250,000 represents the amount necessary to complete the program of establishing the bases being acquired from Great Britain. The total estimated cost of naval projects at these bases is $116,050,000. This total amount, as will be seen from the accompanying table, may be broken down as follows: Already appropriated and allocated from the President's emergency fund $50,000,000; authorization originally in this bill $7,800,000; amount to complete authorization for these projects $58,250,000. The

Summary of estimate for immediate and future development of facilities at proposed United States naval bases in British possessions — Revised Feb. 17, 1941

	IMMEDIATE		FUTURE	TOTAL
	$50,000,000 Program	Title VI Estimates		
Naval air station, Newfoundland	$15,450,000	$1,600,000	$3,260,000	$20,310,000
Naval air station and protected anchorage, Bermuda . . .	10,150,000	1,100,000	18,390,000	29,640,000
Naval air station and protected anchorage, Trinidad . . .	12,755,000	5,100,000	32,100,000	49,955,000
Naval air station, British Guiana	1,800,000	——	——	1,800,000
Naval air station, Jamaica .	2,750,000	——	4,500,000	7,250,000
Naval air station, Antigua . .	2,920,000	——	——	2,920,000
Naval air station, St. Lucia .	1,625,000	——	——	1,625,000
Naval air station, Bahamas (temporarily deferred) . .	2,550,000	——	——	2,550,000
Total	50,000,000	7,800,000	58,250,000	116,050,000

---

[1] *Authorizing the Secretary of the Navy to Proceed with the Construction of Certain Public Works . . . Report to accompany H.R. 3325* (House Report No. 85, 77th Cong., 1st sess.).

committee are of the opinion that the appropriations for the total estimated cost of these bases should be authorized at this time rather than in piecemeal fashion.

In most cases the appropriations authorized would be for the extension of shore activities already in existence, and in those cases the breakdown of contemplated expenditures is self-explanatory. The committee have deemed it wise, however, to explain further the situation with respect to those activities being established, or to those where the contemplated expenditure is sufficiently great to modify the character or radically increase the importance of the activity.

For military reasons, the exact nature of the expenditures at the bases being acquired from Great Britain is not given in this report. The table on p. 702, however, shows the total estimated expenditures at each base.

It has occurred to the committee that although the recent transfer of certain of our destroyers to Great Britain in exchange for leases on certain land has to all intents and purposes been consummated, this exchange has not yet been sanctioned by the Congress, and therefore authorizations for appropriations for naval air stations not authorized by the Congress might not be in order. For this reason the committee have amended the bill to authorize the establishment of naval air stations at the places leased from Great Britain, the effect of which will be congressional ratification of the exchange.

. . . .

NAVAL STATION, TUTUILA, SAMOA

With the rapid development of aircraft, Samoa is assuming increasing importance in the strategy of the Pacific. Generally speaking it is a sort of South Pacific crossroads, lying close to the direct route from Hawaii to New Zealand and Australia, and from Panama to Australia. It is 2,300 miles from Hawaii, 2,400 miles from Sydney, and 2,500 miles from Auckland.

Samoa was established as a naval station by Executive order in 1900 and since that time has continued to be administered under the jurisdiction of the Navy Department. At the present time it has no defenses or aircraft facilities. The bill under consideration proposes to authorize the construction of limited aviation and defense facilities at Samoa. The proposed authorization of $8,100,000 represents the estimated amount to complete the project.

At the present time we have in existence or in process of construction a string of aviation and light-force bases extending from Kodiak and

Unalaska southward through Midway, Oahu, Johnston Island, Palmyra Island, together with a Pan American Airways base at Canton Island. The proposed development of aircraft facilities at Samoa will complete this defensive system, and thereby permit the establishment of air patrols to safeguard our lines of communication throughout the entire area.

Samoa will also provide a base for the operation of surface craft in protection of our line of communications, and a safe refuge for merchant vessels operating in this area should raiders become active in the South Pacific.

NAVAL STATION, GUAM

Guam is rapidly assuming greater importance as an air terminal for trans-Pacific travel. If and when the Philippines become an independent nation, Guam would then become the western terminal of our commercial air lines — the Grand Central Station, so to speak, in the Western Pacific, for transfers to Japan, China, the Philippines, Dutch East Indies, and all points beyond.

At the present time harbor facilities are practically nonexistent, and heavy swells at times prevent safe take-off by heavily loaded seaplanes. The purpose of this authorization is to provide a small breakwater, to remove coral heads from the seaplane runways, and to dredge a channel through the reef by which vessels may enter the inner lagoon and unload cargo in safety.

The attention of the House is particularly invited to the fact that this authorization contains no items of a military nature, other than provisions for certain passive defense features, such as bombproofing; and that the more extensive development of Guam, as recommended by the Hepburn board,[1] and previously debated by the Congress, is not included herein.

FLEET OPERATING FACILITIES — SECURITY OF FLEET ANCHORAGE — VIEQUES, P. R.

There is an urgent need for the development of a naval base in the Caribbean area, strategically located, and capable of providing ample and secure anchorage to the United States Fleet. No such base now exists. Guantanamo and San Juan are small, and incapable of development to the required extent.

After careful consideration and thorough investigation of the available sites, the Navy Department has recommended a location on Vieques Sound, at the southeastern end of Puerto Rico, as being the most desirable.

[1] See n. 2, p. 705.

This area, the most easterly possession of the United States, forms the keystone of the Caribbean arch. It is centrally located with respect not only to the island chain forming the outer rim of the Caribbean, but also to the line of communication from the United States to South America. It is approximately equidistant from the Azores and Cape Verde Islands, and dominates the approaches to the Panama Canal and to the southeastern portion of the United States. The strategic location of Vieques is illustrated by the following table of distances:

	Miles
Vieques to New York	1,422
to Para, Brazil	1,018
to Canal Zone	1,600
to Guantanamo	584
to Trinidad	512
to Azores	2,278
to Cape Verde Islands	2,200
to Pernambuco, Brazil	2,250
to St. Johns, Newfoundland	1,890

Construction of a drydock here has previously been authorized, and the ultimate development will require the installation of minimum facilities for fleet supply, repair of battle damage, and the construction of landing fields for carrier aircraft.

(2) *Authorizations for Naval Establishments Outside of the United States*

The Navy Department, Bureau of Yards and Docks, has charge of constructing public works for naval purposes. The Bureau of the Budget reported its expenditure for the fiscal year 1940 at $64,398,550 and the estimate for 1941 at $268,128,475. The increase indicates the expansion taking place both in providing for larger forces and for strategic developments.

Additions to naval establishments for the national defense program called for enlargement of facilities to take care of increased men and matériel and preparation of establishments more particularly of a strategic character. Establishments outside of the continental United States are of the latter type. A comprehensive examination of such facilities and their requirements was provided for in sec. 10(a) of the act of May 17, 1938 [1] and the Statutory Board on Submarine, Destroyer, Mine and Naval Air Bases, 1938, of which Rear Admiral Andrew J. Hepburn was senior member, rendered its report to the Secretary of the Navy, December 1, 1938.[2]

Public Laws 21 and 22, both approved March 23, 1941, carried appropriations for new construction amounting to about $350,000,000 as compared with a budget estimate of $268,000,000. So much of the Acts as relates to construction outside of the United States proper is given as an indication of the extent of naval establishments.

[1] *Documents, I, 1938–39*, p. 509.

[2] *Report on Need of Additional Naval Bases to Defend the Coasts of the United States, its Territories and Possessions. Letter of the Secretary of the Navy transmitting Report* (H. Doc. No. 65, 76th Cong., 1st sess.).

(*a*) *An Act to Authorize the Secretary of the Navy to Proceed with the Construction of Certain Public Works, and for Other Purposes, Approved March 23, 1941, 11 a.m., E.S.T.*[1]

[Excerpt]

Be it enacted by the Senate and House of Representatives of the United States of America in Congress assembled, That the Secretary of the Navy is hereby authorized to proceed with the construction of the following public works projects, with which shall be included the authority to acquire land, at a cost not to exceed the amount stated after each item enumerated:

Naval Ammunition Depot, Oahu, Hawaii: Additional ammunition storage facilities, including purchase of land, $815,000.

Naval Air Station, Kaneohe Bay, Hawaii: Seaplane hangar, $773,000.

Naval Air Station, Midway Island: Seaplane hangar, $741,783.

Naval Air Station, San Juan, Puerto Rico: Quarters and accessories for bachelor officers, $200,000. Additional aviation facilities, including buildings and accessories and breakwater, $972,000.

Naval Air Station, Johnston Island: Additional aviation facilities, including buildings and accessories and equipment, $3,480,000.

Naval Air Station, Kaneohe Bay, Hawaii: Additional aviation facilities, including buildings and accessories and equipment, $3,446,500.

Naval Air Station, Kodiak, Alaska: Additional aviation facilities, including buildings and accessories and equipment, $5,266,500.

Naval Air Station, Palmyra Island: Additional aviation facilities, including buildings and accessories and equipment, $3,489,000.

Naval Air Station, Pearl Harbor, Hawaii: Additional aviation facilities, including buildings and accessories and the development of outlying fields, $4,395,000.

Naval Air Station, Sitka, Alaska: Additional aviation facilities, including buildings and accessories and equipment, $4,305,000.

Naval Air Station, Unalaska, Alaska: Additional aviation facilities, including buildings and accessories and equipment, $5,030,000.

(*b*) *An Act to Authorize the Secretary of the Navy to Proceed with the Construction of Certain Public Works, and for Other Purposes, Approved March 23, 1941, 12 m., E.S.T.*[2]

[Excerpt]

Be it enacted by the Senate and House of Representatives of the United States of America in Congress assembled, That the Secretary of the Navy

[1] Public Law 21, 77th Cong.; originating as H. R. 3155 from Committee on Naval Affairs, February 18, 1941; House Report No. 115; Senate Report No. 96; House (conference) Report No. 277.

[2] Public Law 22, 77th Cong.; originating as H.R. 3325 from Committee on Naval Affairs, February 17, 1941; House Report No. 85; Senate Report No. 72; House (conference) Report No. 278.

is hereby authorized to establish or develop the following shore activities by the construction of the public works projects hereinafter indicated at a cost not to exceed the amount stated after each item enumerated:

Navy Yard, Pearl Harbor, Hawaii: Housing and messing facilities for crews of ships undergoing overhaul, repair, and fitting out, improvement of water supply, bombproofed break-down power supply and extension of storage facilities, $6,827,000.

Naval station, Guam: Fleet operating facilities, additional power, recreational facilities, and bombproofed shelters for communication and personnel, $4,700,000.

Naval station, Guantanamo, Cuba: Additional fleet operating facilities, bombproofed shelters for communication and personnel, and limited ship repair facilities, $5,747,500.

Naval station, Tutuila, Samoa: Expansion of naval station facilities, including buildings and accessories and the development of defense facilities, including housing, landplane and seaplane operating facilities, and acquisition of land, $8,100,000.

Naval operating base, Balboa, Canal Zone: Fleet operating and repair facilities, including buildings and accessories, Balboa and Cristobal, $2,765,000.

Submarine operating facilities, Balboa, Canal Zone: Additional submarine operating facilities, including buildings and accessories, piers, and dredging, $1,855,000.

Submarine base, Charlotte Amalie, Virgin Islands: Additional submarine operating facilities, including buildings and accessories, $1,270,000.

Submarine base, Coco Solo, Canal Zone: Additional submarine operating facilities, including buildings and accessories, $1,010,000.

Submarine base, Kodiak, Alaska: Submarine operating and limited repair facilities, including piers and buildings and accessories, $4,002,000.

Submarine base, Midway Island: Submarine operating and limited repair facilities, including piers and buildings and accessories, $4,115,000.

Submarine base, Pearl Harbor, Hawaii: Storehouse and housing for submarine training devices, $125,000.

Naval air station, Sitka, Alaska: Surface craft berthing facilities, including extension of pier, dredging, and storage facilities, $592,000.

Naval air station, Unalaska, Alaska: Surface craft berthing facilities, including piers and storehouse, $1,050,000.

Tenth Naval District, San Juan, Puerto Rico: Surface craft operating facilities, including buildings and accessories, berthing, and housing for personnel, $737,500.

Fleet operating facilities — Security of fleet anchorage, Vieques, Puerto Rican area: Protected fleet anchorage, including breakwaters, dredging, development of limited repair facilities, and buildings and accessories, $35,000,000.

Naval air station, Coco Solo, Canal Zone: Additional aviation facilities, including buildings and accessories, $450,000.

Naval air station, Kaneohe Bay, Hawaii: Additional aviation facilities, including buildings and accessories and equipment, $1,014,500.

Naval air station, Kodiak, Alaska: Additional aviation facilities, including buildings and accessories and equipment, $3,077,500.

Naval air station, San Juan, Puerto Rico: Additional aviation facilities, including buildings and accessories and breakwater, $1,575,000.

Naval air station, Sitka, Alaska: Additional aviation facilities, including buildings and accessories and equipment, $499,000.

Naval air station, Unalaska, Alaska: Additional aviation facilities, including buildings and accessories and equipment, $4,086,500.

Naval air station, Wake Island: Additional aviation facilities, including buildings and accessories and equipment and the development of entrance channel, $2,954,500.

Naval air stations, Trinidad, Newfoundland, Bermuda, British Guiana, Jamaica, Antigua, Saint Lucia, and the Bahama Islands: Aviation facilities, including buildings and accessories, $66,050,000.

Naval hospital, Balboa, Canal Zone: Development of temporary hospital facilities, including buildings and accessories, $500,000.

Naval hospital, Coco Solo, Canal Zone: Extension of hospital facilities, including buildings and accessories, $700,000.

Naval hospital, Guantanamo, Cuba: Additional hospital facilities, including buildings and accessories, and quarters for corpsmen and nurses, $610,000.

Naval hospital, Pearl Harbor, Hawaii: Development of hospital facilities, including buildings and accessories, and acquisition of land, $2,600,000.

General: Additional underground fuel storage facilities at various locations outside continental limits of the United States, $5,000,000.

Marine barracks at Parris Island, Pearl Harbor, Quantico, and San Diego: Additional housing, storage, and recreation facilities, including buildings and accessories and facilities, $3,500,000.

Tenth Naval District: Acquisition, improvement, and development of Puerto Rican drydock, including berthing and limited repair facilities, $2,500,000; bombproofing communication centers, bombproofed shelters for personnel, and recreation facilities, $650,000.

C. Executive Orders Establishing Naval Defensive Sea Areas Around and Naval Airspace Reservations Over Certain Bays and Islands, February 14, and March 22, 1941 [1]

(1) Kiska and Unalaska, etc.

No. 8680. By virtue of the authority vested in me by the provisions of section 44 of the Criminal Code, as amended (U.S.C., title 18, sec. 96), and section 4 of the Air Commerce Act approved May 20, 1926 (44 Stat. 570, U.S.C., title 49, sec. 174), the territorial waters between the extreme high-water marks and [2] the three-mile marine boundaries surrounding the islands of Kiska and Unalaska are hereby established and reserved as naval defensive sea areas for purposes of national defense, such areas to be known, respectively, as "Kiska Island Naval

[1] Executive Orders Nos. 8680, 8681, 8682, 8683, 8684, 6 Fed. Reg., p. 1014.

[2] Correction made in Nos. 8680, 8682 and 8683 by Executive Order No. 8729, April 2, 1941 (6 Fed. Reg., p. 1791).

Defensive Sea Area," and "Unalaska Island Naval Defensive Area"; and the airspaces over the said territorial waters and islands are hereby set apart and reserved as naval airspace reservations for purposes of national defense, such reservations to be known, respectively, as "Kiska Island Naval Airspace Reservation," and "Unalaska Island Naval Airspace Reservation."

No. 8681: . . . The territorial waters within Kaneohe Bay between extreme high-water mark and the sea and in and about the entrance channel within a line bearing northeast true extending three nautical miles from Kaoio Point, a line bearing northeast true extending four nautical miles from Kapoho Point, and a line joining the seaward extremities of the two above-described bearing lines, are hereby established and reserved as a naval defensive sea area for purposes of national defense. . . .

No. 8682: . . . The territorial waters between the extreme high-water marks and the three-mile marine boundaries surrounding the islands of Palmyra, Johnston, Midway, Wake, and Kingman Reef, in the Pacific Ocean, are hereby established and reserved as naval defensive sea areas for purposes of national defense. . . .

No. 8683: . . . The territorial waters between the extreme high-water marks and the three-mile marine boundaries surrounding the islands of Rose, Tutuila, and Guam, in the Pacific Ocean, are hereby established and reserved as naval defensive sea areas for purposes of national defense. . . .

No. 8684: . . . The territorial waters between the extreme high-water mark and the three-mile marine boundary surrounding the island of Culebra, Puerto Rico, are hereby established and reserved as a naval defensive sea area for purposes of national defense. . . .

No. 8717: [1] . . . The territorial waters between extreme high-water mark and the three-mile marine boundary adjacent to the eastern portion of Kodiak Island, Alaska, in and about Women's Bay to the westward within a line bearing true north and south tangent to the eastern extremity of High Island, are hereby set apart and reserved as a naval defensive sea area for purposes of the national defense, such area to be known as "Kodiak Island Naval Defensive Sea Area."

No. 8718: [1] . . . The territorial waters within Subic Bay, Philippine Islands, between extreme high-water mark and the sea and in and about the entrance channel within a line bearing true southwest extending three nautical miles from Panibatujan Point, a line bearing true southwest extending three nautical miles from Sanpaloc Point, and a line joining the seaward extremities of the above two bearing lines, are hereby set apart and reserved as a naval defensive sea area for purposes of the national defense, such area to be known as "Subic Bay Naval Defensive Sea Area"; and the airspace over the said territorial waters and over the Subic Bay Naval Reservation, Olongapo, Philippine Islands, is hereby set apart and reserved as a naval airspace reservation for purposes of the national defense, such reservation to be known as "Subic Bay Naval Airspace Reservation."

[1] 6 *Fed. Reg.*, p. 1621. Executive order dated March 22, 1941.

No. 8749: [1] . . . The territorial waters within Guantanamo Bay, Cuba, between high-water mark and the sea and in and about the entrance channel within a line bearing true south extending three nautical miles from the shore line of the eastern boundary of Guantanamo Naval Reservation, as laid down in the Agreement between the United States of America and the Republic of Cuba signed by the President of Cuba on February 16, 1903, and by the President of the United States on February 23, 1903, a line bearing true south extending three nautical miles from the shore line of the western boundary of said Naval Reservation, and a line joining the seaward extremities of the above two bearing lines, are hereby set apart and reserved as a naval defensive sea area for purposes of the national defense, subject to the right of vessels engaged in Cuban trade to have free passage through the waters as provided for in said agreement, such area to be known as "Guantanamo Bay Naval Defensive Sea Area"; and the airspace over the said territorial waters, and over the Guantanamo Naval Reservation, is hereby set apart and reserved as a naval airspace reservation for purposes of the national defense, such reservation to be known as "Guantanamo Bay Naval Airspace Reservation."

At no time shall any person, other than persons on public vessels of the United States, enter either of the naval defensive sea areas herein set apart and reserved, nor shall any vessel or other craft, other than public vessels of the United States, be navigated into either of said areas, unless authorized by the Secretary of the Navy.

At no time shall any aircraft, other than public aircraft of the United States, be navigated into either of the naval airspace reservations herein set apart and reserved, unless authorized by the Secretary of the Navy.

The provisions of the preceding paragraphs shall be enforced by the Secretary of the Navy, with the cooperation of the local law enforcement officers of the United States and of the Territory of Alaska; and the Secretary of the Navy is hereby authorized to prescribe such regulations as may be necessary to carry out such provisions.

Any person violating any of the provisions of this order relating to the above-named naval defensive sea areas shall be subject to the penalties provided by section 44 of the Criminal Code as amended (U.S.C., title 18, sec. 96), and any person violating any of the provisions of this order relating to the above-named naval airspace reservations shall be subject to the penalties prescribed by the Civil Aeronautics Act of 1938 (52 Stat. 973).

This order shall take effect ninety days after date hereof.

FRANKLIN D. ROOSEVELT

THE WHITE HOUSE
February 14, 1941

[1] 6 *Fed. Reg.*, p. 2252; Executive order dated May 1, 1941.

6. THE DEFENSE AID PROGRAM

A. The "Lend-Lease Act" and Its Enactment

In consequence of the German invasions of foreign countries in April 1940 and following, the demand for active "aid to Britain" became general in the United States. The passive aid which consisted of British purchases in the United States with British funds had accelerated from the outbreak of war in September 1939 and in the summer of 1940 the approaching exhaustion of British exchange resources appeared as a disturbing factor. The exchange of notes of September 2, 1940 (see p. 203) effecting the transfer of destroyers to the United Kingdom and providing for United States acquisition of naval and air bases was well received and pointed to the possibility of further transactions of a cooperative character. A long-standing opposition to intergovernmental and even private loans constituted another factor of psychological importance. Possibilities of further assistance to the democracies within these conditions were the subject of frequent colloquies at the President's press conferences.

On January 10, 1941, a week after the convening of the 77th Congress, the Democratic floor leaders in the House and Senate introduced "a bill further to promote the defense of the United States, and for other purposes," which by chance in the House fell to receive a significant serial number, and became famous as H.R. 1776.[1] Public attention was concentrated on the matter for two months owing to hearings in the two committees and the debates in the House and Senate. In the hearings, the Secretaries of State, Treasury, War and Navy made statements both concerning the form of the bill and its operation. The House Committee on Foreign Affairs and the Senate Committee on Foreign Relations each sent out the bill, amended with a carefully reasoned report concerning its provisions and with minority views of a different and generally critical character. The House committee held hearings on H.R. 1776 from January 15 to 29, 1941[2] and reported it out on January 30[3] to the House of Representatives which amended and passed it on February 8 by a vote of 260 yeas, 165 nays.

The Senate committee held hearings from January 27 to February 11[4] and reported[5] H.R. 1776 with amendments to the Senate on February 13. The debate in the Senate closed with the adoption of some amendments and the passage of the bill itself on March 8 by a vote of 60 yeas, 31 nays. As passed by the Senate, H.R. 1776 embodied 12 amendments not in the text passed by the House. Formal conference proceedings were waived and on March 11 the House by H. Res. 131 agreed to all Senate amendments by a vote of 317 yeas, 71 nays. The act was approved and its machinery set in motion on March 11.

[1] The identic Senate bill was S. 275.

[2] U. S. Congress, House of Representatives, Committee on Foreign Affairs, *Lend-Lease Bill; Hearings* . . . 77th Cong., 1st sess., on H.R. 1776. Washington, 1941. 692 p.

[3] U. S. Congress, House of Representatives, Committee on Foreign Affairs, *Lend-Lease Bill. To Promote the Defense of the United States* . . . *Report to accompany H.R. 1776* (House Report No. 18, 77th Cong., 1st sess.). Minority views printed as part 2 at p. 13–16.

[4] U. S. Congress, Senate, Committee on Foreign Relations, *To Promote the Defense of the United States; Hearings* . . . 77th Cong., 1st sess., on S. 275. Washington, 1941. 914 p. (consolidated print).

[5] —— —— *Promoting the Defense of the United States* . . . *Report to accompany H.R. 1776* (Senate Report No. 45, 77th Cong., 1st sess.). Minority views, printed as part 2.

The Act Further to Promote the Defense of the United States, and for Other Purposes, approved March 11, 1941 (the Lend-Lease Act) empowers the President, "in the interest of national defense," to make available to governments whose defense he deems vital to the defense of the United States "defense articles," as defined; those transactions involving use of public funds are limited by the fund available for that purpose, and the act puts limits upon current expenditures under it. The basic principle of the act meets the conditions envisaged by the terms sanctions, collective security and prevention of aggression.

As the passage of the act raised questions of many different kinds, it is deemed appropriate here to set forth the text at the various stages of its evolution.

(1) *"The Lend-Lease Act."* An Act Further to Promote the Defense of the United States, and for Other Purposes, Approved March 11, 1941 [1]

Be it enacted by the Senate and House of Representatives of the United States of America in Congress assembled, That this Act may be cited as "An Act to Promote the Defense of the United States."

SEC. 2. As used in this Act —

(*a*) The term "defense article" means —

(1) Any weapon, munition, aircraft, vessel, or boat;

(2) Any machinery, facility, tool, material, or supply necessary for the manufacture, production, processing, repair, servicing, or operation of any article described in this subsection;

(3) Any component material or part of or equipment for any article described in this subsection;

(4) Any agricultural, industrial or other commodity or article for defense.

Such term "defense article" includes any article described in this subsection: Manufactured or procured pursuant to section 3, or to which the United States or any foreign government has or hereafter acquires title, possession, or control.

(*b*) The term "defense information" means any plan, specification, design, prototype, or information pertaining to any defense article.

SEC. 3. (*a*) Notwithstanding the provisions of any other law, the President may, from time to time, when he deems it in the interest of national defense, authorize the Secretary of War, the Secretary of the Navy, or the head of any other department or agency of the Government —

(1) To manufacture in arsenals, factories, and shipyards under their jurisdiction, or otherwise procure, to the extent to which funds are made available therefor, or contracts are authorized from time to time

[1] Public Law 11, 77th Cong.; originated as H.R. 1776. See headnote for history.

by the Congress, or both, any defense article for the government of any country whose defense the President deems vital to the defense of the United States.

(2) To sell, transfer title to, exchange, lease, lend, or otherwise dispose of, to any such government any defense article, but no defense article not manufactured or procured under paragraph (1) shall in any way be disposed of under this paragraph, except after consultation with the Chief of Staff of the Army or the Chief of Naval Operations of the Navy, or both. The value of defense articles disposed of in any way under authority of this paragraph, and procured from funds heretofore appropriated, shall not exceed $1,300,000,000. The value of such defense articles shall be determined by the head of the department or agency concerned or such other department, agency or officer as shall be designated in the manner provided in the rules and regulations issued hereunder. Defense articles procured from funds hereafter appropriated to any department or agency of the Government, other than from funds authorized to be appropriated under this Act, shall not be disposed of in any way under authority of this paragraph except to the extent hereafter authorized by the Congress in the Acts appropriating such funds or otherwise.

(3) To test, inspect, prove, repair, outfit, recondition, or otherwise to place in good working order, to the extent to which funds are made available therefor, or contracts are authorized from time to time by the Congress, or both, any defense article for any such government, or to procure any or all such services by private contract.

(4) To communicate to any such government any defense information, pertaining to any defense article furnished to such government under paragraph (2) of this subsection.

(5) To release for export any defense article disposed of in any way under this subsection to any such government.

(b) The terms and conditions upon which any such foreign government receives any aid authorized under subsection (a) shall be those which the President deems satisfactory, and the benefit to the United States may be payment or repayment in kind or property, or any other direct or indirect benefit which the President deems satisfactory.

(c) After June 30, 1943, or after the passage of a concurrrent resolution by the two Houses before June 30, 1943, which declares that the powers conferred by or pursuant to subsection (a) are no longer necessary to promote the defense of the United States, neither the President nor the head of any department or agency shall exercise any of the powers conferred by or pursuant to subsection (a): except that until July 1, 1946, any of such powers may be exercised to the extent necessary to carry out a contract or agreement with such a foreign government made before July 1, 1943, or before the passage of such concurrent resolution, whichever is the earlier.

(d) Nothing in this Act shall be construed to authorize or to permit the authorization of convoying vessels by naval vessels of the United States.

(e) Nothing in this Act shall be construed to authorize or to permit the authorization of the entry of any American vessel into a combat area in violation of section 3 of the Neutrality Act of 1939.

SEC. 4. All contracts or agreements made for the disposition of any defense article or defense information pursuant to section 3 shall contain a clause by which the foreign government undertakes that it will not, without the consent of the President, transfer title to or possession of such defense article or defense information by gift, sale, or otherwise, or permit its use by anyone not an officer, employee, or agent of such foreign government.

SEC. 5. (a) The Secretary of War, the Secretary of the Navy, or the head of any other department or agency of the Government involved shall, when any such defense article or defense information is exported, immediately inform the department or agency designated by the President to administer section 6 of the Act of July 2, 1940 (54 Stat. 714), of the quantities, character, value, terms of disposition, and destination of the article and information so exported.

(b) The President from time to time, but not less frequently than once every ninety days, shall transmit to the Congress a report of operations under this Act except such information as he deems incompatible with the public interest to disclose. Reports provided for under this subsection shall be transmitted to the Secretary of the Senate or the Clerk of the House of Representatives, as the case may be, if the Senate or the House of Representatives, as the case may be, is not in session.

SEC. 6. (a) There is hereby authorized to be appropriated from time to time, out of any money in the Treasury not otherwise appropriated, such amounts as may be necessary to carry out the provisions and accomplish the purposes of this Act.

(b) All money and all property which is converted into money received under section 3 from any government shall, with the approval of the Director of the Budget, revert to the respective appropriation or appropriations out of which funds were expended with respect to the defense article or defense information for which such consideration is received, and shall be available for expenditure for the purpose for which such expended funds were appropriated by law, during the fiscal year in which such funds are received and the ensuing fiscal year; but in no event shall any funds so received be available for expenditure after June 30, 1946.

SEC. 7. The Secretary of War, the Secretary of the Navy, and the head of the department or agency shall in all contracts or agreements for the disposition of any defense article or defense information fully protect the rights of all citizens of the United States who have patent rights in and to any such article or information which is hereby authorized to be disposed of and the payments collected for royalties on such patents shall be paid to the owners and holders of such patents.

SEC. 8. The Secretaries of War and of the Navy are hereby authorized to purchase or otherwise acquire arms, ammunition, and implements of war produced within the jurisdiction of any country to which section 3 is applicable, whenever the President deems such purchase or acquisition to be necessary in the interests of the defense of the United States.

SEC. 9. The President may, from time to time, promulgate such rules and regulations as may be necessary and proper to carry out any of the provisions of this Act; and he may exercise any power or authority conferred on him by this Act through such department, agency, or officer as he shall direct.

SEC. 10. Nothing in this Act shall be construed to change existing law relating to the use of the land and naval forces of the United States, except insofar as such use relates to the manufacture, procurement, and repair of defense articles, the communication of information and other noncombatant purposes enumerated in this Act.

SEC. 11. If any provision of this Act or the application of such provision to any circumstance shall be held invalid, the validity of the remainder of the Act and the applicability of such provision to other circumstances shall not be affected thereby.

(a) *H.R. 1776 as Introduced January 10, 1941, Showing Amendments Proposed by the Committee on Foreign Affairs, House of Representatives, January 30, 1941* [1]

[Omit the part struck through and insert the part printed in italic.]

Be it enacted by the Senate and House of Representatives of the United States of America in Congress assembled, That this Act may be cited as "An Act to Promote the Defense of the United States."

[1] The amendments are explained and the whole bill discussed in House Report No. 18, 77th Cong., 1st sess., which with the minority report of 8 members of the Committee on Foreign Relations was submitted to the Committee of the Whole House on the State of the Union.

SEC. 2. As used in this Act —

(a) The term "defense article" means —

(1) Any weapon, munition, aircraft, vessel, or boat;

(2) Any machinery, facility, tool, material, or supply necessary for the manufacture, production, processing, repair, servicing, or operation of any article described in this subsection;

(3) Any component material or part of or equipment for any article described in this subsection;

(4) Any other commodity or article for defense.

Such term "defense article" includes any article described in this subsection: Manufactured or procured pursuant to section 3, or to which the United States or any foreign government has or hereafter acquires title, possession, or control.

(b) The term "defense information" means any plan, specification, design, prototype, or information pertaining to any defense article.

SEC. 3. (a) Notwithstanding the provisions of any other law, the President may, from time to time, when he deems it in the interest of national defense, authorize the Secretary of War, the Secretary of the Navy, or the head of any other department or agency of the Government —

(1) To manufacture in arsenals, factories, and shipyards under their jurisdiction, or otherwise procure, any defense article for the government of any country whose defense the President deems vital to the defense of the United States.

(2) To sell, transfer, exchange, lease, lend, or otherwise dispose of, to any such government any defense ~~article~~ *article, but no defense article not manufactured or procured under paragraph (1) shall in any way be disposed of under this paragraph, except after consultation with the Chief of Staff of the Army or the Chief of Naval Operations of the Navy, or both.*

(3) To test, inspect, prove, repair, outfit, recondition, or otherwise to place in good working order any defense article for any such government.

(4) To communicate to any such government any defense information, pertaining to any defense article furnished to such government under paragraph (2) of this subsection.

(5) To release for export any defense article to any such government.

(b) The terms and conditions upon which any such foreign government receives any aid authorized under subsection (a) shall be those which the President deems satisfactory, and the benefit to the United States may be payment or repayment in kind or property, or any other direct or indirect benefit which the President deems satisfactory.

(c) *Neither the President nor the head of any department or agency shall, after June 30, 1943, exercise any of the powers conferred by or pursuant to subsection (a), except to carry out a contract or agreement with such a government made before July 1, 1943.*

(d) *Nothing in this Act shall be construed to authorize or to permit the authorization of convoying vessels by naval vessels of the United States.*

SEC. 4. All contracts or agreements made for the disposition of any defense article or defense information pursuant to section 3 shall contain a clause by which the foreign government undertakes that it will not, without the consent of the President, transfer title to or possession of such defense article or defense information by gift, sale, or otherwise, or permit its use by anyone not an officer, employee, or agent of such foreign government.

SEC. 5. (*a*) The Secretary of War, the Secretary of the Navy, or the head of any other department or agency of the Government involved shall, when any such defense article or defense information is exported immediately inform the department or agency designated by the President to administer section 6 of the Act of July 2, 1940 (54 Stat. 714), of the quantities, character, value, terms of disposition, and destination of the article and information so exported.

(*b*) *The President from time to time, but not less frequently than once every ninety days, shall transmit to the Congress a report of operations under this Act except such information as he deems incompatible with the public interest to disclose. Reports provided for under this subsection shall be transmitted to the Secretary of the Senate or the Clerk of the House of Representatives, as the case may be, if the Senate or the House of Representatives, as the case may be, is not in session.*

SEC. 6. (*a*) There is hereby authorized to be appropriated from time to time, out of any money in the Treasury not otherwise appropriated, such amounts as may be necessary to carry out the provisions and accomplish the purposes of this Act.

(*b*) All money and all property which is converted into money received under section 3 from any government shall, with the approval of the Director of the Budget, revert to the respective appropriation or appropriations out of which funds were expended with respect to the defense article or defense information for which such consideration is received, and shall be available for expenditure for the purpose for which such expended funds were appropriated by law, during the fiscal year in which such funds are received and the ensuing fiscal year.

SEC. 7. The Secretary of War, the Secretary of the Navy, and the head of the department or agency shall in all contracts or agreements for the disposition of any defense article or defense information fully protect the rights of all citizens of the United States who have patent rights in and to any such article or information which is hereby authorized to be disposed of and the payments collected for royalties on such patents shall be paid to the owners and holders of such patents.

SEC. 8. The Secretaries of War and of the Navy are hereby authorized to purchase or otherwise acquire arms, ammunition, and implements of war produced within the jurisdiction of any country to which section 3 is applicable, whenever the President deems such purchase or acquisition to be necessary in the interests of the defense of the United States.

SEC. 9. The President may, from time to time, promulgate such rules and regulations as may be necessary and proper to carry out any of the provisions of this Act; and he may exercise any power or authority conferred on him by this Act through such department, agency, or officer as he shall direct.

(*b*) *H.R. 1776 as Passed by the House February 8, 1941, Showing Amendments Reported to the Senate by Its Committee on Foreign Relations, February 13, 1941* [1]

[Omit the part struck through and insert the part printed in italic.]

Be it enacted by the Senate and House of Representatives of the United States of America in Congress assembled, That this Act may be cited as "An Act to Promote the Defense of the United States."

[1] The amendments were described and the bill analyzed in Senate Report No. 45, 77th Cong., 1st sess. The minority views of one member of the committee, printed as part 2 of the report, discussed questions of general policy.

SEC. 2. As used in this Act —

(a) The term "defense article" means —

(1) Any weapon, munition, aircraft, vessel, or boat;

(2) Any machinery, facility, tool, material, or supply necessary for the manufacture, production, processing, repair, servicing, or operation of any article described in this subsection;

(3) Any component material or part of or equipment for any article described in this subsection;

(4) Any other commodity or article for defense.

Such term "defense article" includes any article described in this subsection: Manufactured or procured pursuant to section 3, or to which the United States or any foreign government has or hereafter acquires title, possession, or control.

(b) The term "defense information" means any plan, specification, design, prototype, or information pertaining to any defense article.

SEC. 3. (a) Notwithstanding the provisions of any other law, the President may, from time to time, when he deems it in the interest of national defense, *to the extent to which funds are made available or contracts are from time to time authorized by Congress*, authorize the Secretary of War, the Secretary of the Navy, or the head of any other department or agency of the Government —

(1) To manufacture in arsenals, factories, and shipyards under their jurisdiction, or otherwise procure, any defense article for the government of any country whose defense the President deems vital to the defense of the United States.

(2) To sell, transfer, exchange, lease, lend, or otherwise dispose of, to any such government any defense article, but no defense article not manufactured or procured under paragraph (1) shall in any way be disposed of under this paragraph, except after consultation with the Chief of Staff of the Army or the Chief of Naval Operations of the Navy, or both. The value of defense articles disposed of in any way under authority of this paragraph, and procured from funds heretofore appropriated, shall not exceed $1,300,000,000.

(3) To test, inspect, prove, repair, outfit, recondition, or otherwise to place in good working order any defense article for any such government.

(4) To communicate to any such government any defense information, pertaining to any defense article furnished to such government under paragraph (2) of this subsection.

(5) To release for export any defense article to any such government.

(b) The terms and conditions upon which any such foreign government receives any aid authorized under subsection (a) shall be those which the President deems satisfactory, and the benefit to the United States may be payment or repayment in kind or property, or any other direct or indirect benefit which the President deems satisfactory.

~~(c) Neither the President nor the head of any department or agency shall, after June 30, 1943, exercise any of the powers conferred by or pursuant to subsection (a), nor shall such powers be exercised if terminated by a concurrent resolution by both Houses of the Congress, except that until July 1, 1946, such powers may be exercised to the extent necessary to carry out a contract or agreement with such a government made before July 1, 1943.~~

(c) *After June 30, 1943, or after the passage of a concurrent resolution by the two*

Houses before June 30, 1943, which declares that the powers conferred by or pursuant to subsection (a) are no longer necessary to promote the defense of the United States, neither the President nor the head of any department or agency shall exercise any of the powers conferred by or pursuant to subsection (a); except that until July 1, 1946, any of such powers may be exercised to the extent necessary to carry out a contract or agreement with such a foreign government made before July 1, 1943, or before the passage of such concurrent resolution, whichever is the earlier.

(d) Nothing in this Act shall be construed to authorize or to permit the authorization of convoying vessels by naval vessels of the United States.

(e) Nothing in this Act shall be construed to authorize or to permit the authorization of the entry of any American vessel into a combat area in violation of section 3 of the Neutrality Act of 1939.

SEC. 4. All contracts or agreements made for the disposition of any defense article or defense information pursuant to section 3 shall contain a clause by which the foreign government undertakes that it will not, without the consent of the President, transfer title to or possession of such defense article or defense information by gift, sale, or otherwise, or permit its use by anyone not an officer, employee, or agent of such foreign government.

SEC. 5. (a) The Secretary of War, the Secretary of the Navy, or the head of any other department or agency of the Government involved shall, when any such defense article or defense information is exported, immediately inform the department or agency designated by the President to administer section 6 of the Act of July 2, 1940 (54 Stat. 714), of the quantities, character, value, terms of disposition, and destination of the article and information so exported.

(b) The President from time to time, but not less frequently than once every ninety days, shall transmit to the Congress a report of operations under this Act except such information as he deems incompatible with the public interest to disclose. Reports provided for under this subsection shall be transmitted to the Secretary of the Senate or the Clerk of the House of Representatives, as the case may be, if the Senate or the House of Representatives, as the case may be, is not in session.

SEC. 6. (a) There is hereby authorized to be appropriated from time to time, out of any money in the Treasury not otherwise appropriated, such amounts as may be necessary to carry out the provisions and accomplish the purposes of this Act.

(b) All money and all property which is converted into money received under section 3 from any government shall, with the approval of the Director of the Budget, revert to the respective appropriation or appropriations out of which funds were expended with respect to the defense article or defense information for which such consideration is received, and shall be available for expenditure for the purpose for which such expended funds were appropriated by law, during the fiscal year in which such funds are received and the ensuing fiscal year; *but in no event shall any funds so received be available for expenditure after June 30, 1946.*

SEC. 7. The Secretary of War, the Secretary of the Navy, and the head of the department or agency shall in all contracts or agreements for the disposition of any defense article or defense information fully protect the rights of all citizens of the United States who have patent rights in and to any such article or information which is hereby authorized to be disposed of and the payments collected for royalties on such patents shall be paid to the owners and holders of such patents.

SEC. 8. The Secretaries of War and of the Navy are hereby authorized to purchase or otherwise acquire arms, ammunition, and implements of war produced within the jurisdiction of any country to which section 3 is applicable, whenever the President deems such purchase or acquisition to be necessary in the interests of the defense of the United States.

SEC. 9. The President may, from time to time, promulgate such rules and regulations as may be necessary and proper to carry out any of the provisions of this Act; and he may exercise any power or authority conferred on him by this Act through such department, agency, or officer as he shall direct.

Passed the House of Representatives February 8, 1941.

Attest: SOUTH TRIMBLE,
                                                                            Clerk
                                          By H. NEWLIN MEGILL

(c) H. R. 1776 as Passed by the Senate March 8, 1941, and Agreed to by the House of Representatives in Adopting H. Res. 131 on March 11, 1941 [1]

[Amendments of the Senate printed in italic and numbered.]

Be it enacted by the Senate and House of Representatives of the United States of America in Congress assembled, That this Act may be cited as "An Act to Promote the Defense of the United States."

SEC. 2. As used in this Act —

(a) The term "defense article" means —

(1) Any weapon, munition, aircraft, vessel, or boat;

(2) Any machinery, facility, tool, material, or supply necessary for the manufacture, production, processing, repair, servicing, or operation of any article described in this subsection;

(3) Any component material or part of or equipment for any article described in this subsection;

(4) Any (*1*) *agricultural, industrial or* other commodity or article for defense.

Such term "defense article" includes any article described in this subsection: Manufactured or procured pursuant to section 3, or to which the United States or any foreign government has or hereafter acquires title, possession, or control.

(b) The term "defense information" means any plan, specification, design prototype, or information pertaining to any defense article.

SEC. 3. (a) Notwithstanding the provisions of any other law, the President may, from time to time, when he deems it in the interest of national defense, authorize the Secretary of War, the Secretary of the Navy, or the head of any other department or agency of the Government —

(1) To manufacture in arsenals, factories, and shipyards under their jurisdiction, or otherwise procure, (*2*) *to the extent to which funds are made available therefor, or contracts are authorized from time to time by the Congress,*

---

[1] The Senate's passage of the act, on calendar day March 8, is recorded as of the legislative day February 13. The Senate vote was 60 yeas, 31 nays; the House vote (on H. Res. 131) was 317 yeas, 71 nays.

or both, any defense article for the government of any country whose defense the President deems vital to the defense of the United States.

(2) To sell, transfer (3) *title to*, exchange, lease, lend, or otherwise dispose of, to any such government any defense article, but no defense article not manufactured or procured under paragraph (1) shall in any way be disposed of under this paragraph, except after consultation with the Chief of Staff of the Army or the Chief of Naval Operations of the Navy, or both. The value of defense articles disposed of in any way under authority of this paragraph, and procured from funds heretofore appropriated, shall not exceed $1,300,000,000. (4) *The value of such defense articles shall be determined by the head of the department or agency concerned or such other department, agency or officer as shall be designated in the manner provided in the rules and regulations issued hereunder.* (5) *Defense articles procured from funds hereafter appropriated to any department or agency of the Government, other than from funds authorized to be appropriated under this Act, shall not be disposed of in any way under authority of this paragraph except to the extent hereafter authorized by the Congress in the Acts appropriating such funds or otherwise.*

(3) To test, inspect, prove, repair, outfit, recondition, or otherwise to place in good working order (6), *to the extent to which funds are made available therefor, or contracts are authorized from time to time by the Congress, or both,* any defense article for any such government (7), *or to procure any or all such services by private contract.*

(4) To communicate to any such government any defense information, pertaining to any defense article furnished to such government under paragraph (2) of this subsection.

(5) To release for export any defense article (8) *disposed of in any way under this subsection* to any such government.

(*b*) The terms and conditions upon which any such foreign government receives any aid authorized under subsection (*a*) shall be those which the President deems satisfactory, and the benefit to the United States may be payment or repayment in kind or property, or any other direct or indirect benefit which the President deems satisfactory.

(9) ~~(c) Neither the President nor the head of any department or agency shall, after June 30, 1943, exercise any of the powers conferred by or pursuant to subsection (a), nor shall such powers be exercised if terminated by a concurrent resolution by both Houses of the Congress, except that until July 1, 1946, such powers may be exercised to the extent necessary to carry out a contract or agreement with such a government made before July 1, 1943.~~

(*c*) *After June 30, 1943, or after the passage of a concurrent resolution by the two Houses before June 30, 1943, which declares that the powers conferred by or pursuant to subsection (a) are no longer necessary to promote the defense of the United States, neither the President nor the head of any department or agency shall exercise any of the powers conferred by or pursuant to subsection (a); except that until July 1, 1946, any of such powers may be exercised to the extent necessary to carry out a contract or agreement with such a foreign government made before July 1, 1943, or before the passage of such concurrent resolution, whichever is the earlier.*

(*d*) Nothing in this Act shall be construed to authorize or to permit the authorization of convoying vessels by naval vessels of the United States.

(*e*) Nothing in this Act shall be construed to authorize or to permit the authorization of the entry of any American vessel into a combat area in violation of section 3 of the Neutrality Act of 1939.

SEC. 4. All contracts or agreements made for the disposition of any defense article or defense information pursuant to section 3 shall contain a clause by which the foreign government undertakes that it will not, without the consent of the President, transfer title to or possession of such defense article or defense information by gift, sale, or otherwise, or permit its use by anyone not an officer, employee, or agent of such foreign government.

SEC. 5. (a) The Secretary of War, the Secretary of the Navy, or the head of any other department or agency of the Government involved shall, when any such defense article or defense information is exported, immediately inform the department or agency designated by the President to administer section 6 of the Act of July 2, 1940 (54 Stat. 714), of the quantities, character, value, terms of disposition, and destination of the article and information so exported.

(b) The President from time to time, but not less frequently than once every ninety days, shall transmit to the Congress a report of operations under this Act except such information as he deems incompatible with the public interest to disclose. Reports provided for under this subsection shall be transmitted to the Secretary of the Senate or the Clerk of the House of Representatives, as the case may be, if the Senate or the House of Representatives, as the case may be, is not in session.

SEC. 6. (a) There is hereby authorized to be appropriated from time to time, out of any money in the Treasury not otherwise appropriated, such amounts as may be necessary to carry out the provisions and accomplish the purposes of this Act.

(b) All money and all property which is converted into money received under section 3 from any government shall, with the approval of the Director of the Budget, revert to the respective appropriation or appropriations out of which funds were expended with respect to the defense article or defense information for which such consideration is received, and shall be available for expenditure for the purpose for which such expended funds were appropriated by law, during the fiscal year in which such funds are received and the ensuing fiscal year (10); *but in no event shall any funds so received be available for expenditure after June 30, 1946.*

SEC. 7. The Secretary of War, the Secretary of the Navy, and the head of the department or agency shall in all contracts or agreements for the disposition of any defense article or defense information fully protect the rights of all citizens of the United States who have patent rights in and to any such article or information which is hereby authorized to be disposed of and the payments collected for royalties on such patents shall be paid to the owners and holders of such patents.

SEC. 8. The Secretaries of War and of the Navy are hereby authorized to purchase or otherwise acquire arms, ammunition, and implements of war produced within the jurisdiction of any country to which section 3 is applicable, whenever the President deems such purchase or acquisition to be necessary in the interests of the defense of the United States.

SEC. 9. The President may, from time to time, promulgate such rules and regulations as may be necessary and proper to carry out any of the provisions of this Act; and he may exercise any power or authority conferred on him by this Act through such department, agency, or officer as he shall direct.

(11) SEC. 10. *Nothing in this Act shall be construed to change existing law relating to the use of the land and naval forces of the United States, except insofar as such use relates to the manufacture, procurement and repair of defense articles, the communication of information and other noncombatant purposes enumerated in this Act.*

(12) SEC. 11. *If any provision of this Act or the application of such provision to any circumstance shall be held invalid, the validity of the remainder of the Act and applicability of such provision to other circumstances shall not be affected thereby.*

Passed the House of Representatives February 8, 1941.

Attest:

SOUTH TRIMBLE,
Clerk

By H. NEWLIN MEGILL

Passed the Senate with amendments March 8 (legislative day, February 13) 1941.

Attest:

EDWIN A. HALSEY,
Secretary

B. "Defense Aid Supplemental Appropriation Act, 1941"

The President transmitted a budget estimate of $7,000,000,000 to the Congress on March 12, 1941, to carry out the provisions of the Lend-Lease Act, approved the previous day. The Subcommittee on Deficiencies of the House Committee on Appropriations held hearings on the estimate March 13–15, the principal witnesses being the Secretaries of State, War, and Navy, the Director of the Bureau of the Budget, and the Chairman of the Office of Production Management. The Committee on Appropriations reported H.R. 4050 on March 18 and the House of Representatives passed it March 19. It was received by the Senate under order on March 17, referred to the Senate Committee on Appropriations, and rushed through all stages without amendment. The act was approved March 27 at 10 : 50 A.M.

(1) *The President (Roosevelt) to the Speaker of the House of Representatives (Rayburn), March 12, 1941* [1]

THE WHITE HOUSE,
Washington, March 12, 1941.

HON. SAM RAYBURN,
Speaker, House of Representatives,
Washington, D. C.

MY DEAR MR. SPEAKER: This Nation has felt that it was imperative to the security of America, that we encourage the democracies' heroic resistance to aggressions, by not only maintaining but also increasing the flow of material assistance from this country. Therefore, the Congress has enacted and I have signed H.R. 1776.

Through this legislation our country has determined to do its full part in creating an adequate arsenal of democracy. This great arsenal will

[1] House Doc. No. 135, 77th Cong., 1st sess.

be here in this country. It will be a bulwark of our own defense. It will be the source of the tools of defense for all democracies who are fighting to preserve themselves against aggression.

While the defense equipment produced under H.R. 1776 remains under the control of the United States until it is ready for disposition, it is the fixed policy of this Government to make for democracies every gun, plane, and munition of war that we possibly can.

To accomplish these objectives I am transmitting an estimate in the amount of $7,000,000,000, the details of which are set forth in the accompanying letter [1] from the Director of the Bureau of the Budget. I strongly urge the immediate enactment of this appropriation.

Respectfully,

FRANKLIN D. ROOSEVELT

(2) *Conditions and Extent of Aid. Report from House Committee on Appropriations, March 18, 1941* [2]

[Excerpt]

The committee invites attention to the remarks of the Secretary of State at the opening of the hearing on these appropriations. They are a clear and cogent restatement of the policy and purpose of our Government in approving an Act to Promote the Defense of the United States and of the urgency of providing the appropriations called for by the bill. The following excerpt epitomizes the statement:

Secretary Hull. * * * . Our safety and the success of the course upon which we have set ourselves demand the courage and the wisdom to go full out in furnishing adequate material aid to the nations whose defense is necessary to our defense. When we do this, we take the most effective step possible in the circumstances to keep war away from our hemisphere, from our own Nation. Doing this, we act in defense of our homes, our institutions, our liberties, our way of life.

In this task, half measures will not suffice. There is much to be done and the task is urgent. We must strive with all our will, all our power, and all our resources. To be content with less would be to invite disaster. No people in history have had such opportunity to learn from the tragic example of others. We cannot stint and we must not falter.

.   .   .   .   .   .

There has been speculation on the part of some that the production of such vast amounts of defense articles for assistance to other countries

[1] The act repeated the recommendations of the letter from the Director and is therefore not reproduced.

[2] *Defense Aid Supplemental Appropriation Bill, 1941 . . . Report to Accompany H.R. 4050*, p. 3–5 (House Report No. 276, 77th Cong., 1st sess.).

might injure our own defense. The committee desires to quote from the very pertinent testimony of the Chief of Staff of the Army in response to a question from Representative Ludlow:

Mr. LUDLOW. General, I want to ask whether, in your opinion, providing these articles in aid to Britain will in any way endanger our own defense?

General MARSHALL. No, sir; on the contrary I think that as we now have matters arranged, the result will be to our advantage. Our own actual resources will not be diminished until the finished products come off the production line and are ready for shipment. Increased production will add to our strength until the time for distribution begins. I will go further and say this; that I would be a much happier man today if I thought we had reached a point in our production development where we actually had more capacity than we required. That would be the most favorable situation possible for us, in view of present conditions.

The committee has also been advised with respect to the utilization by the United States of the defense articles to be procured with these funds in the event they are not disposed of for aid to any country whose defense is vital to the United States.

Secretary Stimson made this statement, which shows very commendable planning by the War Department and very commendable cooperation by the British:

* * * Of the War Department items, practically all or 95 per cent are those which can be used for our own Army purposes and which would be vitally useful in case Britain should fall. Only 5 per cent represent purely British types of weapons, including the facilities to be erected for such weapons, as distinguished from our American types and their facilities. And even in the case of this last 5 per cent, the plant facilities necessary for construction — that is, the tools and the plants for these purely British items — could be used by us on very short notice.

In other words, as you are doubtless familiar, I might give as an example that the British use the .303-caliber rifle. The facilities for the construction of that rifle which they are using in this country today, under their contracts for its creation, could be transferred so as to manufacture the .30-caliber rifle which we use, I am informed, in about 2 months. And, in the same way, the facilities for the ammunition could be transformed. And that is true largely of other British items.

The committee has received from the Director General of the Office of Production Management a résumé from last June to date of the progress of our own defense efforts. Contracts placed for matériel total $12,600,000,000. Contracts for construction on 302 Government plants total $1,574,000,000. A total of 421 privately financed prime contractors' plants have been certified for assistance in the amount of $393,000,000. The total for facilities, governmental, or privately owned assisted with

Federal funds, is $2,138,000,000 on a total of 723 plants. In addition the British Government has financed 61 plants for a total of $171,000,000.

. . . . . .

The committee has also made inquiry as to British resources and orders placed in this country. The total of such orders placed by the British Purchasing Mission to January 1, 1941, is $2,700,000,000. Payments on these orders to March 12 totaled $1,682,000,000, consisting of $1,300,000,000 paid prior to January 1, 1941, and $382,000,000 paid during the period January 1 to March 12, 1941. All goods delivered under these orders have been paid for in cash and some goods not delivered have been partially paid for in advance. The committee has been assured that none of the $7,000,000,000 contained in the bill will be used to pay for materials under any orders heretofore placed by the British Government and that sufficient existing dollar resources and dollars to be acquired by them will be available to pay for those orders. The estimated British holdings in the United States as of January 1 last consisted of $616,000,000 of marketable securities, $900,000,000 in direct investments, $292,000,000 in gold, $54,000,000 in official dollar balances, and $305,000,000 in private dollar balances. These figures necessarily have changed as these resources have been drawn upon between January 1 and March 12 by $382,000,000 to meet payments for the goods ordered. The committee is also advised that the British assets in this country insofar as they are not needed for payment on their orders here will be given as security on defense articles which the United States may furnish to them.

Britain is engaged in a terrific struggle. The expenditures of the United Kingdom and the Dominions are currently amounting monthly to $1,750,000,000, of which $1,500,000,000 is by the United Kingdom and $250,000,000 by the Dominions. Canada will spend $1,400,000,000 in the fiscal year 1941–42 on her direct war effort, which is 25 per cent of her expected national income.

The agreements with the governments to be assisted under "An Act to Promote the Defense of the United States" rest with the President of the United States. His is the responsibility to determine the terms and conditions under which the nations receiving this aid should make a return to the United States. A nation engaged in a death struggle with a mortal enemy needs, in addition to the tools of war, the maintenance of its own economy and financial stability in order to pursue successfully its efforts. If the United States furnishes Great Britain with defense articles but upsets her economy the aims and purposes of our assistance would be defeated.

(3) *An Act Making Supplemental Appropriations for the National Defense to Provide Aid to the Government of Any Country Whose Defense the President Deems Vital to the Defense of the United States, and for Other Purposes, Approved March 27, 1941, 10:50 a.m., E.S.T.*[1]

Be it enacted by the Senate and House of Representatives of the United States of America in Congress assembled, That to enable the President, through such departments or agencies of the Government as he may designate, to carry out the provisions of An Act to Promote the Defense of the United States, approved March 11, 1941, and for each and every purpose incident to or necessary therefor, there is hereby appropriated out of any money in the Treasury not otherwise appropriated, the following sums for the following respective purposes, namely:

(a) For the procurement, by manufacture or otherwise, of defense articles for the government of any country whose defense the President deems vital to the defense of the United States, including services and expenses in connection therewith, as follows:

(1) Ordnance and ordnance stores, supplies, spare parts, and materials, including armor and ammunition and components thereof, $1,343,000,000.

(2) Aircraft and aeronautical material, including engines, spare parts, and accessories, $2,054,000,000.

(3) Tanks, armored cars, automobiles, trucks, and other automotive vehicles, spare parts, and accessories, $362,000,000.

(4) Vessels, ships, boats, and other watercraft, and equipage, supplies, materials, spare parts, and accessories, $629,000,000.

(5) Miscellaneous military equipment, supplies, and materials, $260,000,000.

(6) Facilities and equipment, for the manufacture or production of defense articles, by construction or acquisition, including the acquisition of land, and the maintenance and operation of such facilities and equipment, $752,000,000.

(7) Agricultural, industrial, and other commodities and articles, $1,350,000,000.

(b) For testing, inspecting, proving, repairing, outfitting, reconditioning, or otherwise placing in good working order any defense articles

---

[1] Public No. 23, 77th Cong.; originated as H.R. 4050; House Report No. 276; Senate Report No. 135.

U. S. Congress, House of Representatives, Committee on Appropriations, Subcommittee on Deficiencies, *Defense Aid Supplemental Appropriation Bill, 1941; Hearings* . . . 77th Cong., 1st sess.

for the government of any country whose defense the President deems vital to the defense of the United States, including services and expenses in connection therewith, $200,000,000.

(c) Not to exceed 20 per centum of any of the foregoing eight appropriations may be transferred by the President to any other such appropriation, but no appropriation shall be increased by more than 30 per centum.

(d) For necessary services and expenses for carrying out the purposes of such Act not specified or included in the foregoing, $40,000,000.

(e) For administrative expenses, $10,000,000.

(f) In all, $7,000,000,000, to remain available until June 30, 1943.

SEC. 2. If any defense article procured from an appropriation made before March 11, 1941, is disposed of, under such Act of March 11, 1941, by any department or agency to the government of any country whose defense the President deemed vital to the defense of the United States, the President may transfer, from the appropriations made by this Act to the appropriate appropriation of such department or agency, an amount equivalent to the value (as computed for the purposes of the $1,300,000,000 limitation contained in section 3 (a) (2) of such Act of March 11, 1941) of the defense article so disposed of, but not to exceed in the aggregate $1,300,000,000.

SEC. 3. Any defense article procured from an appropriation made by this Act shall be retained by or transferred to and for the use of such department or agency of the United States as the President may determine, in lieu of being disposed of to a foreign government, whenever in the judgment of the President the defense of the United States will be best served thereby.

SEC. 4. No part of any appropriation contained in this Act shall be used to pay the salary or wages of any person who advocates, or who is a member of an organization that advocates, the overthrow of the Government of the United States by force or violence: *Provided,* That for the purposes hereof an affidavit shall be considered prima facie evidence that the person making the affidavit does not advocate, and is not a member of an organization that advocates, the overthrow of the Government of the United States by force or violence: *Provided further,* That any person who advocates, or who is a member of an organization that advocates, the overthrow of the Government of the United States by force or violence and accepts employment the salary or wages for which are paid from any appropriation in this Act shall be guilty of a felony and, upon conviction, shall be fined not more than $1,000 or imprisoned for not more than one year, or both: *Provided further,* That the above penalty clause shall be in addition to, and not in substitution for, any other provisions of existing law.

Sec. 5. This Act may be cited as the "Defense Aid Supplemental Appropriation Act, 1941."

C. Administration of the Lend-Lease Program

(1) *Cessation of Liaison Committee. The Secretary of the Treasury (Morgenthau) to the President (Roosevelt), March 12, 1941* [1]

MARCH 12, 1941.

MY DEAR MR. PRESIDENT:

As I indicated to you in my letter of March 5, it is my opinion that, with the signing of the Lend-Lease Bill, there will no longer be any need for the Liaison Committee which you established on December 6, 1939, to coordinate foreign military purchases with our domestic program.

The Committee has handled approximately 2,000 requests between July 1940, and March 1941. Of these, over 1,000 were British, and some 700 Dutch, with the balance representing the American Republics and a few other countries, such as Russia, Portugal and Iran.

It is my understanding that purchasing operations by all countries in the war zone will come under the lend-lease procedure, although in certain instances, such as the Dutch East Indies, the country itself may continue to buy for cash. The purchasing operations of foreign countries not included in this lend-lease area depend basically on questions of foreign policy rather than upon questions of production. This is specifically true in the case of Russia, and it is also true with respect to all the American Republics.

Because of this situation it is my recommendation that the Liaison Committee be disbanded and that all foreign countries outside the lend-lease area desiring to purchase military supplies in this country be advised to submit their needs to the Secretary of State.

I believe I can be most useful as a member of your new advisory committee and the members of my office experienced in handling British purchasing operations can be of the greatest assistance if they are instructed to devote their full energies to assisting Harry Hopkins in the detailed problems involved in the lend-lease administration. They already have instructions to assist him in any way and to the full extent he desires.

I would appreciate it if you would notify the Secretary of War and the Secretary of the Navy that the original Liaison Committee has been

[1] Department of State, *Bulletin*, IV, p. 479.

dissolved and that all foreign purchasing operations outside of the lend-lease area will henceforth be the responsibility of the Secretary of State.

Faithfully,

HENRY MORGENTHAU, Jr.

(2) *The President (Roosevelt) to the Secretary of the Treasury (Morgenthau), April 14, 1941* [1]

APRIL 14, 1941.

DEAR MR. SECRETARY:

Thank you for your letter of March 12 concerning the operations of the Liaison Committee for the coordination of foreign and domestic military purchases.

I would like to thank this committee for the work which it has done in the past year, and may I express my appreciation to you for your sincere and continuous efforts to make war materials available to those countries defending themselves against aggressor nations.

The work of the Liaison Committee as a coordinating body for foreign and domestic military purchases is no longer useful since the signing of the Lend-Lease Act and will be dissolved. Purchasing operations by all countries in the Lend-Lease area will be supervised by Harry Hopkins, and such operations by all other countries which must necessarily involve consideration of foreign policy will be processed by the Department of State.

Sincerely yours,

FRANKLIN D. ROOSEVELT

(3) *Coordination of Activities of the Department of State. Department of State Order No. 939, April 30, 1941* [2]

Mr. Lynn R. Edminster, in addition to such other duties and responsibilities as may be assigned to him, shall have responsibility for coordinating the activities of the Department relating to the administration of the Act of March 11, 1941 (the Lend-Lease Act). In carrying out this function, Mr. Edminster shall have responsibility for enlisting the collaboration of the interested divisions and offices of the Department, particularly those charged with functions involving the formulation of policies; for initiating and coordinating action; and for establishing and maintaining effective liaison with other interested departments and agencies of the Government. When appropriate, he shall represent the Department on such interdepartmental committee or committees as may be established or maintained for the purpose of coordinating the activities of the interested departments and agencies of the Government in the administration of the Act of March 11, 1941.

[1] Department of State, *Bulletin*, IV, p. 479.   [2] *Ibid.*, p. 533.

The provisions of this Order shall be effective as of April 1, 1941, and shall supersede the provisions of any existing Order in conflict therewith.

(4) *Creation of Division of Defense Aid Reports in the Office for Emergency Management of the Executive Office of the President. Executive Order No. 8751, May 2, 1941* [1]

[Excerpt]

1. There is established within the Office of Emergency Management of the Executive Office of the President the Division of Defense Aid Reports, at the head of which shall be an Executive Officer appointed by the President. . . .

2. Subject to such policies and directions as the President may from time to time prescribe, the Division of Defense Aid Reports shall perform and discharge the following described duties and responsibilities:

(*a*) Provide a central channel for the clearance of transactions and reports, and coordinate the processing of requests for aid under the Act.

(*b*) Maintain such system of records and summary accounts to be approved by the Bureau of the Budget, as may be necessary for adequate administrative and financial control over operations under the Act and as will currently reflect the status of all such operations.

(*c*) Prepare such reports as may be necessary to keep the President informed of progress under the Act; assist in the preparation of reports pursuant to Section 5 (*b*) of the Act; and serve generally as a clearing house of information for agencies participating in the program.

(*d*) Perform such other duties relating to defense aid activities as the President may from time to time prescribe.

D. Operations Under the Lend-Lease Act

(1) *Message of the President (Roosevelt) Transmitting First Report, June 10, 1941* [2]

To THE CONGRESS OF THE UNITED STATES:

SECTION 5 (*b*) of Public Law No. 11, Seventy-seventh Congress, approved by me on March 11, 1941, provides in part as follows:

The President from time to time, but not less frequently than once every ninety days, shall transmit to the Congress a report of operations under this act except such information as he deems incompatible with the public interest to disclose.

---

[1] 6 *Fed. Reg.*, p. 2301. A military order of May 6, 1941 (*ibid.*) designated Major General James H. Burns as executive officer of the Division.

[2] *Operations under Lend-Lease Act. Message from the President of the United States Transmitting, Pursuant to Law, First Report under the Act of March 11, 1941* . . . (Sen. Doc. No. 66, 77th Cong., 1st sess.).

In compliance with this provision I am submitting this report.

We have supplied, and we will supply, planes, guns, ammunition and other defense articles in ever-increasing quantities to Britain, China and other democracies resisting aggression.

Wars are not won by guns alone, but wars are not won without guns. We all know this full well now. Beginning with the outbreak of the war the American public began to realize that it was in our own national interest and security to help Britain, China and other democratic nations.

Beginning with the outbreak of the war British and French orders began to be placed. But dollars could not be immediately turned into airplanes and ships and guns and ammunition.

In those dark days when France was falling, it was clear that this government, to carry out the will of the people, had to render aid over and above the matériel coming off the assembly line. This government, therefore, made available all that it possibly could out of its surplus stocks of munitions.

In June of 1940, the British Government received from our surplus stocks rifles, machine guns, field artillery, ammunition, and aircraft in a value of more than $43,000,000. This was equipment that would have taken months and months to produce and which, with the exception of the aircraft, cost about $300,000,000 to produce during the World War period. Most of this matériel would not have been usable if we had kept it much longer. This equipment arrived in Britain after the retreat from Dunkirk, where the British had lost great quantities of guns and other military supplies. No one can appraise what effect the delivery of these supplies had upon the successful British resistance in the Summer and Fall of 1940 when they were fighting against such terrific odds.

Since June 1940, this government has continued to supply war matériel from its surplus stocks, in addition to the matériel produced by private manufacturers. The fifty over-age destroyers which Britain received in exchange for the defense bases were a part of the aid supplied by the government.

By the turn of the year 1941, the British commitments in this country for defense articles had reached the limit of their future dollar resources. Their striking power required the assurance that their munitions and equipment would steadily and certainly be augmented, not curtailed.

The will of our people, as expressed through the Congress, was to meet this problem, not only by the passage of the Lend-Lease Act but by the appropriation of 7 billion dollars made on March 27 of this year to carry out this task.

In the ninety days since the Lend-Lease Act was passed, and in the seventy-four days since the funds were appropriated, we have started in motion the vast supply program which is essential to the defeat of the Axis powers.

In these seventy-four days, more than $4\frac{1}{4}$ billion dollars out of the 7 billion dollars have been allocated to the War, Navy, Agriculture and Treasury Departments and to the Maritime Commission to procure the aid authorized. Contracts have been let for long-range bombers, ships, tanks and the other sinews of war that will be needed for the defense of the democracies. The balance of less than $2\frac{3}{4}$ billion is being rapidly allocated.

To be effective, the aid rendered by us must be many sided. Ships are necessary to carry the munitions and the food. We are immediately making available to Britain 2 million gross tons of cargo ships and oil tankers.

But this is not enough. Adequate shipping for every day to come must be reasonably assured. Since the Appropriation Act was passed, 550 million dollars has been allocated for the construction of new ships under the Lend-Lease Act. Contracts have been let and the new ways required to build these ships are now nearing completion. Allied ships are being repaired by us. Allied ships are being equipped by us to protect them from mines, and are being armed by us to protect them as much as possible against raiders. Naval vessels of Britain are being repaired by us so that they can return quickly to their naval tasks.

The training program of 7,000 British pilots in our schools in this country is under way. Valuable information is being communicated, and other material assistance is being rendered in a mounting benefit to the democracies.

Millions of pounds of food are being and will be sent. Iron and steel, machine tools and the other essentials to maintain and increase the production of war materials in Britain are being sent and received in larger quantities day by day.

Since September 1939, the war goods sent to Britain have risen steadily. The over-all total exports to the British Empire have greatly increased in 1941 over 1940. What is more important, the increase of those things which are necessary for fighting have increased far beyond our other exports. In the first five months of this year we have sent more than twelve times as many airplanes to Britain as we did in the first five months of 1940. For the first four months of this year the dollar value of explosives sent to the British Empire was about seventeen times as much as for the first months of 1940. Ninety times as much in dollar value of firearms and ammunition was sent to Britain during the first four months of this year as for the first four months of 1940.

With our national resources, our productive capacity and the genius of our people for mass production we will help Britain to outstrip the Axis powers in munitions of war, and we will see to it that these munitions get to the places where they can be effectively used to weaken and defeat the aggressors.

In the report that follows facts and figures are given to the extent advisable without disclosing military secrets to benefit the Axis powers. These facts describe the past and portray the present status of our aid to those nations so gallantly fighting the aggressors. They do not present the most important fact of all — the strong will of our people to see to it that these forces of aggression shall not rule the world.

We have before us a constant purpose not of present safety alone but, equally, of future survival.

FRANKLIN D. ROOSEVELT

THE WHITE HOUSE,
  June 10, 1941.

(a) Transfers of Defense Articles as of May 31, 1941 [1]

CLASSIFICATION	FROM APPROPRIATIONS MADE PRIOR TO MARCH 11, 1941	FROM ACT OF MARCH 27, 1941	TOTAL
Ammunition for small arms and artillery, explosives, etc.	$9,760,361.08	——	$9,760,361.08
Ordnance, arms and miscellaneous	20,580,109.13	——	20,530,109.13
Aircraft	2,572,570.67	$1,455,726.16	4,028,296.83
Vehicles	3,005,807.00	399,911.45	3,405,718.45
Watercraft, etc.	26,155,193.89	27,000.00	26,182,193.89
Clothing and medical supplies, etc.	616,000.00	——	616,000.00
Signal and chemical equipment, etc.	1,782,700.00	21,866.10	1,804,566.10
Agricultural products . .	——	7,998,261.67	7,998,261.67
Machinery, etc.	——	242,181.28	242,181.28
Raw materials and metals .	——	497,806.82	497,806.82
Miscellaneous	——	86,930.62	86,930.62
Total	$64,472,741.77	$10,729,684.10	$75,202,425.87

[1] *Operations Under the Lend-Lease Act. Message from the President of the United States Transmitting, Pursuant to Law, First Report under the Act of March 11, 1941,* p. 7 (Sen. Doc. No. 66, 77th Cong., 1st sess.).

(b) Allocations Under the Appropriation Act of March 27, 1941 [1]

(As of May 31, 1941)

Ordnance and ordnance stores	$880,176,863.00
Aircraft and aeronautical material	1,938,823,489.00
Tanks and other vehicles	318,502,800.00
Vessels and other water craft	551,414,140.00
Miscellaneous military equipment	119,172,013.00
Facilities and equipment	137,134,818.00
Agricultural, industrial and other commodities	280,314,697.50
Testing, reconditioning, etc., of defense articles	48,385,880.00
Services and expenses	3,042,605.00
Administrative expenses	445,574.00
Total	$4,227,412,879.50

Outline of Procedure [2]

Operations under the Lend-Lease Act conform, so far as possible, to the normal procedure of United States administrative, executive and procurement agencies. Accounting and statistical records, for instance, are kept according to standard practice. This summary, therefore, sketches only the special organizations and their functions.

The Division of Defense Aid Reports in the Office for Emergency Management of the Executive Office of the President is the organ primarily concerned with the operation of the act. On its establishment by Executive Order No. 8751 (p. 731) of May 2, 1941, it succeeded to administrative functions performed during the preceding 12 months by the President's Liaison Committee. Its work falls into six categories:

1. Processing of requirements;
2. Fiscal accounts, embracing every angle of defense aid operations;
3. Statistical operations, including analysis of procurement facilities, progress of orders and final records;
4. Transportation coordination;
5. Liaison between governmental agencies and foreign governments;
6. Legal problems, involving the whole range of the varied and complicated ramifications of the program.

The processing of requirements is initiated by formal requisitions for specific defense articles or defense services submitted by foreign governments which have given the assurances required by secs. 4 and 7 of the Lend-Lease Act and which are subject to an agreement fixing the terms and conditions under sec. 3 (b) upon which they receive the aid. Requisitions originate with the representatives of foreign governments after conferences with the departments or agencies

[1] *Operations Under the Lend-Lease Act;* see p. 734, n. 1.
[2] These notes are a summary of the *First Report under the Act of March 11, 1941*, p. 14–16, 25–39 (Sen. Doc. No. 66, 77th Cong., 1st sess.).

of the United States Government which are best qualified to deal with the specific proposal. For the purpose of these negotiations the War Department on April 8, 1941, instituted the Division of Defense Aid, Office of the Under Secretary of War, out of the personnel of the Army Section, Clearance Committee, Army and Navy Munitions Board.[1] Subordinate to this Division are Defense Aid Requirements Committees of varying formation but always having a nucleus of personnel of four members who include the chairman of the British Supply Council or other foreign supply service.[2] The five committees decide on matériel requirements as to type, quantity and destination for these arms and services: Ordnance, Chemical, Signal, Engineer, Quartermaster. The recommendation, duly approved in the Department, goes to the White House and as a requisition at the Division of Defense Aid Reports secures a Presidential directive authorizing its execution.

Actual procurement may be by transfer of stock or production under contract. The War, Navy, Treasury and Agriculture Departments and the Maritime Commission have participated directly as procurement agencies, and the Office of Production Management and the Departments of State, Justice and Interior have contributed to the program in an advisory capacity. Over 2,000 requisitions were received during the period March 11 to June 1, 1941.

7. PROCUREMENT AND SUPPLY OF WAR MATERIALS

A. Strategic and Critical Materials

(1) *Revolving Pool of Strategic and Critical Materials. Amendment of Act of June 7, 1939 by Act Approved May 28, 1941* [3]

The Act of June 7, 1939 [4] in providing for a stock pile of strategic and critical materials appropriated $100,000,000 for a limited time for the purpose. The use of the materials would have resulted in the depletion of the stocks unless provision was made for their replenishment. Proceeds resulting from sales were therefore allocated by the Amending Act of 1941 to that purpose. See also *Documents, II, 1939–40*, p. 781 for Public No. 664, 76th Cong., approved June 25, 1940.

SEC. 6.[5] For the procurement, transportation, maintenance, rotation, and storage of the materials to be acquired under this Act, there is

[1] For the organization and functions of the Army and Navy Munitions Board see *Industrial Mobilization Plan Revision of 1939;* a study of methods for the effective and equitable utilization of the industrial resources of the United States in time of war, p. 13–17 (Sen. Doc. No. 134, 76th Cong., 2d sess.).

[2] The two groups of countries benefiting by general export licenses (p. 493) are indicative of the eligible governments.

[3] *An Act to Appropriate the Proceeds of Sales or Other Dispositions of Strategic and Critical Materials Acquired under the Act of June 7, 1939 (53 Stat. 811), in Order to Prevent Depletion of the Stocks of Such Materials Available for National-Defense Purposes, Approved May 28, 1941*, Public Law 76, 77th Cong.; originated as S. 994; Senate Report No. 136; House Report No. 529.

[4] *Documents, I, 1938–39*, p. 513; 53 Stat. 811; U. S. Code, title 50, sec. 98a.

[5] The last sentence was added by the Act of May 28, 1941.

hereby authorized to be appropriated the sum of $100,000,000, out of any money in the Treasury not otherwise appropriated, during the fiscal years June 30, 1939, to and including June 30, 1943, to be expended under the joint direction of the Secretary of War and the Secretary of the Navy. Any funds heretofore or hereafter received on account of sales or other dispositions of materials under the provisions of this Act shall be deposited to the credit, and be available for expenditure for the purposes, of any appropriation available at the time of such deposit, for carrying out the provisions of sections 1 to 6, inclusive, of this Act.

(2) *Stockpiling of Strategic and Critical Materials. Report of the Federal Loan Administrator (Jones), May 7, 1941* [1]

(a) *Rubber Reserve Company*

In aid of the defense program the RFC [Reconstruction Finance Corporation] has made commitments aggregating approximately $1,635,000,-000. These include the creation on June 28, 1940, of the Rubber Reserve Company to acquire a reserve supply of raw rubber. $5,000,000 was subscribed to the capital stock of this Company, and with the approval of the Reconstruction Finance Corporation it has agreed with the International Rubber Regulation Committee,[2] which controls the world output of raw rubber, to purchase up to 430,000 tons of Far Eastern crude rubber, costing approximately $190,000,000, and, in addition, has agreed to purchase up to 24,000 tons of Brazilian rubber in the years 1941 and 1942 at a maximum cost of $10,752,000. On April 30, 1941, ninety-seven thousand nine hundred and forty-seven (97,947) tons had been delivered, 13,710 tons were in transit, and 37,533 tons await shipment. The balance of the Far Eastern rubber should be accumulated in 1941. In order not to interfere with the requirements of the rubber industry, the Rubber Reserve Company is buying in cooperation with the industry at approximately 20¢ a pound. The industry agreed with the Company to carry not less than 150,000 tons to meet current needs. It is doing this, and, in addition, as of March 31, 1941, had accumulated an excess of 60,000 tons. In order to accumulate this reserve supply, the International Rubber Regulation Committee by agreement with the Company has

---

[1] Excerpt from the *Report of the Federal Loan Administrator on Aid to the Defense Program*, May 7, 1941.

[2] The Committee was established by an agreement of the rubber-producing countries signed on May 7, 1934 and amending protocols (League of Nations, *Treaty Series*, CLXXI, p. 203; *ibid.*, CLXXXI, p. 469.

The Rubber Reserve Company operations are additional to the 85,000 tons acquired by the cotton-rubber agreement of June 23, 1939 (*Documents, I, 1938–39*, p. 519).

authorized increases of approximately 50 per cent in the normal world output.

(b) Metals Reserve Company

On June 28, 1940, the Reconstruction Finance Corporation created the Metals Reserve Company with a capital of $5,000,000 to acquire a reserve supply of critical and strategic materials. Purchases of such materials are in excess of current requirements.

To the close of business April 30, 1941, the Metals Reserve Company, with approval of the Reconstruction Finance Corporation, had made commitments to acquire the following metals at approximately the costs stated:

	Tons Delivered	Tons Afloat	Tons On Order	Amount
Antimony				
Chinese	6,796			$1,903,000.00
Domestic	250		2,750	780,000.00
Asbestos			1,560	215,000.00
Chrome Ore				
South African, etc. . .	12,457	11,950	138,593	4,039,000.00
Philippine			148,000	3,166,000.00
Copper				
Latin-American . . .	106,722		393,777 [1]	140,110,000.00
Graphite				
Madagascar	411		4,500	486,000.00
Manganese Ore				
Far Eastern	172,866	48,450	393,940	20,533,000.00
Latin American . . .	16,149		439,945	15,023,000.00
Domestic			1,490,000	53,155,000.00
Mica			489	400,000.00
Tungsten Trioxide				
Domestic			1,250	2,875,000.00
Tin				
Far Eastern	30,375	6,275	113,350 [2]	168,000,000.00
Bolivian			90,000	100,000,000.00
Zinc			50,000	8,250,000.00
Antimony, Wolframite and Tin — Chinese (respective quantities undetermined) . . .				90,000,000.00
				$608,935,000.00

[1] Includes 198,160 tons for which purchase contract is not yet executed.
[2] Includes 93,024 tons for which purchase contract is not yet executed.

(c) Defense Supplies Corporation

On August 29, 1940, Defense Supplies Corporation,[1] was created with an authorized capital of $5,000,000 to acquire and carry a reserve supply of critical and strategic materials and supplies which may be necessary in the national defense program.

The Corporation is transporting to and storing in this country 250,000,000 pounds of Australian wool. The estimated cost of the transportation and storage of the wool is approximately $12,000,000, to be provided by the President from the "Emergency Fund for the President" contained in the Military Appropriation Act, 1941 [2] (Public No. 611–76th Congress). As of April 30, 1941, approximately 46,860,000 pounds of wool had been received and several cargoes were afloat. The wool belongs to Great Britain, but the United States Government has the right to use any part of it that it may need.[3]

The Corporation has contracted for the purchase of 300,000 tons of nitrate of soda from Chile at a cost of $5,400,000. It has also made arrangements for the purchase of 6,000 diamond dies for use in the wire drawing industry, at an estimated cost of $155,000.

At the request of the National Defense Commission, the Corporation made arrangements for financing the purchase of 7,500,000 barrels of high-test aviation gasoline to cost approximately $50,000,000 and 10,000,000 gallons of toluol to cost $3,250,000. Such arrangements have been canceled.

(3) Exchange of Notes Concerning the Strategic Reserve of Australian Wool

(a) The British Secretary of State for Foreign Affairs (Halifax) to the American Chargé d'Affaires (Johnson), December 9, 1940 [4]

FOREIGN OFFICE, S. W. 1,
9th December, 1940.

No. W11985/79/49

SIR:

I have the honor to inform you that in order to enable the Government of the United States of America to establish in the United States a reserve of Australian wool against a possible emergency shortage of wool supplies

[1] Total commitments of the Defense Supplies Corporation reported on May 7, 1941 were $119,202,814. The charter of the Corporation is at 6 Fed. Reg., p. 2972, 3363.

[2] See p. 671 and Documents, II, 1939–40, p. 780.

[3] See the following exchange of notes.

[4] Executive Agreement Series No. 195; Department of State, Bulletin, III, p. 555.

in the United States, the Government of the United Kingdom of Great Britain and Northern Ireland are prepared to enter into an agreement with the Government of the United States in the following terms:

(1) The Government of the United Kingdom shall make available to the United States Government (or an agency acting on its behalf) two hundred and fifty million pounds of Australian wool as a strategic reserve for the United States Government against a possible emergency shortage of wool supplies in the United States. The wool shall be transported to the United States where it shall be stored in bonded warehouses. The Government of the United Kingdom shall retain title to the wool, but all or any part of the wool may be purchased by the United States Government (or an agency acting on its behalf) for use in the United States or may be sold to the United States domestic trade, if and when it has been determined by the United States Government that an emergency shortage of wool exists in the United States.

(2) The Government of the United Kingdom may withdraw wool from the reserve for shipment to the United Kingdom or other British territory in the case of emergency shortage of supplies in such territory, or in the contingency of an interruption of wool textile production in the United Kingdom for the manufacture of textiles in the United States to meet United Kingdom emergency textile requirements, provided that (a) replacements for wool so withdrawn are on the way to the United States and (b) at no time the total of the reserve in the United States is temporarily depleted by more than 20 per cent by such withdrawals.

(3) At any time after the signing of a general armistice between the United Kingdom and Germany, the Government of the United Kingdom shall be at liberty to dispose of the wool remaining in the reserve, but the United States Government and the Government of the United Kingdom shall consult together with a view to ensuring that the disposal of any such wool in the United States shall be effected under conditions which will avoid a dislocation of normal wool marketing there.

(4) The wool for the reserve shall be made available by the Government of the United Kingdom f.o.b. at Australian ports, and the United States Government (directly or through an agency acting on its behalf) shall thereafter accept responsibility for the safe custody of the wool and shall pay transport, handling, storage, insurance including war risk, and other charges in connection with the establishment and maintenance of the wool reserve. Payments shall be made between the United States Government and the Government of the United Kingdom on sale of wool from the reserve to offset any savings secured by the Government

of the United Kingdom owing to the wool having been transported to and stored in the United States by the United States Government and any loss incurred by the Government of the United Kingdom by reason of depreciation in the value of the wool stored in the United States as a result of deterioration of the wool or by reason of the position in which the wool is stored in the United States, provided that (a) in the case of sales in the United States no payment shall be made which would reduce the receipts by the Government of the United Kingdom for the wool in question below the amount which would have been received on sale f.o.b. Australia at the same date, and (b) in the case of sales outside the United States any payments as between the two Governments shall not involve the Government of the United Kingdom in any net expenditure of United States dollars in respect thereof.

(5) It is tentatively agreed that the 250,000,000 pounds of Australian wool which will be made available by the Government of the United Kingdom for the reserve shall be composed of the following: 270,000 bales of 58/60s of types normally imported into the United States and of good topmaking Bradford styles; 290,000 bales of 60s and finer of types normally imported into the United States and of good topmaking Bradford styles; 190,000 bales of 60s and finer of good to average Bradford styles; balance (to make up 250,000,000 pounds) of 60s and finer of average Bradford styles; two thirds of all the 60s and finer wools to consist of 64/60s. The counts are as normally understood in the United States. Although this tentative agreement on grades and types is subject to modification following consultation between the two Governments after examination of samples of the wool by the United States authorities, it shall become definitive if the examination of samples indicates that the grades and types of wool included in the above mentioned general categories are such that they could be readily used in American mills without interruption of or delays in the production of the mills. It is understood that the Government of the United Kingdom in estimating the quantities available for the reserve have provided for the retention of sufficient supplies in Australia to ensure that the commercial demand can be met. It is also understood that both the total quantity estimated to be available for the reserve after providing for sales abroad and shipments to the United Kingdom, and the distribution by types and descriptions, have been based upon the results of the 1939–40 clip, and that should the results of the 1940–41 clip differ it may be necessary to vary the supply for the reserve.

(6) Space on established British shipping lines running between Australia and the United States shall be used for the transport of the

wool so far as available. The wool will be made available in Australia as rapidly as possible, provided that the sale of wool from Australia on commercial account or its shipment to the Wool Control in the United Kingdom or Canada shall not be prejudiced, and every endeavor shall be made to complete the allocations in Australia by the end of March 1941.

2. If the Government of the United States are prepared to accept the foregoing provisions, I have the honor to propose that the present note and your reply to that effect be regarded as constituting an agreement between the two Governments which shall come into force immediately.

I have [etc.]   HALIFAX

(b) The American Chargé d'Affaires (Johnson) to the British Secretary of State for Foreign Affairs (Halifax), December 9, 1940 [1]

No. 2662   LONDON,
                                                        December 9, 1940.

MY LORD:

I have the honor to acknowledge the receipt of your note no. W11985/79/49 of December 9, 1940, in which Your Lordship is good enough to inform me that in order to enable the Government of the United States of America to establish in the United States a reserve of Australian wool against a possible emergency shortage of wool supplies in the United States the Government of the United Kingdom of Great Britain and Northern Ireland is prepared to enter into an agreement with the Government of the United States in the following terms:

[Here follow items (1) to (6), from the British note.]

In reply to numbered paragraph two of Your Lordship's note, I have the honor to confirm under instructions of my Government that Your Lordship's statement of our understanding as set forth above is agreed to by my Government and that the present exchange of notes is to be regarded as constituting an agreement between the two Governments which shall come into force immediately.

I have [etc.]

HERSCHEL V. JOHNSON
Chargé d'Affaires ad interim

[1] Department of State, *Bulletin*, III, p. 556.

B. Obligatory Orders of Defense Material by the War and Navy Departments

(1) *Amendment of Sec. 8 of Act of June 28, 1940* [1] *by Sec. 9 of the Act of September 16, 1940* [2]

SEC. 9. The President is empowered, through the head of the War Department or the Navy Department of the Government, in addition to the present authorized methods of purchase or procurement, to place an order with any individual firm, association, company, corporation, or organized manufacturing industry for such product or material as may be required, and which is of the nature and kind usually produced or capable of being produced by such individual, firm, company, association, corporation, or organized manufacturing industry.

Compliance with all such orders for products or material shall be obligatory on any individual, firm, association, company, corporation, or organized manufacturing industry or the responsible head or heads thereof and shall take precedence over all other orders and contracts theretofore placed with such individual, firm, company, association, corporation, or organized manufacturing industry, and any individual, firm, association, company, corporation, or organized manufacturing industry or the responsible head or heads thereof owning or operating any plant equipped for the manufacture of arms or ammunition or parts of ammunition, or any necessary supplies or equipment for the Army or Navy, and any individual, firm, association, company, corporation, or organized manufacturing industry or the responsible head or heads thereof owning or operating any manufacturing plant, which, in the opinion of the Secretary of War or the Secretary of the Navy shall be capable of being readily transformed into a plant for the manufacture of arms or ammunition, or parts thereof, or other necessary supplies or equipment, who shall refuse to give to the United States such preference in the matter of the execution of orders, or who shall refuse to manufacture the kind, quantity, or quality of arms or ammunition, or the parts thereof, or any necessary supplies or equipment, as ordered by the Secretary of War or the Secretary of the Navy, or who shall refuse to furnish such arms, ammunition, or parts of ammunition, or other supplies or equipment, at a reasonable price as determined by the Secretary of War or the Secretary of the Navy, as the case may be,

[1] *An Act to Expedite National Defense, and for Other Purposes, Approved June 28, 1940;* Public No. 671, 76th Cong.; *Documents, II, 1939–40,* p. 804.

[2] *Selective Training and Service Act of 1940,* approved September 16, 1940, Public No. 783, 76th Cong., see above p. 672.

then, and in either such case, the President, through the head of the War or Navy Departments of the Government, in addition to the present authorized methods of purchase or procurement, is hereby authorized to take immediate possession of any such plant or plants, and through the appropriate branch, bureau, or department of the Army or Navy to manufacture therein such product or material as may be required, and any individual, firm, company, association, or corporation, or organized manufacturing industry, or the responsible head or heads thereof, failing to comply with the provisions of this section shall be deemed guilty of a felony, and upon conviction shall be punished by imprisonment for not more than three years and a fine not exceeding $50,000.

The compensation to be paid to any individual, firm, company, association, corporation, or organized manufacturing industry for its products or material, or as rental for use of any manufacturing plant while used by the United States, shall be fair and just: *Provided*, That nothing herein shall be deemed to render inapplicable existing State or Federal laws concerning the health, safety, security, and employment standards of the employees in such plant.

The first and second provisos in section 8 (*b*) of the Act entitled "An Act to expedite national defense, and for other purposes," approved June 28, 1940 (Public Act Numbered 671, Seventy-sixth Congress), are hereby repealed.

C. Requisition of Military or Naval Equipment or Munitions

(1) *An Act to Authorize the President to Requisition Certain Articles and Materials for the Use of the United States, and for Other Purposes, Approved October 10, 1940* [1]

This act of October 10, 1940 gave authority to make effective the export control system under the act of July 2, 1940. Its purport and the method of its execution were explained in a White House release of October 15, 1940 as follows:

" . . . Many applications for licenses have been refused as a result of decisions by the Administrator of Export Control that the proposed exportation would be contrary to the interests of the national defense. The articles or materials for which export licenses have been refused have in many cases been already sold and the title has passed to a foreign purchaser. It has been found that, in some of these cases, purchasers did not desire to sell the article or material in the United States or, because they were acting in a representative capacity, they were not legally in a position to do so. This situation has been particularly acute in the case of some exportations of machine tools. A great many of these

[1] Public No. 829, 76th Cong., 3d sess.; H.R. 10339 reported from Committee on Military Affairs, August 15, 1940; House Report No. 2854; Senate Report No. 2097.

tools for which export licenses have been refused are especially needed to meet national defense requirements.

"The President today issued an Executive Order [1] directing the Secretary of War and the Secretary of the Navy, acting jointly through the agency of the Army and Navy Munitions Board, to determine the necessity for the requisitioning of any equipment, munitions, or machinery, tools, materials, or supplies necessary for the manufacture of munitions, or the servicing, or operation of facilities for the National Defense, and to determine whether in any case it is in the public interest to sell, or otherwise dispose of, any of the articles and materials so requisitioned. The administration of the other provisions of the Act has been vested in the Administrator of Export Control."

An act of April 20, 1918 (40 Stat. 533; U. S. Code, title 50, secs. 101–103) provides for punishment for wilful injury or destruction of war material or of war premises or utilities used in connection with war material, and defines those terms. An act of November 30, 1940 (Public 886, 76th Cong., chap. 926, 3d sess.) amends the act of 1918 so as to extend its provisions to the wilful injury or destruction of "national defense" materials, premises or utilities, identically defined.

Be it enacted by the Senate and House of Representatives of the United States of America in Congress assembled, That whenever the President determines that it is necessary in the interest of national defense to requisition and take over for the use or operation by the United States or in its interest any military or naval equipment or munitions, or component parts thereof, or machinery, tools, or materials, or supplies necessary for the manufacture, servicing, or operation thereof, ordered, manufactured, procured, or possessed for export purposes, the exportation of which has been denied in accordance with the provisions of section 6 of the Act approved July 2, 1940 [2] (Public, Numbered 703, Seventy-sixth Congress), he is hereby authorized and empowered to requisition and take over for the said use or operation by the United States, or in its interest, any of the foregoing articles or materials, and to sell or otherwise dispose of any such articles or materials, or any portion thereof, to a person or a corporation of the United States whenever he shall determine such action to be in the public interest. Any moneys received by the United States as the proceeds of any such sale or other disposition of any such articles or materials or any portion thereof shall be deposited to the credit of that appropriation out of which was paid the cost to the Government of the property thus sold or disposed of, and the same shall immediately become available for the purposes named in the original appropriation: *Provided, however*, That nothing in this section shall modify or repeal section 14 of Public Law Numbered 671, 76th Congress, approved June 28, 1940.[3]

[1] No. 8567, 6 *Fed. Reg.*, p. 4121; regulations, p. 4122.
[2] Quoted in Proclamation No. 2413, p. 474.
[3] *Documents, II, 1939–40*, p. 793.

SEC. 2. Whenever the President shall requisition and take over any article or material pursuant to the provisions of this Act, the owner thereof shall be paid as compensation therefor such sum as the President shall determine to be fair and just. If any such owner is unwilling to accept, as full and complete compensation for such article or material, the sum so determined by the President, such owner shall be paid 50 per centum of the sum so determined by the President and shall be entitled to sue the United States for such additional sum as, when added to the sum already received by such owner, such owner may consider fair and just compensation for such article or material, in the manner provided by sections 41 (20) and 250, title 28, of the Code of Laws of the United States of America: *Provided*, That recovery shall be confined to the fair market value of such article or material, without any allowance for prospective profits, punitive or other damages.

SEC. 3. The authority granted in this Act shall terminate June 30, 1942, unless the Congress shall otherwise provide.

(2) *Exchange of Notes Concerning the Requisition of Planes Ordered by Sweden*

The Swedish Government in 1939 placed orders with the Seversky Aircraft Corporation (now reorganized as the Republic Aviation Corporation), Farmingdale, Long Island, N. Y., for 60 type EP–1 single-seater pursuit airplanes and 50 2–PA single-seater bombers, complete with engines, spare parts, accessories, etc.

The Administrator of Export Control determined that the proposed exportation of these planes to Sweden would be contrary to the interests of the national defense. As a result of this decision the licenses which had been issued by the Department to authorize the exportation of some of these planes were revoked and applications for further licenses to export these shipments were denied.

The appropriate authorities of this Government having determined that these planes were required by the Army Air Corps for national defense purposes endeavored to negotiate and purchase these planes from the Swedish Government. These endeavors having failed, requisition was decided upon in accordance with the Executive order and the President's regulations issued on October 15, 1940,[1] pursuant to the Requisition Act approved October 10, 1940.

The Swedish Legation in Washington, acting under instructions from its Government, protested to the Department against the proposed requisition proceedings.

(a) *The Secretary of State (Hull) to the Swedish Minister (Boström), October 18, 1940* [2]

SIR: OCTOBER 18, 1940.

I have the honor to acknowledge the receipt of your note of October 16, 1940,[3] stating that you have been instructed by your Government to

[1] See p. 745 for citation.   [2] Department of State, *Bulletin*, III, p. 339.
[3] Not printed.

make earnest representations to this Government against the requisition of war materials ordered in this country by your Government.

In reply, I have to inform you that the interests of the national defense have made it necessary for this Government to refuse, in the instances to which you refer, to issue licenses authorizing the exportation of war materials to Sweden. I am informed that some of these materials — in particular certain airplanes — are urgently needed by the armed forces of this country for their own use. You will understand, I am sure, that in these circumstances this Government must exercise the right which inheres in all governments to requisition the war materials within its jurisdiction which are required for its own defense. I may add that, although this procedure may cause unavoidable inconvenience to your Government, it is my understanding that, when war materials are requisitioned pursuant to the Act to which your note refers, fair and just compensation will be paid to the owners after discussions in which the owners will be given every opportunity to set forth their claims.

Accept [etc.] CORDELL HULL

(b) The Secretary of State (Hull) to the Swedish Minister (Boström), October 21, 1940 [1]

OCTOBER 21, 1940.

SIR:

I have the honor to refer to my notes of October 15, and October 18, 1940, and previous correspondence in regard to the possible requisition by this Government of airplanes and other war materials purchased in this country by the Swedish Government, and have to inform you that in accordance with the Executive Order of October 15, 1940, and the President's regulations of the same date, issued pursuant to the Requisition Act of October 10, 1940, the appropriate authorities of this Government have requisitioned airplanes, the property of your Government, as follows:

60 Type EP1, single-seater pursuit airplanes, complete with engines, spares, accessories, equipment, and technical data, located at Republic Airplane Factory, Farmingdale, New York.

50 Type 2PA single-seater bombers, complete with engines, spares, accessories, equipment, and technical data, located at Republic Airplane Factory, Farmingdale, New York.

I have been informed by the Administrator of Export Control that owners of articles or materials requisitioned pursuant to the Act of October 10, 1940, will be given full opportunity to present evidence of the cost of these articles, and that this evidence will be accorded full

[1] Department of State, *Bulletin*, III, p. 339.

consideration in the determination of the reimbursement to be paid by this Government.

Accept [etc.]   CORDELL HULL

D. Procurement of Foreign Supplies of Food and Clothing

The question of exclusive domestic supply of food for the army has arisen a number of times, especially in the matter of Argentine canned beef, which American meat producers regard as competitive with their product. The conditions under which foreign articles of food or clothing may be procured by the War Department are defined in the Fifth Supplemental National Defense Appropriation Act, 1941.

(1) *"Fifth Supplemental National Defense Appropriation Act," Approved April 5, 1941* [1]

[Excerpt]

Clothing and equipage, Army: For clothing and equipage, $79,418,000, to remain available until June 30, 1942, of which not to exceed $50,700,000 shall be for payments under contracts authorized under this head in the Second Supplemental National Defense Appropriation Act, 1941: *Provided,* That no part of this or any other appropriation contained in this Act shall be available for the procurement of any article of food or clothing not grown or produced in the United States or its possessions, except to the extent that the head of the department concerned shall determine that articles of food or clothing grown or produced in the United States or its possessions cannot be procured of satisfactory quality and in sufficient quantities and at reasonable prices as and when needed, and except procurements by vessels in foreign waters and by establishments located outside the continental United States, except the Territories of Hawaii and Alaska, for the personnel attached thereto.

.   .   .   .   .   .

E. Priorities

(1) *An Act to Extend the Power to Establish Priorities and Allocate Material, Approved May 31, 1941* [2]

The President delegated to the Office of Production Management by Executive Order No. 8629 of January 7, 1941 his authority to establish priorities under

[1] Public Law 29, 77th Cong.; originating as H.R. 4124; House Report No. 301; Senate Report No. 150; House (conference) Report No. 368. Hearings on the bill were held by the subcommittee of the House Committee on Appropriations, March 5–11, 1941.

[2] Public Law 89, 77th Cong., *An Act to Amend the Act Approved June 28, 1940,* entitled *"An Act to Expedite the National Defense, and for Other Purposes," in Order to Extend the Power to Establish Priorities and Allocate Material;* originated as H.R. 4534; House Report No. 460; Senate Report No. 309; House (conference) Report No. 603.

sec. 2(a) of the act of June 28, 1940 and a Director of Priorities was appointed in that Office. The Army and Navy Munitions Board establishes the order of importance of materials by so-called Directives, which specify the schedule of ratings applicable to its Priorities Critical List. The Director of Priorities issues four types of preference rating certificates for those materials. Certificates for army and navy contracts under the act of June 28, 1940 are mandatory in form. Certificates for foreign governments, other United States Government and civilian contracts were voluntary in form. The acceleration of the production program and the enlarged orders for foreign governments under the Lend-Lease Act made it desirable to extend the mandatory authority. The amending act of May 31, 1941 accomplishes the following six purposes:

1. Permits the assignment of mandatory priorities to contracts or orders of any foreign government which the President brings within the terms of the Lend-Lease Act.

2. Permits the assignment of mandatory priorities to any contract or order of a Government agency other than the Army or Navy or of private industry which is of vital importance to the defense program.

3. Makes clear that mandatory priorities may be extended to subcontracts and suborders for parts, supplies, and materials which enter directly or indirectly into the fulfillment of the prime contracts which are subject to mandatory priorities.

4. Permits control of the distribution of those products and materials in which shortages appear by reason of the impact of the defense program and to permit the allocation of such products and materials to defense and to the most important civilian needs in preference to less important uses.

5. Permits adequate information to be obtained to operate the priorities system.

6. Protects persons complying with priority orders against liability for damages.

Be it enacted by the Senate and House of Representatives of the United States of America in Congress assembled, That section 2 [1] of the Act approved June 28, 1940 (Public, Numbered 671, Seventy-sixth Congress), as amended, is amended by inserting " (1) " after "SEC. 2. (a)" and by adding at the end of subsection (a) thereof the following:

" (2) Deliveries of material to which priority may be assigned pursuant to paragraph (1) shall include, in addition to deliveries of material under contracts or orders of the Army or Navy, deliveries of material under —

" (A) contracts or orders for the Government of any country whose defense the President deems vital to the defense of the United States under the terms of the Act of March 11, 1941, entitled 'An Act to promote the defense of the United States';

" (B) contracts or orders which the President shall deem necessary or appropriate to promote the defense of the United States; and

" (C) subcontracts or suborders which the President shall deem necessary or appropriate to the fulfillment of any contract or order as specified in this section.

[1] For text see *Documents, II, 1939–40,* p. 802.

Deliveries under any contract or order specified in this section may be assigned priority over deliveries under any other contract or order. Whenever the President is satisfied that the fulfillment of requirements for the defense of the United States will result in a shortage in the supply of any material for defense or for private account or for export, the President may allocate such material in such manner and to such extent as he shall deem necessary or appropriate in the public interest and to promote the national defense. The President shall be entitled to obtain such information from, require such reports by, and make such inspection of the premises of, any person, firm, or corporation as may be necessary or appropriate, in his discretion, to the enforcement or administration of the provisions of this section. No person, firm, or corporation shall be held liable for damages or penalties for any default under any contract or order which shall result directly or indirectly from his compliance with any rule, regulation, or order issued under this section. The President may exercise any power, authority, or discretion conferred on him by this section, through such department, agency, or officer of the Government as he may direct and in conformity with any rules and regulations which he may prescribe."

(2) *Announcement of the National Defense Advisory Commission, Priorities Board, November 8, 1940* [1]

The Priorities Board today announced that the British Purchasing Commission will be permitted to negotiate orders for 12,000 airplanes with the American aviation industry.

These planes will be built in existing plants and in other facilities now developing.

Under plans being devised by the Priorities Board it is intended to gear construction of the British planes to American production in such a way as to prevent interference with our own requirements.

The question of delivery priorities is being studied. They will be filled at appropriate times as production progresses.

(3) *List of Formal Mandatory Priorities on Materials*

The Division of Priorities, Office of Production Management, has imposed formal mandatory priorities for national defense on the following materials:

[1] *New York Times*, November 9, 1940, p. 1. At the President's press conference he discussed the scope of the decision as setting up a 50–50 allocation of United States' production and indicated that it was intended to set up a rule-of-thumb allocation slightly increasing the deliveries of planes to the United Kingdom.

Aluminum, February 28, 1941
Machine tools, February 28, 1941
Magnesium, March 3, 1941
Nickel, March 7, 1941
Neoprene, March 7, 1941
Tungsten, March 27, 1941
Nickel-bearing steel, April 11, 1941
Borax and boric acid, June 10, 1941
Zinc, June 11, 1941
Coffee, May 29, 1941
Cork, May 31, 1941
Synthetic rubbers, June 9, 1941
Polyvinyl chloride, June 9, 1941

For the Priorities Critical List as revised to June 17, 1941 see Office for Emergency Management, *Defense: Official Weekly Bulletin,* June 17, 1941, p. 9. The list is determined by the Army and Navy Munitions Board and is a compilation of the items on orders for which the appropriate Army and Navy representatives may issue preference rating certificates automatically.

F. Participation of the Reconstruction Finance Corporation in the National Defense Program

(1) *Sec. 5d, par. 4, of the Reconstruction Finance Corporation Act Amended by Act Approved June 10, 1941* [1]

Sec. 5d of the Reconstruction Finance Corporation Act was further amended [2] by Public Law 108, approved June 10, 1941, which a second time authorized the borrowing authority to be "increased by $1,500,000,000." This act exempted several organizations from taxation, including the Defense Plant Corporation, the Defense Supplies Corporation, the Metals Reserve Company and the Rubber Reserve Company. In addition it added to the national defense functions of the Corporation by new provisions in sec. 5d of the Act which enable the Reconstruction Finance Corporation to make loans to foreign Governments, banks and persons with the approval of the President. These provisions are valid until January 22, 1947.

[1] *An Act to Extend the Operations of the Disaster Loan Corporation and the Electric Home and Farm Authority, to Provide for Increasing the Landing Authority of the Reconstruction Finance Corporation, and for Other Purposes,* Public Law 108, 77th Cong., approved June 10, 1941; originated as S. 1438; Senate Report No. 292; House Report No. 616, pts. I and II; House (conference) Report No. 737; also H.R. 4674; House Report No. 514.

[2] For the Amendment of the Act of June 25, 1940 (*Documents, II, 1939–40,* p. 781) by the Act of September 26, 1940, Public No. 792, 76th Cong., 3d sess., see p. 550.

[Excerpt]

In order to aid the Government of the United States in its national defense program, the Corporation is authorized —

(2) To make loans to, or, when requested by the Federal Loan Administrator with the approval of the President, purchase the capital stock of, any corporation (*a*) for the purpose of producing, acquiring, and carrying strategic and critical materials as defined by the President, and (*b*) for plant construction, expansion and equipment, and working capital, to be used by the corporation in the manufacture of equipment and supplies necessary to the national defense, on such terms and conditions and with such maturities as the Corporation may determine; and

(3) [1] When requested by the Federal Loan Administrator, with the approval of the President, to create or organize, at any time prior to July 1, 1943, a corporation or corporations, with power (*a*) to produce, acquire, carry, sell, or otherwise deal in strategic and critical materials as defined by the President; (*b*) to purchase and lease land, purchase, lease, build, and expand plants, and purchase and produce equipment, facilities, machinery, materials, and supplies for the manufacture of strategic and critical materials, arms, ammunition, and implements of war, any other articles, equipment, facilities, and supplies necessary to the national defense, and such other articles, equipment, supplies, and materials as may be required in the manufacture or use of any of the foregoing or otherwise necessary in connection therewith; (*c*) to lease, sell, or otherwise dispose of such land, plants, facilities, and machinery to others to engage in such manufacture; (*d*) to engage in such manufacture itself, if the President finds that it is necessary for a Government agency to engage in such manufacture; (*e*) to produce, lease, purchase, or otherwise acquire railroad equipment (including rolling stock), and commercial aircraft, and parts, equipment, facilities, and supplies necessary in connection with such railroad equipment and aircraft, and to lease, sell, or otherwise dispose of the same; (*f*) to purchase, lease, build, expand, or otherwise acquire facilities for the training of aviators and to operate or lease, sell, or otherwise dispose of such facilities to others to engage in such training; and (*g*) to take such other action as the President and the Federal Loan Administrator may deem necessary to expedite the national-defense program, but the aggregate amount of the funds of the Reconstruction Finance Corporation which may be outstanding at any one time for carrying out this clause (*g*) shall not

---

[1] The first four sentences of subparagraph (3) inserted by sec. 4 (*b*) of Public Law 108, 77th Cong., approved June 10, 1941.

exceed $200,000,000: *Provided*, That nothing in this subsection shall be construed to authorize the Corporation to take any action, directly or indirectly, with respect to the proposals, heretofore considered by the Congress and known as the Great Lakes-St. Lawrence seaway, Passamaquoddy, Florida ship canal, and Tombigbee River projects, or to the project known as the Nicaragua Canal. The powers of every corporation hereafter created or organized under this subsection shall be set out in a charter which shall be valid only when certified copies thereof are filed with the Secretary of the Senate and the Clerk of the House of Representatives and published in the Federal Register, and all amendments to such charters shall be valid only when similarly filed and published. The charters of corporations heretofore so created or organized shall be so filed and published before July 1, 1941, and amendments thereto shall be valid only when certified copies thereof are hereafter so filed and published. No corporation heretofore or hereafter created or organized by the Corporation pursuant to this subsection shall have succession beyond January 22, 1947, except for purposes of liquidation, unless the life of such corporation is extended beyond such date pursuant to an Act of Congress.[1] The Corporation may make loans to, or purchase the capital stock of, any such corporation for any purpose within the powers of the corporation as above set forth related to the national-defense program on such terms and conditions as the Corporation may determine.

(4) [2] When requested by the Federal Loan Administrator, with the approval of the President, and subject to such conditions and limitations as may be set forth in such request, to make loans, notwithstanding the provisions of any other law, to any foreign governments, to their central banks, or to any person, commission, association, corporation, or bank acting for or on behalf of such government, for the purpose of achieving the maximum dollar exchange value in the United States for the securities or property of any such government, central bank, person, commission, association, corporation, or bank. Such loans may be made only upon the security of bonds, debentures, stocks, or other such obligations of (a) the Government of the United States or any State, municipality, or political subdivision of any State, or (b) any private corporation organized under the laws of the United States or any State.

Any corporation created or organized by the Corporation under the preceding paragraph is also authorized, with the approval of the Presi-

---

[1] The remainder of subparagraph (3) enacted by Public Law 664, 76th Cong., 3d sess., approved June 25, 1940.

[2] Added by sec. 4(a) of Public Law 108, 77th Cong., approved June 10, 1941.

dent, to make payments against the purchase price to be paid for strategic and critical materials in advance of the delivery of such materials. Whenever practicable, the Corporation may require the payments so made to be used for purchases of raw or manufactured agricultural commodities to be exported from the United States.

8. UNLIMITED NATIONAL EMERGENCY

(1) *Proclaiming That an Unlimited National Emergency Confronts This Country, Which Requires That Its Military, Naval, Air and Civilian Defenses Be Put on the Basis of Readiness to Repel Any and All Acts or Threats of Aggression Directed Toward Any Part of the Western Hemisphere, May 27, 1941* [1]

BY THE PRESIDENT OF THE UNITED STATES OF AMERICA

A Proclamation [No. 2487]

WHEREAS on September 8, 1939 because of the outbreak of war in Europe a proclamation [2] was issued declaring a limited national emergency and directing measures "for the purpose of strengthening our national defense within the limits of peacetime authorizations,"

WHEREAS a succession of events makes plain that the objectives of the Axis belligerents in such war are not confined to those avowed at its commencement, but include overthrow throughout the world of existing democratic order, and a worldwide domination of peoples and economies through the destruction of all resistance on land and sea and in the air, AND

WHEREAS indifference on the part of the United States to the increasing menace would be perilous, and common prudence requires that for the security of this nation and of this hemisphere we should pass from peacetime authorizations of military strength to such a basis as will enable us to cope instantly and decisively with any attempt at hostile encirclement of this hemisphere, or the establishment of any base for aggression against it, as well as to repel the threat of predatory incursion by foreign agents into our territory and society,

Now, THEREFORE, I, FRANKLIN D. ROOSEVELT, President of the United States of America, do proclaim that an unlimited national emer-

---

[1] 6 *Fed. Reg.*, p. 2419; Department of State, *Bulletin*, IV, p. 654. The proclamation was issued at the time of the President's address of May 27, and the announcement of its issuance was the conclusion of that analysis of United States policy. See p. 48.

[2] *Documents, II, 1939–40*, p. 645. Both proclamations are unusual in that they are based upon a recitation of facts rather than a citation of authority.

gency confronts this country, which requires that its military, naval, air and civilian defenses be put on the basis of readiness to repel any and all acts or threats of aggression directed toward any part of the Western Hemisphere.

I call upon all the loyal citizens engaged in production for defense to give precedence to the needs of the nation to the end that a system of government that makes private enterprise possible may survive.

I call upon all our loyal workmen as well as employers to merge their lesser differences in the larger effort to insure the survival of the only kind of government which recognizes the rights of labor or of capital.

I call upon loyal state and local leaders and officials to cooperate with the civilian defense agencies of the United States to assure our internal security against foreign directed subversion and to put every community in order for maximum productive effort and minimum of waste and unnecessary frictions.

I call upon all loyal citizens to place the nation's needs first in mind and in action to the end that we may mobilize and have ready for instant defensive use all of the physical powers, all of the moral strength and all of the material resources of this nation.

IN WITNESS WHEREOF I have hereunto set my hand and caused the Seal of the United States of America to be affixed.

DONE at the City of Washington this twenty-seventh day of May, [SEAL] in the year of our Lord nineteen hundred and forty-one, and of the Independence of the United States of America the one hundred and sixty-fifth.

FRANKLIN D. ROOSEVELT.

By the President:

CORDELL HULL
Secretary of State.

———

The proclamation of an "unlimited national emergency" revived speculation with respect to the extent of executive powers. Senate Resolution 185, 76th Cong., 2d sess., September 28, 1939, requested the Attorney General (Jackson) to report "what executive powers are made available to the President under his proclamation of national emergency [of September 8, 1939], and what other extraordinary powers, if any, are made available to the Executive under existing statutes in emergency or state of war." In declining "to give an opinion to the Senate on legal phases of the subject matter," the Attorney General said in his letter of October 4, 1939: [1]

———

[1] *Executive Powers under National Emergency: Letter from the Attorney General Transmitting with Reference to S. Res. No. 185 Information as to Extraordinary Powers Available to the President during a National Emergency or State of War* (Sen. Doc. No. 133, 76th Cong., 2d sess.).

"This time-honored position should not, in my opinion, be departed from. However, desiring to be of all possible assistance to the Senate, I have prepared and am transmitting herewith a list of statutes which, by their terms, grant to the executive branch of the Government powers which may be exercised in emergency or state of war.[1] It is not claimed that this list is complete — indeed accuracy in this respect can be assured only by careful and painstaking search of the entire body of the Federal statutory law — statutes of this class having been enacted from time to time since the beginning of the Government.

"You are aware, of course, that the Executive has powers not enumerated in the statutes — powers derived not from statutory grants but from the Constitution. It is universally recognized that the constitutional duties of the Executive carry with them the constitutional powers necessary for their proper performance. These constitutional powers have never been specifically defined, and in fact cannot be, since their extent and limitations are largely dependent upon conditions and circumstances. In a measure this is true with respect to most of the powers of the Executive, both constitutional and statutory. The right to take specific action might not exist under one state of facts, while under another it might be the absolute duty of the Executive to take such action."

Appended to the letter was a list of "Statutes which by their terms grant powers that may be exercised by the President 'in emergency or state of war.'"

In the House of Representatives, Stephen Pace, Ga., proposed to reprint this list on May 28, 1941, but Earl C. Michener, Mich., made available to him a later list compiled by the Library of Congress, Legislative Reference Service, which under the title "Acts of Congress applicable in time of emergency" was published in *Congressional Record*, Vol. 87, p. 4605–12 (daily edition, May 28, 1941).

9. AIRCRAFT AS PRIZES OF WAR

(1) *An Act to Amend Sections 4613 and 4614 of the Revised Statutes of the United States to Include Captures of Aircraft as Prizes of War, Approved June 24, 1941* [1]

Be it enacted by the Senate and House of Representatives of the United States of America in Congress assembled, That sections 4613 and 4614 of the Revised Statutes of the United States (U.S.C., title 34, secs. 1131 and 1132) be amended to read, respectively, as follows:

"SEC. 4613. The provisions of this title (title LIV) shall apply to all captures of vessels, including aircraft, made as prize by authority of the United States or adopted and ratified by the President of the United States: *Provided,* That the terms 'vessel' and 'ship' as used in this title (title LIV) shall include aircraft, and that the term 'master' as used in this title (title LIV) shall include the pilot or other person in command of such aircraft: *Provided further,* That nothing herein con-

[1] Public Law 127, 77th Cong., originating as S. 992; Senate Report No. 287; House Report No. 749.

tained shall be construed as affecting, or in any way impairing, the legal right of the Army of the United States or any component part thereof, while engaged in hostilities, to capture any enemy property or neutral property used or transported in violation of the obligations of neutrals under international law, wherever found, and without prize procedure.

"SEC. 4614. The term 'vessels of the Navy' as used in this title (title LIV) shall include all armed vessels, including aircraft, officered and manned by the United States and under the control of the Department of the Navy."

CHAPTER XII

DEPARTMENT OF STATE AND THE FOREIGN SERVICE

1. ORGANIZATION OF THE DEPARTMENT OF STATE

The Department of State, below the Secretary and Under Secretary, was officered by the Counselor and three Assistant Secretaries until the post of Counselor was left vacant by the death of R. Walton Moore on February 8, 1941. Previous to Mr. Moore's appointment as Counselor on May 20, 1937 there were four Assistant Secretaries. Changes of function in the interval led the Secretary of State to leave the post of Counselor vacant and to reassign duties among four Assistant Secretaries of State.

(1) *Department of State Order No. 922, March 4, 1941* [1]

There is hereby delegated to the Assistant Secretaries of State, respectively, the supervision of functions of the Department of State as hereinafter enumerated:

Assistant Secretary Berle

Coordination of financial questions with questions of major policy.

General supervision of Canadian affairs and affairs relating to Greenland.

General supervision of the following units of the Department, including, except as otherwise provided, the signing of correspondence with respect to the work thereof: Passport Division; Division of International Conferences (except fiscal); Division of International Communications (aviation only); Division of Foreign Activity Correlation; and the Translating Bureau.

Assistant Secretary Long

Coordination of matters relating to the formulation and execution of foreign policies assigned to him by the Secretary of State.

General liaison work with the Senate and the House of Representatives

---

[1] Department of State, *Bulletin*, IV, p. 271.

and general representation of the Department of State at hearings before Congressional committees, excepting the legislative activities relating to the duties and administrative functions of the Assistant Secretary and Budget Officer.

General supervision of the following units of the Department of State, including, except as otherwise provided, the signing of correspondence with respect to the work thereof: Visa Division; Special Division; Office of Philippine Affairs; and the Division of International Communications (except aviation).

General supervision, under the direction of the Secretary of State, of work relating to special problems arising from international armed conflicts; and of affairs relating to international fisheries problems.

Assistant Secretary Acheson

Coordination of commercial and economic questions with questions of major policy.

General supervision of the following units of the Department of State, including, except as otherwise provided, the signing of correspondence with respect to the work thereof: Division of Commercial Treaties and Agreements; Division of Controls; Treaty Division; Division of Commercial Affairs; and the Editor of Treaties.

Assistant Secretary Shaw

General supervision of the following units of the Department of State, including, except as otherwise provided, the signing of correspondence with respect to the work thereof: Office of Fiscal and Budget Affairs; Division of Personnel Supervision and Management; Division of Accounts; Division of Communications and Records; Division of Foreign Service Administration; Division of Foreign Service Personnel; Foreign Service Officers' Training School; Foreign Service Buildings Office; Division of Research and Publication; Division of Protocol (fiscal only); and Division of International Conferences (fiscal only).

It shall be understood that for budgetary purposes and in relation to expenditures of government funds, all of the divisions, offices and bureaus of the Department of State, including those specifically so indicated in this order, are subject to the fiscal supervision of the Assistant Secretary and Budget Officer.

The provisions of this order supersede the provisions of all orders or parts of orders in conflict therewith.

CORDELL HULL

(2) *Chart on Organization of the Department of State* [1]

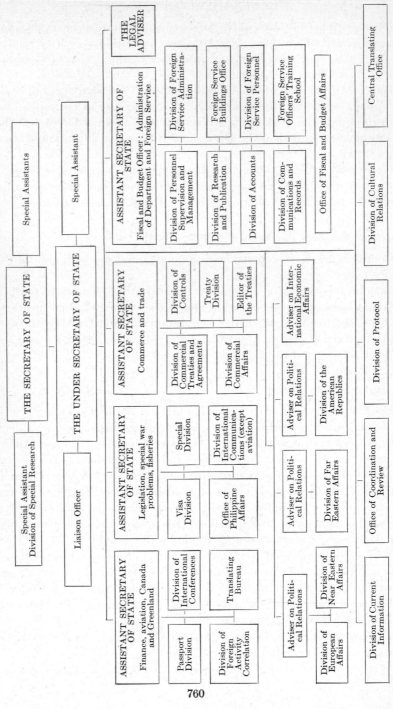

760

[1] Department of State, *Bulletin*, IV, p. 754.

(3) *Department of State Appropriations for Fiscal Year 1942 Compared With 1941* [1]

The Department of State Appropriation Act for the fiscal year ending June 30, 1942 is Public Law 135, approved June 28, 1941. The total is a gross sum, being offset to the extent of some $4,000,000 by receipts incidental to the functions of the Department, principally passport and visa fees. Included under the heading International Obligations are the sums payable by the Government of the United States for which the Department of State is the appropriate channel.

For a table of the International Obligations under treaty, law or other authority which are payable through the Department of State, see Department of State, *Bulletin*, V, p. 47.

Appropriation Title	Appropriations for 1942	Appropriations for 1941	Increases (+), Decreases (−) for 1942
Department Proper	$3,318,440	$3,272,580	+ $45,860
Foreign Service (exclusive of Emergency Fund).	13,681,900	13,559,500	+ 122,400
Emergency Fund	500,000	1,225,000	− 725,000
Foreign Service Buildings	450,000	300,000	+ 150,000
International Obligations	3,548,900	3,733,000	− 184,100
GRAND TOTAL	21,499,240	22,090,080	− 590,840
Deduct appropriations included above in 1941 column which were provided in supplemental appropriation acts.	——	− 1,968,500	+ 1,968,500
TOTAL OF APPROPRIATIONS CONTAINED IN ANNUAL APPROPRIATION ACTS.	21,499,240	20,121,580	+ 1,377,660

2. CONFERENCES IN WHICH THE UNITED STATES GOVERNMENT PARTICIPATED, JULY 1, 1940–JUNE 30, 1941

Continues lists in *Documents I, 1938–39*, p. 471; *II, 1939–40*, p. 822. See also *American Delegations to International Conferences, Congresses and Expositions and American Representation on International Institutions and Commissions, with relevant Data. — Fiscal Year ended June 30, 1940* (Department of State, Conference Series 49, Publication 1587).

Second Meeting of the Ministers of Foreign Affairs of the American Republics for Consultation Under the Inter-American Agreements of Buenos Aires and Lima; Havana, Cuba, July 21–30, 1940.

This Meeting, the second in a series inaugurated at Panama in 1939 following the outbreak of the European war, was held in accordance

[1] Department of State, *Bulletin*, V, p. 45.

with procedure established at the Inter-American Conference for the Maintenance of Peace (Buenos Aires, 1936) and elaborated at the Eighth International Conference of American States (Lima, 1938), providing for consultations of the Ministers of Foreign Affairs of the American Republics or their representatives whenever a state of emergency shall exist or whenever the peace of the Western Hemisphere shall be threatened.

Inter-American Maritime Conference, Washington, D. C., November 25–December 2, 1940.

The Inter-American Maritime Conference met in Washington at the invitation of the Inter-American Financial and Economic Advisory Committee, which was established in accordance with a resolution of the First Meeting of Ministers of Foreign Affairs of the American Republics held at Panama in September 1939. The Advisory Committee was established for the purpose of providing a convenient means of discussion of the serious crises in the economic field as a consequence of the outbreak of the European war.

North American Regional Radio-Engineering Conference, Washington, D. C., January 14–30, 1941.

Pursuant to the North American Regional Broadcasting Agreement signed at Havana, Cuba, on December 13, 1937, an informal meeting of representatives of the Governments of Canada, Cuba, Dominican Republic, Haiti, Mexico, and the United States was held at Washington, D. C., from January 14 to January 30, 1941. The purpose of the meeting was to harmonize the action of the radio administrations of the participating governments so that the assignment of frequencies to broadcasting stations in the standard broadcasting band would be in conformity with the provisions of the Agreement.

Second Pan American Congress of Endocrinology, Montevideo, Uruguay, March 5–8, 1941.

The principal purposes of the Pan American congresses of endocrinology are to promote the development and improvement of this branch of medicine and to encourage closer collaboration among the specialists throughout the Americas.

Third General Assembly of the Pan American Institute of Geography and History, Lima, Peru, March 30–April 8, 1941.

The Institute was established pursuant to a resolution of the Sixth International Conference of American States held at Havana, Cuba, in 1928, and maintains permanent headquarters in Mexico City. The Institute collects and disseminates geographical and historical material, and has conducted numerous explorations and surveys in the fields of anthropology, archaeology, volcanology, geology, et cetera. The Second General Assembly of the Institute was held in Washington in October 1935.

Third Meeting of the Inter-American Union of the Caribbean, Port-au-Prince, Haiti, April 22–29, 1941.

The Inter-American Union of the Caribbean was organized for the purpose of convening meetings "to further closer relations and to contribute toward the development of cultural as well as economic and tourist relations among the nations in this portion of the New World."

3. DIPLOMATIC REPRESENTATION

Shifts in diplomatic representation occurred since the outbreak of war in Europe as follows:

Diplomatic representation withdrawn from Tirana, Albania, September 16, 1939.

Diplomatic representation withdrawn from Brussels, Belgium, July 15, 1940; the Ambassador Extraordinary and Plenipotentiary to Poland was confirmed by the Senate on February 10, 1941 to be concurrently Ambassador Extraordinary and Plenipotentiary near the Government of Belgium, established in London.

Diplomatic representation withdrawn from Luxemburg July 15, 1940; the Envoy Extraordinary and Minister Plenipotentiary to Canada was confirmed by the Senate on February 10, 1941 to be concurrently Envoy Extraordinary and Minister Plenipotentiary near the Government of Luxemburg, established in Canada.

Diplomatic representation was withdrawn from Oslo, Norway, July 15, 1940; the Ambassador Extraordinary and Plenipotentiary to Poland was confirmed by the Senate on February 10, 1941 to be concurrently Envoy Extraordinary and Minister Plenipotentiary near the Government of Norway, established in London.

Diplomatic representation was withdrawn from The Hague July 15, 1940; the Ambassador Extraordinary and Plenipotentiary to Poland was confirmed by the Senate on February 10, 1941 to be concurrently Envoy Extraordinary and Minister Plenipotentiary near the Government of the Netherlands, established in London.

Diplomatic representation at Belgrade withdrew with the Yugoslav Government in April 1941; the Ambassador Extraordinary and Plenipotentiary to Poland was confirmed by the Senate on July 29, 1941 to be concurrently Envoy Extraordinary and Minister Plenipotentiary near the Government of Yugoslavia, established in London.

The American Legations at Kaunas, Lithuania, Tallinn, Estonia, and Riga, Latvia, including the consular sections of each, were closed as of September 5, 1940.

The American Embassy in London and the British Embassy in Washington were strengthened in February 1941 by the addition of an officer of ministerial rank to assist the Ambassador at the head of the mission. The personnel of the two Embassies was increased in other respects.

4. UNITED STATES CONSULAR OFFICES OPENED, JULY 1939–JANUARY 1941 [1]

1. Acapulco de Juarez, Mexico..................Vice consulate
2. Aruba, Netherlands West Indies.............Consular agency
3. Bahia Blanca, Argentina....................Vice consulate
4. Canberra, Australia........................Legation
5. Coatzacoalcos, Mexico......................Consulate
6. Dakar, Senegal, French West Africa.........Consulate
7. Florianópolis, Brazil......................Consulate
8. Fortaleza, Brazil..........................Vice consulate
9. Freetown, Sierra Leone, British West Africa....Consular agency
10. Georgetown, British Guiana.................Consulate
11. Godthaab, Greenland........................Consulate
12. Horta, Fayal, Azores.......................Consulate
13. Königsberg, Germany........................Consulate
14. La Paz, Baja California, Mexico............Vice consulate
15. Manáos, Brazil.............................Vice consulate
16. Manzanillo, Mexico.........................Vice consulate
17. Martinique, French West Indies.............Consulate
18. Medellín, Colombia.........................Consulate
19. Natal, Brazil..............................Consulate
20. Nouméa, New Caledonia......................Vice consulate
21. Paramaribo, Surinam........................Consulate
22. Puerto de la Cruz, Venezuela...............Vice consulate
23. Punta Arenas, Chile........................Vice consulate
24. Reykjavik, Iceland.........................Consulate
25. Ríohacha, Colombia.........................Vice consulate
26. São Luiz, Brazil...........................Consular agency
27. São Vicente, Cape Verde Islands............Vice consulate
28. Suva, Fiji Islands.........................Vice consulate
29. Tananarive, Madagascar.....................Consulate
30. Valdivia, Chile............................Vice consulate
31. Vladivostok, U. S. S. R.[2]................Consulate general

[1] U. S. Congress, House of Representatives, Committee on Appropriations, *Department of State Appropriation Bill for 1942; Hearings* . . . 77th Cong., 1st sess., p. 176.

[2] A Department of State release of December 9, 1940 (Department of State, *Bulletin*, III, p. 551) said:

"A Consulate General of the United States of America will be opened at Vladivostok in the immediate future. Mr. Angus I. Ward, who has served for approximately six years as Consul and Secretary in the American Embassy at Moscow, has been ordered to Vladivostok in order to complete arrangements for the opening of the Consulate General and to act temporarily as Consul in charge. . . . At the present time this Government maintains no consulates in the Soviet Union; American consular affairs in that country are handled by the Consular Section of the American Embassy at Moscow.

"The last American Consulate at Vladivostok, which was opened in 1898, was closed on May 15, 1923 by Mr. Summerville Pinkney Tuck."

APPENDIX

The *Statistical Abstract of the United States* published by the Department of Commerce is the standard annual official collection of data concerning the United States. Certain statistics pertaining particularly to the relations of the United States and its nationals to foreign governments and peoples are here brought together from various sources.

I. AMERICAN CITIZENS LIVING ABROAD [1]

	As of Jan. 1, 1940	As of Jan. 1, 1941
South America	16,502	17,787
Mexico and Central America	23,881	24,769
West Indies and Bermuda	12,605	13,407
Canada and Newfoundland	181,773	164,977
Europe	63,235	50,901
Africa	5,056	4,944
Asia	33,118	28,946
Fiji Islands and Society Islands . . .	199	28
Australasia	2,240	2,125
Total	338,609	307,884

II. PASSPORT STATISTICS

OBJECT OF TRAVEL

	Calendar Year	
	1939 [2]	1940 [3]
Commerce	5,265	3,628
Education	3,689	601
Employment	5,399	3,439
Family affairs	3,597	706
Health	869	185
Personal business	23,790	5,414
Pleasure	42,541	10,380
Profession	2,479	446
Religion	1,861	1,352
Science	360	102
Total	89,850	26,253

[1] Compiled from Department of State, *Bulletin*, IV, p. 602, and also *Documents, II, 1939–40*, p. 825.   [2] Department of State, *Bulletin*, II, p. 122.   [3] *Ibid.*, IV, p. 129.

II. PASSPORT STATISTICS (*cont.*)

APPLICANTS

	CALENDAR YEAR	
	1939	1940
Native	57,896	22,963
Naturalized	31,954	3,290
Male.	48,820	16,661
Female	41,030	9,592

ADDITIONAL PERSONS INCLUDED IN PASSPORTS

Adults	13,200	2,325
Minors	10,431	2,712

PREVIOUS PASSPORTS

Number of applicants having been previously issued American passports . .	31,048	8,882

DESTINATION

Africa	1,074	396
All countries	460	——
Australia and New Zealand	1,207	570
Bermuda	——	1,945
Canada and Newfoundland	44	728
Eastern Europe	4,018	48
Far East	5,409	5,291
Latin America	13,951	15,508
Near East	4,997	607
Western Europe	65,163	1,528
Total	96,323	26,621

III. NET CAPITAL MOVEMENT, JANUARY 2, 1935 – OCTOBER 2, 1940 [1]

[In thousands of dollars. Capital inflow or capital outflow (−)]

	Grand Total	United Kingdom	France	Germany	Italy	Netherlands	Switzerland	Other Europe	Total Europe	Canada	Latin America	Asia	All Other
Movement in Short-Term Banking Funds	$3,866,421	$ 586,178	$546,707	$169,124	$30,233	$183,881	$452,481	$665,594	$2,634,198	$376,046	$370,382	$428,602	$57,193
Movement in Brokerage Balances	101,563	16,302	18,845	− 161	132	12,347	19,196	8,065	74,726	11,216	9,146	5,755	720
Movement in Transactions in Domestic Securities	1,044,341	271,131	74,538	−28,831	26,157	230,669	365,367	64,464	1,003,495	−20,652	26,610	22,047	12,841
Movement in Transactions in Foreign Securities	793,266	130,541	42,954	36,136	28,074	31,025	47,358	195,881	511,969	20,713	197,642	50,072	12,870
Net Capital Movement	$5,805,591	$1,004,152	$683,044	$176,268	$84,596	$457,922	$884,402	$934,004	$4,224,388	$387,323	$603,780	$506,476	$83,624

[1] Bulletin of the Treasury Department, December 1940, p. 36.

IV. MUNITIONS LICENSES TO THE BRITISH COM-
MONWEALTH OF NATIONS, 1935–MAY 1941 [1]

Since the issuance of Proclamation No. 2413 of July 2, 1940 (p. 474) trade in arms, ammunition and implements of war has been subject to export control as well as to the license system of the National Munitions Control Board, which dates from November 6, 1935. That trade in consequence became concentrated with the British Commonwealth of Nations and the British Empire, countries associated with them and the American Republics. Of the several technical categories of arms, ammunition and implements of war, the demand for aircraft and parts was some two-thirds of the total in 1939 and 1940. Full details of the licensing system are contained in the biennial reports of the National Munitions Control Board.

From the beginning in 1935 through May 1941 licenses for exports amounting to $1,853,975,500 worth of arms, ammunition and implements of war had been issued; of this total over $1,496,000,000 had been issued to the British group.

In five years through 1940 licenses amounting to over $1,000,000 had been issued for export to each of the following: Argentina, Australia, Belgium, Brazil, Canada, Chile, China, Colombia, Czecho-Slovakia, Finland, France, Germany, Gold Coast, Great Britain, Greece, India, Iran, Iraq, Japan, Mexico, Netherlands, Netherlands Indies, New Zealand, Norway, Peru, Poland, Portugal, Rumania, South Africa, Soviet Union, Straits Settlements, Sweden, Thailand, Turkey, Venezuela and Yugoslavia.

From the entry of the system into force on November 6, 1935 to December 31, 1940 there were 522 persons and companies registered as manufacturers, exporters or importers of arms, ammunition or implements of war, of which 490 registrations were in effect on December 31, 1940. During the year 1940 a total of 4,800 licenses were issued. Licenses issued are subject to revocation by the Board or to cancellation upon request of the licensee. Statistics of licenses issued in past years are net and show the values exported thereunder. Later statistics of licenses issued may not correspond to the exports effected during the period owing to revocations, cancellations or amendments of the licenses or, increasingly, to the delay between the licensing and the execution of the transaction.

	TOTAL LICENSES	CANADA	UNITED KINGDOM
1935	$ 1,550,587.78	$ 8,231.05	$ 60,805.80
1936	24,182,929.36	792,439.38	572,298.88
1937	46,102,119.21	2,172,923.77	1,526,996.87
1938	83,641,308.29	2,851,180.85	23,060,337.41
1939	143,743,900.79	5,824,783.82	19,129,162.05
1940	873,064,658.26	48,448,158.41	675,470,249.57
Jan.–June	270,060,420.24	20,196,993.75	138,407,826.91
1941, Jan.–May [2] . .	681,689,996.28	$667,581,328.88 [3]	

[1] Compiled from *National Munitions Control Board, Fifth Report . . . for the Period January 1, 1940 to June 30, 1940* (House Doc. No. 876, 76th Cong., 3d sess.); *Sixth Report . . . for the Year Ended December 31, 1940* (House Doc. No. 127, 77th Cong., 1st sess.).

[2] Department of State, *Bulletin*, V, p. 28.

[3] Combined total for British Commonwealth of Nations, the British Empire, British mandates, and the armed forces elsewhere of Great Britain and its allies.

V. PACIFIC ISLANDS NEAR PANAMA CANAL

The following table is reconstructed from a memorandum of the Navy Department, Hydrographic Office, to the late Senator Ernest Lundeen, dated June 19, 1939 and published in the *Congressional Record*, July 17, 1939.

| NAME | LOCATION | SOVEREIGNTY | DISTANCE IN MILES FROM | |
			Panama	Corinto
Perlas Islands . . .	Gulf of Panama	Panama	——	550
Galapagos Islands, including Culpepper and Wenman Islands	Off coast of Ecuador	Ecuador	850	810
Malpelo Island . .	Off coast of Colombia	Colombia	300	600
Cocos Islands . . .	West of Panama	Costa Rica	480	400
Isla Coiba ⎫ Isla Jicaron ⎪ Isla Montuosa ⎪ Isla Parida ⎬ . . Isla Afuera ⎪ Islas Conteras ⎪ Islas Secas ⎪ Islas Ladrones ⎭	Off northwest coast of Panama	Panama	150 to 200	400 to 450
Isla Caño	Off coast of Costa Rica	Costa Rica	270	300
Clipperton Island . .	Off coast of Mexico	France	1930	1320
Revilla Gigedo Islands	Off coast of Mexico	Mexico	2150	1560

VI. DECLARATIONS OF WAR OR OPENING OF HOSTILITIES

The following list in tabular form is calculated to present the time of declarations of war or their current equivalents in recognition of the existence of a state of war and the opening of hostilities under various guises. The country first listed in the first column took the initiative indicated in the second column, where the time notations refer to the locality of the action.

Fuller details of the declarations of war, through November 15, 1940, are given in a table published in Department of State, *Bulletin*, IV, p. 224.

COUNTRIES	DECLARATION OR ACTION	UNITED STATES NEUTRALITY PROCLAMATION	UNITED STATES PROCLAMATION UNDER "NEUTRALITY ACTS" OF MAY 1, 1937, AND/OR Nov. 4, 1939
Japan — China	Attack, July 7, 1937		
Germany — Poland	Invasion, Sept. 1, 1939, dawn	Sept. 5, 1939	Sept. 5, 1939

Countries	Declaration or Action	United States Neutrality Proclamation	United States Proclamation under "Neutrality Acts" of May 1, 1937, and/or Nov. 4, 1939
United Kingdom — Germany	Ultimatum expired Sept. 3, 1939, 11 A.M.	Sept. 5, 1939	Sept. 5, 1939
France — Germany	Notification, as of Sept. 3, 1939, 5 P.M.	Sept. 5, 1939	Sept. 5, 1939
India — Germany	Proclamation of Governor-General, Sept. 3, 1939	Sept. 5, 1939	Sept. 5, 1939
Australia — Germany	Proclamation, Sept. 3, 1939	Sept. 5, 1939	Sept. 5, 1939
New Zealand — Germany	Statement as of Sept. 3, 1939, 9 : 30 P.M.	Sept. 5, 1939	Sept. 5, 1939
Union of South Africa — Germany	Proclamation, Sept. 6, 1939	Sept. 8, 1939	Sept. 8, 1939
Canada — Germany	Proclamation, Sept. 10, 1939	Sept. 10, 1939	Sept. 10, 1939
Germany — Norway	Invasion April 9, 1940; decree for exercising authority, April 24, 1940	April 25, 1940	April 25, 1940
Germany — Denmark	Occupation, unresisted, without acquiescence, April 9, 1940, dawn		
Germany — Belgium	Invasion, May 10, 1940, dawn	May 11, 1940	May 11, 1940
Germany — Luxemburg	Invasion, May 10, 1940, dawn	May 11, 1940	May 11, 1940
Germany — Netherlands	Invasion, May 10, 1940, dawn; Netherlands "at war" 3 hours after engaging invader	May 11, 1940	May 11, 1940
Italy — France	June 11, 1940; note delivered, June 10, 4 : 30 P.M.	June 10, 1940	June 10, 1940
Italy — United Kingdom	June 11, 1940; note delivered, June 10, 4 : 45 P.M.	June 10, 1940	June 10, 1940

Countries	Declaration or Action	United States Neutrality Proclamation	United States Proclamation under "Neutrality Acts" of May 1, 1937, and/or Nov. 4, 1939
Canada — Italy	Proclamation, as and from June 10, 1940		
New Zealand — Italy	Statement, "at war" from June 11, 1940, 10 : 30 A.M.		
Australia — Italy	Notification, as from June 11, 1940, 9 A.M.		
Union of South Africa — Italy	Proclamation, as from June 11, 1940		
Italy — Greece	Ultimatum expiring Oct. 28, 1940, 6 A.M.	Nov. 15, 1940	Nov. 15, 1940
Greece — Italy	Notification (Nov. 12), as from Oct. 28, 1940, 5 : 30 A.M.	Nov. 15, 1940	Nov. 15, 1940
Germany — Greece	Note advising of action to Greek minister at Berlin, April 6, 1941, 6 : 30 A.M.; invasion at 5 : 15 A.M.		
Germany — Yugoslavia	Note advising of action to Yugoslav minister at Berlin, April 6, 1941; attack at dawn		April 10, 1941
Italy — Yugoslavia	Announcement of collaboration with Germany, April 6, 1941		April 10, 1941
Bulgaria — Yugoslavia	Frontier attacks, April 8, 1941; relations severed April 15; occupation of Uskub, April 19		April 24, 1941
Hungary — Yugoslavia	Troops ordered into Yugoslavia, April 10, 1941		April 15, 1941

Countries	Declaration or Action	United States Neutrality Proclamation	United States Proclamation under "Neutrality Acts" of May 1, 1937, and/or Nov. 4, 1939
Rumania — Yugoslavia	Artillery exchange near Orsova, April 12, 1941		
Bulgaria — Greece	Relations severed, April 23, 1941; occupation in Thrace, April 25, 1941		April 24, 1941
Germany — Soviet Union	Note delivered, June 22, 1941, dawn		
Italy — Soviet Union	Note delivered, June 22, 1941, 5:30 A.M.		
Rumania — Soviet Union	Order to army, June 22, 1941		
Slovakia — Soviet Union	Notice to Germany, June 24, 1941, 12 m.; proclamation to army		
Finland — Soviet Union	Unanimous vote of confidence by Eduskunta to resist "repeated attacks," June 25, 1941		
Hungary — Soviet Union	Relations severed, June 23, 1941; full powers to government, June 25; "at war" announcement, June 26		
Albania — Soviet Union	Decree, state of war, June 28, 1941, issued at Rome, June 30		

Moreover, France severed relations with the Soviet Union on June 28, 1941 and blocked Soviet funds on July 1. Denmark also severed relations with the Soviet Union on July 12. Both countries, under the pressure of German occupation, have permitted the recruiting of soldiers for service against the Soviet Union.

VII. FOREIGN MERCHANT VESSELS REQUISITIONED BY THE UNITED STATES, UP TO JUNE 30, 1941 [1]

The United States requisitions foreign vessels under two conditions: (1) Forfeiture of vessels in case of sabotage in American waters by officers or crew following court proceeding pursuant to the provisions of U. S. Code, title 50, sec. 193; (2) requisition by the Maritime Commission of foreign shipping with payment of compensation under the act of June 6, 1941 (p. 631). The form of order for this type of requisition is printed at p. 635.

Some of the ships in the following list were among those taken into protective custody on March 30, 1941 (p. 621).

VESSEL	NATIONALITY	GROSS TONNAGE	D. W. TONNAGE	DATE OF TAKING 1941
SS JUTTA	Danish	1,549	2,700	June 16
MV NORA	Danish	2,937	4,500	June 16
SS MARNA	Danish	1,700	2,900	June 16
SS JONNA	Danish	1,517	2,183	June 16
SS RITA MAERSK	Danish	1,889	3,450	June 16
SS HERTA MAERSK . . .	Danish	1,890	3,500	June 16
SS CLARA [2]	Italian	6,131	8,560	June 18
MV EMMA MAERSK . . .	Danish	8,278	13,580	June 20
MV CAROLINE MAERSK . .	Danish	7,691	12,725	June 23
SS IRCANIA [2]	Italian	4,815	8,250	June 24
SS CONFIDENZA [2]	Italian	6,458	10,750	June 24
MV MANGALIA	Rumanian	3,495	5,000	June 25

[1] List supplied by the United States Maritime Commission.

[2] Proceedings for the forfeiture of these vessels on account of sabotage pursuant to the provisions of U. S. Code, title 50, sec. 193, have been instituted by the Department of Justice.

INDEX

A

Acheson, Dean, functions of, as Asst. Secy. of State, 759

Acting Secretary of State. *See* Welles, Sumner.

Advisory Commission, Division of Labor. *See* National defense.

Afuera, Isla, 769

Agrarian properties in Mexico, 133

Agreements, international. *See* Treaties *and* Trade agreements.

Aggression, fight against, resolution, 444

Agriculture:
Agricultural Adjustment Act, 462
Coffee Marketing Agreement, Inter-American, 98
division under Office for Emergency Management, 667

Aircraft (*see also* National defense):
capture as prizes of war, act in revised statutes to include, 756

Albania:
Soviet Union, declaration of war with, issued at Rome, 772

Albany River Basin, diversion of waters in Great Lakes System, 181

Aliens in U. S.:
documents required for entry in U. S., 596
escaped prisoners of war, Dept. of Justice instructions regarding treatment of, 600
limitation and control of visas, 598
registration of, 576, 601
exemption of foreign government officials, 602
refusal of visas to certain aliens, 608
restrictions on departure and entry during national emergency and in wartime, 607
waiver of passport and visa requirements for certain aliens, 595

Allied Governments:
address of Prime Minister Churchill at meeting of, 445
resolution on fight against aggression, 444

Aluminum, export of, 475

American citizens:
attack on, in Anglo-Egyptian Sudan, 421–3
evacuation from —
Europe, 580
Far East, 582
living abroad, as of Jan. 1, 1940 and Jan. 1, 1941, 765

American foreign policy. *See* Policy.

American holdings in foreign countries, 547

American legations and embassies in occupied territories, 763

American Legion, U. S. Army transport:
announcement of sailing, 581
safety of vessel not guaranteed by Germany:
German refusal, 410
statement to German Foreign Office by American Chargé d'Affaires, 411

American property, Italian air attack on, in Anglo-Egyptian Sudan, 421–3

American Red Cross:
amendment of Neutrality Act of 1939, Sec. 4, dealing with ships under control of, 649
food relief for Unoccupied France, 516
role in coordination of relief activities, 610
vessels in combat areas under direction or control of, travel of American citizens on, 656–7

American Republics. *See* Inter-American relations.

American ships. *See under* Neutrality *and* Shipping.

American states, international conferences of. *See* Inter-American relations.

Ammunition. *See under* National defense.

Anderson, John Z., U. S. Representative, letter from Secy. Hull regarding German representation in the U. S., 414

Anglo-Egyptian Sudan, Americans attacked by Italian airmen in, 421–3

775

Antigua, naval and air bases, lease from Great Britain, 226

Antilles, French Islands of, 95

Appropriations, Department of State, 761

Appropriations for national defense. *See* National defense: appropriations and authorizations.

Arbitration:
offer of friendly offices of Argentina, Brazil and the U. S. in boundary dispute between Ecuador and Peru, 157

Argentina:
air mission of U. S., agreement, 148
continental defense, attitude on, 138
reservation on convention for the provisional administration of European colonies and possessions in the Western Hemisphere (1940), 91
stabilization agreement with U. S., joint statement, 120
trade agreement with U. S., proposed negotiations for, 459

Arica-Santos transoceanic railway (Final Act of Havana), 72

Armistice Day, 1940:
address by Pres. Roosevelt, Arlington, 15

Arms, ammunition and implements of war. *See under* Neutrality *and* National defense.

Army registration day, proclamation, 682

Army, U. S. (*see also* National defense): strength, June 1941, 695

Attorney-General of the U. S.:
executive agreement, letter to Secy. Hull on memorandum of legal adviser of State Dept., 198
executive powers of President, declination of opinion on, requested by Senate, 755-6
instructions regarding treatment of escaped prisoners of war, 600
opinion on agreement between U. S. and Canada regarding Great Lakes–St. Lawrence Deep Waterway, 198

Australia:
Germany, proclamation of war against by Governor-General, and application of U. S. neutrality proclamations, 770
Italy, notification of war on, 771

wool reserve, exchange of notes with U. S. on, 739-42

Avenol, Joseph. *See* League of Nations Secretariat.

Aviation. *See* Aircraft *and* National defense.

Azores, 51, 53

B

Bahamas, naval and air bases in, lease from Great Britain, 204, 206, 215-6

Balance of international payments:
1939-40, 527, table
U. S. 1940, summary prepared by Dept. of Commerce, 519

Balances, brokerage, 767

Baltic republics (*see also* Latvia, Lithuania, *and* Estonia):
blocking of funds by U. S., 429
statement of Acting Secy. Welles on Soviet aggression, 429
treaties of nonaggression with Soviet Union, 429

Barter trade, German, 409

Belgium:
costs of occupation by German authorities, 448-9
German invasion of, and application of U. S. neutrality proclamations, 770

Belize, question of (Final Act of Havana), 79

Belligerents. *See individual countries and under* Far Eastern situation.

Berle, Adolf A., Jr., Asst. Secy. of State, functions of, 758

Bermuda, naval and air bases in, lease from Great Britain, 226

Blockade practices:
British Admiralty notice, 503
German Govt. notices, 504

Bolivia:
interoceanic railway from Arica to Santos, 72
reservation to resolution on Inter-American Neutrality Committee, 2d meeting Foreign Ministers of American Republics, 65

Brazil:
European colonies and possessions in the Western Hemisphere, convention on, ratification, 90
military and air mission of U. S. to, agreement, 149

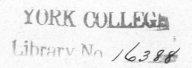